Introducing
Human Resource
Management

Sixth Edition

Margaret Foot
Caroline Hook

FT Prentice Hall
FINANCIAL TIMES

An imprint of **Pearson Education**

Harlow, England • London • New York • Boston • San Francisco • Toronto
Sydney • Tokyo • Singapore • Hong Kong • Seoul • Taipei • New Delhi
Cape Town • Madrid • Mexico City • Amsterdam • Munich • Paris • Milan

Pearson Education Limited

Edinburgh Gate
Harlow
Essex CM20 2JE
England

and Associated Companies throughout the world

Visit us on the World Wide Web at:
www.pearsoned.co.uk

First published under the Longman Group Limited imprint 1996
Second edition published under the Addison Wesley Longman imprint 1999
Third edition published 2002
Fourth edition published 2005
Fifth edition published 2008
Sixth edition published 2011

ISBN: 978-0-273-74098-8

British Library Cataloguing-in-Publication Data
A catalogue record for this book is available from the British Library

Library of Congress Cataloging-in-Publication Data
Foot, Margaret.
 Introducing human resource management / Margaret Foot,
Caroline Hook.—6th ed.
  p. cm.
 ISBN 978-0-273-74098-8 (pbk)
 1. Personnel management. 2. Employee rights. I. Hook, Caroline, 1946– II. Title.
  HF5549.F5875 2011
  658.3—dc22
                                2011002659

10 9 8 7 6 5 4 3 2
14 13 12

Typeset in 9.5/13 Giovanni by 73
Printed and bound by Rotolito Lombarda, Italy

Brief contents

Contents

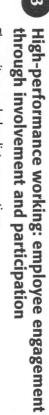

Contents

Supporting resources

Visit **www.pearsoned.co.uk/foothook** to find valuable online resources

Companion Website for students

- A Variety of tests for every chapter, including multiple-choice, fill in the blank and true false questions.
- Crossword and word puzzles to help test your understanding.
- Answers are provided to help you check your understanding.

For instructors

- Complete, downloadable Instructor's Manual
- PowerPoint slides that can be downloaded and used for presentations

Also: The Companion Website provides the following features:

- Search tool to help locate specific items of content
- E-mail results and profile tools to send results of quizzes to instructors
- Online help and support to assist with website usage and troubleshooting

For more information please contact your local Pearson Education sales representative or visit **www.pearsoned.co.uk/foothook**

Quick guide to employment legislation and related documents

Preface

Managing people is an important part of all managers' jobs whether they are line managers or HR specialists. Successful management and leadership make a huge difference to the performance of teams and to the achievement of strategic objectives. We have written this book primarily as an introductory text for students who are working towards management positions and who have started their career strategy by studying for a degree such as a BA in HRM, Business Studies or Business Management. It is also suitable for students on a Higher National Diploma or a foundation degree programme in Management or Business Studies. Students on the Chartered Institute of Personnel and Development's professional courses will also find this text useful, especially for the Certificate in HR Practice. The textbook has also proven its worth in the workplace. Students on business placements and graduates in their first jobs have reported back to us that they turn to the book for a quick and accessible review of a variety of people management concepts.

The content represents an introduction to the philosophical and legal framework of people management strategies aimed at achieving a high-performance workplace. The book further examines the basic operational areas and good practice associated with HRM. Chapter 1 provides an overview of current issues in the field of HR, which are taken up in more detail in the rest of the book. Chapters 2–5 review aspects of strategy and the philosophy and legal underpinnings of people management, including an exploration of employment relations issues such as the psychological contract and employee engagement. Together with in-depth coverage of diversity and equality, the discussion of these issues provides a background to the areas dealt with in Chapters 6–11. Here we focus on the functional areas that, if executed well, can add value for both employers and employees. We examine strategic and good practice issues in recruitment, selection, performance management, learning and talent development, reward systems, and health, safety and wellbeing. The final two chapters consider how to deal with situations where problems develop in the employer–employee relationship with an examination of discipline, grievance, dismissal, redundancy and outplacement. This new, sixth edition also offers a regular review of cross-cultural or international aspects of HRM.

The book is divided into 13 chapters to provide a topic each week for a modular course, but if your tutor wishes to involve you in more skills development work, or to go into these areas in more detail, the subject matter in the chapters may be spread over two terms. Each chapter starts with a list of objectives. These are important as they list the concepts that you should know or the skills you should be able to apply by the time you have finished the chapter. When you have finished the chapter, look back at the objectives and ensure that you have achieved them.

We intend that you should become actively involved in your own learning as you progress through the book, and to this end, as well as the list of learning objectives, there are activities for you to undertake and opportunities to pause and think about issues raised in each chapter. We recommend that you have a pen and paper beside you as you read the book, so that you can complete the activities. Reflection is important, so resist any temptation to skip these exercises.

Discussion about specific points raised in the activities is often an integral part of the text, but we have also occasionally referred you to the companion website for our thoughts on these issues. This should encourage you to think things through on your own first, and using the website should provide some variety in your approaches to learning. There are short-answer or multiple-choice questions at the end of each chapter so that you can check your own understanding and go back, if necessary, to points that you may not be clear about. There are also review questions and activities designed to help you examine key learning points in more depth. We have included an article from the *Financial Times* in each chapter to provide some real-life scenarios and information relevant to the concepts introduced there, together with suggested questions to stimulate discussion. Your tutor should have a further set of activities and case studies to help with the main learning points in each chapter, and you can gain further practice by trying out the exercises on the companion website at **www. pearsoned.co.uk/foothook**. You can also take your studies to a higher level by trying out the 'What next?' exercise at the end of each chapter.

The Fabric Brothers, Hookworth Department Stores, Spartan Insurance Company, and the Sheffley Company, which appear in activities and case studies in this text, are fictional organisations. The scenarios are based on real-life situations, but none of the people or organisations named in them actually exists. Details have been drawn together from a number of events to create totally fictional, although realistic, situations. Real organisations are, however, mentioned in the text, particularly where they serve as examples of good practice, and the *Financial Times* articles obviously describe real-life people, events and organisations.

Margaret Foot and Caroline Hook
March 2011

Acknowledgements

The authors wish to acknowledge the help and support they have received from Robert Foot and Stephen Papworth.

Robert has had to go for long walks on his own while Margaret was glued to her computer. He then returned to prepare wonderful meals for which she is very grateful.

Stephen is also a whizz in the kitchen, for which Caroline is very grateful. Both authors also wish to thank Stephen for the work he has done on the book and the companion website.

Publisher's acknowledgements

We are grateful to the following for permission to reproduce copyright material:

Logos

Logo 9.2 from Yahoo! Inc. Delicious logo. Reproduced with permission of Yahoo! Inc. © 2011 Yahoo! Inc. DELICIOUS and the DELICIOUS logo are registered trademarks of Yahoo! Inc.; Logo 9.2 from Facebook

Tables

Table on pages 409–10 adapted from *Tackling Stress – The Management Standards Approach. Adapted from HSE (nd) What are the Management Standards?*, Health and Safety Executive (2005) © Crown Copyright 2011

Text

Box on page 28 from The winner Baringa Partners, *UK's Best Workplaces: Special Report*, May, pp. 8, 9 (Finn, W. 2010), Great Place to Work Institute UK; Box on page 86 from Tesco staff enjoy share windfall, *People Management*, 22 February, p. 11 (2007), This article first appeared in People Management on 22 February 2007 and can be accessed on www.peoplemanagement.co.uk/pm/articles/2007/02/tescostaffenjoysharewind-fall.htm; Box on page 88 from Are your employees in the office or volunteering today?, www.hrzone.co.uk, HRzone.co.uk, part of SiftMedia, accessed 18.01.2010; Box on page 91 from Milburn J (2010) Employees give scathing report on UK management, www.managers.org.uk, accessed 13.04.2010. With permission of Chartered Management Institute; Box on page 110 from Department for Business, Innovation

xvi

Acknowledgements

and Skills (2009) Simplification Plan 2009. Delivering a Better Business Environment, BIS. www.bis.gov.uk, accessed 02.08.2010. © Crown Copyright 2011; Box on page 119 from Potential unauthorised absence; and the reply: Unlawful deduction from wages, Any Answers, www.hrzone.co.uk, HRzone.co.uk, part of SiftMedia, accessed 01.03.2010; Box on page 324 from Rethinking learning, HR Zone (Skillsoft 2010), www.hrzone.co.uk; HRzone.co.uk, part of SiftMedia, accessed 11.08.2010; Box on page 340 from The Gangmaster's Licensing Authority, Health and Safety Executive (2007) © Crown Copyright 2011; Box on page 353 from Eliminating discrimination: systems and policy reviews, equal pay for work of equal value, Equal Opportunities Commission Hong Kong Annual Report 2001-2 (Hong Kong Equal Opportunities Commission 2003), www.eoc.org.hk//EOC/GraphicsFolder/Information-center/ Annual/default.aspx?year=2001; accessed 24.06.2004. Equal Opportunities Commission, Hong Kong; Box on page 390 from Karoshi – Death from overwork: Occupational Health Consequences of the Japanese Production Management, International Journal of Health Services (Nishiyama, K. and J. Johnson 1997), www. workhealth.org/whatsnew/lpkarosh.html; accessed 17.09.2010. Baywood Publishing Co. Inc.; Box on page 392 from 2010 Myths, Health and Safety Executive www. hse.gov.uk; accessed 7.9.2010. © Crown copyright 2011; Box on page 409 from How to tackle work-related stress (Health and Safety Executive 2009) www.hse.gov.uk; accessed 06.08.2010. © Crown copyright 2011; Box on page 411 from Statistics: Stress-related and Psychological Disorders (Health and Safety Executive 2009) www.hse.gov.uk, accessed 17.09.2010. © Crown Copyright 2011; Box on page 415 from Dangerous liaisons, People Management, pp. 26–7 (Hammond, D. 2001). This article first appeared in People Management on 30 May 2001; Box on pages 451–2 from Recruitment: Social networking and workplace discipline, Financial Times, 08/11/2007 (Richard Donkin), Reproduced with permission; Box on page 458 from HR Zone online (2010) Lessons to be learned from Facebook sacking, www.hrzone.co.uk/topic/managing-people/lessons-be-learned-facebook-sacking 101835, HRzone.co.uk, part of SiftMedia, 25.03.2010; accessed 4.4.2010; Boxs on page 461, page 463 from Annual Report and Accounts 2008–2009, Advisory, Conciliation and Arbitration Service (2009). Crown Copyright is reproduced with permission under the terms of the Click-Use Licence.

The Financial Times

Box on pages 32–34 from A good name is beyond price, Financial Times, 07/06/2010 (Sarah Murray), Reproduced with permission; Box on pages 65–66 from Companies jostle to hire in Australian rebound, Financial Times, 31/03/2010 (Peter Smith), http://ft.com/cms/s/0/b5e49e10-3c5d-11df-b316-00144feabdc0.html; reproduced with permission; Box on pages 94–96 from Share the power, FT.com, 22 March (Stefan Stern 2010), Reproduced with permission, © The Financial Times Ltd.; Box on pages 128–130 from A different way of working: By Alison Maitland, http://www.ft.com/cms/s/0/0672069a-3549-11df-9cfb-00144feabdc0,s01=1.html, FT.com, 22 March 2010; reproduced with permission, © The Financial Times Ltd.; Box on pages 155–156 from Ethnic diversity: 'New Canadians' expand markets. By Christopher Mason, http:www.ft.com/cms/s/0/7581dc14-b6bd-11de-8a28-00144feab49a.html, FT.com, 13 October 2009. Reproduced with permission, © The Financial Times Ltd.; Box on pages 241–2 from how can you tell the best job candidate is not the best liar?, http://www.ft.com/cms/s/0/50e1a000-8c57-11de-b14f-00144feabdc0.html, © The Financial Times Ltd; Box on pages 372–3 from Bonuses may be the back door to a widening pay gap, *Financial Times*, 24/05/2010 (Tony Jackson), Reproduced with permission; Box on pages 419-20 from Workforce health on a par with profits and dividends, *Financial Times*, 19/02/2010 (Paul Betts), Copyright The Financial Times Limited (FT.com) Reproduced with permission; Box on pages 483–4 from the safe way to sack a baby boomer, *Financial Times* (Patti Waldmeir), Copyright The Financial Times Limited 2010.

In some instances we have been unable to trace the owners of copyright material, and we would appreciate any information that would enable us to do so.

Guided tour

Activities get you to apply what you're reading about to the real world.

Chapter objectives summarise what you will be able to do by the end of the chapter.

Case studies help you think about what you would do in certain scenarios and also come with a set of questions to help test your understanding of the case.

Did you know? and **Pause for thought** boxes provide a thought-provoking fact or question to keep you interested and keep you thinking.

Review questions reinforce what you have learnt in the chapter and

Self-check questions let you test your understanding. Answers are provided at the back of the book.

The **HR in the news** feature contains articles from the *Financial Times* and promotes discussion of real examples of HR in practice. These also come with a set of questions to help you critically evaluate the article.

What next? Features encourage you to find out more about a topic.

Comprehensive **References** and annotated **Further Study** boxes point you in the direction of wider reading.

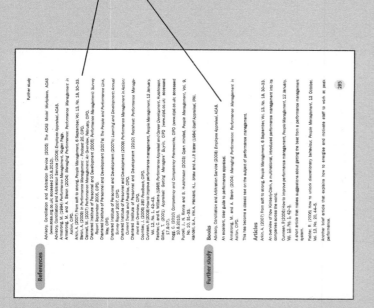

A variety of resources such as true or false questions, **Match the phrase** questions and **Crossword puzzles** can be found on the Companion Website at **www.pearsoned.co.uk/foothook**

CHAPTER 1

Introducing human resource management

Objectives

By the end of this chapter you will be able to:

- define what is meant by the term 'human resource management'
- understand the roles of line managers and human resource managers in managing people
- outline the range of activities with which practitioners of human resource management are likely to be involved
- demonstrate how human resource management can make a difference by adding value to an organisation
- outline some of the current issues facing HR managers.

HRM? What's it all about?

This book is designed as an introductory text for students studying human resource management (HRM) either with a view to becoming HR specialists themselves, or for those who are starting or hoping to start a career in management. As you will discover, people management forms a large part of every manager's job, whether they work in a large multinational organisation, a not for profit organisation or a small charity. Organisations also increasingly aim for all employees to be motivated and involved, so an understanding of the subject is important for everyone.

As stated in the preface, we intend that you should become actively involved in your own learning as you progress through the book. Even though you are just beginning this subject, you may already have ideas about some of the topics that you are about to study and you may even have a general idea of the role and functions of the human resource management or personnel department in an organisation. Your ideas may not all be right but, after all, that is why you are studying the subject. Many students talk of studying HRM because they would 'like to work with people,' and they seem to think of human resource management as a cosy job that involves being nice to people at all times. While this view is not entirely accurate, it is certainly a career which provides a wealth of variety and great deal of job satisfaction. It is also a career which is constantly changing as the role evolves in response to changing social, political, economic and demographic issues and we shall examine some of the ways the profession is developing in response to these later in this chapter.

According to the Chartered Institute of Personnel and Development (2005) when HR managers were asked whether they would choose a career in HR if they had the opportunity to start again, 'the vast majority (81%) said "yes". The reasons people give for enjoying their HR careers related to variety, challenge and interest, and the view that HR is at the heart of the business and can make a difference.'

We shall discuss in this book the variety of roles and tasks that modern HR professionals cover but it is important to note that it is not just the HR professionals who work in these areas: line managers are also involved. Therefore, this book is also written as an introduction to HRM for them.

Let us start with an activity to help you focus on your ideas about human resource management. You can compare your answers with the answer that we give at the end of the chapter. Later in the chapter we shall also look at what researchers and HR practitioners say HR is about.

ACTIVITY 1.1

What do you think are the main areas in which a human resource manager is likely to be involved? Make a list of these areas. For each of the areas on the list, indicate the type of involvement of the human resource practitioner and whether other managers are also likely to have a role in handling this activity (use Table 1.1). We have completed the first row of Table 1.1 to start you off. Our suggestions for this Activity are given at the end of the chapter in Table 1.3.

Table 1.1 The main activities of human resource practitioners

Main areas of activity of human resource management specialist	Type of involvement of the human resource management specialists	Type of involvement of line manager
Recruitment and selection	Design of policies and procedure for fair recruitment and selection in order to contribute to the fulfilment of the organisation's corporate strategy. Carry out interviews or monitor and give advice on interview technique or on terms and conditions of employment.	Carry out interviews.
Learning and talent development.		

The main activities of human resource management

The areas that we would list are as follows:

- recruitment and selection
- learning and talent development
- human resource planning
- provision of contracts
- provision of fair treatment
- provision of equal opportunities
- managing diversity
- motivating workers to achieve improved performance
- employee counselling
- talent management
- employee wellbeing
- payment and reward of employees
- health and safety
- disciplining individuals
- dealing with grievances
- dismissal
- redundancy
- negotiation
- encouraging involvement and engagement
- adding value
- ethics and corporate responsibility
- knowledge management
- change management
- managing cross-cultural issues or international HRM.

You may have included some slightly different activities since human resource managers, as you can see from this list, do become involved in a wide range of issues and it is difficult to predict the exact nature of the job in any particular enterprise. We have selected the main topics with which we feel most human resource managers are likely to be involved, but this will vary from organisation to organisation and may also depend on the way the function itself is organised. The type of involvement of the HR specialists will also vary. Some HR specialists operating at a high level in the organisation will be concerned with the provision of clear strategic direction for HR and linking this to the strategic objectives of the organisation. Others will be concerned to provide specialist advice, while still others will focus on the provision of administration and support. All will be concerned in some way to ensure that HRM activities add value by helping the organisation achieve its strategic objectives. They will focus on ensuring that the overall HR policies and procedures support the strategic objectives and that there is consistency in approach and implementation across the organisation.

However, for each activity it is likely that other managers will also be involved to some extent. Line managers will be concerned with the actual implementation of the policies and procedures in so far as they affect their team, whereas the HR specialists will also be involved in the bigger picture, although the extent of the differences in role will vary between organisations.

Pause for thought 1.1

A line manager is a person who has direct responsibility for employees and their work. Since line managers seem to have such a large part to play in people management, to what extent do you think they need human resource managers at all?

The fact that aspects of managing the human resource are an element of every manager's or supervisor's job is an important point for you to keep in mind. Many of you will find that your career may take you from line management to human resource management and then back to line management, or vice versa. In a survey of HR managers carried out by the CIPD (2005) 'only about a quarter (26%) of respondents started out in HR' and at some point in their careers 'eighty-three percent of respondents have worked outside HR, the most frequently cited functions being sales, marketing and retail'.

Obviously, we consider that line managers do need to call on the services and expertise of human resource specialists. If you look at our discussion of Activity 1.1 in Table 1.3 at the end of this chapter, you will see that although a great deal of work can be devolved to line managers, there is also a role for a person skilled in human resource management to establish policies, standards and procedures, to integrate these with the organisation's objectives to ensure that they contribute to the organisation's strategic objectives, to provide expert advice and consistency, and to coordinate and provide training and development. Human resource practitioners will also often be involved in initiating company-wide programmes such as promoting employee engagement, communication and consultation. The exact nature of their involvement will vary from one organisation to another, as will the range of activities they cover. The human resource department may carry out some administrative work and maintain central records on people and may also provide advice and expertise for other managers to draw on. In some organisations the human resource department may carry out all the activities listed above, while in others many or most of these functions may be an important part of the jobs of other managers. Increasingly more and more aspects of the HR function are being carried out by line managers and you will find as you work through the book that we emphasise the roles of line managers in HR activities.

Even among human resource managers there will be differences in the scope of their job, so it is also important to consider the ways in which HR jobs are organised as specialist or generalist roles. Does an organisation employ its own HR practitioners inhouse, or is the HR department outsourced and provided by a form of shared services for other divisions of the same organisation or with other organisations? Are the individuals themselves consultants or business partners or do they have some other job title such as employee champion? Is their role dealing with issues just in one country or is it a multinational? We shall deal with some of these issues about the variety of roles in HRM and the ways in which HRM can be organised later in this chapter.

Cross-cultural issues will provide another dimension to be considered in relation to each of these tasks. Multinational organisations have to consider both expatriates and host-country nationals employed by them around the world as well as their home-country-based employees. Recently several of our students who have graduated from the BA Human Resource Management degree at the University of

Huddersfield have taken up first jobs in HR which have involved them working at least for some of their time in other countries and this has meant that they needed an awareness of cultural issues in human resource management quite early in their careers. The expansion of the European Union with the entry of several Eastern European countries such as Poland has also meant an increase in workers from these countries coming to the UK to seek employment, and while in the current economic climate this trend my not be so pronounced it is still important, so an awareness of cross-cultural issues is also of value to HR managers, even if they work exclusively in the UK.

Given the changes to the way organisations are operating in terms of their recruitment, you may find yourself working with migrant workers in this country, recruiting internationally or working in another country yourself in an international organisation. We shall therefore consider later in this chapter some of the cross-cultural or international issues in HRM and in some later chapters we shall also touch briefly on cross-cultural or global dimensions.

The background to human resource management

The role of HR manager has changed in response to social, economic and political conditions and to advances in technology and it is still developing dynamically. The relative importance of many of the activities has changed as external circumstances have affected the needs of organisations and it is still a dynamic area where the roles and ways of organising the HR function continue to change and develop.

It may help you to understand the diversity of roles that are sometimes adopted by human resource managers if we look briefly at the development of the profession. A variety of names have been used to describe those who specialise in managing people. In this book we have chosen to use the terms *human resource manager* or *people manager* as these are increasingly the main terms used but you will also find other terms such as *personnel manager* or *employee champion* used and we shall discuss some of these other job titles later in this chapter. However, while it is important to have some idea of the background of HRM it is of even greater importance to examine current roles and issues and to consider possible developments in HR of the future, in the world in which most of you will find yourselves working. We shall discuss recent and possible future developments in more detail later in this chapter.

Industrial welfare

The earliest activity with which the HR practitioner was involved was welfare work. During the nineteenth century the conditions of work for men, women and children in the factories were generally appalling compared to today's accepted standards. There were some enlightened employers who wanted to try to improve working conditions for their employees and adopted schemes to improve the lot of their workforce as part of their company policy. Among these were several Quaker organisations, and it is generally held that the first personnel officer, referred to at that time as an industrial welfare officer, was Miss Mary Wood who was appointed by

Rowntree's in York in 1896. She was appointed to be a type of social worker for the factory, with responsibility for ensuring the wellbeing of women and children in the workforce and watching over their health and behaviour.

Although Mary's first day at work over 100 years ago is very different from the type of work that we associate with human resource managers of today, welfare and the wellbeing of the workforce is still an area in which many HR practitioners will be involved. High levels of absenteeism are expensive, so modern organisations which are proactive in encouraging a healthy workforce have also shown benefits in reduced levels of absence with consequent saving for the organisation.

Recruitment and selection

The early industrial welfare workers met with great success, and Mary Wood and others were soon asked to start recruiting girls, which was the beginning of the development of the role of recruitment and selection. (Remember this was well before equal opportunities had been thought of!) During the First World War there was rapid development in many fields of personnel management, largely as a result of government initiatives to encourage the best possible use of people, and also because of legislation.

Acquisition of other people management activities

In 1921 the National Institute of Industrial Psychologists was established, and its members published results of studies on selection tests, interviewing techniques and training methods so providing an academic rationale for some aspects of people management.

During the Second World War the work spread from welfare, recruitment and selection to training, improving morale and motivation, discipline, health and safety, joint consultation and often wages policies. This expansion of duties required the establishment of an adequate personnel department with trained staff.

Employee relations

Joint consultation between management and workforce spread during the Second World War, and personnel departments became responsible for its organisation and administration. There was an increased emphasis on health and safety and a need for specialists to deal with employee relations, so that gradually the personnel manager became the usual spokesperson for the organisation in discussion with trade unions and shop stewards. This aspect of their role gained further impetus in the 1970s, where in many organisations the personnel manager had executive authority to negotiate deals about pay or other collective issues.

● Legislation

During the 1970s the growth in the amount of employment legislation resulted in the personnel function often adopting the role of specialist adviser, ensuring that managers did not fall foul of the law and that cases did not end up at industrial tribunals, as they were then called.

● Flexibility and diversity

In the 1990s there was a major trend for employers to seek increasingly flexible arrangements in the hours worked by employees, with a growth in the number of employees who worked part time or on temporary contracts, and an increase in distance working and working from home. This trend has continued in the early years of the twenty-first century. The workforce and patterns of work are becoming increasingly diverse and this presents its own challenges to HR managers.

The development of the human resource management approach

The concept of human resource management first appeared in the 1980s and the use of the term grew in the 1990s. Initially, writers in the field focused on trying to distinguish between personnel management and HRM, but according to Boxall and Purcell (2008) HRM has, in spite of the lack of clarity over definition, become the most popular term to refer to the activities of managers in relation to people management.

The major characteristics of the HRM approach to people management have been identified as follows:

- The importance of adopting a strategic approach is emphasised.
- Line managers play a predominant role.
- Organisational policies must be integrated and cohesive in order to better project and support the central organisational values and objectives. Along with this, communication plays a vital role.
- An underlying philosophy is adopted that emphasises the achievement of competitive advantage through the efforts of people. This can variously be interpreted into actions that are known as hard HRM or those that are known as soft HRM (see page 10).
- A unitarist rather than a pluralist approach prevails in the relationship between managers and employees.
- All people who work in an organisation are important whether they are part-time or full-time employees or not employees of that organisation at all. In this way agency staff and consultants, or volunteers in a charity, are all perceived to be important to the organisation.

● Focus on strategy

Throughout the 1980s and 1990s business leaders came to accept more and more that competitive advantage could be achieved only through the efforts and creativity of the people employed by them. In companies that follow through with the logical conclusions to this statement rather than simply paying lip service to the rhetoric, developing strategies for their human resources will inevitably play a prominent role when they are formulating the corporate strategy, and senior managers will want to call on the expertise of a specialist to get the best input possible. Thus strategic activity becomes a major focus for specialists in HRM, but probably only those acting at the higher levels will be involved in board-level meetings where strategic alternatives are discussed. It should also be noted that in order to have effective input into the corporate strategy, the HRM specialist will require a high level of business acumen in addition to knowledge of people strategies and programmes. It is this recognition that people are a resource to be managed as efficiently and effectively as any other resource that has led to the term human resource management.

Role of the line manager

We have defined strategic involvement as being a key characteristic of HRM and noted that this means a focus on strategic activity for high level HRM practitioners. However, the HRM approach recognises the centrality of the human resource for all business activities, and therefore consideration of the people management aspects would be expected in the strategic planning input from managers in all business functions (e.g. production, marketing, etc.). Likewise, the importance of active management of people matters becomes more clearly an integral part of every line manager's job. Line managers must combine their commitment to the technical aspects of task completion with attention to people aspects and recognise the symbiotic nature of these two elements of the managerial role.

This means that some activities that might traditionally have been undertaken by specialist personnel management staff are now undertaken by line managers. Increased line involvement in training and recruitment and performance management can be cited as areas where this has occurred. There is still, however, a substantial role for human resource specialists, as you discovered when you completed Activity 1.1, in designing strategic HR solutions, in leading, advising and disseminating information about evolving people management programmes to line managers, in ensuring consistency in the treatment of employees company-wide and, in general, in being supportive partners to managers in their efforts to achieve company goals.

The pivotal role of the line manager is one of the most often cited characteristics of human resource management but line managers do not always see things this way. Finding ways of educating and encouraging line managers to take responsibility for the people management aspects of their job is in many organisations still one of the key challenges that face HR specialists though in other organisations it is already seen as the norm. According to the CIPD (2010b) line managers are already making a difference and are often involved and contributing in positive ways to training and coaching, performance management, employee appraisal, and are also vital to ensure that workers know that their contribution is recognised by the organisation.

Integrated policies and effective communication

Proponents of HRM emphasise that policies across the whole HR spectrum (recruitment, selection, reward, employee relations) must be fully integrated and consistent

The development of the human resource management approach

with the organisation's culture. This is logically consistent with the strategic, forward planning nature of HRM. Effective communications are a pivotal aspect of this as they constitute a means of conveying senior management's values and commitment to their goals (Legge 1995, p. 75). It is also an important aspect of knowledge management.

● Competitive advantage through people

The balanced scorecard

At this point it is appropriate to introduce the concept of the balanced scorecard (BSC). This concept emanates from work done on business strategy by Kaplan and Norton (1992, 1996) in the Harvard Business School which emphasises the role of the human resource in the achievement of business strategy. The BSC has become a well-established technique used extensively not only in the USA, but also worldwide, including some UK companies, for instance Tesco (see Industrial Relations Services 2000).

The essential idea behind the balanced scorecard is the notion that businesses must measure the success of their plans in order to validate their actions, identify and evaluate their successes, and build on them for the future. Traditionally businesses have focused mainly if not exclusively on financial results to evaluate the success of their strategy, but Kaplan and Norton propose that measuring success in only one area is inadequate for a number of reasons. One argument is that financial results are always a retrospective measure of past success and do not necessarily indicate that similar actions in the future will meet with similar achievements. Also, although financial gains may be the ultimate desired outcome, it is imperative to know exactly what factors contributed to this outcome and in what way they contributed.

A more satisfactory approach to formulating strategic initiatives, and subsequently evaluating their success, is to take a more balanced approach, which is represented by the balanced scorecard. The scorecard is a flexible tool, which can be adapted according to the nature of the business adopting it, but the original model proposes four elements that should be evaluated in order to achieve a balanced overview of what contributes to a company's success:

● financial results
● customer relations
● internal processes
● learning and development.

The examination of financial results is, of course, still a necessary part of evaluating business success but, according to Kaplan and Norton, this focus needs to be balanced out by taking the other criteria into consideration. Each of the three other criteria contributes to financial success, and purposively focusing on them helps to shift managerial awareness to the role each plays. Typically, the formulation of a corporate strategy would start with a goal to increase shareholder value, and a strategy that focuses on the customer's perspective is most likely to succeed in achieving this aim (Kaplan and Norton, 2000). A company must then examine its internal processes and adapt them where necessary. This in turn goes hand in hand with the development of the human resource that will deliver the strategy. An organisation's capacity for learning and development is regarded as being one of the key factors contributing to success in today's competitive environment.

Just as the balanced scorecard is used to formulate the overall corporate strategy and measure its success, it can also be used to plan for the component parts and measure their contribution to the achievement of company strategy. Thus, while the examination of internal processes must be carried out throughout the organisation and constitutes one component of the balanced scorecard used to measure the whole company's performance, the BSC can also be used to guide and evaluate each individual's performance. That is, the development of individuals becomes explicitly tied in to the key issues addressed in the BSC at corporate strategy level, and in appraising each individual, the question is asked to what extent the individual contributed to the financial success of the company, to customer relations, to the improvement of internal processes, and to learning and growth. The Halifax is one company in the UK that has used a balanced scorecard to evaluate its employees' performance.

The adoption of the balanced scorecard by Tesco also served to strengthen and re-define the role of the stores' personnel managers. The scorecard highlighted the importance of all employee contribution to the success of the company, and therefore the importance of people management issues. To complement this, personnel managers in Tesco stores are also expected to be fully involved in the day-to-day running of the stores, thus enhancing their business awareness and their credibility (IRS, 2000).

Hard and soft HRM

The basic requirement of HRM to serve the corporate strategy and achieve corporate aims by means of a high-performance workforce can be read in two ways:

● The primacy of business needs means that human resources will be acquired, deployed and dispensed with as corporate plans demand. Little regard is paid to the needs of those human resources and the emphasis is on quantitative aspects. This is known as hard HRM.

● In order to gain a competitive advantage through the workforce, regardless of whether they are full- or part-time, temporary or contract staff, all potential must be nurtured and developed, and programmes that pay due notice to knowledge about the behavioural aspects of people at work are developed. This is characterised as soft HRM.

The emphasis in our text lies mainly with soft HRM, but as Legge (1995, pp. 66–67) argues, the two are not mutually exclusive, and you will detect elements of hard HRM in the discussion of human resource planning.

Unitarist and pluralist approaches to management–employee relations

Human resource management is identified as being a unitarist rather than a pluralist approach (Legge, 1995, pp. 72–73). Briefly, the unitarist stance is characterised as a senior management assumption that all members of the organisation are dedicated to the achievement of a common goal with no conflict from personal interests. Pluralism, on the other hand, recognises that within a large group of people there are inevitably a variety of interests and that these have to be managed. The adoption of one or other of these two philosophies obviously has a major impact on the way that managers treat the workforce.

We explore the concepts of unitarism and pluralism in greater depth in Chapter 3 where we come to the conclusion from observing current rhetoric that we may now be witnessing a merging of the two stances in the development of the partnership theme. This promotes the idea that managers and employees can pursue common goals while still recognising that diverging interests exist. The common purpose of the unitarists is pursued in a pluralist framework.

We refer throughout the text to the key characteristics described here and their links with specific activities. In particular, we emphasise the role of the line manager in all of the activities we discuss, but in addition we focus on the theme of strategy in Chapter 2 where we examine the human resource planning activity, and the topics of employee involvement/engagement and communication as a part of high-performance working in Chapter 3.

Current issues in HRM

The political and economic environment

The state of the national and global economy has a direct impact on all types of organisation and will inevitably influence their people practices and strategies. In the simplest of terms, consumer spending power dictates what goods and services need to be produced, which has an impact on employers' employment decisions and intentions. The CIPD (2009b) emphasise the need for HR practitioners to understand the economy and its impact on the labour market. The economy is affected by the interplay of a wide variety of factors including rates of unemployment, the demand for goods and services as reflected by consumer decisions on spending and saving, the costs of importing and exporting goods, and the policies of the political party in power on issues such as inflation. The ability of the Government to influence employment decisions and consumer spending as strategies to improve the economic outlook has been a matter of debate in recent years.

Pause for thought 1.2 Statistics on factors such as consumer spending choices and employment rates are also open to interpretation, and therefore cannot be taken as direct indicators of the health of the economy. Take unemployment rates as an example! Lower levels of unemployment would normally indicate a healthier economy. But are the figures artificially lowered because numbers of people who would normally be counted as available for work but unemployed have opted for further study instead and are therefore not counted as unemployed?

The global economy became a major focus of everyday news reports and financial analysis in 2008 and the following years. The national economy of many countries in the developed world was affected by the so-called credit crunch. Following a period of growth that had persisted for a number of years, many of these countries, including the UK, went into a recession in 2008. Reporting in the final quarter of 2009 and the first half of 2010 has circled around the possibility of renewed economic growth, with the main questions being how strong the indicators of growth are, and how strong the recovery will be if and when it materialises. Improvements in employment rates are cited as a positive indicator, but some commentators sound a note of caution, pointing out, for example, that public authorities are expected to reduce their numbers of employees during 2011.

The outcomes associated with an improved economy cannot be taken for granted. A better economy would normally go hand-in-hand with heightened recruitment intentions. The CIPD (2010c) indicates, however, that the expected upturn in 2010 does not translate into expectations of increased recruitment. This ties in with the view expressed in *The Economist* (2009) that the economy is expected to return to growth, but at a lower level and rate than it had achieved prior to the recession. *The Economist* designates this as a 'new normal' which the economy is expected to reflect.

There is also a public/private sector difference whereby most reductions in staffing are expected in the public sector while the private sector predicts some increases in recruitment.

There are many mixed messages in the analyses of the current and expected economic situation, so this is a difficult but crucial area for employers to factor in to their decision-making. Business leaders who think strategically must also strive to focus on future needs as well as the demands of current circumstances. This means, for example, that while recessionary effects may require the contraction of business and reduction in the numbers of employees in the immediate term, the organisation also has to be ready for potential future growth in the event of a recovery, and be in a position to seize the opportunities this may bring. This is indeed a difficult balancing act.

As reported by Faccini and Hackworth (2010), it has been a typical reaction in previous recessions for employers to reduce their numbers of employees through redundancies. In the crisis of 2008 and the following years, however, many adopted an alternative approach of wages cost control by reducing the number of hours employees worked and adopting a policy of wage restraint. One of the problems that arise from recessions is that the skills needed to deal with demand in an upturn are lacking due to rising levels of unemployment. Keeping people at work during the recessionary period certainly helps to retain the skills needed for the return to growth.

In terms of human resource management, it has also been affirmed that good practice continues to be important during a downturn since survival becomes crucial and will depend to a great extent upon the efforts of the workforce. The need for a high level of performance and the concomitant quality do not diminish just because the quantity of output diminishes. This ongoing need for quality during a recession together with the potential future need for skills at recovery confirm the crucial role played by HR practices which attract, retain and engage high-quality workers.

We have established in this section the central role that the economy plays in business decision-making and performance, and the need for managers, including people managers, to be aware of economic circumstances and factor their impact into their decision-making. HR appears to have been largely successful in adapting to the changing economic circumstances and in a 2010 IRS survey it was found that overall HR managers felt HR had increased its influence during this period due in part to the fact that their expertise has been essential for restructuring organisations in positive ways and, where redundancies had been necessary, by handling those in as effective and positive ways as possible (Murphy, 2010).

ACTIVITY 1.2

1 Review the cited article by Faccini and Hackworth (2010). The authors give some detail on possible contributing factors to employer decisions to retain employees during the 2008–2009 recession rather than make them redundant. Summarise the arguments presented by Faccini and Hackworth.

2 Review a number of news sources to form a picture of the current UK economy. How is the economy being described? Is it experiencing growth? Is this growth weak or strong? What factors are addressed to explain the state of the economy?

3 What is the impact of the economy on the current labour market and labour market predictions?

● Social and demographic trends

Though understandably the economic situation has taken precedence recently there are other social and demographic factors that also have an effect on the HR department and the HR techniques it uses. Most western countries are experiencing falling birth rates which combined with improvements in health and medical advances results in an ageing workforce. The age at which individuals will be able to access their pensions in the UK is due to increase between 2010 and 2020 so that men and women's state pension age will equalise at 65 by November 2018. The previous Labour government wanted to increase the state pension age further by stages and set this out in the Pensions Act 2007 so that by 2046 the state pension age would rise to 68. However, the Coalition government feels that this should happen even sooner and recent legislation has already abolished the default retirement age and made it illegal to dismiss workers just because they reach a certain age. The pension age for everyone increases to 66 on 6 April 2020. According to Churchard (2010) the Pensions Policy Institute has indicated that the state pension age would need to rise even further to 72 by 2030 to maintain the balance between the numbers of retirees and those still working. According to the Office for National Statistics (2009) by 2033 the working population aged 40 or over will outnumber the under 40 working population by 1.4 million.

There are now several different generations of workers who, it is claimed, have different attitudes to work and who will consequently be motivated by different things. Writers have used various terms to describe these groups. The following are the terms used by Allen (2010):

● *Baby boomers* who are those who were born after 1946, or according to some definitions after 1948. This group currently amounts to 30% of employees and it is claimed that they are loyal and long-serving.

● *Generation X* consists of those born between 1964 and 1978 and amounts to 32% of the workforce. They are supposed to be used to uncertainty as they moved into the workforce at the worst time for jobs since the Depression. It is claimed that they are very focused on achieving results.

● *Generation Y* were born between 1979 and 1991 and amounts to 27% of the UK workforce. According to Allen (2010) this is the most technologically aware generation and they are highly desirable to employers. Penna and CIPD (2008) also found this generation to be more technologically aware and more ethnically diverse than previous generations and they are also multi-taskers who like to work collaboratively. They also need rapid two-way communication, fairness and flexibility and are concerned about the organisation having a meaningful policy for corporate and social responsibility.

However, while Generation Y should be desirable to employers, they are also the group which has suffered most from the recent recession which impacted disproportionately on employment for the under 25s. While it is understandable that those in this generation, who have experienced periods of unemployment or have been unable to find a job at all, are likely to be highly dissatisfied it also appears that those who are working are a particularly unhappy group who experience low levels of job satisfaction (CIPD, 2010d). This dissatisfaction appears to be the result of contributing factors: this generation has not experienced economic problems before as they grew up in times of relative affluence; they are also unhappy with the provision of opportunities to learn new skills and lack of progress at work, but a stagnant job market also limited opportunities for progression (CIPD, 2010d).

While these are all stereotypes of different generations of workers if there is any truth at all in them it does mean that HR and managers will need to be very flexible in their approaches if they are to lead, motivate and retain these groups and they will need to adapt their HR processes accordingly. In the rest of the text we shall briefly address the impact of a changing political and economic, and social and demographic climate on the specific aspects of HRM as they occur in each chapter.

Employee retention

Even with the difficult economic circumstances discussed here some 69% of employers were still experiencing problems with the retention of their employees, with managers and professionals being the most difficult to retain (CIPD, 2010a). Organisations keen to keep their staff so that they could benefit from their skills and expertise as the economy improved frequently took action to boost retention of staff. In the CIPD survey (2010a) the most frequently cited retention strategies included increasing opportunities for learning and development (47%), making improvements to the organisation's induction programme (45%), increasing pay (42%) and making improvements to the selection process (42%). Moreover, 72% of the participants in the survey felt that improving the HR skills of line managers was also an effective retention technique but there was a mismatch between what they said and did, with only 39% of the sample actually doing this.

Clearly there needs to be a mixture of techniques used if the stereotypes of the different generations are to be believed with Generation Y in particular needing fast access to information technology and good Corporate Social Responsibility (CSR) if they are to be motivated and encouraged to stay working for an organisation while for older workers more flexible approaches to work are needed.

Information technology

If you glance through any journal relating to human resource management nowadays, you will find countless advertisements relating to the various ways that information technology (IT) can assist those in the HR department to do their jobs. These include: systems for e-recruitment, online shortlisting of applicants, online performance management and appraisals, e-learning, online psychometric testing, as well as IT systems to help with payroll, employment data, recruitment administration, references and pre-employment checks. There are also some large organisations which use HR shared service centres where they bring many of the HR services together and use technology such as email, a company intranet or telephones to provide HR information in order to deal with HR queries and provide expert advice for people working at various sites, sometimes in different countries.

More recently developments with web 2.0 have meant more involvement is possible from employees and this too is having an effect in some organisations on approaches to recruitment and selection, and learning and talent development, with organisations using Facebook or second life as a part of their HR approach. As well as being a means for controlling or reducing costs through using IT there is also the potential to get better quality information, better decision-making and with the latest developments, increased involvement and engagement of the workforce which may also prove attractive to Generation Y workers.

Pause for thought 1.3

How do you think the increased use of information technology will affect the job of the HR manager and line manager? Will it enable them to get rid of the routine jobs by delegating them to IT systems or by outsourcing them to specialist organisations, or will it mean that more people end up in routine jobs working with computers? What effect will blogs or social networking sites have?

The increasing use of information technology is already having all of these effects, at least to some extent. For many HR managers, using IT for routine tasks frees them from more mundane tasks, so they have more time to think strategically. Increasing use of IT has also ensured a much greater amount of information is available on which to base decisions and to plan for the future.

Teleconferencing and teleworking mean that people no longer have to be in the same place to hold a meeting or to work in the same building. E-learning means people are often able to learn at their desks or via their smart phone. All such developments raise issues and pose different problems about the ways staff should be managed and these will be of concern to both the HR manager and line manager.

Some people will be in high value jobs, using their expertise to design these labour-saving IT systems. Others may find that, perhaps for part of their career, they are dealing with completion of basic tasks using computers; or, on the other hand, they may use their knowledge and expertise in people management to deal with HR queries from around the world, via computers or telephones in shared service centres.

● Human capital

By the early 2000s several new areas were starting to be of concern to those involved in managing people. The term 'human capital' was being discussed and, in particular, ways to measure human capital was an area of concern to some employers. The government set up a strategy group to examine the concept of human capital and created the Accounting for People Task Force to investigate it.

15

Professor Scarborough and the CIPD Human Capital Task Force (2003) defined the term 'human capital' as 'the contribution of people [their skills and knowledge] in the production of goods and services.'

An article in *People Management* (2003) by Professor Scarborough discussed the TV series *Jamie's Kitchen* and said, 'we witnessed "human capital" in action, when a group of unemployed young people were transformed on TV into top-class chefs.' Jamie Oliver tried to pass on many of his culinary, business and professional skills to a group of unemployed 16 to 24-year-olds and used a variety of methods from coaching to hectoring and pleading to achieve this. He was successful with many members of the group and created within them a desire to perform at a high level, although in the TV series it often seemed to be harder than he had imagined it would be. However, according to Scarborough 'this blending of new skills and attitudes into high performance sums up exactly what human capital can be and why it is so important to business.' In 2007 Channel 4 showed a sequel to the original programme, *Jamie's Chef*, which followed four of the initial trainees as they went on and tried to start their own businesses. Since the first programme there have been five intakes of trainees from unemployed or disadvantaged backgrounds to the restaurant *Fifteen London* and similar projects and restaurants have been established in Amsterdam, Cornwall and Melbourne, Australia (Oliver, 2010).

The concept of human capital also encourages organisations to move beyond just training people to do their jobs, although doing the job they are employed to do is of course still important. It is about encouraging organisations to make use of the whole range of abilities that people bring to the organisation and, as such, it is also linked to ideas about performance management discussed in Chapter 8 and about learning and talent development discussed in Chapter 9. Measuring human capital is an attempt to measure the difference that people make to the organisations and those facing tough economic decisions need to make these on the basis of sound information.

Added value

Another related concept that has gained in popularity in recent years is that of 'added value.' This is also concerned with making a difference and in difficult economic times this may be of even greater importance. This concept aims to show how the HRM function or other related functions make a difference to the organisation and how they can help to shape the organisation's business strategy. Once again one of the concerns is for measurement of the difference the people initiatives have made. According to Harrison (2002), in order to add value, HRM or human resource development (HRD) must 'achieve outcomes that significantly increase the organisation's capability to differentiate itself from other similar organisations, and thereby enhance its progress. It must also achieve these outcomes in ways that ensure, through time, that their value will more than offset the costs that they incurred.' So, they have to make a difference to the organisation but do so in a way that is also cost-effective.

Green (1999) had criticised HR professionals for not having sufficient awareness of the effects that new HR interventions would have on the organisation, and maintained that in order to provide added value, people professionals needed to provide three things:

- *alignment* – pointing people in the right direction
- *engagement* – developing belief and commitment to the organisation's purpose and direction

- *measurement* – providing the data that demonstrate the improved results achieved (Green, 1999).

We can also use the TV series *Jamie's Kitchen* and the later series *Jamie's Chef* as examples of added value. Jamie Oliver put his life savings into a venture to establish a top-class restaurant in London called *Fifteen*. In doing so he wanted to create a business with a very strong sense of corporate and social responsibility that would make a difference to unemployed and disadvantaged young people by giving them the opportunity to train as chefs. He added value to the trainees themselves by using, perhaps without knowing, the series of techniques which Green (1999) referred to as alignment, engagement and measurement.

Alignment

Both in *Jamie's Kitchen* and later in *Jamie's Chef*, Jamie tried to point the trainees in the right direction in several ways. These included conventional on-the-job training, off-the-job training and team-building exercises on outward-bound programmes. He also used many student-centred approaches such as coaching, mentoring, counselling and sometimes cajoling, hectoring or pleading, and he drew attention to the fact that the business aim was to create a top-class restaurant and that all the trainees needed to work effectively in order to achieve this.

Engagement

Jamie tried to develop belief in and commitment to the organisation's purpose and direction. He tried to instil in the unemployed youngsters some sense of purpose and the idea that they had responsibilities to themselves, the team and the organisation. He tried to point them in the right direction; in this case to become experts in culinary skills so the restaurant would be successful. A further aim of his efforts to engage the group was that they would work effectively together as a team to achieve the excellent standards required by what he hoped would be a top restaurant.

Measurement

For the first group of 15 trainees the measurement was partly undertaken by the TV programme itself as it provided a visual record of their developing skills. The trainees and the viewing public could clearly see the extent to which some individuals changed, but many other measures such as restaurant reviews by food critics, numbers of bookings and repeat bookings, numbers of complaints and amount of praise also helped to quantify the added value. In the later TV series some of the original trainees even went on to set up and run their own restaurants which provided a further visible indicator of the skills that had been developed and the value that had been added.

A further longer-term measure of success is that the experiment has been successfully repeated again and again and, as stated above, there have now been five intakes of trainees to the *Fifteen* restaurant in London. Jamie established the Fifteen charity and puts profits from his 2006 cookbook *Cook with Jamie* into the Foundation so that unemployed and disadvantaged youngsters can continue to receive training to become top chefs. Several of the trainees have been very successful, in spite of their initial unpromising backgrounds, and all of the restaurants have gone on to meet with great success (Oliver, 2010).

Jamie Oliver was successful in adding value to most of the young people he took into his kitchen. They developed from being unemployed youngsters who had very little sense of purpose into highly trained and skilled workers who were able to work together to achieve the level of cookery skills required by the organisation. From the original group of 15, four went on to work in top restaurants and one opened his own catering business in Australia. However, in spite of the high-profile nature of the experiment there were still some youngsters who did not become motivated by any of the techniques used and preferred to drop out, showing that it can be difficult to always add value in all circumstances and emphasing the point that HR managers have to be flexible in their approach to motivating and engaging different groups of workers.

Knowledge workers

In the UK there has been a decline in traditional manufacturing industry and a growth in areas of work such as the service sector or knowledge economy, where the workers are sometimes referred to as knowledge workers. The management guru Peter Drucker (1999) identified the growth and management of knowledge workers as being one of the key issues for the twenty-first century. According to the IRS (2006) knowledge workers will be very selective about who they want to work for and will want to establish, before joining any organisation, whether it will be suitable for them and whether their work will be valued and they, like applicants from Generation Y, will be concerned to know whether or not the organisation's ethos and values are similar to their own. The way organisations share and manage knowledge and motivate their knowledge workers may be a critical factor in attracting and retaining this group and will also be crucial in determining the success of organisations in the twenty-first century. This is likely to be an issue for many involved in managing people. However, as we said earlier, all workers are vital for an organisation if it is to be successful and all workers should be managed in ways that will motivate them and help them to contribute to the achievement of their organisation's objectives.

There are varying views about the importance of knowledge workers and how they should be managed. Suff (2006) says that 'knowledge workers can be highly challenging to manage effectively. She says that the defining feature for knowledge workers is their attitude to work and the value their employer attributes to them. They are primarily motivated by career and personal development and need full involvement in issues that affect them and their work or they may become alienated and leave to join an organisation that appreciates them more.

Talent management

Talent management has been defined by the CIPD (2010e) as 'the systematic attraction, identification, development, engagement/retention and deployment of those individuals who are of particular value to the organisation, either in view of their "high potential" for the future or because they are fulfilling business/operation-critical roles.' This definition shows that talent management is a process that uses many different HR techniques and as such it will be discussed in more detail in several chapters of this book, in particular recruitment, selection, performance management, reward and learning and talent development.

The definition also seems to imply a fairly exclusive approach to talent management as being just for those who have been identified as of particular value to the organisation and when there are tough financial constraints it is easy to see the attraction of this rather limited approach. However, a broader interpretation of talent management can be and is used in many organisations as all employees should be making a contribution to the organisation and should have talents: if the employee wants to develop in ways that will contribute to the organisation, there should be opportunities for that development. While the term talent management does nowadays seem to have a variety of interpretations, according to Clake and Winkler (2006), there is broad agreement that 'talent management is not just about upward career moves. Horizontal career moves that broaden an individual's experience are also an integral part of many processes. For many, detailing a talent management strategy has seen a deliberate increase in the "sharing" of talent within an organisation and opportunities to gain experience in other departments or to work shadow are comparatively cheap ways of giving people opportunities to develop.'

The number of organisations which were involved in some form of talent management activities decreased slightly between 2006 and 2009 due to the recession, but one trend that emerged from the survey showed that those organisations using it were doing so in a more effective way and were linking talent management clearly to the organisation's strategic objectives (Sheppard, 2009). A year on and more organisations appear to be seeing the business case for talent management and according to CIPD (2010e) this is in response to a 'potent mix of external supply issues and internal organisational demands such as increasingly competitive global markets, skills shortages, demographic trends and corporate governance and business strategy.' The term 'talent management' is now widely used and even where there is currently a high level of unemployment many organisations still complain of being unable to fill their vacancies and the idea of attracting and keeping talented workers as a way of achieving the organisation's strategic objectives is becoming increasingly important. In this sort of economic environment it is important not only to attract but to develop and retain talented workers and the war for talent and talent management affects all aspects of HR from recruitment and selection to reward and motivation, and learning and development. Generation Y workers in particular may feel that the opportunity to develop their talent is vital if they are to be attracted to an organisation and to stay with it, but it is also important to ensure fairness and consistency and that relevant stakeholders are asked to contribute to designing the process.

Knowledge management

Another related area of concern nowadays is in knowledge management. All workers possess a great deal of knowledge which can be easily lost to the organisation when systems change or when there is a reorganisation and, of course, when people leave an organisation. HR specialists today also therefore have a role to play in trying to ensure that knowledge is shared and retained since this knowledge is a great source of competitive advantage. This presents issues about the best ways of communicating and sharing knowledge but also raises other issues about retention of workers.

Cross-cultural issues in HRM

Some organisations are multinational and produce and sell their goods or services in other countries. Others may use overseas workers in call centres to deal with queries in the UK or in other parts of the world. Even when there is unemployment there are still many jobs which prove unattractive to local workers and consequently are difficult to fill. There are also many jobs where there are skills shortages and just insufficient people with the right skills.

Evidence of the extent to which some parts of the UK are now multicultural was provided on 7 July 2005 when terrorists in London killed 52 people who were in the main just on their way to or from work and who happened to be using the London transport system. Those killed came from 13 different countries including the UK. While not all areas of the UK can claim to have as culturally diverse a population as London, it is the case that many areas are becoming increasingly culturally diverse, so issues around cross-cultural management are important. In the twenty-first century, managing people who come from a culture different to their own is likely to be a part of every manager's job even if they do not consider themselves to be working in an international organisation. According to French (2007), 'it is now possible to present a strong case that all managers should possess cross-cultural sensitivity at the level of managing people at work.'

There is no one theory of cross-cultural management that covers all issues but certain approaches have been very influential. Professor Gert Hofstede's (1980, 1997) research has been instrumental in helping organisations and individuals to understand cultural differences and, according to him, 'For those who work in international business, it is sometimes amazing how different people in other countries behave. We tend to have a basic human instinct that "deep inside" all people are the same – but they are not. Therefore, if we go into another country and make decisions based upon how we operate in our own country – the chances are we'll make some very bad decisions.'

Hofstede conducted a study of values in the workplace and how these are influenced by culture. He used the following dimensions: power distance index, individualism versus collectivism, masculinity versus femininity, uncertainty avoidance and, later, long-term orientation versus short-term orientation. All of these have some effect on how people behave in organisations and will impact on the ways HR managers need to manage people.

These categories are listed and described in Table 1.2, together with some examples of which countries tended high or low scores on the various values.

Hofstede's work is not to be applied as a model which will solve all problems that stem from intercultural differences, but it does serve to highlight various issues which may affect work relationships. At the very least, an awareness of these differences as potential sources of misunderstanding or conflict provides a basis from which to work towards more effective relationships. For instance, Western approaches towards performance management rest heavily on managers and subordinates being very

Table 1.2 Hofstede's cultural characteristics

Power distance		Uncertainty avoidance		Individualism/Collectivism		Masculinity/Femininity		Long-term orientation/short-term orientation	
The extent to which people accept authority structures, i.e. acceptance that it is right for some to make decisions and for others to follow their lead.		Tolerance of ambiguity. The extent to which people desire certainty about what to do in various circumstances or about future events. People with high uncertainty avoidance would welcome rules and regulations.		The extent to which people's actions are determined with reference to their own individual benefit or benefit of the community.		The importance that is placed on material outcomes (masculinity) versus the quality of relationships (femininity).		This relates to values associated with a long-term orientation such as thrift and perseverance as opposed to values more frequently associated with a short-term orientation such as respect for tradition, fulfilling social obligations and protecting one's 'face.'	
High power distance	Low power distance	High uncertainty avoidance	Low uncertainty avoidance	High individualism	High collectivism	High masculinity	High femininity	High long-term orientation	Low long-term orientation
Malaysia	USA	Greece	India	USA	Japan	Japan	Sweden	China	UK
Philippines	Great Britain	Portugal	Malaysia	Great Britain	Greece	Great Britain	Portugal	India	USA
Mexico	Sweden	Japan	Great Britain	Sweden	Malaysia	USA	France		
India		Germany	Sweden	France	Pakistan	India			
France				Germany					
Japan									

open with each other in analysing plans for the future and possible weaknesses on the employee's part. Indeed, upward and 360-degree appraisal require constructive criticism of managers by their subordinates. A person from a high power distance country would probably experience extreme discomfort if asked to do this.

In a multicultural society like that in the UK, one is likely to encounter elements of different ethnic cultures even in the domestic workplace, and the influx of migrant workers with the expansion of the EU has added to this cultural diversity.

Cross-cultural issues are becoming increasingly important not just in multinational organisations but also in organisations that recruit to fill skills gaps from workers in the expanded EU and elsewhere. Other issues relating to the treatment of migrant workers in the UK and of workers in third world countries are equally important. In the UK we have become used to comparatively cheap clothes and food but this also has implications for the way in which we pay and treat workers both within the UK and the third world (Lawrence, 2007; McVeigh, 2007). The issue of pay and conditions for migrant workers in the UK and also for suppliers of products from third world countries has been raised in national newspapers and will be discussed in more detail in later chapters. There is clearly a strong moral and ethical issue here which links with the next topic, corporate social responsibility.

Corporate social responsibility (CSR)

This is an area that is becoming of increasing interest and importance to organisations and to the people in them. Frequently the interest has been generated by public scandals and mismanagement such as in the world of finance, or by the great disparity in salaries of directors in some organisations who get hefty rewards even though their organisation has not done well under their leadership. It also includes issues about fairness and ethics as well as environmental concerns about the threat of global warming and about ways organisations can help to minimise their carbon footprint. According to the CIPD (2009c), 'CSR covers all aspects of company governance. It is about how companies conduct their business in an ethical way, taking account of their impact economically, socially, environmentally and in terms of human rights.'

As such it affects everyone and not just those who are the core stakeholders in the business: the shareholders, the workforce, suppliers and customers. There are other stakeholders such as local communities which may be affected by the action or inaction of businesses and their impact on the community or its environment. If some of its goods are produced in another country the organisation may have global responsibilities towards the workforce in terms of their fair treatment as well as to its suppliers and the local communities. An organisation's actions can even affect future generations.

There are a great many areas in CSR in which HR can become involved, although clearly others will also need to be part of any form of organisational culture change such as this. HR can play an important part in initiating and coordinating ideas or by providing a forum for discussion as many of the best ideas will come from the workforce. HR can also contribute through training, communication and support and by setting objectives for change. For CSR ideas to be acted upon, they also need to make business sense and many simple ideas (for example switching off lights in offices or installing time controls on water coolers to switch them off at night) help the environment and also save organisations money.

CSR is increasingly of importance to people when choosing which organisation they want to work for and for some of you this may be a strong guiding factor in your choice. According to the CIPD (2009c) CSR helps by 'building credibility and trust with current and potential customers and employees. It can help significantly with recruitment, engagement and retention of employees.' People, especially generation X and younger, don't want to work where there is a clash with their personal values. Present and future employees are placing increasing value on the credibility of an organisation's brand. Employers are using the positive aspects of their brand in recruiting, motivating and retaining highly skilled people.'

Clarke (2006) goes further and suggests that 'there is evidence that tapping into this interest and engaging staff is also likely to benefit the company brand and reputation. The recent Carbon Trust survey showed that more than three quarters of employees considered it important to work for a company that had an active policy to reduce its carbon emissions.' As organisations increasingly incorporate their ideas about CSR into their company brand image, using it in effect as a marketing tool, it is important that HR professionals utilise the benefits too in all aspects of people management. However, it is not sufficient just to have policies about the environment and corporate social responsibility if they are not implemented. According to Emmott (2005), 'Companies that want to build or protect their brand also need to think about their employer brand, and there is evidence that more and more people want to work for organisations that they respect. No company competing in the "war for talent" can afford to ignore this advice.'

Other approaches to HRM

Roles of HR specialists

Another way to try to establish what is meant by HRM and what roles HR managers and line managers take in managing people-related issues is to look at research into possible roles that HR practitioners have. Ulrich and Brockbank (2005) have been very influential in trying to clarify the roles of HR specialists and some large organisations have restructured along the lines of the Ulrich model of HRM. He originally envisaged the HR function in large organisations as having four main streams in order to deliver value to the organisation. According to Arkin (2007) these were:

- transactional HR carrying out administrative work through service centres
- embedded HR working directly with business leaders
- centres of expertise providing specialist advice
- corporate HR, which oversees the whole function, implementing organisation-wide initiatives and working with the top business leaders.

Ulrich's earlier work listed four roles to go with these structures: the business partner, administrative expert, employee champion and change agent, and according to Arkin (2007) 'a growing number of CIPD members now describe themselves as "HR business partners", a title sometimes prefixed with the word "strategic". A quick survey of the titles used in job advertisements in *People Management* in early 2010 revealed that the most popular titles advertised were for HR managers, Heads of HR, HR directors and then Business Partners but there were also smaller numbers of advertisements for HR advisers, coordinators and consultants and for a few HR administrators. This was virtually the same result as in 2007. It does appear that the title HR Business Partner is popular but it still has not overtaken the titles of HR Manager or Director in popularity, at least in the editions of the magazine reviewed.

In 2005 Ulrich and Brockbank updated these HR roles for the twenty-first century saying that their new descriptions reflected the changing roles in the organisations in which they occur. They said that 'all HR professionals aspire to add value but it is not always easy for the provider of a service to see what contribution they are making. To help our profession to get a better handle on this, we have tried to explain it in terms of the mastery of certain roles.' They list these as follows: employee advocate, functional expert, human capital developer, strategic partner and HR leader.

1 Employee advocate

This role focuses on the current needs of the workforce and on employee relations issues. Caring for, listening to employees and understanding their viewpoint is important in this role. However, the employee advocate also has to understand the points of view of other stakeholders and be able to communicate these to employees so they can in turn contribute to achieving value. Developing policies and procedures for fairness and diversity and rooting out discrimination are also key to this role and they could also be involved in developing policies for corporate and social responsibility. Keeping employees in touch with competitive realities and dealing with issues such as discipline or dismissal in a fair way are also important. Increased involvement in employee relations issues and negotiations about pay and conditions of employment are also likely to be important as government imposes constraints and as the economy recovers. According to Ulrich and Brockbank (2005) this role consumes about 19 per cent of the HR professional's time.

2 Functional expert

This role is one where the role holder concentrates on increasing the administrative efficiency of the HR department by using his or her expertise to design HR policies and procedures. The use of technology has been influential in changing this role from that of the administrative expert of the 1990s. Ulrich and Brockbank (2005) say that this role involves HR professionals in accessing a body of knowledge so that they act with insight and make well-informed and more effective decisions. They divide the role of the functional expert in two and say that it involves knowledge of both foundational and emerging HR practices.

Foundational HR practices are described as the practices for which HR departments have direct responsibility such as recruitment and selection, learning and development and reward, in fact many of the things that you will have associated with HR when you completed Activity 1.1 earlier in this chapter. They describe as emerging HR practices the types of things that will have a big impact on HRM but which may not be directly under the influence of the HR department. These are things such as process design, internal communications, sharing information and organisational design and restructuring. According to Ulrich and Brockbank (2005), 'By mastering the concepts and research of these foundational and emerging practices and ensuring their alignment with the key business priorities HR professionals will optimize their impact on business performance.' Besides possessing knowledge and expertise in HR areas, HR professionals also need to be knowledgeable about other areas of the organisation in order to be able to see things from other managers' points of view and to be able to discuss their specific business needs with them. This role may also fit with the concept of knowledge management, which we mentioned earlier.

3 Human capital developer

This role is about developing the workforce so that they are successful in the future. This could involve developing individual workers but also could involve the development of teams so the focus is on learning and talent development and on identifying approaches that can help people to learn appropriate skills, knowledge, behaviour and attitudes using approaches such as coaching in a cost-effective way to contribute to the organisation's strategic objectives.

4 Strategic partner

This role operates at a high level within the organisation and could involve several things such as being an expert in the business, thinking and planning strategically, or it could be someone who acts as a consultant or is a knowledge manager. Ulrich and Brockbank (2005) say that 'In their role as a strategic partner, HR professionals bring know-how about business, change, consulting and learning to their relationships with line managers.' They basically see the role as divided into three main areas: strategy formulators, strategy implementers and facilitators.

Ulrich and Brockbank (2005) see the sub-role of strategy formulator being divided into three areas also. First, HR strategic partners should act as devil's advocate and ask awkward questions about an organisation's strategy and about its ability to fulfil it. This, however, while important, is a purely reactive role.

Second, they should play a more proactive role in which they design the strategies based on their own knowledge of existing and future customer needs and ensure resources are aligned to those needs. Finally, according to Ulrich and Brockbank (2005), they should play a role in developing and improving the standards of strategic thinking among managers.

In terms of strategy implementers and change agents, they are involved in ensuring that all the HR systems and policies and procedures are aligned with the organisation's vision and goals so that they help these to be fulfilled. They plan for the future and make the future happen.

In the third variant of the role of strategic HR manager, they facilitate the work of managers and teams to help them achieve their aims and this also involves them in sharing knowledge and spreading it between people. Once again this links with the idea of knowledge management as explained earlier.

5 The HR leader

This involves all of the other four roles and also involves leading the HR function and working with other business functions in setting standards for strategic thinking and corporate governance. However, Ulrich and Brockbank (2005) envisage the leadership role as being so important that it needs to be a role in its own right. The effective HR leader will establish goals and show results in relation to the added value for workers, shareholders, customers and the managers. Ulrich and Brockbank also emphasise the fact that it is not just those at the top of HR who should be leaders but that every HR manager should also exercise personal leadership.

Ulrich and Brockbank (2005) do emphasise the point that not everyone operates at a strategic level and that all the roles are important within an organisation, although it appears to have been the role of business partner or strategic business partner that has captured the imagination of HR practitioners. While all HR managers need to be aware of the need to think strategically and to align HR policies and procedures with the organisation's strategic objectives, many, particularly when starting out in their careers, are likely to act in roles such as employee advocate. As Ulrich and Brockbank (2005) say, 'Some argue that HR should move exclusively to strategic partnering, to help business leaders define and deliver financial and customer goals. We disagree. Employee advocacy is not merely window dressing; it contributes to building the human infrastructure from which everything else in the organisation flows.'

The people and performance model

A different approach was adopted by John Purcell and a team of researchers from the University of Bath who carried out studies sponsored by the CIPD over a three-year period to try to ascertain what aspects of HRM actually make a difference to performance within organisations (Purcell *et al.* 2003).

They found that on their own, good HR policies were not sufficient to create an effective organisation but excellent policies about recruiting, developing and retaining the people in the organisation were important. Purcell *et al.* (2003) referred to this as the 'human capital advantage'. Much of this book will address ways to achieve this type of human capital advantage. However, the other key factor that distinguished effective organisations from those that were less effective was the way they 'worked together to be productive and flexible enough to meet new challenges'. We also emphasise this approach throughout this book.

The researchers identified two vital ingredients in effective organisations. According to Purcell *et al.* (2003) these are:

- First, they had strong values and an inclusive culture.
- Second, they had enough line managers who were able to bring HR policies and practices to life.

Strong values and an inclusive culture

Purcell and his team of researchers found that organisations that developed a strong and inclusive culture usually had what they called a 'big idea.' This was always something that was clearly communicated to everyone in the workforce and that could be easily understood.

The big ideas the researchers identified were ideas such as the 'pursuit of quality' at Jaguar cars, 'living the values' at Tesco and the 'principles of mutuality' at Nationwide Building Society. Everyone shared and understood these ideas and they became the foundation for all the HR policies and procedures, enabling everyone to see why they were necessary.

Line managers who could bring the policies to life

We have already mentioned the importance of line managers in the HRM approach to the management of people and here we have recent research that substantiates this view. In the research by Purcell and his team (Purcell *et al.*, 2003) the line managers were found to be the other vital ingredient in making an effective organisation. The line managers had not only to see the relevance of the HR policies and procedures to themselves, but also to see how they could use them to contribute to an effective organisation.

Pause for thought 1.4

The researchers from Bath University said, 'It's better to ensure that HR policies are properly implemented than to try to develop new policies' (Purcell *et al.*, 2003). As you work through this book and learn more about HR policies and procedures, remember that the way they are introduced into an organisation is also very important and worker involvement and excellent communication are also crucial to the effectiveness of the organisation.

The ACAS model

Donaghy (2005) makes a similar point in the foreword to the ACAS model workplace and says that 'Our experience tells us that the way you do something is just as important as what you do. Having the right policies and procedures is vital but they won't work properly unless they are introduced and used in the right spirit.' ACAS have developed a model to help organisations improve the effectiveness of their people management. This shows some similarities to the findings of Purcell *et al.* but is based on 30 years of experience on the part of ACAS in assisting organisations with people management issues. They list the following as key issues:

Formal procedures for dealing with disciplinary matters, grievances and disputes that managers know about and use fairly.

Ambitions, goals and plans that employees know about and understand.

Managers who genuinely listen to and consider their employees' views so everyone is actively involved in making important decisions.

A pay and reward system that is clear, fair and consistent.

A safe and healthy workplace.

People to feel valued so they can talk confidently about their work and learn from both successes and mistakes.

Everyone to be treated fairly and valued for their differences as a part of everyday life.

Work organised so that it encourages initiative, innovation and people to work together.

An understanding that people have responsibilities outside work so that they can openly discuss ways of working that suit personal needs and the needs of the business or elsewhere.

A culture where everyone is encouraged to learn new skills so they can look forward to further employment whether in the business or elsewhere.

A good working relationship between management and employee representatives that in turn helps build trust throughout the business.

(Advisory Conciliation and Arbitration Service, 2005)

Many of the principles outlined in the ACAS model workplace were also identified by Purcell and his team as of importance in achieving high performance and they are also to be found in organisations that have been judged as some of the best places to work. According to Will Hutton, Executive Vice-Chair of the Work Foundation (2010), the work of researchers means that we now know much about 'what makes for good work and good workplaces. It is in the mix of performance, engagement and fairness: a steely commitment to excellence and quality; a sense of integrity and high trust in working relationships; and developing the practices, structures and (whisper it) terms and conditions of employment that help people feel valued and well-treated and facilitate their participation in the life and objectives of organisations.'

It should not be surprising that organisations that have been judged by their employees to be excellent places to work have also been among some of the most successful organisations to survive or even expand during the recent recession (Paton, 2010). In the following chapters we examine many of the key HR policies, practices and procedures that can contribute towards making an effective workplace that will

Did you know?

In 2010 Baringa Partners, a management consultancy specialising in the energy and utilities markets and financial services industry, won the award of the best workplace in Britain. Its success was due in part to its ability to support and grow talented and motivated staff but it also had a friendly recruitment process, a non-hierarchical organisation structure with excellent sharing of information and a sustainability programme which enabled employees to become actively involved in CSR programmes.

(*Source*: Finn, 2010)

hopefully also be one of the best places to work, and we have tried to emphasise the roles of both the specialists in HR and line managers in implementing these in ways which will benefit the organisation. We have already shown how the role of HR practitioners has evolved and the importance of the role of line managers in HRM issues.

● The changing HR function

Reality does not always match the theories, as a two-year CIPD-sponsored research project led by Reilly (2007a) into *The changing HR function* showed. According to Reilly (2007b), 81 per cent of the 781 organisations that responded said that they had recently reorganised or restructured their HR departments but less than 20 per cent had adopted the Ulrich model in full. A quarter of the organisations surveyed had a single HR team, but the remainder had central teams with operational HR staff aligned to specific business units. In this sample shared service centres were only found in large organisations that employed more than 5,000 employees and in most instances these were not outsourced to other organisations, although they were sometimes in-sourced to separate parts of the organisation.

There was a widespread use of HR business partners but the survey found a wide variation in their roles. Some were solo operators, concentrating on strategic issues, while others were team members, focusing on operational work: some reported to HR directors while others reported to heads of business units.

Some organisations created centres of HR expertise. The most common centres of expertise specialised in learning and development followed by those centres that focused on recruitment/resourcing, reward and employee relations/employment law. If there was no centre of expertise then the work was usually done within the business unit so it could reflect specific challenges to that unit, although sometimes the work was done in the corporate centre itself.

The research showed that many organisations were trying to make the HR function more strategic and in larger organisations many of the administrative functions were being consolidated and often routine functions are becoming automated. More recent research shows increasing success in making the HR function more strategic. A survey of 253 HR practitioners conducted by IRS 2010 showed that increasingly HR departments had clearly documented HR strategies that had been developed as an integral part of and at the same time as the organisation's main strategy, rather than later as a result of it (Murphy, 2010).

The IRS survey also showed HR departments becoming more effective at putting in place HR processes and then identifying ways to measure their success and two-thirds of those surveyed felt that the influence of the HR department had increased during the last two years. This increased influence was due in part to success in restructuring and handling redundancies and in meeting the business challenges caused by the recession. There had also been greater representation of HR at board level, an improvement in relationships between HR and management and HR initiatives having been successful in making a difference in tangible ways to the organisation. Of the HR professionals surveyed 68.3 per cent measured the efficiency of their HR departments and used a range of measures. These included using metrics from absence management, staff turnover data and results of staff surveys to measure improvements in HR effectiveness (Murphy, 2010).

The CIPD (2010g) have also conducted recent research into the changing roles of HR and have developed what they refer to as a profession map as a tool for helping HR professionals identify what they need to know, do and deliver at various points in their career. They have focused on 10 professional areas but at the heart of these are two areas that they see as of vital importance to all. They too have focused on strategic issues and the role of HR and have identified 'strategy, insights and solutions' and 'leading and managing the human resource function' as two key areas of importance to the future of HR. Both will be of importance in the current economic climate and for organisations to make a strong recovery: the CIPD (2010g) see them as being 'central to understanding the organisation and delivering an HR function that believes in success.' The focus is still very much about the added value HR can deliver and the contribution it can make to the organisation's strategic objectives. There is also a recognition that HR needs to lead as well as manage; this is increasingly important with age diverse and culturally diverse workforces and will affect the different HR strategies that are needed to motivate workers which we shall discuss in the other chapters of the book.

The other eight areas of the HR profession map show what the CIPD (2010g), from their research, have identified as the activities HR professionals performed or supported others such as line managers in performing, and each of these areas is described at four different levels so people just starting in a career, or those further into their careers, know what they have to do as a part of their own career development. These areas are:

1 Resourcing and talent planning
2 Learning and talent development
3 Performance and reward
4 Employee engagement
5 Employee relations
6 Service delivery and information
7 Organisational design
8 Organisational development.

Not all HR managers will be involved in all aspects of these and we have chosen to focus in this book on the topics most likely to be of importance to those starting to study HR with the intention of either becoming HR managers or managers in other functions who will have an increasing level of responsibility for HR. The CIPD (2010g) underpin their 10 professional areas with eight underlying skills, behaviours and knowledge. They say that those working in HR should be or become curious, decisive, skilled in influencing, driven to deliver, collaborative, a role model for others, brave enough to challenge issues and personally credible. We hope that working through this book will help you to start to develop some of these underpinning skills, behaviours and knowledge.

Conclusion

In this chapter we have briefly discussed the background to HRM and introduced some of the areas in which HR managers are currently working, and introduced you to some of the discussions and debates about the ever-changing roles of HR specialists. We have chosen to focus on current thinking and research about HRM and the extent to which various HRM strategies contribute to the organisation being effective. We have also emphasised the fact that line managers nowadays play important roles in many aspects of managing people.

In reality, HR roles are very diverse and no one model explains them completely. In small or medium-sized organisations there will be HR practitioners who will deal with all aspects of HRM and who will regard themselves as generalists. In larger organisations there may be a much greater degree of specialisation and some will use business partners and may adopt a shared services approach alongside this. The survey *The Changing HR Function: Transforming HR?* led by Reilly (2007a) showed the wide variety of roles being adopted as HR departments adapted to meet new demands and continued to search for ways to add value to their organisations and contribute to their strategic objectives. This will continue as organisations find and adapt different HR strategies to help them to achieve success in response to the economic circumstances in which they find themselves and as ways of leading and motivating their own often diverse workforces in situation specific ways.

In the next chapter we focus on some of the issues relating to strategy. Since each organisation will have different strategic objectives, it is actually not surprising that they do not just adopt one approach to the way they organise and provide leadership in their HR departments, and rather than looking to one model of 'best practice' we should be considering different approaches to 'good practice' depending on what works for specific organisations in the context in which they operate. We shall continue in the next chapters to explain the key aspects of areas of HRM and will take into account when doing so other important issues in the way these topics are handled, such as economic circumstances, social and demographic trends, cross-cultural issues and issues relating to ethics and corporate social responsibility.

REVIEW QUESTIONS

1 We include here a pictorial representation of this chapter in the form of a mind map (Figure 1.1). Use the key words we have included to refresh your memory of what we have covered in this chapter. Add your own key words or drawings to this mind map to reinforce your learning.

2 Identify at least three issues that currently engage the attention of people managers. Explain why each of these is important.

3 Examine three job advertisements for HR specialists. Compare these with the roles listed by Ulrich and Brockbank (2005) of employee advocate, functional expert, human capital developer, strategic partner and HR leader. To what extent do the job advertisements relate to Ulrich and Brockbank's roles?

4 Interview a human resource specialist about their job and main duties. Does this person think of themselves as a business partner to the organisation? How do the results from your interview compare with the roles and main duties we described in this chapter?

Figure 1.1 Mind map of Chapter 1

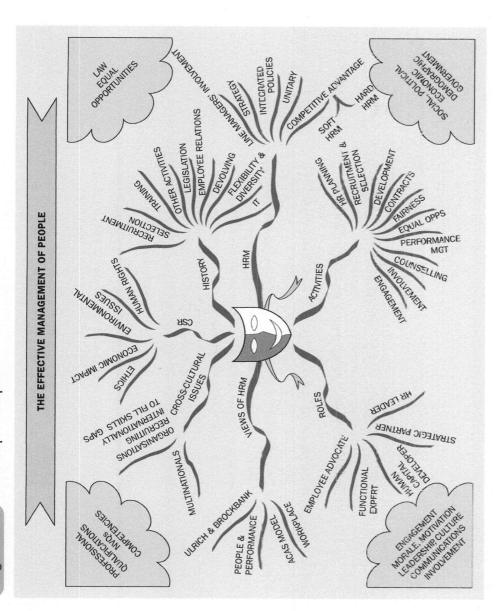

THE EFFECTIVE MANAGEMENT OF PEOPLE

SELF-CHECK QUESTIONS

Answer the following multiple-choice questions. The correct responses are given on page 487 for you to check your understanding of this chapter.

1 To which of the following do the letters CIPD refer?
   (a) The Chartered Institute of Professional Development.
   (b) The Constitutional Institution for the Progress of Devolvement.
   (c) The Chartered Institute of Personnel and Development.
   (d) The Community Institute of Personal Development.

2 Which of the following is not identified in this chapter as a current issue of major importance in the field of people management?
   (a) The need to attract and retain good employees.
   (b) The need to demonstrate how people management activities add value.
   (c) The need to apply advances in IT to improve people management.
   (d) The need to keep wages low to improve competitive advantage.

3 Which of the following statements best sums up the role of the human resource manager in managing people?

(a) The human resource manager is the sole person who should be involved in all people management activities.

(b) Both the human resource manager and line manager are likely to be involved in differing ways in managing people.

(c) The line manager always acts alone in all organisations in dealing with people management activities.

(d) The human resource manager is only concerned with people management at the day-to-day level.

4 Which of the following statements would be true of the human resource management approach to managing people at work?

(a) It tackles issues in a piecemeal way.

(b) It relies on traditional forms of communication.

(c) There is not much involvement of the workforce in decision making.

(d) It is strategic.

5 Which of the following sums up an underlying theme in the philosophy of HRM?

(a) People are important whether they are full-time or part-time employees, permanent or temporary, or contract workers who are actually employed by another company.

(b) People are important only if they are full-time, permanent employees.

(c) People are important whether they are full-time or part-time employees so long as they are permanent and are employed by your company.

(d) People are important whether they are full-time or part-time, permanent or temporary so long as they are employed by your company.

HR IN THE NEWS

FT

A good name is beyond price

By Sarah Murray

This year's Business in the Community's Awards for Excellence are accompanied by research revealing that companies managing and measuring their corporate responsibility appear to be able to recover from recession faster than their FTSE 350 peers.

Yet the financial meltdown and, more recently, the BP oil spill in the Gulf of Mexico have shaken trust in the ability of companies to behave responsibly.

The oil spill has increased pressure for tighter regulation of the private sector, with BP coming under attack for its safety record and its handling of the accident.

Meanwhile, the global financial crisis shook public trust in companies, particularly those in the banking sector.

According to the 2010 Trust Barometer produced by Edelman, the public relations company, trust in UK banks fell 20 points between 2007 and 2010.

Such developments have called into question the effectiveness of the voluntary approach to corporate responsibility that is being celebrated by the BITC awards.

Nevertheless, if the awards are anything to go by, many companies are making sincere efforts to behave responsibly.

The awards – which rank businesses' impact on the community, the environment, the market-place and the workplace – have found that of the 117 companies participating in the Corporate Responsibility Index, 111 won a place in the annual ranking.

However, while accolades are one thing, demonstrating that good behaviour is rewarded with higher profits is another. BITC has taken steps to do so. In research conducted by Ipsos Mori for the organisation, it has emerged that companies with strong environmental, social and governance standards have outperformed the FTSE 350 and the FTSE All-Share indexes on total shareholder return for seven of the past eight years.

The research also found that total shareholder return for these 28 companies recovered more quickly in 2009, compared with that of their FTSE 350 and FTSE All-Share peers.

The BITC rankings take two forms. While the CR Index assesses companies on their overall management approach and processes, the awards are focused on the impact of specific pro-grammes, such as environmental leadership or skills development.

Meanwhile, two separate awards celebrate the company of the year and small company of the year.

Utilities claim half of the top 10 positions in the Platinum Plus rankings of the CR Index this year.

Two of these accolades go to accounting and consulting firms, KPMG and PwC. Also in the top 10 are BT Group, the telecoms company, the Co-operative Group, the UK retailer and Unilever, the Anglo-Dutch consumer products group.

Within the CR Index and the Big Tick awards, different areas of focus emerge. A strong theme this year is the corporate role in employability, with BITC recognising companies that are contributing to the employment prospects and the employability skills of the communities in which they operate.

Marks and Spencer, for example, has employed more than 3,500 people via its Marks & Start programme. Part of Barclays' Business Action on Homelessness initiative is to build employability skills and find work placements for homeless individuals.

Corporate performance on health and wellbeing in the workplace is also featured in the awards, with BITC reporting that 65 per cent of the companies completing the CR Index say they report publicly on this.

Mori research commissioned by BITC agrees, showing that in FTSE 100 companies, public reporting on the health and wellbeing of employees has risen sharply from 68 per cent in 2007 to 85 per cent in 2009.

Attention to this issue appears to pay off for companies. Research in Motion, the maker of the BlackBerry, has a healthy workplace programme called Healthy@RIM. It has found its annual employee turnover rates in the region studied are less than 6 per cent, compared with an indus-try average of 15 per cent.

Meanwhile, Northern Foods' Fit4life campaign – which includes a free annual health check – has contributed to falling absenteeism and a cut of 15 per cent in the company's sick pay costs.

Perhaps unsurprisingly, the drive towards a low carbon economy is a prominent part of com-panies' strategies as the corporate sector recognises the link between carbon efficiency and financial efficiency, with seven companies receiving awards in the climate change category.

A new theme in the awards this year is the role of companies in accelerating progress to-wards meeting the Millennium Development Goals, the list of eight targets drawn up by the United Nations in 2000.

In recognising companies for this, BITC is acknowledging growing interest from the corporate world in contribution to the health, education and economic independence of some of the world's poorest people through business strategies rather than with philanthropic efforts.

Two of the companies in the Platinum Plus ranking provide good examples of how this can be done.

Unilever has long pursued a strategy of bringing smallholder farmers in developing countries into its supply chains.

Meanwhile, at the Co-operative Group, a policy of stocking supermarkets with a large number of Fairtrade products helps give smallholders access to UK consumers, boosting rural incomes. Fairtrade products are an example of another trend highlighted by this year's awards – influencing consumer behaviour.

When asked whether they engaged with customers on the social and environmental impacts of the company and its products and services, 83 per cent of participants in this year's CR Index affirmed that they did this across the business, with a further 80 per cent saying they encourage positive customer behaviour on these issues.

This, argues BITC, brings companies several benefits, including differentiation from competitors, increased customer loyalty and the creation of new markets for sustainable products and services.

BITC points to the case of J Sainsbury, which worked with the Marine Conservation Society (MCS) on a customer tool to rate the sustainability status of the different fish species that it sells. Using a traffic light ranking system, it removed red-rated fish from its shelves.

It also set itself a target of doubling sales of MCS-certified fish by 2009. As a result, the company has found its share of cod sales rise from 19 per cent to 21 per cent, and haddock from 26 per cent to 28 per cent.

Such initiatives may be behind the findings of the 2010 Edelman Trust Barometer, which – with the exception of the banks – found trust in companies up slightly, with the credibility of chief executives recovering from the previous survey, rising by 13 points in the UK.

Yet, winners in this year's BITC awards should not be tempted to brag to their customers. In 20 countries, Edelman found that corporate or product advertising remains the least credible source of information about a company.

And anyone doubting this result should take note from BP's present woes. Neither the company's numerous environmental awards – nor its logo, advertising campaigns and web pages celebrating the environment – are having much effect, as it struggles to minimise the fallout from the disastrous Gulf of Mexico oil spill.

(Financial Times, 7 June 2010. Reproduced with permission.)

Questions

1 Which approaches to building corporate and social responsibility are listed here?

2 What are the main benefits for those organisations that are actively involved in developing strong attitudes towards corporate and social responsibility?

3 In your view should corporate and social responsibility be voluntary or should there be some form of compulsion from governments?

4 To what extent would the corporate and social responsibility record of an organisation determine whether or not you would buy something from that organisation?

5 To what extent would the organisation's record on corporate and social responsibility influence your decision as to whether or not to apply to work for that organisation?

6 Do you think that it is true that this is a particular concern for those known as Generation Y, those born between 1979 and 1991, rather than for other generations?

WHAT NEXT?

Now that you have read the first chapter and completed the exercises, you may want to go further and test your understanding.

1 There are exercises that will help you to do this on our website at **www.pearsoned.co.uk/foothook.**

2 Listen to the following podcasts to gain a further understanding of the social, political and ethical issues that face HR managers as they try to build capacity and competence in a global economy. Go to **www.cipd.co.uk** and listen to

Podcast 36: Next Generation HR and Podcast 45: Building HR Capability. Each of these involves HR managers discussing the changing role of HR.

If your library, or organisation, subscribes to the XpertHR database, listen to Noelle Murphy discussing the results of the IRS 2010 survey into the roles of HR and compare this with the views expressed in the two CIPD podcasts. Go to www. xperthr.co.uk and search for IRS podcasts in the 2010 list.

3 Go to www.acas.org and examine in more detail the ACAS Model Workplace mentioned earlier in this chapter. Use the model as a checklist. Think of an organisation you know well and compare the way they manage people with the ACAS checklist.

4 Go to www.greatplacestowork.co.uk and read about the organisations that have been judged to be great places to work. How many of the criteria used compare with the ACAS model workplace or with Purcell's work?

5 Students in the UK can view *Jamie's Kitchen* and *Jamie's Chef* on 4oD at www. channel4.com. See for yourselves the extent to which you think Jamie Oliver adds value to the trainees in these programmes and discuss the extent to which you think that the *Fifteen* restaurants were created to have a sense of corporate and social responsibility. Do you think that is a part of the reason for their success?

Table 1.3 The main activities of human resource practitioners (Activity 1.1 answer)

Main areas of activity human resource/people management specialist	Type of involvement of the human resource/people management specialist	Type of involvement of line manager
Recruitment and selection	Design of policies and procedure for fair recruitment and selection in order to contribute to the fulfilment of the organisation's corporate strategy. Commission online recruitment activities. Carry out interviews or monitor and give advice on interview technique or on terms and conditions of employment.	Prepare and carry out interviews and other selection tests. Participate in selecting the successful candidate(s).
Learning and talent development	Involved in planning learning and development opportunities for the whole organisation, to meet the needs of the organisation as expressed in its strategic plan and to meet the needs of individuale. These could be formal training courses, online materials or less formal approaches such as coaching or mentoring. May design and organise training courses for groups and sometimes run them. May keep training records centrally and request information from line managers as part of planning exercise or to monitor success of training and development.	May also be involved in planning and provision of training and talent development opportunities to meet the needs of individuals and their departmental needs linked to the organisation's strategic plan, primarily for employees in their own department. May provide training and may also keep records of training and provide information to central HRM department.
Human resource planning	Depending on the level of appointment they are likely to be involved to various degrees in contributing to the strategic plan. Collection and analysis of data, monitoring targets for the whole organisation. Providing information to managers. Conducting exit interviews and analysing reasons for leaving.	Collect information on leavers and provide information on anticipated requirements for employees for their department.
Provision of contracts	Provide written statement of particulars for new employees and issue them to these employees, having checked that the detail is correct. Keep copies of all documentation relating to the employee and advise on any alterations to the contract.	Possibly issue documents and get signature of new employee.

Table 1.3 Continued

Main areas of activity	Type of involvement of the human resource/people management specialist	Type of involvement of line manager
Provision of fair treatment	Involvement in design of policies and procedures for the whole organisation to encourage fair treatment at work. Inform and train people in these policies and procedures. Monitor the success of these policies.	Responsible for fair treatment of people in their department to ensure all treat others in a fair way. Listen and respond to grievances as an initial stage in the grievance procedure or informally before someone gets into the grievance procedure. May contribute suggestions about design of policies.
Equal opportunities	Involvement in design of policies to encourage equal opportunities. Train and inform managers and all employees throughout the organisation in these. Monitor the effectiveness of the equal opportunities policies by collecting and analysing information.	May also be involved in, and contribute to, the design of policies. Will be responsible for ensuring that all employees for whom they are responsible do not suffer from any form of unfair discrimination while at work.
Managing diversity	Developing policies about diversity and promoting and ensuring a diverse workforce so that the organisation can benefit from ideas generated by individuals from a range of different backgrounds.	Line managers need to actively encourage diversity to be valued within their own team or department.
Motivating workers to achieve improved performance	Involvement in design and implementation of techniques to assess effectively performance of employees in a way that links clearly with the organisation's strategic plan. Review all HR policies to ensure strategic integration with the strategic plan. Train, inform and involve people in performance management techniques and encourage line managers to work towards a high-performance workplace. Monitor the effectiveness of the procedures. May maintain central records about performance of individual employees.	Contribute to achievement of a high-performance workplace by taking an active role in people management and performance management of their own department. Assess performance of those in own department. Involve teams and individuals in setting and agreeing targets and monitoring performance. Monitor their success and give feedback.
Employee counselling	Establish appropriate system, either in-house or by external consultants, for employee counselling or for employee assistance programmes. May be involved in counselling employees with problems or may have to refer them to specialised counselling service.	May be involved in the initial counselling of employees in their own section, or may need to suggest alternative sources of counselling if they do not feel qualified to deal with the situation.
Employee welfare	Establish appropriate systems for employee welfare in accordance with the objectives of the organisation. Monitor the cost and effectiveness of this provision.	Ensure the well-being of employees in their department and draw their attention to, and encourage use of, any provisions designed by the organisation to improve their welfare.
Payment and reward of employees	Establish appropriate payment and reward systems for all employees in order to support achievement of aspects of the organisation's strategic plan. Monitor the success of these. Collect comparative data for other organisations in area or nationally. Deal with individual problems about pay. May be involved in negotiation about payment or reward systems. Tell individuals of their level of pay when they join the organisation or change jobs. May deal with individual problems or complaints about pay.	May be involved in, and contribute views about, appropriate systems of payment or reward to be used in the organisation. May be involved in negotiation to some extent over issues relating to own department. May deal with problems concerning pay raised by employees in their department in the first instance.

Table 1.3 Continued

Main areas of activity human resource/people management specialist	Type of involvement of the human resource/people management specialist	Type of involvement of line manager
Health and safety	Involvement in design and implementation of the organisation's health and safety policy in order to contribute to the organisation's strategic plan and ensure policies are integrated with other HR policies. Monitor the effectiveness of this. May sit on safety committee or may have line management responsibilities for safety officer or organisation's nurse. Involvement in promotion of health and safety and encouraging the involvement of others throughout the organisation.	Responsible for health and safety of employees working in their department. Encourage the involvement of individuals and teams in health or safety promotion activities. Monitor activities of own staff. Carry out regular safety inspections in own department. May take initial disciplinary action against those who infringe health and safety rules.
Disciplining individuals	Design of disciplinary procedure. Monitor the effectiveness of the procedure. Give advice to line managers on disciplinary problems. Organise training for line managers and employees about disciplinary issues to ensure they comply with organisation's policy and with the law. In some organisations they may still issue warnings in later stages of disciplinary procedure. Maintain central records of disciplinary action taken.	Conduct informal disciplinary interviews with own staff if necessary. Issue formal warnings as outlined in disciplinary procedure. Maintain records of warnings issued. Ensure compliance both with the organisation's policy and with the statutory discipline, dismissal and grievance procedures.
Dealing with grievances	Participate in the design of grievance procedure and encourage the involvement of others in this. Inform and train people in grievance handling and in the requirements of the statutory procedure. Monitor the effectiveness of the grievance procedure. May deal with some stages in the grievance procedure or appeals.	Deal initially with grievances raised by employees in their department. This may be handled informally at first or as part of the formal grievance procedure. Deal with grievances within specified time limits and ensure that these are dealt with in accordance with the organisation's policy and the statutory procedures.
Dismissal	Review procedures for dismissal to ensure that they comply with legislation. Provide advice and guidance on fair dismissal procedure. Provide training for all who may be involved in the dismissal process. May dismiss employee.	In many organisations the actual dismissal will be handled by someone from the HR department with the manager being present. However, nowadays managers in many organisations will also be fully trained to take full responsibility for dismissing an employee in their section in a fair way.
Redundancy	Is likely to be involved in consultation with appropriate people with regard to redundancy. Is likely to be involved in selection of those to be made redundant. May inform employee of redundancy and amount of pay and rights. May organise provision of more generous redundancy payment if this is in line with organisation's policy. May organise provision of outplacement facilities either in-house or by consultants.	Is likely to be involved in selection of those to be made redundant from their department. May be involved in telling them of the decision to make them redundant.
Negotiation	Is likely to be involved in negotiation on a wide range of organisation-wide issues.	Is likely to be involved in negotiation on a wide range of issues that affect employees in their department.

Table 1.3 Continued

Main areas of activity human resource/people management specialist	Type of involvement of the human resource/people management specialist	Type of involvement of line manager
Encouraging involvement and engagement	Will have an extremely important role in creating a culture within the organisation in which employees are encouraged to be involved in decision-making and engaged in working towards the organisation's objectives. Will be involved in designing policy and procedures to encourage employee involvement in line with strategic plan. Will also provide training to encourage employee involvement.	Will contribute to organisation's policies and will encourage involvement of employees in their department.
Adding value	Ensuring that all HR activities help to add value to the organisation by helping it achieve its objectives and become a high-performance workplace.	Ensuring that all HR activities help to add value to their department or section by ensuring they contribute to its objectives.
Ethics and corporate responsibility	HR managers are concerned with all issues relating to fairness whether or not this is covered by legislation. Increasingly they are becoming involved in design of policies and procedures which take account of the impact of their business economically, socially, environmentally and in terms of human rights. They may challenge the way things have been done to draw attention to the corporate and social responsibility issues. They are likely to play an important role in support of environmental issues.	Ensure that all activities in their own section comply with the organisation's policies on corporate and social responsibility and that they always act in a way consistent with these.
Knowledge management and talent management	HR specialists are likely to be involved in devising polices and strategies to encourage the sharing of knowledge within the organisation and to try to ensure that the organisation keeps its knowledge workers and has communications systems that facilitate the sharing of knowledge so it is not lost to the organisation if someone leaves. They will also play a key role in identifying talent and nurturing it within their team.	Line managers will need to manage knowledge workers in sensitive ways to ensure they stay with the organisation. They should encourage the sharing or knowledge within their team. They will also be concerned to identify and develop talent.
Change management	HR specialists will deal with the people aspects of change and will have a role to design policies and procedures to support change. They will also ensure that there is clear communication, consultation, involvement and engagement with the workforce with any changes that are planned. They are likely to be involved in designing learning and development initiatives to support the changes.	The line manager will be involved in implementing the changes but will also play an important part in communicating issues relating to the changes to their team and in communicating concerns about the changes upwards to senior management. They will run learning and development activities to support the changes.
Managing cross-cultural issues or international HRM	The HR specialist may be involved in recruitment drives in other countries or in managing cross-cultural issues within this country as workers from many differing ethnic origins are employed. Policies and procedures will need to take account of cross-cultural issues and if working in a multinational organisation there will also need to be decisions made about the way HR policies are implemented within each country. They are likely to have involvement in learning and development initiatives to support this.	The line manager will deal with day-to-day issues arising form cross-cultural issues in the workplace, whether they are working in their home country or working in another country with host country nationals and expatriate workers.

References

Advisory, Conciliation and Arbitration Service (2005) *The ACAS Model Workplace*, ACAS, 4–5.

Allen, A. (2010) Generational divide, *UK's Best Workplaces: Special Report*, May, Great Place to Work Institute UK, 28–29.

Arkin, A. (2007) Street smart, *People Management*, 5 April, Vol. 13, No. 7.

Boxall, P. and J. Purcell (2008) *Strategy and Human Resource Management*, 2nd edition, Houndsmills: Palgrave McMillan.

Chartered Institute of Personnel and Development (2005) *Survey Report 2005. HR: Where is Your Career Heading?* CIPD (www.cipd.co.uk; accessed 6.4.07).

Chartered Institute of Personnel and Development (2009a) *CIPD Annual Report 2008–2009*, CIPD (www.cipd.co.uk; accessed 18.8.10).

Chartered Institute of Personnel and Development (2009b) *Understanding the Economy and Labour Market*, CIPD (www.cipd.co.uk; accessed 08.03.10).

Chartered Institute of Personnel and Development (2009c) *Corporate Social Responsibility*, CIPD.

Chartered Institute of Personnel and Development (2010a) *Overview of CIPD Surveys: A Barometer of Social Trends*, CIPD (www.cipd.co.uk; accessed 16.8.2010).

Chartered Institute of Personnel and Development (2010b) *The Role of Front Line Managers in HR*, CIPD (www.cipd.co.uk; accessed 21.8.2010)

Chartered Institute of Personnel and Development (2010c) *Labour Market Outlook. Quarterly Survey Report, Winter 2009–2010*, CIPD (www.cipd.co.uk; accessed 20.03.10).

Chartered Institute of Personnel and Development (2010d) *Gen Y or Gen Lost? The Effect of the Recession on Our Future Workforce*, CIPD (www.cipd.co.uk; accessed 21.8.2010).

Chartered Institute of Personnel and Development (2010e) *Talent Management: An Overview*, CIPD (www.cipd.co.uk; accessed 18.8.2010).

Chartered Institute of Personnel and Development (2010f) *Taking the Temperature on HR Skills for Survival*, CIPD (www.cipd.co.uk; accessed 16.8.2010).

Chartered Institute of Personnel and Development (2010g) *The HR Profession Map*, CIPD (www.cipd.co.uk; accessed 19.8.2010).

Churchard, C. (2010) State pension age of 72 'would balance costs'. *People Management Magazine Online*, 20 August (www.peoplemanagement.co.uk).

Clake, R. and V. Winkler (2006) *The Change Agenda: Reflections on Talent Management*, CIPD (www.cipd.co.uk; accessed 9.4.07).

Clarke, E. (2006) Power brokers, *People Management*, 18 May, Vol. 12, No. 10.

Donaghy, R. (2005) Foreword to *ACAS Model Workplace*, ACAS.

Drucker, P (1999) *Management Challenges for the Twenty-first Century*, Harper Business.

Emmott, M. (2005) CSR laid bare, *People Management*, Vol. 11, No. 16, 11 August, 38–40.

Faccini, R. and C. Hackworth (2010) Changes in output, employment and wages during recessions in the United Kingdom, *Bank of England Quarterly Bulletin*, Q1, Vol. 50, No. 1, 43–50.

Finn, W. (2010) The winner Baringa Partners, *UK's Best Workplaces: Special Report*, May, Great Place to Work Institute UK, 8–9.

French, R. (2007) *Cross-cultural Management in Work Organisations*, CIPD.

Green, K. (1999) Offensive thinking, *People Management*, Vol. 5, No. 8, 27.

He, H. (2009) Stealing cyber veggies thrives in a lonely world, *South China Morning Post*, 12 December.

Harrison, R. (2002) *Learning and Development*, CIPD.

Hofstede, G. (1980) *Culture's Consequences: International Differences in Work Related Values*, McGraw-Hill.

Hofstede, G. (1997) *Cultures and Organisations: Software of the Mind*, revised edition, McGraw-Hill.

Hutton, W. (2010) Foreword, *UK's Best Workplaces: Special Report*, May, Great Place to Work Institute UK, 4.

Industrial Relations Services (IRS) (2000) In-store personnel managers balance Tesco's scorecard, *IRS Employment Trends*, May, 13–16.

Industrial Relations Services, (2006) Recruiting knowledge workers, *IRS Employment Review*, 859, 17 November, IRS.

Kaplan, R.S. and D.P. Norton (1992) The balanced scorecard – measures that drive performance, *Harvard Business Review*, January–February, 71–79.

Further study

Books

Armstrong, M. and A. Baron (2007) *Human Capital Management: Achieving Added Value Through People*, Kogan Page.

This is an extremely useful book for those interested in finding out more about human capital and added value. Describes how human capital management provides a bridge between human resource management and strategy.

Kaplan, R.S. and D.P. Norton (1996) *The Balanced Scorecard: Translating Strategy into Action*, Harvard Business School Press.

Kaplan, R.S. and D.P. Norton (2000) Having trouble with your strategy? Then map it, *Harvard Business Review*, September–October, 167–176.

Lawrence, F. (2007) The miracle of cheap fresh food depends on illegality, *The Guardian*, Comment and Debate, Thursday 17 July.

Legge, K. (1995) *Human Resource Management: Rhetorics and Realities*, Macmillan Business.

McVeigh, K. (2007) Asda, Primark and Tesco accused over clothing factories, *The Guardian*, Monday 16 July.

Murphy, N. (2010) HR roles and responsibilities: the 2010 IRS survey, *IRS Employment Review*, 22.2.2010, IRS (www.xperthr.co.uk accessed 11.8.2010).

Niven, M. (1978) *Personnel Management 1913–63*, IPM.

Office for National Statistics (2009) Statistical bulletin, *National Population Projections: 2008 Based*, 21 October, 2–6. (www.statistics.gov.uk; accessed 18.8.2010).

Oliver J. (2010) *The Jamie Oliver Webpage* (www.jamieoliver.com; accessed 22.8.2010).

Paton, N. (2010) Preparing for the upturn, *UK's Best Workplaces: Special Report*, May, Great Place to Work Institute UK, 6–7.

Penna and the Chartered Institute of Personnel and Development (2008) *Gen Up: How the Four Generations Work Together*, Joint survey report, September, Penna (www.cipd.co.uk accessed 21.8.2010).

Purcell, J., N. Rinnie, S. Hutchinson (2003) Open minded, *People Management*, Vol. 9, No. 10, 31–33.

Reilly, P. (2007a) *The Changing HR Function: Transforming HR?* CIPD.

Reilly, P. (2007b) HR transformation: Facing up to facts, *People Management*, Vol. 13, No. 19.

Scarborough, H. (2003) Recipe for success, *People Management*, Vol. 9, No. 2, 32–35.

Scarborough, H. and the CIPD Human Capital Task Force (2003) Human capital: external reporting framework, *The Change Agenda*, CIPD (www.cipd.co.uk; accessed 16.9.04).

Sheppard, G. (2009) The rise and fall of talent management, *Personnel Today*, 27 October, RBI (www.xperthr.co.uk accessed 5.8.2010).

Suff, R. (2006) Managing knowledge workers, *IRS Employment Review*, 861, 15 December, IRS (www.xperthr.co.uk accessed 22.8.2010).

The Economist (2009) The long climb. A special report on the world economy, 3 October, 2–28.

Ulrich, D. and W. Brockbank (2005) Role call, *People Management*, 16 June, Vol. 11, No. 12, 24–28.

Journals

Human Resource Management Journal.
Quarterly, contains articles on a wide range of HRM issues of interest to practitioners and academics alike.

International Journal of Human Resource Management.
A monthly publication that focuses on the changing role of HR in a fast-changing global environment.

People Management.
Twice-monthly journal produced on behalf of the CIPD with topical articles relating to personnel management issues.

Personnel Review.
Journal produced six times per year with in-depth articles on personnel topics.

Personnel Today.

Contains topical articles on personnel management but is now only available online at www. xperthr.co.uk.

Articles

Rickard, C. and A. Boroughs (2009) Dos and Don'ts in a downturn, *People Management*, 15 January, 38–9.

One of *People Management*'s 'How to . . .' series: concise overviews of topical issues.

Internet

There are numerous useful sources of information from around the world relating to human resource management. We have found the following to be particularly useful:

The Advisory, Conciliation and Arbitration Service www.acas.org.uk
Useful articles, news and lists of ACAS publications.

The American Society for Human Resource Management www.shrm.org
The website for a US body that represents HRM managers. This includes topical people-related issues in America and video clips and podcasts.

The Australian Human Resource Institute www.ahri.com.au
Many articles relating to human resource management in Australia.

Chartered Institute of Personnel and Development www.cipd.co.uk
This is the website of the professional body that represents most personnel and development professionals in the UK. It includes a wide range of information, including podcasts, but some of the information is only accessible to CIPD members.

Department for Business, Innovation and Skills www.bis.gov.uk
Many useful publications, discussion documents and booklets can be found on this site, particularly in the 'Employment Matters' section.

The Government www.direct.gov.uk
Useful information site covering a wide range of employment-related topics such as holiday entitlements, disability issues etc.

Great Places to Work UK www.greatplacestowork.co.uk
This organisation has a set of criteria that it feels makes for a great place to work and it reviews UK and European workplaces against these criteria, making annual awards to organisations.

Incomes Data Services Limited www.incomesdata.co.uk
Some very useful articles on a range of HRM topics, including a section on management pay and remuneration, plus lists of contents for IDS publications.

People Management www.peoplemanagement.co.uk
Journal produced on behalf of the CIPD with topical articles relating to personnel management issues.

Trades Union Congress www.tuc.org.uk
This gives the TUC's views on many current HRM issues and new legislation in Britain.

Workforce online (US) www.hrhq.com
Another American site that provides useful information about HRM in the USA.

Xpert HR www.xperthr.co.uk
This is an extensive database of HR resources and includes some publications that are now only available on-line such as the *IRS Employment Review* and *Personnel Today.*

CHAPTER 2

Human resource strategy and planning

Objectives

When you have studied this chapter you will be able to:

- describe the three basic levels of strategic planning
- explain the concept of strategy formulation
- explain the need for human resource strategies in work organisations
- describe the stages involved in human resource planning
- identify and describe the issues that have an impact on human resource supply and demand forecasts
- use basic mathematical techniques to produce forecast supply figures
- describe the skills shortages encountered by employers, their causes and possible solutions
- comment on the use of IT systems in strategic HRM.

The chapter introducing human resource management (HRM) established that a key characteristic of the HRM approach is the involvement of the people management function at a strategic level. We will now look briefly at the different levels at which strategy can be formulated and the generic types of strategy that are encountered, and comment on the links between the formulation of business strategy and consideration of human resource issues. You must remember that we shall be looking at the ideal situation or models of how corporate/business strategy and HR considerations could interact. What we describe as an ideal is not always found in reality, or, indeed, the specific circumstances in which a business is operating might call for a different approach. You will find that occasionally throughout the text we refer to contingency approaches, which means that there is no one right way to manage human resources in an organisation.

Following an overview of corporate/business and human resource strategies, we examine the activities that underpin the development of HR strategies, namely the techniques involved in human resource planning and the factors which have a major impact on planning decisions. This chapter ends with a discussion of the role of IT in supporting strategic human resource management (SHRM) endeavours, and a brief overview of some relevant aspects of people management in the international sphere.

Strategy

Strategy can be defined as a plan of action for the future, answering the questions, first, of *what* to do, then, of *how* to do it. The three commonplace questions used to give a simple explanation of the strategic process are: Where are we now? Where do we want to be? How do we get there? A strategic plan should have a long-term focus, business plans usually being developed around a five-year perspective. The aim of designing and following a strategic plan is to create a competitive advantage, and all efforts in the formulation and implementation processes will be directed towards this. As far as work organisations are concerned, strategy can be formulated and implemented at different levels, and there are recognised generic forms of strategy that organisations or sub-divisions of organisations might adopt.

Levels of strategy

The levels at which strategy is formulated and implemented are most frequently identified as corporate, business and functional or operational (see, for example, Anthony *et al.* 1996; Boxall and Purcell, 2008; Greer, 2001; Lynch, 2003; Marchington and Wilkinson, 2005).

Corporate and business strategies

Corporate strategy is concerned with the overall direction that an organisation will follow. For large corporations, this is a question of which lines of business they will choose to be engaged in. These organisations would then develop separate business level strategies for their divisions, each of which might be engaged in producing very different products or services. As Anthony *et al.* (1996) point out, corporate and business strategy would be one and the same thing for a small organisation dealing only with one line of products or services, and it follows that you will sometimes find writers using the terms interchangeably when they are discussing these two levels of strategy.

Functional strategy

The functions represented in an organisation depend on the type of business, its size and structure, but may include production, marketing, sales, finance, research and development, and human resources. Each of these functional areas needs to be following strategic plans that are consonant with the corporate and business plans adopted by their organisations. The strategic plans adopted by all these functional departments must be integrated, however, to ensure the success of the organisation; they are interdependent and cannot be formulated in ignorance of each other. Indeed, it can be stated incontrovertibly that the human resource is an integral part of every one of the above-named functions.

The strategy formulation process

You will find throughout the discussion of the strategic planning process that there is a great deal of emphasis on gathering information as a basis for decision making.

There is a need to focus on relevant information, but it is also imperative to be comprehensive so you do not miss something that could have an impact. Since planning implies forecasting future actions, there is always the potential for developments that you may not have foreseen. This means that planning becomes a rolling process, and that a five-year plan developed in 2011 cannot be followed slavishly until the year 2016, but will probably need to be adjusted on an ongoing basis to account for unforeseen developments. Indeed, the credit crisis of 2008 necessitated radical change to the business plans of many organisations.

What kinds of information might senior managers in a company manufacturing and distributing consumer goods need to consider in order to formulate strategic plans?

You may have considered a variety of factors and kept in mind the types of changes that businesses in general are facing. Your list may include some of the following:

- **Product life cycle:** Is the product or service a new one with room for development and an expanding potential market? Is the product something that is bought once or do customers replace it? Is the product mature and not likely to attract more customers? Are customers likely to look for an alternative to the product or service?

- **Changing consumer tastes and requirements:** How are these likely to affect the demand for the product? Are there changes in customer expectations that organisations need to respond to?

- **The economy:** What are the prospects for disposable income in the UK and overseas?

- **Expansion of business into other countries:** Are there opportunities to sell your product or service abroad?

- **Competition:** What are the threats from competitors and the opportunities to compete? What will be the impact of new issues such as the growth of global competition, for instance increasing competition from countries like China?

- **Technological developments:** Will new technology affect the design of products, work processes and costs?

- **Legislation:** What regulations are in the pipeline and what are the associated implications for costs, work processes and product standards?

These are just some of the factors that affect business planning, and you may be able to identify even more. Information about all of these factors will influence what managers see as threats and opportunities and will therefore affect the strategic choices made and formulation of the strategic plan.

Keeping an eye on all of these issues is referred to as environmental scanning, and the acronym PEST or its alternative forms of PESTEL, PESTLE or EPISTLE are commonly used as a reminder of the issues that businesses need to take into consideration when formulating their strategies. The initials in PEST stand for political, economic, social and technological issues. The E and L in variations of the basic acronym variously stand for European, environmental and legislative issues.

ACTIVITY 2.1

Think of some current examples in these categories which may be of particular import to business strategists. Go to the companion website at www.pearsoned.co.uk/foothook to compare your suggestions with ours.

In summary, then, a strategic approach implies a *long-term view*, encompassing *global information* from *all relevant perspectives*, and focusing on an *ultimate goal of corporate success* through achieving and exploiting a position of *competitive advantage*. Furthermore, a strategic approach requires the *integration of activities and processes* throughout an organisation, all *aligned* to the *organisation's goals*.

Generic types of corporate and business strategy

There are a number of recognised generic types of strategies that companies may choose to follow. The overarching corporate strategies are generally cited as being growth, stability and retrenchment (Millmore *et al.*, 2007), but there are a number of ways of pursuing each of these. Growth can be achieved, for instance, through the development of new products, by acquiring a larger share of the market for existing products, through mergers and acquisitions. Glaister (1995) also lists internationalisation as a possible generic strategy that organisations might wish to follow. These strategic directions (i.e. growth, stability and retrenchment) are normally associated with the life cycle stages of products and markets (Johnson *et al.*, 2006) and the idea behind the BCG matrix put forward by the Boston Consulting Group in the 1970s is that large corporations would aim to have a balanced portfolio of businesses encompassing a range of these (see Lynch, 2003).

The work of Michael Porter (1980) is frequently cited in discussions of business-level strategies. The generic concepts he developed are cost leadership, differentiation and focus. One or a combination of these can be adopted in order to achieve the chosen corporate strategy. In adopting a strategy based on cost, companies will attempt to improve efficiency by reducing staffing and production costs. A strategy of differentiation means emphasising the distinctiveness of one's products or services, for example by being known for consistent high quality. A market or niche focus approach entails concentrating on a particular segment rather than the whole industry. As Glaister comments, this strategy can be pursued in combination with either cost leadership or differentiation. Innovation as a strategic direction can also provide a major focus (see, for instance, Johnson and Johnson's website at www.jnj.com) and Guest *et al.* (1997) make the point that all business strategies need an element of innovation.

Human resource strategies

Human resource strategies arise from the adoption of a strategic approach to people management which is aligned with the business strategy and which is reflected in a set of HR policy initiatives specifically designed to achieve the strategic goals of the business. This implies that an appropriate HR strategy is being 'read off' the

Did you know?

An IRS survey (2007) revealed that although almost all organisations surveyed recognised the need for strategic action, they still had not achieved an acceptable level of formal alignment between corporate and HR strategies. The analysis of the survey results comes to the conclusion that there is still a lot of work to be done in this area for organisations to achieve the full potential of adopting a strategic approach.

corporate strategy to provide the 'best fit' between the two levels of strategy (discussed in detail by Marchington and Wilkinson, 2005, pp. 106–113). Ideally, however, human resource considerations should inform the corporate strategy and affect what is included in it (CIPD, 2010c). The costs of the HR strategies and the probability of their success should have been a factor in the decision to pursue the particular business strategic goal in the first place.

HR strategies reflect the philosophy of senior management with regard to the treatment of human resources and address the various activities related to their management. The underlying premise of this is that the HR function supports corporate goals by developing and implementing people management practices which engage employees and encourage them to direct their efforts towards the achievement of organisational goals (CIPD, 2005). The most tangible aspect of strategic HRM is, therefore, the set of HR policies and processes in existence in an organisation, and these would normally address the various aspects of people management such as recruitment, diversity management, development, reward and employee relations. In other words, rather than being able to identify *the* human resource strategy of an organisation, one will encounter an organisation's recruitment strategy or its diversity strategy or its reward strategy, either explicitly addressed as a strategy or reflected in the organisation's policies and processes. For many organisations, the main focus of their HR strategies is to acquire, develop and maintain an engaged workforce, and this is dealt with in Chapter 3.

As environmental factors change, different issues may assume critical strategic importance. One example of this which is examined later in this chapter (see the discussion of skills shortages) and in other parts of the book is the issue of the war for talent. Because of increased competition for skilled employees in a wide variety of positions, many organisations across the globe have developed a talent management strategy or talent management processes (CIPD, 2010d; Ready and Conger, 2007; Wooldridge, 2006), and the need to acquire and/or retain highly competent employees has not been diminished by the economic downturn of 2008/2009. The strategic approach to the various aspects of people management mentioned in this and the preceding paragraph is covered in the relevant chapters throughout this text.

Because there are so many important aspects of people management strategy, it becomes essential that these various strategies are coherent and supportive of each other as well as being aligned with the overall business strategy. Other crucial aspects of successful strategic HRM are effective communication and change management (CIPD, 2005). In order to be motivated to achieve an organisation's goals, its people need to understand what is expected of them and how their efforts contribute to their organisation's success; hence the need for excellent communication systems. Also, of necessity, operating in a strategic fashion means dealing with change since the definition of a strategic approach involves planning for the future and adjusting to a turbulent business environment. The CIPD (2005, p. 3) poses a number of questions for HR strategists to consider when embarking on the strategy formulation, development and implementation processes. Some examples of these questions are: Will line managers support strategy initiatives and do they have the skills to implement them? How are staff generally likely to react to the strategy? Can any difficulties be anticipated, and if so, how can they be dealt with? These questions help the practitioner to focus on more general aspects of project and change management processes as well as developing the HR strategies *per se*.

The discussion of strategic HRM and HR strategies so far has emphasised the role of the HR practitioner as a business partner, one of the roles in HR described by Ulrich (CIPD, 2010c). The devolution of people management responsibilities to line managers at all levels in an organisation is, however, recognised as a basic element of the HRM approach (Storey, 2007), so line involvement in the development and implementation of HR strategies is essential. Hutchinson and Purcell (2003) emphasised that front-line managers, defined as line managers with no managerial staff reporting to them, play a crucial role in ensuring that HR strategies are carried out effectively, and ongoing research into aspects of people management continues to affirm the key role that line managers play. You can find examples of this in the research reports on employee engagement published by the CIPD (2010b) and the government (Macleod and Clarke 2009). Strategic HR practitioners, therefore, need to incorporate line management views into the HR strategy planning process, nurture the relationship between the HR function and line managers, and ensure that line managers are actively engaged with the people management strategy. Unfortunately, the achievement of this goal of mutual understanding between HR strategists and line managers has been identified as problematic (Smethurst, 2005). This is obviously another instance where improvements in communication and change management are required.

Human resource planning

Whatever the strategy adopted by an organisation, it is recognised that an unrelenting and increasing rate of change is an unavoidable phenomenon of today's workplace. The implication is that tomorrow's workplace will not be the same as today's. Employment patterns are changing, as we discuss in more detail in Chapter 4 on the employment relationship, and changing work methods, arising, for instance, from technological advances, give rise to requirements for different and new skills and for flexibility from existing employees to acquire these new skills or adapt to new methods of working. This highlights the need for human resource planning which responds to this situation by taking a long-term view and works towards preparing an organisation to cope with its future requirements and achieve its strategic objectives. The information acquired through the process of human resource planning provides the foundation for the development of human resource strategies.

The next few sections of this chapter examine the stages involved in the human resource planning process, the types of issues and information that need to be considered, and techniques for processing that information.

Did you know?

Research completed by the CIPD in 2010 led to the recognition of a resurgence of interest in human resource planning in a wide variety of organisations, including public sector organisations, and small and medium-sized enterprises as well as large private sector companies. As a result, the CIPD has compiled a guide to what it calls workforce planning. The guide covers many of the issues addressed in this chapter and so represents excellent further reading for anyone interested in consolidating and deepening their understanding of this area. Six case studies also provide information on the approach adopted by various organisations.

(*Source*: Baron, A., R. Clarke, P. Turner and S. Pass (2010) *Workforce Planning: Right People, Right Time, Right Skills. A Guide*, Spring, CIPD; available at www.cipd.co.uk)

Estimating the demand for human resources

Whatever the goals of the corporate/business plan are, they can be achieved only by the application of human skill and effort. One of the primary stages in the human resource planning process is therefore to estimate what will be required in terms of skills and numbers of people to achieve the corporate goals, i.e. the demand for human resource inputs. Let us take some examples of corporate goals so that we can envisage what this exercise might entail.

ACTIVITY 2.2

Examine the following two scenarios, and evaluate what will be required in terms of human resources in order to achieve the goals stated in each case. What factors would have to be considered in making forecasts of requirements?

1 A UK distributor of women's clothing wishes to expand its customer base into Germany, France and Spain. It intends to open a warehouse and distribution depot in France.

2 A regional building society and a national bank are set to merge.

Discussion of Activity 2.2

In order to assess the requirements for human resources in the above scenarios, you would have to envisage:

● what tasks need to be done
● the skills required to complete these tasks
● how the tasks could be grouped together to form jobs, taking the skills requirements into consideration
● how many people would be required to complete the volume of work.

First, then, there is a matter of the identification of discrete work tasks, followed by the organisation of those work tasks into jobs (i.e. a collection of tasks that somehow belong together and could reasonably be carried out by one individual), and a qualitative analysis of the skill base required to perform those jobs and achieve the organisation's goals. The records that document tasks and skills in an organisation are the job descriptions (JDs) and person specifications, and the information contained in these documents is collected and organised through the processes of job analysis and job design, which are discussed more fully in Chapter 6, which deals with recruitment. Alternatively, an organisation might use a competency framework to describe the skills and attributes required and create job profiles based on this (see pages 172–5). Second, there is the task of quantifying the numbers of people required.

In scenario 1 you will have identified the need for the staff to run the warehousing and distribution processes in the new depot in France. This will include a manager, picking and packing staff, administrative staff and drivers. You may further have considered the need for language skills among some of these staff to cope with communications with the customers in Spain and Germany and with the home base in the UK. The expansion of business into these countries might also mean adding new tasks and skill requirements to existing posts in the home base, or it may mean recruiting a new manager and/or administrative staff who have the requisite language skills and knowledge of marketing and business processes in those countries. At the very least, the expansion of business into new countries implies a need for someone to coordinate the activities with headquarters. You would need additional information about the expected volume of business to be able to calculate how many people will be required in each category of employee.

Scenario 2 requires an examination of where skills and functions overlap within the two types of business, which might imply that some duties can be merged and not all of the existing posts will be needed. Alternatively, because the new, merged organisation will cover a wider range of tasks than either of the separate organisations had, there may be a new requirement for people who can combine skills and manage tasks in both areas.

Quantitative aspects of estimating demand

Having worked out what is required in terms of tasks to be done and skills needed to complete those tasks, an analysis is required of how many people are needed for the volume of work.

Pause for thought 2.2 Imagine you are a manufacturer who is going to export clothes to mainland Europe. You have estimated that you will require sewing machine operators to produce an additional 10,000 blouses in the first year. What methods could you use to estimate how many people you would need for this task?

If you have no previous measures of how much work is produced by your employees, you can engage in work study techniques This involves determining how the task can be performed most efficiently and timing the operation. You would then calculate how many blouses can be sewn at this rate in one year by one operator and divide your production target of 10,000 by this number to get the number of employees required.

If prior data do exist, you can use past production figures and calculate the ratio of operatives to the number of blouses produced by taking the total figure of blouses produced divided by the total number of operatives engaged in this or similar work. You might also apply managerial judgement by basing your calculations on a task that is similar to producing a blouse.

Another historical figure employers might use is the ratio of various categories of personnel to the volume of sales or the number of customers. For instance, if a distribution company has one invoice clerk for every 10,000 customers, and it intends to increase its customer base by 10,000, the historical ratio indicates a need for one additional invoice clerk.

You would need to take account of the fact that new employees might not work at full capacity until fully trained, or you might envisage savings from economies of scale or from changing work methods or the technology used. In other words, even when statistical methods are used to calculate the demand for human resources, managerial judgement will also be a factor.

Estimating the internal supply of human resources

As with estimating the demand for human resources, organisations need to combine qualitative data based on managerial judgement with quantitative data to assess whether the requisite resources will be available.

A properly designed human resource information system (HRIS) will provide data on the numbers of existing employees in various categories of posts (the internal supply of human resources), and personal data that may have an impact on how long they are likely to be with the organisation. There are some simple statistical techniques that enable employers to forecast fluctuations in their workforce numbers. The basic figure that most employers calculate is the labour turnover rate, sometimes referred to as the wastage rate or the separation rate, which represents the proportion of employees who leave in a given period of time, usually a year or a quarter. This figure is calculated as a percentage by dividing the number of leavers by the total complement of staff and multiplying this figure by 100. If the requirements for staff vary during the time period, the total complement can be calculated as an average of the number required at the beginning of the period and the number required at the end. This would give an overall turnover rate for an organisation, but it is usually more useful to calculate the rate for specific categories of staff such as secretarial staff, systems analysts, employees in specified production areas, etc.

For example, if a company requires 50 machinists throughout the year, and five of these have left in one year, then the turnover rate is $(5/50) \times 100 = 10$ per cent. The average turnover rate experienced over a period of time can be used as a trend to forecast requirements for the future. For instance, if the turnover rate for machinists in our example company has been fairly stable at about 10 per cent over the past three years, then this employer knows that it is likely to be necessary to recruit five machinists next year to maintain his or her supply. If the demand forecast implies that additional machinists will be needed over the next few years, the 10 per cent turnover rate should be factored into the recruitment calculation.

ACTIVITY 2.3

At the end of 2011, the employer in question decides that she will require 10 additional machinists in each of the next three years. The additional machinists are to be recruited at the beginning of each year. How many machinists will she have to recruit during each year to maintain the workforce?

Discussion of Activity 2.3

These figures are best calculated by tracking the base figure required each year, the increase in personnel required, and an adjustment for the expected turnover. As you can see, the manufacturer needs not only to recruit the additional 10 employees each year, but also to cover the turnover on the new base figure. With a typical labour turnover rate of 10 per cent, in 2012, five of the original employees may leave, and perhaps one of the new employees. The figures are presented in Table 2.1.

Table 2.1 Estimated recruitment figures adjusted for labour turnover

	Number of machinists required	Increase over previous year	Projected turnover during year	Number to recruit during year
End of 2011	50			
2012	60	10	6	16
2013	70	10	7	17
2014	80	10	8	18

Another calculation that can be made is known as the stability index. This also gives an indication of turnover, but provides information additional to the base turnover figure and is calculated as follows: (Number of people currently employed with one year or more of service/number of people employed one year ago) × 100.

ACTIVITY 2.4

This is a simple activity that will help you to focus on the information that can be gleaned by analysing the same data in different ways.

1 You are asked to perform a simple calculation for each of three situations.

(a) Your organisation has 20 drivers. In one year, 5 of these drivers leave and have to be replaced. Calculate the turnover rate.

(b) Your organisation has 20 drivers. At the end of one year, you still have 19 of those drivers with you, but you have had to recruit 5 times to keep your staff complement up to 20. Calculate the turnover rate and the stability index.

(c) Your organisation has 20 drivers. In one year, 5 drivers leave. Each of them had 2 to 5 years of service. You have had to replace each of them and your new recruits are still with you. Calculate the turnover rate and the stability index.

2 What do these turnover and stability index figures tell you?

Discussion of Activity 2.4

You should have calculated a turnover figure of 25 per cent for each of these circumstances. On its own, the turnover figure reveals nothing about the underlying causes of turnover, and this is emphasised by the fact that you have the same figure for the two very different circumstances described as (b) and (c) above. The turnover rate on its own becomes meaningful only if you can compare it with rates experienced by your organisation in the past or by other organisations in your industry for similar categories of staff. Then you can deduce whether you are performing in a competitive way in terms of retaining staff, or whether there are problems you need to investigate. This is, however, not a straightforward exercise as employers may include or exclude various categories of leavers, such as employees who have been dismissed for misconduct, redundant staff or retirees.

The stability index figures, 95 per cent in scenario (b) and 75 per cent in scenario (c), are much more revealing. The similarity among all three scenarios in the exercise is that there have been five recruitment actions in each case; the stability index, however, reveals that the situations are different and the reasons for the vacancies differed. The higher figure, which means that the turnover is not occurring among the longer-serving employees, indicates that there is a problem with retaining new recruits. The lower figure indicates that the problem lies with the retention of longer serving employees. Each problem requires different action to remedy it, and this will be very important when you arrive at the stage of formulating human resource management action plans.

Pause for thought 2.3

In the discussion of Activity 2.4, we mentioned that comparing your turnover to that experienced by your competitors might prompt you to analyse retention problems. If your turnover rate was unfavourable in such a comparison, what might some of the problems and remedies be?

Some of the problems and remedies associated with excessive turnover are represented in Table 2.2.

Table 2.2 Labour turnover: causes and remedies

Cause	Remedy
Poor handling of new recruits	Design and implement induction process
Unfavourable salary/terms and conditions of employment	Revise reward strategies
Job dissatisfaction	Improve job design
Low morale	Organisational culture change
	Employee involvement and engagement practices
	Employee opinion surveys
Recruits not equipped for work demands	Improve recruitment and selection practices
	Improve training

There are some other factors that have an impact on the turnover rate. Some of these might be reflected in long-term trends and others may cause occasional fluctuations. One such factor is the age of employees. Retirement may account for a certain percentage of leavers on an ongoing basis, but it also sometimes happens that an organisation has a large number of people due to retire at the same time, which will temporarily increase the turnover rate. This continues to be a consideration even if one pays due attention to the changing regulations with regard to the normal retirement age discussed in Chapter 5, 'Diversity and equality'. Factors such as this need to be taken into consideration in forecasting the supply of human resources and when adjusting the estimates to reflect the effects of labour turnover. To achieve successful strategic planning, the HRIS should be set up so that it can provide this information.

In addition to information about numbers, the analysis of various aspects of the workforce can highlight a range of problems or issues that deserve consideration. Some of the analyses that could be obtained pertaining to both leavers and retained workers are:

- the male/female distribution of personnel across the whole workforce or in each category of employee
- the distribution across the workforce or by employee category of members of specified ethnic minority groups
- age profiles
- length of service for each of the above.

These analyses of human capital could help managers to see where new approaches or policies are needed to help the organisation reach its goals.

A further factor that may have an impact on future internal supply is the fact that people often have skills that their employer may not have required them to use in their current post. These could include facility in foreign languages, computer knowledge, training skills and interpersonal skills. In order to have a full picture of skills available from the current workforce the organisation needs to develop a skills inventory, with each individual's competencies recorded on their personal record, which will form part of the organisation's HRIS. The skills inventory should list skills that are available but not being used in addition to those that are being used.

Assessing the external supply of human resources

At the same time as analysing their internal supply of human resources, employers need to be aware of the availability of potential employees externally in case the internal supply falls short of what is required. If the internal supply of employees cannot meet the demand, managers must know whether there are problems with the availability of workers from outside the organisation. Indeed, the Industrial Relations Services (2001) reported that competition for new recruits was likely to be a major problem for employers throughout the first decade of the twenty-first century. The ongoing problems with skills shortages, reported later in this chapter, indicate that this has in fact proven to be the case, even taking the effects of the recession into account.

The labour force is defined as the number of people aged 16 and over, and who are either in employment or available for work. As such, those members of the labour force who are not currently employed by a particular employer constitute that employer's external labour market. Sometimes separate figures are given for people of working age, but since some people continue working past the state retirement age, figures for persons in their late sixties and seventies are included in estimates of the total labour force. Changes to the state retirement age also mean that working life is being extended. Current plans mean that the state retirement age will be 66 for men from 2016, and 68 for everyone by 2046.

Pause for thought 2.4   There are many factors that have an impact on:

- the size of the labour force in general
- the availability of employees from the labour force to any particular employer.

Before you go on to read about these factors, make a list of as many of them as you can think of. You may also wish to consider what employers might have to do to counteract any problems you identify.

● Size and composition of the labour force

British labour force projections for the years 2006–20, as reported in *Labour Market Trends* (Madouros, 2006), included the following data:

- Between 2006 and 2020 the labour force is set to increase, but the rate of increase will decline over that period. The labour force is projected to consist of 32.1 million economically active people in 2020.

- The working age is defined here as 16–64 years old, but a growing number of people *above* the age of 64 are expected to continue to be economically active, and, as noted earlier, there will be compelling reasons for people to opt for this as the state retirement age increases.
- The proportion of people in the labour force aged under 50 will fall to 69 per cent by 2020. By comparison, it was 75 per cent in 2005.
- 50 to 54-year-olds will constitute the largest economically active group in 2020.
- The activity rates of women will increase over this period, partly because, by 2020, women will have to work until the age of 65 before they can claim the state pension. Again, note the changes expected by 2046 which will reinforce this phenomenon.
- The proportion of women in the labour force increased noticeably in comparison to the proportion of men in the 1970s and 1980s. These relative proportions are now stabilising: 54.2 per cent male and 45.8 per cent female in 2005, expected to be 53.3 per cent male and 46.7 per cent female in 2020. So female participation in the labour force is still expected to increase but at a slower rate than previously.

Changes in the numbers of people in the labour force are caused by a combination of population effects and activity rate effects. Increasing numbers of young people are choosing to study full time which, together with birth rate effects, account for the lower numbers of people in the lower age groups available for work. However, this may be offset by an increase in the numbers of students who work on a part-time basis. The ageing of the labour force is a noticeable phenomenon, and there is an expectation that more older people will wish to extend their participation in the workforce until a later age, many of them for financial reasons such as poor pension provision. The important issue from the point of view of analysing the external labour market is the extent to which employers are noting this shift and adjusting their recruitment strategies in response. As will be seen later, skills shortages are a continuing challenge for employers, even in recessionary times, and if the people available in the labour market belong increasingly to an older age group, this may call for different strategies in attracting them, a different approach to training may be required, and older employees may have different requirements with regard to flexibility in their working arrangements.

Economic activity rates also affect the size and composition of the labour force. Increasing numbers of young people are choosing to study full time which, together with birth rate effects, account for the lower numbers of people in the lower age groups available for work. There was a peak birth rate around 1964 which accounts for some of the increase in the 45 and over age group in the projection period, and the birth rate was particularly low in the years 1973–79 (Armitage and Scott, 1998). Further demographic changes which affect the projections of the labour force are increased life expectancy and migration.

The numbers of people presenting themselves as being economically active can also be affected by the state of the economy. Increased numbers of people were reported to have become economically *inactive* in 2010 when job opportunities in some areas were so scarce that people stopped looking for vacancies.

The growing proportion of women in the labour force is attributed in part to socio-economic influences such as the greater availability of part-time work and the social acceptability of women in employment as well as the raising of the state pension age for women. All of the factors discussed in this section have implications particularly for employers who have a traditional view of whom they might employ, for instance in positions thought of as being suitable for school leavers. The changing demographic structure of the external labour market may oblige employers to adopt more open approaches to recruitment and to consider the necessity of providing training.

The figures provided by surveys of the national labour force are important in providing a broad indication of factors to be considered in human resource planning. There are, however, some limitations on their usefulness. The statistics are only estimates, projections of the numbers of people expected to be economically active in the future. As such, they have to be predicated on some basic assumptions linked with patterns of economic activity observed at the time the analysis is performed. Obviously, unexpected events can occur which may have a sizeable impact on the validity of the projected figures. The IDS study, *The Future Workforce* (1996), provides some useful guidelines on how to interpret statistical data culled from workforce surveys, and the CIPD (2009c) provides some insight into the complexity of broader economic factors.

Tight and slack labour markets

As the CIPD (2009c) explains, the interplay of many factors in the economy may result in a tight labour market or one that has more slack in it. Examples of these factors are the demand for goods and services, employers' recruitment intentions, how much employers have to pay to attract people. Also, as we have already indicated, the number of migrants who choose to come here to look for work has an impact on the number of people who are economically active in the UK.

Rates of unemployment and the prevalence of redundancies have an obvious impact on the numbers of people looking for work. This does not necessarily mean, however, that meeting one's requirements for human resources is automatically easier in times of high unemployment. Redundant jobseekers may have a range of skills, but not necessarily in the areas required by other employers. There is also resistance among newly redundant people to accepting a large immediate drop in earnings. The existence of large numbers of unemployed or newly redundant people, therefore, does not equate directly with a ready supply of human resources.

The existence of competitors that also need people with the same skills will obviously influence the availability of human resources. This may have a direct impact on recruitment and pay strategies as employers try to attract the best people in direct competition with other companies. For the purposes of human resource planning, it will be important to be informed about existing competitors and to assess the likelihood of new competitors arriving on the scene.

If the labour market is tight, this means that employers experience difficulties in recruiting and the term 'skills shortages' is used to describe this. A slacker labour market means that there are plenty of appropriate human resources on the market and employers can fill their vacancies more easily. Skills shortages can arise for a variety of reasons and this term does not necessarily imply that the required skills are actually in shortage. They may not be available to employers for other reasons which we shall explore later.

Skills shortages

The issue of skills shortages fluctuates over time. They were regarded as a serious and widespread issue in the early years of the twenty-first century, but, as the CIPD

(2007a) reported, fewer employers reported these difficulties in 2005, probably because of the large influx of migrants after the enlargement of the EU in 2004 and because this was a difficult year in terms of economic growth so demand was suppressed to some extent. Problems with recruitment increased again in 2006 with a stronger economy, and with 84 per cent of employers reporting recruitment difficulties in 2006, it obviously continued to be an issue of some concern. Even when recruitment levels decreased in 2008 and 2009, a large number of recruiting organisations, 81 per cent according to the CIPD (2010a), still reported skills shortages. Admittedly, a smaller number was reported in the 2010 resourcing and talent planning survey report (CIPD 2010d), but still 68 per cent of employers declared recruitment problems. This coincides with reports of large numbers of unsuitable applications for vacant posts (CIPD 2010d), reaffirming the point that higher levels of unemployment do not necessarily equate with greater ease of recruitment. Several sources also confirm that employers are likely to face renewed levels of skills shortages on the arrival of an economic upturn (Confederation of British Industry (CBI) 2010; Craig 2009).

It is vital that organisations take steps to counteract skills shortages as they have a detrimental impact on operational effectiveness. The IRS (2000) reports that one major result of recruitment difficulties, together with the problem of skill gaps identified in internal staff, is a poorer level of customer service. Lost business and an inability to develop new products as planned are also identified as consequences of skills shortages and skill gaps. The UK Commission for Employment and Skills (UKCES, 2010) refers to a heavier workload for colleagues as being the most frequently reported negative effect of skills gaps, along with higher costs, problems with quality standards and difficulties in introducing new working methods. Employees can suffer too, as HR specialists and line managers might have to neglect 'other areas' such as training and development, coaching and general employee welfare issues' (Sloane, 2007) to spend more time on difficult recruitment campaigns. As a counterpoint to this stand the reports that employers are focusing much more effort on retention of employees with a major emphasis on training (CIPD, 2009b). This inevitably places some stress on the capabilities of HR specialists and line managers. These business repercussions highlight the effect of skills shortages on strategy formulation both at the corporate and the functional HR level.

Examples of skills shortages reported

The CIPD (2009b, p. 6) states that employers surveyed about their recruitment experiences report skills shortages in the 'necessary specialist skills' and a lack of sufficient experience, but they also reported a problem with 'higher pay expectations'. All sectors reported some level of recruitment difficulty (manufacturing and production; voluntary, community and not-for-profit; private sector services; public sector), and the types of jobs that were difficult to fill included managers and professionals, senior managers and directors. Lower figures were cited for administrative, secretarial and technical positions, services (including customer and sales services) and manual and craft workers (CIPD, 2009b, p. 6).

The UKCES (2010, p. 24) reports on a lack of 'technical, practical and job-specific skills' as well as customer-handling, problem-solving and team working skills. Both the UKCES (2010) and the CBI (2009) emphasise that employers are observing a lack of appropriate literacy and numeracy levels, with the CBI pinpointing this as being a problem with school leavers and to a lesser extent with graduates. Employers are also looking for improvements in business awareness and time management skills in these groups.

Reasons for skills shortages

As indicated previously, there can be a variety of factors that contribute to any one employer's recruitment problems. It might be that there is an actual lack of specific skills available in the labour market. The CBI (2009) report, for instance, alludes to failure of the educational system to prepare young people properly for business life. Recruitment difficulties might be a regional issue connected to the cost of living and travel in different parts of the country. It might be that the terms and conditions, pay and benefits offered by a particular employer are less attractive than those offered by a competitor.

The organisation's reputation in general might attract some people and not others. Public perceptions of what a job entails will make occupations seem more attractive or less so. Social work, particularly work involving the care of children, has notoriously suffered in this way for some years. In the first decade of the twenty-first century alone, two horrific cases of child abuse and death have hit the newspaper headlines in the UK: Victoria Climbié, who died in February 2000, and Baby Peter in August 2007. There has been massive negative publicity about the social workers involved in these cases (as well as other professionals who were involved in the care of these children), and indeed, for the whole decade, difficulties in recruiting people into social work have persisted.

With so many potential causes for skills shortages, it is self-evident that there could be a variety of solutions, and an appropriate solution or mix of responses will be necessary to address the problem.

Solutions to skills shortages

Provide training

If employers recognise that the required skills actually are not available, one solution is to recruit people who can be trained up. Organisations may also look to their own current employees (their internal supply of human resources) for skills they do not have. This is known as a 'skills gap', and again, provision of training can be the answer. The CIPD's survey (2009b) indicates that the provision of training is the preferred response to skills shortages, with 74 per cent of respondents providing training for new recruits and 75 per cent training up their current employees. This approach is seen as leading to improved retention of existing staff, in which case employers would have less need for recruitment activities in the first place, and the focus on development continued to be reported in the 2010 survey.

Some organisations have even gone to the extent of setting up their own educational establishment and qualifications to ensure a supply of skills at the appropriate level. Arcadia Group founded a Fashion Retail Academy in 2006, and in 2005 the BBC founded a College of Journalism (CoJo), supported by online learning opportunities, to raise the level of skills and knowledge in its reporters and newsreaders in areas such as writing skills, politics and the law. Visit **www.bbc.co.uk/journalism** to see how this innovative approach works.

Recruiting overseas/targeting migrant workers/offshoring

Subject to immigration laws, it is possible for employers to turn to other countries and recruit people there to come and work in the UK. 36 per cent of employers surveyed by the CIPD (2009b) felt this approach was beneficial, although only 18 per cent engaged in it. Almost equally useful (32 per cent) but actually used slightly less (13 per cent) was targeting migrant workers from the extended EU. It must be noted that the relationships between these figures tend to fluctuate in tune with economic circumstances and government regulations. Although often undertaken for reasons of costs, skills shortages could also be addressed by relocating jobs to countries such as India and China where resources are in plentiful supply. The CIPD (2007a, p. 19) reported the following countries as attracting the highest levels of offshoring from the UK: India (favoured by 53 per cent of the survey respondents), China (27 per cent) and Poland (18 per cent).

Diversity and the labour market

The problem of skills shortages can be alleviated by eliminating entrenched stereotypical ideas about who might be suitable for particular types of jobs. In spite of legal obligations to provide equality of opportunity in the workplace, there are still some occupations where barriers need to be broken down to facilitate access for particular groups of people, and sometimes individuals too have stereotyped ideas about the suitability of certain occupations. A BBC Radio 4 (2007) section of Woman's Hour examined the persistence of the stereotyping of some occupations as men's jobs (construction; engineering) and others as women's jobs (hairdressing; nursing; caring). The programme highlighted the need for improved standards in careers advice and training for careers advisers, while acknowledging the role of attitudes and cultural influences on career choice. The consensus was that steps need to be taken to ensure that women are better equipped to make informed decisions about career choices.

Employers can engage in targeted recruitment to encourage applications from groups who do not normally apply for certain jobs. In recent years, some metropolitan police forces have had recruitment campaigns encouraging Asians to apply to join the police, and B&Q was a well-known example of making a point of recruiting older employees long before age discrimination regulations were in force (IDS, 2004). It is also advisable to re-visit the person specification for jobs to confirm that all the requirements listed there for qualifications and experience are really necessary. Indeed, the CIPD (2009b) reported a marked increase in the numbers of employers willing to consider a broader range of candidate qualities during recruitment rather than focusing on formal qualifications alone.

Further examples of innovative approaches to easing recruitment difficulties through the promotion of diversity come from the judiciary and the utilities sector. *The Times* reported that Judge Geoffrey Kamil was one of 45 circuit judges visiting their local community groups to speak to them about how the judicial system works, which might even result in increased interest in working in the system (Gibb, 2007). *Personnel Today* (2007) reported on steps taken by the water companies, including going out to schools and offering a qualification as part of the GCSE course, targeting people leaving the Armed Forces, and focusing on training for ex-offenders.

Employer branding

Among other things, being known as an employer that is committed to diversity is very much a part of creating an employer brand which will attract applicants. Being an employer of choice would also entail things such as good pay and working conditions, but equally important are the less tangible aspects of the workplace such as ensuring that employees have a voice and that they are fully engaged. Employers must obviously treat employees appropriately on an ongoing basis to deserve and maintain their employer brand, but it is important to communicate this, partly through advertising, to attract prospective employees. A total of 85 per cent of employers identify their mission, culture and values as being the essence of their employer brand (CIPD, 2007b), but many also recognise the significance of other aspects of their organisation for their reputation as an employer of choice. These include the quality of the career and development opportunities and the reward packages they offer, their commitment to supporting work–life balance and diversity, and their stance on corporate social responsibility.

Although it is only one of a list of the attributes of an employer brand, it is worth highlighting the importance of the work–life balance issue, which we also address in more detail in Chapter 4 on the employment relationship. We have addressed diversity in the workforce here and in Chapter 5, and diversity of necessity brings about a requirement for greater flexibility in working arrangements to respond to the varying needs of people from different cultures and at differing stages in their lives. If employers wish to obtain the benefits offered by diversity, they must make reasonable efforts to accommodate their employees' needs and help them to achieve an acceptable balance between their work and their non-work lives.

● Summary

All the factors that affect the labour force are important to employers. Similar to the need for environmental scanning that was described regarding the formulation of corporate or business strategy, up-to-date information is the key to effective human resource planning. Managers need to be aware of local, regional, national and global trends and be able to integrate this knowledge into their strategic plans. Knowledge of the key issues will enable organisations to assess the threats and opportunities in their environment, and to evaluate their ability to respond with their existing and available resources.

Comparing demand and supply forecasts

A comparison of your expected demand for human resources and your expected supply will identify what you need to accomplish in your human resource plans in order to achieve your corporate goals, or, as already mentioned, there may be an indication that the corporate/business plan needs some adjustment. You can be faced with a number of situations:

- internal supply = demand
- internal supply > demand
- internal supply < demand
- internal plus external supply < demand.

Since there are so many changes affecting organisations, as we have already discussed, and since this is likely to continue for the foreseeable future, internal supply is not likely to equal demand. This is more likely to occur in very stable conditions. If internal supply is greater than demand, human resource plans will need to focus on eliminating the surplus through redeployment or redundancy or through other adjustments to working arrangements. In response to recessionary pressures in 2008–2010, it has been noticeable that employers have opted to retain employees through adjustments to their working hours rather than losing them by declaring redundancies. This reflects long-term thinking in terms of a desire to be ready for an economic upturn. When internal supply is less than demand, an organisation will be involved in recruitment or other methods of acquiring the necessary skills such as outsourcing tasks. In the final instance, where internal supply plus external supply is inadequate to meet demand, the solutions we have just described with regard to combating skills shortages come into play, or organisational goals must be revisited and adjusted to reflect the resourcing problems.

Developing and implementing human resource strategies

In Chapter 1 we presented a long list of the major people management activities, and these can be categorised into four broad areas: resourcing, development, reward and employment relations. It is useful to refer to these categories to identify the areas in which it is necessary to develop human resource strategies and action plans.

Resourcing

If demand exceeds supply, the organisation will have to develop plans to acquire the additional skills it needs. This may involve recruitment activities, but there may also be a need for career and succession planning for existing employees, and the organisation may consider subcontracting work. If internal supply exceeds demand, the organisation may have to release staff, but consideration should first be given to redeployment and to providing the training that this might entail.

Development

If skills gaps exist, meaning that the competencies the organisation needs are not present in its current workforce, managers should make plans to develop those skills through training, team and individual development, and performance management. The provision of opportunities for development is identified by the CIPD (2009b and 2010d) as one of the major retention initiatives undertaken by employers.

Reward

A review and restructuring of the reward system might enable an organisation to attract and retain the required complement of human resources. The organisation should examine its pay levels and the attractiveness of its benefits packages and terms and conditions compared with those of competitors. Action plans should also address the issue of linking both financial and non-monetary rewards properly to the achievement of corporate goals.

Employment relations

Improvements in the contribution that employees make to their employing organisation can often be achieved through developing better employment relations. Areas to consider include consultation, communications, employee involvement and engagement, and the development of a partnership approach.

All of the functional areas mentioned briefly above are discussed in greater depth in the chapters that follow. The major aspects of the strategic human resource planning process are captured in the model presented as Figure 2.1. You should be able to track the elements of this model back to the discussion contained in this chapter.

Information technology systems and HR

Some comment about HR uses of computerised information systems is apropos at this juncture. We have established the need for a broad spectrum of information to manage HR activities in a strategic fashion and to make the business case, but still observers of HR in practice are reporting that a majority of HR experts are unable to pull the requisite figures together with an acceptable level of speed and accuracy (Twentyman, 2006). As mentioned in Chapter 1, HR specialists are increasing their use of IT systems for many operational activities such as recruitment and development, and this is reflected in much of the published material about how organisations are using IT in the context of people management (CIPD, 2006; IRS, 2006; Twentyman, 2007).

The use of IT is seen as being instrumental in the successful delivery of a number of people management strategies once these have been formulated, e.g. facilitating the level of communication needed to support employee voice and engagement (CIPD, 2006). This is still, however, an operational use of IT. There are also suggestions that these transactional uses of IT free up HR experts to engage in more activities at a strategic level (CIPD, 2006; CIPD, 2007c). Where they need to make greater strides, however, is in the provision of HR metrics to inform and support strategic decision making (CIPD, 2009a).

Twentyman (2006) gives some examples of strategic analyses using business intelligence tools. She reports on Rotherham Metropolitan Borough Council and how it has used its HRIS to compile its best value performance indicators with regard to the achievement of strategic diversity objectives. Other potential and real applications reported are a breakdown of the workforce by strategically important variables such as availability of specified skills, employers' use of information to benchmark themselves against other organisations, analyses based on 'what if' scenarios, modelling the impact of proposed changes. There are some indicators elsewhere that HR may be

Figure 2.1 Model of the human resource planning process

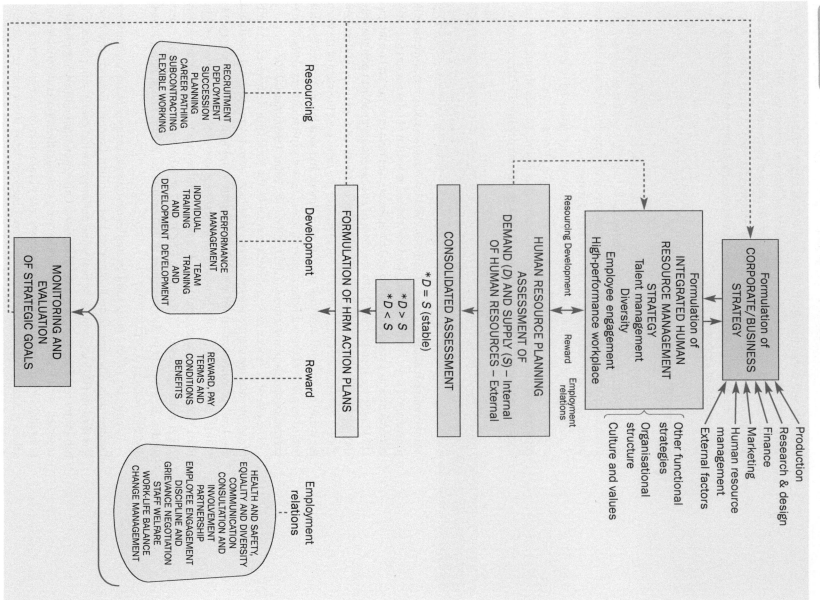

making such use of IT, but the evidence is not strong. The CIPD (2006a), for instance, mainly addresses operational uses of IT, but it does also allude to HR undertaking 'more strategic work as business partners . . . by providing the managers with quantifiable data to drive this strategy' (p. 11). They further state that 'HR can also play an important role in the formulation of strategy by making explicit the human capital resources required to support various strategies and strategic initiatives' (p. 12).

The CIPD (2006) comes to the conclusion that the technology-driven changes in HR roles 'will undoubtedly lead to a change in the skills needed as their role shifts towards more strategic issues' (p. 12). The CIPD (2009a) still comments, however, that 'HR data is more often collected for administrative rather than evaluation purposes', and that 'HR people do not always have the skills to interpret data to evaluate the contribution of people to business performance'. These statements imply that the HR profession still has some way to go before it is fully effective at the strategic level, and that the potential of IT systems is yet to be fully exploited.

International issues

Skills shortages

Offshoring and recruiting overseas have been mentioned above as potential solutions for skills shortages and the level of migration has been identified as a factor which has an impact on the size of the labour force. It should be noted that this applies to migration out of the UK as well as migration into the country. All of these eventualities raise issues in terms of the management of language and communication competencies, cultural differences and diversity.

Looking at things on a global scale, employers must also be aware that their solution to skills shortages might well be someone else's problem and that this might lead to further developments which will have to be managed. The ethics of recruiting nurses from less developed countries to come to the UK was raised as an issue in the early years of the twenty-first century, and the NHS, which was suffering from a shortage of nurses and other medical professionals at that time, pledged not to recruit from those countries. Economic issues other than corporate social responsibility can also arise. The emigration of Polish workers into the UK and other parts of Europe in the mid-2000s meant that Poland itself was facing skills shortages, particularly in terms of resourcing the European Football Championships to be held there in 2012. Berry (2007) reported that Poland would need to attract 200,000 workers to return to Poland from the UK and Ireland to get ready for this event. Not an inconsiderable number of people!

There are other examples of skills shortages being reported around the world. For example, as our chosen HR in the News article indicates, the skills shortages issue we have described in this chapter is also a concern in Australia, albeit that we provide here a very specific example.

Wooldridge (2006) produced a special report for *The Economist* with a subheading 'Talent has become the world's

Did you know?

The Adlon. The Kempinski. The Dorint. Three luxury hotels in Berlin, and where do they get their laundry done? In Poland, according to an article in a German TV magazine in 2006. Even with the time and cost needed for transport between the two locations, the service provided in Poland is superior and personnel with the required skills are more readily available. An update on this phenomenon occurred in 2009 with the appearance of a documentary film directed by Hans-Christian Schmid with the title *Die wundersame Welt der Waschkraft* (*The Wondrous World of Laundry*). Reviews indicate, however, that the film focuses on the availability of cheap labour in Poland rather than an appreciation of superior skills. You can see a trailer of the film at www.bavaria-film-international.de.

(*Sources:* Ernst, F. (2006) Waschtag in Polen, *HÖRZU*, Nr 11, 10.03, 18–19; Grabowska, K. (2009) *The Wonderous [sic] World of Laundry: Forgiving Free Market in Berlin and Warsaw*, available at www. cafebabel.co.uk, accessed 08.05.2010)

most sought after commodity' (p. 3), emphasising that the war for talent is a worldwide issue. These news stories are all evidence of the fact that labour supply can be a truly global issue, that labour markets are dynamic and subject to change, and that organisations have constantly to acquire information to stay ahead of the game.

An ageing workforce

The increasing proportion of the population represented by older people is not just occurring in the UK. In 2007, the 6th Munich Economic Summit focused on the demographic challenge that business faces in Europe, i.e. the ageing of the workforce. Among others involved were the CEOs of BMW and Siemens as well as EU politicians. The summit was attended by representatives from 22 countries including Germany, France, Italy and The Netherlands. The issues discussed there echoed some of the problems we have highlighted in this chapter, especially the impact of what those attending the summit referred to as the 'double ageing of Europe', i.e. low birth rates combined with greater life expectancy. The business representatives, however, saw some positive angles to this. Both Siemens and BMW forecast an increased demand for their products, and in terms of people management, the representative from BMW stated that using their 'programme "Today for Tomorrow", the company keeps up the productivity of its employees. The programme includes health prevention measures, ergonomic work spaces and a good age balance among working teams, which makes it possible for older employees to pass on their wealth of experience to younger employees, thus enabling life-long learning' (**www.munich-economic-summit.com**).

Shacklock *et al.* (2009) address issues to do with the ageing of the workforce in Australia and the need for business to devise strategies to retain older workers in order to combat potential skills shortages. The authors examine factors such as the importance of work to the individual and perceptions of autonomy at work. The role of work-life balance provisions and the opportunity for social interactions were also examined. The study found that the importance of work, flexibility and interests outside of work have an impact on decisions whether or not to continue working irrespective of gender. The importance of work factor was, however, of greater significance for men whereas lack of opportunity to develop meaningful relationships at work was of greater significance for women. The study concludes that employers need in general to develop retention strategies for older workers, but that they could also benefit from addressing gender differences.

Did you know?

The ageing of the workforce is a phenomenon that is not restricted to the UK or Europe. The Society for Human Resource Management (SHRM) website makes it clear that employers in the USA are also facing similar developments. The SHRM expressed concerns in 2003 that US employers were not preparing adequately for this demographic shift. The website contains a lot of later information about employer retention strategies for older workers, but also indicates that fewer employers have developed recruitment strategies targeted at this group.

(*Source:* www.shrm.org)

REVIEW QUESTIONS

You will find brief answers to these review questions on pages 487–488.

1 Describe the different levels of strategy found in organisations, and comment on their interconnecting nature.

2 Outline the major stages of the human resource planning process, and comment on the major considerations at each stage.

3 'Information is crucial as a basis for decision making in the human resource planning process.' Comment on this statement, and describe the sources of information available to management.

4 Explain what is meant by the terms 'skills shortages' and 'skills gaps'. Why do they arise and what can employers do about them?

SELF-CHECK QUESTIONS

Answer the following multiple-choice and short-answer questions. The correct responses are given on page 488 for you to check your understanding of this chapter.

1 Name the three major generic strategies available at the corporate level.

2 Name the three business level strategies described by Porter.

3 A local supermarket employs 50 sales assistants on a part-time basis. Over the past year the personnel department has had to recruit 25 new employees to keep the establishment full. Of the assistants who were hired over a year ago, 40 are still working with the supermarket in the same position. Calculate the turnover rate.

4 Calculate the stability index for the situation in question 3.

5 What does the stability index indicate?

6 Which stage has been left out of the following brief description of the human resource planning process?

● development of corporate strategy
● estimation of the demand for human resources
● formulation of human resource management plans.

7 How are IT systems predominantly used in HR: for strategic or for operational purposes?

8 Which countries are facing issues to do with an ageing workforce?

HR IN THE NEWS

Companies jostle to hire in Australian rebound

By Peter Smith

The post-recession scramble for jobs in the coal-exporting hub of Gladstone, a port near the southern tip of Australia's Great Barrier Reef, is unlike most round the world.

Here, welders, pipefitters, electricians and construction workers are not desperately battling for scarce employment. The fights are between companies as executives struggle to fill long vacancy lists.

The city in Queensland is benefiting from record demand for Australia's biggest exports – iron ore and coal – while the region's bauxite and alumina industries are booming, and liquefied natural gas (LNG) is proving a new frontier, with Gladstone named as the designated export centre for the state's burgeoning industry.

Across the country, companies are gearing up to spend more than A\$100bn (\$92bn, €68bn, £61bn) on a slew of large labour-intensive resource projects, including more than a dozen in LNG and several schemes to convert underground reserves of coal-bed methane into LNG.

'There's no doubt more inter-state and overseas migrants will be needed,' Julia Gillard, Australia's deputy prime minister, said this week during a visit to the biggest single project – the A\$43bn Gorgon development off the coast of Western Australia by Chevron and partners.

Western Australia's Chamber of Commerce and Industry estimates that the state alone will need hundreds of thousands of extra workers by 2017.

Officials in Gladstone estimate that 12,000 more employees will be needed to develop the local LNG industry – a large number for a city with a population of barely 50,000 and an unemployment rate of 4.6 per cent, compared with Australia's already low – by international standards – national rate of 5.3 per cent.

For example, Santos, an energy company, has forecast that its total workforce will swell by 50 per cent to more than 3,000 people as a direct result of its Gladstone LNG project. During the project's peak construction phase in 2012 it says it will need an extra 5,000 contractors and employees.

'There is a lot of strategic planning going on to find who might be available,' says Roger Kennett, an executive at the Santos-Petronas joint venture company.

Bosses are looking to hire both at home and overseas.

Bala Pandurangan, 30, from Chennai, India, who arrived in Australia four years ago as a qualified welder, says 'good money and good weather' attracted him to Gladstone.

Working for a mid-sized contracting company, he says he is able to earn a wage almost a third higher than if he worked in a big city such as Brisbane.

'In Chennai, I can earn in a month what I earn in Gladstone in a week,' he says, adding that welders' annual pay in Gladstone is near A\$120,000.

It was not always like this. Rio Tinto, the Anglo-Australian mining group that is Gladstone's main employer, was among those that cut jobs as it shrank operations during the recession. But those days are now long gone.

To attract employees, Rio is offering 'lifestyle packages', including a nine-day working fortnight and free golf club and gym memberships.

Yet such benefits may not keep the labour poachers at bay. Carlos Oria, an instrument design engineer at Queensland Alumina, majority owned by Rio, says his boss got another job offer on the golf course.

'He was offered big money,' he says.

The federal government is also in the market for workers as it ramps up spending on infrastructure projects, including a A\$43bn national broadband telecoms network. In such market conditions, companies are finding it hard to retain workers.

Mr Pandurangan is being sponsored by his current employer as he seeks permanent residency. But he says he would be happy to entertain better offers when LNG operators build their facilities.

Lincoln Crawley, of big recruitment company Manpower, says a lack of skilled workers will hamper efforts to develop the resources sector, while wage inflation will cut productivity.

'There are significantly more projects than there ever have been before and the skills training and development is not keeping up,' says Mr Crawley. 'Other countries that are better organised will steal a march on Australia.'

He says urgent and co-ordinated action is needed between Australia's state and federal governments and industry to address the shortages.

'We need to grow apprenticeship schemes [and] attract more women and older workers back into the workforce,' he says, adding that targeted immigration would also help. 'People also need to have flexible skills that are relevant to different industries. The last thing we want to see is another bubble in the labour market.'

Financial Times, 31/03/2010 (Peter Smith), http://ft.com/cms/s/0/b5e49e10-3c5d-11df-b316-00144feabdc0.html; Reproduced with permission.

Question

1 Identify the concepts covered in Chapter 2 which are illustrated in this article.

WHAT NEXT?

In this chapter we have looked at the factors that affect the external labour market and the impact this can have on employers in resourcing their strategic plans. One aspect that should be evident is that the supply of labour can fluctuate from year to year, bringing ever-changing opportunities and threats to employers. It is important to keep up to date on developments, and regular perusal of the following publications can assist you in doing this.

Economic and Labour Market Review, a monthly journal published by the Office for National Statistics, formerly published as *Labour Market Trends*.

Labour Market Outlook, a quarterly review published by the CIPD together with KPMG.

We have referred a number of times to the CIPD annual survey of recruitment, retention and turnover. The survey report provides a good statistical overview of employers' experience of labour turnover, skills shortages, retention etc., but it also gives informed comment on and explanations of the major issues. The most recent report available at the time of writing was the 2010 edition, reporting on experiences from 2009 and renamed as the *Resourcing and Talent Planning Survey*. By the time this text is published, the 2011 report should soon be available to download on the CIPD website. Go to www.cipd.co.uk/surveys to find and read the most recent reports available. It will help you to stay in the know about labour market issues.

References

Anthony, W.P., P.L. Perrewe and K.M. Kacmar (1996) *Strategic Human Resource Management*, 2nd edition, Harcourt Brace.

Armitage, B. and M. Scott (1998) British labour force projections: 1998–2011, *Labour Market Trends*, June, 281–291.

Baron, A., A. R. Clarke, P. Turner and S. Pass (2010) *Workforce Planning: Right People, Right Time, Right Skills. A Guide*, Spring, CIPD; (available at www.cipd.co.uk).

BBC Radio 4 (2007) *Woman's Hour News: Career Advice*, 27/08 (podcast downloaded at www.bbc.co.uk; accessed 27.08.07).

Berry, M. (2007) Poland needs to lure 200,000 workers back home to get facilities ready for 2012 European Football Championships, *Personnel Today*, 17 May (available at www.personneltoday.com; accessed 11.07.10).

Boxall, P. and J. Purcell (2008) *Strategy and Human Resource Management*, 2nd edition, Palgrave Macmillan.

Chartered Institute of Personnel and Development (2005) *HR Strategy: Creating the Framework for Successful People Management*, CIPD (CIPD tool available at www.cipd.co.uk; accessed 03.05.10).

Chartered Institute of Personnel and Development (2006) *HR and Technology: Beyond Delivery*, CIPD (Change Agenda available at www.cipd.co.uk; accessed 11.07.10).

Chartered Institute of Personnel and Development (2007a) *A Barometer of HR Trends and Prospects 2007. Overview of CIPD Surveys*, CIPD.

Chartered Institute of Personnel and Development (2007b) *Recruitment, Retention and Turnover. Annual Survey Report 2007*, CIPD.

Chartered Institute of Personnel and Development (2007c) *Technology In HR: How to Get the Most out of Technology in People Management*, CIPD (HR tool available to members at www.cipd.co.uk; accessed 11.07.10).

Chartered Institute of Personnel and Development (2009a) *Human Capital*, CIPD (Factsheet available at www.cipd.co.uk; accessed 20.05.10).

Chartered Institute of Personnel and Development (2009b) *Recruitment, Retention and Turnover. Annual Survey Report 2009*, CIPD.

Chartered Institute of Personnel and Development (2009c) *Understanding the Economy and Labour Market*, CIPD (Factsheet available at www.cipd.co.uk; accessed 07.05.10).

Chartered Institute of Personnel and Development (2010a) *A Barometer of HR Trends and Prospects 2010. Overview of CIPD Surveys*, CIPD.

Chartered Institute of Personnel and Development (2010b) *Creating an Engaged Workforce*, CIPD (research report available at www.cipd.co.uk; accessed 01.03.10).

Chartered Institute of Personnel and Development (2010c) *HR Business Partnering*, CIPD (factsheet available at www.cipd.co.uk; accessed 03.05.10).

Chartered Institute of Personnel and Development (2010d) *Resourcing and Talent Planning: Annual Survey Report 2010*, CIPD.

Confederation of British Industry (2010) *Ready to Grow: Business Priorities for Education and Skills. Education and Skills Survey 2010*, CBI.

Craig, T. (2009) The recession lesson: Reed research findings, *Personnel Today*, 21 September (available at www.personneltoday.com; accessed 27.10.09).

Gibb, F. (2007) Out of the ivory towers and into mosques, *The Times* (Law section), 26 June.

Glaister, K. (1995) Introduction to the strategic management process, in C. Clarke-Hill and K. Glaister (eds) *Cases in Strategic Management*, 2nd edition, Pitman Publishing.

Greer, C.R. (2001) *Strategic Human Resource Management: A General Managerial Approach*, 2nd edition, Prentice Hall.

Guest, D. J. Storey and W. Tate (1997) *Innovation: Opportunity through People. Consultative Document*, Institute of Personnel and Development, June.

Hutchinson, S. and J. Purcell (2003) *Bringing Policies to Life: the Vital Role of Front Line Managers in People Management*, CIPD.

Incomes Data Services (1996) *IDS Focus: The Future Workforce*, No. 80, December, IDS.

Incomes Data Services (2004) Cultural diversity at B&Q, *IDS Diversity at Work*, No. 5, November, 7–10.

Industrial Relations Services (IRS) (2000) Responding to the challenge of skills shortages, *Employee Development Bulletin* 130, October, 4–9.

Industrial Relations Services (IRS) (2001) Be prepared: forecasts for recruiters' needs to 2020, *Employee Development Bulletin* 139, July, 5–7.

Industrial Relations Service (IRS) (2006) HR management systems move online as the web matures, *IRS Employment Review* 855, 22/9 (available at www.xperthr.co.uk; accessed 11.07.10).

Industrial Relations Service (IRS) (2007) Aligning HR with the business: two steps forward, one step back, *IRS Employment Review* 866, 20/3 (available at www.xperthr; accessed 11.07.10).

Johnson, G. K. Scholes and R. Whittington (2006) *Exploring Corporate Strategy*, 7th edition, Financial Times Prentice Hall.

Lynch, R. (2003) *Corporate Strategy*, 3rd edition, Financial Times Prentice Hall.

Macleod, D. and N. Clarke (2009) *Engaging for Success: Enhancing Performance through Employee Engagement*, Crown Copyright.

Madouros, V. (2006) Projections of the UK labour force, 2006–2020, *Labour Market Trends*, January, 13–27.

Marchington, M. and A. Wilkinson (2005) *Human Resource Management at Work: People Management and Development*, 3rd edition, CIPD.

Matthews, V. (2009) Reversing a negative image: debt collection *Personnel Today*, 24 February (available at www.xperthr.co.uk; accessed 02.03.09).

Millmore, M., P. Lewis, M. Saunders, A. Thornhill and T. Morrow (2007) *Strategic Human Resource Management: Contemporary Issues*, Financial Times Prentice Hall.

Personnel Today (2007) Water companies consider radical recruitment drive to avoid looming skills crisis, *Personnel Today*, 27 February (available at www.xperthr.co.uk; accessed 11.07.10).

Porter, M.E. (1980) *Competitive Strategy*, Free Press.

Ready, D.A. and J.A. Conger (2007) Make your company a talent factory, *Harvard Business Review*, June, 68–77.

Shacklock, K. Y. Brunetto and S. Nelson (2009) The different variables that affect older males' and females' intentions to continue working, *Asia Pacific Journal of Human Resources*, 47(1), 79–101.

Sloane, W. (2007) We put in an infrastructure more efficiently ourselves, *The Sunday Times*, 14 January (available at www.timesonline.co.uk; accessed 22.01.07).

Smethurst, S. (2005) HR roles: the long and winding road, *People Management*, 28 July, 25–29.

Storey, J. (2007) *Human Resource Management: A Critical Text*, 3rd edition, Thomson.

Twentyman, J. (2006) Show me the numbers, *Personnel Today*, 5 December (available at www.xperthr.co.uk; accessed 11.07.10).

Twentyman, J. (2007) Expanding HR: How forward planning and investing in technology can help, *Personnel Today*, 20 February (available at www.xperthr.co.uk; accessed 11.07.10).

UK Commission for Employment and Skills (2010) *National Employer Skills Survey for England 2009: Key Findings Report*, UKCES.

Wooldridge, A. (2006) A survey of talent, *The Economist*, 7 October, 3–20.

www.jnj.com; accessed 13.05.10.

www.munich-economic-summit.com; accessed 11.07.10.

Further study

Books

Advisory, Conciliation and Arbitration Service (2010) *Managing Attendance and Employee Turnover*, ACAS (available at www.acas.org.uk; accessed 08.05.10).

Chartered Institute of Personnel and Development (2007) *HR and Technology: Impact and Advantages*, CIPD.

A research report produced for the CIPD by a team of researchers at Cranfield School of Management. The report includes a number of interesting case studies.

Incomes Data Services (IDS) (2008) *IDS HR Studies 863: Improving Staff Retention*, IDS.

Looks at the use of various labour turnover metrics to identify problems, what the implications of the resulting figures might be and how to devise a retention strategy. Provides case studies of how six organisations have addressed retention problems, including Trinity-Chiesi Pharmaceuticals, First Group and BUPA Care Homes.

Joseph Rowntree Foundation (2006) *Findings: Central and East European Migrants in Low Wage Employment in the UK*, Joseph Rowntree Foundation.

Examines the experiences of migrant workers and the views of their employers both before EU enlargement in 2004 and afterwards. The findings and the full report can be downloaded at www.jrf.org.uk where you will also find other reports of research on social issues.

Articles

Capelli, P. (2008) Talent management for the twenty-first century, *Harvard Business Review*, March, 74–81.

An innovative take on approaches to calculating the demand for and supply of human capital.

Clancy, G. (2009) Labour demand: The need for workers, *Economic and Labour Market Review*, Vol. 3, No. 2, February, 21–29.

Clancy, G. (2009) The labour market and the economy: 20 years reviewed, *Economic and Labour Market Review*, Vol. 3, No. 2, February, 17–20.

Two articles which provide a good overview of the main labour market measures of interest to human resource strategists. The *Economic and Labour Market Review* is a monthly journal produced by the Office for National Statistics. Contains statistical analyses of various aspects of the workforce, and articles and news items about issues of current interest. Essential reading for keeping up to date.

Gregg, P. and J. Wadsworth (2010) Employment in the 2008–2009 recession, *Economic and Labour Market Review*, Vol. 4, No. 8, August, 37–43.

Analyses the various factors that have had an impact on the labour market during the recession.

Industrial Relations Services (IRS) (2007) Labour turnover trends, rates and sources 2007/2008, *IRS Employment Review 870*, 10/4.

Provides links to a set of articles which constitute the IRS guide to labour turnover for 2007/2008. Separate articles address how to collect and use labour turnover information, the costs of labour turnover, the latest trends and an overview of what is happening on a national scale. Available at www.xperthr.co.uk; accessed 08.05.10.

Jenkins, J. (2010) The labour market in the 1980s, 1990s and 2008/09 recessions, *Economic and Labour Market Review*, Vol. 4, No. 8, August, 29–36.

Compares the changes in the labour market during the recessionary times named in the title.

Morrow, P. and J. McElroy (2007) Efficiency as a mediator in turnover-organizational performance relations, *Human Relations*, Vol. 60(6), 827–849.

An American research article examining how labour turnover affects organisational efficiency in the banking sector.

People Management.

Produced for the Chartered Institute of Personnel and Development, this magazine is aimed at keeping HR practitioners informed, and frequently contains articles on HR strategy. A good source of case studies.

Suff, R. (2010) Labour turnover rates and costs: IRS survey 2010, *IRS Employment Review*, 14/06.

Provides definitions and information on labour turnover rates and associated costs. Available at www.xperthr.co.uk; accessed 06.07.10.

Internet

Chartered Institute of Personnel and Development   **www.cipd.co.uk**

The CIPD site provides a wide range of useful information on HR strategy and uses of technology. The tool on technology in HR, available to members, includes a number of interesting case studies of organisations, including Cancer Research UK and BSkyB. The CIPD has also produced a podcast on workforce planning, No. 46 in its series, added to the website in September 2010. It includes interviews with HR experts explaining the role that workforce planning plays in achieving their business goals. The organisations are Harrod UK, a sports equipment manufacturer, the Royal Navy and the insurance company AXA.

CHAPTER **3**

High-performance working: employee engagement through involvement and participation

Objectives

When you have studied this chapter you will be able to:

- explain what is meant by the terms 'unitarism' and 'pluralism'

- understand the key employment relations concepts of partnership, participation, employee involvement, commitment, engagement and high-performance working

- describe developments in EU legislation relating to employee rights to information and consultation

- appreciate the importance of communication and consultation in the employment relations arena

- name and describe the techniques that can be used to enhance employee involvement

- describe the concepts of commitment and employee engagement, and explain how they are connected to employee involvement and high performance working.

Chapter 1 established that the HRM approach to managing employees entails developing strategies and using techniques that result in employees reaching their full potential and giving their best efforts for the success of the organisation. This approach to management recognises that the contribution of an organisation's people is critical to the creation of a competitive advantage. Employers acknowledge that their organisations will flourish if they can engage their employees, meaning that they will be fully motivated to give of their very best to their employer, and indeed many adopt a strategy of employee engagement in order to achieve the high-performance workforce that will give them this edge. Sisson (2007, p. 21) even goes so far as to say that 'employee engagement can make or break a business', and ACAS (2009b) reviews research that indicates the continuing importance of engagement to firms in recessionary times, both so that employees provide the high level of performance necessary for organisations to survive, and so that they are retained and ready for the rigours of an eventual upturn.

Other chapters examine specific functions that can be performed in such a way as to acquire such employees (HR planning, recruitment and selection), retain them (payment systems), and develop them (performance management, training), HR practices which, if carried out with strategic forethought, ought to result in the desired high-performance workplace (EEF/CIPD, 2003). The willingness of employees to contribute their best efforts, however, can be affected pervasively by the way they are treated on a day-to-day basis, by their relationships with managers and by the attitude they perceive management in general to have towards them. This is largely a matter of organisational culture which develops in part from the philosophical stance of senior managers and the owners of enterprises as to the role they expect employees throughout the organisation to play in the life of the organisation.

This chapter reviews major concepts from the field of employment relations that have developed over several decades, including a review of the current discussion of employee engagement. We examine the basic stances that managers can adopt towards the workforce, looking at the concepts of unitarism and pluralism, which provide a framework for an examination of partnership, participation and employee involvement (EI). The techniques of participation and employee involvement are believed to enhance the willingness and ability of employees to contribute to the achievement of their organisation's goals, and the levels of commitment and engagement that are expected to arise from these approaches are fundamental in the creation of the high-performance workplace.

Pause for thought 3.1   Given that the aim of human resource management is to use the potential of employees, how would you expect this to be achieved in terms of general management attitude towards employees and their place in the decision-making process?

In keeping with basic concepts of motivation theory, you have probably stated that employees are more likely to produce greater effort if they have a sense of responsibility and a feeling of achievement from their work. According to Herzberg *et al.* (1959) and later work by Hackman and Oldham (1980), one of the ways to achieve this is by job enrichment. One method of enriching jobs is to shift responsibility for making some decisions from supervisors to more junior employees. This is known as a vertical job loading factor, designed to improve motivation. Employee empowerment became a business buzzword in the 1990s, and this too involves devolving the responsibility for decision making through all levels in the organisation.

The fact that we can talk about the *devolution* of decision making implies that it lay elsewhere before it was devolved. Traditionally owners and managers have regarded the right to make decisions as being theirs, an attitude reflected in the ideas of Frederick Winslow Taylor (1911). In Taylor's concept of scientific management, managers were to plan and control the work and give orders, while other employees were meant simply to carry out these orders. Taylor's ideas were underpinned by a view that workmen (at that time Taylor's work was primarily involved with men rather than men and women together in the workplace) were motivated only by money and the possibility of gaining financial incentives for producing more work.

Later theories of motivation, such as those of Herzberg, moved away from this concept of money being the only motivating factor for employees, but in spite of a growing acceptance of the fact that people look for responsibility, achievement and a sense of autonomy at work, the debate over the managerial prerogative to make decisions has continued. The ability or willingness of managers to share their decision-making powers with employees at a lower level in the organisation's hierarchical structure will be very much influenced by those managers' general attitude towards management–workforce relationships. The two major philosophical stances have been described as unitarism and pluralism, and another important concept, i.e. partnership, became the focus of debate in the late 1990s. Recent and ongoing legislative developments emanating from the EU have also meant that there is a heightened need to address employees' rights to information and consultation about what is happening in their workplace.

The unitary and pluralist perspectives

The type of relationship that will develop between employer (as represented by managers) and employee, and the techniques that are utilised to regulate this relationship, are influenced by the beliefs of the employer. You will see that a unitary stance is likely to result in a workplace culture that is different from what you would expect to find in an organisation headed by pluralists. These concepts were developed in the work of Fox (1974).

The unitary perspective

Unitarists believe that all members of an organisation have the same interests, that they will all accept the organisation's goals and direct all their efforts towards the achievement of these goals. This implies that there is no conflict in such organisations; if conflict were to arise, it would be attributed to some misunderstanding of what the goals are or to deliberate trouble-making on the part of some individual. The unitarist stance also implies that the person or persons leading the organisation have decided what the goals are, and there is an expectation that everyone who joins the organisation will internalise those goals. Unitarist organisations, therefore, depend on strong leadership from the top and are likely purposefully to recruit like-minded members. The signature of this philosophy is the belief that there is a common goal and that everyone is directing their efforts towards the achievement of this goal.

The pluralist perspective

Pluralists, on the other hand, believe that in any organisation a range of interests are likely to be represented among the members. One example of this is that employees are likely to be interested in increasing the pay they receive for a unit of work, whereas managers and owners will be concerned to increase profits. This is a clear example of differing objectives or a plurality of interests in the workplace. The existence of different interests means that conflicts are likely to arise as the various parties pursue their interests, and pluralists accept that this is natural and needs to be managed. These conflicts should be managed in such a way that they do not disrupt the running of the organisation, or even so that they potentially contribute to its success.

Unitary employers are more likely to resist unionisation; pluralist employers are likely to accept unionisation more readily. Unionisation implies the existence of different sets of interests and the will to set up mechanisms for resolving these differences. Pluralists accept the existence of these differences and the need to work towards their resolution, whereas unitarists expect everyone to have the same goals. According to unitarists there should be no conflict, and therefore no need to have mechanisms for representing differing interests in the workplace will have an impact recognise from the outset that differing interests in the workplace will have an impact on the achievement of organisational goals, and therefore need to be incorporated into the decision-making process. This is an important point to bear in mind when you read about the methods employers can adopt for involving employees in decisions.

Partnership, participation and employee involvement

As well as the effects that involvement in decision making has on employee motivation, as discussed earlier, there is also a broader philosophical debate about the role of owners, managers and employees as players in the employment relations scene. Are owners and managers the only participants in the workplace with the right to make decisions? Are the providers of capital the only ones with a vested interest in the success of an enterprise? The concept of stakeholders suggests that the success of an organisation does not affect only those who have a financial stake in it, but that a range of people have a direct interest in what an organisation does. Everyone who is affected in any way by the actions and decisions of an enterprise is a stakeholder, including:

- employees, who depend on their organisation for their livelihood and for the pleasantness or otherwise of their work life
- customers, who have their own requirements of the organisation and who expect organisations to take their concerns into consideration
- suppliers, who depend for their own livelihood on the success of client organisations
- the community, which depends on organisations to protect the environment.

This raises again the question of managerial prerogative in deciding what should happen in the workplace versus the right or the desire of employees to have their interests represented. Arguments for maximising employees' input include their democratic right to have a say in any decisions that will affect them directly, their vested interest in the success of the organisation and, on another level, the fact that it makes sense to use the expertise that is available throughout the organisation.

The preceding discussion touches on major political and ethical questions to which there are no easy answers, and certainly no one answer that everyone will accept. In the discussion of the role that employees should play in an enterprise there is often perceived to be a tension between economic and social imperatives (McGlynn, 1995). Improvements in employee consultation, especially if they are legislated and therefore compulsory, are frequently seen as essentially social measures that impose unnecessary costs on businesses. But it is congruent with HRM thinking to see these improvements as measures leading to economic success; that is, you can attain a competitive edge by maximising the contribution of your employees, and the contribution of employees is greater the more they are consulted on, and therefore involved and engaged in, what is happening in the organisation. These arguments lead us into a discussion of the various ways in which employees' input can be solicited: partnership, involvement and participation.

Partnership

Coupar and Stevens (1998) make some interesting comments about the long-established pedigree of partnership, but the partnership concept in modern times emerged more clearly as part of the employee relations agenda in 1997, and the terminology appeared with increasing frequency throughout 1998, although an IPA (Involvement and Participation Association) paper on the benefits of partnership had already appeared earlier, in 1992. A clear link can be seen between a strategic goal of innovation and partnership as a method of engaging the full commitment of employees (Allen, 1998), and the Labour Government, first elected in 1997, quickly aligned itself with the idea of partnership (*Fairness at Work* 1998, Chapters 1 and 2), presenting it as one of the 'three pillars' which supported its 'strategy for achieving competitiveness' (s1.3). So, obviously, partnership was placed well and truly on the employee relations agenda for the duration of the Labour Government.

Pause for thought 3.3 Government policy has an effect on employment relations and at least will seek to provide a direction with the ultimate goal of economic growth. At the time of writing, the Labour Government, which had been in power for 13 years, had just been replaced by the Conservative Liberal coalition, and their employment relations policy has yet to be fully developed and publicised. You should investigate what developments have been established by the time you read this text. The website for the Department for Business, Innovation & Skills (www.bis.gov.uk) or the business link website (www.businesslink.gov.uk) are good places to start.

As with HRM, partnership is an evolving concept and several commentators in the late 1990s observed that there was at that time no accepted definition of what partnership was and what it encompassed (Beardwell, 1998; Marchington, 1998). As the Labour Government pointed out in its *Fairness at Work* paper, businesses should be free to adopt a contingency approach and develop whatever programmes suit their particular circumstances and, indeed, the IRS (2004) assert that companies tend to adopt their own definition of partnership. It may be, then, that the search for an authoritative definition of partnership is not a productive exercise.

We have gathered a number of descriptions of partnership from several publications, and present them here, followed by a comment on the similarities that emerge.

Employers and employees working together jointly to solve problems.

(ACAS, 1997, p. 13)

Key components might include high degrees of communication, personal development, employment security and an emphasis on ethical people management.

(Beardwell, 1998, p. 36)

Individual representation; consultation and communication; values; and understanding and promoting the business.

(Allen, 1998, p. 41, describing the partnership deal agreed between Tesco and Usdaw)

- Employment security and new working practices.
- Giving employees a voice in how the company is run.
- Fair financial rewards.
- Investment in training.

(Monks, 1998, p. 176)

1 A commitment to working together to make a business more successful.
2 Understanding the employee security conundrum and trying to do something about it.
3 Building relationships at the workplace which maximise employee influence through total communication and a robust and effective employee voice.

(Coupar and Stevens, 1998, p. 157)

- Commitment to the success of the enterprise.
- Building trust.
- Recognising legitimate roles and interests.
- Employment security.
- Information and consultation.
- Sharing success.
- Training and development.

(Industrial Relations Services, 2003a, p. 9 and 2004, p. 15)

- Commitment to the success of the enterprise.
- Recognizing the existence of different interests.
- Employment security.
- Quality of working life.
- Genuine sharing of information and consultation.
- Added value from both partners.

(Gennard and Judge, 2005, pp. 224–5)

Relations . . . conducted on the basis of a common interest in the success of the organisation.

(ACAS, 2009d, p. 20)

Common themes that emerge among these definitions are the importance of security, the common aim of business success and the concept of employee voice.

Of these three components, the one which is probably the most contentious is security, implying, as it seems to, that employees are promised their jobs will be safe no matter what happens. The numbers of redundancies declared in the first decade of this century are an indicator of how difficult it has been for many organisations to comply with such a promise, and the threat of redundancy continues at least for some workers. The CIPD (2010c) reported that 29 per cent of employers surveyed in the Spring 2010 *Labour Market Outlook Survey* were considering redundancies with public sector employees affected more so than those in the private sector. On the other hand, as John Monks points out: 'Security in exchange for positive work flexibility is at the heart of the partnership approach' (1998, p. 176). You will note, however, that Monks and Beardwell, as cited above, both refer to *employment* security rather than *job* security, and this distinction is important to the concept of partnership and the modern psychological contract. Employment security implies that employees will be developed in such a way that, should an employer ultimately have to declare redundancies, the employees affected will be highly skilled and therefore their chances of employment elsewhere will be enhanced. Nonetheless, redundancies can still pose a problem for the effectiveness of the partnership approach, a fact that we shall return to in our concluding comments on partnership.

In their review of the literature on partnership up to 2008, Johnstone *et al.* (2009) also identify employee voice as a common, and indeed central, theme in definitions of partnership. The combination of a 'common aim of business success' and the concept of 'employee voice' is interesting, given our previous discussion of unitarism and pluralism. Working in partnership calls for the recognition of a mutually desirable goal (business success), but seems to imply at the same time that employees may have different opinions from management and that therefore some mechanism is needed to facilitate 'employee voice'. We shall return to this point after our initial overview of participation and involvement.

Some further interesting points to note about partnership before investigating ways in which it can be achieved are as follows:

- The Labour Government of 1997–2010 emphasised the development of a satisfactory work–life balance for employees as being another key feature of effective partnership.
- Partnership can be achieved in both a unionised and non-unionised environment. There is nothing to stop a non-unionised organisation from making arrangements with its employees to consult with elected representatives on a wide range of issues and indeed, as described in more detail later in this chapter, the scope of all employees' statutory rights to information and consultation is increasing.

There is a definitive link between partnership and employee participation which can be the channel for employee voice, and between partnership and employee involvement initiatives in that these can represent the way to achieve partnership. Coupar and Stevens (1998, p. 157) state that 'the IPA sees partnership as a unique combination of employee involvement processes which has the potential to maximise the benefits to the company and to employees in the process of change.' They also comment (1998, p. 151) on the previously mentioned phenomenon, that 'companies typically use a very wide range of differing activities to develop the mix needed to gain staff commitment and achieve success in the marketplace.'

We shall now provide an overview of the difference in approach implied by the terms employee involvement and participation, sometimes referred to together as EIP (Marchington and Cox, 2007) although commentators at the same time make a distinction between the two. We shall also comment again on the concept of partnership in that context before continuing with a more detailed exploration of EIP.

Employee involvement and participation (EIP)

The main purpose of EIP is to make workers feel like active participants in what happens in the workplace. There are numerous practices aiming to achieve this, and these have been categorised as *representative* methods and *direct* methods. Representative methods mean that workers are not involved in communications and decision making directly and individually, but through elected representatives who will put forward the workers' views. This sort of representation is often referred to as workers having a *voice*, and practices involving employee representatives are typically categorised as *participation*. Often, such participation is supported by legal structures as in the case of European Works Councils (EWCs), addressed by the Transnational Information and Consultation of Employees Regulations 1999 together with amending regulations in 2010, and the national councils formed under the Information and Consultation of Employees (ICE) Regulations 2004.

Direct methods are those typically described as constituting *employee involvement*, and they include communications targeted straight at employees (i.e. not cascaded by representatives) and other techniques that involve individuals or groups of workers. Employee involvement practices focus on the agenda set by management and attempt to get employees to understand the importance of organisational goals and commit to them.

Employee participation recognises that groups within an organisation will have different points of view, and allows for input on those differences, giving employees a voice during the decision-making process at higher levels. In accepting the validity of the existence of differing interests, employee participation is pluralist in nature. Employee involvement calls for commitment to decisions managers have made and the organisational goals they have set, so it is essentially unitary in nature.

Commentators on the employment relations scene in the UK state that a combination of direct and representative approaches is likely to work best (Sisson, 2007; Earls, 2007; Coupar, 2007), although they also indicate that direct practices are likely to predominate (Coupar, 2007; Marchington and Cox, 2007). As the ICE Regulations become more embedded in the UK employment relations scene, we may witness a strengthening of representative participation for workers, but that remains to be seen.

It is certainly true of a partnership approach, however, as we have described it, that it comprises both employee involvement and participation. It can be said, then, that partnership exemplifies a blend of some aspects of unitarism with some aspects of pluralism: we can have the pursuit of the unitarist common goal within a pluralist framework. Appealing as this may be, some critics question the viability of partnership agreements, pointing to the imbalance of power between management and worker representatives so that the management agenda is likely to prevail (Smith, 2006; IRS, 2006b).

We shall now review in more detail the concept of worker participation, developments with regard to regulatory information and consultation rights, and a variety of employee involvement practices that have been identified in a number of companies.

EU rights to information and consultation

● European Works Councils

Participative structures have been a subject of debate for many years among the member states of the European Union, and a number of directives were proposed but subsequently failed to be adopted. These include the Vredeling Directive and the Fifth Company Law Directive, which each contained broad proposals on consultation and information. On 22 September 1994 a Directive of more limited scope was adopted, and this is the European Council Directive on the establishment of a European Works Council or other procedure in Community-scale undertakings or Community-scale groups of undertakings for the purposes of informing and consulting employees. The main background details of the Directive, features of the works councils and further regulatory developments are described in the following paragraphs. A fuller outline of events that preceded the adoption of the Directive and of the development of European thought on employee consultation and information can be found in Gold and Hall (1994) and Mill (1991).

The key issues in the Directive are that employees should be properly informed and consulted about major issues that will have an impact on them. The Directive refers to transnational undertakings where decisions could be made in one country that would affect employees in another country. In such circumstances, it seemed essential to most member states in the European Union that proper mechanisms should be in place in order to ensure that employees in the different countries of a transnational operation receive equal treatment with regard to information and consultation. This is the objective of the European Works Council Directive.

When the Maastricht Treaty on European Union was ratified in 1993, the UK Government opted out of the agreements on social policy, but the Protocol on Social Policy and Agreement on Social Policy, which are annexed to the Treaty, allowed the other member states to adopt social policy measures without having to consult or gain agreement from the UK. This was the background against which the Directive on European Works Councils was developed.

Approximately 100 UK-owned undertakings were affected by the Directive because they have establishments in other member states that meet the threshold requirements. They were obliged to adhere to the Directive for employees located in other member states, but this obligation did not extend to employees located in the UK. That is, they did not have to establish works councils in relevant UK establishments, but they could do so if they chose to. Two UK-owned multinationals that quickly decided to establish works councils in their undertakings in the UK were BP Europe and United Biscuits (see *Industrial Relations Review and Report*, December 1994, cited in the further study section, for more details).

The date set for the implementation of the Directive was 22 September 1996. If companies established a transnational agreement on information and consultation covering the whole workforce before this date, the Directive would not apply; i.e. companies that made an agreement by then would not be constrained by the terms of the Directive. This is, in fact, what companies such as BP Europe and United Biscuits opted to do.

By the end of 1997, this scenario had changed, when the Labour Government ended the UK's opt-out from the Social Chapter by signing the Treaty of Amsterdam. This meant that the Directive on European Works Councils now applied fully to relevant companies in the UK. The Directive was implemented in the UK as the Transnational Information and Consultation of Employees Regulations 1999.

The essential characteristics of the regulations and the prescribed process for developing and implementing a European Works Council (EWC) at that time are listed below.

Characteristics

- The threshold at which employers come under the terms of the regulations is that they have at least 1,000 employees within the member states and at least 150 employees in each of any two member states.
- The terms of the regulations come into effect either when management initiates action or when a written request is made by at least 100 employees or their representatives in at least two undertakings in at least two member states.

Process

- Management and labour meet each other in order to establish a procedure for consultation about the issue of an EWC.
- There are four possible outcomes of this consultation process:
  - the parties establish an EWC
  - if they decide against an EWC, they may establish an alternative procedure for information and consultation on transnational issues
  - the parties agree not to have a specific procedure relating to transnational issues
  - the parties fail to reach agreement.
- The regulations establish a framework for handling confidential information.
- If the parties fail to reach agreement, there are minimum standards that will be applied: an EWC will be established and will meet management once a year, or more often if necessary, to be informed and consulted on any matters that will significantly affect the employees. Matters that the EWC will consider include the structure of the undertaking, its financial situation and the future development of the business. These issues set down in the minimum standards are a good indicator of the kinds of issues the ministers from the member states felt employees should be consulted on.

Even at this stage, it is evident that a complex set of circumstances was likely to arise. Arrangements by managers outside of the regulations were permissible; management could voluntarily organise an EWC within the regulations; employees could request an EWC; the coverage of the EWCs could vary extensively. In 2010, the scenario changed again with the publication of new regulations, the Transnational Information and Consultation of Employees (Amendment) Regulations 2010, known as TICE 2010, to be implemented as of 5 June 2011. To add to the complexity, these regulations affect companies differently, depending on whether they adopted a voluntary EWC prior to the implementation of the 1999 regulations or set one up under the terms of these regulations. An exceedingly complicated picture has emerged which is dealt with in detail in the Department for Business, Innovation & Skills (2010) publication, and summarised by the CIPD (2009). The CIPD (2009) identifies some of the new aspects of the amended regulations, including:

● The requirement to set up a Special Negotiating Body (SNB) to organise the establishment of an EWC. The SNB will include employee representatives whose task is to negotiate with management on what issues the EWC will cover.
● A broader scope of issues is identified in the new regulations, including a new right for training for the EWC employee representatives to enable them to carry out their role; the need to amend EWC agreements following any corporate re-structuring.

● Information and Consultation of Employees: Works Councils and Employee Forums

The EU Directive on Information and Consultation of Employees was finally adopted and came into force on 23 March 2002 after many years of discussion about its content and wording. The Department of Trade and Industry (as it was called at that time) engaged in extensive consultation to establish the context of communication and consultation that already existed in the UK in order to provide a suitable framework for the national regulations. These came into force on 6 April 2005 as the Information and Consultation of Employees (ICE) Regulations 2004.

A phased introduction of the regulations took effect as follows:

● 2005 – establishments with 150 or more employees
● 2007 – establishments with 100 or more employees
● 2008 – establishments with 50 or more employees.

The establishment of these regulations introduced employee rights to consultation on matters likely to affect the economic status of their employer, and any proposed changes that might affect their employment status. Among the issues for information and consultation which are likely to lead to a successful arrangement, Hall *et al.* (2008) list consultation on ways of handling new legislation, on the 'impact and implementation of business decisions', on strategic plans such as acquisitions or the sale of a part of the business, on the restructuring of the organisation. Consultation should include the provision of timely and accurate information to employees from management, opportunities for employees to put forward their views, a managerial response to these views together with reasons for their response, and an attempt to reach agreement on decisions. A request from 10 per cent of the workforce will trigger the obligation for management to set some formal mechanism for the provision of information and consultation. The mechanisms have been variously referred to as national works councils (IRS, 2001; IDS, 2002a), consultation committees, company councils (IDS, 2002b), forums and staff councils (IDS, 2004b), works councils, employee forums (IRS, 2006a), and collectively as ICE bodies (Hall *et al.* 2008).

The IRS (2006a) reports that only 19 per cent of employers surveyed said that they had made changes to

Did you know?

The Bank of Ireland provides a good example of an organisation which has a well-established and highly effective works council. Their Partners' Council focuses on eliciting information from all workers on key aspects of employee engagement (involvement in decision making, availability of resources, communication, employment policies such as development opportunities, and wellbeing). Feedback is synthesised to provide a 'Barometer' of engagement levels to senior management.

(*Source*: Involvement and Participation Association (2010) Bank of Ireland employee forum drives engagement agenda, *IPA Bulletin*, No. 88, January; available at www.ipa-involve.com; accessed 30.07.10)

their information and consultation processes as a direct result of the ICE Regulations, but 31 per cent had introduced changes since their implementation anyway. Later IRS research compiled by Wolff (2008) indicates some slow progress in the development of formal information and consultation arrangements, with 69 per cent of organisations surveyed reporting the establishment of a works council.

Luckhurst (2007) points out that it can be difficult to get workers to take on the role of employee representative and to ensure that discussions are properly focused. His suggestions for these two problems are that the agenda in meetings must be management driven and focused on important strategic issues so that the meetings do not dissolve into discussions of 'tea and toilets' issues (p. 1). The research conducted by Hall et al. (2008) also confirms lack of weight in the subjects up for discussion as a major problem in a minority of the organisations they surveyed (4 out of 15) as well as lack of training for representatives. They do, however, also state that it is important that domestic issues ('tea and toilets') not be overlooked; they just should not be the major focus of meetings. Luckhurst (2007) further gives guidance that full explanations of decision-making processes should be given, exploring, for instance, what the alternatives were, so that employees fully understand why certain decisions have been made, leading to greater trust and more willingness to participate as representatives of the workforce.

Employee involvement (EI) and high-performance working (HPW)

As described previously, direct methods of employee involvement are widely used to achieve employee commitment and engagement, leading to the high-performance workplace which is necessary to maintain and improve levels of productivity. Our focus in the rest of this chapter is first on a detailed overview of employee involvement practices, followed by an explanation and comment on the concepts of commitment and engagement.

Pause for thought 3.5

Make a list of at least three techniques that could be used to promote the involvement of employees in decisions relating directly to their work or in general to make employees feel more that they are an equal partner in the workplace whose contribution is sought after and valued. As you read through the next section you can check your list against the practices that are discussed here.

In 1994, the Department of Employment (DoE), as it was then called, used six categories, each with a range of initiatives, to describe employee involvement and they are still useful as a basis for a structured examination of EI practices. These are summarised in Table 3.1, but extended and updated to include more recent developments such as the focus on employee wellbeing, and discussed in more detail below. The practices listed by the DoE remain representative of the bundles of HRM practices described by later researchers and commentators such as the EEF and the CIPD (2003), Incomes Data Services (2004a, 2004b and 2007), the Involvement and

Employee involvement (EI) and high-performance working (HPW)

Table 3.1 Employee involvement categories and practices

Category	EI practices
Sharing information	Team briefing
	Employer and employee publications
	Company videos
	Company website, intranet and email
	Roadshows
Consultation	Employee suggestion schemes
	Employee opinion surveys
	Works committees
	Health and safety committees
Financial participation	Profit-related pay
	Employee share schemes
	Share incentive plans
Commitment to quality	Continuous improvement
	Teamwork
	Total quality management
	Quality circles
	Self-managed project groups
	Employee award schemes
Developing the individual	Performance management
	Appraisal schemes
	Employee development programmes
	Investors in People
	A qualified workforce
Health and wellbeing	Line manager relationship
	Wellbeing programmes
Beyond the workplace	The community
	The environment

Participation Association (2007), Rankin (2008) for the Industrial Relations Services, MacLeod and Clarke (2009), reporting to the Government, and Alfes *et al.* (2010) for the CIPD. We shall refer to these and other sources as we review the various practices identified by the DoE. The Department of Employment's categorisation is not an all-inclusive definition, i.e. you do not have to be involved in all the listed activities at the same time to say you are practising employee involvement. Different combinations of practices will be suitable for different businesses, and Edwards (2007) draws attention to the fact that it may be difficult, for example, to adapt HPW practices for small businesses which are so important to the UK economy. Marchington and Cox (2007) also allude to the fact that EI practices work well in combination with each other, depending on the circumstances, and that often one practice will support the effectiveness of another.

It must be stressed again that various combinations of these measures are taken up by organisations at different times (IRS, 2003b; MacLeod and Clarke 2009; Alfes *et al.* 2010). Research conducted by Marchington *et al.* (1993) revealed that individual managers tended to adopt their preferred measures, which might well be dropped when they moved on. This is an unfortunate aspect of the voluntary and flexible nature of involvement arrangements. As you will see in the discussion of the initiatives, a longer-term commitment on the part of managers is needed if the techniques are to work to best effect. Formal partnership deals agreed between managers and employees may introduce an element of continuity into this scenario.

Sharing information

- team briefing
- employer and employee publications
- company videos
- company website, intranet and email
- roadshows.

Keeping people informed is often described as one of the cornerstones of employee involvement, and in fact provides the foundation on which many of the individual techniques can be built. Without information it is impossible for people to develop and contribute their own ideas. A commitment to sharing information is an essential component of involvement and engagement, and the list of associated practices gives an indication of some of the vehicles that can be used to get information to employees: face-to-face in small, regular meetings (team briefing), materials that could use the written word, graphics or electronic systems such as a company's intranet (company and staff newsletters, notices, posters), and videos. Wolff (2008) lists organisations that have extended or improved their use of a number of these communication methods, including the intranet and roadshows. These include John Bell & Croyden, West Kent Housing Association, Hoya Lens UK, and London Borough of Tower Hamlets/Primary Care Trust. Careful consideration should be given to choosing the form of communication most appropriate to the type of message.

Marchington and Cox (2007) report on research that shows that team briefings and mass meetings with the workforce are by far the most popular methods chosen by organisations to involve their employees: 91 per cent of organisations surveyed in 2004 used this method, up from 85 per cent in 1998. Wolff (2010) confirms that face-to-face team meetings continue to be popular (96 per cent) in spite of technological developments. So, not only is this the most used method, but its use is also on the increase. With more legal pressures to inform and consult employees, for instance because of the ICE Regulations, we can expect to see even more attention being paid to this area of employment relations.

Consultation

- employee suggestion schemes
- employee opinion surveys
- works committees
- health and safety committees.

Along with sharing information, consultation is a key concept in developing good employee relations, and much of the ongoing debate about the development of mechanisms to improve the employer-employee relationship centres on the employee's right to information and consultation. Of the information-sharing techniques we have discussed in the preceding section, briefing sessions allow for some immediate feedback from employees, but most of the other vehicles encourage only one-way communication. ACAS (2009a) emphasises that effective communication requires a two-way flow of information and ideas. The consultation mechanisms named in this section essentially provide a route for employees to feed ideas back to their employers. These vehicles only represent true consultation, however, if there is an honest willingness to consider the ideas proffered and to incorporate reasonable suggestions into the decision-making process. As the regulations on information and consultation continue to bed in, the use of those of the consultation mechanisms described here which are voluntary will be further supported by regulatory measures.

Most staff suggestion schemes are linked with a reward for successful suggestions, especially those where a cost saving for the organisation or other improvements in productivity can be identified. The reward does not, however, have to be financial for people to feel encouraged to contribute their ideas. Often people wish merely to see their expertise recognised, gaining a sense of achievement from this, and they need only to be encouraged by the introduction of a recognised scheme. The reward for successful suggestions could be linked to information vehicles from the first category, i.e. a mention in the company or staff newsletter.

Employee opinion surveys are an excellent method of collecting honest feedback from employees about what they see as the important issues, and what aspects of the workplace affect their levels of commitment and engagement both positively and negatively. The surveys obviously need to be constructed properly, addressing relevant issues, and employees need to see that their feedback is taken seriously and leads to identifiable action, otherwise the system of obtaining employee feedback will fall into disrepute and cease to be taken seriously by the employees. A further important aspect of employee opinion surveys is that not everyone is motivated by the same things (Gratton, 2007), and analysing employee feedback can enable management to tailor their EI practices to the needs of different groups of employees.

Works committees to promote information and consultation involve meetings of management and employee representatives who may be elected directly or nominated through the trade unions. Their terms of reference can be tailored to the requirements of individual organisations, and may vary widely from one organisation to another. In its work with companies, ACAS very often establishes joint working committees to solve a variety of problems. Works councils may have been established in some organisations on a voluntary basis, but the Information and Consultation of Employees (ICE) Regulations now also provide a framework for the constitution and remit of such councils. Employers who have already established information-sharing and consultation committees in their organisation may apply to the Central Arbitration Committee to have them recognised as valid arrangements under the ICE Regulations. One caveat, however, is that such arrangements must apply to all employees (Pickard, 2004). You will find information about health and safety committees in Chapter 11.

All of the methods in this category of EI practices involve upward communication, a chance for employees to put forward their point of view and ideas, an opportunity to be heard. We have already noted that this is referred to as *employee voice*, an important concept in modern employment relations. Several commentators emphasise the crucial nature of employee voice in achieving successful employee involvement leading to engagement (IDS, 2007; Purcell, 2006; MacLeod and Clarke 2009). The CIPD (2006b, p. 14) goes so far as to say that: 'Allowing people the opportunity to feed their views and opinions upwards is the single most important driver of engagement.'

Financial participation

- profit-related pay
- employee share schemes
- share incentive plans.

Although mentioned less frequently than other EI practices, a number of share schemes, often with tax relief approved by HM Revenue and Customs, exist to provide employees with financial participation in their organisations. The schemes include group or individual bonuses (which *are* subject to income tax) linked to the company's profit performance, and ownership of shares.

Again, various schemes exist in relation to share owner-ship. In some schemes, shares may be bought by a trust for employees, usually at no direct cost to them, and are later distributed to them; other schemes give employees the opportunity to buy shares directly. A variety of arrangements exist regarding the percentage of shares that employees can hold, what happens to the shares when an employee leaves the company, and, very importantly, whether the shares are voting or non-voting shares. If ownership of the shares gives employees a voice at shareholders' meetings, this is essentially a form of employee participation as it has been defined in this chapter. The Incomes Data Services study on all-employee share schemes (2001) contains excellent information on the types of plan brought in by the Finance Act 2000. These schemes are now known as Share Incentive Plans or SIPs (IDS, 2010a). XpertHR (2007) and IDS (2010a) both identify 'sharesave', also known as Save As You Earn (SAYE), as being amongst the most popular schemes, and these have existed since the 1980 Finance Act.

As intimated above, financial participation is certainly recognised as an EI practice, but it is not used as frequently as other methods. Lloyd and Payne (2007) mention profit sharing in passing, and O'Connell *et al.* (2007) point out that foreign-owned companies operating in Ireland are more likely to use performance-related financial incentives. That recognition and reward in general have a place in EI is mentioned by several observers (Brown *et al.*, 2007; CIPD, 2007), but the 2004 Workplace Employment Relations Survey (Kersley *et al.*, 2005) reports that only 21 per cent of private sector workplaces have an employee share scheme in place as part of the reward package.

Commitment to quality

- continuous improvement
- teamwork
- total quality management
- quality circles
- self-managed project groups
- employee award schemes.

The human resource management approach and modern ideas about employee motivation go hand-in-hand with an emphasis on the social aspects of work. Human beings on the whole work better in groups, they respond to the stimulation of feedback on their achievements, and there are synergies in terms of improved ideas and methods of working to be gained from having people work in teams rather than as isolated individuals. All these factors are reflected in the techniques listed above.

The idea that benefits can be gained from the formation of teams and self-managed groups is addressed in the work done by Trist and Murray at the Tavistock Institute (1993). You may have encountered their concept of sociotechnical systems in your course on organisational behaviour. Basically this theory says that organisations must pay attention to the social systems in the workplace as well as the technical systems when designing jobs. ACAS (2005) also addresses the value of teamwork as a motivational tool.

Total quality management emphasises the responsibility of each individual for ensuring the quality of their work and de-emphasises the role of supervision or inspection. This puts responsibility firmly with each individual employee. If this is combined with employee award schemes, it heightens an individual's awareness of the contribution they can make to the organisation and of the extent to which this is valued. The term 'quality circles' is linked with an approach adopted by Japanese companies, but the method stems from the work and thinking of an American, Dr W. Edwards Deming. Essentially, quality circles involve having a group of people, usually from one work area, meet away from the shop floor to discuss improvements that could be made in the work systems. The group analyses data and sets up proposals which are presented to senior managers who consider the new ideas and report back to the quality circle, either accepting the proposal or explaining why it is rejected. Since this requires a greater level of analytical skill than the employees may need for their jobs, quality circles often have a facilitator who provides assistance in the presentational aspects but does not contribute ideas as far as content is concerned.

Continuous improvement is an umbrella term for any programme that focuses on identifying and solving problems or exploring opportunities to improve the organisation's performance. These programmes often focus on an improved response to customer requirements or a reduced rate of errors which can be targeted by a combination of initiatives such as teamwork, quality management and problem-solving groups.

According to the IDS (2010b), giving awards to employees through recognition schemes can play an important role in employee motivation and engagement. Awards can take the form of non-cash gifts or may simply be a formal thank-you or recognition as employee of the month.

Developing the individual

- performance management
- appraisal schemes
- employee development programmes
- Investors in People
- a qualified workforce.

All the employee involvement techniques that we have discussed contribute to the development of employees: better communication means that people are well informed; encouragement to share ideas through consultation equates with encouragement to develop ideas rather than accept the status quo; financial participation increases awareness and knowledge of the economic performance of the organisation. Employee development extends the boundaries of knowledge, interest and understanding and enables each employee to feel more involved and more able to participate in decisions. Chapters 8 and 9 explore in detail all the practices listed above related to developing people and the contribution that these practices make to the organisation.

Health and wellbeing

The CIPD (2010a) factsheet on employee engagement refers to a research finding from as early as 2004 that the level of engagement felt is in part affected by employees' perceptions of managerial concern with their health and wellbeing. ACAS (2009c) makes a strong connection between wellbeing and engagement practices in general, and MacLeod and Clarke (2009) confirm the important role of line managers' showing concern for employee wellbeing. An article on the hrzone website (2009) took this idea further by suggesting that employers could improve engagement and business results by proactively developing health and wellbeing programmes. These programmes include offering regular health screenings, health, fitness and lifestyle consultations, and the opportunity to attend keep-fit sessions.

Beyond the workplace

- the community
- the environment.

The Department of Employment (1994) proposed that attempts to make employees feel more committed should not be limited to activities at work. We have stated in other contexts, for instance with regard to human resource planning, that employers need to be aware of the community within which they operate, and this can mean the global community as well as the local community. A number of employers have empowered their staff to become involved in community initiatives such as working with schools or with disabled persons. This has the effect of increasing the loyalty of employees and strengthening the organisation's public image.

Did you know?

hrzone reports on the volunteering programme available to employees at BT, where volunteers may work on community programmes or offer their professional skills to help charitable organisations. Leaders at BT see the programme as tying in with corporate social responsibility and employee engagement, and thus their employer brand.

(Source: Are your employees in the office or volunteering today?, www.HRzone.co.uk accessed 18.01.10)

Additional influences

In addition to the practices described above, the CIPD (2006a and b) comment on the importance of providing flexibility for employees, and state that employees who achieve a good work–life balance are more likely to be engaged. Richman et al. (2008)

A similar argument is extended to environmental issues. If employers show concern for the environment and enlist employees in methods of protecting the environment, this is likely to gain loyalty and make employees proud to be associated with the organisation.

also provide research evidence that flexible working practices can contribute to engagement and retention. The CIPD (2010b) also takes a broader look at the impact of reward systems on the employer brand, and how this can affect employee commitment and engagement. The relevant concept of total reward addresses issues such as pay incentives, bonuses and benefits in addition to the forms of recognition, development and financial participation we have described in this chapter. Flexible working arrangements and work–life balance are addressed in more detail in the next chapter, and you can read more about total reward in Chapter 10.

Commitment

As intimated previously, the reason for pursuing a programme of employee involvement is the expectation that improvements in productivity levels will follow, leading to a high-performance workplace. By informing and consulting with employees and using other techniques to make them feel more involved in the workplace, workers will be enabled and feel empowered to add more value to their organisations. An important concept in terms of the expected motivational outcomes of EI is employee commitment. The direct effect of involvement in the organisation is expected to be an increase in the individual employee's commitment to colleagues, the workplace or the job, which will be reflected in increased productivity, lower labour turnover and reduced absenteeism.

The human resource management approach is intent on maximising the contribution of employees as a critical success factor, and increasing employee commitment through involvement is seen as a way to do this. There may, however, be some problems with the contention that involvement arrangements result in increased commitment. Commitment is an attitude, and the connection between attitudes and behaviour is not a straightforward one. Behaviour depends on a variety of influencing factors, including values and beliefs and what each individual sees as motivating factors, so attitudes are not always reflected in behaviour. For instance, if a person has a positive emotional reaction to a management innovation, we could say that that person may feel greater commitment to the job or the organisation. If, however, that person is influenced by co-workers who are not like-minded, and the person values their relationship with those co-workers, then the positive attitude may not be reflected in subsequent behaviour. In fact, the person may attempt to rationalise the positive feelings away. EI practices could therefore engender a positive attitude in some people and not in others, and even where it does result in positive attitudes, it is only one feature of the workplace and other influences could result in this positive attitude not being reflected in the behaviour managers are hoping for.

There has been considerable interest in commitment among academic researchers in recent years, including Wright and Kehoe (2008), Elias (2009) and Conway and Monks (2009). Wright and Kehoe provide a good overview of recent research examining types of commitment and their links with HR practices and productivity, and Elias examines the interplay between change and organisational commitment. Conway and Monks focus on the point we have made that individual employees may react in different ways to particular HR practices.

This discussion of attitudes and behaviour is included just to sound a cautionary note that increases in commitment and productivity are not a foregone conclusion. In general, however, the introduction of EI initiatives is welcomed by the workforce and results in a positive response. Some reactions will depend on the culture and relations that have traditionally existed either in the organisation or in a particular industry. If employees do not trust management, they will greet management initiatives with scepticism. If employers wish to encourage change in these circumstances, they will have to build trust, which can only be achieved in the long term.

● Engagement

Employee engagement is recognised as being the stage beyond commitment. Employees may feel committed to their colleagues, clients, work or employer, and yet not expend the sought after discretionary effort expressed in those well-known HRM phrases such as 'going the extra mile' and 'working beyond contract'. It is when employees display these behaviours that they can be said to be engaged (Coupar, 2007). The IDS (2007) uses phrases such as 'passionate about their job' (p. 2) and a firm's 'ability to ignite enthusiasm' (p. 3) as indicators of engagement.

All of the practices we have described as participation and involvement can contribute to the creation of commitment. As Woodruffe (2006, p. 9) states: 'Engagement has become something of a vogue word, eclipsing commitment and involvement in the management literature.' Edwards (2007, p. 55) expresses a similar idea with regard to the related concept of the high-performance work system: 'The HPWS is not new. It is that employees need to be given the ability to contribute to the performance of the firm together with the means and the incentive to do so. This principle can be found in the Quality of Working Life movement of the 1960s, and indeed earlier.'

In spite of the long-established pedigree of EI practices and the much vaunted recognition of the crucial importance of engagement to business, surveys of the level of engagement in the UK report poor results. The CIPD (2006a, p. 3) reports that 'three in ten employees are engaged in their work' and that 'levels of engagement among the under-35s are significantly lower than those in older age groups'. The PeopleIndex (2007) reports a more favourable level at 52 per cent, yet calls this an alarming figure. These statistics raise questions about why EI practices are not more effective, and indeed the current focus of debate on these issues revolves around the question about what are the crucial elements that drive employees from commitment to engagement. Observers of employment relations repeatedly emphasise the prime importance of communication and leadership, and the CIPD (2007) confirms this view by identifying the psychological contract and relationships as being the key issues with regard to achieving a high-performance workplace.

We have already established that various forms of communication, and in particular employee voice, are major and essential components of EI. Beyond actually communicating, organisations need to demonstrate that they are fully committed to the processes involved and provide evidence that employee voice is being taken seriously.

Employee involvement (EI) and high-performance working (HPW)

Among a number of writers on EI, Marchington and Cox (2007) emphasise the importance of line managers in creating engagement. Managers may make choices about the extent to which they wish to subscribe to and encourage EI practices, which will obviously have an impact on the effectiveness of EI programmes within an organisation. Marchington and Cox allude to 'informal EIP' (p. 189), and link this with management style. Other commentators also draw attention to the importance of adopting an appropriate management style to encourage involvement, commitment and engagement (Earls, 2007), and to the need to ensure that managers have the appropriate skills to be able to provide leadership in this area (Gratton, 2007). Alfes *et al.*

(2010, p. 3) conclude that close attention must therefore be paid 'to the selection, development and performance management of line managers to ensure they maximize their potential to be engaging leaders'.

CASE STUDY 3.1 Employee engagement through involvement and participation

You are the head of HR at the headquarters of a national chain of supermarkets. The stores have always operated with a very hierarchical structure and a set of rigid rules. Major decisions about the business are made centrally by a board of senior executives in Birmingham, and only information that is deemed necessary is passed down the line to the next level of staff who then cascade information further down the line as they see fit. The normal chain of command consists of a regional manager, a store manager, department managers and unit supervisors. Personnel at each level deal only with the level above them. Shop assistants expect explicit instructions from their supervisors, and will refer all matters to a supervisor if a question arises on which they have not been briefed. The extent of each person's authority is strictly defined, e.g. shop assistants cannot deal with returned items; unit supervisors are responsible for deciding when displays will change, what to display, and for maintaining the general tidiness of their area. All employees know their role and their limits, and managers and supervisors do not ask for opinions from their subordinates. The company also has a rigid wage structure with a standard rate allocated to each type of job, and no deviations from this are allowed. All of this is accepted by all staff members, and everyone who has been with the company for any length of time is used to the way things are done.

A new chief executive has recently joined the company, and she is not pleased with the current way of running things. She asks you to investigate ways of changing the culture to improve the contribution from every employee, and to prepare a confidential report for her.

Questions

1 Draw up a list of the changes that could be made and how these changes would be implemented.

2 List the benefits to be gained if you try to implement your suggested changes, and the problems that may be encountered.

Conclusion

We have discussed a range of management approaches to the workforce, and the implications that different philosophies have for the ways in which, and the extent to which, employees might be encouraged to participate in the decisions made in the workplace. The development of employee involvement initiatives and partnership deals and a focus on engagement are likely to be found in organisations that espouse the tenets of human resource management. Through the use of involvement and partnership practices, these organisations will attempt to maximise their employees' contribution to the achievement of organisational goals and their ability to add value through high-performance working while also directly benefiting the employees themselves.

International issues

The range of articles available on engagement and related topics such as commitment and high-performance working indicates that these issues are high on the business and research agenda overseas as well as in the UK. This is logical, given the global exigencies of a poor economy and the recognition that organisational performance can be improved through employee engagement. Common themes emerge in the research conducted in a variety of countries.

Chalofsky and Krishna (2009) examine the importance of the meaningfulness of work for current workers in the USA. Their finding that this is an important driver of engagement is echoed by Alfes et al. (2010) in their research conducted in the UK for the CIPD.

Beltrán-Martín et al. (2008) examine the relationship between high-performance work systems (HPWS) and the expected outcome of improved performance in a study of 226 Spanish firms. Their research focuses on the role of worker flexibility in this relationship, i.e. the workers' capacity to develop and apply new skills, knowledge and behaviours in response to changing demands. The authors conclude that HPWS do lead to improved performance because approaches such as development and performance management allow workers to develop greater flexibility in their working methods.

Macky and Boxall (2008) studied 775 New Zealand workers in the context of high involvement work systems, but with a special focus on employee wellbeing. Their research again confirmed the link between high involvement and improved performance, but they caution about the possibility of increased work intensification where workers may feel compelled to work long hours and experience work overload.

And finally, Welz and Fernández-Macías (2008) provide an interesting overview of the extent to which various European member states have embraced financial participation. Their overall conclusion about the use of financial participation schemes is that it remains relatively low.

REVIEW QUESTIONS

Brief answers to these review questions are provided on page 488.

1 Describe the two main philosophical approaches underlying management–employee relations, and comment on the likelihood of each of these espousing worker participation or employee involvement initiatives.

2 Explain the connections between employee involvement, employee commitment, engagement and high-performance working.

3 Describe the history of initiatives to improve employee consultation and information in the European Union.

4 Name the major components of partnership, and comment on its aims.

SELF-CHECK QUESTIONS

Answer the following multiple-choice and short-answer questions. The answers are provided on page 489 for you to check your understanding of this chapter.

1 Which of the following statements best describes the unitary perspective?
   (a) Managers expect all employees to espouse the organisation's goals. There are occasional conflicts of interest which managers settle by negotiation.
   (b) Managers espouse the organisation's goals and recognise that employees are likely to have their own set of interests. Differences in interests are regulated by negotiated agreements.
   (c) Managers expect all employees to espouse the organisation's goals. There are no conflicts of interest.

2 Participation is the method that you are most likely to find in unitarist organisations. TRUE or FALSE?

3 What is the threshold number of employees at which the Transnational Information and Consultation of Employees Regulations 1999 obliges a community-scale company to establish a European Works Council?

4 Which of the following statements is true?
   (a) Partnership deals can only be made when the workforce is not unionised.
   (b) Partnership deals can be made in both unionised and non-unionised companies.
   (c) Partnership deals can only be made in a unionised environment.

5 Which of the following was NOT named specifically by the Department of Employment as a technique for promoting employee involvement?
   (a) quality circles
   (b) peer appraisal
   (c) team briefing
   (d) financial participation.

6 Managers can confidently expect that employee commitment to work will be a direct result of employee involvement initiatives and will lead to improved motivation and productivity. TRUE or FALSE?

7 What does the acronym SAYE stand for?

8 Which techniques are listed in your textbook as being part of sharing information?

9 Which of the following has NOT specifically been identified as a standard component of partnership agreements?

   (a) improvements in employment security

   (b) fair wages for employees

   (c) consultation on matters affecting employees

   (d) provision of flexible benefits.

10 Name two elements that have been identified as crucial for the creation of employee engagement.

HR IN THE NEWS

FT

Share the power

By Stefan Stern

Management is a practical task. It is about getting things done, not speculating about what you might do. Managers tend to be happier with concrete, tangible procedures or situations, rather than abstractions. So it is hardly surprising if mention of the term 'employee engagement' can be met, on occasion, by some rather blank looks. To some people, the idea that employees should need to feel engaged with their work remains quaint and sentimental at best, and downright soft-headed at worst.

An explanation for this inability, or unwillingness, to engage with engagement was provided 50 years ago by Douglas McGregor, the US psychologist. In his book The Human Side of Enterprise, he argued that, in general, managers subscribe to one of two theories about the people they have to deal with: they adhere to either Theory X or Theory Y.

Theory X is based on a fairly grim view of human nature. It holds that people are essentially lazy and uncomfortable with the idea of bearing too much responsibility for anything. They only turn up to work for the pay. Employees have to be supervised rigorously in a strict hierarchy, otherwise nothing will get done.

Theory Y, on the other hand, suggests people may be capable of something more positive – that they will seek out responsibility and try to get better at their jobs, from which they can derive significant personal satisfaction. Theory Y managers have high expectations of their people. They are also much more likely to develop a truly engaged workforce.

As businesses struggle to emerge from the recession, and public sector organisations endeavour to maintain and improve services with limited and possibly diminishing resources, the commitment of employees will be vital. A new Ipsos Mori poll of 100 board-level directors from the 500 biggest companies in the UK confirms that business leaders realise they need more from their staff right now.

According to this survey, 'attracting, motivating and retaining the best employees' is the number-one priority for businesses, beating even greater efficiency or having the right strategy. If the bosses surveyed by Ipsos Mori had an extra half-day a week, they would choose to be more visible and find more time to speak to their colleagues, ahead of any other measure.

For some business leaders, these ideas are not controversial. Justin King, chief executive of J Sainsbury, the retailer, says his company's efforts to encourage greater engagement are based on having open, two-way communication in the business.

'For me, colleague engagement is about helping colleagues to want to do a better job every day,' he says. 'The more they feel committed to what we are trying to achieve, the greater PR ambassadors they become for the company in everything they do and say.'

But it is not enough just to listen to colleagues, he says. They need to know their opinions matter and that suggestions will be acted upon. 'The "Tell Justin" scheme enables colleagues to raise ideas and suggestions. So far we have had more than 30,000 entries, with many being taken up,' he says.

At O2, the mobile phone company, engagement has been a priority for some time. Kay Winsper, head of employee involvement and experience, says O2 wants its employees to be emotionally and rationally committed. They should feel proud to work for the company, and realise it makes financial and professional sense not to change employers.

'All of our internal communications are couched in terms of "fans". It's part of our language and the way we think and behave. We measure internal engagement with the brand against a range of external factors, including financial performance. Our quarterly performance is measured on a "fanometer", and our brand-new recognition programme, "Fanclub", makes peer-to-peer as well as manager-to-peer recognition easier, tapping into the closeness of teams and the relationship between managers and their teams.'

At the John Lewis Partnership, engagement is a central part of the culture and distinguishes the business from its competitors. Patrick Lewis, the 'partners' counsellor' at John Lewis, says leaders are encouraged to seek out the views of colleagues in order to sustain that culture.

'Our ownership model is a huge reinforcer for engagement,' he says. 'On difficult issues, such as changes in the way we work or to our pension scheme, the fact people are listened to is vital. Leaders are effectively working for their owners. And the commitment we get from partners can be very impressive.'

Both sides of industry have high hopes for the emergence of a more engaging style of leadership and management. Brendan Barber, general secretary of the Trades Union Congress, says: 'Employers who are serious about employee engagement recognise the value that unions can bring to the workplace. During the recession there were examples of unions and employers working together to save jobs and cut costs so the company is in a competitive position as the economy starts to recover.'

Ruth Spellman, chief executive of the Chartered Management Institute, says: 'Organisations across the UK are hampered by poor management skills, with leaders who have an inability to let go and allow staff to take ownership of their work. The end result is talented people becoming frustrated and disengaged at best, or ready to leave, at worst . . . By investing in the development of staff through training and development, and acknowledging their achievements, employers have a better chance of taking advantage of the upturn.'

Managers are starting to see what a more engaged workforce could achieve. But true engagement goes deeper than mere 'morale-boosting' communication efforts or staff attitude surveys. It arises only when the leadership's behaviour – words, attitudes and actions – encourages belief and commitment from the staff.

A matter of motivation

What does employee engagement look like in practice? John Smythe, from the Engage for Change consultancy, offers two scenarios to illustrate it.

Imagine two different employees, called Ruby and Geraldine, who work for different businesses. In the first scenario, Ruby is invited to attend a morning meeting titled 'Help our recovery'.

'The invitation confirms recent open communication about the poor performance of all parts of the company, and that its parent is unable to subsidise it, let alone provide more cash for investment, and that fast action must be taken to stabilise the situation,' Mr Smythe explains. 'But it also says there are no secret pre-hatched plans for radical action. It says: "We want you and your colleagues to take ownership with management to solve the crisis, recognising that unpalatable options will have to be on the table."'

Ruby is both concerned and flattered. She arrives at the meeting, feeling like a player rather than a spectator. A two-month timetable is laid out in which she and her colleagues are invited to use their knowledge to find achievable cost savings without harming key business areas.

In this process, Mr Smythe says, there are three good questions employees can be asked. What would they do if they had a free hand in their day job? What would they do if they were a director of the company? What would they do if they had survived a takeover but were given two months by the acquirer to propose small but radical changes? In this way, employees can own the decisions that are necessary, and not become disengaged or demotivated even as tough measures are put in place.

The alternative scenario, which concerns Geraldine, is less appealing. She is also invited to a meeting described as a 'cascade briefing'. Rumours have been spreading, directors have gone to ground and communication from the company has been sparse.

'At the "cascade", her fears are confirmed when, in a PowerPoint presentation, the full extent of the dire state of the business is revealed for the first time,' Mr Smythe says. 'Detailed top-down plans for restructuring and efficiencies are revealed. The focus is all on reduction with no hint of new business opportunities. Geraldine feels less like a spectator and more like a victim. To varying degrees, her colleagues leave the meeting in shock and immobilised.'

These examples are based on real situations, he says. 'The first adult-to-adult example resulted in very fast action from a large group of workers, who all, or nearly all, felt they were driving change where they worked, and fast results were achieved. The second disenfranchised those who could contribute, resulting in a huge task of execution by an overworked "change team",' he says.

'When have you have felt most engaged, most valued and most implicated in a successful project or period at work?' he asks. 'Absolutely none of us is going to report that it was more like Geraldine's experience.'

Engagement means sharing power, which can scare some managers. It also means developing a culture of 'distributed leadership': selecting and developing leaders at every level who engage people in the decision-making and change process.

'A culture of distributed leadership means challenging assumptions about the primacy and effectiveness of a command-and-control approach to leadership,' Mr Smythe says. 'It primarily means individual leaders assessing how they have learnt to make decisions, how they engage others in decision making and how they transition from being a "god" with all the answers to being a "guide" helping to liberate the creativity of others.'

FT.com, 22/03/2010 (Stefan Stern 2010), Reproduced with permission, © The Financial Times Ltd.

Questions

1 List the factors that are identified as contributing to the development of an engaged workforce.

2 What style of leadership or management is likely to hinder employee engagement, and why is this so?

3 What are the outcomes of employees' becoming engaged? Why is employee engagement regarded as being important?

WHAT NEXT?

One of the major messages in this chapter has been about the important role that commitment plays in leading to engagement. Questions of commitment and its effects are, of course, also of interest in other countries. We have found a number of research articles investigating these issues: one focuses on three countries, Germany, China and Romania, examining individual workers' leanings on the cultural dimension of collectivism and the effect that this has on feelings of commitment. The second examines cultural differences and the effect of these on organisational commitment by analysing data gathered in a large multinational company covering 29 nations. The third examines the effects of managerial practices on commitment in two Indian organisations, one from the public sector and one from the private sector. An interesting aspect of this article is that it includes an examination of the effects of ethical practices. These three articles will give you an idea of international aspects of commitment, engagement and retention.

Felfe, J., W. Yan and B. Six (2008) The impact of individual collectivism on commitment and its influence on organisational citizenship behaviour and turnover in three countries, *International Journal of Cross Cultural Management*, Vol. 8(2), 211–237.

Gelade, G. A., P. Dobson and K. Auer (2008) Individualism, masculinity, and the sources of organisational commitment, *Journal of Cross-Cultural Psychology*, Vol. 39, No. 5, 599–617.

Mohapatra, M. and B. R. Sharma (2008) Drivers of organizational commitment among managers of industrial organizations: a case study, *Global Business Review* 2008, Vol. 9, No. 1, 51–63.

References

Advisory, Conciliation and Arbitration Service (1997) *Annual Report*, ACAS.

Advisory, Conciliation and Arbitration Service (2005) *Teamwork: Success through People*, ACAS (available at www.acas.org.uk; accessed 20.07.10).

Advisory, Conciliation and Arbitration Service (2009a) *Employee Communications and Consultation*, ACAS (available at www.acas.org.uk; accessed 19.07.10).

Advisory, Conciliation and Arbitration Service (2009b) Employee engagement: is it still relevant in a recession?, *Employment Relations Matters*, 13, Winter, 5–7 (available at www. acas.org.uk; accessed 24.03.10).

Advisory, Conciliation and Arbitration Service (2009c) Healthy work, healthy lives, *Employment Relations Matters*, 13, Winter, 3–5 (available at www.acas.org.uk; accessed 24.03.10).

Advisory, Conciliation and Arbitration Service (2009d) *Representation at Work*, ACAS (available at www.acas.org.uk; accessed 30.07.10)

Alfes, K., C. Truss, F. Soane, C. Rees and M. Gatenby (2010) *Creating an Engaged Workforce: Research Report*, CIPD.

Allen, M. (1998) All-inclusive, *People Management*, 11 June, 36–42.

Beardwell, I. (1998) Voices on, *People Management*, 28 May, 32–36.

Beltrán-Martín, I., V. Roca-Puig, A. Escrig-Tena and J. C. Bou-Llusar (2008) Human resource flexibility as a mediating variable between high performance work systems and performance, *Journal of Management*, Vol. 34, No. 5, 1009–1044.

Brown, A., M. Roddan, S. Jordan and L. Nilsson (2007) The time of your life, *People Management*, 26 July, 40–43.

Chalofsky, N. and V. Krishna (2009) Meaningfulness, commitment, and engagement: The intersection of a deeper level of intrinsic motivation, *Advances in Developing Human Resources*, Vol. 11, No. 2, 189–203.

Chartered Institute of Personnel and Development (2006a) *Change Agenda: Reflections on Employee Engagement*, CIPD.

Chartered Institute of Personnel and Development (2006b) *How Engaged are British Employees? Annual Survey Report 2006*, CIPD (available at www.cipd.co.uk; accessed 20.07.10).

Chartered Institute of Personnel and Development (2007) *Employee Engagement*, CIPD (podcast available at www.cipd.co.uk; accessed 20.07.10).

Chartered Institute of Personnel and Development (2009) *European Works Councils*, CIPD (factsheet available at www.cipd.co.uk; accessed 06.07.10).

Chartered Institute of Personnel and Development (2010a) *Employee Engagement*, CIPD (factsheet available at www.cipd.co.uk; accessed 27.07.10).

Chartered Institute of Personnel and Development (2010b) *Employer Branding and Total Reward. Research Report March 2010*, CIPD.

Chartered Institute of Personnel and Development (2010c) *Labour Market Outlook, Quarterly Survey Report, Spring 2010*, CIPD.

Conway, E. and K. Monks (2009) Unravelling the complexities of high commitment: An employee-level analysis, *Human Resource Management Journal*, Vol. 19, No. 2, 140–158.

Coupar, W. (2007) Employee involvement and high performance, in Involvement and Participation Association, *High Performance Working*, IPA.

Coupar, W. and B. Stevens (1998) Towards a new model of industrial partnership: beyond the 'HRM versus industrial relations' argument, in P. Sparrow and M. Marchington (eds), *Human Resource Management: The New Agenda*, Financial Times Pitman.

Department for Business, Innovation & Skills (2010) *The Transnational Information and Consultation of Employees (Amendment) Regulations 2010 – Guidance*, Crown Copyright.

Department of Employment (1994) *The Competitive Edge: Employee Involvement in Britain*, Department of Employment.

Earls, J. (2007) Good work: an agenda for trade unions and employers, in Involvement and Participation Association, *High Performance Working*, IPA.

Edwards, P. (2007) The high performance work system and the small firm, in Involvement and Participation Association, *High Performance Working*, IPA.

EEF/CIPD (2003) *Maximising Employee Potential and Business Performance: the Role of High Performance Working*, EEF/CIPD.

Elias, S. M. (2009) Employee commitment in times of change: assessing the importance of attitudes toward organizational change, *Journal of Management*, Vol. 35, No. 1, February, 37–55.

Fairness at Work, Government White Paper, May 1998 (paper available at www.berr.gov.uk; accessed 30.07.10).

Fox, A. (1974) *Beyond Contract: Work Power and Trust Relations*, Faber and Faber.

Gennard, J. and G. Judge (2005) *Employee Relations*, 4th edition, CIPD.

Gold, M. and M. Hall (1994) Statutory European Works Councils: the final countdown? *Industrial Relations Journal*, Vol. 5, No. 3, September, 177–186.

Gratton, L. (2007) *Why Some Companies Buzz with Energy and Others Don't* (MBA Podcast available at www.timesonline.co.uk; accessed 13.07.07).

Hackman, J.R. and G.R. Oldham (1980) *Work Redesign*, Addison Wesley.

Hall, M., S. Hutchinson, J. Parker, J. Purcell and M. Terry (2008) *Implementing Information and Consultation: Early Experience under the ICE Regulations – Interim Update Report. Employment Relations Occasional Paper*, Department for Business, Enterprise & Regulatory Reform.

Herzberg, F., B. Mausner and B. Snyderman (1959) *The Motivation to Work*, Wiley.

HRzone (2009) Workplace Wellbeing: Alternative Rules of Engagement (available at www.hrzone.co.uk; accessed 22.09.09).

Incomes Data Services (2004b) Information and consultation: nine months to go, *IDS HR Studies Update 776*, June, 1–9.

Incomes Data Services (2001) *IDS Study 712: All-Employee Share Schemes*, IDS.

Incomes Data Services (2002a) *IDS Studies 722: European Works Councils*, IDS.

Incomes Data Services (2002b) *IDS Studies 730: Company Councils*, IDS.

Incomes Data Services (2007) Employee engagement, *IDS HR Studies Update 846*, May.

Incomes Data Services (2010a) *IDS HR Study 909: Employee Share Schemes*, IDS.

Incomes Data Services (2010b) *IDS Study 914: Employee Recognition Schemes*, IDS.

Incomes Data Services (2001) Common position reached on national works councils text, *European Industrial Relations Review 330*, July, 13–15.

Incomes Data Services (2003a) An open relationship, *IRS Employment Review 779*, 4 July, 8–21.

Incomes Data Services (2003b) *IDS Studies 741: Internal Communications*, IDS.

Incomes Data Services (2004a) *IDS HR Studies Plus 777: Employee Attitude Surveys + Guide to Suppliers*, IDS.

Industrial Relations Services (2003b) Raising productivity: policy and practice, *IRS Employment Review 776*, 23 May, 10–15.

Industrial Relations Services (2004) We're all in this together – partnership at work, *IRS Employment Review 801*, 4 June, 15–17.

Industrial Relations Services (2006a) A two-way process: informing and consulting employees, *IRS Employment Review 859*, 17/11 (available at www.xperthr.co.uk; accessed 20.07.10).

Industrial Relations Services (2006b) Unions in search of a new role in employee engagement, *IRS Employment Review 860*, 1/12 (available at www.xperthr.co.uk; accessed 20.07.10).

Involvement and Participation Association (2007) *High Performance Working*, IPA.

Johnstone, S., P. Ackers and A. Wilkinson (2009) The British partnership phenomenon: a ten year review, *Human Resource Management Journal*, Vol. 19, No. 3, 260–279.

Kersley, B., C. Alpin, J. Forth, A. Bryson, H. Bewley, G. Dix and S. Oxenbridge (2005) *Inside the Workplace: First Findings from the 2004 Workplace Employment Relations Survey*, DTI.

Lloyd, C. and J. Payne (2007) High performance work organisation – a driver for the high skills vision, in Involvement and Participation Association, *High Performance Working*, IPA.

Luckhurst, D. (2007) The five key steps to engagement, *IPA Bulletin*, No. 67, July, 1 and 4 (available by email via www.ipa-involve.com; accessed 30.07.10).

Macky, K. and P. Boxall (2008) High-involvement work processes, work intensification and employee well-being: a study of New Zealand worker experiences, *Asia Pacific Journal of Human Resources*, Vol. 46, No. 1, 38–55.

MacLeod, D. and N. Clarke (2009) *Engaging for Success: Enhancing Performance through Employee Engagement: A Report to Government*, Crown Copyright.

Marchington, M. (1998) Partnership in context: towards a European model? in P. Sparrow and M. Marchington (eds), *Human Resource Management: The New Agenda*, Financial Times Pitman.

Marchington, M., A. Wilkinson and P. Ackers (1993) Waving or drowning in participation? *Personnel Management*, March, 46–50.

Marchington, M. and A. Cox (2007) Employee involvement and participation: structures, processes and outcomes, in J. Storey, *Human Resource Management: A Critical Text*, 3rd edition, Thomson.

McGlynn, C. (1995) European Works Councils: towards industrial democracy? *Industrial Law Journal*, Vol. 24, No. 1, March, 78–84.

Mill, C. (1991) The long road to employee involvement, *Personnel Management*, February, 26–27.

Monks, J. (1998) Trade unions, enterprise and the future, in P. Sparrow and M. Marchington (eds), *Human Resource Management: The New Agenda*, Financial Times Pitman.

O'Connell, L., W. Liu and P. Flood (2007) Ireland's national workplace strategy: high performance through partnership: An examination of the evidence, in Involvement and Participation Association, *High Performance Working*, IPA.

Peopleindex (2007) *Employee Engagement Benchmark* (www.yougov.com; accessed 28.08.07; no longer available on-line).

Pickard, J. (2004) Informed decision, *People Management*, 16 September, 31–34.

Purcell, J. (2006) Building better organisations, in CIPD, *Change Agenda: Reflections on Employee Engagement*, CIPD.

Rankin, N. (2008) The drivers of staff retention and engagement, *IRS Employment Review 901*, 01/07 (available at www.xperthr.co.uk; accessed 20.07.10).

Richman, A.L., J. T. Civian, L. L. Shannona, E. J. Hill, and R. T. Brennanc (2008) The relationship of perceived flexibility, supportive work-life policies, and use of formal flexible arrangements and occasional flexibility to employee engagement and expected retention, *Community, Work and Family*, Vol. 11, No. 2, May, 183–197.

Sisson, K. (2007) Right challenge – wrong conclusion, in Involvement and Participation Association, *High Performance Working*, IPA.

Smith, A. (2006) 'Partnership' at work? *Work, Employment and Society*, Vol. 20(4), 811–817.

Taylor, F.W. (1911) *The Principles of Scientific Management*, Harper.

Trist, E. and H. Murray (eds) (1993) *The Social Engagement of Social Science: A Tavistock Anthology*, Vol. II: The Socio-Technical Perspective, University of Pennsylvania Press.

Welz, C. and E. Fernández-Macías (2008) Financial participation of employees in the European Union: much ado about nothing?, *European Journal of Industrial Relations*, Vol. 14, No. 4, 479–97.

Wolff, C. (2008) Survey: employee communications, *IRS Employment Review 903*, 26/08 (available at www.xperthr.co.uk; accessed 19.07.10).

Wolff, C. (2010) Employee communications: the 2010 IRS survey, *IRS Employment Review*, 28/06 (available at www.xperthr.co.uk; accessed 06.07.10).

Further study

Books

Advisory, Conciliation and Arbitration Service (2009) *Employee Communications and Consultation*, ACAS (available at www.acas.org.uk; accessed 19.07.10).

Gives detailed coverage of the uses, benefits and methods of communication and consultation in the workplace.

Advisory, Conciliation and Arbitration Service (2009) *Representation at work*, ACAS (available at www.acas.org.uk; accessed 30.07.10).

Covers the various ways in which workers may be supported or involved through the use of employee representatives.

Incomes Data Services (2006) *IDS HR Study 824: European Works Councils*, IDS.

Gives an overview of the legislation, the operation of an EWC, and case studies of six organisations.

Incomes Data Services (2008) *IDS Studies 868: Suggestion Schemes*, IDS.

Overview of how to design an effective suggestion scheme, with case studies of seven organisations, including Boots UK, the Driver and Vehicle Licensing Agency and Sellafield.

Incomes Data Services (2010) *IDS HR Study 909: Employee Share Schemes*, IDS.

Reviews the main facets of sharesave and share incentive plans, and provides case studies of 16 companies that offer these schemes to their employees. These include AstraZeneca, Rolls-Royce and Wincanton.

Johnson, M. (2004) *The New Rules of Engagement: Life-Work Balance and Employee Commitment*, CIPD.

Based on conversations with a number of people, and written in a lighter tone than standard academic publications, this book provides a readable overview of aspects of employee engagement and some insights most readers will identify with. There are some trenchant messages for managers here.

Sparrow, P. and M. Marchington (eds) (1998) *Human Resource Management: The New Agenda*, Financial Times Pitman Publishing.

Part 2 of this book, 'Developing partnership and employee voice', contains six excellent chapters giving different perspectives on partnership.

Woodruffe, C. (2006) From 'Whatever' to 'My pleasure': how can employers increase engagement? in CIPD, *Change Agenda: Reflections on Employee Engagement*, CIPD.

Wright, P. M. and R. R. Kehoe (2008) Human resource practices and organizational commitment: a deeper understanding, *Asia Pacific Journal of Human Resources*, Vol. 46, No. 1, 6–20.

XpertHR (2007) Employee share schemes and employee share ownership plans, *Employment Law Reference Manual* (available at www.xperthr.co.uk; accessed 23.07.10).

Articles

First British European Works Councils established (1994) *Industrial Relations Review and Report*, No. 574, December, 4–7.

A description of the EWCs set up by BP Oil Europe and United Biscuits, involving UK employees even before the directive was adopted by the UK.

Industrial Relations Services (2000) Buy in or sell out? *IRS Employment Trends* 716, November, 6–11.

A review of what happens after union–management partnership agreements. Provides references to 12 IRS case studies.

Industrial Relations Services (2000) Towards commercial consciousness raising, *IRS Employment Trends 718*, December, 12–16.

HR specialists' views on the link between enhanced communication with employees and improved performance.

Johnstone, S., P. Ackers and A. Wilkinson (2009) The British partnership phenomenon: a ten year review, *Human Resource Management Journal*, Vol. 19, No. 3, 260–279.

Summarises the major points made in the literature on partnership from 1998 to 2008.

Nohria, N., B. Groysberg and L-E. Lee (2008) Employee motivation: a powerful new model, *Harvard Business Review*, July–August, 78–84.

A very readable article which presents an overview of motivation in terms of four drives (to acquire, bond, comprehend and defend), and links these to outcomes such as engagement, commitment and retention. The article offers advice on practical ways to achieve these outcomes, but stresses both that *all* drives must be addressed simultaneously and that senior and line managers contribute greatly to the potential success of any initiatives.

Park, R., E. Appelbaum and D. Kruse (2010) Employee involvement and group incentives in manufacturing companies: a multi-level analysis, *Human Resource Management Journal*, Vol. 20, No. 3, 227–43.

Park *et al.* examine group incentives and other employee involvement practices separately to discover differences in the effect of these techniques on commitment and turnover intentions. They find that employee involvement is more effective in capital-intensive companies whereas group incentives are more effective in labour-intensive companies.

Ramaswamy, E. A. (2009) Labour management partnership: how to make it work? *Global Business Review*, 10, 1, 103–121.

Ramaswamy presents the case of a company in India, trying to establish a partnership approach to its work, and the problems encountered along the way. Three professors from Indian Universities, E. M. Rao, Debi S. Saini, and Narendra Nath Akhouri, then present their responses to the issues raised in the case study. This is an interesting opportunity to review a realistic situation in an Indian context, and to attempt to think through solutions before reviewing others' responses.

Internet

Advisory, Conciliation and Arbitration Service   **www.acas.org.uk**

Provides good practice advice on how to implement the ICE Regulations. Also has a downloadable advisory booklet on communications in the workplace and an e-learning course on informing and consulting.

Chartered Institute of Personnel and Development   **www.cipd.co.uk**

Information on consultation and information, employee voice and high-performance working. The website also has a number of downloadable podcasts related to the topic of employee engagement, including podcast number 43 from June 2010 on distributed leadership and number 37 on employee engagement. The podcasts include interviews with representatives from a number of organisations, giving a good insight into their views and activities in the context of engagement.

Department for Business, Innovation and Skills   **www.bisgov.uk**

Provides masses of information on employment matters.

Involvement and Participation Association   **www.ipa-involve.com**

A rich source of information on partnership, employee involvement, high-performance working, information and consultation. Sign up for their monthly e-bulletin, and you can keep informed about a wide range of employment relations issues.

CHAPTER 4

The employment relationship

Objectives

When you have read this chapter you will be able to:

- understand and describe the rights and obligations of both parties to the employment relationship

- understand the basis of the contract of employment and describe the terms that should constitute a basic contract of employment

- describe the main employment rights provided by legal statute

- outline a variety of flexible working arrangements and assess their usefulness and impact for both employers and employees

- describe the issues to be considered when an employee leaves an organisation.

The relationship between employers and their employees can be described in many ways. To get a clear picture of what this might entail, think first of any relationship between people, including personal relationships between friends, life partners and relatives; that is, think about relationships, but not necessarily in the context of employment. Any relationship is formed within a context of rights, expectations and obligations on the part of each party to the relationship. These rights etc. may be individualised for each pair of individuals as in marital relationships, or it may be that a group of people see themselves together as forming one party to a relationship and that they therefore have shared interests that they wish to see represented on a collective basis. Some of these rights, expectations and obligations are unspoken: you assume that your close friends will not purposely do anything to harm you, but you do not feel that this needs to be said explicitly. In other things, you may need to negotiate and reach agreement; in spite of the much heralded concept of the equality of the sexes, the division of labour in the household can still be a contentious area in heterosexual relationships. Beyond what individuals agree among themselves, both implicitly and explicitly, there is a legal framework that imposes obligations and guarantees rights, such as the division of possessions when a marital relationship fails. Relationships are also affected by cultural norms, custom and practice, views on what is and is not acceptable and the balance of power. These influences may be relatively stable for long periods of time, but the twentieth century was recognised as a period of great and rapid change, a phenomenon which will no doubt continue in the twenty-first century.

Pause for thought 4.1

Stop to consider the last two sentences in the preceding paragraph. Can you identify examples of these issues either in your own life or in those of people you know? What are the determinants of power in personal relationships? What changes in these areas can you identify? Discuss this with a group of fellow students, and you will probably identify a surprising number of influences and changes.

If you accept that this complex framework applies to personal relationships, it should not come as any surprise that the employment relationship is governed by a complex mix of individual and collective agreements, implicit and explicit understandings, and rights and obligations enshrined in legal statutes, and that other influences such as culture and the balance of power apply to it too. This chapter will attempt to give an overview of the many threads that weave together to create the canvas of the employment relationship, and will also look at how trends within it can be monitored. In particular we shall examine the legal aspects of the employment relationship, together with some cultural and psychological factors and the concept of flexibility in working arrangements. We shall also look briefly at what happens on the termination of the employment relationship.

Rights and obligations of the two parties

Balance of power

The extent to which one party in a relationship has rights and the extent to which that party has obligations depend in some measure on the balance of power between the two parties.

Pause for thought 4.2

Put aside for the moment the notion that as a proponent of the HRM approach you would be seeking to develop a workforce that shared a common purpose with management and with which there was therefore little conflict. If you regard an individual employee or a group of employees as having some areas of conflict with a manager, who would you judge to have more power than the other? List your reasons. What are the implications of this balance of power for the relationship between workforce and managers?

In spite of legislation that protects a range of employee rights, the general feeling in the industrial relations arena in the 1990s was that the balance of power lay with the employer. These sentiments had been fuelled by legislation throughout the 1980s and early 1990s which progressively curtailed the powers of the trade unions, and by high levels of unemployment and frequent redundancies which undermined many employees' sense of job security. There were also a large number of redundancies in the early years of the twenty-first century, many attributed to the global effects of the slowdown in the American economy at that time. The credit crunch and poor economy of 2008–2009 brought further fears of potential redundancy situations and job losses.

The implications of this for the relationship between employees and their managers lie in the areas of trust, openness, willingness to cooperate and amenability to different points of view. Where there is an imbalance of power, these areas of a relationship can suffer or at least they can be difficult to maintain. In the workplace this means that managers will have to find ways of reassuring employees that they will be treated as equal partners in the relationship. Managers will attempt to do this of their own volition if they believe that an employee relationship based on partnership is in fact a contributory factor in the success of their organisation. We have already explored this belief more fully in our examination of employee involvement and engagement in Chapter 3.

The Labour Government of 1997–2010 produced a programme of employment measures emphasising the development of fairness at work and a partnership approach to the relationship between employer and employee. Some of its original proposals have subsequently been enshrined in the Employment Relations Act 1999 and other regulations. These include improved regulations on union recognition, enhanced rights to time off work, and rights to request serious consideration of flexible working arrangements to support people in combining their family life commitments with work. The implementation of EU legislation on consultation and information is also shifting the focus more firmly towards employees' rights. We have discussed some of these issues in Chapter 3 in our detailed discussion of partnership, participation and employee involvement. These developments all strengthened workers' rights in the workplace. This chapter attempts to build up a fuller picture by addressing more of the elements that combine to create our employment relations climate, but it should be noted that the employment policies of the Conservative–Liberal Coalition Government, in power since May 2010, have yet to be fully developed and implemented.

Expectations of the two parties: the psychological contract

The concept of the psychological contract aroused much interest among observers of HRM in the late 1990s, and interest in the concept and its impact on the employment relationship continues (CIPD, 2010). Attributed initially to Argyris (1960), the concept was further developed by Schein (1978), among others. It concerns the expectations that each party holds with regard to the other, and is recognised as having an impact on the way people behave in the workplace. The psychological contract is akin to the implied terms in a legal contract, i.e. much of it will be assumed and unspoken, but whereas implied terms in a contract would be fairly standard across organisations, the psychological contract is more likely to vary. It includes factors that result in feelings such as loyalty and perceptions of fair treatment, and many intrinsic factors that affect motivation. Much of the debate in the 1990s was about expectations of job security as an element of the psychological contract and the extent to which organisations could or could not continue to offer reassurance with regard to job security. Guest and Conway (1997) refer to the *new* psychological contract where the focus has shifted to employment security or employability rather than job security. This means that if employees can no longer expect their employer to guarantee them a job for life, they might instead expect their employer to support their development to make them more employable.

The nature of the psychological contract and the motivation of the individual can be influenced by the culture of an organisation and its predominant management style, and can be seen as coercive, calculative or cooperative (Handy, 1985). Coercion, where people are motivated to expend effort in order to avoid punishment, is generally regarded as unproductive and inappropriate for today's work organisations. A calculative contract will come into being where the connection between effort and reward is explicit, and each employee can calculate the value to themselves of expending extra energy on the organisation's behalf. The cooperative contract arises when individuals identify with the goals of their organisation. The latter is the kind of psychological contract one would expect to find in an organisation that espouses the human resource management approach towards maximising the contribution of its employees through the use of practices that involve and engage them.

The cooperative contract implies a more participative style of management and greater employee involvement in decisions in the workplace. Individuals differ, however, in what they perceive as motivating, as Handy points out, and he goes on to say that managers may sometimes be disappointed at a lack of response when they try to change from, say, a calculative contract to a cooperative contract. However, if an organisation is run on participative lines, it is likely to engender positive attitudes in new employees, and perseverance with new techniques may help to alter attitudes among existing staff. The renewed emphasis of the late 1990s on fairness at work and partnership between employers and employees tied in well with this concept of a cooperative contract, and the work by Guest and Conway (1997) also highlights the link between a climate of employee involvement, as described in the preceding chapter, and a positive psychological contract.

More recently, reflective analysis from the Chartered Institute of Personnel and Development (CIPD, 2005) has highlighted important aspects of the psychological contract. The paper as a whole strongly emphasises the importance of the role of line managers in establishing a positive psychological contract, the effects of stress and wellbeing, and developments in attitudes towards career expectations. The CIPD (2010) in its factsheet on the psychological contract makes the point that most workers in large organisations identify their line manager as the employer as this is the person with whom they have contact on a day-to-day basis. As such, line managers and their management style therefore have the most immediate impact on perceptions of the psychological contract.

Both Woodruffe (2005) in the set of reflections on the psychological contract and the CIPD (2010) point out that different employees may be motivated by different things. Woodruffe writes of graduates as being 'the talent pool from which the future senior management of an organisation will be drawn' (p. 8) and suggests that their need for independence will require careful management in order to retain them. The CIPD (2010) state that while employees in general may be concerned with security, 'many younger people are not interested in the concept of a job for life, being more likely to move around jobs and change careers'.

This brings us to a final point about flexible working practices and work–life balance. You will learn from later sections in this chapter that flexible working arrangements are addressed as a contractual matter and that certain groups have a statutory

The legal framework

● Contract and common law

Contract and common law, the latter being law established by judges' decisions rather than by statute, are important components of the legal framework that delineates the employment relationship. The first question that arises is whether or not a person is regarded in the eyes of the law as being an employee in the first place, and this has implications for a person's ability to claim the right to the protections provided by statutory employment law.

As with many legal questions, there are instances where there is no straightforward answer to the question of whether two parties have the relationship of employer and employee, and it is up to the courts to interpret the law and come to a decision. There is also no single definitive test that will give a conclusive answer, but some combination of the following factors can be considered in order to conclude whether a person is rendering services as an employee or on a self-employed basis. In deciding on the relationship between two parties, the courts will subject the relationship to a number of tests, including whether:

● the employer is entitled to exercise control over what the employee does and how they do it
● the employee is integrated into the structure of the organisation
● there is a mutual obligation to supply and accept work.

A person who is performing work for someone on a self-employed basis is not entitled to the rights enshrined in statutes such as the Employment Rights Act 1996 since such a person is not an employee in the eyes of the law.

The situation is further complicated, however, by the use of another term, i.e. 'worker'. A worker may be under some sort of contract, but may fail on one or more of the tests applied to determine whether the person can be classed as an employee. In a website table (member access only) showing the entitlements of employees and workers, the CIPD (**www.cipd.co.uk**) indicates that both workers and employees would be covered by certain pieces of legislation (for example the Working Time Regulations, meaning workers too are entitled to holiday pay, and the National Minimum Wage Act), but that workers would not have all of the statutory rights that can be claimed by those classed as employees (such as unfair dismissal rights, a right to statutory redundancy pay and the right to request flexible working arrangements). People working for an organisation in a transitory fashion tend to be those classed as workers unless they are, in fact, self-employed, but the distinction between 'worker' and 'employee' status can be difficult to identify and ultimately only an Employment Tribunal can pass a definitive judgement if there is a disagreement on this. Also, as the CIPD points out, the term 'worker' is being used more and more in developing legislation.

right to request flexible working. There is, however, still a fair amount of managerial judgement involved in deciding whether or not to adopt various patterns of flexibility and how to manage them. This means that access to flexible working patterns and the related outcomes in terms of the quality of work–life balance may vary and so are also part of what constitutes the psychological contract.

The contract of employment

It is a common misapprehension that the letter offering employment or the written documentation supplied by an employer to an employee constitutes the contract of employment. A contract is basically an agreement, and despite the saying that 'an oral contract is as good as the paper it is written on', if a person offers you employment over a cup of coffee in a restaurant and you accept the offer, you have a contract with each other. The written statement is evidence or proof that a contract exists, but it is not a contract *per se*; it is a statement of what has been agreed.

Implied and express terms

Contracts are made up of express terms and implied terms. As the phrases indicate, an express term is something that is regarded as important enough to be dealt with specifically and agreed on. Some terms may be assumed and not stated explicitly. For example, it may be stated how much notice an employee is to give if they wish to terminate the contract of employment, but if it is not explicitly stated, the implied term would be whatever is customary in that particular industry or line of work. There is a statutory minimum as far as the amount of notice that an employer should give is concerned, so if there is no explicit mention of this in the contract, the statutory minimum will be the implied term.

On the whole it is best for employers to be explicit about any terms they require, for example with regard to mobility. If you are likely to require an employee to work at various locations, particularly if you already have establishments in various geographically dispersed locations, it is advisable to include this requirement as an express term in the contract. Even then, the enforcement of such contract terms is not without difficulties; you have to be able to show that the term is justified and it has to be applied in a reasonable fashion. In a case involving a British Council requirement of its employees to work anywhere in the UK on promotion to a certain grade, *Meade-Hill v. British Council*, it was held that this could amount to indirect sex discrimination unless the broadly stated requirement could be justified. Such a clause could be seen as indirect discrimination because fewer women would be able to comply with it than men.

Implied terms include:

- on the part of the employer
  - the duty to maintain mutual trust and confidence
- on the part of the employee
  - the duty to obey lawful and reasonable orders
  - the duty of fidelity
  - the duty to work with due diligence and care.

The duty of fidelity can be explained as the obligation to act in good faith in dealings with an employer or on behalf of an employer. For example, submitting a tender for a contract that your employer is pursuing could be construed as breaching the implied duty to give faithful service. The employee also has an implied duty not to disclose confidential information, and a duty to cooperate with the employer, i.e. not to deliberately cause disruptions.

Variation of the terms of a contract

An employer must give written notice to an employee of any intended changes in the terms of the contract. The employer does not, however, have the right to vary unilaterally the terms of the contract, but must consult with employees and if possible obtain their agreement to the changes. If an employer tries to enforce a change without the agreement of an employee, this may be taken as a fundamental breach of contract which has the effect of repudiating the contract. In these circumstances, the employee may, after following the internal grievance procedure, resign, claiming constructive dismissal, and pursue compensation at an employment tribunal. We have mentioned at various times in this edition that many employers have attempted to avoid redundancies by altering the working pattern of employees to cut costs and save jobs. Reducing a person's hours would normally be to the detriment of employees if they had not sought this change themselves. Both Adams and Stakim (2008) and Doran (2010) point out, however, that such a variation is more likely to be acceptable to employees if they are properly consulted and realise that this is an alternative to redundancy.

● Employment law

A variety of employee rights are protected by legal statute, but it is beyond the scope of this text to provide a comprehensive description of employment law. We shall give a brief explanation of how European Union law affects UK legislation, and then focus on some of the issues that have been of recent interest and that you are likely to be asked about as either a line manager or a human resource practitioner. Remember that the law can be very complex and its interpretation most difficult. To assist employers to understand and keep up to date with legislation, a number of professional journals, such as *People Management*, publish regular briefings which help employers to interpret the law, especially in the light of new decisions on tribunal or court cases. Professional and government websites also provide guidance on various aspects of the law, and some even provide interactive tools which take the user through questions addressing individual cases. Web pages showing FAQs are also often particularly useful. Several of these sites are listed at the end of this chapter. We shall be looking at some aspects of employment law in greater detail, but remember that if you are in any doubt about an employee's or worker's rights, it is best to consult a solicitor.

You should also keep in mind the fact that the law usually states the minimum entitlement of an employee, and in most circumstances employers can decide to enhance the legal entitlement with more generous contractual provision. Enhancing entitlements may be a way of attracting and retaining employees with superior abilities, and so may be a consideration in pursuing the corporate strategy, particularly one of growth or innovation. All employees and workers should ensure that they are aware of their contractual provisions, but as a line manager or HR practitioner, you are likely to be asked for explanations.

We have dealt with certain employee rights in other chapters, so we shall not repeat that information here. You will find a discussion of the equality legislation in Chapter 3, certain aspects of the right to consultation and information in Chapter 5, dismissal and redundancy rights in Chapter 13 and health and safety regulations in Chapter 11. Our discussion here will focus on:

- the statement of particulars of employment
- notice of termination of employment
- employee rights to time off work
- guaranteed payments
- the written statement of reasons for dismissal
- maternity and other parental rights
- the rights of part-time staff
- working hours
- protection of employee data.

In addition to the issues we have chosen to address, readers should be aware of the Transfer of Undertakings (Protection of Employment) Regulations 2006 (TUPE, 2006). The regulations protect the terms and conditions of employees in cases of a transfer of ownership of a trade or business, and state that dismissal because of the transfer is unfair. The original 1989 regulations were updated in 2006 to incorporate the many developments that had occurred over the intervening years. This is a very complex area of legislation which is beyond the scope of this introductory textbook.

The European Union (EU) and UK employment law

EU law takes effect in a number of ways, the most important being regulations, which have direct effect in member states (i.e. they override domestic law) and directives, which have to be implemented through national legislation. Some directives, for example those that encourage improvements related to health and safety, can be adopted by qualified majority voting, which means that they must be enacted by all member states, including the minority that voted against them. An example of this is the European Working Time Directive which was adopted in 1993 with dissension from the then Conservative Government of the UK. As the directive was considered to be a health and safety measure, the UK was obliged to accept and implement it. This contrasts with directives concerning the social rights and interests of employees, which require unanimity and from which individual member states can opt out. For example, the Conservative Government in the UK opted out of several social measures that were adopted by the rest of the EU at the time of the Treaty on European Union 1992 (the Maastricht Treaty). Subsequently, however, the Labour Government signed up to the Social Chapter which is now integrated into agreements made in the Treaty of Amsterdam 1997.

Employees in the public service sector can rely upon the direct effect of directives, i.e. if the directive has not been implemented, this group of employees can take their case to the European Court. National courts also take account of the purpose of directives when interpreting national legislation. This gave rise, for example, to the House of Lords finding in 1994 that the two-year threshold, in force at that time, to be able to claim a range of employment protection rights should apply to all employees irrespective of the number of hours worked, in spite of the fact that this was not stated explicitly in UK law at the time of the finding. (See the later section in this chapter on part-time employees for more detail, and note that this two-year threshold was itself later reduced to a one-year qualifying period.)

Written statement of particulars of employment

Although the documentation referred to in this section does not constitute a contract as such, an employer is bound by law to issue a statement of terms and conditions to most employees, and the content of these documents serves as proof of the existence of a contract and evidence of the terms that were agreed. The legislation covering this statement is to be found in part I of the Employment Rights Act 1996, an Act which consolidates various individual employment rights which had previously been enshrined in a number of pieces of older legislation. The Act sets out what kinds of information employees are entitled to receive about their contract with their employer, and the time frame within which this should be issued, i.e. within two months of the commencement of employment. This entitlement includes all employees contracted to work for one month or more irrespective of the number of hours worked. Parts of the documentation may be given in instalments within that two-month period.

The statement should contain certain details and at least refer to other documents so that employees are aware of their existence and know where they may examine them. The details to be made explicit in the statement are:

- the names of the parties to the contract
- date of commencement of employment
- date of commencement of period of continuous employment
- hours of work
- location of the workplace and an indication if there could be a requirement to work elsewhere
- details about pay – rate of pay or how it is calculated; frequency of payments (weekly, monthly, etc.)
- job title or a brief description of the duties
- holiday entitlements

- arrangements about sick pay and sick leave
- details about any company pension plan
- entitlement to receive notice of termination of employment and obligation to give notice
- date employment ends if the contract is for a fixed term
- any terms of a collective agreement that affect working conditions.

Employees are entitled to be notified in writing of any changes to be made to any of these terms.

Details about sick pay, notice periods and pension arrangements may be given to employees by referring them to other documents, but again any subsequent changes in these documents must be notified directly to individual employees. Employees should also be referred to documents outlining the disciplinary rules, procedure, named person or position of person to whom appeals against decisions can be made, grievance procedures and name or position of person to whom a grievance should be referred in the first instance.

Notice of termination of employment

Employers may have their own schedule of the notice they require from employees and are prepared to give to employees, but the statutory rights of employees as stated in part IX of the Employment Rights Act are:

- 1 week's notice after 1 month and up to 2 years' service
- 2 weeks' notice after 2 years and up to 3 years' service, continuing to increase by one week for every completed year of service to a maximum of 12 weeks' notice.

Employee rights to time off work

The Employment Rights Act provides for employees to have a right to time off work in various circumstances. This may be unpaid or paid, depending on the circumstances, and includes time off for:

- union officials, in a union recognised by the employer, to complete certain duties such as taking part in negotiations with the employer (paid)
- members of a recognised union to participate in certain activities (unpaid)
- public duties such as acting as a magistrate (unpaid)
- employees selected for redundancy to look for work or make arrangements for training (paid; 2 years' service required)
- antenatal care (paid).

This is not a comprehensive list, but gives you some idea of existing entitlements to time off, and it should also be noted that new rights can be introduced too. In 2010, an amendment of the Employment Rights Act came into force, giving employees with 26 weeks of service a right to request time off for training which they feel will lead to an improvement of their skills and business productivity. In 2010, this applied to employers of 250 or more people, and in 2011 this is to be extended to cover all employing organisations.

The phrase that is applied to the entitlement to time off is that it should not be unreasonably refused, and in some circumstances, for example those related to the performance of public duties, employers are entitled to give consideration to business needs in assessing what a reasonable amount of time off work would be.

The Employment Relations Act 1999 also introduced rights to time off which had been addressed in the *Fairness at Work* White Paper (1998): revised maternity rights and rights to paternity leave (both dealt with later in this chapter), and entitlement for all to time off for dependants, i.e. unpaid leave in cases of emergency to arrange for care for any person who is dependent on the employee to do so. The Department for Business, Innovation and Skills offers guidance on the meaning of 'dependants' on its website (**www.bis.gov.uk**), and includes an elderly neighbour in its definition as well as family members, but explicitly excludes tenants or boarders.

Guaranteed pay

Under the Employment Rights Act, employees are entitled to five days' pay within any three-month period for workless days if the employer cannot provide work as contracted.

Written statement of reasons for dismissal

Employees with one year of service are entitled to receive a written statement of reasons for dismissal on request. As noted in the following section, however, different rules apply to anyone dismissed during pregnancy or maternity leave.

Maternity and other family support rights

Support for family life to enable people with family commitments to continue working is an issue that has evidently been of continuing importance in terms of public policy, so HR professionals need to ensure they are aware of the latest developments. The following sections give an overview of parental and other family support rights as they stand at the time of writing (August 2010), but since this is an area of continuing change, any practitioner responsible for interpreting related rules and policies will need to study this area in more depth and check for the latest status of the regulations.

Beginning with the Maternity and Parental Leave etc. Regulations 1999, a number of enhancements in maternity and other parental rights have come into effect in the years since 1999. The major piece of recent legislation in this area is the Work and Families Act 2006 which brought in key changes with regard to rights connected with maternity, paternity, and some other family relationships. A crucial consideration with regard to the employment rights of pregnant employees is that it is a complex area and one in which there will be many individual circumstances to take into account. Note that we have simplified matters by using the terminology relating to birth parents. The rights we describe apply to same-sex relationships too, and a broadly similar range of rights to leave and pay (standard rate as described below) apply to adoptive parents. The Department of Business, Innovation and Skills website pages on maternity and parental rights are a good starting point for more detailed information (www.bis.gov.uk; accessed 02.08.10). The key points are as follows.

Antenatal care

As mentioned earlier, pregnant employees have a right not to be unreasonably refused paid time off work for antenatal care, regardless of length of service and hours worked.

Dismissal or selection for redundancy

Dismissal for a matter related to pregnancy or childbirth is automatically unfair. There is no qualifying period of employment or threshold of hours worked attached to this right. It is also unlawful to select a woman for redundancy on grounds of pregnancy or childbirth.

Written statement of reasons for dismissal

An employee dismissed during pregnancy or maternity leave is entitled to receive a written statement explaining the reasons for the dismissal. The employee does not have to request the statement in these circumstances, and again there is no qualifying length of service or number of hours worked.

Maternity leave

All pregnant employees are entitled to 52 weeks of maternity leave, regardless of length of service or hours worked: 26 weeks of this leave is called *ordinary* maternity leave, and the rest is *additional* maternity leave.

Women who have been on maternity leave are also entitled to return to work at the end of this leave period. The Department for Business, Enterprise and Regulatory Reform (now BIS) 2009 booklet *Pregnancy and Work*, written for employees, explains that women have the right to return to their job after ordinary maternity leave on the same pay and conditions as they would have received if they had been at work during that period. However, if the employer cannot reasonably accommodate a return to the same job after the longer period of absence involved in additional maternity leave, then the employee must be given a similar job without any detriment with regard to terms and conditions.

Keeping in touch days

The Work and Families Act 2006 introduced the concept of keeping in touch days. During their maternity leave, employees can go back into the workplace without affecting their entitlement to maternity leave and pay. The purpose of these days might be for training, to do a day's work or to be kept informed about developments. The keeping in touch days should not exceed 10 days in total and the employee is not obliged to undertake them.

Maternity pay and conditions

During both ordinary and additional maternity leave, an employee continues to benefit from all the terms and conditions of her contract except for remuneration. This means, for example, that she continues to accrue holiday entitlement and the maternity leave period counts as continuous service.

All qualifying pregnant employees are entitled to 39 weeks of statutory maternity pay (SMP). The qualifications are that they have worked for their employer for at least 26 weeks by the qualifying week (i.e. the 15th week before the week of expected childbirth) and their average weekly earnings are relevant for national insurance contributions. The qualifying period of employment essentially means that the employee already worked for her employer before she became pregnant. SMP is 90 per cent of the employee's average weekly earnings during the first six weeks of the maternity leave, and the remaining 33 weeks are paid at the standard rate, which was £124.88 from 4 April 2010 (or 90 per cent of the employee's weekly earnings if this is a smaller amount). Additional maternity leave beyond the 39 weeks is currently unpaid but some employers may wish to offer better contractual terms.

Employers can recoup 92 per cent of the SMP they have paid out, and small employers can recoup 104.5 per cent if they qualify for Small Employer's Relief. More information on this is available from the employers' information pages on the website of HM Revenue and Customs (www.hmrc.gov.uk; accessed 03.08.10). Pregnant employees who do not qualify for SMP may be eligible for the maternity allowance paid by Jobcentre Plus.

Paternity leave

The spouse or partner of a new mother has an entitlement to two weeks of ordinary paternity leave, paid at the SMP rate, during the two months following the birth of a child. This entitlement applies to unmarried as well as married partners, and to same-sex as well as opposite-sex partners. ACAS (2009c, p. 23) suggests that it might be better to think of 'paternity leave' as 'maternity (or adoption) support leave'. Organisations might consider using such non-discriminatory terminology in their policies. An additional criterion applied to employees requesting this type of leave is that they must, alongside the mother's responsibilities, have the main responsibility for the upbringing of the child.

The Additional Paternity Leave Regulations 2010 and Additional Statutory Paternity Pay Regulations 2010 established a facility to transfer up to 26 weeks of the mother's (unused) maternity leave and statutory maternity pay to her partner for employees with an expected childbirth date of 3 April 2011 onwards. A qualifying employment period also applies to paternity leave and pay rights, essentially that the employee should have been with the employer before the start of the pregnancy.

Parental leave

Parents of children under the age of 5 are entitled to 13 weeks of unpaid parental leave or 18 weeks for disabled children under the age of 18. This leave may be taken up until the 5th, or respectively 18th, birthday of the child, but there is a qualifying period of 1 year of service for this entitlement. The leave can be taken in blocks of 1 week up to a maximum of 4 weeks per year or in blocks of 1 day in the case of a disabled child, and the leave must be for the purpose of taking care of the child.

Right to request flexible working arrangements

Parents of children under the age of 16 (or 18 for a disabled child) have the right to request flexible working arrangements so they can give adequate attention to their family responsibilities while continuing to work. This right formerly applied to parents with children under the age of 6, but this was extended to 16 by the Employment Act 2008. Qualifying employees with at least 26 weeks of service are entitled to request a change in the hours they work or in their place of work. Employers must give such requests serious consideration, but they are entitled to deny a request if there is a valid business reason for doing so, including the cost involved, the impact on the organisation's ability to meet its customers' needs, structural issues such as the potential for redistributing the employee's work to others or the availability of recruits with the appropriate skills and knowledge. These rights and obligations were introduced in the Employment Act 2002, supplemented by the Flexible Working (Eligibility, Complaints and Remedies) Regulations 2002 and the Flexible Working (Eligibility, Complaints and Remedies) Regulations 2002.

The Industrial Relations Services (IRS, 2004) give a detailed overview of this legislation and its implications, explanations of how to put it into practice, and what issues need to be considered.

ACTIVITY 4.1

The IRS article cited above lists other relevant pieces of legislation for employers to keep in mind when applications for flexible working are made under these regulations and responses are delivered, and maybe when changes to the employee's contract are initiated. Think about the processes involved and which other pieces of legislation might be relevant and require some action or thought, and compare your ideas to those listed in the article.

The right to request flexible working arrangements has been extended by the Work and Families Act 2006 to cover employees who are carers of certain adults. The caregiving relationships specified are spouse, partner, civil partner and close relative. Macpherson (2007) states that 'employees who care for an adult living at their home address will also have the right to make a request'. The Conservative–Liberal Coalition Government has declared its intention to extend the right to request flexible working arrangements to all employees, following consultation on how best to achieve this (Cabinet Office, 2010), and indeed Wolff (2010c) reports that 'three-quarters of the 162 employers in the 2010 IRS flexible working survey will consider a request to work flexibly from any employee, regardless of whether or not they have a legal right to have the request considered'.

Contractual enhancements

Maternity and paternity leave and pay, similar arrangements with regard to adoption, and considering requests for flexible work arrangements are all areas where employers may choose to adopt family-friendly policies which are more generous than the minimum requirements of the law. The Incomes Data Services (IDS 2009b) review 21 organisations which offer enhancements on various aspects of these regulations, such as giving full pay for some or all of the maternity leave, and Silcox (2010) reports that 40 per cent of 179 organisations surveyed by the IRS have introduced enhancements. Macpherson (2007) also suggests that employers might consider extending the right to request flexible working arrangements to groups of employees not covered by the legislation in order to promote good working relationships and a sense of fairness in the workplace, and the IDS (2009b) report that most of the employers in their review do so.

Part-time employees

The treatment accorded to part-time employees in the UK was traditionally inferior to that given to full-time employees. However, as employers came to depend more on employees to be flexible, and to recognise the benefits organisations can gain from employing people on non-standard contracts, they also had to recognise the necessity of addressing the needs of these employees and treating them fairly. The statutory rights of part-time employees were strengthened in the mid-1990s by a ruling from the House of Lords, and subsequent legislative developments have also bolstered their position.

Prior to 1994, part-time employees had to work for considerably longer than full-time employees to acquire the employment protection rights then enshrined in the Employment Protection Consolidation Act 1978. In March 1994 the House of Lords held that the UK had been in breach of Article 119 of the Treaty of Rome and the Equal Pay and Equal Treatment Directives. The existence of differing thresholds to obtain a variety of employment protection rights amounted to indirect sex discrimination since the majority of part-time employees are women. The right of part-time employees to claim statutory protection against unfair dismissal and redundancy should be the same as that of full-time workers, i.e. a two-year qualifying period at that time. In response to this judgment, the Government implemented the Employment Protection (Part-Time Employees) Regulations 1995 (now incorporated into the Employment Rights Act 1996) which created equality between full- and part-timers in terms of statutory employment rights. The qualifying period with regard to unfair dismissal was subsequently reduced to one year.

Part-time staff also have rights to membership of pension schemes as outlined in the Pensions Act 1995 ss 62–66 and the Occupational Pension Schemes (Equal Treatment) Regulations 1995. Their rights have been strengthened more recently by the adoption of the EU Part-Time Work Directive which was implemented on 1 July 2000. The Part-Time Workers (Prevention of Less Favourable Treatment) Regulations 2000 give part-timers equal rights to the full array of contractual terms, including rights to staff discounts, and access to training and promotion opportunities. A major aspect of the regulations is that it is unlawful to discriminate against a person because of their part-time status, and part-time workers may request a written explanation if they feel they have been subjected to detrimental treatment. Naturally, cases can be taken to an Employment Tribunal.

Working time

The Working Time Regulations 1998 came into force in October 1998. The key features are described here in brief.

Working hours

Essentially the regulations provide for a maximum of 48 weekly working hours averaged over a period of 17 weeks. It should be noted that there are provisions in the regulations for employers to reach agreement with employees to work longer hours while the legislation protects employees from being obliged to work longer hours. The IRS (2001a, p. 2) reported that 'a significant minority of workers are opting out of the maximum 48-hour working week'. This opt-out provision has been the subject of much debate at EU level, and some observers expected that it would be rescinded in a subsequent review of the regulations. Arrowsmith (2004) points out that basic working hours in the countries that joined the EU in 2004 were in general longer than the European average, resulting in a sudden change to the overall picture, which may have accounted for the less decisive approach of the European Commission to this issue at that time. The Department for Business, Innovation and Skills website reports on negotiations which failed in 2009, and concludes that 'the Directive will remain as it is now – keeping the individual's right to opt-out' (**www.bis.gov.uk**; accessed 03.08.10). This phrasing makes the position sound quite definite, but the European Commission website put up a document asking for views on this issue among others in March 2010 (**www.ec.europa.eu**; accessed 03.08.10). The question of the opt-out has therefore seemingly not been put to rest.

ACTIVITY 4.2

Check the employment pages on the BIS website to find out whether there have been any developments with regard to the UK opt-out or any other aspect of the Working Time Regulations.

Rest breaks

Employees should have 11 consecutive hours of rest in any 24-hour period, and a 24-hour rest in every seven days. There is also an entitlement to a 20-minute break if the work day exceeds 6 hours.

Annual leave

Until the advent of this legislation there was no legal obligation for employers to provide paid annual leave for their employees, other than arrangements for statutory holidays. Of course, the vast majority of employers did make such provision, and annual leave has often been part of collective bargaining agreements between employers and trade unions. Even now, many employers will provide more than the basic entitlement, but at least this legislation guarantees a basic entitlement, which was three weeks in the first year that the legislation was introduced and four weeks after November 1999.

The Work and Families Act (2006) gave the Government power to extend the entitlement to annual leave because the Government was concerned to make it clear that the entitlement to four weeks did not include statutory bank holidays. Promulgated through the Working Time (Amendment) Regulations 2007, the enhancement of annual leave took effect on a phased basis, with an entitlement to 4.8 weeks (24 days) from 1 October 2007, rising to 5.6 weeks (28 days) from 1 April 2009. This entitlement may include statutory bank holidays. Part-timers will have this entitlement on a pro rata basis.

Derogations and subsequent amendments

There were some groups of workers who were not originally covered by these regulations, including workers involved in air, sea and road transport, junior hospital doctors and people who have autonomous decision-making powers, such as senior managers. These exemptions arose where the nature or location of the work made the regulations unfeasible, such as oil rig workers working in remote locations or people whose working hours are not usually measured such as executive directors. The CIPD website law pages (www.cipd.co.uk; accessed 20.09.10; available to CIPD members only) point out that the excluded groups are progressively being brought under the regulations, albeit with some adjusted clauses to do with the averaging of hours and entitlements to breaks. For instance, the averaging period for offshore workers is 52 weeks rather than the normal 17 weeks. This allows for intermittent periods of longer hours, which, however, must ultimately be balanced out. The NHS is also still allowed to require more hours of its junior doctors, i.e. 52 hours per week. According to the CIPD, this is because of an extension of the exemption from the Working Time Regulations granted to the NHS until 31 July 2011, and the CIPD states that some NHS Trusts have developed schedules based on this 52-hour working week. Much of the furore that has surfaced in news reports and letters to the editor of newspapers such as the *Times* in September 2010 focuses on the 48-hour working week prescribed for junior doctors in the European Working Time Directive as of August 2009. Some have argued that it is not possible for doctors to achieve all the training they need in a 48-hour working week; others have argued that it is because of administrative systems that the training targets cannot be achieved and that it is unreasonable to expect doctors in training to work longer hours. This is obviously an issue on which we can expect further development in the next few years.

The CIPD website points out that amendments have been made to the Working Time Directive almost every year since it first came into effect.

Data protection

Employers gather and keep a wide range of personal information about employees, and employees have a right to expect that those data will be kept confidential and that a high standard of accuracy will be maintained. The Data Protection Act 1984 provided for some assurances with regard to computerised information, and since 1 March 2000, when the Data Protection Act 1998 came into effect, information relating to individuals which is kept on paper, or in any other format, is also covered. Whistleblowers have also gained some protection via the Public Interest Disclosure Act of 1998, while the Human Rights Act 1998 applies to aspects of an individual's privacy. The Freedom of Information Act 2000 provides a statutory right of access to 'recorded' information held by public authorities and this Act came fully into force from January 2005. The Information Commissioner has responsibilities for providing an integrated role relating to both the Freedom of Information Act 2000 and to the Data Protection Act 1998.

The Data Protection Act 1998

The Data Protection Act 1998 covers all the stages involved in the management of data, from collection, safe storage, use and disclosure to destruction. The Act applies to personal information used in the workplace, including recruitment and selection, employment records, monitoring at work and information about workers' health. The legislation applies to any filing systems kept by managers as well as to centralised HR record systems.

The provisions of the Data Protection Act 1998 were originally applied in stages, but since 24 October 2001 they have applied to all manually stored records that have been collected since 24 October 1998, and also to all computerised record systems.

The Information Commissioner's Office (ICO, 2009) has produced a guide, covering the handling of personal data in the areas noted above. The purpose of the guide is to enable employers to understand better their obligations under the Data Protection Act 1998.

The Act includes eight principles:

- Data must be handled and processed in a fair and lawful manner.
- The reasons for obtaining these data must be legal and have been clearly specified. The data must only be used for the reasons specified.
- Data collected must be sufficient and relevant for the specified purpose. There should be no excessive collection of data.
- Any data collected must be accurate and be updated regularly.
- It should not be kept for any longer than is necessary, so data need to be regularly reviewed so that out-of-date information is removed.
- Data should be processed in accordance with the rights of individuals.
- The data must be kept secure.
- Data may only be transferred to countries that have adequate data protection.

We said earlier that this applies to personal data held by all managers, not just HR managers, and consequently most organisations need to complete an audit to establish exactly what data is kept and by whom. Many managers and other professionals such as lecturers maintain their own filing systems and may store out-of-date personal data. Someone in the organisation, possibly from within the HR department, has to take on the role of data controller and ensure that everyone who keeps personal data also complies with the eight data protection principles. Personal data means information which identifies an individual. Information which, for instance, reviews salary structures for a whole workforce or for particular groups of staff is not likely to be deemed personal information.

Data subjects have the right to know what information is kept about them and can ask to see the data. Employers can charge a fee for this, but must supply the information within 40 days. The data controller may be liable if there are breaches in the security of information, or if losses occur as a result of such a breach, but the ICO guide (2009) states that even where an individual is given this responsibility, the organisation is still the data controller in the terms of the ICO.

Statutory rights: a concluding statement

As well as understanding the rights and obligations of both employers and employees already established in law, it is essential to be aware that this is an area where issues develop and change very rapidly. These changes can arise, as we explained earlier, from formal consideration of statutes in Parliament, perhaps following on from discussions at EU level, or because new understanding of various circumstances arises when judgments are handed down on cases in the courts. In 1995 the *Walker* case, among others, focused attention on employer obligations with regard to the mental health of employees. Lobbying on behalf of disabled people engendered changes in the mid-1990s in statutory law regarding their rights to equal opportunity in employment. One way of staying informed about developments in employment law is to read the legal update articles that appear in journals such as *People Management*, *Personnel Today* and *Equal Opportunities Review*.

It is essential to review and update policies and practices to reflect the law as new requirements come into effect. The willingness of employers to offer employees more than the minimum that is required by the law might also contribute to improved employment relations and so enhance the contribution that employees are willing to make.

Did you know?

The *Any Answers* section on the HRzone website allows practitioners to raise issues they are facing at work and fellow HR specialists can endeavour to provide a helpful response. One practitioner wrote about a medical certificate which had been provided and seen but then mislaid following on from an initial certificate which had been posted but not received. The question related to whether or not the absence could be regarded as unauthorised in the circumstances. The advice that ensued included the point that the medical certificate that had been received was sensitive personal information and this had not been handled with the level of care required under the Data Protection Act. In fact, the employee would be in a position to complain about this if they wished to do so.

(*Source*: Potential unauthorised absence; and the reply: unlawful deduction from wages, *Any Answers*; available at www.hrzone.co.uk; accessed 01.03.10)

ACTIVITY 4.3

The Employment Law at Work section on the CIPD website, a resource for CIPD members, has links to frequently asked questions on a wide range of topics such as family-friendly working, maternity, paternity and adoption leave and pay, and working time regulations. Look at some of the FAQs and formulate your own response before checking out what the CIPD says. Go to www.cipd.co.uk and follow the links to the Employment Law at Work and FAQs pages (accessed 03.08.2010).

119

Flexible working arrangements

The traditional image of working patterns involved workers' spending Monday to Friday in a workplace with contractual provisions for a 36 to 40-hour full-time working week and something like four weeks' holiday. There are, however, many new patterns evolving to suit both the changing requirements of businesses, some of them due to increasing pressures to provide goods and services on a 24/7 basis, and employees' needs to balance their family and personal life commitments with their availability for work. Supermarkets now open on Sundays, and the once restrictive Sunday licensing hours for public houses have also been relaxed. Some people are working fewer hours to provide flexibility, and some are working more to cope with the pressures of work. During the 2008–2009 economic downturn, organisations have also used flexible working patterns as a way of avoiding redundancies. Wolff (2010b) reports that 40 out of 162 (24.7 per cent) employers surveyed had instituted or were about to bring in flexible working schemes specifically to enable them to cut costs. There were 147 schemes, mostly voluntary but some compulsory, in place, including reduced working hours, sabbaticals without pay and job-sharing.

ACTIVITY 4.4

List and describe as many flexible working arrangements as you can think of. Look at the IRS article cited here to see if you can extend your list by adding any of Rankin's suggestions.

Rankin, N. (2008) *Good Practice Guides. Good Practice: Flexible Working*, 26.11, XpertHR (available at **www.xperthr.co.uk**; accessed 02.03.10)

The new working patterns include numerous variations on shift work, part-time employment, contracting-out of work, arrangements for flexitime, and contracts based on annual or even zero hours. All this variety and change suggests that for some part of your working life you are as likely to be working under flexible conditions as in a supposedly traditional arrangement.

The mix of working arrangements can mean that employers have the flexibility to call on people's services only when they need them. The emphasis in this case is on developing arrangements to increase flexibility in the availability of human resources and the organisation's ability to respond rapidly and well to changing requirements. Meeting the needs of business can, however, be synonymous with meeting employee needs if an organisation wishes to use flexibility as a strategy to attract and retain valuable workers. Of the 162 employers surveyed by the IRS in 2010 (Wolff 2010a), almost all of them (161) had flexible working practices of some kind in place. Retention of employees was one of the major benefits reported (73 per cent) along with improved ability to provide cover (65 per cent).

Since the late 1990s there has been growing recognition of the importance of achieving a good balance between work and private commitments. A good work–life balance can meet both employer and employee needs in terms of stress management, health, productivity and, of course, employers must respond to the right of eligible parents and carers to request flexible working arrangements as described earlier.

These aspects of employee wellbeing are very much a part of a positive psychological contract and the level of engagement among employees. Indeed, 63 per cent of respondents to the 2010 IRS survey (Wolff 2010a) rated employee engagement as a business benefit of flexible working practices.

We shall review some of the important developments in flexible working, looking specifically at annual hours contracts, job sharing, fixed-term contracts and teleworking.

Annual hours

Instead of contracting employees to work, say, a 40-hour week regularly throughout the year, which might entail periods of under-employment and periods of overtime for which the employer pays at an enhanced rate (usually one and a half times or double the normal rate), the employer estimates the number of hours he or she will need an employee over the period of a year, and contracts the employee to work those hours at the standard rate but according to an agreed, irregular pattern that corresponds better to fluctuating business needs. This means that, subject to agreed arrangements, the employer can call on the services of employees when they are needed, and most importantly does not pay employees for their presence at times when they are not needed. Employees are guaranteed payment for the hours that they have been contracted for, and normally the salary would be paid in equal amounts spread over the year.

Terms that would usually need to be imposed on this arrangement would be agreements on things such as the maximum number of hours an employee could be expected to work in a given number of days, entitlement to a consecutive number of days off, notice of a call in to work. The arrangements should be such that employers are able to cover both scheduled and unscheduled requirements. The IDS (2009a) report that reserve hours are often factored into annual hours schemes to allow for emergencies, and these hours may or may not be worked, but they will be paid for.

A number of organisations have found that annualised hours work to their advantage, but the IDS (2009a) caution that care needs to be taken when introducing such a scheme and organisations must ensure that workers understand the advantages that they too will enjoy. Annual hours schemes should reduce the need for overtime work and payment significantly, but effective rostering of hours should mean that workers have longer periods of time away from work.

The IDS (2009a, p. 3) report that the health and social work sector makes the most use of annualised hours with almost 118,000 full-time workers on annual hours contracts. On the other hand, they also state that many annual hours workers are manual workers, and a high percentage of those working on such contracts in the manufacturing sector are involved in continuous operations in production areas.

Job share

The concept of having two people share the tasks designated as constituting one post probably grew out of the recognition that some women did not wish to return to full-time work after maternity leave but would prefer to continue in their careers, working a reduced number of hours. Some employers developed job-sharing schemes partly to accommodate this desire, but also because they recognised that this was one way of retaining scarce talent and benefiting from the investment they had made in employees who no longer wished to work full time. As we explained in the section on parental rights, it has also become increasingly clear that there is an obligation on all employers to at least consider the viability of flexible arrangements such as this.

Job sharing requires additional arrangements to ensure coordination between job-share partners, which has implications for their managers, but there are numerous benefits: it can bring additional flexibility in terms of availability of staff when required for extra work; it shows that the employer is willing to consider new arrangements that accommodate staff needs; the talents and ideas of two people are applied to one job; and it is good for morale. In fact, it is an arrangement that can clearly bring mutual benefit. Also, although we stated earlier that the arrangement probably grew out of the wishes of women returning from maternity leave, job share is not just of benefit to women. Men can also have responsibilities as the primary care givers in their families and welcome the opportunity to work part time, and job share is also attractive to people who wish to combine a steady income with freelance consultancy activities.

Fixed-term contracts

Fixed-term contracts are addressed specifically in part XIII, s 197 of the Employment Rights Act 1996, but other sections of the Act also apply, such as the need to issue a written statement of employment particulars to anyone hired for longer than one month. Fixed-term contracts obviously offer some flexibility to employers in terms of adjusting the numbers of employees at different times to suit fluctuating business needs. There has been some concern about the rights of employees on fixed-term contracts, however, and the European Directive on Fixed Term Work required the member states to address these issues. The Fixed-term Employees (Prevention of Less Favourable Treatment) Regulations 2002 came into effect on 1 October 2002 and provided extra protection for employees on such contracts. The issue of consecutive fixed-term contracts to an employee is now limited to a period of four years, after which the position must be made permanent. Employers are also not entitled to include a redundancy waiver in the terms of a fixed-term contract.

The major features of fixed-term contracts are as follows:

- They state the maximum period of the contract, giving the date on which the contract will end.
- Non-renewal at the end of a fixed-term contract is a dismissal.
- A contract for a specific purpose is now included in the definition of a fixed-term contract.
- Service over a series of fixed-term contracts can be aggregated to constitute continuity of service.

Teleworking/homeworking

The work arrangements we are referring to as teleworking are not to be confused with the kind of low-paid piece work that involves activities such as stuffing envelopes. Teleworking has evolved with the rapid developments in information technology and telecommunications. With the advent of fax and email, people do not need to be in the same building to transmit written documents and reports instantaneously. Distance working is also used as a term for employees who no longer need to go into an office to do their work, 'tele' being the Greek root meaning 'far'. In other words, the term can be used for people who mainly use technology to produce reports, but also for people out on the road seeing customers. Orders can be relayed using information technology, and often it is more sensible for such employees to use their home as their base rather than an office in a town centre. Jobs are no longer equated with a desk in the office.

Pause for thought 4.4   Make a list of what you think the advantages and disadvantages of teleworking are. For every disadvantage you identify, suggest a solution.

Advantages

- A wider range of people can be gainfully employed, for instance those who have care duties and cannot leave home for prolonged periods of time but who can organise their time at home to include periods of work.
- Flexibility in working hours: some people like to work at three in the morning while others sleep, and teleworking gives them the opportunity to do so.
- Working at home cuts down on travelling time and on costs of office accommodation and furniture.

Disadvantages

- Social factors may be the source of disadvantages, but that simply means that the social system needs to be managed properly. Teleworkers may suffer from isolation and a feeling of not being part of an organisation. An antidote for this is to arrange training sessions and regular briefing sessions when employees can get together and review common problems, and to use communication channels to keep people in touch. If some isolation cannot be avoided, recruiters should attempt to select people who will be suited to the type of work.
- Some managers, particularly those who adopt a control style, may be uncomfortable supervising teleworkers. It is possible to institute regular reporting mechanisms and control the volume of work done in a period of time, but on the whole the development of teleworking calls for a different style of management and a higher level of trust. The emphasis is definitely on the fact that the work gets done rather than on imposing controls on when and where it is done. Again, appropriate competencies should be stipulated and tested during the recruitment and selection of managers who will work with teleworkers. Management development could also include a focus on the requisite skills.
- Research by Golden (2007) also indicates that the prevalence of teleworking may have a negative impact on the job satisfaction of non-teleworking co-workers who may feel that their own flexibility is decreased and their workload increased the more they are expected to work with teleworkers. This may even influence their intentions to leave. The research suggests that the number of teleworkers

and the amount of time they spend away from the main workplace are factors that need to be managed carefully with an eye on their impact on non-teleworkers. Enhancing face-to-face contact when workers are all together in the workplace, and increasing decision-making autonomy are also suggested as appropriate management practices to alleviate any potential conflict between teleworkers and non-teleworkers.

Employers who develop teleworking arrangements should be aware of their duties with regard to the health and safety of employees. They will need to conduct a risk audit of the employee's home-based workplace – information about this is readily available from the Health and Safety Executive (see Chapter 11 for information about access to HSE information).

ACTIVITY 4.5

Your class will conduct a survey to establish what kinds of working patterns are in existence and whether these meet the needs of the employees concerned. You should decide who your target population will be. For example, you may wish to survey only local businesses and residents, or to include the friends and relatives of students to extend your geographical coverage. You may wish to target a particular industry, for example, the manufacturing sector or retail outlets. You should probably exclude full-time students from your survey, as they have an obvious need to work only part time.

1 Work out in class what you want to find out and what questions you need to ask to gather this information. You will want to include some of the following issues. Establish what basis each person is employed on: part time, permanent, temporary, etc. Establish whether they are satisfied with this or would prefer some other arrangement. What are the main reasons for their levels of satisfaction or dissatisfaction?

2 Each student will conduct a survey of five to ten people who have some sort of employment and make an analysis of this small sample. Compare your findings with those of others in your class.

3 Work in groups of five and compile an analysis of your pooled information. Report your results to the class and compare your results with those of the other groups in your class.

4 Establish which patterns of employment and employee attitudes have emerged.

5 Discuss how this information might be used by employers to improve their human resource management practices.

Termination of employment

Employees leave their organisations in a variety of ways and a number of circumstances, and for a number of reasons. Stop for a moment and make a list of as many of these circumstances as you can think of.

In making your list you may have categorised the reasons for employee exit into those that signify voluntary exit and those that are involuntary. Voluntary reasons include:

● to take up another post
● retirement or early retirement
● voluntary non-employment, often due to a change in circumstances including parenting or studying.

The involuntary reasons you have listed may include:

● redundancy
● dismissal, including dismissal due to ill-health.

For each of these reasons for exit, there is a range of circumstances that apply, except perhaps for retirement, which is essentially age-related. People taking up another post, for example, may be doing so for a number of reasons, such as:

● personal reasons for moving to another geographical area
● because they have been offered more pay or better conditions for doing the same work with another employer
● opportunities for promotion
● to escape from uncongenial managers or colleagues
● a desire for a change of career.

If you have read the chapter on human resource strategy and planning (Chapter 2), you will realise that it is essential for employers to understand why people leave their organisations so that appropriate recruitment and retention plans can be devised as part of the talent management strategy. For this reason, many employers gather information from staff who are leaving, especially those leaving for voluntary reasons, by conducting an exit interview with them.

Exit interviews and employee opinion surveys

It is important to gather data on any problems connected with aspects of the employment relationship so that employers can take action to remedy any arrangement that might potentially cause more valuable employees to leave. The areas usually covered in an exit interview include:

● the reason for leaving, particularly if the person is going to another job – is it for better pay/career or development opportunities/some other benefit?
● relationships with supervisors and co-workers
● working conditions in general and specific ones that might be problematic, such as shift work.

With the expansion of equality legislation, ACAS (2009a, b and c) suggest the inclusion of questions about whether a person has ever felt harassed in the workplace with regard to any of the types of harassment covered in the relevant regulations in force at that time (i.e. age, religion or belief and sexual orientation, now all covered by the Equality Act 2010).

Exit interviews are usually conducted by someone in the human resource management department since employees, even when they are leaving an organisation, may be more willing to talk about problems with a person who does not work directly with them. The interviewer should ensure confidentiality and explain that information gained from exit interviews is normally used to identify trends rather than to act on information from any individual. These reassurances can make people open up. It should be noted, however, that any references to bullying or harassment do need to be followed up as it would not be acceptable to ignore reports of unlawful harassment.

A good process will include a form that the employee can complete in advance of the interview, and the interview can then be used to clarify details. You will find a similar process recommended for appraisal interviews in Chapter 8.

ACTIVITY 4.6

Design an exit interview form and process, either generic or for an organisation of your choice. Refer to Chapter 7 to read about interview questioning techniques and apply some of the techniques you learn about there in formulating your questions, particularly open and closed questions in this case. You can also get some excellent guidance on the design of questionnaires and types of questions from an IRS (2001b) article on separation questionnaires.

Rather than waiting to gather information from employees who have decided to leave, employee opinion surveys can be used to assess the levels of satisfaction within an existing workforce in a variety of work conditions. It is well recognised that management must demonstrate a willingness to take action on the issues raised, or at least respond to these issues in some way, if they wish to retain the trust of their employees and have employees take any subsequent surveys seriously.

Retirement

One of the benefits that employers can offer their employees is preparation for retirement through some kind of formal pre-retirement programme. Moving from working life to retirement requires a big adjustment, and can be achieved more successfully with careful planning, in terms of coping with a changed financial situation as well as increased leisure time. Financial advice on pensions is a complex subject beyond the scope of this text. It is sufficient to note that this is another area that can be affected by changing legislation.

Employers can further consider programmes for keeping in touch with people who have retired from employment with them. It can be a low-cost benefit to arrange occasional social gatherings for past and present employees and to send the organisation's newsletter to past employees, and the returns in terms of morale and commitment from current employees who witness this evidence of their employer's concern for employee welfare may well repay these costs many times over.

International issues

In recent years, there has been substantial interest among researchers in the topic of work–life balance (WLB), especially with regard to Australia, New Zealand and the USA. This has even culminated in two special editions of journals dedicated to this subject: *Asia Pacific Journal of Human Resources* 2008, volume 46, issue 3 and *Human Relations*, 2010, volume 63, issue 3. A review article by Bardoel *et al.* (2008) identified the major themes of research on WLB in Australia and New Zealand to be:

- organisational work–life policies, focusing on policies set up to improve WLB
- work hours and workload, highlighting the tendency toward a long-hours culture
- wellbeing, stress and burnout.

Kossek *et al.* (2010) provide an overview of the developing interest in WLB in the USA since the 1970s, and argue that WLB policies, though well established, are still not regarded as a core aspect of people management. That is, they may still be regarded primarily as accommodating workers' needs rather than as a strategic management tool with inherent business benefits, and those taking advantage of flexible working arrangements may be regarded as less committed to work than others. The authors also compare the US with the situation in Europe where, they argue, there is more legislated support for WLB practices, but even here, it is observed that such practices still need to be better integrated into the mainstream approach to people management.

Further articles in the *Human Relations* special issue also take up the theme of conflicting views on where the benefits of WLB policies really lie, focusing on the USA and the EU (including the UK). Adopting the interesting approach of examining employer representations of their WLB policies on their corporate websites, Mescher *et al.* (2010) looked at British, American, Dutch, Australian and global websites, and their overall conclusion was that though WLB was ostensibly supported, there were implicit indications that such arrangements were really a privilege and readers were discouraged from thinking that they were an entitlement for all.

Conclusion

We have seen that the relationship between employer and employee consists of rights and obligations on both sides, and that these are determined by law and various other agreements. Innovations in terms, conditions and working arrangements are a sign of the times as organisations attempt to respond to increasing competitive challenges, global economic developments and to social changes such as growing expectations of an acceptable work–life balance. The likelihood of further developments in legislation also guarantees that this will continue to be an area of change in the future, and recent research indicates that WLB ideas need to be more holistically embraced as a strategic business approach.

REVIEW QUESTIONS

You will find brief answers to the review questions on page 489.

1 Peruse the 'Law at work' sections in *People Management* or the court cases listed in the Industrial Cases Reports for the last three months or so. Select the articles or cases that are concerned with contractual issues and review them. Summarise the major hot topics of the day. Have these issues arisen because of any changes in legislation?

2 We mentioned that employment legislation usually sets out minimum provisions for employee rights. Can you identify a number of areas where some employers are known to provide more than the minimum?

3 Explain what the purposes of making flexible working arrangements are. Describe at least two forms of flexible working arrangement, and comment on the benefits of each for both the employer and the employee.

SELF-CHECK QUESTIONS

Answer the following multiple-choice and short-answer questions. The correct responses are given on page 489 for you to check your understanding of this chapter.

1 Which of the statements below best describes the psychological contract?

(a) Managers will do nothing to destroy the relationship of trust they have with their subordinates.

(b) Employers will do all they can to promote the mental well-being of employees, for instance by providing facilities for counselling on personal problems.

(c) The expectations that managers and employees have of each other can lead to a relationship based on coercion, a calculation of reward for effort, or cooperation.

2 Explain the difference between implied and express terms in a contract.

3 Name the terms that are implied in an employment contract on the part of an employee.

4 Joe Biggins has worked for Actwell Company for nine years. There is nothing in his contract about how much notice he should get if his job is terminated. The company is now moving to another location and, following appropriate consultation, has had to dismiss all its employees. How much notice should Joe receive?

5 Annie Creston has been with Actwell for only two months. How much notice should the company give her?

6 Which piece of legislation contains the duty of an employer to supply employees with a written statement of their particulars of employment?

7 How many weeks constitute ordinary maternity leave?

8 A woman needs to have two years of service before the expected birth in order to qualify for additional maternity leave. TRUE or FALSE?

9 An annual hours contract means that employees are not allowed to work over-time. TRUE or FALSE?

10 What major problems were identified related to teleworking?

HR IN THE NEWS

FT

A different way of working

By Alison Maitland

Lee Summersgill was initially concerned when he heard that his employer, KPMG, the professional services firm, wanted staff to volunteer for a four-day week to help minimise job cuts in the recession. The news coincided with the birth of his daughter in January last year, and he was worried about a reduction in hours and pay.

Then he considered the benefits of a change to his working week so that he could share the childcare with his partner, a health visitor. Now he puts away his BlackBerry every Thursday night and spends Friday with his two young children.

'I've been doing it for a year and it's worked really well,' says Mr Summersgill, who advises clients on public-private housing and regeneration projects. 'You have to be really disciplined and try to fit everything into four days. I think it makes you more loyal. Would any other firm have the same level of flexibility and understanding? In the market I'm in, I don't think that would be there.'

Mr Summersgill's experience illustrates two growing trends: fathers wanting greater flexibility to accommodate family life, and employers using flexibility to keep employees motivated, improve productivity and avoid large-scale job cuts.

Business leaders around the world have remained concerned about retaining good people, even in the depths of recession. In December 2008, a global survey by Hay Group, a consultancy, concluded: 'While employees fear losing their jobs, organisations fear the loss of top talent and critical skills.'

Amid signs of economic recovery, but with cost constraints continuing, employers are looking at alternatives to financial incentives. Offering employees greater control over working time and location is one such option.

KPMG, for example, is examining new approaches, after the success of its 'Flexible Futures' programme in signing up employees for sabbaticals or reduced weeks. Roughly 85 per cent of the 10,000 UK staff, and 95 per cent of partners, volunteered at the start of last year. Approximately 800 people moved temporarily to four-day weeks, with the heaviest use of the programme last May and June. The firm saved £4m last year, or the equivalent of 100 full-time jobs, says Michelle Quest, UK head of people.

When the programme was relaunched for this year, 71 per cent volunteered. 'One of the softer benefits is moving the whole idea of flexible working up the agenda for everybody,' says Ms Quest. The firm is now considering more active promotion of job sharing, because this type of arrangement provides all-week cover for clients.

The business benefits of alternative working patterns are increasingly well documented by both large and small employers. A survey of small firms by the British Chambers of Commerce found most of those that had introduced flexible working reported a positive effect on employee relations, retention and productivity.

Benefits also include extended customer service cover, more efficient use of office space, reduced absenteeism, and access to new employees who need such flexibility to work.

Many employers still see flexible working as an employee benefit – and therefore a cost – rather than a tool to improve the business. They remain nervous about allowing staff greater flexibility, and managers fear losing control of employees if they work from home or on the move.

Yet nearly 60 per cent of people who work from home at least some of the time say they are definitely more productive than in their workplace, and more than 20 per cent say they are probably more productive, according to a recent online survey. The main reasons are being able to work uninterrupted, saving time on commuting and being able to fit work around other commitments. Twelve per cent say their output at home is at least 50 per cent higher.

'In a time of unsteady recovery from recession, employers from all sectors must look for continued improvements in efficiency,' says Peter Thomson, director of research at the Telework Association, which conducted the survey. 'Ultimately, the organisations that do not adopt new ways of working, including home working, will lose not just good people, but also high performers. Those that do allow people to work at home will reap the benefits of substantial increases in output.'

UK government policy has focused on extending parents' and carers' right to request flexible working. However, some large and small employers offer flexibility to all their employees, arguing this is more productive and less divisive.

A desire for flexibility unites workers of different ages. Research by the Equality and Human Rights Commission's 'Working Better' project found parents' top priority for improving work-life balance was to have a wider range of flexible jobs, and that it was harder for men to access such jobs. Another commission survey, published in January, found significant demand among workers over 50 for flexibility in hours and location of work.

At Centrica, owner of British Gas, roughly 60 per cent of employees work a variety of non-standard arrangements, most of them informal. Research by Cranfield School of Management found that Centrica employees working flexibly scored significantly higher than non-flexible workers on job satisfaction and fulfilment, commitment to the company and empowerment.

At the other end of the scale in terms of size is Clock, a digital agency in Hertfordshire employing about 30 people, mostly men. Syd Nadim, chief executive, offers flexibility to attract and keep skilled web designers and developers. Managers set staff objectives and give them leeway to meet these as they think best.

Flexible start and finish times mean the agency's office is staffed from 8am to 9pm, while employees are also available to clients on their mobile phones.

'We're successful and we're making money while creating an environment for people to enjoy their lives,' says Mr Nadim.

Read business advice on new ways of working at: www.equalityhumanrights.com/advice-and-guidance/here-for-business/working-better

Family responsibility

The rights of parents and carers in the UK to take leave and request flexible working have increased progressively in the past decade under the Labour government. New mothers are now entitled to 52 weeks' leave, of which 39 weeks are paid at a level below their full salary, while new fathers have the right to two weeks' paid paternity leave.

However, there is pressure for further reform to address the low level of statutory maternity and paternity pay, as well as the emphasis on rights for mothers rather than both parents. The government is proposing to extend fathers' rights from next year to give them three months' paid leave and three months' unpaid leave, which would be taken from the mother's leave allocation if she chose to return to work early.

The Equality and Human Rights Commission last year called for an overhaul of leave policies to enable fathers to play a bigger role in looking after children in their early years. Currently, 45 per cent of fathers fail to take even two weeks' paternity leave after the birth of their child.

Comparing policies around the world, the commission said fathers were most likely to take leave if it was not transferable: if it carried an incentive such as a 'use it or lose it' condition; if they received at least 60 per cent of full pay; and if their allocation was added to mothers' leave, rather than replacing it. In Norway, a use-or-lose-it condition increased paternity leave take-up from less than 4 per cent among new fathers to 45 per cent in the year after it was introduced.

Meanwhile, European Commission proposals to give all new mothers at least 18 weeks' maternity leave on full pay have met resistance from some governments and business groups, including some in the UK. Opponents say the move would cost too much at a time of weak public finances.

British law now gives the 'right to request' flexible working to parents of children up to 16 and disabled children up to 18, and to carers of adult relatives. The Conservative party has said it will go further if it wins this year's general election, making the right to request available to parents of all children up to 18.

Some European Union countries, including France, Germany and the Netherlands, give all employees a right to work reduced hours, regardless of the reason. However, the range of flexible working options is wider in the UK, the human rights commission found.

FT.com, 22/03/2010 (Alison Maitland 2010), http://www.ft.com/cms/s/0/0672069a-3549-11df-9cfb-00144feadc0,s=1.html. Reproduced with permission. © The Financial Times Ltd.

Questions

A different way of working

1 Which flexible working practices are identified in the article?

2 What are the benefits of flexible working to employers and employees?

3 What are the perceived disadvantages of flexible working?

4 On balance, which outweighs the other: benefits or disadvantages? What evidence does the article provide, and how would you argue the case?

Family responsibility

1 What is the current situation with regard to parental rights on all of the issues raised in this article?

WHAT NEXT?

Relax and listen to the CIPD's latest podcast on employment law. Episode 33 from August 2009 addresses a variety of issues raised by HR professionals, including a question about an employer's liability under the Working Time Regulations if an employee takes a second job with another employer. Podcasts are available at **www.cipd.co.uk**.

In late 2009, the Department for Work and Pensions set up a taskforce to investigate aspects of flexible working, including business benefits and how flexible working arrangements could be developed to improve business success in the UK. The report of the taskforce and the response of the Government at that time provide an interesting overview of the major issues to do with flexible working. Of course, these documents were prepared during the tenure of the Labour Government, so while they present a picture of modern circumstances in the UK, the Conservative–Liberal Coalition will set its own priorities. You should check Government websites to keep up-to-date on any further developments.

Department for Work and Pensions (2010) *Flexible Working: Working for Families, Working for Business. A Report by the Family Friendly Working Hours Taskforce*, Crown Copyright.

Department for Work and Pensions (2010) *Flexibility for the Future: The Government's Response to the Recommendations of the Family Friendly Working Hours Taskforce*, Crown Copyright.

These documents are available from **www.dwp.gov.uk**; accessed 04.08.10.

References

Adams, B. and C. Stakim (2008) How to use flexible working to avoid redundancies, Employers' Law, 01.10 (available at www.xperthr.co.uk; accessed 17.11.08).

Advisory, Conciliation and Arbitration Service (2009a) *Age and the Workplace: Putting the Employment Equality (Age) Regulations 2006 into Practice*, ACAS.

Advisory, Conciliation and Arbitration Service (2009b) *Religion or Belief and the Workplace: A Guide for Employers and Employees*, ACAS.

Advisory, Conciliation and Arbitration Service (2009c) *Sexual Orientation and the Workplace: A Guide for Employers and Employees*, ACAS.

Argyris, C. (1960) *Understanding Organisational Behaviour*, Dorsey Press.

Arrowsmith, J. (2004) Counting the hours, *People Management*, 16 September, 37–41.

Bardoel, E. A., H. De Cieri and C. Santos (2008) A review of work-life research in Australia and New Zealand, *Asia Pacific Journal of Human Resources*, Vol. 46, No. 3, 316–333.

Cabinet Office (2010) *The Coalition: Our Programme for Government*, Crown Copyright.

Chartered Institute of Personnel and Development (2005) *The State of the Employment Relationship. Reflections on Employee Well-Being and the Psychological Contract*, CIPD.

Chartered Institute of Personnel and Development (2010) *The Psychological Contract*, CIPD (factsheet available from www.cipd.co.uk; accessed 02.08.10).

Department for Business, Enterprise and Regulatory Reform (2009) *Pregnancy and Work: What You Need to Know as an Employee*, DBERR (available at www.direct.gov.uk; accessed 02.08.10).

Doran, N. (2010) *Topic of the Week: Varying Contracts*, 02.08 (available at www.xperthr.co.uk; accessed 02.08.10).

Fairness at Work, Government White Paper, May 1998 (paper available at www.berr.gov.uk; accessed 30.07.10).

Golden, T. (2007) Co-workers who telework and the impact on those in the office: understanding the implications of virtual work for co-worker satisfaction and turnover intentions, *Human Relations*, Vol. 60, No. 11, 1641–1667.

Guest, D. and N. Conway (1997) *Issues in People Management No. 21: Employee Motivation and the Psychological Contract*, IPD.

Further study

Handy, C. (1985) *Understanding Organizations*, 3rd edition, Penguin.

Incomes Data Services (2009a) *IDS HR Study 908: Annual Hours*, IDS.

Incomes Data Services (2009b) *IDS HR Study 907: Maternity and Parental Leave*, IDS.

Industrial Relations Services (2001a) Changing working time patterns prompt smarter ways of working, *IRS Employment Trends* 729, June, 2.

Industrial Relations Services (IRS) (2001b) Separating retention fact from fiction, *Employee Development Bulletin* 136, April, 3–7.

Industrial Relations Services (IRS) (2004) Flexible working – avoiding the legal pitfalls, *IRS Employment Review* 801, 4 June, 51–60.

Information Commissioner's Office (2009) *The Guide to Data Protection*, ICO (available at www.ico.gov.uk; accessed 03.08.10).

Kossek, E. E., S. Lewis and L. B. Hammer (2010) Work–life initiatives and organizational change: overcoming mixed messages to move from the margin to the mainstream, *Human Relations*, Vol. 63, No. 1, 3–19.

Macpherson, K. (2007) Flexible working for carers, *HR Zone*, 5 July (available at www.hrzone.co.uk; accessed 06.08.10).

Mescher, S., Y. Benschop and H. Doorewaard (2010) Representations of work–life balance support, *Human Relations*, Vol. 63, No. 1, 21–39.

Schein, E.H. (1978) *Career Dynamics: Matching Individual and Organisational Needs*, Addison Wesley.

Silcox, S. (2010) Maternity provision and return to work: the IRS survey, *IRS Employment Review*, 04.01 (available at www.xperthr.co.uk; accessed 22.03.10).

Wolff, C. (2010a) IRS flexible working survey 2010: benefits, issues and making it work, *IRS Employment Review*, 22.03 (available at www.xperthr.co.uk; accessed 05.08.10).

Wolff, C. (2010b) IRS flexible working survey 2010: combating the recession, *IRS Employment Review*, 22.03 (available at www.xperthr.co.uk; accessed 22.03.10).

Wolff, C. (2010c) IRS flexible working survey 2010: take-up and employee requests, *IRS Employment Review*, 22.03 (available at www.xperthr.co.uk; accessed 22.03.10).

Woodruffe, C. (2005) Commitment and satisfaction: the true state of the psychological contract, in Chartered Institute of Personnel and Development, *Relationship. Reflections on Employee Well-Being and the Psychological Contract*, CIPD.

www.bis.gov.uk; accessed 11.08.10.

www.cipd.co.uk; accessed 11.08.10.

www.ec.europa.eu; accessed 03.08.10.

www.hmrc.gov.uk; accessed 11.08.10.

Books

Advisory, Conciliation and Arbitration Service (2009) *Personnel Data and Record Keeping*, ACAS.

An advisory booklet, this reviews the types of information an employer may need to obtain from employees, and explores ways of storing the data. Also includes sample forms and a brief overview of the data protection regulations.

Incomes Data Services (2008) Homeworking, *IDS HR Studies* 864, February, IDS.

Provides a general overview of homeworking and addresses the issue of health and safety in the home. Presents six case studies, including HBOS and the Foreign and Commonwealth Office.

Incomes Data Services (2010) Shift pay, *IDS HR Studies* 925, September, IDS.

Provides an analysis of shiftworking in practice, outlining various forms such as three-shift patterns, alternating day and night shifts, shift-swapping. Also examines health and safety implications. Presents case studies of 22 organisations, detailing their shift patterns and premia, including Argos Distribution, Jaguar Cars and United Utilities.

Lewis, D. and M. Sargeant *Essentials of Employment Law*, CIPD.

Selwyn, N. *Law of Employments*, Butterworths.

Willey, B. *Employment Law in Context: An Introduction for HR Professionals*, Financial Times/Prentice Hall.

Three excellent sources of information on employment law. Make sure you refer to the latest edition available.

Articles

Industrial Relations Services (2007) The right to request flexible working, *IRS Employment Review* 869, 21/3 (available at www.xperthr.co.uk; accessed 03.04.07).

A good, concise overview of the various rights and how requests should be handled.

'Law at work' is a regular feature in *People Management*.

The authors offer readable interpretations of employment laws and regulations, addressing specific issues that are of current concern to HR practitioners and line managers.

Zagenczyk, T. J., R. Gibney, C. Kiewitz and S. L. D. Restubog (2009) Mentors, supervisors and role models: do they reduce the effects of psychological contract breach? *Human Resource Management Journal*, Vol. 19, No. 3, 237–259.

This research article provides a readable explanation of the psychological contract and explores the importance of mentors and line managers in maintaining it.

Internet

There are many Internet sites that can give you access to legal information and related employment matters. We have listed only a selection here for you to try. Most of them have numerous linked sites that you can click on to get more specific information.

Advisory, Conciliation and Arbitration Service   **www.acas.org.uk**
In addition to advisory booklets, the website has e-learning courses on working parents and contracts and written statements.

Business Link   **www.businesslink.gov.uk**
A government-sponsored website with lots of employment-related information for employers. There is also an interactive tool to guide employers through queries specific to an individual employee's circumstances with regard to issues such as maternity leave and pay, annual leave entitlement etc.

Chartered Institute of Personnel and Development   **www.cipd.co.uk**
A number of legislation-related factsheets are available to all visitors to the CIPD website as is the employment law podcast which covers a range of issues. The Employment Law at Work subject area, for members of the CIPD, links to many interesting and informative pages. The CIPD provides a succinct summary of how UK law is made, including an explanation of statutory instruments (SIs), how to find the most recent court decisions and how to cite case law. There are also lists of forthcoming employment statutes and regulations, SIs in force etc., and a list of law-related factsheets and surveys. The pages on records also address which ones have to be kept to fulfil statutory obligations and for how long.

Department for Business, Innovation and Skills   **www.bis.gov.uk**
A fount of information on employment matters with links to other sites. Extensive guidelines for both employers and employees on maternity and other parental rights are available.

Equality and Human Rights Commission   **www.equalityhumanrights.com**
The Commission prepared a very interesting document in 2009 presenting guidance for managers with regard to flexible working practices. It outlines the business benefits and presents a number of cases including IBM, Sainsbury's and National Grid. Look for *Working Better: A Manager's Guide to Flexible Working* at www.equalityhumanrights.com/hereforbusiness.

HM Revenue and Customs   **www.hmrc.gov.uk**
Here you will find help for employers in dealing with statutory maternity pay and related issues.

hrzone   **www.hrzone.co.uk**
A wide assortment of articles on various aspects of HR, including legal issues.

CHAPTER 5

Diversity and equality

Objectives

When you have studied this chapter you will be able to:

- explain the concept of workforce diversity and how to manage it successfully
- understand the issues relating to equality of opportunity in the workplace
- describe the legislation that addresses equality
- explain the practical implications of the equality legislation with regard to recruitment and selection.

Diversity in the workplace

● Definitions of diversity

Diversity and equality are recognised as being of strategic importance in the workplace (Incomes Data Services (IDS), 2010). Initiatives directed towards improving diversity and equality have a demonstrable impact on productivity and costs, and contribute in a variety of ways to business success. This chapter examines workforce diversity first, reviewing key concepts of what drives an organisation to adopt diversity initiatives, and the managerial imperatives of how to obtain the advantages expected from having a diverse workforce. We then turn our attention to the related topic of equality, examining the equality legislation in detail and reviewing the practicalities of equality in the workplace.

When describing diversity, the CIPD (2006a and b, and 2007) frequently emphasises that each one of us is different from the next person in some way, and that these differences should be valued and celebrated. It is through recognising, responding to and managing these differences, drawing out each individual's unique potential, that diversity can thrive and make a contribution to organisations. Wolff (2007) reinforces some of this terminology when describing Arriva's approach to diversity: '. . . diversity is about valuing differences in staff and customers in terms of all aspects of difference. This includes not only colour, religion, birthplace, gender, sexual orientation and age, but also which school people have been to, what they like and do not like, what they believe in and what is important to them.' Organisations can, of course, benefit from general diversity in their workforce, but the case studies presented in various publications (e.g. Trades Union Congress and the Confederation of British Industry (TUC and CBI), 2008; IDS, 2010) often reflect a tendency to focus on attempts to improve diversity by attracting members of specific under-represented groups such as people with disabilities, gender-specific diversity, age diversity etc.

Drivers of diversity

In general it is accepted that there are solid business reasons for attempting to build and maintain a diverse workforce (IDS, 2010). Strong business case arguments are reflected in the major reasons cited for pursuing diversity initiatives by respondents to a CIPD survey (2006b). The following drivers were each identified by 60–68 per cent of respondents: legal pressures, better recruitment and selection, corporate social responsibility (CSR) goals, being seen as an employer of choice, it makes business sense and it is morally right. This list implies that complying with the law is still a major driving force behind diversity initiatives, but as the CIPD also points out, at least four of the drivers identified here are to do with business objectives. Our research has identified the predominance of four major areas of business advantage to be gained from promoting diversity in the workforce: recruitment and retention; employee satisfaction and productivity; employer brand; customer orientation and product innovation. The following sections review these business case factors in more detail.

Recruitment and retention

Skills shortages, due in part to population change, were examined in Chapter 2 along with the resulting focus of organisations on talent management. Aiming for a diverse workforce means that organisations are recruiting from a wider pool of applicants and are more likely to gain access to the talent they require. The TUC and CBI (2008) also identify lower staff turnover with the concomitant reduction in recruitment costs as an outcome of greater diversity in the workplace.

Employee satisfaction and productivity

The reduction in staff turnover combined with lower recruitment costs mentioned above can also be taken as indicators of higher employee satisfaction. The TUC and CBI (2008) comment on organisations' experience that improved diversity results in fewer disciplinary problems and lower absence rates, perhaps as an outcome of the improved management skills of line managers and the promotion of teamwork which are key components of successful diversity management. The IDS (2010) link diversity with successful employee engagement and retention.

Employer brand

Being seen as an employer that believes in and promotes equality is likely to contribute to the organisation's image, thus bringing the business benefits of diversity that relate to CSR and being recognised as an employer of choice.

Customer orientation and product innovation

The words from the article by Wolff (2007) cited above give a clue to at least one business argument for diversity: being responsive to customers. A workforce which reflects the diversity of an organisation's customers should enable the organisation to understand and better respond to its customers' needs and wishes. Combined with this, organisations can expect greater creativity and access to a wider range of ideas from a diverse workforce. This has been known to result in product and marketing innovations (see, for example, the account of B&Q's experiences in IDS, 2004) and even gaining access to new markets (TUC and CBI, 2008; IDS, 2010).

Management of diversity

We now turn to the question about initiatives employers may need to engage in specifically to achieve their diversity objectives. As with the other people management issues we address in this book, line managers play a front-line role in the delivery and achievement of objectives. Senior management commitment to diversity and the goals they wish to achieve through such initiatives need to be communicated to line managers. Godwin (2005) suggests that line managers' performance objectives and reward should be linked to diversity to underline the organisation's commitment. Furthermore, line managers need to be trained in understanding what the organisation aims to gain from diversity, and in managing people in such a way that they can achieve their full potential.

Of course line managers are not the only people involved in making diversity work; everyone is. Bentley (2006) suggests that providing diversity training to everyone might be too costly, but recommends that organisations should lay out their expectations to all employees, for instance as part of an induction programme. We also have anecdotal evidence that can be used to illustrate the importance of this. A friend of the authors recounted that senior management in his firm were keen on diversity and had made efforts to recruit people who could bring different skills and attitudes to the workplace. This had resulted, however, in two separate groups of workers who each pursued their own ideas and who did not communicate well with each other. The company obviously was not reaping the promised benefits of diversity as outlined above, and this example illustrates the need to manage a diverse work group properly in order to obtain those advantages.

Recruitment, however, is a major source of diversity, and a broader approach to recruitment must be adopted to ensure that a full range of people are attracted to the organisation. Positive action that allows disadvantaged groups to compete during the recruitment process such as application forms in Braille or information printed in different languages can be used to enhance the recruitment process. Furthermore, employers may consider taking proactive measures to make adjustments that will enable access to jobs to candidates with a disability.

Another issue for employers to consider is the need to offer flexible working arrangements to accommodate the inevitable differing needs of a diverse workforce. Various employees will require leave at different times for religious observances, some employees will need to adapt their working hours to fit in with child care or care of elderly or infirm dependants, and yet others may wish to take extended study leave. Offering such flexibility can itself engender further benefits for employers, as reported in *Personnel Today* (2007) referring to a survey on work-life balance: 'Increased retention was perceived to be the greatest factor in favour of offering flexible working (cited by 87% of respondents), followed by workers being happier in their jobs (82%) and increased productivity (65%)'. A variety of flexible working arrangements are dealt with in detail in Chapter 4.

McCartney and Worman (2010) offer advice on how to set about building and strengthening diversity initiatives in the workplace. The pragmatic approach outlined below is based on their project plan (p. 2) and involves the following steps:

- Get the buy-in of the leadership team by persuading them of the business benefits to be gained from a diversity strategy.
- Integrate diversity goals into plans for recruitment and selection, performance management, development and reward. Targeting under-represented groups in recruitment and making general adjustments to the workplace or working practices to enable access for people with disabilities are examples of initiatives that might be considered.
- Involve the whole range of stakeholders from the beginning of the initiative: board members, team leaders, employees. This requires clear communication of the goals and objectives of the programme, including how everyone is affected and how everyone can gain from diversity.
- Challenge negative behaviours and encourage people to think the issues through. Offer relevant training and keep the communication lines open.
- Monitor and evaluate progress. Appropriate metrics on recruitment, selection, performance, promotion and retention could provide feedback on the success of diversity initiatives, and employee opinion surveys could be used to measure job satisfaction and to identify any areas needing attention.

The IDS (2010) further suggest that employers could benchmark their programmes against those of other organisations to identify areas of good practice and ideas for improvement. Obviously, all of these actions entail a cost, but not always a substantial cost. And organisations such as those profiled by the TUC and CBI (2008), the IDS (2010) and McCartney and Worman (2010), all of which have a track record of successful diversity, demonstrate that the rewards in terms of business benefits outweigh the costs of their diversity programmes.

Equality and diversity

Equality and diversity are major issues that affect everyone in the workplace. All employees, current and potential, have a right not to be discriminated against unfairly and blocked in their careers for reasons that have nothing to do with their abilities in relation to their work. Legislation exists to protect the interests of groups of people who may have historically been discriminated against in terms of employment and services, and employers have a duty to ensure that this legislation is upheld in their organisations. Beyond the need for compliance with legislation, however, there are also business arguments for equality and diversity as described above.

The distinction between equality of opportunity and the management of diversity has often been described in terms of equal opportunity being driven by legislation and applying to specified groups whereas diversity refers to all differences among people (e.g. Kandola and Fullerton, 1998). This way of making a distinction between the two terms has become more and more tenuous as the equality legislation has expanded to encompass ever more segments of society. One way of coming to grips with the two terms is to reflect that, logically, compliance with the equality laws will inevitably lead to a diverse workforce, and the CIPD (2006a) strengthens this notion with the neat phrase 'diversity takes equality forward'. If we accept that compliance with equality legislation leads to a diverse workforce, it becomes important to have a thorough understanding of this area of law, given all the advantages that can accrue to an organisation from having a diverse workforce.

There have been many developments in equality legislation during the first few years of the twenty-first century and activity in this area continues apace. The many strands of previous discrimination legislation, developed over more than a quarter of a century, have been consolidated into a single equality act, the Equality Act 2010. Part of this process was the establishment of a single equality commission, the Equality and Human Rights Commission, to have oversight of all equality issues. The new Commission took up its full mandate in October 2007, and the separate commissions relating to gender, race and disability were all subsumed under this one body. The aim, as with the formation of the single equality Act, was to create a higher level of simplicity so that organisations and individuals could receive better and more coordinated guidance on an integrated framework of equality legislation. However, the publications of the individual commissions are still available on the new consolidated website, and their documents can still be found at **www. equalityhumanrights.com.**

ACTIVITY 5.1

Check the website for the Equality and Human Rights Commission (www. equalityhumanrights.com) to get an overview of the extent of fascinating information provided there.

The previous Acts and Regulations that provided protection against unfair discrimination, together with just a selection of subsequent amendments, and the areas they cover are summarised in a table which has been placed on the companion website to this textbook should any readers wish to review the equality legislation from a historical perspective. Go to **www.pearsoned.co/foothook** if you wish to look at this material.

Given the benefits that can be gained from having a diverse workforce, it may seem strange that legislation is required to ensure equal treatment for various groups in the workplace. We thought it would be interesting, therefore, to describe a range of discrimination cases that have gone to the Employment Tribunal in the last few years to set the scene before engaging in a description of the Equality Act 2010. We have tried to be brief, just to give a flavour of the types of discrimination that may be encountered. If you track down the records of the actual proceedings for these and other cases, you will find that the courts' deliberations are in fact very complex.

Discrimination cases

● Sex discrimination

Furlong v. BMC Software Ltd ET/2701283/09

Ms Furlong's case involved the use of lap dancing clubs by the company to entertain clients, and the company's refusal to properly consider grievances she raised when remarks were made to her commenting on how she might have been expected to participate, had she attended certain visits to such clubs. There was also an instance of inappropriate sexual conduct (groping of Ms Furlong), which was not appropriately addressed by her managers and sexual rumour-mongering. The Employment Tribunal (ET) found in her favour with regard to direct sex discrimination, victimisation and harassment, and awarded a total of £34,618 in compensation plus interest.

● Race discrimination

Amnesty International v. Ahmed [2009] IRLR 884 EAT

Ms Ahmed, a woman of Sudanese extraction, was already working with Amnesty International when she applied for a job as a researcher on the Darfur conflict in Sudan. Some members of management were concerned about the security risks involved in having her work in this area and so rejected her application for the position. The Employment Appeal Tribunal (EAT) was clear that even though management's motivation may have been for the safety of Ms Ahmed, their rejection of her job application was primarily driven by considerations of her ethnic origins, and therefore constituted direct race discrimination.

● Disability discrimination

Fareham College Corporation v. Walters [2009] IRLR 991, EAT

Johnston v. Chief Constable of Humberside Police [2009] ET/1804303/08

Many disability discrimination cases centre on the failure of the employer to make reasonable adjustments to enable a disabled person to either commence or continue employment. Ms Walters developed medical conditions which necessitated long periods of absence, and she was dismissed following the College's absence management procedures, but without any adjustments having been put in place. The EAT held that in the circumstances, the dismissal itself could constitute a failure to make a reasonable adjustment.

In the case of *Johnston v. Chief Constable of Humberside Police*, the employer had gone through a process of making adjustments to accommodate Mr Johnston's dyslexia. His

---

Did you know?

The CIPD website has information on how to cite court cases properly on the members only employment law at work section. There is more than one method of citing cases, but you may find the following in some publications: the names of the parties are given, separated by v. (standing for *versus*, which in Latin means against); the next piece of information is the year in which the case was heard in square brackets; an abbreviation for the legal reports publication in which a description of the case can be found plus page number; an abbreviation for the court at which the case was heard may also appear. Some of our cited cases were reported in the *Industrial Relations Law Reports* (IRLR).

Cases which have not been reported in the law reports may have the abbreviation for the court and a number indicating the case number for that court and the year of the hearing.

The Employment Law at Work section also contains a description of key cases going back to 2005.

XpertHR also provides 'summaries of thousands of employment law cases' on the case reports section of its employment law pages. Look for the monthly update articles, such as 'In the employment tribunals: September 2010'.

Both the CIPD and XpertHR provide a commentary on the cases and address implications for employers and their approach to equality issues, and these websites were used as sources of information for the cases we have described here.

(*Sources:* www.cipd.co.uk; accessed 12.09.10; www.xperthr.co.uk; accessed 12.09.10)

disability was in the process of being diagnosed while he was a probationer constable on the force. However, his case was ultimately badly handled by an HR person who, while waiting for the diagnosis of dyslexia to be completed, had implied he would be out of a job if he did not accept a position as a PCSO and relayed this information to a third party, not a member of the police force, but in fact Mr Johnston's wife, on the phone. The ET held this to be direct discrimination.

Age discrimination

Growcott v. Home Office NIFET/85/09

The Northern Ireland Fair Employment Tribunal (NIFET) found that Mr Growcott had been subjected to direct age discrimination. Some ageist banter had occurred in Mr Growcott's workplace, including exchanges with the HR administrator, and he had not found this offensive. However, when he applied for a more senior post, he received an email from the HR administrator, saying he was too old. Whether or not this was meant as banter, the fact that it occurred during a recruitment process made it totally unacceptable. Although it did not find this particular incident to constitute harassment, the NIFET included as part of its judgement comment that the organisation had not taken proper steps to ensure that age-related harassment was not taking place.

Wilkinson v. Springwell Engineering Ltd (unreported, ET/2507420/07 25 February 2008, ET)

Eighteen-year-old Miss Wilkinson was dismissed after her probationary period as an office worker. She claimed she had been told she was too young for the position, whereas the company claimed her work had been below standard. The company had not, however, made adequate attempts to provide training, and it had not followed a proper dismissal process. The ET held, therefore, that the company was unable to prove that age had not been a factor in the dismissal. The compensation awarded to Miss Wilkinson for injury to feelings and loss of earnings totalled more than £16,000.

Sexual orientation discrimination

English v. Thomas Sanderson Blinds Ltd [2009] IRLR 206 CA

Note that Mr English's case was upheld on appeal by the Court of Appeal (CA) after an ET had dismissed his case, and the EAT had not upheld his initial appeal. The case raised a complex area of the law. Mr English had been harassed through name-calling by a small group of co-workers after they found out, among other things, that he had been educated in a boarding school. These co-workers started taunting him with homophobic names. The complexity of the case arose from the fact that they actually knew that Mr. English was not homosexual, and Mr English was aware that his co-workers knew this. Given the fact that Mr English was not gay, and this was known to the harassing co-workers, the legal question was whether or not this amounted to harassment on the grounds of sexual orientation. The CA, in a majority judgement, decided that the law could be interpreted in that way.

Religion or belief discrimination

McFarlane v. Relate Avon Ltd (unreported, [2010] EWCA Civ B1 29 April 2010, CA)

Mr McFarlane was a relationships counsellor with Relate, but he refused to deal with same-sex couples as he felt such relationships were in conflict with his Christian beliefs. He was dismissed because of this refusal on the grounds that his behaviour infringed on Relate's equal opportunities policies. The ET and EAT rejected Mr McFarlane's claims that he had been discriminated against because of his religion, arguing that any other employees who refused to deal with same-sex couples would also have been dismissed regardless of their religious beliefs. The dismissal came about because of a refusal to follow the employer's equality policies, not because of the employee's religion. The Court of Appeal refused Mr McFarlane the right to further appeal.

Equal pay discrimination

City of Edinburgh v. Wilkinson and others (unreported, EATS/0002/09 14 April 2010, EAT)

A group of women working in a variety of locations in schools, hostels and libraries, for example, brought a claim for equal pay, comparing themselves with gardeners and refuse collectors working for the same local authority.

Gibson and others v. Sheffield City Council (unreported, [2010] EWCA Civ 63, 19 February 2010, CA)

A group of women working as carers and in school meals claimed for equal pay with men working for the Council as street cleaners and gardeners. The Council's case for the difference in pay rates hinged on a bonus scheme which applies to the male worker groups, but the CA judged the bonuses to be discriminatory.

Gutridge and others v. Sodexho and another [2009] IRLR 721, CA

A group of female cleaners from a hospital who had been transferred to an external provider of services under a transfer of undertakings brought a claim for equal pay by comparing themselves with a group of male hospital employees, maintenance assistants, who had not transferred. A major question in this case was whether such a comparison was allowable, and the CA held that it was.

It is noticeable from the few equal pay cases described here, that many such cases involve groups of women working for public service organisations. Such organisations usually employ people in a wide range of jobs, and so are a prime example of an employer's need to ensure that pay systems are fair. You can read more about pay systems in Chapter 10.

Equality

As already stated, legislation exists in the UK to protect the interests of groups of people that have historically been discriminated against in terms of employment and services. The core aspects of the Equality Act 2010 were set to come into force from October 2010, with a few aspects still under consideration and potentially due to come into force in 2011, e.g. s. 14 dealing with combined discrimination (based on dual characteristics) and s. 159 dealing with positive action in selection and promotion. Discrimination in general is a matter of treating certain groups less favourably than others because of a particular characteristic of members of that group, e.g. being a woman, being regarded as too old or too young, being of a particular religious persuasion. Areas of discriminatory behaviour that are prohibited with regard to work apply to employees and applicants in terms of the arrangements made for deciding to whom to offer work, the terms of work offered, the decision whether or not to offer work. These types of discrimination typically occur when a person is refused employment, promotion or training opportunities or is dismissed.

We shall outline the characteristics which are covered by the Equality Act 2010, the ways in which discrimination can occur, the issues of combined discrimination and positive action, how an individual might raise a complaint about discrimination, and good practice employers can engage in to ensure they are achieving equality goals. Because of historical developments in Northern Ireland, certain statutes apply there that differ from the rest of the UK, and at the time of writing (September 2010) the equivalent legislation to the Equality Act 2010 is under consideration in Northern Ireland. ACAS (2010, p. 2) provides a very useful table showing where discrimination has changed or remains the same with the advent of the Equality Act 2010.

A further group of people who may be prone to discriminatory treatment are those with prior criminal convictions. The Rehabilitation of Offenders Act 1974, which provides some protection for this group, is also described briefly.

The Equality Act 2010

● Protected characteristics

The characteristics which are protected under the Equality Act 2010 are listed as:

Age
Disability
Gender reassignment
Marriage and civil partnership
Pregnancy and maternity
Race
Religion or belief
Sex
Sexual orientation

In general, the Act harmonises the treatment of members of these protected groups, but certain groups are not specified in particular sections. For instance, s. 159, dealing with combined discrimination, addresses neither marriage and civil partnership nor pregnancy and maternity, and s. 149, dealing with the public sector equality duty, omits marriage and civil partnership from the list of protected characteristics. These omissions imply that discrimination based on these characteristics is dealt with to better effect in other sections of the Act.

Age

The Act protects people against discrimination at both the younger and the older ends of the age spectrum. Since 2006, when age was added into the previous regulations as a protected characteristic, the equality legislation has emphasised for employers the need to focus on competencies when making selection decisions and the need to avoid making stereotypical judgements about people's capabilities according to their age. Although these regulations affect all aspects of the employment relationship like any other aspect of equality, their immediate impact has been in the area of recruitment and selection. Much guidance has been offered to organisations in terms of redesigning their application forms and other parts of the recruitment and selection processes to comply with the legislation (see, for instance the Employers Forum on Age at **www.efa.org.uk**; the Age Positive publications on the Department of Work and Pensions website at **www.dwp.gov.uk**; ACAS, 2009a).

The Conservative–Liberal Coalition Government further strengthened the age discrimination provisions in 2010 by removing the default retirement age of 65.

Disability

Disability is defined under the Act as a mental or physical impairment which has a substantial and long-term adverse effect on a person's ability to carry out normal day-to-day activities. This definition is very broad and open to interpretation. Decisions on whether a person is disabled may hinge, for example, on judgements about the meaning and applicability of the terms 'substantial', 'long-term' and 'normal day-to-day activities'. 'Long-term' is defined in the Act as having lasted or being likely to last for at least 12 months, including being likely to last for the rest of the person's life (Schedule 1, part 1 s. 2). A range of impairments may, depending on the circumstances, contribute to a person's being deemed disabled: severe disfigurement, sight or hearing impairments, cancer, multiple sclerosis, muscular dystrophy and HIV infection, people who are certified as blind or partially sighted. Cancer and HIV are covered by the legislation from the point of diagnosis, i.e. before a person's abilities may begin to be impaired by their symptoms.

Employers must make reasonable adjustments in any arrangements or to work premises in order that disabled people can apply for and carry out work. This may include consideration of flexible hours to accommodate the needs of a disabled person, or modifying equipment. Employers are compelled at least to consider these matters seriously and be prepared to justify their decisions with regard to their reasonableness. In order to fulfil this duty, it is reasonable for employers to ask at the application stage whether an applicant requires any adjustments to be made to enable them to make an application (such as an application form in large script), attend an interview or participate in any scheduled assessments. It is not permissible, however, to issue a pre-employment health questionnaire at this stage or to ask questions about a person's absence record. These issues may be raised once a job offer is being considered, and the emphasis should be on the reasonable adjustments that may be required to enable the person to take up the work on offer.

Gender reassignment

This characteristic refers to persons planning to undergo, in the process of undergoing or who have undergone procedures to change their sex from male to female or *vice versa*. Such persons are also referred to as transsexuals.

Marriage and civil partnership

A person who is married or a civil partner.

Pregnancy or maternity

The Act refers to the employment rights to ordinary and additional maternity leave. Section 74 deals with aspects of maternity pay.

Race

Characteristics protected against discrimination include colour, nationality and ethnic or national origins, and membership of a racial group.

Religion or belief

Any religion or belief, including lack of religion or belief. Although the Act refers to 'philosophical or religious belief' in s. 10(2), it otherwise only refers to 'belief', and it had been established under previous regulations that this could be widely interpreted. A belief such as humanism is recognised as being covered by this provision, but allegiance to a political party is not.

Sex

Protection applies to both men and women. Issues of equal pay for equal work, with reference to like work, work of equal value, and work rated as equivalent, are a matter of sex equality.

Sexual orientation

Sexual orientation is defined as a person's orientation towards persons of the same sex, of the opposite sex, of both the same sex and the opposite sex. Note that the legislation addresses sexual orientation and not sexual practices, where existing law continues to apply. Sexual orientation refers to gay and lesbian preferences, heterosexuality and bisexuality. Criminal issues such as non-consensual sex, paedophilia, etc. are not covered by the Equality Act 2010.

It is worth noting that remarks about a person's family members or friends with regard to their sexual orientation can also constitute harassment, i.e. not just remarks pertaining to the individual themselves. Also, even if a person's sexual orientation has been falsely interpreted, derogatory comments can still constitute harassment.

Types of discrimination

Discrimination can occur in four basic ways:

● direct discrimination
● indirect discrimination
● victimisation
● harassment.

Direct discrimination occurs when someone is treated less favourably for a reason directly to do with his or her sex, age, race or racial origin, etc., and in comparison to how a person without that protected characteristic would be treated. Examples of this would be to refuse a woman a job as a truck driver simply because she is a woman, and to refuse a Chinese person a job in a school kitchen simply because all the other employees are white European and the employer fears that a person from a different racial background will not 'fit in'.

Exceptions may apply in the case of age discrimination if it can be proven that a decision was made as a proportionate means to achieve a legitimate aim. Special treatment given to women because of pregnancy or childbirth cannot be construed as sex discrimination against a man.

With regard to the protected characteristics and discrimination, it does not matter whether or not the person actually has the characteristic that is the focus of the discrimination. So, for instance, if an employer refuses to hire a woman because the employer thinks she is a lesbian (and that is the reason for the rejection), this is discrimination because of the applicant's sexual orientation whether she is a lesbian or not. This is known as perceptive discrimination. Another form of direct discrimination is associative discrimination. This may occur, for instance, in cases where a person is treated unfairly because they have to take time off to care for a disabled person and the employer makes no attempt to discuss the possibility of making reasonable adjustments to help the employee with his or her responsibilities. The unfair treatment would not be connected to a disability of the individual concerned but it could still be discrimination because of disability due to his or her connection to a disabled person.

Indirect discrimination occurs when someone is treated unfairly because of some provision, requirement or condition that would disproportionately exclude the particular group that person belongs to, and when the requirement cannot be objectively justified. For example, if you wished to hire someone to clean the windows in your building, and you stipulated that applicants must be six feet tall, could this requirement be justified in terms of the skills and abilities required to do the job? Which groups might such a requirement discriminate against? Fewer women than men, for instance, are six feet tall. This requirement therefore discriminates indirectly against female applicants.

Informal practices can also constitute indirect discrimination. For instance, if an informal workplace culture has grown, such that it is well known that promotion in the company depends on employees being willing to entertain clients by taking them out for drinks late in the evening, there are some groups of people who would be less able or willing than others to participate in such outings, e.g. women with small children, members of religious groups which ban alcohol.

ACTIVITY 5.2

Can you think of any other instances of indirect discrimination and identify how various groups might be affected by them?

Look through the records of cases heard by employment tribunals and you will find some examples. To find reports of such cases you can use several sources:

- A number of human resource management journals have a section that gives updates on the law and describes recent cases. Look, for instance, in *People Management* and *Personnel Today*.

- You can look in the subject index of the *Legal Journals Index*, for instance under the heading 'sex discrimination'. This will give a brief summary of the major points of the case, and refer to a journal in which you can read more about the case.

- There are also numerous cases reported in the *Equal Opportunities Review* and some issues of the *IRS Employment Review*, both publications of XpertHR.

- CIPD members have access to descriptions of numerous tribunal cases in the Employment Law at Work section of the CIPD website (www.cipd.co.uk).

You may wish to compare the instances you find with those found by others in your class.

Victimisation occurs when someone is treated less favourably because that person has, in good faith, made a complaint or indicated an intention to make a complaint about discrimination or given evidence to support someone making a complaint. An example of this might be a woman who has raised a grievance about lack of promotion in comparison to similarly qualified men and who is subsequently dismissed unfairly.

Harassment is defined as unwanted conduct that intimidates or humiliates an individual, affecting their dignity or creating a hostile work environment. The behaviour in question can be verbal or physical, including unwanted conduct of a sexual nature, and it is important to note that the target individual's perception of the effect of the conduct can contribute to the behaviour being deemed to be harassment, i.e. if a person thinks their behaviour is harmless, but another person complains of this behaviour being harassment, then the complaint must be taken seriously.

Combined discrimination

The Act includes a new provision for a person to complain of discrimination on a combination of two factors. For instance, an employer may accept white male applicants, black male applicants and white female applicants, but reject black female applicants. Since this employer hires black males, there is no particular evidence of race discrimination, and since white females are hired, there is no overall sex discrimination. But if black females are excluded as a group, then they are being subjected to combined discrimination. This form of discrimination could be a combination of any two of the protected characteristics with the exclusion of marriage and civil partnership and pregnancy and maternity.

Simpson (2010) provides some interesting sample scenarios of possible dual discrimination, making it clear that a case that may fail on a claim of discrimination based on a single protected characteristic may in contrast succeed if it is based on a combination of two characteristics. One of his examples of a case of combined sex and age discrimination is based on a putative stereotype of older women being poor drivers. If an older woman was refused a job as a driving instructor because of such a prejudice, a complaint based purely on sex discrimination is likely to fail because the company would probably have (younger) female driving instructors, and a complaint based on age discrimination might fail because the company had older male driving instructors. If the rejection of the job applicant did reflect a prejudice against older women, a complaint of combined discrimination would be more likely to succeed.

● Occupational requirement

In exceptional circumstances there may be a requirement for an employee to be of a particular sex, racial background, religion, sexual orientation or age etc. These are known as occupational requirements, which are addressed in Schedule 9, Work: Exceptions Part 1 occupational requirements; in this case, a requirement to have a particular protected characteristic. This provision applies to all of the protected characteristics.

Section 60(8) refers, for example, to the possibility that having a specific disability may be designated as an occupational requirement and s. 193(3a) states that a charity providing supported employment may give preference to a person with a relevant disability. The application of an occupational requirement must be a proportionate means of achieving a legitimate aim.

Such requirements have traditionally been acceptable in instances where authenticity is required, say in entertainment, modelling (for instance male or female fashion clothes) or serving food in ethnic restaurants to create a specific ambience, and where privacy and decency in the provision of personal services are concerned. An example of an occupational qualification would be to advertise for a female care attendant to provide personal services to a female stroke victim. A further example might be an organisation that offers support and advice on relationships to bisexual persons and may wish to recruit bisexual counsellors who may be more able to empathise with their clients.

Note that the presence of an occupational requirement means not only that persons from the specified group are being invited to apply, but also that only such a person will be selected. This is often confused by less informed job-seekers with encouragement for members of under-represented groups to apply for vacancies so they can be considered along with all other qualified applicants in the selection process. You can read more about the recruitment of under-represented groups in Chapter 6, under the heading 'Targeted recruitment'.

● Positive action in recruitment and promotion decisions

Section 159 of the Equality Act 2010 extends the previous concept of positive action to selection decisions, meaning that an employer, when faced with two equally qualified applicants for a post, could lawfully give preference to a member of an under-represented group in order to help overcome or minimise the disadvantages that members of that group had previously suffered. This section is currently under consideration by the Coalition Government, and may not be put into effect.

The equality duty of public sector employers

The Equality Act 2010 reconfirms the duty of public authorities actively to promote improvements in equality among all the listed groups. Public authorities include organisations such as local councils, the police and fire service, educational establishments and the NHS, but the Government is currently consulting on which specific duties might be imposed and which public bodies might be included in the list.

The equality duty of public sector employers goes further than simply prohibiting discrimination and responding to claims of discrimination. These organisations have a duty to promote equality for the designated groups and are expected to take positive action in various ways to do this and to eliminate discrimination. The legislation refers to the provision of services as well as employment, but our focus here is naturally on employment.

Some local authorities have approached their race equality duty, for example, by forging relationships with community groups to examine what their problems and requirements are. Public sector employers customarily prepare a scheme showing which actions they intend to take to fulfil the equality duty. The groups concerned are usually involved in the design of these schemes, and the authorities review and assess the impact of the steps they have taken to promote equality.

Burden of proof in discrimination cases

From 2001, a number of regulatory amendments introduced a shift in the burden of proof into the equality legislation, meaning that the burden of proof is shared between the complainant and the respondent employer if anyone takes a case of discrimination to an employment tribunal. Once a tribunal is satisfied that an applicant has provided *prima facie* evidence of discrimination (that is, it considers that on the balance of probabilities, discrimination may have occurred), it is then up to the employer to provide positive evidence that it did not discriminate, and that its decisions and actions were not discriminatory. XpertHR (2010a) describes an example of the EAT finding that a company's reference to age in the phrase a 'younger, entrepreneurial profile' in its person specification was sufficient to shift the burden of proof to the employer.

Taking the recruitment and selection processes as an example, positive evidence of non-discrimination could include copies of the documentation used throughout these processes, including equality policies, non-discriminatory job descriptions and person specifications, and evidence that only non-discriminatory questions were used during interviews. Further evidence to support an employer's claim to have acted in a non-discriminatory fashion might include notes made during interviews, the results of non-biased tests, analysis of data collected for monitoring purposes, evidence of how the position was advertised and a description of equality training that is provided to managers and others involved in the selection process.

The Government's Equalities Office (**www.equalities.gov.uk**) provides information about the procedure to follow to obtain information if a person feels he or she may have been discriminated against, together with forms which can be used for this purpose. The ET might make inferences from failure to complete the questionnaire, or an evasive or equivocal answer.

As the European Commission (2003) points out, it is the managers making decisions who have the full information behind why a particular decision was made and who are therefore best placed to demonstrate that it was made on a non-discriminatory basis. Of course, claims of discrimination could also relate to issues such as harassment in the workplace; they are not necessarily restricted to events during recruitment and selection.

Concluding comment on the Equality Act 2010

Although a major goal of the Equality Act 2010 was to streamline and simplify the discrimination legislation, this is, nonetheless, a complex area of law. Some sections of the Act are subject to further debate and some of these may or may not be implemented: for example, positive action in selection decisions; combined discrimination. Already at the time of writing (September 2010), secondary legislation has been enacted to support aspects of the Equality Act 2010 (XpertIR, 2010c). As with all major pieces of legislation, we can expect amending regulations in the next few years as the law beds in and questions of interpretation arise.

ACTIVITY 5.3

Check the website for the Equality and Human Rights Commission (www.equalityhumanrights.com) and the Government Equalities Office (www.equalities.gov.uk) to find out what the most recent developments are with regard to equality legislation.

Good practice in equal opportunities

Essentially, to operate within the spirit of the equality legislation, all actions and documents involved in HR processes must be free of any criteria that could be interpreted as being discriminatory within the terms of the legislation. As ACAS (2009b and 2009c) points out, the existence of an up-to-date equality policy signals an organisation's intention to follow good practice with regard to all discrimination issues covered by the law. A good policy establishes a framework that enables current employees to know how they are expected to behave with regard to these issues and that they themselves will be treated fairly. Prospective employees may also be attracted to an organisation that demonstrates its intentions to treat employees fairly. It must be noted, however, that the mere existence of an equality policy is not enough to signify that an employer is serious about equality of opportunity. Communication of the policy and training of line managers in implementing it are crucial. The Industrial Relations Services (XpertHR, 2010b) emphasise the benefits an employer can obtain from having a policy established in this way. Benefits include the recruitment and retention of excellent staff, leading to an enhanced ability to compete and avoidance of discrimination complaints.

The equality legislation has practical implications for all aspects of people management, and some of these are dealt with in other chapters. For instance, the role of flexible working was dealt with in Chapter 4 on the employment relationship; equal pay will be addressed in Chapter 10. To illustrate the practical implications of equality here, we shall take a look at some examples from the area of recruitment.

Advertisements, job descriptions and person specifications, documents which are explained more fully in Chapter 6, must not include anything that could be construed as an intention to discriminate on an unlawful basis. Except in the case of an occupational requirement, as described earlier, advertisements should not include words that might imply a preference for hiring females rather than males, or indicate a preference for waitresses as this would imply that men could advertise for waitresses as this would imply that men could not apply for these posts. This would be direct discrimination on the basis of sex. The same stricture applies to the other groups protected by legislation.

The advent of the age discrimination regulations brought with it a lot of discussion about words which might imply a preference for persons from a particular age group. To advertise for 'young people' would quite obviously be unlawful, but practitioners were also discussing the viability of other terms such as 'mature' (which might imply a preference for an older person) or energetic (which might imply that a younger person was being sought). Whether or not these and similar terms suggest that unlawful age discrimination is intended, the wording of an advertisement is certainly something which employers need to think about carefully. The implications of age discrimination for the design of application forms are addressed in the next chapter.

The existence of a good person specification or competency framework can help an employer to avoid inadvertent sex, race or other unlawful discrimination when advertising for a post and carrying out the selection process. The design and use of person specifications is discussed more fully in Chapter 6 with specific reference to recruitment. Direct discrimination is rarely overtly expressed ('We really don't think a woman can do this job'). The intention to discriminate can be inferred from various events, and introducing new criteria after the person specification has been agreed is one such event. If a post involves an occupational requirement to have a particular protected characteristic, this should be decided before the post is advertised and made clear to everyone through the person specification and the job advertisement.

Positive action during the recruitment process is allowed under the discrimination legislation in terms of providing assistance to underprivileged groups to enable them to compete on a more level playing field. This might involve assistance with the completion of application forms or the provision of training for specified groups. Final hiring decisions must, however, be made on the basis of each individual's ability to do the job with some possible exceptions if s. 159 comes into effect, allowing for positive action in the selection decision.

With regard to harassment, it is necessary to make it clear to all employees that so-called banter can be regarded as offensive by individuals and should be avoided. Communications with employees and the creation of a culture of tolerance and acceptance of diversity have become even more important in the twenty-first century with the broadening of the equality law and growing recognition of the business case for diversity.

In terms of equal pay, the law provides for members of one sex to claim equal pay with a member of the opposite sex who is doing like work, or work of a different nature which can be shown to be similar in terms of the requirements for skill and effort, i.e. work of equal value. Equal pay is dealt with in more detail in Chapter 10, which examines payment systems and the evaluation of jobs. The major point to be made here is that it would be unlawful to advertise different pay rates for men and women doing the same work, or to offer employees of one sex disadvantageous terms and conditions.

Organisations that wish to promote equality of opportunity can also introduce complaints procedures, so that applicants who feel they may have been discriminated against can appeal in the first instance to the organisation concerned. This would normally mean that at least one staff member would be designated as responsible for the promotion of equal opportunities, so that applicants felt they were approaching a committed but unbiased person.

Monitoring of equality and the extent to which it is reflected in an organisation is also regarded as being crucial to the achievement of goals in this area (IRS, 2006). Most organisations place an emphasis on monitoring during the recruitment and selection processes, but it can also be carried out with regard to training, appraisals, grievance, discipline and dismissal, promotions and resignations (IRS, 2006). By monitoring their HR processes to measure any apparently adverse treatment of any particular group, organisations can identify any areas that require investigation and action.

Rehabilitation of Offenders Act 1974

The Rehabilitation of Offenders Act 1974 stipulates a range of time periods after which convictions for various offences are regarded as being spent. This means that past offenders should not be expected to reveal their offence once the conviction is spent, and should not be denied employment because of this previous offence. An offence that attracts a sentence of life imprisonment or a sentence of more than 30 months' imprisonment is never spent. The time periods over which convictions do become spent vary, and include 7 years for imprisonment for less than 6 months, 10 years for a prison sentence of 6 to 30 months, 1 year for a probation order (longer if the order covers a longer period) and the period of a disqualification for a driving offence. A number of exceptions to these rules about spent convictions apply to people who in the course of their jobs have unsupervised access to minors or other groups of vulnerable people, meaning that for this category of employee certain convictions can never be regarded as spent. Issues relating to employer access to criminal records will be explored more fully in Chapter 7.

Did you know?

Nacro, the National Association for the Care and Resettlement of Offenders, launched a new campaign, *Change the Record*, on 13 September 2010. Jonathan Aitken, himself a high-profile ex-offender, spoke to John Humphrys on BBC 4's *Today* programme about the campaign. He opined that the law had not been adjusted to take sentence inflation into account, and that ex-offenders who declare unspent convictions are not getting job interviews. The time limits before convictions become spent, e.g. 10 years for a 2-year sentence, are considered by Nacro to be too long and too obstructive in terms of rehabilitation and reintegration into society. It may be possible to hear the interview on the *Today* archive on the BBC Radio 4 website.

(*Sources*: www.nacro.org.uk; accessed 13.09.10; www.bbc.co.uk; accessed 13.09.10)

CASE STUDY 5.1 Discrimination

Mrs Meninder Patel applied for a post as a careers adviser with a local authority. The advertisement and person specification for the post had listed three years' experience in careers advice as one of the criteria being sought, and Mrs Patel had worked as a careers adviser in local schools for four years. The careers service received a number of good applications and the selection panel had difficulty in shortlisting a small number of applicants to call for interview. After some deliberation they decided that they would interview those candidates who had experience dealing with adults, because the careers service was going to expand into this area and the panel decided that this specific experience would be valuable. Mrs Patel was not one of the applicants called to interview. She felt that she was well qualified for the post according to the advertisement and the job description and person specification that had been sent to her. Mrs Patel felt that she must have been discriminated against unfairly and decided to pursue the matter.

Comment on the equal opportunities implications of this case. Why might Mrs Patel feel that she has been the victim of unlawful discrimination? What should the local authority do?

Discussion of case study

In times of high unemployment it is common to find large numbers of people applying for vacancies. It is difficult to achieve the correct balance between a tight person specification and one that excludes people unnecessarily. However, introducing criteria after applications have been submitted could be seen as an attempt to exclude people for covert reasons, for example to exclude women or certain racial groups. Depending on who was ultimately hired for this post, Mrs Patel could believe that she had been discriminated against because of her sex or ethnic origin or a combination of these.

Let us assume that there was no discriminatory intent on the part of the selection panel and that they were merely seeking a device to enable them to carry out the shortlisting exercise after receiving an unexpectedly large number of applications from well-qualified people. The case points out the importance of developing a good person specification in the first place, and the equal opportunities implications that this can have.

The local authority should ensure that there is an adequate internal mechanism for dealing with Mrs Patel's query. The fact that an employer tries to address any problems of this nature in a sincere fashion would be recognised by the Equality and Human Rights Commission as part of good equal opportunities practice. Of course, local authorities are also subject to the duty to promote equality in terms of race, gender and disability etc., so this employer should also have the relevant policies in place.

The employer should also ensure that training is provided to all employees involved in recruitment and selection to ensure that they understand the importance of each element of the process.

International issues

One of the main concerns for international organisations with regard to equality is that laws may differ in other countries. International HR specialists would need to be familiar with the legislation in force in other countries and ensure that they abide by the appropriate regulations. They also need to consider their commitment to diversity initiatives and decide how far these can be carried out in overseas locations, taking cultural differences into consideration. In terms of selecting employees for overseas assignments too, Brewster *et al.* (2007) highlight the issue of the levels of participation of women in foreign assignments, and state that it is necessary to improve on the current situation if the benefits of diversity are to be obtained.

Research articles from Australia and New Zealand indicate that gender equality continues to be a problem in those countries in spite of equality legislation and the adoption of sex equality programmes by employing organisations. Knox (2008) and French and Strachan (2007) examine gender equality respectively in the luxury hotel sector and in financial services in Australia. Both articles come to the conclusion that the segregation of women into lower paid and lower quality work continues. Knox's research identifies inconsistencies in the commitment of line management to equal opportunity measures across all aspects of hotel work as a major contributing factor to this. Another factor is the fact that gender stereotyping remains prevalent among applicants and customers; for instance, the fact that few women apply for portering roles, and some customers refused the services of a female porter. French and Strachan (2007) find that women continue to be under-represented in managerial positions in financial services. Handy and Davy (2007) examine combined age and sex discrimination in employment agency practices in Auckland, New Zealand, and come to the conclusion that there is the potential of a double whammy for older women seeking work in a predominantly female sector, in this instance, clerical and secretarial office work. The discrimination that the women in the study faced emanated from stereotypical views about the appearance expected from front-line clerical staff (stereotypically young, fashionable and attractive) and the way they would fit into the team (older women might be perceived as a challenge to the authority of younger male managers). The competency of the women in the study was in no way called into question.

A number of reports and research articles identify age as a further strand of equality issues which are important in a North American context. Posthuma and Campion (2009) present a meta-analysis of 117 American research articles and books on age stereotypes in the workplace, demonstrating that the ageing workforce is indeed an issue in the USA. Their recommendations focus on helping managers to recognise and avoid ageist stereotyping. Eyster et al. (2008) produced a report for the US Department of Labor, reviewing the changes that employers might need to make in their employment practices to cope with the challenges of an ageing labour force. They place some emphasis on the provision of part time work and flexible schedules along with arrangements for phased retirement. Armstrong-Stassen (2008) also identifies the ageing population as an issue for employers in Canada, and her research confirms the findings that employers who adapt their HR practices to the needs of older workers will be the most successful in attracting and retaining this group. Again, opportunities to work part time and on a flexible work schedule proved to be the most significant factors for retirees returning to work.

A set of three articles in the February 2009 issue of the American journal *Advances in Developing Human Resources* reveals that equal treatment in the workplace with regard to sexual orientation is currently an issue in the US. A search of several websites leads to a complex picture of relevant regulations in the US (the Human Rights Campaign at **www.hrc.org**, and the Equal Employment Opportunity Commission at **www.eeoc. gov**), but the basic picture is that while there is protection for employees in the federal government and in some states under state laws, there is currently no overall law that provides protection to this group consistently in the whole of the US.

Kormanik (2009) researched levels of awareness among employees on a range of sexual factors in the workplace: sex discrimination, sexual harassment, sexual attraction, sexual orientation and gender identity. His results indicated lower levels of understanding of sexual orientation and gender identity, which has implications for diversity management around these factors in the workplace. Kormanik identifies

Did you know?

The Equal Employment Opportunity Commission in the US does not have direct jurisdiction over cases of sexual orientation discrimination in the whole of the US, but since 2009, it does enforce protection against discrimination based on genetic information. Such discrimination refers, for instance, to use of people's genetic test results or the genetic test results of their family members to refuse employment, and is covered under Title II of the Genetic Information Nondiscrimination Act (2008). This came into effect on 21 November 2009.

(Source: www.eeoc.gov)

this as an area that HRD practitioners should focus on with awareness development programmes. In an article which refers to a wealth of background material but does not offer further empirical research, Hill (2009) makes a case for HRD practitioners to be aware of possible resistance to diversity initiatives related to sexual orientation and gender identity. Davis (2009) presents a very personal view of transgender issues as a tool which HRD experts can use to help others develop an understanding.

The International Labour Organization (ILO) conducts research on equality standards on a global basis. They find that improvements are still needed in many countries, and state that: 'Despite advances, in particular the considerable progress in women's educational attainments, women continue to earn less than men everywhere, and the unequal burden of family responsibilities places them at a disadvantage in finding full-time employment' (ILO, 2007, ix). To combat this and other persistent types of discrimination, the ILO promotes the development of 'active labour market policies' (xi) including training and job creation programmes.

REVIEW QUESTIONS

You will find brief answers to the review questions on pages 489–90.

1 Explain the concept of workforce diversity and outline the business benefits to be gained from a diverse workforce.

2 Comment on what is needed in terms of the management of diversity.

3 Outline the protected characteristics listed in the Equality Act 2010.

4 Explain the following terms and give examples: direct discrimination; indirect discrimination; victimisation; harassment.

SELF-CHECK QUESTIONS

Answer the following multiple-choice and short-answer questions. The correct responses or page references are given on page 490 for you to check your understanding of this chapter.

1 Diversity means the same thing as equality. TRUE or FALSE?

2 What is the name of the Commission that provides guidance on aspects of the Equality Act 2010?

3 How many protected characteristics are named in the Equality Act 2010?

4. Which of the following is a form of direct discrimination?
   (a) connective
   (b) associative
   (c) reflected

5 Genetic information is one of the protected characteristics in the Equality Act 2010. TRUE or FALSE?

Ethnic diversity: 'New Canadians' expand markets

By Christopher Mason

Nytric, a small product development consultancy in suburban Toronto, owes its existence and growth prospects to Canada's cultural diversity.

Two-thirds of the company's 22 staff are foreign-born and speak a broad range of languages that help the company bridge cultures.

Chinese companies learn from Nytric's Mandarin and Cantonese-speaking staff how to break into North American markets, while North American clients learn from Nytric's Asian developers how their product can be reconfigured to suit much larger Asian markets.

'A lot of people from outside Canada that we deal with don't realise how diverse Canada is until they actually come here,' says British-born Anthony Gussin, head of business development at Nytric.

The company is based in Mississauga, a fast-growing Toronto-area suburb where more than half of the 665,000 residents are immigrants.

Nytric illustrates the seamless way an increasing number of companies are incorporating Canada's cultural diversity into their business plans.

Canada's 33m people are scattered across a massive land mass. But what it lacks in density, Canada makes up for in diversity. It is home to newcomers from all corners of the planet, with immigrants now accounting for the bulk of population growth.

A growing number of companies recognise this and are tapping into 'new Canadian' communities to expand their markets, recruit fresh international talent and provide a springboard to markets in the home countries of new Canadians.

Declining birthrates are not keeping pace with the demands of the growing economy, so immigrants are expected to account for virtually all net labour force growth by 2011, and for all net population growth by 2030, according to Statistics Canada, the national statistical agency. The marked shifts allow immigrants greater sway and greater freedom to retain ties to their cultures.

Ethnic diversity is not spread equally across the country. Rural regions remain largely populated by descendants of Europeans. But the big picture illustrates the degree of overall diversity. Fully 19.8 per cent of Canada's population was born outside Canada, compared with 13 per cent in the US and 10.1 per cent in the UK in 2006, according to a survey by the Organisation for Economic Co-operation and Development.

Much of that diversity is centred in the cities, especially Toronto, Montreal and Vancouver.

Montreal is home to vibrant French-speaking Haitian, Lebanese and west African communities, while only about 40 per cent of children in Vancouver's school system speak English as their first language.

More than half of Toronto's 2.5m inhabitants were born outside Canada and some 115,000 immigrants arrive in the city each year.

'You need to have people on board who understand that market intuitively so you can develop products that meet the market's needs,' says Elizabeth McIsaac, executive director of the Toronto Region Immigrant Employment Council (Triec).

Larger employers, especially, have the resources to incorporate large-scale approaches to ethnic diversity. Banks in particular have seized the opportunity, as immigrants offer one of the few sources of domestic retail growth.

At the Royal Bank of Canada, one of Canada's five largest banks, some 26 per cent of the workforce is made up of visible minorities. The bank is actively reaching out to immigrant communities through such services as an International Remittance account and by sponsoring cricket programmes in schools to tap into the ethnic markets.

They and other banks also try to establish relationships with immigrants even before they come to Canada.

RBC has set up workshops and seminars abroad that teach those preparing to come to Canada about the country's financial system. Attendees can then set up a bank account, obtain a credit card and perhaps even be approved for a mortgage before they leave for Canada.

'When it comes to newcomer clients, it became clear to us that you want to get to them before they come to Canada,' says Zabeen Hirji, chief human resources officer for RBC and a native of Tanzania.

Not all is easy for newcomers to Canada. Many in professional fields such as medicine and engineering find it difficult to get their foreign credentials recognised in Canada, and language barriers can exist for those who do not speak English or French.

But the labour shortage facing the country means governments are increasingly gearing programmes and training to suit the needs of newcomers, giving hope that the foreign credentials issue will be resolved.

'It has been on the radar of several subsequent governments,' Ms McIsaac of Triec says.

Despite some of the challenges that come with doing business in Canada, such as its dispersed population and regionalised markets, Mr Gussin of Nytric says the Canadian demographic is an ideal stepping stone for companies looking to increase their global presence.

'If I were a Russian investor or if I were a British or French investor looking to set up an operation anywhere outside my home country, Canada is the first place I'd come,' Mr Gussin says.

FT.com, 13/10/2009 (Christopher Mason 2009) http://www.ft.com/cms/s/0/7581dc14-b6bd-11de-8a28-001144feab49a.html. Reproduced with permission, © The Financial Times Ltd.

Questions

1 What are the business opportunities and benefits of diversity identified in this article?

2 What is the nature of the ethnic diversity in Canada?

3 What are companies doing to embrace the ethnic diversity present in Canada?

WHAT NEXT?

One focus you could adopt for further study is gender equality, and you might wish to examine developments in this area from a more global perspective. In 2010, the International Labour Organization published an in-depth report about gender equality developments in the workplace on a global basis. The report, which can be downloaded at www.ilo.org, is entitled *Women in Labour Markets: Measuring Progress and Identifying Challenges*. The report finds that although there is in general increasing participation of women in the labour market, more women are still forced to take lower paying jobs than are men. Reading this report will give you a global perspective on gender equality issues, and specific profiles of 10 countries are also presented, including Argentina, Finland, Spain, Sri Lanka and the United Republic of Tanzania.

References

Advisory, Conciliation and Arbitration Service (2009a) *Age and the Workplace: Putting the Employment Equality (Age) Regulations 2006 into Practice*, ACAS.

Advisory, Conciliation and Arbitration Service (2009b) *Religion or Belief and the Workplace: A Guide for Employers and Employees*, ACAS.

Advisory, Conciliation and Arbitration Service (2009c) *Sexual Orientation and the Workplace: A Guide for Employers and Employees*, ACAS.

Advisory, Conciliation and Arbitration Service (2010) *The Equality Act: What's New for Employers*, ACAS.

Armstrong-Stassen, M. (2008) Organisational practices and the postretirement employment experience of older workers, *Human Resource Management Journal*, Vol. 18, No. 1, 36–53.

Bentley, R. (2006) Diversity training: Different strokes for different folks, *Training & Coaching Today*, 1 February (available at www.xperthr.co.uk; accessed 20.09.10).

Brewster, C., P. Sparrow and G. Vernon (2007) *International Human Resource Management*, 2nd edition, CIPD.

Chartered Institute of Personnel and Development (2006a) *Diversity: An Overview* (factsheet available from www.cipd.co.uk; accessed 20.09.10).

Chartered Institute of Personnel and Development (2006b) *Diversity in Business: How Much Progress Have Employers Made? First Findings*, CIPD.

Chartered Institute of Personnel and Development (2007) Diversity in Business: A Focus for Progress, Survey Report March 2007, CIPD.

Davis, D. (2009) Transgender issues in the workplace: HRD's newest challenge/opportunity, *Advances in Developing Human Resources*, Vol. 11, No. 1, 109–120.

European Commission (2003) *Annual Report on Equality and Non-Discrimination 2003: Towards Diversity*, Office for Official Publications of the European Communities.

Eyster, L., R. W. Johnson and E. Toder (2008) *Current Strategies to Employ and Retain Older Workers*, The Urban Institute.

French, E. and G. Strachan (2007) Equal opportunity outcomes for women in the finance industry in Australia: evaluating the merit of EEO plans, *Asia Pacific Journal of Human Resources*, Vol. 45, No. 3, 314–32.

Godwin, K. (2005) Promoting diversity – the role of line managers, *Equal Opportunities Review*, Issue 147, 1/11 (available at www.xperthr.co.uk; accessed 20.09.10).

Handy, J. and D. Davy (2007) Gendered ageism: older women's experiences of employment agency practices, *Asia Pacific Journal of Human Resources*, Vol. 45, No. 1, 85–99.

Hill, R. J. (2009) Incorporating queers: blowback, backlash, and other forms of resistance to workplace diversity initiatives that support sexual minorities. *Advances in Developing Human Resources*, Vol. 11, No. 1, 37–53.

Incomes Data Services (2004) Cultural diversity at B&Q, *IDS Diversity at Work*, No. 5, November, 7–10.

Incomes Data Services (2010) *IDS HR Study 921: Managing Diversity in the Workplace*, July, IDS.

Industrial Relations Services (IRS) (2006) Equality structures: an EOR survey, *Equal Opportunities Review*, Issue 157, 1/10 (www.xperthr.co.uk); accessed 20.09.10).

International Labour Organization (2007) *Equality at Work: Tackling the Challenges*, ILO.

Kandola, R. and J. Fullerton (1998) *Diversity in Action: Managing the Mosaic*, 2nd edition, IPD.

Knox, A (2008) Gender desegregation and equal employment opportunity in Australian luxury hotels: are we there yet?, *Asia Pacific Journal of Human Resources*, Vol. 46, No. 2, 153–72.

Kormanik, M. B. (2009) Sexuality as a diversity factor: an examination of awareness, *Advances in Developing Human Resources*, Vol. 11, No. 1, 24–36.

McCartney, C. and D. Worman (2010) Opening Up Talent for Business Success. Integrating Talent Management and Diversity, CIPD

Personnel Today (2007) The Work and Families Act: what are employers doing in practice about flexible working? *Personnel Today*, 27 March (available at www.personneltoday.com; accessed 20.09.10).

Posthuma, R. A. and M. A. Campion (2009) Age stereotypes in the workplace: common stereotypes, moderators, and future research directions, *Journal of Management*, Vol. 35 No. 1, February, 158–188.

Simpson, S. (2010) Equality Act 2010: 10 example dual discrimination scenarios, *XpertHR*, 08.09 (available at www.xperthr.co.uk; accessed 10.09.10).

Trades Union Congress and the Confederation of Business Industry (2008) *Talent not Tokenism: The Business Benefits of Workforce Diversity*, CBI.

Wolff, C. (2007) Arriva: dramatic results on diversity, *Equal Opportunities Review*, Issue 160, 1/1 (available at www.xperthr.co.uk; accessed 20.09.10).

XpertHR (2010a) Age discrimination: 'Younger' in job specification enough to shift burden of proof to employer, *XpertHR Case Law Stop Press*, 14.09 (available at www.xperthr.co.uk; accessed 14.09.10).

Further study

Books

Advisory, Conciliation and Arbitration Service (2010) *The Equality Act: What's New for Employers*, ACAS.

An excellent booklet which provides a concise and readable summary of the new legislation.

Macleod, A., D. Worman, P. Wilton, P. Woodman and P. Hutchings (2010) *Managing an Ageing Workforce: How Employers are Adapting to an Older Labour Market*, Chartered Institute of Personnel and Development and Chartered Management Institute.

Presents results from a survey conducted in 2010, and an overview of what some employers are doing to deal with an increasingly older labour force. Focuses on key areas, including recruitment, training and development, and flexible working practices.

Selwyn, N. (latest edition) *Law of Employment*, Butterworths.

This is an excellent reference book on employment law. The book is updated fairly frequently, so you should always make sure you are working with the latest edition.

Articles

Fredman, S. (2001) Equality: a new generation? *Industrial Law Journal*, Vol. 3, No. 2, June, 145–168.

A very readable overview of the then current and planned status of equality legislation in the EU and its implications for the UK. Still valuable as an interesting discussion of the values underpinning attitudes towards equality though subsequent changes in the law should be kept in mind when reading this article.

Wolff, C. (2007) Arriva: Dramatic results on diversity, *Equal Opportunities Review*, Issue 160, 1/1 (available at www.xperthr.co.uk; accessed 03.04.07).

Provides a very interesting case study of how Arriva approaches the management of diversity and what it sees as the benefits.

Internet

Advisory, Conciliation and Arbitration Service   **www.acas.org.uk**

ACAS offers e-learning courses on the sexual orientation, religion or belief, and age discrimination regulations.

Chartered Institute of Personnel and Development   **www.cipd.co.uk**

The CIPD website contains a wealth of information on various aspects of equality and the law. The website provides a podcast on equality and the podcast on employment law also contains relevant sections on parental rights and age.

Department for Work and Pensions   **www.dwp.gov.uk**

Age Positive documents can be found here as well as other equality information relevant to recruitment.

XpertHR (2010b) Avoiding discrimination – policies and monitoring, *Employment Law Reference Manual*, 8/7 (www.xperthr.co.uk; accessed 20.09.10).

XpertHR (2010c) Equality Act 2010: new secondary legislation supports definition of disability, *XpertHR Upfront*, 01.09 (available at www.xperthr.co.uk; accessed 07.09.10).

www.dwp.gov.uk (accessed 20.09.10).

www.eeoc.gov (accessed 20.09.10).

www.efa.org.uk (accessed 20.09.10).

www.equalities.gov.uk (accessed 20.09.10).

www.hrc.org (accessed 20.09.10).

Employers' Forum on Disability   www.efd.org.uk

A fount of information for employers, including guidelines and factsheets, information on events and awards, and links to many more sites.

Equalities Unit   www.equalities.gov.uk

Provides information on all aspects of the Equality Act 2010.

Equality and Human Rights Commission   www.equalityhumanrights.com

The Equality and Human Rights Commission has been established to deal with all equality issues. The website offers a series of extensive guidance booklets for both employers and individuals on aspects of the Equality Act 2010.

Xpert HR   www.xperthr.co.uk

Access to a wealth of articles to stay updated on developments in equality legislation and employment practices.

CHAPTER 6

Recruitment

Objectives

When you have read this chapter you will be able to:

- explain the aims of recruitment and describe how specified policies and procedures contribute to these aims

- understand the role of human resource managers and line managers in the recruitment process

- describe and design support documentation for the recruitment process – job description, person specification, job advertisement, application form, letters to applicants

- understand the role of competencies and a competency framework

- evaluate and draft recruitment policies and procedures

- identify a range of recruitment methods.

Organisations recognise the crucial part their people play in achieving and sustaining a competitive edge, and they are therefore aware of the need to attract people of the right calibre. Although recruitment intentions inevitably declined during the recession in 2008–9, there were more optimistic reports in 2010, especially with regard to the private sector (CIPD, 2010a). Most companies had turned their major focus onto the engagement and retention of current employees rather than recruiting new employees, but 65 per cent reported that they intended to recruit staff in 2010, and 68 per cent still reported encountering skills shortages. Although there is an inevitable increase in redundancies during a recession, there are still areas where recruitment continues to take place. For instance, the hotel, catering and leisure industry still reported a labour turnover rate of 34 per cent in 2008, the last time this was reported as a separate figure (CIPD, 2009c). Seventy six per cent of organisations also reported that the recession meant they were increasingly likely to receive applications from people who did meet their requirements (CIPD, 2010a). All of these data argue for continued good practice in recruitment to ensure that organisations attract the most suitable applicants in the most cost-effective way.

Because of continuing skills shortages and the resultant 'war for talent', as described in Chapter 2, talent management has become well established as an HR priority and continues to be recognised as being of strategic importance even during difficult economic times (CIPD, 2009d). Talent management focuses largely on the development and retention of employees, but in order to achieve business strategic goals, an organisation has to attract and hire people with the appropriate competencies in the first place. This confirms the strategic importance of recruitment and, as discussed in Chapter 1, the expected recovery from the recession is likely to put added pressure on organisations' ability to attract appropriately skilled human resources. Competition for the best resources, coupled with a need to reduce costs which became even more crucial during the recession, also means that organisations have to be innovative in their recruitment methods, and examples of some recent innovations will be presented in this chapter.

The processes of recruitment and selection are closely linked. Both activities are directed towards obtaining employees with the requisite competencies and attitudes, and recruitment activities lay the groundwork for the selection process by providing the pool of applicants from whom the selectors may choose. However, although the two activities are closely connected, each requires a separate range of skills and expertise, and may in practice be carried out by different individuals. The recruitment activity, but not normally the selection decision, may even be outsourced to an agency. It makes sense, therefore, to treat each activity separately. This chapter will deal with recruitment processes, actions, policies and procedures which, of course, should be designed to meet the strategic objectives of the organisation.

Recruitment is commonly referred to as the attraction phase (e.g. Murphy, 2008b) and can be further defined as:

- all activities directed towards locating potential employees
- stimulating the interest of potential applicants
- attracting applications from suitable candidates.

The aims of recruitment

Organisations do not operate in a vacuum, and recruitment drives are one of the times when an organisation has direct contact with the outside world. Other factors affecting recruitment are the framework imposed by legislation and the fact that no organisation will want to spend money on unnecessary activities. In light of this and the definition of recruitment given above, the aims of recruitment are:

- to obtain a pool of suitable candidates for vacant posts
- to use a fair process and be able to demonstrate that the process was fair
- to ensure that all recruitment activities contribute to organisational goals and a desirable organisational image
- to conduct recruitment activities in an efficient and cost-effective manner.

These statements intimate that a number of judgements have to be made about how recruitment is carried out. What is meant by a 'suitable candidate', and who decides this? Does the organisation have a process for evaluating the need to fill a post? What is a fair recruitment process and in what terms can fairness be evaluated or demonstrated? What recruitment actions can contribute to, or damage, an organisation's image? What are the costs involved in recruitment and how can they be managed to

Figure 6.1 Mind map of recruitment considerations

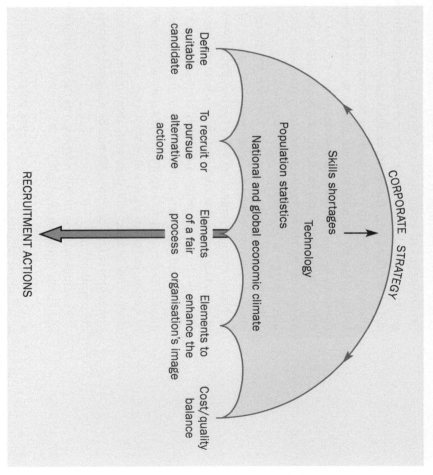

maximise the efficiency of the process? Acting as an umbrella to all of these consider-ations is also the need to tailor recruitment action to the corporate strategic plan, which itself should have incorporated factors in the environment such as skills short-ages, technological advances, etc. Figure 6.1 is a mind map of some of the factors that need to be considered in a systematic recruitment process.

Most human resource management issues can be analysed in terms of legal, moral and business considerations. With reference to the stated aims of recruitment, these considerations could be said to be:

● *legal* – to comply with anti-discrimination legislation
● *moral* – to avoid unfair discrimination for moral reasons as well as legal reasons
● *business* – to ensure that all efforts are directed towards achieving corporate goals.

To achieve all these aims, and because recruitment is likely to involve a wide range of people within an organisation, it is important to have a systematic approach so that all steps of the recruitment and selection process are conducted in line with:

● the organisation's human resource strategy
● equality goals.

The first step towards ensuring that the recruitment process achieves these aims in a coordinated manner is to develop and implement appropriate policies and procedures.

Recruitment policies

A policy is simply a statement of intent on the part of an organisation; it outlines the approach everyone is expected to adopt and the standards they should achieve in carrying out an organisation's business. A recruitment policy enables all employees involved in the process to direct their efforts towards achieving the organisation's goals and to know that they are acting in the spirit intended by the organisation.

A basic recruitment policy should at the very least include statements about the organisation's stance on:

● the overall goal of recruitment
● equality of opportunity.

To show that they value their employees, wish to retain them and want to provide them with every opportunity to develop, organisations may also adopt a policy of giving preference to suitably qualified internal applicants over external applicants, and this too would need to be stated explicitly in the organisation's recruitment policy. Such a policy would have implications for the way that recruitment procedures are developed.

One argument that is sometimes raised against internal recruitment policies is that they may lead to entrenching any equality problems that exist. That is, if the organisation has not previously hired from a particular ethnic group, for example, then it will not improve its record by hiring from within. A counter-argument to this is that if current employees are moved to new positions, presumably they eventually leave a vacancy that must be filled by external candidates. Organisations following good equality policies would be able to address any problems at this stage.

Organisations that wish to take the human resource management approach to enhancing the contribution and commitment of their employees should certainly consider adopting a policy on internal recruitment.

Pause for thought 6.1 Imagine you are in a company that has decided to formulate a recruitment policy which reflects its commitment to equality of opportunity along with an intention to give preference to internal candidates. Before you read on, consider what might be included in a recruitment policy for this company.

The following is an example of how such a policy might be worded:

This company aims to employ the person best suited for each post without regard to sex, marital status, racial origin, disability, sexual preference, religion, age or any other factor that cannot reasonably be construed as being related to a person's ability to do the job.

The company values the contribution of its employees and so will seek wherever possible to help employees develop new skills so that they may be considered for promotion opportunities. The company will advertise vacancies externally only if there are no suitably qualified internal candidates for transfers or promotions.

163

Recruitment procedures

The first step in the recruitment process is to assess the need for additional human resources and decide whether or not you have a vacancy you wish to fill. The vacancy may be a new post that has been identified through the development of the corporate strategic plan, or it may have arisen because an employee has resigned, retired or been dismissed. The latter are sometimes referred to as replacement posts to distinguish them from new posts. You may also decide to recruit a job-share partner for an established employee who no longer wishes to work full time.

Filling vacancies which arise because an employee has decided to leave or creating new posts should be part of a careful planning process, scrutinised in terms of how the action contributes to the organisation's strategic goals. When a jobholder leaves, HR and line managers should take the opportunity to examine the work done and consider whether it can be covered in another fashion. Here are some of the factors that could be considered:

- Are all the tasks necessary?
- Can some tasks be incorporated into another post?
- Should the job be redesigned to include more interesting and challenging work?
- Can some tasks be completed in other ways, e.g. by machine, by computer?
- Can the work be done on a part-time, flexitime or job-share basis?
- Is there a permanent need for the output of the post or should it be filled on a temporary basis or even contracted out?

A systematic approach to recruitment as recommended by the CIPD (2009b) includes:

- preparation of all supporting documents such as job descriptions and person specifications or competency profiles
- guidelines on actions to be taken such as writing and placing advertisements, and administrative procedures related to contacting prospective candidates.

Documentation to support the recruitment process

● Job descriptions and person specifications/competency profiles

In organisations that engage fully in human resource planning there will be on-going work dedicated to producing and maintaining job descriptions and person specifications/competency profiles, since these documents contain much of the information required for the planning process. Job analysis is the name of the process which is followed to produce these documents. However, even in organisations that do not engage fully in human resource planning, it is essential to produce job descriptions and person specifications/competency profiles for all existing posts as a basic framework for recruitment and, later, selection activities. These documents contain the information around which the job advertisement and the assessment of candidates will be structured and they can also be used to provide evidence of a fair process.

Job analysis

Job analysis is a process of gathering together all data about an existing job, which activities are performed, what the expected outcomes of tasks are, and what skills are needed. Some decisions, as described in the next section, need to be made about who will carry out the job analysis most effectively. The collected data are then structured to create job descriptions and person specifications or a job profile related to a competency framework. A similar process can be carried out to create this documentation for new posts though this would inevitably rely more on managerial knowledge and judgement.

The following aspects of job analysis need to be considered:

- What techniques can be used for gathering the information required?
- Who can best provide the information?
- Who can best gather the information?
- Who should write the job description and person specification?

What techniques can be used for gathering the information?

A range of techniques are available for performing job analysis, including observation, critical incident analysis and the use of questionnaires and interviews.

Observation involves shadowing employees and observing what they actually do. Obviously this can be very time-consuming and could stretch over a long period if, for instance, some tasks were performed infrequently. This technique is therefore most appropriate in the case of routine jobs with a narrow range of repetitive tasks.

Critical incident analysis involves getting a number of jobholders and their supervisors to describe events that showed successful behaviour on the job and events that showed unsuccessful behaviour. The analyst collects a large number of such anecdotes and condenses out of them a list of dimensions that represent the job. The advantage of this is seen as being that it focuses on behaviours, i.e. what people actually do, but the process is very time-consuming and may miss some of the more routine aspects of the job.

A sound approach for gathering information would involve written questionnaires and face-to-face interviews. A structured questionnaire can be used to gather initial information from the jobholder, supplemented with details from the line manager. The job analyst can then interview both and obtain clarification on the details outlined in the questionnaire. The draft job description should then be submitted to the jobholder and line manager for further comment. A structured questionnaire will guide people into giving relevant and adequate information.

Pause for thought 6.2 If you were asked to design a form in order to conduct a job analysis, what questions would you include?

The questions on a job analysis form might be dictated to some extent by the type of company you are working in. For instance, if you worked in a bank which is closed in the evening, you would not include questions about night shift work, whereas if you worked in a chemical plant with a 24-hour process, you obviously would ask questions about shift patterns. If we ignore such differences between organisations, however, there are some basic data that you would want to include in any job analysis. These would include such details as:

● a description of the duties performed
● the expected outcome of the tasks, i.e. what is the jobholder expected to achieve?
● the most important or responsible duties
● time spent on each duty
● how often each duty is performed (daily/weekly/monthly/annually)
● levels of supervision/independence
● the skills and skill levels needed to perform each task
● any special conditions related to the performance of these tasks.

The questionnaire and interview should be designed so that information needed for each section of the job description will be obtained. If employees and their managers are asked to describe ways in which they think their jobs will change, this adds information to the job analysis beyond what is already observable about the job. Pearn and Kandola (1993) provide a detailed description and evaluation of a wide variety of job analysis methods.

Although many people are happy to talk about their job, some people do not respond well to questioning or they may lack good powers of expression. The person performing the job analysis needs to develop good interviewing techniques to extract all the relevant information. Interviewing skills are an essential part of many aspects of human resource management and you will find more information about relevant techniques and skills development in Chapter 7 on selection.

Who can best provide the information?

Before you read on, stop and ask yourself: 'Who knows most about any particular job?' Most people would probably respond by saying: 'The person who actually does the job.' The postholder is, therefore, a good source of information about any post. But is the postholder the best source, or the only source? The direct line manager will also know the job requirements intimately, and will probably have a better perspective on how the job fits into the wider context of the company. Gathering information from both of these individuals will create a better picture of the post than gathering information from only one of them.

HR specialists too are often in a position to develop detailed knowledge of the tasks performed throughout the company, and in fact must do so particularly if they are involved in the human resource planning process, so they can bring an even wider perspective to the description of an individual post. To that extent they can also provide input to the job description, but their major role as far as job descriptions are concerned is about structuring, standardising and maintaining them rather than providing content-based information.

ACTIVITY 6.1

Information given by any person will be influenced by their perceptions and self-interest. Consider the pros and cons of involving the postholder and the line manager in the production of job descriptions and make a list of these before you continue reading.

Your list might include the following points:

1 The postholder:
- knows the job in detail
- may wish to inflate the importance of certain duties as a matter of status or self-image
- may represent preferred duties as more important duties
- may have incorrect perceptions of the level of authority they can exercise
- may not have the specialised skills needed to gather information and compose job descriptions
- may be reluctant to spend the time necessary to develop a good job description.

2 The line manager:
- knows the job well, but may not know every step the jobholder takes to complete the job
- can give information about how the job fits in with other functions performed in the company
- may sometimes be reluctant to define which tasks their subordinates have full authority for
- may not have the specialised skills needed to gather information and compose job descriptions
- may be reluctant to spend the time necessary to develop a good job description.

Who can best gather the information?

A human resource specialist is probably in the best position to fulfil this role. Although line managers may often put job descriptions to good use, most of them would not consider the production of JDs to be part of their duties, and there is no reason to assume that line managers in a wide range of functions would necessarily have the skills needed in order to produce a good job description. The human resource management function would normally provide this as a service to line management, and of course people with the requisite skills would be recruited and selected to perform this duty. It is rare to see an HR position totally devoted to job analysis, but depending on the structure of the HRM division, the task could be allocated to a recruitment specialist or an HR generalist.

Who should write the job description?

Again the HR specialist can probably best perform this task because of the writing skills required and the opportunity to become familiar with jobs throughout the organisation. This means that all job descriptions will be written in a uniform manner, providing an excellent database of all tasks performed within the organisation, thus facilitating a range of HR tasks such as the human resource planning activities described in Chapter 2. The various uses of JDs are examined later in this chapter.

How to write a job description
Structure and content

Since a collection of job descriptions can serve as a database of all tasks performed within an organisation, it makes sense to adopt a standard format for all job descriptions. This will ensure that the same types of information are gathered for each post, and will make the information more accessible to the reader and facilitate coding if the data are to be entered onto a computerised information system. The following elements are commonly found in job descriptions:

- job title
- reporting structure:
  - reports to
  - responsible for
- purpose of job
- major duties.

These are the essential elements of a job description, but you will find an assortment of other dimensions included in some job descriptions, for example: contacts, working conditions, salary grade, performance standards. Each organisation must decide what factors should be included in a job description, and this will depend on the nature of the business. For instance, some local authorities include a description of the contacts their employees are expected to deal with because they have complex internal structures, and contact with the public is an important part of their operation. The four elements listed above, however, are the basic information you would expect to find in any job description. Figure 6.2 shows a sample job description.

Most JDs contain a summary description of the post or, as we have called it, an outline of the purpose of the post. This is a brief paragraph encapsulating what the job is all about – what the jobholder contributes to the organisation. The major part of any JD is the list of major duties, itemising in detail the activities the jobholder undertakes and what they are meant to achieve.

Torrington *et al.* (2008) demonstrate the inclusion of performance standards in job descriptions. This can certainly enhance a job description by giving more information about what is expected from the jobholder. For instance, the second duty in our sample JD might read: 'Answer phone queries within three rings.'

Writing style

One important pointer when you are writing a job description is to use verbs to describe what a person is doing. For instance, the phrase 'responsible for letters' does not indicate what this employee would actually be doing. It is much better to employ a verb and say: 'writes letters'; 'sorts and distributes letters'; 'replies to letters'.

You should also, where possible, avoid the temptation to use the phrase 'assists with', as again this does not give a clear picture of what an individual employee is actually doing. Take, for example, the phrase: 'assists the manager with invoices'. It must be possible to get a clearer idea of which duties have been delegated to the employee and what activities are retained by the manager. 'Sorts the invoices by date'; 'processes invoices and forwards them to appropriate departments'; 'checks that invoices have been processed and payment made': each of these indicates a different activity and a different level of responsibility, and each is certainly more meaningful than 'assists the manager with invoices'.

Uses of the job description

It has been mentioned previously that job descriptions can be used for a number of purposes. These will be dealt with more extensively in other chapters, but it is worth

Figure 6.2   Sample job description

JOB DESCRIPTION

Job title: Receptionist

Reports to: Office Services Manager

Responsible for: Assistant receptionists (2)

Purpose of post: To ensure that visitors to the company are received in a welcoming fashion, to answer routine queries and to ensure that all other queries are handled expeditiously by the appropriate staff member. To ensure that all telephone queries are handled in the same manner.

As the first point of contact for the company, the receptionist must maintain high standards of customer care.

Contacts: All customers and other visitors to deal with initial and routine queries. All members of staff to pass on queries as appropriate.

Major duties: ● Greet walk-in visitors and ascertain purpose of their visit. Handle or redirect queries as appropriate.

● Answer phone queries as above.

● Answer all initial queries about receipt of payments using the online payment receipts system.

● Open and sort incoming post by department. Organise delivery of post by assistant receptionists.

● Perform clerical tasks assigned by departments in agreement with the Office Services Manager.

● Supervise assistant receptionists and delegate work as appropriate.

● Perform other duties as assigned by the Office Services Manager or other authorised manager.

---

pausing here to reflect briefly on what the applications of job descriptions are and whether they have any implications for how job descriptions are compiled and written. The major uses of job descriptions are as follows:

● human resource planning
● recruitment and selection
● day-to-day performance management
● long-term performance management/performance appraisal
● identification of training needs
● job evaluation.

Can one description provide all the information needed for the whole range of these activities? Some HR managers may argue that different input is needed, for example, for the job evaluation process. More detailed information may be needed about the amount of freedom that employees have to make decisions independently, the impact their actions have on other colleagues, or the financial implications of their work. The question arises of whether a different job description is needed for the purposes of job evaluation. You can form a better opinion on this when you read about these other activities and the uses of job descriptions to support them.

ACTIVITY 6.2

1 Design a generic questionnaire that could be used to solicit adequate information from an employee to draft a job description. (It might help you if you have one or two posts in mind while you design the questionnaire: what sorts of question would you need to ask in order to elicit all the relevant information? You may also wish to work with a group of fellow students to pool your ideas about the questionnaire design.)

2 Test your questionnaire on a friend, relative or other willing volunteer, and follow up with an interview to fill in the gaps.

3 Analyse this process and make recommendations for improvement.

4 Draft the job description from the information you have gathered.

Person specifications

The person specification is a document that outlines the knowledge, skills and qualities a person would need to have in order to be able to do the tasks or achieve the outcomes required on the job description. Drawing up a person specification requires a fair amount of judgement in assessing what level of skill is necessary. To ensure equality of opportunity, care must be taken *not* to inflate these requirements, especially with regard to academic qualifications and length of experience. The requirements detailed in a person specification should be the minimum standards required for a person to be able to perform the job. There should be an expectation that any person will improve performance while doing a job, and the fact that training could be provided should also be considered.

How to write a person specification

Several models of person specifications are available, those designed by Alec Rodger in 1952 and John Munro Fraser in 1978 being the most widely known. We shall briefly describe the criteria set out in these two models, with some indication of how you might interpret the recommended dimensions in modern circumstances, and then we shall apply a simplified model to our sample job description.

Rodger developed the seven-point plan which described people in terms of:

● *Physical make-up*: any particular physical requirements of the job, such as visual acuity

● *Attainments*: education and training

● *General intelligence*: it is difficult to make a meaningful statement about intelligence unless you intend to test for it

● *Special aptitudes*: verbal, numerical and diagrammatical abilities related to the job

● *Interests*: current wisdom is that private interests are not good indicators of job performance

Documentation to support the recruitment process

- *Disposition*: job-related behaviours such as persuasiveness
- *Circumstances*: only job-related circumstances such as availability for shift work.

The criteria suggested by Fraser are known as the five-fold framework:

- *Impact on others*: similar to Rodger's physical make-up and disposition
- *Qualifications and experience*: education, training and skills developed through work experience
- *Innate abilities*: similar to intelligence in Rodger's plan
- *Motivation*: difficult to apply for recruitment and selection purposes since differing motivational structures can lead to equally good performance
- *Emotional adjustment*: Relevant personality factors such as the ability to cope with the demands of the job.

In essence, the person specification should cover three areas of requirements:

- knowledge
- skills
- personal attributes or qualities.

These three dimensions have long been used to create person specifications in North America where they are referred to as KSAs.

The person specification can be drawn up by examining each task in the job description and determining:

1 what each task requires in terms of knowledge, skills and personal qualities
2 how these skills, knowledge and personal qualities might be acquired.

As mentioned earlier, a high level of judgement is needed to decide on relevant criteria, and one person's judgement may differ from another's. You must be able to justify any requirement you make and be ready to explain why it is reasonable, particularly when the specification is to be used later in recruitment and selection. You should also take care to avoid meaningless clichés like 'a sense of humour', when what is really required is the ability to deal calmly with challenging situations.

Once you have a list of the criteria you are looking for, they must be arranged in a logical and understandable fashion:

- Similar criteria, e.g. all skills and knowledge involving numeracy, should be grouped.
- Criteria can be designated as essential for the post or merely desirable.

The sample person specification in Table 6.1 relates to the sample job description in Figure 6.2.

Table 6.1 Sample person specification

Post: Receptionist

	Person specification	
Attributes	Essential	Desirable
Knowledge	Knowledge of clerical systems	Knowledge of the company
Skills	Experience of clerical work Experience in handling queries in person and over the telephone	Supervisory experience
Personal qualities	Polite manner Ability to work under pressure	

Pause for thought 6.3

One of the major requirements for the job described in Figure 6.2 has been missed out of the model person specification in Table 6.1. Can you identify it? What can you add to the person specification to cover this requirement?

The job description mentions use of an online system to answer queries about receipt of payment, yet there is no requirement for computer skills in the person specification. Obviously a low level of skill is required. It would not, for instance, be appropriate to ask for programming skills, but it would be reasonable to require the 'ability to extract information from a computerised database'.

ACTIVITY 6.3

Draft a person specification for the job description in Figure 6.2 using the models provided by Alec Rodger and John Munro Fraser. Compare your drafts with those of other students and incorporate the best ideas into a final version.

Competency frameworks

Competencies are work-related behaviours that have been identified as necessary for successful performance at work. Rather than designing a person specification for each post, perhaps using new vocabulary each time to describe the skills, knowledge and personal attributes required, it may be possible to design a schematic or framework of competencies that can be applied to all jobs performed in a particular company. At least it should be possible to identify a set of core competencies required of all employees, with more specialised competencies attached to the job descriptions of particular posts. With the broadening of equality legislation, the focus in setting requirements during recruitment and selection is shifting firmly towards the use of competencies. The use of competencies means that the assessment of candidates centres on their abilities, not on aspects of their background, such as length of work experience or non-essential academic qualifications, that may tie in with their sex, race, age, etc. Requirements for particular qualifications or a number of years of work experience can take attention away from an evaluation of actual competencies.

Setting up a competency framework is a complex endeavour, and organisations that wish to introduce one into their HRM systems would normally call on the services of a firm of occupational psychologists to assist in the design and implementation processes. Competency frameworks come in many shapes and sizes, and the issues that would typically need to be addressed in designing a system include the following:

- Should we adopt a framework geared towards particular categories of employee (e.g. managers) or design one that can be applied to all employees in the organisation?
- What are the competencies relevant to our enterprise? How many should we include to build a comprehensive but manageable representation of the skills, knowledge and personal qualities required in the organisation?
- Which competencies can be grouped together as clusters, how many performance levels should there be for each competency and how will these levels be described?

- How do these competency clusters, individual competency and levels of competency relate to individual jobs in the organisation?

An example of a competency cluster, individual competency and levels of competency should help you to recognise the significance of these issues and appreciate the potential usefulness of a competency framework. Typical competencies that are required by organisations include things like communication skills, analytical abilities, ability to work in a team, leadership, and ability to plan work.

Let us take the employees in a supermarket as an example. Most of these employees would at some time come into contact with the public, so 'working with people' might well be a major area of competence which would subsume a cluster of related competencies. 'Working with people' therefore becomes a competency cluster, and the competencies included under this designation might include communication, customer service and teamwork. These competencies might be applied to all jobs in the supermarket, including managerial, supervisory, office and shop-floor employees. Obviously, different levels of these competencies would be expected from employees working in different functions and at different levels in the organisation. Thus a description of the level of competence in teamworking required of a manager would probably allude to the ability to devise and implement new structures that enhance productivity, whereas the level of competence expected of a shelf stacker would probably involve statements such as 'assists other team members when own work is completed' or 'helps other team members solve queries'.

The Incomes Data Services (IDS, 2008) review examples of the frameworks used in a number of organisations and provide some useful excerpts. Rankin (2008) reviews the ways employers are using competencies and provides some guidelines on how to avoid problems in developing and using them.

ACTIVITY 6.4

The competencies we have just outlined in our supermarket example are presented in a grid in Figure 6.3. Provide descriptions of the levels of competency left blank for all the competencies, and indicate which jobs these would apply to.

The job description in the recruitment context

The four basic elements of the job description are: the job title; the reporting structure, i.e. the job title of the person to whom the postholder reports and the number and categories of the people the postholder is responsible for; a statement of the purpose of the post; and a description of the major duties. Taken together, they should provide a job applicant with a good idea of what the job entails.

The job title, such as sales assistant, warehouse supervisor, marketing department manager or nurse, already contains a lot of information about the position. In choosing a job title you should be careful not to inflate the level of the job, for instance by the inappropriate use of words such as executive or director, and you should avoid any potentially biased language such as waitress and foreman.

The information given in the sections on reporting structure enables applicants to see where the job fits into the organisation's structure and whether the post has any supervisory responsibilities. If there are particularly pertinent details about terms and

Figure 6.3 Competency framework exercise

	LEVEL 1	LEVEL 2	LEVEL 3	LEVEL 4	LEVEL 5
WORKING WITH THE TEAM	• Demonstrates willingness to help other members of the team complete their work	• Uses knowledge to help other team members solve problems		• Designs and implements new team work structures to improve efficiency and effectiveness	
CUSTOMER SERVICE					
COMMUNICATION SKILLS					

conditions, such as shift work or a requirement to work on Sundays, they should also be included since this will enable candidates to judge whether they are willing to take on such responsibilities.

The person specification/competency profile in the recruitment context

The very fact that an employer draws up a person specification/competency profile demonstrates an attempt to introduce some objectivity into what can otherwise be a very subjective process. Rather than relying on instinctive personal judgements about the knowledge, skills and qualities the successful candidate should possess, the employer with a person specification/profile is following a much more methodical and reasoned process. It is also a much more open process, since the specification is a written record of what the employer is basing his or her selection decision on. These written records can be requested by employment tribunals should anyone complain of unfair treatment, but many employers now share this information openly with applicants for posts, so applicants also know in detail what the employer is looking for in a candidate.

Care should therefore be taken that no one is unfairly excluded from being considered for a position because the requirements were set unnecessarily high. This could constitute indirect discrimination, as certain disadvantaged groups may have more difficulty in acquiring some qualifications or competency levels. Care should also be taken that none of the criteria set are directly unlawfully discriminatory.

The information about skills, knowledge and personal qualities should be summarised and included in advertisements for the post.

As mentioned above, the person specification/competency profile can be included with the information sent to candidates to give them more details about requirements. It is an excellent practice to design and send to candidates a form showing each requirement and

Table 6.2 Assessment of person specification criteria

Post: Receptionist

Attributes	Criteria	How assessed
Knowledge	Knowledge of clerical systems	Application form Interview Work sample test
	Knowledge of the company	Interview
Skills	Experience of clerical work	Application form Interview Work sample test
	Experience of handling queries in person and on the telephone	Application form Interview
	Ability to extract information from a computerised database	Application form Interview
	Supervisory experience	Application form Interview
Personal qualities	Polite manner	Interview
	Ability to work under pressure	Interview

how it will be assessed, for example from information included on the application form, at the interview or from references. Table 6.2 shows an example of this, based on the person specification for a receptionist which was given earlier in this chapter (Table 6.1).

Recruitment methods

Job advertisements

Once you know you have a vacancy to fill, you must decide what is the best way to let people know about it. The following are some methods of advertising the existence of vacancies:

- on-site noticeboards
- local/national newspapers
- professional journals
- minority group newspapers and magazines
- recruitment agencies
- university/college/school careers centres
- job centres
- radio/television (including text pages)/cinema
- Internet sites
- set up a stall at a recruitment fair or exhibition.

Deciding where to place an advertisement

You will need to assess the available advertising methods in terms of their appropriateness for a particular vacancy. Considerations will include: the likelihood of finding people with particular skills in a particular geographical location; the type of qualifications you are seeking and which publications people with those qualifications are likely to read; salary level and whether you are likely to be able to attract someone to move to your area for the salary you are offering. Obviously some judgement is required to make these decisions, but one should always be wary of making assumptions about what people will do given their personal circumstances, and one should strive to keep recruitment open and fair. It may be unfair, for example, to restrict applications to your geographical area as there may be good candidates who would be willing to move to your area for the sake of the job. That should remain the personal decision of the prospective candidate.

The costs of advertising are also a factor. You may be more willing to spend a large portion of your advertising budget on a senior post than on a junior one. However, you may have a relatively junior post that requires skills not readily available in your locality, or you may have a large number of low-paid posts and the need to fill these posts may call for the willingness to spend more on advertising.

Word-of-mouth advertising is often listed in textbooks as a possible method of recruitment, and it is used to varying extents in some organisations. It is mentioned here for clarification but excluded from the recommended list because of its potentially discriminatory effects. Organisations that recruit heavily by word of mouth run the risk of perpetuating the make-up of their workforce in terms of gender, age and ethnic origin, etc. In general, employees tend to recommend people like themselves from among their family and friends. For example, in general, if an organisation's workforce were all white Europeans, word-of-mouth recruitment would tend to bring in more white Europeans. A commitment to equality of opportunity means that this cycle has to be broken, and one way of doing this is to advertise in the ethnic press.

Designing recruitment advertisements

First consider what the objectives of a job advertisement are, and what techniques might be used to achieve those objectives. The overall aim of the advertisement is to secure sufficient applications from suitably qualified persons with the end result that the employer will find 'the best person for the job'. Note that advertisers wish to obtain a reasonable number of applications, but not an overwhelming number. The first principle of writing job advertisements is therefore to *give sufficient information about the post so that suitable candidates will apply but also so that unsuitable candidates will be discouraged from applying.*

What will attract good applicants to a post? Consider these factors and also consider how they should be incorporated into an advertisement to achieve maximum impact. For example, is salary a major selling point for your organisation? Should salary figures be included or excluded? Should they be displayed at the top of the advertisement, in the body of the text or at the end? A job advertisement is an opportunity to tell people what you can offer as well as what you require. The following are some suggestions of the kind of factors you may wish to include in a job advertisement:

- organisation name and information
- job title and major duties
- competencies required
- opportunities and challenges
- salary and benefits
- statement of policy on important issues such as equality of opportunity
- how to apply.

Organisation name and information

Obviously people need to know which organisation they are applying to. Information about the organisation's prospects and what it can offer as an employer can be a selling point: several IRS articles by Murphy and Suff in 2008 and 2009 refer to the importance of the employer brand in recruitment. Murphy (2008b) reports that more than 48 per cent of employers surveyed by the IRS were focusing more on presenting information about their organisations which showed that they were a good place to work. Another of her articles (2008a) reviews how to create an employer brand by soliciting information from both current employees and applicants about how the organisation is seen as an employer, examining areas in which improvements can be targeted, and then communicating the overall profile to potential employees. Benefits of this approach are the attraction of a larger and more diverse group of applicants, and aiding self-selection among applicants since they will have a better idea of what the company is like to work for. Suff (2009b) profiles Paul UK, makers of bread, cakes and pastries, and describes how they used their employer brand in their recruitment to help combat the high labour turnover they were experiencing. Their recruitment literature now illustrates their pride in their product and the staff benefits available to employees, including opportunities for development and performance rewards. You can get a good idea of Paul's employer brand by visiting their website at **www.paul-uk.com**.

Job title and major duties

The job title should be the one used in the job description, and the main duties should be summarised for the advertisement to give potential applicants a good idea of what the job entails.

Competencies required

The person specification/competency profile will provide a good basis for summarising the abilities you are looking for. Job advertisements should contain enough detail to allow suitable and unsuitable candidates to identify themselves. Enabling self-selection in this way at this early stage of recruitment makes an important contribution to the cost-effectiveness and overall success of the process.

Opportunities and challenges

The tasks in a job can be described as requirements, but it is much more appealing to most people if you emphasise the opportunities a job will offer them to use their skills and feel a sense of achievement, and the challenges that will provide them with a chance to develop.

Salary and benefits

Every organisation will have records of the salary ranges and benefits that are attached to each job. An organisation might have a particularly attractive range of benefits that could be the deciding factor for someone deliberating on whether or not to apply for a position. You can read more about salaries and benefits in Chapter 10.

Did you know?

One way of promoting one's employer brand would be to achieve a three-star listing as a 'best company' to work for in the *Sunday Times* listings. Factors that can get you into the list include offering a fair deal, recognition, good leadership and management, good communication and providing opportunities for development, and a complete set of eight factors combine to represent the art of engagement. Companies that made it into the list in 2010 include Nando's, Mothercare and Boots Opticians. You can find out more at **www.best-companies.co.uk**.

Did you know?

Sathnam Sanghera provides an interesting example of a company tailoring its advertisement placement and content to the job in question. The advert for an expert in social media marketing was placed on **www.craigslist.org**, and interested parties were instructed to apply using tweets and staying within the Twitter word limit. A veritable test of the competencies required for the job!

(*Source:* Sanghera, S. Start-up gets down to nitty-gritty in recruitment, *The Times*, 18 January 2010, p. 42)

How to apply

A range of possibilities exist, and the most appropriate will depend on the particular post being filled, the volume of applications expected or desired, and the systems and capabilities of the department receiving the applications. You may request interested applicants to do any of the following:

- call in person
- attend an open day interview event
- phone/leave a message on a 24-hour answer machine requesting an application form
- write a letter applying for the post; apply by e-mail
- contact a particular person
- request and return an application form
- request further information
- send a curriculum vitae (CV) and covering letter
- send a CV or acquire and return an application form
- apply for an application form online
- apply by a certain date.

Style of writing

The style of writing that is appropriate for a job advertisement depends on the nature of the position. Traditionally, advertisements were written in a very formal style, using phrases like: 'The successful candidate will possess a university degree and two years of directly related work experience.' In recent years, most advertisements have been written in a less formal and more direct style, using 'you' as if the recruiter were speaking directly to the prospective applicant.

Other techniques that have been used to attract the reader's attention are the use of questions and bold or controversial statements such as:

> **Are you looking for your next challenge and an opportunity to develop your project management skills?**

or

> **You'd have to be crazy to take on this job!**

or

> **We can offer you long hours and tiring days . . . but plenty of rewards too.**

These are acceptable techniques for producing job advertisements, but care should be taken that they are not overused, thereby losing their freshness and impact. A list of questions at the start of an advert can become tedious. Once you have caught your reader's attention, you should proceed swiftly to giving information. You should also avoid using hackneyed phrases, clichés or essentially meaningless phrases. Most employers would like to employ enthusiastic, intelligent, well-motivated and outgoing people. However, since practically no one is likely to admit to not being any of these, it seems pointless to include them as criteria in a job advertisement as they help neither qualified persons to identify themselves nor unsuitable persons to screen themselves out.

Use of colour and graphics

Organisations often use colour and graphics to draw attention to their advertisement. A company logo may be part of promoting the employer brand, and photographs can convey an impression of an organisation's culture or maybe its commitment to diversity.

Job advertisements: whose responsibility?

Depending on its particular circumstances, every organisation needs to decide who should be responsible for producing job advertisements.

There are several contingencies to consider. For instance, is the post of a routine nature, with simple duties or a job description that has not changed much? Does a previous advert exist that can be used without much change? A junior member of the HRM department could handle this or the administrative staff in any unit where this activity has been devolved to line management.

If the post is new or has changed considerably, the line manager should be more involved in deciding the content, and more expertise in composing advertisements will be needed so someone with more experience in this area and well-developed writing skills should take on the task.

If the post is difficult to recruit for (maybe due to a local skills shortage), you may consider using the specialised skills of a recruitment advertising agency. The additional cost of this would be a factor to weigh against the cost of unsuccessful recruitment attempts. Some organisations save costs by maintaining a list of preferred suppliers and negotiating special deals with them in return for putting more work their way. The general consensus about using recruitment agencies, however, seems to be that the major benefits come from a faster recruitment and selection process as these agencies may handle applications and carry out the initial sifting process, and the process may be more efficient and effective since the agencies have specialist knowledge of recruitment such as where to tap into supplies of scarce skills (CIPD, 2007; IRS, 2007b).

If you have any doubts about your writing ability, get help! Advertisements are very expensive and very public, and can contribute to the public image of your organisation. If the requisite skill is not available within your organisation, you may have to consider using the services of an advertising agency.

Online recruitment

As the twenty-first century progresses, the use of the Internet to advertise posts and deal with recruitment processes is becoming ever more well established, and developments in Web 2.0 technology are opening up more opportunities for innovative approaches. Vacancies for a wide range of posts are listed by some organisations on their own website, in other cases by recruitment agencies, on job boards such as fish4jobs (**www.fish4.co.uk**) and on the online jobs pages of newspapers and journals. Throughout the early years of the twenty-first century, the CIPD annual surveys of recruitment have shown an increasing usage of online methods. The reports on practices used in 2005 and 2006 (CIPD, 2006 and 2007) already indicated increasing usage of e-recruitment, the latter making the point that online advertising on companies' own websites had grown to equal their respondents' usage of local newspaper advertising. The reports from the following three years (CIPD, 2008, 2009c and 2010a) consistently show that use of the corporate website for advertising vacancies has outstripped the popularity of local newspapers. Several commentators report that the increased use of online advertising during 2009 could at least in part be interpreted as a way of reducing recruitment costs during the recession (O'Reilly, 2009; Rankin, 2009; Suff, 2009a).

Did you know?

Some of the companies that report using online recruitment successfully include Ernst & Young (accountancy), BSkyB (broadcasting), PricewaterhouseCoopers (accountancy), and Accenture (IT consultancy).

(*Source:* Griffiths, J. (2009) A new tool for talent spotters. Social networking sites are proving indispensable, *The Times* (Graduate career section), 16 September)

Reduced costs are, indeed, regarded as being a benefit to be accrued from recruiting online, particularly through organisations' own corporate websites; there are, however, a number of other advantages to online recruitment. One of the major reasons for using the Internet for recruitment is that it provides access to a large pool of applicants (CIPD, 2009a). The increased access to a large pool of applicants is not, however, unproblematic: the CIPD (2009a) posits that Internet recruitment could lead to an increased number of unsuitable applicants. Henkes (2007) emphasises the importance of the design and content of web-based advertising if organisations hope to make their recruitment process more effective and efficient. The issue of diversity is addressed in potentially contradictory ways. Williams (2009) reports that diversity is enhanced because of the broader reach of online advertising, but the CIPD (2009a) cautions that Internet recruitment could act as a barrier to the recruitment of older workers.

Further expected advantages from e-recruitment processes are improved speed in completing the recruitment and selection processes, enhancement of employer brand for those employers seen to be using modern and innovative techniques, flexibility and ease of use for applicants, better informed candidates, particularly when applicants are driven to an organisation's own website. Murphy (2007) also makes the interesting point that the information presented on websites, particularly video clips showing the experience of current employees, can operate like a realistic job preview and help to eliminate any misapprehensions held about a particular line of work. You may remember that we addressed this problem in our discussion of skills shortages and potential employer solutions in Chapter 2.

The Sunday Times (2007) distributed a special supplement on uses of technology for recruitment which reviewed a number of recent innovations including: company presence on social networking sites such as Facebook and My Space; the production of podcasts offering careers advice; employee video blogs included in company websites; virtual tours of a company's premises so people can see what the physical environment looks like. Other commentators have reported on further technological advances in recruitment processes such as using text messages to inform potential applicants of vacancies (*People Management*, 2006) and candidates' use of video CVs to present themselves (Chynoweth, 2009).

(Sources: *PM Guide to Recruitment Marketing*, July 2010, distributed with *People Management* magazine; www.armyjobs.mod.uk, accessed 06.09.10)

> **Did you know?**
>
>
>
> The Army provides an excellent example of innovative use of a corporate website for recruitment purposes. In the 2010 CIPD Recruitment Marketing Awards, the Army won the Grand Prix, plus awards in four other categories: campaign of the year, digital recruitment, recruitment website and recruitment effectiveness. The site uses video clips of successful recruits to explain various aspects of working in the army, information about the range of jobs available and the competencies required, an opportunity to try out samples of the tests that applicants have to pass with an online soldier guide to talk the visitor through what is required, and a chance to chat online.
>
> See for yourself at **www.armyjobs.mod.uk**.

> **ACTIVITY 6.5**
>
> One advantage of using a website for recruitment purposes is that organisations can provide easy access to a lot of information for prospective candidates. You can easily find some current job advertisements in the print media that include an Internet address, or you can locate companies with job vacancies via a search engine online.
>
> Visit a selection of these websites to see for yourself how employers are using the World Wide Web for recruitment.

Rankin (2009) reports that most employers are not fully exploiting the range of possibilities that have been explored here. Human resource managers need to be aware of these issues and developments to maximise the effectiveness of their organisation's recruitment process.

Targeted recruitment

The Equality Act 2010, described in detail in Chapter 5, is essentially designed to protect specified groups against unfair discrimination in employment. A controversial aspect of this Act is contained in s. 159 which allows for preferential treatment to be accorded to members of under-represented groups as long as they are equally qualified in comparison with people who are not members of that group. This is known as positive action. Employers are not obliged to adopt this approach in making selection decisions, but the Act introduces this as a new possibility if an employer has the legitimate aim of trying to address a previous imbalance. It must be noted, however, that this section was not due to come into effect before 2011, and, since it is subject to Government consultation, may not ultimately come into effect at all.

Targeted recruitment is somewhat different to positive action, and has a long pedigree as an acceptable approach to equitable recruitment and selection. Targeted recruitment is a method of encouraging previously disadvantaged groups to apply for vacancies but, in keeping with the basic intention of equality legislation, any subsequent selection must be based on merit only.

Targeted recruitment can be drawn to potential applicants' attention in job advertisements in several ways:

- A statement that encourages under-represented groups to apply for a post, for example: 'We welcome applications from people with disabilities, women, and members of black and ethnic minority groups as they are under-represented in the company in positions at this level.'
- A statement not targeted at any particular specified group, but emphasising that diversity is valued and that all candidates will be assessed on merit without reference to sex, race, age, etc.
- Photographs and text that show people in non-traditional roles, thus emphasising an employer's desire to receive applications from groups that do not traditionally apply for particular posts.
- An assurance that qualified candidates with a disability will be invited to interview.
- Photographs showing a mix of men, women and members of various racial groups, ages, etc.

Employers who engage in targeted recruitment have recognised that good, able people have become discouraged from even applying for certain jobs because of a history or perception of discrimination. A number of such companies were profiled in a seminal *Personnel Management* article (Paddison, 1990). The experience of these companies was that targeted recruitment attracted a much greater pool of suitable candidates, and not only from the specified groups. There was an overall improvement in the quality of applications. Targeted recruitment, then, speaks loudly about an organisation's level of commitment to equality, and may help the organisation address equality issues *per se*, but a side-effect is that it also attracts applications from better candidates in general.

ACTIVITY 6.6

Review a number of job advertisements from a variety of sources, and comment on what you regard as poor and good factors with regard to the elements described in this chapter. For example:

● What caught your eye?
● How complete is the information about tasks, skills requirements, salary, etc.?
● Does the advert appropriately assist the reader in self-selection?
● Are important aspects of organisational culture presented, such as equality and diversity policies?

You may wish to discuss your findings with others in your class in small groups, and present your combined findings to the whole class.

Application forms

Once you have provided people with information about your vacancy, you must decide on the best way for interested candidates to present information about themselves. The major choices are:

● application form ⎫
● curriculum vitae (CV) ⎪
● letter of application ⎬ submitted on paper or electronically
● handwritten/typed submission ⎪
● personal call. ⎭

Many organisations prefer to use their own application form because of the advantages this can offer. Application forms can be designed to elicit information specific to the types of work done in your organisation. The information can be arranged so that very important information is seen first, for example, academic qualifications or membership of professional bodies which are regarded as being essential for particular posts. One advantage of application forms over CVs is that the organisation controls the information that is given, not the applicant. In this way the organisation can ensure that the same types of information are gathered from all applicants, the information is relevant to the work the organisation can offer, and information that could potentially lead to unlawful discrimination is excluded.

The application form is a bridge between the recruitment process and the selection process. Once a completed form has been received, it can be used as a basis for the initial selection exercise, but until this occurs, it is part of the recruitment process and its design should be subject to recruitment considerations. A poorly designed form – one, for example, that requests inappropriate information – could alienate potential applicants and discourage some from applying.

The design of the content and layout of an application form must also take several other factors into consideration. We have mentioned the avoidance of unlawful discrimination above, but the age discrimination regulations further sharpened the focus on the need to redesign application forms so that they would be age neutral. Forms should also address issues such as making arrangements to assist people with disabilities, monitoring for equality and diversity purposes, data protection issues, and other legalities.

Questions regarding disabilities

According to the IRS (2007a), it is permissible to ask questions on the application form about an applicant's disability, with an emphasis on what arrangements might be necessary to facilitate the application process and enable the candidate to perform the work in question.

It is also regarded as good practice to offer alternative ways of applying to accommodate disabilities. The IRS (2007a) give the following examples: application forms in Braille, on audio tape, electronic submission of applicant details.

Age neutral application forms

The age discrimination regulations renewed the focus on competencies in the recruitment and selection process instead of concentrating on qualifications and experience. These two latter factors continue to be important, but HR and employers are being encouraged to shift their attention more simply to an assessment of a person's capabilities rather than depending, for instance, on length of experience as a yardstick. The Employers Forum on Age (EFA, n.d.) has interesting information on its website about eliminating dates from the application process so that employers will focus on competencies rather than making judgements based on information that is linked to age. Although much of the information on this website is now only accessible by those who have paid for a corporate membership, the template and guidance for an age neutral application form is still generally accessible at **www.efa.org.uk/data/files/publications/507/Getting-Recruitment-Right.pdf** (accessed 07.09.10).

Equality and diversity monitoring

Many application forms now contain an equality monitoring section so that employers can evaluate their success in attracting applications from qualified members of designated groups, and also monitor the handling of these applications at all stages of the selection process. The information on this form should be used only to provide feedback to the organisation that it is operating in a non-discriminatory fashion, and should not be used as part of the selection process. It is essential that candidates are informed about why the information is being requested and how it will be used. They should also be informed that it is not compulsory to provide this information and that this will not be detrimental to their application.

It is best if the monitoring form can be detached from the application form so that it is clear to applicants that the monitoring and selection processes are completely separate. Monitoring forms usually request information about factors which are directly addressed in the legislation on discrimination. ACAS (2009a and 2009b) recommends that employers give a great deal of thought to whether and how they introduce new categories of information into their monitoring forms as many people may feel sensitive about issues such as sexual orientation and religious belief and regard any queries about these as an invasion of privacy. It is also regarded as good practice to invite applicants to specify any special requirements that may need to be met to enable them to attend an interview (e.g. avoidance of a clash with timing of a religious festival or time of religious observance).

Data protection and other legal issues

Employers inevitably gather a lot of personal information about their candidates, so the design and handling of application forms is subject to the Data Protection Act 1998. The principles of data protection are described in more detail in Chapter 4 on the employment relationship, but the principles that obviously apply here are that the information collected should be appropriate for its intended use, it should be used only for the purpose for which it was collected and it should be handled in a secure fashion. Application forms should contain a statement to this effect and indicate that applicants should sign indicating acceptance of the organisation's stated use of their data. A sample data protection statement can be seen on the age neutral application form template on the EFA website, and the issue is also addressed by the IRS (2007a). There is also detailed guidance available from the Information Commissioner's Office (2005).

All employers need to be sure that potential employees have the right to work in the UK, so application forms must request confirmation of this. This is dealt with in more detail in Chapter 7.

ACTIVITY 6.7

- Choose an employer and design an application form that could be used for all posts within that organisation. Check that your form elicits all relevant information from applicants. Consider the design and layout of your application form: is it easy to complete; is it easy for selectors to locate relevant information?
- Compare your application form with the sample form given on the website of the Employers Forum on Age at www.efa.org.uk/data/files/publications/507/Getting-Recruitment-Right.pdf (accessed 07.09.10).

Equality implications

In order to promote access to jobs, employers may wish to assist those with poor language skills in completing application forms. There are many posts where the duties to be performed do not require the levels of reading, writing and language ability that are necessary for a person to be able to complete an application form. Positive measures to ensure that such people are not unfairly excluded from such posts would be an example of good practice and could lead to an organisation acquiring committed employees who might otherwise have been excluded. Employers who are genuinely interested in equality and diversity would also naturally include a statement on their application forms to this effect as part of their employer branding efforts.

CVs

Although we have presented the advantages of using an application form, there are some advantages to using CVs too. If an advertisement required all applicants to submit a CV, the organisation would have eliminated the steps, and therefore the cost, of designing, producing and sending out application forms. It must be remembered, however, that preparing a CV requires a fairly good standard of writing skills, so it would not be appropriate to require this for all positions. Many advertisements for managerial posts request interested candidates to apply by sending in a CV.

Administrative procedures

The final aspect of the recruitment process we need to consider is how you are going to handle applications in addition to any data protection requirements. You will need to design administrative procedures that address the following issues:

- accepting applications by phone/walk in/electronically
- sending forms/information
- acknowledgement of applications received.

In deciding on the appropriate administrative procedures you will need to address questions about what you want to achieve, but also the question of cost. There is a public relations element in every recruitment exercise, as your organisation will have contact with many people who will not become employees, but who may be potential customers and will certainly relate to others how you treated them. You will want to create a good impression with every applicant, but the desire to do this must be tempered by the question of cost. Many organisations are now alerting potential applicants that they will not receive an acknowledgement of receipt of their application form due to rising postal costs and the number of applications expected (IRS, 2003a). A sample letter can be found in Appendix 6.1, but one alternative is to include a statement on the application form.

Global issues in recruitment

The first point to make about global recruitment issues is that the recruitment and retention of personnel, particularly in crucial leadership positions, has been reported in the first decade of the twenty-first century as one of the key issues in people management, not only on a national but also on a global basis (Ready and Conger, 2007; Woolbridge, 2005). Major ongoing CIPD research into what makes organisations sustainable (CIPD, 2010b) includes several international companies among its case studies (Pfizer, Standard Chartered Bank and Xerox), and lists leadership as one of the three main characteristics which are essential to organisational ability to sustain high performance. Ready and Conger (2007) write about the talent management strategies employed by two major companies to address this challenge. For one of them, Procter and Gamble, the company's HRIS provides rapid access to 'a global database of talent profiles' (p. 70) which means that positions can readily be filled by internal talent. The system is also designed to report on the achievement of diversity goals.

Organisations recruiting for international operations can make choices about where they wish to focus their recruitment efforts. The four approaches identified by Perlmutter and Heenan (1974) are ethnocentric, polycentric, regiocentric or geocentric or indeed a combination of these.

An ethnocentric approach means that senior, and perhaps other managerial positions in overseas locations will be filled by parent country nationals. The assumption underlying such decisions is that the knowledge and expertise needed to make decisions at that level reside only in the parent country. The parent company may also wish to impose its organisational culture on overseas branches.

Polycentrism implies that people local to the particular location would be chosen to occupy managerial as well as operational positions. Regiocentrism means that the best person suited to any job at any level would be selected from within a wider geographical region, e.g. the EU, whereas geocentrism entails recruitment of talent from anywhere in the world.

Each of these approaches will have an impact on the way people in locations around the world are managed on a day-to-day basis, but ethnocentrism in particular might have an inhibiting effect in terms of freeing up the potential of diversity in the workforce. Although the contingency approach to analysing aspects of business life has been emphasised elsewhere in this text, i.e. a belief that there is normally no one interpretation that can be universally applied to business situations, Perlmutter and Heenan (1974) identify ethnocentrism as being problematic in general and something to be avoided. A polycentric approach also does not encourage the benefits of diversity as the emphasis is on local knowledge, expertise and culture. Regiocentric and geocentric approaches obviously encourage greater diversity, but this then needs to be managed in order to gain the maximum benefits.

Conclusion

This chapter has discussed the aims of recruitment and the range of policies and procedures involved in effective recruitment which is a crucial element of talent management. We have emphasised the need for a methodical approach, using job descriptions, person specifications/competency profiles and well-designed advertisements and application forms to support the process. The next chapter will examine the processes and techniques involved in making a selection from the applications you receive.

REVIEW QUESTIONS

You will find brief answers to review questions 2 and 4 on page 490.

1   Choose five current advertisements for job vacancies from different sources. Comment on the structure, content and placement of the adverts, evaluate their effectiveness and suggest improvements.

2   Describe the uses of the job description and person specification/competency profile in the recruitment process.

3   Interview someone about his or her job. Draft a job description, person specification and advertisement for the post.

4   Comment on the approaches to recruitment an employer can adopt in order to create and project a positive public image.

SELF-CHECK QUESTIONS

Answer the following multiple-choice and short-answer questions. The correct responses or page references are given on page 490 for you to check your understanding of this chapter.

1   List three things you would consider when deciding whether or not a vacancy exists.

2 Name three standard methods of advertising vacant posts.

3 List the major components you would include in a job advert.

4 Does targeted recruitment mean that members of under-represented groups will be selected in preference to other candidates? YES or NO

5 Everyone involved in selecting candidates should see the equal opportunities monitoring form. TRUE or FALSE?

HR IN THE NEWS

Computer says: 'You're hired'

By Jessica Twentyman

Edgars Consolidated Stores (Edcon) is something of a national institution in South Africa. Since 1929, the chain of department stores has supplied generations of South Africans with clothing and footwear, from school shoes to funeral suits.

Naturally, keeping a network of more than 1,000 stores in South Africa, Botswana, Namibia, Swaziland and Lesotho fully staffed is a big challenge for the company's human resources department, which oversees a workforce of 20,000 people – especially in the busy run-up to Christmas, when its headcount doubles.

Widespread unemployment in South Africa, meanwhile, means that for every position the company advertises, it receives approximately 100 applications, according to executive HR manager, Andrea Wiehahn.

'We're very aware of the need to handle those applications sensitively,' she says. 'Our job applicants are our customers as well, and even unsuccessful candidates need to be treated with respect, so that they go away from the experience with a positive feeling about the Edcon brand,'

To compound the issue, she adds, economic and political transformation in South Africa means that the company needs to demonstrate compliance with a complex web of government-mandated employment equity policies.

That is a big challenge, but Edcon is evidently handling it well. In a 2005 survey conducted by management consultancy Deloitte, it was named one of the 15 best companies to work for in South Africa and the best company to work for in the retail market.

Edcon makes sure it has the internet on its side. When a store manager has a vacancy to fill, they enter the details of the position on the company's new Softscape Apex HR system. It is automatically forwarded to the relevant senior manager for approval, and from there, it is posted on the career section of the company's website (**www.edcon.co.za**), as well as online job boards, such as Career Junction (**www.careerjunction.co.za**).

The e-recruitment process does not end there. Job seekers submit their applications over the internet via the website, and those applications are subsequently held and managed in the Softscape system. Around three-quarters of all applications Edcon receives are now made over the internet, says Leon Vermaak, Edcon's business integration manager.

The system's talent acquisition tools, meanwhile, enable managers to search applications, retrieve details for prospective employees, contact them and organise interviews, explains Alex Bartfeld, Softscape's director for the EMEA region.

Not only that, the system also holds a wealth of information about the company's recruitment processes, adds Ms Wiehahn, enabling the HR team to report on metrics relating to ethnic diversity in the workforce, as well as calculating the time and cost involved in bringing new hires on board.

Like Edcon, organisations around the world are finding that the internet provides the perfect platform for attracting recruits and streamlining their applications. In fact, it is critical in a world where the job of finding, attracting, selecting and securing top talent has never been more important, according to Peter Cheese, managing partner of management consultancy firm Accenture's 3,500-strong Human Performance practice.

'The thing that's driving attention on recruitment is a general shortfall of skills,' he says. 'The demographics of developed countries are against us, and that's put a great deal of pressure on how companies attract and retain talent,' he says.

Certainly, things have come a long way from the days when job seekers would frequently find that the careers section of a company's website offered no more information than a generic e-mail address for the HR department. 'A whole host of developments are fuelling e-recruitment right now: internet-enabled HR systems, e-mail, online job boards, social networking sites, virtual worlds, and so on. As a term, e-recruitment covers a huge array of tools, but they have one thing in common: the internet,' says Mr Cheese.

Take KPMG, the management consultancy, for example, or the Royal Bank of Scotland, or data storage giant EMC – all three have held careers fairs in Second Life, the online 'virtual world'. And in a recent survey of IT recruiters by the Association of Technology Staffing Companies (ATSCo), 58 per cent said that social networking sites such as LinkedIn, Facebook and MySpace are more useful for recruitment than print advertisements. Eighty-three per cent, meanwhile, said they used those sites to trawl for potential job candidates.

'Sites such as LinkedIn are an incredibly powerful form of recruitment, as it puts the power in both parties' hands – the recruiter in identifying the right candidate and the individual in deciding whether or not to engage in an offer,' says Dan Nye, CEO of LinkedIn.

'Some people are connected to hundreds of professionals across industries and borders, which in turn are connected to thousands more. This immediately places a well-connected recruiter in touch with a large number of possible candidates.'

But it is those organisations that have tightly integrated their e-recruitment tools with their back-end HR systems that have achieved the most notable successes – and that is true whether those back-end systems are hosted in-house or by a third party specialist, under the software-as-a-service (SaaS) model, according to Colin Tenwick, chief executive of hosted talent management software specialist Stepstone, a company that offers both options.

'An all-encompassing e-recruitment tool won't just post vacancies to a website and capture applications,' he says. 'It will provide a robust framework for all the processes that surround bringing new recruits on board, and then managing their performance for as long as they work for you,' he says.

Such systems need to be capable of doing some pretty heavy lifting. Mobile services operator Orange, for example, uses Stepstone's i-Grasp system to process about 80 per cent of the 5,000 applications it receives each year and currently holds 50,000 CVs, says David Roberts, Orange's employer brand manager.

I-Grasp enables Orange's 200-strong HR team to promote the company culture to applicants from the first contact, he says, primarily using the company's careers portal, **www.orange.co. uk/jobs**, as well as a number of retail recruitment microsites.

It also helps to ensure that applicants are kept informed of the progress of their application, via e-mail and text message – and that was certainly welcome to Elly Hallwood, who joined Orange's in-house legal team as senior counsel in August this year, after applying for the job via the portal.

'I was kept informed all the way down the line,' she says. 'Moving from a law firm to an in-house legal department can be quite a transition, but the amount of information that I received from Orange regarding my application made the whole process much less stressful.'

The biggest benefits of effective e-recruitment, however, are encapsulated in two key metrics: time to hire and cost to hire. At Hyatt Hotels, for example, a hosted talent management system from Taleo has cut the process of hiring a front desk employee from four weeks to five days, according to Randy Goldberg, Hyatt's executive director of recruiting. And hotels that have moved both managerial and hourly positions online have reported a 50 per cent reduction in recruitment advertising spending.

But above all, it is quality of candidates that really counts, says Michael Gregoire, CEO of Taleo. 'If e-recruitment means you get people on board quickly and at a lower cost, then that's great, but what companies really need to know is whether they're hiring the kinds of people that have a material positive impact on their organisation,' he says.

That kind of insight, he adds, can only be achieved with a robust set of HR tools that enable companies to manage their ongoing performance in attracting and retaining talent.

Or as Mr Bartfeld of Softscape puts it: 'The story doesn't end when you click on the "hire" button.'

(Financial Times, FT.com, 7 November 2007, © Jessica Twentyman. Reproduced with permission.)

Question
List the ways that e-recruitment can be used to improve the recruitment process.

WHAT NEXT?

Now that you have mastered the introductory level of information presented in this chapter, you may wish to take your studies to a higher level. The article cited below is an American publication, reviewing the major current issues in recruitment and selection, so it is relevant to the next chapter in this textbook as well as this one. Ployhart describes the key issues concisely, but the great joy in reading this article is that he identifies a large number of potential research questions. For example, under the heading 'What We Know,' he states that 'Employer brand image is an effective means to differentiate the firm from competitors' (p. 877). Under the heading 'What We Need to Know,' he identifies gaps in our knowledge with questions such as 'How do organizations best acquire a brand image, present it, and manage it?' and 'How do organizations that lack a familiar brand image compete?' (p. 877).

This article can take you forward on several levels. It gives you an American perspective while reviewing concepts that are also well established in the UK. It stimulates thoughts for those who are interested in conducting research on recruitment and selection or who are maybe seeking a topic for an undergraduate or postgraduate dissertation.

Ployhart, R.E. (2006) Staffing in the 21st century: new challenges and strategic opportunities, *Journal of Management*, 32, 868–97.

References

Advisory, Conciliation and Arbitration Service (2009a) *Religion or Belief and the Workplace: A Guide for Employers and Employees*, ACAS.

Advisory, Conciliation and Arbitration Service (2009b) *Sexual Orientation and the Workplace: A Guide for Employers and Employees*, ACAS.

Chartered Institute of Personnel and Development (2006) *Recruitment, Retention and Turnover. Annual Survey Report 2006*, CIPD.

Chartered Institute of Personnel and Development (2007) *Recruitment, Retention and Turnover. Annual Survey Report 2007*, CIPD.

Chartered Institute of Personnel and Development (2008) *Recruitment, Retention and Turnover. Annual Survey Report 2008*, CIPD.

Chartered Institute of Personnel and Development (2009a) *E-Recruitment*, CIPD (factsheet available at www.cipd.co.uk; accessed 06.09.10).

Chartered Institute of Personnel and Development (2009b) *Recruitment: An Overview*, CIPD (factsheet available at www.cipd.co.uk; accessed 18.02.10).

Chartered Institute of Personnel and Development (2009c) Recruitment, Retention and Turnover, Annual Survey Report 2007, CIPD.

Chartered Institute of Personnel and Development (2009d) The War on Talent. Talent Management under Threat in Uncertain Times, CIPD.

Chartered Institute of Personnel and Development (2010a) Resourcing and Talent Planning, Annual Survey Report 2010, CIPD.

Chartered Institute of Personnel and Development (2010b) Sustainable Organisation Performance: What Really Makes the Difference? Shaping the Future: Interim Report, January 2010, CIPD.

Chynoweth, C. (2009) Smile for the CV camera, The Times: Graduate Career, 16 September.

Employers Forum on Age (n.d.) Getting Recruitment Right, EFA (available at www.efa.org.uk/data/files/publications/507/Getting-Recruitment-Right.pdf; accessed 07.09.10).

Fraser, J.M. (1978) Employment Interviewing, 5th edition, Macdonald and Evans.

Henkes, M. (2007) E-recruitment – Sorting the Wheat from the Chaff, HR Zone (available at www.hrzone.co.uk; accessed 07.09.10).

Incomes Data Services (2008) IDS HR Study 865: Competency Frameworks, March, IDS.

Industrial Relations Services (IRS) (2003) Labour saving devices, IRS Employment Review 774, 18 April, 34–40.

Industrial Relations Services (IRS) (2007a) Job applications, Employment Law Reference Manual, 30/4 (available at www.xperthr.co.uk; accessed 07.09.10).

Industrial Relations Services (IRS) (2007b) Outsourcing the recruitment process: quality gains over quantity, IRS Employment Review 863, 19/1 (available at www.xperthr.co.uk; accessed 07.09.10).

Information Commissioner's Office (2005) Employment Practices Code, ICO.

Murphy, N. (2007) Using employer videos to improve online recruitment, IRS Employment Review 887, 12/12 (available at www.xperthr.co.uk; accessed 07.09.10).

Murphy, N. (2008a) How employer branding can improve recruitment, IRS Employment Review 903, 26/08 (available at www.xperthr.co.uk; accessed 07.09.10).

Murphy, N. (2008b) Trends in recruitment methods in 2006 and 2007 (1): attraction, IRS Employment Review 893, 20/03 (available at www.xperthr.co.uk; accessed 07.09.10).

O'Reilly, S. (2009) Using online recruitment in a cost-effective way, IRS Employment Review, 20/01 (available at www.xperthr.co.uk; accessed 02.03.09).

Paddison, L. (1990) The targeted approach to recruitment, Personnel Management, November, 54–58.

Pearn, M. and R. Kandola (1993) Job Analysis: A Manager's Guide, 2nd edition, IPD.

People Management (2006) Recruiting by text, People Management, 26 October (available at www.peoplemanagement.co.uk; accessed 07.09.10).

Perlmutter, H.V. and D.A. Heenan (1974) How multinational should your top managers be? Harvard Business Review, November–December, 121–131.

Rankin, N. (2008) Competencies in the workplace, IRS Employment Review 906, 06/10 (available at www.xperthr.co.uk; accessed 07.09.10).

Rankin, N. (2009) Using corporate websites for recruitment: the 2009 IRS survey, IRS Employment Review 926, 03/08 (available at www.xperthr.co.uk; accessed 24.08.09).

Ready, D.A. and J.A. Conger (2007) Make your company a talent factory, Harvard Business Review, June, 69–77.

Rodger, A. (1952) The Seven Point Plan, National Institute of Industrial Psychology.

Suff, R. (2009a) The impact of the recession on recruitment: the April 2009 IRS survey, IRS Employment Review 924, 06/07 (available at www.xperthr.co.uk; accessed 14.07.09).

Suff, R. (2009b) Transforming recruitment and retention at Paul UK, IRS Employment Review 916, 02/03 (available at www.xperthr.co.uk; accessed 02.03.09).

The Sunday Times (2007) Recruiting: how technology is shaping the future, 1 July (special supplement distributed with The Sunday Times).

Torrington, D., L. Hall and S. Taylor (2008) Human Resource Management, 7th edition, Financial Times Prentice Hall.

Williams, H. (2009) E-recruitment: Rethinking recruitment, Personnel Today, 09.06 (available at www.personneltoday.com; accessed 10.06.09).

Wooldridge, A. (2006) A survey of talent, The Economist, 7 October, 3–20.

Further study

Books

Advisory, Conciliation and Arbitration Service (2007) *Recruitment and Induction*, ACAS.

One of the advisory booklets that provide succinct advice on good practice. Available at www.acas.org.uk; accessed 25.03.10.

Chartered Institute of Personnel and Development (2010) *Resourcing and Talent Planning. Annual Survey Report 2010*, CIPD.

The annual surveys for several years, previously called *Recruitment, Retention and Turnover. Annual Survey Report*, can be downloaded from the CIPD website so it is possible to analyse developments over time. The CIPD surveys a large number of employers to report on recruitment and selection practices, and comments on trends and key issues.

Incomes Data Services (2008) *IDS HR Studies Update: e-HR*, No. 867, April, IDS.

An overview of the uses of technology in HR, including recruitment and selection, HR management systems, training and development and HR intranets. Presents case studies of six employers, including online graduate recruitment at H J Heinz.

PM Guide to Recruitment Consultancies, June 2010.

PM Guide to Recruitment Marketing, July 2010.

These guides are distributed with *People Management*, and they appear on an annual basis. They offer the latest insights into various aspects of recruitment from specialists in the field.

Articles

Fernandez-Araoz, C., B. Groysberg and N. Nohria (2009) The definitive guide to recruiting in good times and bad, *Harvard Business Review*, May, 74–84.

This article argues for a systematic approach to the recruitment and selection of people for senior posts.

Industrial Relations Services (IRS) (2007) Determining the needs of the job, *Employment Law Reference Manual*, 31/3.

Briefly addresses factors that should be considered when drawing up a job description and person specification, followed by detailed guidance on how to handle genuine occupational qualifications and requirements, these to be renamed simply occupational requirement under the Equality Act 2010.

Suff, R. (2010) Benchmarking competencies: The 2010 IRS survey, *IRS Employment Review*, 23.08 (available at www.xperthr.co.uk; accessed 07.09.10).

Suff, R. (2010) Using competencies in HR practices: The 2010 IRS survey, *IRS Employment Review*, 23.08 (available at www.xperthr.co.uk; accessed 10.09.10).

Two articles from the IRS which provide an overview of current uses of competency frameworks across 168 employers.

Internet

Many recruitment agencies are now using the Internet and many newspapers also have webpages. Interesting sources of information on the Internet that we have checked include the following:

BBC Jobs
www.bbc.co.uk/jobs
The BBC is one example of a large corporation that regularly advertises job vacancies on its company website.

Business Link

www.businesslink.gov.uk

Offers practical advice for employers on a wide range of topics, including aspects of recruitment and employing different types of workers including part-timers, young and older people, the disabled.

Chartered Institute of Personnel and Development

www.cipd.co.uk

The CIPD website contains a wealth of information on various aspects of recruitment, equality and the law.

Department for Work and Pensions

www.dwp.gov.uk

Age Positive documents can be found here as well as other equality information relevant to recruitment.

Equality and Human Rights Commission

www.equalityhumanrights.com

Equality information relevant to recruitment can be found here.

Monster Board

www.monster.co.uk

A worldwide professional employment and job search agency. The site includes a number of company profiles and employer videos, so you can see here how some organisations market themselves as employers.

Total Jobs

www.totaljobs.com and **www.jobability.com**

The main site acts as a recruitment agency, but also has interesting advice for jobseekers on various aspects of the recruitment and selection processes. The company has also developed a site at 'jobability' specialising in information for the disabled applicant.

Appendix 6.1 Sample letter to accompany application form

XYZ Company
1 Company Lane
Companytown
XY1 1YZ

Mr D White
3 Candidate's Close
Everytown
EF3 4GH

March 18, 2010

Dear Mr White

Thank you for your query about the post of Marketing Assistant. Please complete the enclosed application form and return it to us by April 8, 2010.

We regret that we are unable to acknowledge receipt of applications. However, if you wish to enclose a self-addressed and stamped postcard or envelope, we would be pleased to return this to you to indicate that your application has been received.

The selection committee will complete its review of all applications within three weeks of the closing date, and selected candidates will then be notified of an interview date. We intend to hold interviews in the week of May 10, 2010.

If you have not heard from us before May 4, 2010, you should assume that you have not been successful on this occasion.

Yours sincerely

N Barkley

Human Resource Manager

CHAPTER 7

Selection: Interviews and tests

Objectives

When you have studied this chapter you will be able to:

- explain the aims of the selection process
- name and describe the steps that can be taken in the selection process
- decide how to integrate a range of techniques into the selection process
- identify typical interviewer errors and explain how to avoid them
- plan an interview process and formulate appropriate questions
- conduct an interview, assess the candidates and record your evaluation
- suggest a range of work sample exercises and design them
- justify your decision and provide feedback to unsuccessful candidates
- describe the steps to be taken to complete the selection process.

A successful recruitment campaign should result in a good number of applications from people who are suitably qualified for your vacancy, and the next task is to select the most suitable person from this number. Employers must consider who should be involved in this task and provide support in terms of policies, procedures and training. This chapter will examine these factors as well as discussing the expertise needed to participate successfully in the selection process and the wide range of techniques that can be used.

As with all other aspects of people management, organisations can adopt a strategic approach towards selection. Effective selection processes, aligned to the organisation's strategic goals, add value by ensuring the necessary human resources are in place for the achievement of these goals. It is advisable, therefore, to see selection processes within this wider context.

Aims and objectives of the selection process

The ultimate goal of selection is usually expressed as 'to choose the best person for the job'. Selectors attempt to match candidates to the job requirements, predicting how well they will perform if offered the position, but they also need to ensure that the candidates fully understand all major aspects of the job so that new recruits are not likely to become disillusioned and leave within a short period of time. The objectives of the selection process, which will lead to the fulfilment of the main goal, are as follows:

- gather as much relevant information as possible
- organise and evaluate the information
- assess each candidate

in order to:

- forecast performance on the job

and

- give information to applicants

so that

- they can judge whether or not they wish to accept an offer of employment.

Selection policies and procedures

In order to achieve a fair, non-discriminatory outcome, every effort should be made to design a methodical and objective system for selecting employees. Personal factors and perceptions cannot be totally eliminated, but having objective policies and procedures in place can help to obviate any potentially harmful effects of individual persuasions. Good selection policies and procedures provide guidance and support to line managers and others involved in the selection process to carry out this duty successfully, confident that they are following the tenets of best practice.

Selection policies, like recruitment policies, are a statement of an organisation's intentions and should normally address such issues as equality of opportunity, maybe giving information about targeted groups. A selection policy might read as follows:

The objective of the selection process is to obtain employees who will be productive and committed members of staff, working and developing to their full potential. This organisation will select employees on the basis of merit only. Internal and disabled applicants who have the required knowledge and skills are guaranteed an interview.

Selection procedures should address the following issues:

- the stages and techniques that should be used
- who is to be involved in assessing candidates
- administrative processes.

Several factors would be decided on for each of these issues, and relevant guidelines provided. The procedures documentation might, for example, indicate that a shortlist must be prepared and interviews conducted for each vacancy; guidelines might be given on who is to prepare the shortlist and conduct the interviews, and what methods should be used to accomplish these tasks. Further issues to be addressed in selection procedures include: guidelines on non-discriminatory questioning, the appropriateness of testing; whether references should be taken up and when.

According to the CIPD (2009d and f), the most well-established selection methods include:

- shortlisting from information on application forms and CVs
- interviews of various kinds
- tests
- assessment centre
- references.

The CIPD (2009d) has further identified the interview as the most frequently used selection method among those listed.

Selection as a strategic activity

We established in Chapters 1 and 2 that employee selection contributes to the achievement of strategic goals and so is too important an activity to be conducted on the basis of what is familiar or expedient. Organisations may, therefore, depending on the circumstances, need to engage in a broader array of activities rather than simply shortlisting and interviewing alone. Sophisticated selection has been identified as part of the best practice associated with the HRM approach (Marchington and Wilkinson, 2005) and thus a necessary part of a strategic approach dedicated to obtaining the competitive edge that comes from having a superior workforce. The importance of getting the selection decision right is confirmed by the growing emphasis on the crucial contribution to organisations of their talent management processes. As Ready and Conger (2007, p. 68) proclaim: 'Stop losing out on lucrative business opportunities because you don't have the talent to develop them.' The full range of techniques may not be needed for every vacancy, but at least the process should be examined and the appropriate action chosen for each contingency.

This chapter will provide an overview of the full range of selection methods listed at the end of the previous section. Although we address each method in the order given, it should be noted that employers can use considerable flexibility in the design of their selection process. Assessment centres or tests may, for instance, be used early in the process to screen out unsuitable candidates and increase the efficiency of time spent on individual, face-to-face interviews. Alternatively, they may be used to gather further information on candidates who have already had a preliminary interview.

Shortlisting

As mentioned earlier, most employers will wish to interview a number of applicants before offering a position. In many instances, however, a successful recruitment campaign will attract more applicants than it would be possible to interview. The first step is therefore to reduce the applications to a manageable number, a process known as shortlisting. The shortlisting of applicants is, then, a selection procedure that may be performed purely on the basis of the written information that applicants have supplied or which may involve the acquisition of additional information about candidates, for example by conducting a telephone interview.

● Screening written applications

Often candidates for a post give information in their applications which is not required for making a selection decision, and which could lead to accusations of unfair discrimination if it were taken into consideration. For example, candidates might describe their family situation in order to explain a gap in their employment record. Applicants also, obviously, have to give their name so that the organisation can communicate with them. A name, however, can reveal information that is not apropos to the selection process, such as gender and racial origin. A useful technique to avoid being influenced by such information is to assess the application and make notes that refer only to relevant selection criteria. Furthermore, if these notes refer to the candidates only by their initials, any information that might indicate gender or racial origin is eliminated. If the persons shortlisting refer to these notes instead of the original applications when drawing up the shortlist, they will be greatly assisted in eliminating any unconscious biases.

As well as avoiding criteria that have been designated as unlawfully discriminatory, selectors should take care to avoid considering any other criteria that are not strictly related to the candidate's ability to do the job.

Pause for thought 7.1

Before you read on about poor practices in selection, can you suggest a methodical approach to shortlisting that would be fair and effective? That is, how would you decide on the 'relevant selection criteria' referred to above?

Selectors have been known to introduce a wide range of criteria that reflect their own preconceived ideas about people's circumstances and how people are likely to act in those circumstances. This is a matter of imposing one's own assumptions on other people. Some examples of this are selectors who exclude applicants who do not live locally, assuming they will frequently be late for work or will not wish to relocate; selectors who exclude applicants who are currently earning more than the vacancy offers; selectors who exclude people who are currently unemployed. You should even think twice before rejecting an application simply because the writing is difficult to read. Medical practitioners notoriously have poor handwriting (although this is a stereotypical image and as such should be questioned), yet they hold responsible, professional jobs.

So what is the right way to shortlist applicants? If you have read the chapter on recruitment (Chapter 6), you will remember that certain documents should be available to support the whole of the recruitment and selection process. The person specification or competency profile, in particular, plays an important role throughout the selection process. Applications should be assessed against the skills and knowledge requirements listed on the person specification, and where possible against the personal qualities, although it may be more practical to assess the latter at the interview stage. Selectors should note where candidates meet the requirements of the person

Table 7.1 Assessment of CV with reference to person specification for a receptionist

Post: Receptionist		
Attributes	**Essential**	**Desirable**
Knowledge	Knowledge of clerical systems +	Knowledge of the company –
Skills	Experience of clerical work + Experience in handling queries in person and over the telephone ? Ability to extract information from a computerised database –	Supervisory experience –
Personal qualities	Polite manner ? Ability to work under pressure ?	

specification/competency profile and where they lack the required skills and knowledge. Each application could be scored with a series of + and – signs or with numerical grades if you wish to weight the criteria you have selected. To provide you with an example, the CV that appears later in this chapter, in Activity 7.3, has been assessed in relation to the receptionist person specification in Chapter 6 (see Table 7.1).

Pause for thought 7.2

Pause for thought 7.2 Why do you think some of the skills and personal qualities listed in the person specification in Table 7.1 have been marked with a question mark?

A preliminary evaluation of most of the skills of the applicant can be made at the shortlisting stage, but in this particular instance it is not possible to judge the applicant's personal qualities, for instance, based on the information contained in the curriculum vitae. Assessment of these elements will have to be made later in the selection process, and the question marks merely indicate that no assessment can be made at present.

If possible, at least two people should undertake to shortlist from the applications received, and they should do this independently of one another. After the initial selection they can then compare their evaluations of applicants, discuss any discrepancies in their judgements and justify the decisions they have made. If the two shortlisters are following the same objective process, there should be a fair amount of agreement about suitable candidates, but the involvement of two people increases the objectivity of the process and helps to eliminate the effects of individual biases. The shortlisters should end up with a ranked list of candidates using the number of pluses and minuses given to each candidate. Typically they will try to obtain six suitable candidates to be invited for interview for a single vacancy, but this number will vary according to circumstances.

Welch (1998) reported that some organisations were beginning to use the Internet in their shortlisting process for graduates in the late 1990s. By getting students to complete online career and personality questionnaires which were matched against identified competencies, it was claimed that organisations could filter out as many as 90 per cent of applications at a very early stage in the selection procedure. With more experience of this approach, however, it has been recognised that, while electronic techniques can be useful in eliminating a number of unsuitable candidates (CIPD, 2009f), some candidates may potentially also be rejected simply because they did not use the precise terminology that the IT system is set up to search for (CIPD, 2009b). This type of shortlisting software must therefore be used with caution.

A shortlisting checklist

- At least two people to shortlist applications independently.
- Note where applications meet and fall short of the person specification/competency profile.
- Separate all applications according to agreed criteria: suitable/possible/unsuitable.
- Rank the suitable applications.
- Shortlisters to confer on person specification/competency criteria only and select suitable number to call for interview.
- Use IT systems with caution.

Job interviews

It is amazing how many managers still claim to be good judges of character and ability based on very short acquaintance. These managers will tell you that within a few minutes they can tell whether they are going to get on with someone, and whether that person will do well in the job. This kind of overconfidence is a major contributing factor to the low validity of interviews as a selection method. The concept of validity will be discussed in more detail later in the chapter, but it can be stated here that the strategic HRM approach would suggest that employees are too valuable a resource to be selected or rejected in such a subjective and uninformed manner.

Telephone interviewing

Telephone interviewing as an initial part of the recruitment and selection process became more popular early in the twenty-first century, particularly with the growth of call centres. For these employers, telephone skills are an essential requirement for many jobs, and the telephone interview can be used as a legitimate method of testing the telephone manner of applicants (CIPD, 2010a). The Institute cautions, however, that telephone interviews should be monitored to ensure that they are conducted fairly. They should, therefore, be just as structured and focused as face-to-face interviews and not be allowed to degenerate into just a chat over the phone.

The IRS (2007c) state that employers may use telephone interviews as a means of reducing the costs of the selection process. They can be used to provide an initial sifting from a large number of applications or to ensure that applicants satisfy some of the basic criteria for selection before using other selection techniques which might involve more expense.

Face-to-face interviews and the concepts of validity and reliability

Almost every employer includes a face-to-face interview as part of the selection process. The initial selection interview might be delegated to a recruitment agency or a local job centre or might be conducted over the telephone, but most employers would be reluctant to take on new employees without having met them first in person. The face-to-face interview continues to be the most popular and frequently used method of selection, even though research studies have found interviews to be poor predictors of future performance in a job (Makin and Robertson, 1986) depending, of course, on how they are conducted. Poorly conducted interviews can lead to decisions with low predictive validity, which means that they do not test what they purport to test, i.e. ability to perform a job well. The problem of the low validity of interviews is compounded by evidence about poor interviewer reliability, i.e. that two interviewers may form very different opinions about the same candidate. As the CIPD (2010a) points out, these limitations on the validity and reliability of the interview mainly stem from the behaviours of inexpert interviewers. A number of interviewer errors contribute to the low validity of interviews, and awareness of these is one step towards eliminating them or at least reducing their impact.

Interviewer errors

Interviewer errors arise because of the perceptual process we all use to deal with the world around us. From myriad stimuli that surround us, we select those to which we will pay attention. This process is known as perceptual selection, and what we select is determined by our own experience, personality and motivation. This means that we focus on certain aspects of our environment and ignore others. Our own experience might lead us into focusing on inappropriate stimuli in some circumstances and ignoring information that is in fact apposite. A number of such perceptual errors have been identified, and those most relevant to the selection process are described here.

The halo effect

Some candidates for interview make a very strong impression on the interviewers as soon as they enter the room. They may be well dressed and attractive, have a firm handshake and a very confident manner. Research has shown that if interviewers form an initial good impression of a candidate, this has two effects. First, this good impression tends to influence positively their interpretation of everything else that happens in the interview. Second, the interviewers will seek more positive information to confirm their initial judgement. This is known as the halo effect, but it can also happen with an initial negative impression. This is sometimes referred to as the horns effect and can be detected when interviewers start to seek negative information to confirm their first impressions.

Making snap decisions

It is often said of interviewers that they make up their minds about a candidate in the first five minutes and then do not change their assessment of that person's suitability. In terms of the perceptual process this means that interviewers are responding to a limited range of stimuli and not taking the opportunity to elicit a wide range of information.

Hiring people like oneself

There is an innate human tendency to identify with people who are like us and share several of our characteristics. An outgoing person may feel more comfortable with other extroverts and the opposite is true for a more reserved person. These characteristics do not, however, necessarily equate with the ability to perform a job, and it is probably detrimental to an organisation to have only like-minded people on its staff. If interviewers fall prey to this tendency, they are said to be hiring in their own image.

Stereotyping

Allowing one's stereotyped images of people to influence selection decisions is probably the most dangerous of the perceptual errors, and could very often equate to some form of unlawful discrimination. Stereotyping occurs when a person is identified primarily with some group that he or she belongs to and then is assumed to have a range of characteristics that are thought to be common to all members of that group. Some examples of stereotypes are: that Scots are frugal; that students are irresponsible and lazy; that Americans are brash and loud. It is not possible for all members of a group to have the same characteristics, and we should all guard against forming biases of this nature.

Making assumptions

The halo effect, making snap decisions and stereotyping are all specific forms of assumptions based on limited information, but making assumptions can also be a more generalised fault. There are many instances where inexpert interviewers might tend to impose their own personal view of how they would act in particular circumstances, instead of ascertaining how the interviewee would act. One example of this is assuming that women will bear the major responsibility for child care, or that women are less likely to move their families to take up a new post.

Gathering insufficient or irrelevant information

Again, all the specific perceptual errors discussed in this section could be attributed to gathering insufficient or irrelevant information. Interviewers obviously need to be aware of this as a general fault and make sure they use proper techniques to counteract it.

The contrast effect

Imagine yourself in the following scenario. You are a final year student and you have been asked by one of your lecturers to judge presentations being made by students in the first year of your course. You are using a scale of 1–5, with 1 being poor and 5 being excellent. You watch one presentation and the student makes a really poor job of it. The presentation is boring, too long and the student uses no visual aids. You rate this presentation as poor and give it a score of 1. The next student gives a presentation which is somewhat better, and it is a relief to you that this presentation is not as boring. The contrast between the two presentations is likely to have an effect on your judgement, and you will probably rate the second presentation higher than you would have done on some objective measure. If the presentation actually merits a 3, you may rate it as a 4 because of the contrast effect. It means that candidates at interview may be rated more highly than they merit by interviewers because they were preceded by a poor candidate, and by contrast they appear to be better than they are in reality.

Interviewer errors: summary

● Making snap decisions.
● Gathering negative/positive information to support first impressions.
● Hiring in one's own image.
● Stereotyping.
● Making assumptions; imposing one's personal view of how one would act in other people's personal circumstances.
● Gathering insufficient/irrelevant information.
● Contrast effect.

Good practice designed to eliminate interviewer errors

As stated earlier, the very fact that you are aware of interviewer errors can help you to eliminate them if you wish to do so and if you make a conscious effort while you are interviewing. There are also some techniques that you can deliberately employ to diminish the effects of interviewer errors.

Gather sufficient information

This is a general rule that will help to eliminate most interviewer errors. The interviewer should not decide early in the interview that a candidate is unsuitable and then fail to pursue the whole range of information necessary to make a proper decision. Interviewers who persist in gathering information even when a candidate has initially made a poor impression are achieving several goals that may contribute to better decisions:

● They are resisting the halo/horns effect.
● They are making an effort to gather the full range of information.
● They are giving candidates every opportunity to present themselves fully.

Structured interviews

Conducting interviews in a structured fashion will also contribute to the aim of gathering sufficient information on all candidates. Structured interviews involve the following steps:

● Design a set of questions to elicit information relevant to the selection decision.
● Provide all candidates with an opportunity to answer this complete set of questions.

Pause for thought 7.3

How would you go about designing a relevant set of questions? Why should you ask all of the questions of each candidate?

The way to design the basic set of questions for a structured interview is, of course, to refer to the person specification/competency profile and the job description, and to create questions related to the tasks, knowledge, skills and personal qualities listed there. The quality of the information gained will be influenced by the types of question asked, and this is dealt with later in this chapter.

Asking all candidates the same questions means that you will have a similar profile for each candidate which you can compare and use to assess each candidate against the others. Notice that the structured interview gives you a basic set of comparable details; you may wish to supplement this with individualised information on each candidate, clarifying particular details of their experience, etc. In other words, the structured interview guarantees that you will collect certain information, but it is not a straitjacket that restricts you to that information. The CIPD (2010a) refers to this as semi-structured interviewing which allows for the gathering of a wider range of relevant information and which may make candidates feel more comfortable. As well as preparing and using the questions for the structured interview, the interviewer must be adept at using probing questions, as described later.

Giving all candidates an opportunity to respond to a set of questions can also help to diminish the halo effect and gives a nervous candidate time to relax and do better as the interview proceeds. Preparing a set of questions in advance also means that interviewers:

- can relax during the interview and concentrate on the candidates' responses, rather than be thinking about what to ask next
- are less likely to inadvertently ask questions that may be construed as discriminating illegally.

More than one interviewer

In general, the one-on-one interview is not regarded as best practice for selection purposes. The IRS (2007b) identified that 98.7 per cent of employers in their study on selection processes involve at least two interviewers for some of their posts. One reason for this is to do with equal opportunities; the interviewer errors that arise because of individual perceptions are less likely to occur if more than one person is involved in interviewing.

The people involved in the selection process will vary from one organisation to another depending on factors such as size, management philosophy and organisational culture. The IRS (2007b) has, however, identified an increasing trend of devolution of selection responsibilities to line managers. Obviously, line managers know most about the work that needs to be done and are well-placed to judge whether candidates have the appropriate knowledge, skills and personal qualities. However, as the IRS (2007b) also points out, selection interviewing demands particular skills, so most employers recognise the need for training for line managers and others to be able to carry out this duty successfully.

Since human resource management specialists often hold responsibilities for an organisation's equality programmes, they often have some input into the interviewing process even if increased devolution of responsibilities to line managers means that there is not always an HR presence at the interview itself.

Consideration can also be given to involving others affected by the post, such as co-workers or members of other departments. Acceptance of the new employee can be increased if others are involved in the selection process, but this must be balanced against unwieldiness and, of course, everyone involved in interviewing must be trained.

Only trained people involved in interviews

Although the people involved in interviews may have different interests, they should all be working towards the same outcome, i.e. to select the best person for the post in a fair and objective manner. Training for interviewers usually includes an awareness of equality issues and development of questioning skills.

Allow sufficient time for interviews

In 1995 the BBC broadcast a series of programmes showing the recruitment processes followed by a number of organisations; one of the managers who took part in these programmes commented on the length of a selection interview on which one will base the decision about someone one may be working with on a daily basis for many years. He expressed a great sense of unease about the need to make such an important decision on such short acquaintance. Given what we have said in this chapter about the need to gather full information from candidates through careful questioning, it is self-evident that sufficient time must be alloc ated to the interview for this to occur.

Eliminating interview errors: summary

- Gather sufficient information.
- Structured interviews: gather the same, job-related information from all candidates.
- More than one interviewer.
- Only trained people involved in interviews.
- Allow sufficient time.

Interviewer skills

In addition to the techniques you may wish to employ to avoid common interviewer errors, there is a range of skills you can develop to ensure your effectiveness as an interviewer. Since we have established that both HRM specialists and line managers should be involved in selection interviews, these skills are important to both. The skills are presented below, followed by a more detailed discussion:

- Carry out thorough planning and preparation for the interview.
- Put candidates at their ease.
- Keep body language and tone of voice neutral.
- Ask a range of relevant questions.
- Encourage the candidate to talk.
- Record the information.
- Invite and respond to candidates' questions.
- Close the interview.
- Evaluate information and reach a decision.
- Record and justify the decisions.

Planning and preparation

The list of interview skills could almost double as a list of interview stages, and indeed the planning stage entails thinking through and planning the whole process, especially if you are responsible for coordinating it. This includes:

- arranging for the reception of candidates
- ensuring you have a private room available where you will not be interrupted

- reviewing the application forms so that you are properly informed about candidates
- reviewing the job description and person specification/competency profile so you are properly informed about the requirements of the position
- preparing the interview questions
- designing an assessment scheme in order to evaluate the candidates
- ensuring everyone knows what role they are to play in the process.

Put candidates at ease

It is widely acknowledged that most job applicants feel nervous about interviews, and this anxiety may be increased if the candidate is faced by a panel of interviewers or a series of interviews with different people. In some cases, interviewers deliberately subject candidates to stress, arguing that they wish to test the person's ability to handle stress in the job (see Figure 7.1).

A counter-argument to this is that the interview situation is stressful enough anyway, so there is no need to induce stress artificially. If one of the main objectives is to acquire as much information as possible from candidates, it is probably better on balance to try to get candidates to relax and talk freely. It is also worth remembering that for every candidate who eventually joins your organisation, there may be five or more for whom the interview is their only contact with you. It is better for an organisation's public image if these five leave the interview feeling they were treated properly.

Pause for thought 7.4   Make a list of three things you could do to help put interviewees at ease.

Figure 7.1   How not to put candidates at ease

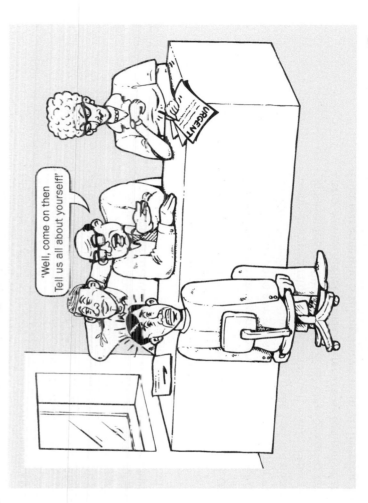

'Well, come on then
Tell us all about yourself!'

The techniques you might use to help put candidates at ease include:

● making introductions and explaining the interview process so that candidates have a chance to settle in before they have to respond to questions

● engaging in small-talk about the traffic difficulties, how the candidate travelled to your location, etc.

● starting the interview with easy questions that entail straightforward description rather than opinion or interpretation, for example: 'What are your major duties in your current post?' rather than 'How do your current duties make you qualified for this position?'

Keep body language and tone of voice neutral

While interviewers should encourage applicants to open up and divulge relevant information, it is important that they do not overly influence candidates during interviews by indicating whether or not the candidate is doing well. This is especially so if a candidate starts out with weak responses, as any sign of impatience or boredom on the part of the interviewer will no doubt make the candidate more nervous, contributing to the horns effect.

Questioning techniques

In addition to using a variety of types of question, there is another component of effective information gathering that is probably just as important as asking the right questions. That is *listening*.

It is difficult to concentrate for prolonged periods of time, and often recruiters will find themselves involved in a series of interviews stretching over many hours or even a number of days. Interviewers need to become practised in the techniques of active listening (Rogers and Farson, 1976) to ensure that they maintain their concentration and gather as much information from the interviewee as possible. In general, active listening refers to the development of listening skills to promote better communication. It includes the use of reflective responses to develop and check understanding, but also involves a range of techniques to reassure the partner in conversation that they are being listened to. Reflective responses are used when the interviewer is trying to gain a better understanding of an interviewee, using a variety of techniques to encourage the interviewee to talk. Reflective responses include silence, non-committal conversational sounds, paraphrasing and asking questions to seek clarification of what an interviewee has said.

Silence; conversational sounds; non-verbal cues

These techniques are meant to encourage the other person to continue talking so he or she may go on to give you additional relevant information. Silence must be used judiciously, since a prolonged silence could lead to embarrassment and would inhibit communication rather than promoting it. Using silences merely means not jumping in too quickly to fill a pause; allow the other person to gather his or her thoughts. The term 'conversational sounds' refers to those companionable sounds we make to reassure someone who is talking that we are in fact listening. We use phrases such as: 'Yes,

I see', 'Mmm', 'Oh, right', often accompanied by a nod of the head, a questioning frown or a smile. Consciously practising these techniques also ensures that you do not do too much of the talking.

Paraphrasing and asking for clarification

Paraphrasing what a person has said demonstrates active listening because you have to have listened carefully in order to do it. Summarising back to a person what you understand them to have said may at times also lead to further clarification as the person confirms or amends your understanding in response. Asking for clarification of a specific point again confirms that you were listening attentively and elicits more information.

Further techniques

As mentioned before, body language is important and can influence the proceedings. Maintaining good, but appropriate, eye contact with the interviewee, looking interested and not yawning or looking bored are all components of active listening.

Actively practising these techniques will help the interviewer to stay alert and concentrate on what the interviewee is saying. A further effect of active listening is that the interviewee is constantly reassured of your attention, which makes him or her more comfortable with the process.

Types of question

There are a number of ways of phrasing a question, and each will have an effect on the likely response. In choosing which type of question to ask, you should consider what the purpose of the question is. What type of information do you wish to elicit from the candidate?

The three basic forms of question are the closed question, the leading question and the open question. The closed question invites a response of 'yes' or 'no'; the leading question indicates to the interviewee what kind of response is expected; the open question is phrased in such a way that interviewees are encouraged to speak freely and give information about themselves. Here are some examples of each type of question, together with a comment on what sort of response might be expected.

Closed questions

● Did you work with a computer at XYZ Ltd?
● Have you had sales experience?

Comment

Each of these questions could be answered by a simple response 'yes' or 'no'. If the interviewer is trying to elicit as much information as possible, these questions are not very useful. Closed questions can, however, be useful for checking the correctness of information. An example might be: 'Did you use Excel on the computer at XYZ Ltd?'

Pause for thought 7.5 Before you go on to read about leading questions and open questions, stop to rephrase the two closed questions in the example above as open questions. That is, how would you put these questions so that an interviewee would be encouraged to speak more freely?

Leading questions

- You do enjoy working with the computer, don't you?
- You have had sales experience, haven't you?

Comment

The phrasing of these questions implies that an affirmative response is expected of the candidate. At the very least this will destroy the confidence of a candidate who answers in the negative. It could also induce a nervous candidate to give false information on the spur of the moment. It is so easy just to answer 'yes' to questions like those above.

Open questions

- What experience have you had of working with a computer?
- Tell me about your experience working with a computer.
- What did you like about working in sales?
- How did you decide to take up a career in HR management?

Comment

None of these questions can be answered with a one-word answer, neither do they indicate what the questioner expects to hear. Open questions usually start with words like what, why or how. Alternatively, the interviewee can simply be asked to talk about something: 'Tell me about . . .'

It should be obvious that the majority of the questions in an interview should be phrased as open questions, with relatively few closed questions to check facts. Leading questions are not very useful and should be avoided.

Situational and behavioural questions

It is a fairly straightforward task to gather information about qualifications and skills by careful questioning and listening and by using a variety of tests. Assessing attitudes and interpersonal skills is more difficult. Situational and behavioural questions are suitable for this purpose, as well as for assessing skills and how these would be translated into behaviour in the workplace. Research has long since indicated that the use of these two types of question improves both the reliability and the validity of selection interviews (Latham *et al.*, 1980; Weekley and Gier, 1987). More recent research from the IRS confirms employers' attempts to improve the effectiveness of their selection processes by using competency-based questions (Murphy, 2008). These are essentially behavioural or situational questions based on a competency framework where such a framework is in place.

Both types of question require an analysis of critical incidents in the job. Interviewers can ascertain what would be critical incidents in the post using methods like those used to draw up a job description or to develop criteria on which to appraise a person's performance or evaluate a post. You will be able to read about the last two issues in Chapters 9 and 10. For the purposes of selection, you will need to design questions that will get candidates to talk about their performance in these areas and the competencies they would call upon (situational) or have demonstrated in the past (behavioural).

Situational interview questions

The interviewee is presented with a situation that represents a typical incident in the job for which he or she being interviewed, and is then asked to describe what he or she would do in this situation.

The responses to a situational interview question need to be assessed carefully in order to achieve increased reliability between interviewers. There should be prior agreement on what constitutes a poor, an acceptable and a good answer to the question. A model of each type of answer should be designed, and points can be assigned to each level of response. Each interviewer then grades the actual answers of interviewees accordingly.

Latham *et al.* (1980) describe a fairly complex manner of designing the graded responses to situational questions, involving knowledge of what was said by previous candidates who turned out to be poor, average or good performers. For most interview situations in practice it is probably adequate for managers to suggest the type of behaviour that they would regard as poor, average and good performance.

An example of a situational question and graded answers for the receptionist post described in Chapter 6 is shown in Figure 7.2.

Figure 7.2   Example of a situational question with graded answers

Critical incident

Dealing with several customer enquiries simultaneously, maintaining a customer centred approach and a friendly manner.

Situational question

One of the assistant receptionists has just gone to the cafeteria for his 15-minute coffee break and the other one is working in a nearby office on some invoices that have to be cleared this morning. You have just answered the phone and the caller has a query to which you don't know the answer. Suddenly a number of people come to the reception desk at the same time, so you have a queue of people wanting assistance. How would you handle this situation?

Ranked answers

3 (poor performance)
- Ask the caller to call back in the afternoon.
- Deal with the people at the reception desk.
- Find out the answer to the phone query.

4 (average performance)
- Ask the caller to hold.
- Deal with the people at the reception desk.
- Find out the answer to the phone query and deal with the phone caller.

5 (good performance)
- Explain the need to find out data to the phone caller, and offer to call back.
- Apologise for the delay to the people at the reception desk, and recall the assistant receptionist to the reception area. Deal with the customers together.
- Find out the answer to the phone query and call the customer back.

Behavioural interview questions

Behavioural questions are normally phrased in a standard way. They are similar to situational questions in that interviewees are presented with a situation that represents a typical incident in the job for which they are being interviewed. The interviewees are then asked to recount what they did in a similar situation in a past position. Candidates may also be informed that competency in a particular area is required, and asked to recount the circumstances in which they have demonstrated that competency. Although this is a very useful approach, there are disadvantages compared to situational interview questions:

- Candidates who do not have any previous experience of the specific incidents will be at a disadvantage. Candidates may also not have had the opportunity to demonstrate a particular skill and yet may well be capable of developing it, given the chance. Interviewers will have to decide whether it is the previous experience that is important or the way people would behave in a given situation.

- It is not possible to design and rank expected answers, as candidates may respond with reference to a wide range of examples of when they encountered similar situations. It should be possible, however, to identify the range of skills and competencies you would expect candidates to allude to in their answers.

An example of a behavioural question for the receptionist post is: 'Tell us about an incident when you had to deal with several things at the same time'

Probing questions

Interviewers need to get over their inhibitions about pursuing information, and practised interviewers often go back to clarify what candidates have said before. The interview is essentially a one-time-only opportunity for both the interviewer and the candidate, and if candidates seem evasive, they may legitimately not realise what you want to know. It is fairer to do all you can to gather relevant information than to superimpose your own assumptions; you should find some polite but insistent way of doing it. It is better to reject someone for something you know than for an assumption made because information was missing.

Within this context it should be noted that interviewers will have to ask individualised questions to obtain clarification related to individual applicants. The set of questions designed for the structured interview is not meant to inhibit the collection of relevant information.

Questions to be avoided

In spite of what we have said about relating interview questions to the job description and person specification for the post, you will still no doubt encounter many interviewers who ask questions that do not seem to have been designed in this way. Some very general questions have almost become standard fare in interviews, such as:

- What are your strengths and weaknesses?
- Where do you see yourself in five years' time?
- Tell me about yourself.

Such questions might elicit relevant information, but they are vague, and given the time constraints of the interview process, it is better for the interviewer to focus more narrowly on essential information.

There are other questions that do not overtly contribute much to the selection process, apart perhaps from attempting to relax a nervous candidate by asking easy questions. These include questions like 'What were your favourite subjects at school?' or 'What do you do in your spare time?' In the limited time available for an interview, there are job-related questions that can be answered in a straightforward fashion which can be used to help candidates relax and which will contribute more to the proceedings. Such a question might be: 'Tell me what you do on a typical day at work.'

It should also be borne in mind that questions about what an applicant does outside of work may be regarded as an infringement of a person's right to respect for their private and family life under the Human Rights Act 1998. Candidates may also feel pressured by such questions into giving information that could potentially be perceived as unlawfully discriminatory, for example if a person is heavily involved in a religious group in their spare time or participates in gay rights campaigns. The widening scope of equality legislation reinforces the fact that employment interviews should focus on work issues and not personal matters. Indeed, the ACAS guidelines on how to implement the sexual orientation regulations (now covered by the Equality Act 2010) recommend the avoidance of questions on a person's social life and the guidelines on the religion and belief regulations (now also covered by the Equality Act 2010) recommend the avoidance of questions on communal involvement (ACAS, 2009a and 2009b).

A third variety of questions of dubious merit consists of those that seem intended to put candidates on the defensive, including statements such as, 'You seem to think very highly of your interpersonal skills.'

All these questions should be judged against what they are meant to achieve. Better results are achieved by interviewers who concentrate on formulating questions related to the job and the skills, knowledge and qualities needed to perform well in the post. It bears repeating here that your questions should be linked to the job description and person specification/competency profile, that you should be able to demonstrate that this is the case and that you should be able to justify why every question is being asked.

Discriminatory questions

If you conduct structured interviews with a planned set of questions that have been designed on the basis of a properly constructed person specification, you are unlikely to ask any questions that are discriminatory in terms of the Equality Act 2010. The implication behind your questions is that if you ask the question, you intend to use the information to make your decision. Avoid any question that would result in your acquiring information on things the legislation or your policies have said would constitute unfair discrimination, for example marital status, race, age of dependants.

One procedure that is often recommended to avoid accusations of unfair sex discrimination is to ask the same questions of all candidates, both male and female. This will supposedly preclude any suspicion of an intention to discriminate against female applicants. However, in today's society there is still generally an expectation that women bear more responsibility for child care than men. If a young woman said she had two children under the age of five, and a young man said the same thing, most people would draw different conclusions about the relative impact of this.

These assumptions are based on each individual's experiences and are not necessarily true for other people. It is best practice, therefore, simply to avoid questions about personal circumstances unless there is some specific element of the job, such as the ability to undertake shift work, where personal circumstances are in fact relevant. Even then, candidates can be asked whether something like shift work will cause them any problems, rather than the interviewers' imposing their own view of whether or not the applicant should undertake such work.

Questions for candidates with little or no work experience

We have firmly established that it is best practice to acquire work-related and job-specific information from applicants to make good selection decisions. However, we must concede that a modified approach may be necessary when dealing with individuals who have no work experience, little work experience or no recent work experience. Typical examples we can identify include:

- school leavers
- students graduating from college and university
- the long-term unemployed.

Asking open questions about work experience related to the tasks involved in the vacancy would obviously not be very productive with this group of applicants. However, it should still be possible to ask about relevant transferable skills. The interviewer might need to give fuller explanations about the requirements of the organisation before asking about the applicant's related knowledge and abilities. You should have identified that situational questions are suitable for people with little experience, so it would make sense to develop such questions in this case rather than behavioural questions. In addition, interviewers faced with people who are not currently accustomed to the working environment might recognise the potential for increased nervousness, and therefore decide to spend more time at the commencement of the interview on putting the applicant at ease.

Before we leave this discussion of the interviewer's questions, we should once again emphasise that it is more important for the candidate to talk than the interviewer. Interview questions are designed as keys to unlock information, and sometimes a pause to allow the candidate time to reflect can be more effective than jumping in with a new question.

Encourage candidates to talk

Proper formulation of questions should ensure that the candidate does most of the talking and not the interviewers. However, it is worth repeating that allowing candidates to talk to obtain the information you need is the objective of the interview, and interviewers should practise due restraint.

For all questions, you should decide in advance what it is you are trying to find out with the question; you can then rephrase and probe if the candidate does not respond with the expected information.

Record the information

You could simply note how each candidate scored on the criteria you are using to assess applicants, but it is much more helpful to have a record of what the candidate actually said. This means that it is necessary for someone to take notes during the interview. It is difficult to take notes, pay attention to what the candidate is saying and keep a normal flow of conversation going, but interviewers develop this skill with experience. Alternatively, roles/tasks can be shared among a panel of interviewers by pre-arrangement. It is also best to explain to candidates what you are doing and why someone is taking notes.

ACTIVITY 7.3

As Office Services Manager, you have received the CV shown in Figure 7.3 for the position of receptionist described in Chapter 6. The HR trainee has prepared three sets of questions, and asked you which set you would like to use in the interviews.

1 Review the following sets of questions and choose the one that you feel would get the best results. Give reasons for your choice and state why you rejected the other two sets.

2 Develop any further questions you would like to ask.

3 Use the chosen, revised set of questions as a basis for mock interviews with members of your class, using the data on the applicant's CV as the interviewee's background. Evaluate whether or not you have obtained sufficient information to make a selection.

Interview questions

Set 1

1 I see you've been with Marvel Appliances for a year. Do you like working there?
2 How do you think your past work experience has prepared you for this job?
3 Can you tell us of a time when you had to deal with several things at the same time?
4 One of our assistant receptionists is male and he's older than you. Do you think you'd have any problems being his supervisor?
5 What do you think contributes to good customer care?

Set 2

1 I see you've been with Marvel Appliances for a year. Can you tell me a little about what you do there on a typical day?
2 How do you think your past work experience has prepared you for this job?
3 I'd like to describe a typical situation you might encounter in this post, then ask you how you would respond to it.

   One of the junior receptionists has just gone to the cafeteria for his 15-minute coffee break and the other one is working in a nearby office on some invoices that have to be cleared this morning. You have just answered the phone and the caller has a query to which you don't know the answer. Suddenly a number of people come to the reception desk at the same time, so you have a queue of people wanting assistance. How would you handle this situation?
4 Can you describe any supervisory experience you have had?
5 What do you think contributes to good customer care?

Set 3

1 I see you've been with Marvel Appliances for a year. Why do you want to leave?
2 How do you think your past work experience has prepared you for this job?
3 Can you tell us of a time when you had to deal with several things at the same time?
4 What do you do in your leisure time, when you're not at work?
5 If we employed you, how long do you think you would stay with us? What about your personal plans for the future?

Go to the student materials for Chapter 7 on the companion website at www.pearsoned.co.uk/foothook to find our comments on these sets of questions.

Candidates' questions

It is good practice in an interview, usually at the end, to allow candidates an opportunity to ask questions about the post. Remember that both parties can benefit from the interview being a two-way process; it is important that prospective employees find out about the job and the organisation so that they can make an informed decision if offered the position. This may help to avoid the situation where someone is hired, only to decide after a short while that they are not suited to the job. As well as responding to candidates' questions, organisations can employ other techniques to supply information to applicants. Some of these, such as supplying job descriptions

Figure 7.3 Example of a curriculum vitae

CURRICULUM VITAE

Joan Reives

Address: 23 Burns Street
                Dorton
                Manchester
                M16 9BF

Telephone: 0161 000 000 (home)   0161 000 000 (work)
                0777 66 000 000 (mobile)

Education:
2008   Stalybridge High School   6 GCSEs incl English and Maths
2010   Stalybridge College   3 A-levels (Business Studies, English and History)

Employment:
July 2010–present   Assistant Receptionist, Marvel Appliances

My duties include welcoming visitors to the company, and calling the person they wish to see to the reception area.
I answer all incoming calls and transfer calls to other employees. I perform clerical and administrative tasks for all departments when reception duties allow.

July–Sept 2009   Sales Assistant, Allgood's Department Store
I assisted customers to choose purchases and completed cash or credit card transactions.

Personal statement:
I have lots of experience as an assistant receptionist and working with customers. I am ambitious and hardworking and I know I could do a good job as a receptionist. I think I am ready for a promotion.

References available on request.

---

and organisational literature, are relevant to the recruitment process, and others, such as realistic job previews, usually take place during the selection process. Realistic job previews are discussed more fully later in this chapter. Company web pages are also an excellent source of information for candidates.

Close the interview

To close the interview, the interviewer should thank the interviewee for attending and inform him or her of what to expect next. This may include a second stage of interviews for selected candidates, a variety of tests, the time frame for the decision and details about how candidates will be informed about the outcome.

Evaluate information

Even if the interview has been carefully structured, with the involvement of several interviewers and the use of a range of well-designed questions, there is still a temptation at this stage to revert to making a decision based on gut feeling or the overall impression that candidates have made. In order to achieve a more objective evaluation of the mass of information that has now been gathered, it is possible to devise a scoring system, either for the answers to interview questions or for the elements of the person specification. Marks can be allocated to each question and questions can be weighted according to their relative importance. It would also be possible to stipulate that a candidate should achieve a pass mark on a question of particular significance in order to be considered further. For example, candidates for an HR position might be rejected for giving an unacceptable answer on a sex or race discrimination issue, no matter how well they performed in the rest of the interview.

A numerical score for each candidate will allow the interviewers to create a ranked order of candidates following an agreed method. Another system that could be used is quite simply to mark the person specification/competency profile for each candidate, + for the criteria that have been met, and − for those that have not. The use of essential and preferred categories implies some weighting of elements.

Record and justify decision

The methodical approach described in the previous section helps the selection panel to justify why they have selected the chosen candidate and why the others have been rejected. All reasons for the decisions reached should be expressed in terms of where candidates did or did not meet the criteria stipulated in the person specification/competency profile.

It is important to keep a written record of these factors for several reasons:

● To be able to present evidence of a proper and fair procedure should a candidate decide to pursue a case under any aspect of the equality legislation.

● To be able to provide feedback to candidates who request it. Increasingly, applicants for posts do this in their quest to make a good impression and to improve their chances of finally securing a post. As you will read in the following sections, there is an obligation to provide information to candidates who have completed psychometric tests, but it is part of an organisation's good image to be able to respond to requests of this nature from rejected applicants in any case.

● To ensure that interviewers follow a rigorous and methodical process.

CASE STUDY 7.1 Recruitment and selection

The Fabric Brothers' recruitment drive

Thomas and Edward Fabric founded a small clothing manufacturing company in the early 1960s in the north of England. Over the years the company has grown and recently the Fabric brothers won a new contract to manufacture dresses for a catalogue company. This has necessitated their taking on 10 new sewing machine operators.

Edward's son, John, has taken care of recruitment since he joined the family enterprise in 1978 when he was 20 years old. The company had functioned very much as a small, family-owned business for many years, and John developed a paternalistic attitude which has never been challenged. He let the 'girls' in the sewing room know that he was looking for some additional employees, and he posted a notice on the factory gates, advertising the vacancies as a good opportunity for, as he put it, 'ladies looking to make some extra money while your children are in school'.

John interviewed a few people who dropped in to ask about the job, and he was able to fill his 10 vacancies with no bother. He was very surprised a few weeks later to get a letter and a questionnaire from two Asian women, who had applied for the post and been interviewed but not selected. They felt that they had been discriminated against on the basis of race, so they had gone to a Citizens Advice Bureau to seek advice about how to pursue this matter. Their questionnaire included questions about whether John had asked the same questions of all applicants and what competencies had been identified as essential for the job. Talking it over with his father, John said: 'Well, I did ask them questions about how long they had been in England and whether they felt their English was good enough for the job, but surely that's not racial discrimination?'

John was actually quite upset because he did not think of himself as a racist. Of course, all the girls in the sewing room were white, but that's just the way things had worked out. Imagine his surprise, then, when a few days later he received another letter and questionnaire from a man he had rejected, indicating that he felt he had been rejected on the basis of sex. This man had once worked as a tailor, so he felt he could not have been rejected on the grounds of competence. He had sought advice from a friend with trade union experience, and he wanted information such as how many men and how many women were employed in the sewing room; how many men and how many women had been interviewed for the recent vacancy; did the company have an equal opportunities policy, and could he have a copy of it.

John knows that you have some background in HR issues, so he has turned to you to explain to him how all this could have happened and to give him some advice about what to do both now in response to these complaints, and in handling recruitment and selection in the future.

Go to the student materials for Chapter 7 on the companion website at www.pearsoned. co.uk/foothook to find our comments on this case study.

Further selection techniques

Thus far in this chapter, we have discussed interviewing techniques in great depth, and this is justified because of the predominance of interviewing as a method of selection. However, there are some strong arguments for developing a broader perspective on the selection process, and these are mainly to do with the validity of the interview as an assessment tool and with the importance of the selection process, as part of talent management, to the achievement of the strategic goals of the organisation. Given the potential strategic impact of selection decisions, it may be a good idea to obtain, in addition to the interview, some objective information, such as test results that can be scored objectively and are not subject to individual interpretation. This would help to counteract any interviewer bias present in the process.

Did you know?

A controversial example of an exercise conducted during a recruitment campaign occurred when the manager at a branch of B&Q was reported to have asked candidates to join in a dance routine during an interview day. The manager claimed that the purpose of the dance was to make candidates feel more relaxed, and the CIPD made a statement supporting the legitimacy of this approach. The authors of this textbook are rather more doubtful about the acceptability of this as part of the selection process for shop-floor staff and find it highly question-able in terms of face validity. What do you think? Reported in *Personnel Today*, 12 January 2007.

motivation to perform the task to the best of their ability. Face validity is therefore something that should be taken into consideration when choosing or designing a test.

The essential criterion in choosing any selection methods is that they should provide information that is directly related to performance on the job. This should be the guiding principle both in choosing off-the-shelf tests and in designing exercises tailor-made for a particular workplace. In their review of assessment centres, the IRS (2007a) stress that tests and exercises used to assess candidates must relate closely to the competencies required in the job they have applied for. In addition to the employer gaining relevant information, a related issue is that candidates can easily see the point of a test that requires them to do something they know will be done on the job. This increases the face validity of the test, making it more acceptable to the candidates, which may in turn affect their willingness to take the test seriously and their

Psychological testing

Psychological testing, sometimes referred to as psychometric testing, is a method of acquiring objective information about a range of individual abilities and traits. Psychological tests are defined as having the following characteristics:

- They are professionally developed and checked for reliability and validity.
- They are administered and scored in a standardised manner.
- They test maximum performance and habitual performance.
- They result in scores that can be compared to norms for relevant populations.

These characteristics will be explained more fully as we examine the various issues surrounding the uses of psychological tests.

The characteristics of psychological tests listed above indicate that their inclusion in the selection process will:

- add an element of objectivity
- increase the predictive validity of selection decisions
- measure some factors that cannot be assessed through the application form and interview.

The standardised administration of tests means that all applicants answer the same test questions in the same conditions, and objective scoring means that the scores are not open to individual interpretation as is the case with interview responses. There is a vast amount of research that underpins the development of commercially produced tests, including proofs of their reliability and validity. If this is properly documented, the user of the tests can rest assured that the tests will improve the validity of the selection process.

Because psychological tests are such complex instruments, they should be used only by people who have had specific training in how to administer them and how to interpret the results, and in fact reputable test providers will only supply commercially developed tests to properly accredited persons with appropriate training. The British Psychological Society (BPS) has approved the standards of training needed to administer and interpret tests at various levels and to give feedback to test-takers, and this training is available from various sources, including the suppliers of tests, who also provide additional training in the use of their own products. The volume of activity in this area led to the creation of a special unit within the BPS, the Psychological Testing Centre (PTC).

In 2009–2010, the PTC was engaged in reviewing its qualifications structure, and at the time of writing was preparing to launch the new standards. The Centre is moving away from the previous levels A and B to a more flexible arrangement based on modular combinations. There will be three levels which grant qualifications in test administration (Level 1), test use (Level 2), and recognition of a specialism in testing (Level 3). According to Bartram (2010), the content of the modules has been developed to match requirements set by the European Federation of Psychologists' Associations (EFPA), which should assist anyone wishing to benchmark these qualifications against the European Qualifications Framework. In addition to achieving these qualifications, test administrators and users need to be enrolled on the BPS Register of Competence in Psychological Testing.

There is a cost implication in this for employers, but the cost of training staff and of staff time for administering tests may be offset by the improved validity of selection decisions. An alternative to having a trained member of staff is to use the services of an occupational psychologist on a consultancy basis when the use of psychological testing seems to be appropriate.

An issue that attracted attention in 2001 (*People Management*), and was regarded at the time as being somewhat controversial, was the use of the Internet to conduct psychological tests. This continued for a time to be an issue where pros and cons needed to be closely examined (Pickard, 2004), but the use of online testing became more firmly established by 2005–06, mainly, it seems, to eliminate unsuitable applications early in the process, especially if a large number of applications are expected (HRzone, 2006; Sloane, 2007). Alternatively, this can be seen as a way to improve the quality of candidates who do make it through to interview following an on-line test, as reported by Yell, the publisher of directories (Wolff, 2008). In general, however, a question mark still hangs over the popularity of on-line testing. The 2007 CIPD survey of recruitment, retention and turnover reported 30 per cent of employers as using on-line tests for selection purposes which indicated an increasing trend, but the figures reported in 2008 and 2009 (CIPD, 2009d), 15 per cent and 17 per cent respectively, imply a decline in popularity. This may, of course, be in part due to changes in employers' recruitment behaviours due to the recession. On-line tests are not listed as a separate category in the 2010 survey (CIPD, 2010b).

The CIPD factsheet on psychological testing (2009c) outlines what to consider when deciding whether to use a test. Their recommendations include, first, that the test should be directly relevant to requirements specified in the person specification/competency profile and should be capable of obtaining additional, pertinent information. There is a very wide selection of tests to choose from, and test suppliers provide brochures outlining the sort of information each test will provide and what types of job each test might be appropriate for. Tests are designed with different groups of people in mind, and test suppliers offer advice about who the tests are suitable for. Some examples of designated groups for whom tests are available are middle to senior managers, administrative/supervisory employees, skilled operatives and staff who have direct customer contact. Second, test suppliers should provide evidence that the test is reliable, valid and free of any bias against any particular group of people. Third, organisations should consider issues around the standard of competence required to administer and interpret the test appropriately. Further indicators of when to use psychometric tests and questionnaires are:

● when a faulty hiring decision would be extremely costly, for example for very senior positions or when employee errors could render employers liable for high financial outlay
● when the selection ratio (the ratio of applicants to the number of positions to be filled) is high and additional information is needed so that the number of candidates can be reduced.

Psychological tests cover a range of human characteristics and may assess:

● intelligence
● ability
● interest
● motivation
● personality.

Intelligence tests

General intelligence tests assess ability in a range of skills such as verbal, arithmetical and diagrammatical reasoning, producing an overall score.

Ability tests

Ability tests focus on specific mental abilities and produce separate scores for the different skills. Sometimes a distinction is made between tests of attainment and tests of aptitude, but in fact it is not always easy to distinguish between the two. Attainment tests assess skills and knowledge that have been acquired through experience and learning, and aptitude tests measure individuals' potential to develop ability. The results of an attainment test, say after learning a foreign language, might also be an indicator of aptitude for learning that language. Since both kinds of tests examine verbal, arithmetical and diagrammatical skills, it is probably more helpful to think of them under the general heading of ability tests.

Work sample tests are an example of an attainment test, and the use of these would not require the special training outlined above. There are aptitude tests for specific occupations such as sales or banking, and test batteries that produce a profile of the candidate over a range of abilities.

Tests of interest and motivation

The relationship between interests and motivation and successful performance is not a straightforward one. For this reason these tests are not used for selection (Smith and Robertson, 1993), but interest tests can be used for career guidance and counselling, and motivation tests can be used for decisions about how best to manage people and enhance their performance by responding to what motivates them.

Personality questionnaires

The expression 'personality questionnaire' has been used in preference to 'personality test', because in terms of measuring personality characteristics there are no right and wrong answers as would be the case in questions of verbal or arithmetical reasoning. Ability tests are examples of tests of maximum performance, meaning that they reflect the best performance an individual is capable of at that point in time in the skill being tested. Personality questionnaires are indicators of habitual performance, meaning that they reflect stable traits that are likely to be revealed in typical behaviour. Of all the assessments that are carried out in the workplace, personality questionnaires are probably the most contentious, especially with regard to acceptance by candidates. For this reason, it is particularly important to explain to applicants how the test is related to performance on the job concerned and to provide feedback on the results. Test users should also monitor results to ensure that tests do not discriminate unfairly.

Personality questionnaires examine aspects of personality that have been shown through research to correlate with performance at work. Murphy and Davidshofer (2001) refer to evidence that some personality characteristics are related to job performance in general, including agreeableness, conscientiousness and openness to experience. Together with extraversion and neuroticism (actually a measure of emotional stability), these traits are known as 'the Big Five', which have been the focus of much interest in recent psychological research (Robertson, 2001; Mol et al., 2005).

Most personality questionnaires are of the self-report variety, where applicants are asked to record how they see themselves on a range of characteristics or traits. Some items may be open-ended questions asking about preferred activities, and some items may be a choice from a number of statements, asking applicants to choose which statement most resembles them or is most unlike them. These measures usually result in a profile of the person on a range of personality dimensions. One of the most well known of these instruments is Cattell's 16 Personality Factor test (16PF). The 16PF test is based on Cattell's work in isolating a range of 16 elements which he believed could be used to describe the whole spectrum of an individual's personality. Cattell's personality dimensions include reserved–outgoing, tough minded–sensitive, conservative–experimenting and relaxed–tense.

Other established tests include the Saville and Holdsworth Occupational Personality Questionnaire and the Myers-Briggs Type Indicator. The Myers-Briggs test is most often used within the framework of training to identify personality types and examine their impact on personal interactions. There are also questionnaires that measure characteristics that predict success in specific occupations.

One of the reasons why personality questionnaires are sometimes regarded with some scepticism is that in self-reporting, candidates may try to give the answers they think are expected. It is also recognised that the situation can affect the responses that people make, so personality test results are not always reliable.

This leads to a very important point with regard to the use of psychological tests in general: they should never be the sole means of assessing candidates, but should always be used as part of a wider process. Rankin (2009), reporting the results of an IRS survey, confirms that the majority of employers using tests, some 85 per cent of the survey respondents, have taken this requirement of good test usage on board.

Work sample tests

As the term suggests, a work sample test consists of getting a candidate to perform some task or element of a task that forms part of the job. You can gain a better understanding of work sample tests by working through the design process using a familiar example.

How to design a work sample test

Let us take an example of a job with which you are all familiar, that of a university or college lecturer. If you were invited to design a work sample test to be used in hiring a new lecturer in human resource management, what preliminary issues would you consider? How would you approach the task?

The first consideration is that a work sample test makes sense only if it demonstrates abilities that are a major and integral part of the job. A critical incident analysis and selection of a critical task are therefore the first step in designing a work sample test. If you think back to the job analysis techniques discussed in Chapter 6, you will realise that you could perform a simplified critical incident analysis by interviewing a number of lecturers and heads of department, and asking them what they consider to be the most important activities that contribute to success in the job. Without doubt most lecturers involved in teaching would identify the ability to conduct a seminar as a critical task.

A second consideration ought to be how the performance of the work sample will be assessed, as this will affect the way the exercise is designed, and it may influence the instructions that are given to candidates.

In deciding on your assessment criteria, you will no doubt have identified the lecturers you regard as being excellent in their seminar delivery, and then you will have identified the competencies and techniques that are part of that excellence. If you have worked with a group of colleagues you may have discussed what each of you considers to be important and agreed on a list. Your criteria will include some of the following:

- choice and relevance of topic
- knowledge of subject; integration of current material
- style of delivery
- use of materials
  - content
  - variety
  - visual aids
- ability to stimulate participation/discussion
- adequacy of preparation
- ability to handle questions.

For some of these criteria, you may also have outlined how each would be judged. Adequacy of preparation, for instance, might be judged by the absence of hesitation, well-ordered notes and materials, observable structure, control of physical equipment.

Some work samples, such as typing tests, can be assessed on an objective basis using a mathematical formula, but assessment of activities like delivering a seminar will still be subjective. It is important to have assessment guidelines to provide some level of standardisation and consequently to improve reliability among the assessors. Assessment criteria should obviously be related to what is regarded as superior performance on the job. This being the case, documentation relating to performance appraisal should be a good source of material to be used when designing work sample tests.

ACTIVITY 7.4

Make a list of the factors on which you would judge the criterion 'style of delivery'. Discuss your list with a group of fellow students and devise a set of assessment criteria for this performance criterion.

Since acceptability of the test to the candidate is an important factor, it may improve the face validity of the test to inform candidates how they will be assessed. You should consider incorporating this into the instructions to be given to candidates. For example, the instructions on conducting a seminar might be phrased as follows:

As part of the selection process you are requested to conduct a seminar in your subject area. The seminar should last one hour and be appropriate for a foundation-level course. Your performance will be judged in terms of the appropriateness of your material, the style of delivery and your ability to stimulate participation.

Assessing performance in the work sample exercise

The assessment criteria will already have been established in the process of designing the work sample. What remains is to ensure that all the assessors involved are fully cognisant of the criteria, and that there is some agreement on what represents acceptable standards of performance. This goal can be facilitated in two ways:

- the involvement of line managers both in the design of the work sample test and in the selection process
- the use of a scoring sheet listing the assessment criteria.

An example of a scoring sheet for the lecturer's work sample test is given in Figure 7.4. We can now summarise the steps you have just worked through to design a work sample exercise:

- Identify key critical factors of performance.
- Choose factors that can be tested appropriately by a work sample.
- Identify assessment criteria.
- Design the work sample exercise.
- Write instructions for the candidate,
- Design the assessment form.
- Train the assessors.

Integration of work sample tests into the selection process

Work sample tests can easily be included in a selection process to provide additional information without necessarily developing a fully fledged assessment centre approach as described in the next section. A written work sample can, for example, be requested along with submission of the application form. This is especially useful if you are expecting a large number of applications for a particular post. Many senior

Figure 7.4 Work sample assessment record

Post: Lecturer in HRM: delivery of a seminar

Assess each of the following criteria on a scale of 1–5, where 1 = poor performance, 3 = acceptable performance, 5 = outstanding performance. An indication of factors you might consider is given for some of the criteria.

	Candidate 1	Candidate 2	Candidate 3	Candidate 4
Choice and relevance of topic				
Knowledge of subject: up-to-date issues included				
Style of delivery: ability to attract and keep attention; natural, conversational tone; use of humour; movement about room				
Use of materials: content; variety; visual aids				
Ability to stimulate participation/discussion				
Adequacy of preparation: absence of hesitation; well-ordered notes and materials; observable structure; control of physical equipment				
Ability to handle questions				
Total				

posts with local and central government require the ability to absorb complex information and compile a written report for dissemination to a wide audience, integrating aspects of new legislation or policy for example.

By asking applicants to submit a written report along with their application form, such employers can potentially gain a vast amount of additional evidence about applicants' capabilities beyond what they would be able to glean from the application form alone. This would include evidence of:

- knowledge – more so than the assumption of knowledge because of academic qualifications and related experience
- report-writing skills
- ability to deliver work under the pressure of deadlines
- attitudes and abilities reflected in the content of the report.

If these factors were included in the job specification, this information would greatly assist the employer in its shortlisting task. The exercise no doubt also brings the additional advantage of discouraging any applicants who were not seriously interested in the post or not willing to make the effort to complete the assignment. Such tests can be designed to incorporate the critical requirements of various posts in any organisation.

ACTIVITY 7.5

Think of three occupations and decide on a job sample test that could be used prior to shortlisting or that could be run within the context of an interview day. Describe the test and explain how it would provide information that could be used to assess a person's suitability for the job.

When you have compiled your own list of three jobs, get together with two other students to compare your lists. Select the best three examples and present these to the rest of the class.

You can also visit the student materials on the companion website to this text at www.pearsoned.co/foothook to review our suggested answers for this activity.

● Assessment centres

As Cook (2009) points out, an assessment centre is a selection method whereby a number of competencies are assessed using a range of approaches. Each organisation can use some flexibility in deciding how many or how few assessment methods to use, but a range of techniques would have to be used to classify a selection event as an assessment centre. The IRS (2007a) report that most assessment centres take place over one day, which means that they are an intense experience for candidates and assessors alike.

Basically then, an assessment centre approach means that a number of people are assessed together by a number of assessors, using a variety of selection techniques. This enables the collection of a range of information and observation and evaluation of how individuals interact with other people. The basic assumption underlying the validity of assessment centres is that the behaviours displayed will be carried over into the workplace. Incomes Data Services (2002) point out that assessment centres are likely to lead to better results if they are designed around competencies that are used right through the recruitment and selection process. Also, the more the assessment exercises reflect aspects of what people would actually be doing in the job, the better the results are likely to be. In this way, assessment centres can also deliver a sort of realistic job preview to the candidates.

The range of activities that can make up an assessment centre include:

● work simulations
  – work samples
  – in-tray exercises
  – role plays
● group exercises and discussions
● psychological tests
● interviews
● peer assessment and self-assessment.

Makin and Robertson (1986) identified group discussion as the kind of exercise most used in assessment centres and the IDS (2002) state that all six of the companies in their study use some form of group exercise, often involving group discussion.

Work simulations

As the phrase suggests, work simulations entail engaging candidates in performing tasks that would actually be done on the job. These exercises can be performed by individuals, as in the in-tray and role-play exercises described below, or in groups if, for example, one of the tasks is to contribute to interdepartmental meetings. One issue to keep in mind when deciding what kinds of exercise to use is that individual exercises such as role plays are more demanding in terms of assessor time, since one assessor will have to be assigned to one individual rather than a group.

Work sample tests are an example of simulation, and have already been discussed in detail. In-tray exercises and role plays should be developed in the same way as we outlined for work samples in terms of isolating critical tasks, setting the assessment criteria, designing the exercise and assessing it. A typical in-tray exercise is to present a candidate for a managerial post with a number of different tasks that a manager would encounter at the beginning of the day, with instructions to prioritise the issues, respond to emails, write memos, make phone calls, etc. The IRS (2007a), however, report a decline in the popularity of in-tray exercises. A role play could be used in situations where the employee would have to deal with customer complaints, and it would be usual for someone already employed with the company to take on the role of the customer.

Group exercises

A variety of tailor-made tests or exercises have been devised by various employers to assess leadership qualities that cannot easily be judged from application forms or straightforward questioning. These tests may be used in designated assessment centre days, but some of them can also be integrated into interview days if a number of candidates are called together. The following are some examples of the kinds of exercises that are used, together with some examples of employers that are known to have used them:

- A group of applicants sit around a table; four or five assessors sit around the room behind the applicants. The lead assessor explains that they have four or five job-related topics (depending on the number of candidates), which will be read out one at a time. When a topic has been announced, one candidate must volunteer to take that topic and conduct a discussion on it. Five minutes will be allowed for the discussion, and the discussion leader will be alerted when four minutes have elapsed. No further information is given to the candidates regarding what is expected of them. (A metropolitan police force; civilian post.)

- Round table interview. The participants are candidates who have passed a preliminary interview. Candidates introduce themselves, and contribute to a discussion of what a manager's job entails. This is followed by a team exercise with instructions to devise an employment strategy for a new store. (A retail outlet selling toys; trainee manager.)

- Candidates engage in teamwork to get equipment across a stream with limited physical resources, sometimes with a designated leader, sometimes as a leaderless group. (The Army; officer.)

As with work sample tests, candidate performance can only be judged fairly if assessors have agreed in advance which competencies and job-related behaviours they are looking for.

Pause for thought 7.8

Look again at the exercise used by the metropolitan police force. What competencies and qualities do you think they were trying to assess?

The assessors would be looking for evidence of negative and positive behaviours: domination of the discussion, assertiveness, who has good ideas, ability to get people discussing a range of ideas, sensitivity to conflicting ideas, ability to incorporate conflicting views.

ACTIVITY 7.6

Think of a number of occupations and come up with four or five topics that could be raised for discussion in a similar selection test.

You can visit the student materials on the companion website to this text at www.pearsoned.co/foothook to review our suggestions.

Issues

Woodruffe (2007) identifies a number of issues that must be considered when deciding to use the assessment centre technique, in designing it, running it, and assessing its effectiveness. Some of the major issues will now be discussed briefly.

As with any other selection technique, all the exercises used in the assessment centre must be designed to identify and measure specific competencies needed in the vacant post. There is a need to involve managers and others such as current postholders in identifying what the critical competencies are. The activities involved in designing assessment centre exercises should be directly linked with the information collated in the context of job analysis that you read about in Chapter 6.

Since assessment centres are very demanding in terms of time and effort, the need for acceptance of the centre by all parties becomes crucial. Line managers are being asked to give their time to the development and the assessment of exercises and to accept that the use of assessment centres will lead to better selection. Line manager acceptance is increased if they are involved at all stages. There is also a need for candidates to feel that the assessment methods used represent a relevant process, especially as the assessment centre is more demanding in terms of their time and energy than a simple interview would be. This can be achieved partly by proper design of the exercises and partly by providing feedback.

We should also briefly consider the pros and cons of assessment centres. Certainly there are identifiable costs associated with assessment centres. These include: the training of a number of assessors; the design of exercises and line manager time devoted to this; arrangements for facilities; the time needed to organise the events and coordinate group activities with individual activities, particularly when one assessor is needed per candidate as in role-play exercises; time spent giving feedback. The argument for assessment centres is that these costs are balanced by the acquisition of additional information, the opportunity to evaluate several candidates together and the increased validity of selection decisions. The importance of talent management, as discussed in this textbook, could serve as a justification for these expenses. The IRS (2007a) also argue that assessment centres are not an unreasonable expense, given the importance of selecting the right people, and that organisations can often use a number of assessment exercises for several posts. An example of this would be if an organisation had core competencies such as communication or customer service, core meaning that an element of these competencies is required in all positions in that organisation.

Whenever a number of assessment techniques are used, there is a need to assign a weight to each technique. This is addressed later in this chapter after all assessment methods have been considered.

References

References are another method of gathering information on applicants, and a number of surveys indicate that the popularity of references as part of the selection process comes second only to the interview (Makin and Robertson, 1986; Newell and Shackleton, 1991). This is so in spite of the reference's poor showing in the validity league table. In their analysis of the accuracy of selection methods, Anderson and Shackleton (1994) found that references rated a correlation coefficient of only 0.13 (0 being equivalent to chance and 1.0 being the equivalent of perfect prediction). These facts seem to suggest that you will find the acquisition of references to be a part of most selection processes you will be involved in, but that great care is needed in their interpretation.

Pause for thought 7.9

At what stage in the selection process should a reference be solicited? Which candidates would you solicit a reference for?

There are no hard and fast rules that provide an answer to these questions, except that it is usual to solicit a reference only for a selection of applicants. There are various circumstances to consider, and this is another area where policy should be formulated to provide guidance to managers.

Most employers recognise that there are costs to providing references, so they would not wish to impose an unnecessary burden on other employers. This means restricting requests for references to an essential minimum. This would imply asking for references at a late stage in the process, after candidates have been assessed using a variety of other techniques. A further argument in support of this approach is that candidates on the whole prefer their current employer not to be approached unless there is a serious possibility that the candidate will be offered the post. The disadvantage of this view is, of course, that some time may elapse before a reference is received and the prospective employer will not want to delay in making the hiring decision.

Some organisations use all their other assessment techniques and make a job offer subject to receipt of a supportive reference. It must be remembered, however, that references are given in confidence, and in this instance, if a job offer is retracted, then the applicant will know it is because of his or her reference. This may have an impact on the extent to which referees are prepared to be truthful. Every organisation needs to think through these implications, design a policy, and stick to it.

In addition to the questions of when to secure a reference and for whom, there are considerations about what information to request, how to interpret the information supplied, and indeed what information to supply to those requesting a reference from you.

Part of the reason for the low validity of references lies in the perceptions and skill of the person writing them or in hidden agendas that may influence what is or is not said. The effects of perceptions that may occur here are similar to the interviewer errors that were discussed earlier in that our opinions of people, even when we have known them for some time, are influenced by our own perceptual set. Lukewarm descriptions of people's abilities may also be due to inadequate powers of expression or reserve on the part of the writer.

Because of the low validity of references, employers are sometimes advised to use them to check factual information only, but references may indicate some serious problem that should be pursued for further clarification or some discrepancy in factual information such as dates of employment which should also be pursued. References should obviously, therefore, be used with caution, and human resource specialists should find ways to improve the quality of the information their organisation receives in response to requests for references.

Requesting a reference

What could you do to improve the quality of references you have solicited?

Referees are able to respond better if you indicate what areas you would like feedback on, such as skills and personal qualities. Since you are seeking information on these as they relate to performance on the job, it would be useful to provide a job description or a brief outline of critical tasks. You might also consider supplying a referee with documents and checklists you will be using to evaluate candidates, such as the person specification or checklists of competencies and behaviours.

Some employers provide a questionnaire to guide the referee and help them to save time when composing a reference. This, together with a covering letter explaining your request, shows courtesy to referees and may contribute to the probability of your receiving a useful response.

Supplying references

Although you are not involved in making the selection decision when you provide a reference, it is worth considering the responsibility of the referee at this stage. In giving a reference to a potential employer, referees owe a duty of care to the receiving organisation. That is, referees would render themselves culpable if they knowingly deceived another organisation and misled it into hiring a person whom they knew to be unsuitable. In the case of *Spring v. Guardian Royal Exchange* (1994), the House of Lords also ruled that an employer has a duty to the employee to provide a reference composed with due care and may be held liable for losses due to negligent misstatement.

The law on discrimination also applies to actions that might be taken subsequent to employment, for example the provision of references. It is, therefore, unlawful to make discriminatory statements in references, for example with regard to a person's actual or perceived sexual orientation or beliefs as covered in the Equality Act 2010. ACAS (2009a and 2009b) provides some guidance on this with reference to the previous regulations which are now incorporated into the new Act.

Criminal record checks

You may remember that the Rehabilitation of Offenders Act was mentioned in Chapter 5. Essentially this Act outlines the concept of offences that are spent and protects offenders from having to reveal these spent offences. There are, however, some offences that are never spent, and some positions for which those guilty of particular offences will not be suitable. For example, any person who has been found guilty of assaulting a child would not be considered suitable for a position working in a school where unsupervised contact with children might occur. Such positions are excepted from the Rehabilitation of Offenders Act, and there are arrangements for organisations such as local authorities to obtain a check of criminal records for individuals applying for posts such as these.

Criminal Records Bureau

The Criminal Records Bureau (CRB) was set up under Part V of the Police Act 1997 and it currently supplies two levels of information relevant to individuals' suitability for certain types of employment or volunteer activities. The levels of certificate available are standard and enhanced. The main characteristics of each, as described on the CRB website **www.crb.homeoffice.gov.uk**, are:

Standard

- All convictions, including spent convictions; cautions, reprimands and warnings held on the Police National Computer.
- Available when people apply for work or volunteer activities with children or vulnerable adults.
- Available only for positions excepted under the Rehabilitation of Offenders Act 1974 (Exceptions) Order 1975.
- The individual's application form is countersigned by the representative of a registered body.
- Certificate is sent to the individual applicant and a copy to the registered body.

Enhanced

- All convictions and cautions including spent convictions as for the standard certificate, but with additional information on non-conviction incidents recorded in local police records.
- A check of the Childrens' and/or Adults' Barred List where requested.
- Available where people will have substantial, unsupervised access to children and vulnerable adults.
- Available only for positions excepted under the Rehabilitation of Offenders Act 1974 (Exceptions) Order 1975.
- The individual's application form is countersigned by the representative of a registered body.
- Certificate is sent to the individual applicant and a copy to the registered body.

As noted above, registered employers may also request information from lists of people barred from working in schools or deemed unsuitable for work with children or vulnerable adults by the Independent Safeguarding Authority (ISA) under the Vetting and Barring Scheme which was introduced in October 2009. From November 2010, registration with ISA will become necessary for all people wishing to start work or change jobs in a regulated activity, for example working in schools or care homes, and this registration will progressively become necessary for all workers in these fields.

The arrangements described here apply to England, Wales and Northern Ireland. Separate equivalent arrangements exist for Scotland. There are charges for organisations which wish to register with the Bureau and for the issue of certificates.

Employer access to records

The reason for the establishment of the CRB was to provide a safer environment for vulnerable groups such as children, the elderly, sick and the disabled, and to set up a system for handling the growing number of requests for information on those wishing to work with these groups. It should be noted that employers requiring a certificate that reveals spent convictions, i.e. a standard or enhanced certificate, must register with the Bureau, supplying it with evidence that such requests are for a legitimate purpose. In essence, this means employers referred to in the Rehabilitation of Offenders Act 1974 (Exceptions) Order 1975.

Employers using the CRB checks also have to abide by the CRB's Code of Practice on the use of such information. This means that the information should be used within the context of a recruitment policy designed to ensure the fair treatment of ex-offenders, i.e. that they should not be rejected for positions where the offence is not a relevant disqualifier. Similar to provisions under the Data Protection Act 1998, the information included in CRB checks should only be used for the purposes for which it was solicited, and it should not be retained indefinitely.

A source of potential difficulty lies with other employers enquiring and making decisions based on a person's past offences. Employers are entitled to ask potential employees the question: 'Do you have a criminal record?' Ex-offenders are protected by the Rehabilitation of Offenders Act 1974 from having to reveal *spent* convictions, but, as the CIPD (2009a) highlights, they may experience a dilemma when faced with having to declare *unspent* convictions to a potential employer. It is an accepted fact that obtaining employment is a major factor in rehabilitation and preventing recidivism, so it is socially desirable that every opportunity to secure suitable employment should be obtainable for ex-offenders. The CIPD therefore urges employers to ask questions about criminal records only where it is relevant to the job, and to handle any information provided with sensitivity. The CIPD provides several documents examining good practice with regard to selection decisions about ex-offenders, and promotes a risk assessment approach for organisations (www.cipd.co.uk/research_offenders).

Making the final selection

In this chapter on selection we have described a number of techniques for your consideration. An important issue to identify and emphasise at this stage is the need to use *all* the information that has been gathered.

There is a tendency to focus on the last stage of the process one has engaged in and to forget prior information, or at least to attribute undue weight and importance to the last stage. For instance, it will often happen that a person who is well qualified on paper but has poor interview skills is eliminated. Is the possession of polished interview skills really a critical success factor for the post in question? Is it wise to allow the interview to be so influential, given the evidence on the reliability and validity of interviews? If you are using a variety of selection techniques, you must decide in advance what each method is going to contribute to the overall assessment. Some things will carry more weight than others, and this should be decided in advance and each component appropriately weighted. Some things will be designated as essential prerequisites, and the lack of other things may be balanced by the presence of something else. For a post managing an accounting unit, for example, good writing skills may be allowed to balance a lack of polished presentation skills, but mathematical ability will be essential. You must decide what to do if there is conflicting evidence, for example if someone performs well in the interview but not in the ability tests or vice versa.

Scoring and ranking

It is, then, important to find some methodical approach to evaluating the information you have gathered, enabling you to rank the candidates in order of preference. There are several approaches to this and a variety of issues to consider:

- Decide on the cut-off percentage score a candidate must achieve in order to be considered.
- Decide which criteria must be met and which can be traded off against each other.
- Use ticks and crosses to record the assessment of candidates.
- Decide on the relative weight of each assessment criterion and assign points accordingly to each factor, amalgamating scores from the various assessment methods. Calculate a total score for each candidate.

Figure 7.5 is a sample form to record and tabulate results.

After all the selection activities have been completed, all the selectors should compare their rankings of the candidates and decide on the best candidate. If there are discrepancies in the ratings, these discrepancies can form the basis of discussion and, if necessary, of further information seeking.

Providing information to aid self-selection

It is often forgotten that applicants for a post also have a decision to make about whether or not they wish to accept the offer of employment. It is risky to assume that merely applying for a job means the applicant will ultimately want the post. If new employees leave shortly after being hired, this can hardly be considered to be successful selection. Just as the selectors gather information on which to base their decision, so the applicants should gather or be given information so that they too will make the right decision.

One obvious way of giving applicants information is to encourage them to ask questions during the interview. In this way you know that you have clarified any points that are important to individual applicants, and these may of course differ

Figure 7.5

Sample candidate assessment form

Key for individual scores:
5 = excellent, 3 = good, 1 = acceptable

POST: _____

ASSESSOR: _____

Minimum acceptable scores
Job knowledge: 38.4/64 (60%)
Total score: 74.5/149 (50%)

	Job knowledge Weight factor: 0.8	Organisational ability Weight factor: 0.6	Experience Weight factor: 0.5	Ability to persuade Weight factor: 0.6
Application form Weight factor: 4	3 × 4 <u>12</u>		4 × 4 <u>16</u>	
Interview Weight factor: 6	4 × 6 <u>24</u>		3 × 6 <u>18</u>	3 × 6 <u>18</u>
Work sample test Weight factor: 6	4 × 6 <u>24</u>	5 × 6 <u>30</u>		
Ability test Weight factor: 4		3 × 4 <u>12</u>		
Personality questionnaire Weight factor: 4				4 × 4 <u>16</u>
Weighted criterion totals	48	25.2	17	20.4

Candidate total score: 110.8
Candidate ranked against others: 2nd of 6

Explanatory notes

The form indicates weightings that would be agreed on some justifiable basis. In this case, job knowledge is weighted higher than the other criteria, and more weight is given to the interview and work sample test than the other assessment methods.

The line under the scores would appear on the blank form to indicate which factors are to be scored under each assessment method.

Any score that fell below the agreed minimum could be ringed on the form to draw attention to the fact that the candidate is no longer to be considered.

from one person to the next. Also, if your interview questions and work sample tests are properly constructed to obtain job-related information from applicants, these questions and tests will have imparted a wealth of information to the interviewee, albeit obliquely. Applicants may, however, still be unaware of certain aspects of the job, and it is incumbent on the selectors to make sure that applicants know about any factors that might influence their decision, and in particular the likelihood of their remaining with the organisation for a reasonable length of time if they do accept an offer of employment.

Very often the factors that cause rapid turnover among new employees are to do with unpleasant working conditions. If recruitment and selection were just about getting people to accept employment with your organisation, it would make sense to hide information about the negative aspects of your workplace. Many organisations have realised, however, that there is a greater likelihood of retaining new recruits if they are open and honest about the less pleasant aspects of their work environment. Offering interviewees information of this nature is known as a realistic job preview.

Did you know?

Rankin (2008) provides examples from companies adopting an innovative approach to delivering information to job applicants. Centrica gives access to graduate employee blogs on its website, so applicants can form a good idea of what these jobs entail. William Hill invites applicants to an open day and a tour of its call centre, along with a realistic work sample test, so potential recruits can form a good idea of work in that area.

Realistic job previews can take the form of oral information given by interviewers either to individual interviewees or in a group session before the interviews, or written documentation provided to candidates, for example statements about the working conditions included in job descriptions. There are, however, some more innovative ways of providing this kind of information.

In 1995 students in the Transport and Logistics department at the University of Huddersfield created a short video film for a distribution company that wanted to alert applicants to the fact that the jobs in its warehouse involved cold, uncongenial working conditions, as most of the work took place in refrigerated areas. This film was made available in job centres so that people who did not wish to work in such conditions would not even apply in the first instance. Realistic job previews can, then, be provided at any stage in the recruitment and selection process, but they are probably most useful at the interview stage, when there is an opportunity to discuss and clarify details.

Additional activities that could be undertaken with the specific purpose of giving information to candidates include a tour of the organisation's premises, which gives applicants a first-hand look at the environment they would be working in and an opportunity to meet prospective colleagues. Letting applicants chat unattended with prospective colleagues means that managers have no control over the kinds of information that will be exchanged; it is rather akin to using the 'sitting at Nellie's knee' method of training you will read about in Chapter 8. However, the exercise would make additional information available to potential employees, and it is worth considering the inclusion of such an opportunity in your selection process. Rankin (2008) confirms that the most effective ways of aiding self-selection are those which provide a job preview, either through a work sample test or a visit to the workplace.

Administrative procedures

Once you have completed your selection process and made a decision about the successful candidate(s), there are a number of things you need to do to close the process:

- The successful candidate(s)
  - offer the position to the successful candidate(s)
  - secure their acceptance of the position
  - agree the details of the appointment
  - confirm the details in writing
  - check essential qualifications
  - initiate new employee processes.
- The unsuccessful candidates
  - inform the candidates of the outcome
  - provide feedback if appropriate.
- Prepare adequate records.
- Monitor the process.

Offer the position and agree details of appointment

Many employers prefer the personal touch of using the telephone to speak directly to the person they hope will be joining their organisation. Some organisations still prefer to make the initial offer in writing. Important details that need to be agreed at this stage include the start date, the starting salary and details about salary progression.

Confirm details in writing

Although an oral agreement can be regarded as a contract, most employers and employees feel more secure about the arrangement if it is put in writing. Usually the employer will write to the candidate to confirm the appointment and in turn require written confirmation of acceptance from the candidate. There is also a legal obligation to give a statement of terms and conditions to most employees, as we discussed in more detail in Chapter 4.

Check essential documents

If specific qualifications are required for the post, for example, a degree, a driving licence or professional certification, the selected candidate should be required to present the documentation as proof that they do in fact possess the relevant qualifications.

A further, general requirement that applies to all employees is, of course, that they are legally entitled to work in the UK. The Asylum and Immigration Act 1996 reinforced the employer's responsibility for ascertaining that every new employee has the appropriate status. If employers selectively check only those applicants who, because of their appearance or a foreign-sounding name, arouse doubts about their citizenship status, such action could be deemed to be unlawful racial discrimination. To avoid this and at the same time fulfil the section 8 requirement to check employees' status, employers need to audit the documentation of all new employees at some stage in the selection process. A record of documented evidence of a person's national insurance number, such as a pay slip issued by a former employer, was originally deemed to be adequate proof of the fact that an employer had carried out this duty, but this was changed with effect from 1 May 2004 with regard to all persons hired from that date on. Section 8 now requires that employers check and copy either one document from a given list (list A) or a specified combination of two documents from a second list (list B). An example from the first list (one document only required) is a document showing that the holder is a national of a European Economic Area country or Switzerland. This must be a national passport or identity card (www.ukba.homeoffice.gov.uk). However, nationals of some countries, including Bulgaria, the Czech Republic and Hungary, may need to be registered with the UK Border Agency and authorised to work in the UK.

The Immigration, Asylum and Nationality Act 2006 came into force in February 2008, and sets out penalties that may apply to employers who unlawfully employ migrant workers. Fines can be up to £10,000 per worker, and deliberately and knowingly infringing on the law in this way is a criminal offence which may attract an unlimited fine and/or a prison sentence of up to two years (www.businesslink.gov.uk). Documents from list B must also now be checked every 12 months.

Employers may also hire asylum seekers, but only if they have an application registration card issued by the Home Office, specifically giving permission to work in the UK. A letter from the Home Office is not sufficient, and the employer must have the registration card checked by the UK Border Agency's Employer Checking Service. This example demonstrates how complex the issues can be, so it is always advisable for employers to check on the Home Office website where they will find a lot of helpful and detailed information and guidance. The website also gives information about documents that are not acceptable, such as a UK driving licence or a utility bill.

Initiate new employee processes

In addition to the appointment letter and check of credentials, there are a number of administrative details that need to be attended to for each employee. These include such things as acquiring details on pension arrangements, ascertaining preferences with regard to benefits (if a cafeteria system of benefits is in place, and employees can choose some benefits in preference to others), acquiring personal details such as bank account data for payroll purposes, and determining whether the person wishes union dues to be deducted from salary if a check-off system is in place. These administrative details will vary from one workplace to another, and it is sufficient here to note that they need to be planned and administered.

Inform the unsuccessful candidates of the outcome

Unsuccessful candidates should be treated with courtesy and informed as soon as possible of the outcome of the selection process, usually as soon as the preferred candidate has accepted the post. We have mentioned before that there is a public relations element in the way that recruitment and selection are performed. It is probably one of the few times that outsiders are invited into your organisation and are able to observe at first hand how you treat people. You will usually reject more people than you hire, and these people could be customers or even still potential employees whom you would not wish to alienate. Most candidates who have made it through the interview stage are serious about wanting the post, and inevitably will be disappointed that they have not succeeded. The rejection message needs, therefore, to be delivered with some sensitivity and, if possible, to avoid implying that these candidates have failed or are of inferior calibre.

Did you know?

The *Telegraph* has reported research on applicants who have become disgruntled about the way their job applications were handled. Some of them were considering taking their custom away from retailers who failed to give feedback about the success or otherwise of an application. Employers who were cited as regarding an effective process as being very important include John Lewis, Unilever and McDonald's.

(Source: Peacock, L (2010) Rejected job applicants shun retail employers and shop elsewhere, *Telegraph*, 9 June)

ACTIVITY 7.7

Compose a standard letter that could be used for informing applicants that they have not been selected for a position. A model letter is given in Appendix 7.1 for you to compare with your proposed letter.

Feedback to candidates

Usually employers do not take the initiative in offering feedback to rejected candidates unless psychological tests have been used, in which case it is considered to be good practice to do so. However, some candidates are aware that asking for feedback can make a good impression with potential employers and that honest feedback might assist them in their further job search. Proper assessment of candidates should enable employers to be ready to give feedback to candidates in a sensitive manner.

Record keeping

The assessment record can form part of the recorded justification of why candidates were selected or rejected. In addition, preparing a summary statement of the reasons for the decisions, i.e. a statement of why the selected candidate was the preferred candidate and why the unsuccessful candidates were rejected, adds some rigour to the process. It is also necessary to keep such records to be able to provide evidence of good practice in case any applicant feels they have been subjected to unlawful discrimination and takes a complaint to an employment tribunal. The burden of proof, which means that employers, when challenged at a tribunal, must provide positive evidence of non-discrimination, is described in more detail in Chapter 5. Since the time limit for presenting a claim of discrimination to an employment tribunal is three months, it would seem sensible to keep detailed records of selection decisions for at least that period of time, and indeed the CIPD (2009e) recommends keeping them for six months to one year.

Monitor the process

The selection process should be monitored for several purposes:

- to ensure that selection is being conducted within the framework of the organisation's policies and equality legislation
- to examine the validity of selection decisions
- to ensure there is an acceptable level of reliability among assessors and interviewers.

A statistical analysis of the candidates who proceed through the various stages of selection will identify trends and provide feedback about how various groups fare throughout the selection process. The data could be analysed in terms of groupings of internal vs external candidates, male vs female, age profiles, racial groups and the disabled, etc. Remember that public sector employers are obliged by law to carry out monitoring of their recruitment and selection processes with regard to all of the equality issues covered by the Equality Act 2010. Monitoring by private sector employers is not prescribed by legislation but is regarded as good practice and may be helpful if decisions are challenged in an employment tribunal.

Another important consideration is whether the selection process results in the acquisition of high-performing employees. Data from performance appraisals and information about promotions could be cross-referenced with the ratings awarded to candidates in the various selection exercises to show whether assessment during the selection process correlates with performance on the job.

The ratings arrived at by individual interviewers and assessors can be compared and the reasons for discrepancies investigated. This information can be used to identify the training needs of those involved in selection.

International issues in selection

It was established in Chapter 6 that recruitment for international operations could be ethnocentric, polycentric, regiocentric or geocentric or indeed a combination of these. Our main focus in this section, because the wider picture is so complex and beyond the scope of this textbook, will be on geocentric expatriate assignments.

It is well established that the success of overseas assignments is regarded as being crucial for organisations as much expense is involved in organising them and settling the employee and potentially their family abroad (IRS, 2000). This is especially so if the assignment is for a considerable length of time (two to five years), usually referred to as an expatriate assignment. Working as an expatriate also means calling on a wider range of competencies than working in the home country environment. Workers posted overseas will need all of the competencies required of a domestic employee in their line of work with additional competencies to cope with working in a foreign environment. A number of researchers have identified a range of these competencies, including flexibility and adaptability, higher levels of communication skills, resilience and intercultural awareness (Edwards and Rees, 2006; Briscoe et al., 2009).

The contribution of selection processes to organisations has been established in this textbook and, given the crucial need for expatriate assignments to succeed, it is obvious that careful selection of employees for these assignments must play an essential role in their success. A sophisticated approach involving psychological tests could be the answer, but Lucas et al. (2006) note that many multinational enterprises will select internal candidates whose competencies they already know well for overseas assignments. They also maintain, however, that increasingly organisations will need to select from a global, external labour market. In the latter case, sophisticated assessment methods will become more important.

Transnational companies draw their employees from all over the world, a geocentric approach, so tests must be capable of measuring the required competencies without ethnic bias. Pickard (2004) has written about the search for psychometric tests which an organisation could use all over the world, and the issue about the transferability of tests across different countries is raised by Brewster et al. (2007). It is an issue identified by these writers as needing further development. A further matter for concern which acquires greater significance in an international context is the use and integrity of Internet-based tests (Lucas et al., 2006).

Conclusion

Now that you have reviewed the approaches you can adopt to find a person who is going to be a productive colleague, you must turn your thoughts to what you can do to help integrate this person into your organisation as quickly and smoothly as possible. You will find a discussion of induction activities in Chapter 9. You should find the case study 7.2 a useful exercise in putting together and applying most of what you have learned about selection methods in this chapter.

CASE STUDY 7.2 Selection

George, the HR Manager, and Ruth, one of the HR assistants, were both conducting preliminary interviews of candidates for the post of PR assistant in the busy public relations department of a large organisation. The PR assistant would have to deal directly with the general public, sometimes with extremely irate people, and would also have to communicate with the press. George and Ruth had decided to interview the candidates separately and then get together to compare their impressions. Ruth was rather inexperienced at interviewing as she was new to the HR office. She was a quiet person who liked to approach work in a calm, methodical manner.

Ruth particularly liked one of the candidates, Jane Marsden. Jane seemed somewhat tense at the beginning of the interview, and Ruth empathised with this as she had recently gone through a number of interviews herself before she got her current job. Ruth got Jane to relax by talking about her interests, and her feeling that Jane was an interesting person was confirmed by the discovery that they shared interests in learning languages and travelling abroad. Ruth went on to tell Jane a little about the job, and Jane said she thought it sounded very interesting. Ruth also confirmed that Jane had actually dealt with customer complaints in previous positions. Ruth noted the following points in her assessment of Jane:

- turned up for the interview well dressed and looking professional
- showed enthusiasm for the job
- has relevant experience.

She also wrote: 'Jane makes a good impression. I'm sure she'll be good at the job.' Ruth reflected that the other two candidates she'd seen that morning hadn't seemed as enthusiastic as Jane, weren't as smart in appearance and hadn't been very expansive about their experience in response to open questions about tasks involved in PR work.

When they got together to discuss the candidates afterwards, Ruth recommended Jane to George, but George responded by saying: 'Well, when I asked her to describe her experience of dealing with an irate customer, she told me that she had always worked in offices dealing only with correspondence. I think some of the other candidates have more suitable experience.'

Questions

1 Identify the perceptual errors that may have occurred in this case.

2 Suggest what George might do to help Ruth to avoid such errors in the future.

3 Assume that the interviews conducted by Ruth and George, followed by line manager interviews, constituted the whole selection process. Suggest how the process could be improved, giving your rationale for your choice of selection methods and the order in which you would use them.

Look at the companion website at www.pearsoned.co/foothook for some suggested answers to these case study questions.

REVIEW QUESTIONS

You will find brief answers to these review questions on pages 491–2.

1 Describe the aims of the selection process and comment on a methodical approach that can be used to achieve these aims.

2 Explain the terms 'validity' and 'reliability' with reference to employment interviews.

3 What factors contribute to the low validity of employment interviews and how can this be overcome?

4 Critically assess the value of different types of questioning in employment interviews.

5 Critically assess the value of using a range of tests in the selection process.

SELF-CHECK QUESTIONS

Answer the following multiple-choice and short-answer questions. The correct responses are given on page 492 for you to check your understanding of this chapter.

1 Which of the following questions is an open question?
   (a) Did you get here by train?
   (b) Don't you enjoy working with computerised files?
   (c) What experience have you had in dealing with after-sales support services?
   (d) So you worked with your last employer for three years?

2 Is the following statement TRUE or FALSE? Of all the selection methods available to employers, interviews have been found to have the highest validity.

3 An interviewer is very impressed by the smart appearance and confident manner of a candidate. The interviewer tends to seek positive information from this candidate and readily overlooks any negative information. This is known as:
   (a) stereotyping
   (b) the contrast effect
   (c) closed questioning
   (d) the halo effect.

4 The validity of an interview can be increased by:
   (a) being aware of potential interviewer errors
   (b) structuring interviews to obtain the same information from all candidates
   (c) having interviews conducted by more than one interviewer
   (d) all the above
   (e) none of the above.

5 Which of the following is the best definition of (i) a situational interview question, (ii) a behavioural interview question?
   (a) The interviewee is asked to describe a situation in which they have performed well.
   (b) The interviewee is presented with a situation that represents a typical incident in the job for which they are being interviewed. The interviewee is asked to recount what they did in a similar situation in a past position.
   (c) The interviewee is presented with a situation that represents a typical incident in the job for which they are being interviewed. The interviewee is asked to describe what they would do in this situation.
   (d) The interviewee is presented with a situation that represents a typical incident in the job for which they are being interviewed. The interviewee is asked to describe what the ideal behaviour would be in this circumstance.

6 What kind of exercise did Makin and Robertson identify as being used most in assessment centres?
   (a) handwriting tests
   (b) group discussion

(c) work sample

(d) information technology skills.

7 Applicants for teaching posts may be asked to teach a class in their subject as part of the selection process. This is an example of:

(a) a leaderless group exercise

(b) a job sample test

(c) a personality test

(d) an attainment test.

8 Is the following statement TRUE or FALSE? The benefit of a realistic job preview is that it persuades people to join the organisation by presenting positive information about the job.

9 References are one of the most valid techniques of acquiring information about candidates. TRUE or FALSE?

10 When an activity has face validity, it means that it:

(a) tests what it purports to test

(b) resembles the activity it is testing for

(c) includes a one-on-one interview together with written tests.

HR IN THE NEWS

How can you tell the best job candidate is not the best liar?

The problem

A recent survey has found that 19 per cent of job applicants to the financial services industry are attempting to deceive their employers with false or misleading information. It suggests that the number of job seekers embellishing their CVs has increased steadily with the onset of the credit crunch. So how do you make sure you employ the best candidate and not the best liar? And how do you discourage people from falsifying their CVs?

The advice

The scientist and the practitioner

Dana Carney & James Palczynski

Through psychological science we know nearly everyone lies every day about all kinds of things. Some lies are attempts to avoid hurt feelings. Others emerge from a human egocentric bias or arise from a flawed or selective memory and, yes, sometimes people set out to deceive purposefully. The survey points to the prevalence of this pattern in human behaviour. Lies are often accompanied by non-verbal and uncontrollable 'tells', particularly when the teller is under pressure or the stakes are high. Creating pressure and reading these tells is a skill that human resource professionals, as well as poker players, would do well to master. Begin an interview with neutral questions to establish a behavioural baseline, then increase stress and watch for distinctive non-verbal tells such as rapid pressing of the lips together and quick one-sided shoulder shrugs, both reactions that can indicate a lie. More traditionally, always ask for references in the job listing and check the candidate's CV. In our experience, salary history and educational performance are two oft-misrepresented items. In today's cut-throat job market, caveat emptor.

Prof Carney is a social psychologist at Columbia University; Mr Palczynski is a director of ICR, a strategic communications consultancy

The CV screener

Alexandra Kelly

We were recently asked to screen a job applicant on behalf of one of our clients. He was interviewing for a senior position in a big City institution working with large amounts of capital and sensitive information. He was highly experienced and sailed through the interviews and was subsequently offered the job, at which point his file ended up with my team. At first glance, his CV and background seemed fine – absolutely nothing there that would cause for suspicion from even an experienced recruitment professional. However, it emerged that this supposedly 'ideal candidate', was in fact an international fraudster convicted of embezzlement in a number of US states. Needless to say, most embellishments by applicants are not quite so extreme, and more often concern the job applicant who conceals that they were fired from their previous role, or who lies about their job responsibilities or the number of people they managed. However, all these scenarios serve to demonstrate that you can never, ever truly know whether an applicant really is exactly who they say they are. Unless, of course, you check.

The writer is managing director of Powerchex, a pre-employment screening company

The recruiter

Tara Ricks

There's a section of *The Apprentice*, [the business reality TV show] where the contestants' wild CV claims are picked apart at interview stage, that I suspect all recruitment experts universally recognise. The truth is, it usually takes a face-to-face chat before credibility can really be verified. CVs have to be one of the most fundamentally flawed concepts, given that they're written by the very person they purport to represent objectively. The CV may say they're a derivatives expert but only an interview can really prove this. Interestingly, it's rare a CV contains complete falsifications – it's more an issue of half truths or over-optimistic euphemisms (such as the candidate who once said he took a career break when really he was detained at Her Majesty's pleasure). This makes it hard to stamp out CV falsification – most people do recognise lying is wrong, but they kid themselves that it's only an odd bit of spin here and there. Professional and academic qualifications can be independently checked but for everything else, like skills and experience, it's down to good old-fashioned detective work at interview.

The writer is managing director of Joslin Rowe recruitment consultants

The executive

Traci Canning

Employers are looking for maximum return on their talent investment, so having a larger candidate pool certainly is a high-grade problem to have. Solid recruitment methodologies and processes ensure the best candidates. The alternative is sifting through stacks of CVs without a clear idea of what one is looking for – a less-than-ideal situation for the employer and a prime opportunity for the candidate with more style than substance. Skills-based job descriptions and competencies-based interviewing both create barriers for the marginally unqualified and the downright dishonest. Communicating a policy of consensual pre-employment screening provides additional layers of protection in the recruitment process. Candidates who have embellished their CVs may remove themselves from consideration once they realise their facts really will be checked.

The writer is managing director of Kroll Background Worldwide, a background screening company

Financial Times, 19/08/2009, http://www.ft.com/cms/s/0/50e1a000-8c57-11de-b14f-00144feabdc0.html. Reproduced with permission. © The Financial Times Ltd.

Questions

1 Critically review the advice given in this article.
2 Present some further advice of your own based on concepts covered in this chapter.

WHAT NEXT?

Because there are so many individual selection methods and combinations to choose from, there are many strands you may wish to follow further. A selection of possibilities is outlined here.

Interviews

Barclay's 2001 research article on behavioural interviewing clearly sets out the advantages of this approach as well as issues that need to be dealt with. The author addresses questions of validity and the place of behavioural interviewing among other selection methods. Of course, Barclay's survey of the extent to which employers were using behavioural interviews is now dated. You can bring this information up-to-date both by reference to information in this textbook and by searching out the most recent data provided by the CIPD or the IRS.

Barclay, J. M. (2001) Improving selection interviews with structure: organisations' use of 'behavioural' interviews, *Personnel Review*, Vol. 30, No. 1, 81–101.

The use of competencies in selection

Kirton and Healy (2009) research the use of competency-based candidate assessment in terms of equality and diversity outcomes. Their focus is on the judiciary, but the article includes a general overview of competencies and some general inferences can be drawn from their conclusions. They also present an interesting insight into assessor and candidate views of the process.

Summarise the pros and cons of competency testing as presented in this article.

Kirton, G. and G. Healy (2009) Using competency-based assessment centres to select judges – implications for equality and diversity, *Human Resource Management Journal*, Vol. 19, No. 3, 302–318.

Personality profiling for international recruitment and selection

Mol *et al.* (2005) look at the Big Five characteristics discussed in this chapter, and review research to determine the relevance of these characteristics for predicted performance in the expatriate context compared with their use in domestic recruitment and selection. The article provides an interesting review of the factors that are important in selecting employees for long-term overseas postings.

Mol, S.T., M.P.H. Born, M.E. Willemsen and H.T. van der Molen (2005) Predicting expatriate job performance for selection purposes: a quantitative review, *Journal of Cross-Cultural Psychology*, Vol. 36, No. 5, September, 590–620.

Psychometric testing for multi-level selection

This article by Burch and Anderson (2008) introduces a concept we have not covered, i.e. multi-level selection. We have focused on matching candidates to the job, but Burch and Anderson extend this matching candidates to the team and the organisation. The authors examine a particular psychological instrument, the Team Selection Inventory, and an additional element of interest in the article is that it focuses on a group of participants in New Zealand.

Burch, G. St J. and N. Anderson (2008) The team selection inventory: empirical data from a New Zealand sample, *Asia Pacific Journal of Human Resources*, 46(2), 241–252.

Impression management

This research report deals with selection issues only in passing and focuses mainly on behaviour in the workplace in general. It does, however, look at a very interesting aspect of human behaviour which illustrates how difficult it is to understand and assess personality. It thus represents good background reading for anyone wishing to acquire a deeper knowledge about the value of personality testing for work purposes. Impression management is about the tendency of human beings to adapt their behaviour according to the circumstances and their perceptions of what is expected of them, even to the extent of suppressing personality traits they would otherwise express.

OPP [n.d.] *Who's Fooling Whom? Exploring the Impact of Impression Management in the Workplace. A Research Report* (www.opp.eu.com; accessed 26.04.10).

References

Advisory, Conciliation and Arbitration Service (2009a) *Religion or Belief and the Workplace: A Guide for Employers and Employees*, ACAS.

Advisory, Conciliation and Arbitration Service (2009b) *Sexual Orientation and the Workplace: A Guide for Employers and Employees*, ACAS.

Anderson, N. and V. Shackleton (1994) Informed choices, *Personnel Today*, 8 November, 33–34.

Bartram, D. (2010) Revision of the UK test user standards and alignment with changes in Europe: Part 3 transitional arrangements, *Assessment & Development Matters*, Vol. 2, No. 1 Spring (www.psychtesting.org.uk; accessed 21.04.10).

Brewster, C., P. Sparrow and G. Vernon (2007) *International Human Resource Management*, 2nd edition, CIPD.

Briscoe, D. R., R. S. Schuler and L. Claus (2009) *International Human Resource Management: Policies and Practices for Multinational Enterprises*, 3rd edition, Routledge.

Chartered Institute of Personnel and Development (2003) *Recruitment and Retention 2003: Survey Report*, CIPD.

Chartered Institute of Personnel and Development (2007) *Recruitment, Retention and Turnover: Annual Survey Report 2007*, CIPD.

Chartered Institute of Personnel and Development (2009a) *Employing People with Criminal Records*, CIPD (www.cipd.co.uk; accessed 12.07.10).

Chartered Institute of Personnel and Development (2009b) *E-recruitment*, CIPD (www.cipd.co.uk; accessed 19.04.10).

Chartered Institute of Personnel and Development (2009c) *Psychological Testing* (www.cipd.co.uk; accessed 19.04.10).

Chartered Institute of Personnel and Development (2009d) *Recruitment, Retention and Turnover: Annual Survey Report 2009*, CIPD (www.cipd.co.uk; accessed 19.04.10).

Chartered Institute of Personnel and Development (2009e) *Retention of Personnel and Other Related Records*, CIPD (www.cipd.co.uk; accessed 19.04.10).

Chartered Institute of Personnel and Development (2009f) *Selecting Candidates*, CIPD (www.cipd.co.uk; accessed 19.04.10).

Chartered Institute of Personnel and Development (2010a) *Resourcing and Talent Planning: Annual Survey Report 2010*, CIPD (www.cipd.co.uk; accessed 12.07.10).

Chartered Institute of Personnel and Development (2010b) *Selection Interviewing*, CIPD (www.cipd.co.uk; accessed 19.04.10).

Cook, M. (2009) *Personnel Selection: Adding Value through People*, 5th edition, Wiley-Blackwell.

Edwards, T. and C. Rees (2006) *International Human Resource Management*, Financial Times Prentice Hall.

HRzone (2006) *Over 200,000 Royal Mail Candidates to be Assessed Online* (www.hrzone.co.uk; accessed 12.07.10).

Incomes Data Services (2002) *IDS Studies 735: Assessment Centres*, September, IDS.

Industrial Relations Services (2000) Working all over the world, *IRS Employment Trends 699*, March, 3–11.

Industrial Relations Services (IRS) (2003) Sharpening up recruitment and selection with competencies, *IRS Employment Review 782*, 15 August, 42–48.

Industrial Relations Services (2007a) Assessment centres: the IRS report, *IRS Employment Review* 877, 16/7 (available at www.xperthr.co.uk; accessed 12.07.10).

Industrial Relations Services (IRS) (2007b) Interviewers' roles, responsibilities and training, *IRS Employment Review* 875, 18/06 (www.xperthr.co.uk; accessed 12.07.10).

Industrial Relations Services (IRS) (2007c) Question styles and formats of job interviewing, *IRS Employment Review* 875, 18/06 (www.xperthr.co.uk; accessed 12.07.10).

Latham, G.P., Saari, L.M., Pursell, E.D. and Campion, M.A. (1980) The situational interview, *Journal of Applied Psychology*, Vol. 65, No. 4, 422–427.

Lucas, R., Lupton, B. and Mathieson, H. (2006) *Human Resource Management in an International Context*, CIPD.

Makin, P. and Robertson, I. (1986) Selecting the best selection techniques, *Personnel Management*, November, 38–40.

Marchington, M. and Wilkinson, A. (2005) *Human Resource Management at Work: People Management and Development*, 3rd edition, CIPD.

McGee, L. (2006) How to interview for engagement, *People Management*, 27 July, 40–41.

Mol, S.T., Born, M.P.H., Willemsen, M.E. and van der Molen, H.T. (2005) Predicting expatriate job performance for selection purposes: a quantitative review, *Journal of Cross-Cultural Psychology*, Vol. 36, No. 5, September, 590–620.

Murphy, K.R. and Davidshofer, C.O. (2001) *Psychological Testing: Principles and Applications*, 5th edition, Prentice Hall.

Murphy, N. (2008) Trends in recruitment methods in 2006 and 2007 (3): selection, *IRS Employment Review* 893, 20/03 (www.xperthr.co.uk; accessed 12.07.10).

Newell, S. and Shackleton, V. (1991) Management selection: a comparative survey of methods used in top British and French companies, *Journal of Occupational Psychology*, Vol. 94, 23–36.

People Management (2001) Frames of mind, 14 June, 26–37.

Pickard, J. (2004) Testing times, *People Management*, 29 January, 43–44.

Rankin, N. (2008) How self-selection can improve recruitment and retention, *IRS Employment Review* 889, 21/01 (www.xperthr.co.uk; accessed 12.07.10).

Rankin, N. (2009) Testing in employment: the 2009 IRS survey, *IRS Employment Review* 930, 05/10 (www.xperthr.co.uk; accessed 22.03.10).

Ready, D.A. and Conger, J.A. (2007) Make your company a talent factory, *Harvard Business Review*, June, 68–77.

Robertson, I. (2001) Undue diligence, *People Management*, 22 November, 42–43.

Rogers, C.R. and Farson, R.E. (1976) *Active Listening*, Industrial Relations Center of the University of Chicago.

Sloane, W. (2007) Online probes to the parts others don't reach, *The Sunday Times: Recruiting* (insert).

Smith, M. and Robertson, I.T. (1993) *The Theory and Practice of Systematic Personnel Selection*, 2nd edition, Macmillan.

Weekley, J.A. and Gier, J.A. (1987) Reliability and validity of the situational interview for a sales position, *Journal of Applied Psychology*, Vol. 72, 484–487.

Welch, J. (1998) Graduate recruitment, *People Management*, 28 May, 14.

Wolff, C. (2008) Yell recruits through Second Life and online behavioural tests, *IRS Employment Review* 890, 04/02 (www.xperthr.co.uk; accessed 12.07.10)

Woodruffe, C. (2007) *Development and Assessment Centres: Identifying and Developing Competence*, 4th edition, CIPD.

www.businesslink.gov.uk; accessed 22.04.10.

www.cipd.co.uk/research_offenders; accessed 12.07.10.

www.equalityhumanrights.com; accessed 26.04.10.

www.ukba.homeoffice.gov.uk; accessed 22.04.10.

Further study

Books

Advisory, Conciliation and Arbitration Service (2009) *Recruitment and Induction*, ACAS.

A concise overview of good practice in recruitment and selection, available at www.acas.org.uk; accessed 12.07.10.

Black, J.S., H.B. Gregersen, M.E. Mendenhall and L.K. Stroh (1999) *Globalizing People through International Assignments*, Addison Wesley.

Although its focus is specifically on HR aspects of dealing with international employees, this book contains some interesting information about recruitment and selection which could have wider applications, including some good examples of open and behavioural questions on the competency areas of perseverance and delegation.

Cook, M. (2009) *Personnel Selection: Adding Value through People*, 5th edition, Wiley-Blackwell.

A thorough review of selection methods and issues, including interviews, tests, assessment centres and validity.

Incomes Data Services (2008) *IDS HR Studies: Assessment Centres*, No. 876, August, IDS.

An overview of how to design an assessment centre. Presents case studies of seven employers, including Mercer and Sainsbury's Supermarkets, giving details of their assessment centres.

Incomes Data Services (2008) *IDS HR Studies Update: e-HR*, No. 867, April, IDS.

An overview of the uses of technology in HR, including recruitment and selection, HR management systems, training and development and HR intranets. Presents case studies of six employers, including online graduate recruitment at H J Heinz.

Smith, M. and I.T. Robertson (1993) *The Theory and Practice of Systematic Personnel Selection*, 2nd edition, Macmillan.

A thorough discussion of all the stages involved in selection, and of issues such as ethical considerations, discrimination and validity of selection methods.

Articles

Industrial Relations Services (2007) Job interviewing: an overview of IRS's research, *IRS Employment Review 875*, 18/06 (www.xperthr.co.uk; accessed 27.06.07).

Lists a number of articles that constitute the 2007 IRS studies on selection interviewing, and provides a further list of useful sources of information on this topic.

Jenks, J.M. and L.P. Zevnik (1989) ABCs of job interviewing, *Harvard Business Review*, July-August, 38–42.

This article discusses how to formulate questions and gives practical guidelines.

Latham, G.P., L.M. Saari, E.D. Pursell and M.A. Campion (1980) The situational interview, *Journal of Applied Psychology*, Vol. 65, No. 4, 422–427.

This article describes research into the validity of situational interviewing, and provides an example of a question used for manual employees.

Rankin, N. (2009) Testing in employment: the 2009 IRS survey, *IRS Employment Review 930*, 05/10 (www.xperthr.co.uk; accessed 22.03.10).

Rankin provides a good overview of how tests are selected and used in the selection process.

Suff, R. (2008) Background checks in recruitment: employers' current methods, *IRS Employment Review 896*, 17/04 (www.xperthr.co.uk; accessed 12.07.10).

This article provides a good overview of employer approaches to soliciting and using references. It also reviews their use of criminal record checks.

Weekley, J.A. and J.A. Gier (1987) Reliability and validity of the situational interview for a sales position, *Journal of Applied Psychology*, Vol. 72, 484–487.

This article describes research into the reliability and validity of interviews, particularly interviews using situational questions. A sample question is provided, together with suggestions on how to assess responses.

Internet

British Psychological Society   www.psychtesting.org.uk

Offers information about psychological tests to test-takers and test-users, as well as general information and pages on current issues. Check out the interesting frequently asked questions and the links to companies which offer practice tests. Look also for the Guidelines and Information section where a number of useful documents on psychological testing, assessment centres and international tests can be downloaded.

The Chartered Institute of Personnel and Development   www.cipd.co.uk

Browse the CIPD's website to find information related to recruitment and selection. Their 2009 factsheet *Psychological Testing* provides a concise guide to the issues involved in choosing to use psychological tests and advice on how to use them in a professional manner. The annual Recruitment, Retention and Turnover survey, renamed in 2010 as the Resourcing and Talent Planning survey, gives an overview of what employers are currently doing in recruitment and selection, highlighting what employers consider to be the main issues affecting the sourcing and retention of employees.

Criminal Records Bureau   www.crb.gov.uk

Describes the work of the CRB and provides recommendations on good practice.

Equality and Human Rights Commission   www.equalityhumanrights.com

Provides a wealth of information relating to equality issues in the selection process.

Immigration and Nationality Directorate   www.homeoffice.gov.uk

This site will give you very detailed information about employers' responsibilities with regard to the Asylum and Immigration Act 1996.

Appendix 7.1

Company name and logo
Company address
Town
PC1 1XX

Ms C Candidate
1 Named Street
Candidtown
PC1 1XX

1 June 2011

Dear Ms Candidate

I regret to inform you that the selection panel has selected another candidate for the position of Human Resource Assistant. I would like to thank you for the time and effort you put into your application for this post and for your participation in our selection process. The panel was impressed with the calibre of the candidates and had a difficult decision to make.

Please do not hesitate to apply again for any suitable position with Company Name.

Yours sincerely

A Barker

Director of Human Resources

Performance management and appraisal

Objectives

By the end of this chapter you will be able to:

- state what is meant by the term 'performance management'
- give examples of techniques used in the management of performance at work
- design a simple performance appraisal system
- discuss some of the key issues of performance management in international organisations.

I t is always important for managers and supervisors to get the best performance from their workforce in terms of levels of production and quality of output. Performance management is concerned to get the best performance from the individual, but goes further in that it also aims to get the best performance from the team and from the organisation as a whole. It aims to improve performance in the workplace in order to achieve the organisation's strategic objectives.

Definition of performance management

Armstrong and Baron (2004), in what is now regarded as a classic work on the subject, define performance management as a process which:

contributes to the effective management of individuals and teams in order to achieve high levels of organisational performance. As such, it establishes shared understanding about what is to be achieved and an approach to leading and developing people which will ensure it is achieved.

How organisations actually carry out the performance management process and the methods they use will vary, but ultimately the aim is to motivate everyone in the organisation and ensure that they are all working towards the same strategic objectives.

Performance management as an integrated and strategic process

As you can see from Figure 8.1, performance management is a process that involves many aspects of people management and each of the topics covered in this book makes a contribution towards it. But simply initiating a new performance management scheme or introducing new HR practices or policies as part of the process will not in itself bring about the desired motivation of workers.

Performance management should be a shared process between managers, individuals and teams in which objectives are agreed and jointly reviewed and in which corporate, individual and team objectives are integrated. All should feel ownership of the process and share a complete understanding of the system (CIPD, 2009). The recent 2009 CIPD survey of 507 HR managers showed they were increasingly aware of this.

This CIPD survey found that demand for effective performance management was even stronger during the recession as HR departments tried to ensure that they achieved the best performance possible so their organisations' strategic objectives were met, while at the same time ensuring fair, objective measurements of performance were used. In the survey most HR managers had continued to use similar processes as part of performance management but had emphasised more strongly its purpose to create and drive a stronger performance culture. They had made clearer the link between individual objectives and strategic objectives and most had used performance management as a way of gaining greater engagement from the workforce.

Because it should also be strategic in nature it should be clearly linked to broad issues and establishing long-term goals. In order to achieve these things managers must ensure that the people or teams they manage:

● know and understand what is expected of them
● have the skills necessary to deliver on these expectations
● are supported by the organisation to develop the capacity to meet these expectations
● are given feedback on performance
● have the opportunity to discuss and contribute to individual and team aims and objectives (Armstrong and Baron, 2004).

According to Cannell (2007), the tools typically used in performance management include the following:

● performance and development reviews
● learning and development
● coaching
● objectives and performance standards
● competences and competencies
● pay
● teams
● 360° feedback
● performance problem solving.

The 2009 CIPD on-line survey, mentioned earlier, about performance management asked for opinions about performance management and what it involved in

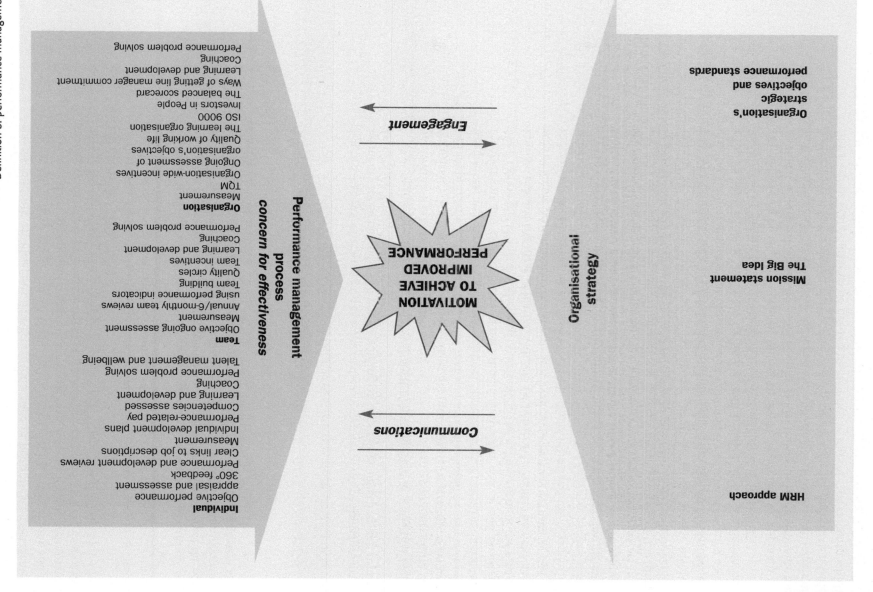

Figure 8.1 Performance management: a dynamic approach

the respondents' organisations. The actual tools used in performance management appear not to have changed much over time with appraisal, objective setting and review and development still being the most popular. A trend to link performance management with a wider range of HR processes was noted and 69.6 per cent of the sample felt that performance management should be aligned with at least four other HR processes (CIPD, 2009).

There was a great deal of variation about which HR processes it should be linked with but there was general agreement among 85 per cent of the sample that learning and development should form a part of performance management. Other HR processes mentioned included career development, coaching and mentoring, and succession planning and talent management was included by 65 per cent of the participants. Performance management was also in some organisations being integrated with a wider range of HR processes designed to promote well-being, engagement and development of potential.

Models of performance

Figure 8.1 shows what we regard as some of the key features of the performance management process but these will vary depending on the strategic objectives and culture of the organisation.

The organisation's strategic objectives need to be expressed in a way that everyone within the organisation understands, in effect by clearly communicating the organisation's vision for the future, or their Big Idea. While the strategic objectives will be primarily formulated by senior management this should be part of a two-way process and the strategic objectives should be agreed after extensive discussion. Involvement and clear communication should mean that everyone in the workforce feels engaged and that they can contribute to the achievement of the organisation's goals or big ideas either individually or as part of a team. The right-hand side of Figure 8.1 lists some of the tools and techniques that can be used as part of the performance management process for individuals, teams and the organisation itself.

While the tools and techniques used in performance management for the individual, the team and the organisation differ slightly, the performance management process itself is very similar for each and can be shown as a cyclical process. Figure 8.2 shows the performance management implementation process in this form. It does not matter whether the focus is on the individual, the team or the organisation as for each the performance management implementation process involves evaluating current levels of performance and assessing them against the desired levels. The aim is to improve performance, add value and contribute to meeting objectives at whatever level. Different techniques will be used in the evaluation and assessment of current levels of performance. Individuals may be assessed against their objectives by using personal development reviews, performance appraisal interviews, or perhaps reports of errors or complaints. For teams or departments the information needed may involve a comparison with team or departmental targets or a summary of faults and complaints for that department. On an organisation-wide basis a great deal of data would need to be collected to indicate the extent to which

Figure 8.2 The performance management implementation process

the whole organisation was meeting objectives and cumulative feedback may be compiled using information from performance appraisals throughout the organisation, or from customer satisfaction surveys. Organisations need individuals to feel engaged in the process and may also conduct surveys to establish the extent to which the workforce feel motivated by various aspects of the performance management process such as the pay and incentives or the learning and development opportunities offered.

In each case the aim is to evaluate the current levels of performance and compare this with the assessment of the performance levels required. These will depend on the organisation's objectives, which in turn feed into departmental objectives, team objectives and individual objectives. In each case it will be necessary to decide whether the aim is to achieve a satisfactory level of performance, whether it is to achieve higher performance levels to add more value to the organisation, or whether the objective is to transform performance levels by encouraging and enabling increasingly new or innovative ways of working.

Once a comparison has been made between desired performance levels and existing performance levels, choices have to be made about how these can be achieved for individuals, teams, departments or organisation-wide. Some of the techniques listed in Figure 8.1 may be chosen for each category and these then need to be implemented. The process on an organisation-wide basis is likely to take a substantial amount of time.

Whatever techniques are chosen as part of the performance management process there should be a review to establish whether or not they have succeeded in meeting the objectives set and this continues into evaluating current performance levels against those required as new objectives are set to meet strategic objectives. Measurement has become increasingly important in assessing whether or not there has been an improvement in performance and according to the CIPD (2010) this should be a continuous process for individuals and teams and it should be integrated into every aspect of running the organisation. The 2009 CIPD survey found that HR managers were in many instances finding it difficult to measure the effects of performance management in isolation from other things that might affect business performance or individual performance. However, HR managers were keen to try to measure performance and were using a wide range of measures such as versions of the balanced scorecard, key performance indicators and measures of level of engagement in employee satisfaction surveys.

As far as the individual is concerned the performance management process could be viewed as starting at the selection stage as individuals are selected because of their skills, knowledge and competencies in order to make a contribution to the achievement of the strategic objectives. When the individual joins the organisation the induction into that organisation will be a way of communicating the organisation's strategic objectives, perhaps in a simpler form of one Big Idea that encapsulates the objectives. It also reinforces the organisation's culture and values. As they find out more about their job they should also discover how they can make a contribution to the performance of the organisation and the achievement of its strategic objectives. Figure 8.3 shows a model of the performance management process for the individual employee.

The induction should also be used as an opportunity to evaluate the individual's skills, knowledge and competencies using a personal development review and to compare these with the organisation's or team's needs. Even though the person has been selected to carry out a specific job they may lack some of the skills, knowledge or competencies needed to work in that job or team. Plans should be made to meet any gaps between the individual's skills, knowledge and competencies and the organisation's or team's requirements for these. Decisions need to be made about the appropriate ways to fill any gaps between the two and this may involve using formal and informal learning and development methods. Individual goals and objectives will be set and the contribution expected by the individual to team or departmental goals and objectives will also need to be discussed. (The topics of induction, and learning and talent development will be dealt with in more detail in the next chapter but they do contribute to the process of performance management.)

In a performance management system there will be regular performance reviews throughout the year and also formal appraisal interviews at regular intervals. Each aims to monitor performance and see how individuals or teams are contributing to and meeting their targets or objectives and they are important in helping to identify learning and development needs. Their aim is to motivate for better performance, but regular reviews could also help to identify poor performance at an early stage. Pay systems are used to reward excellent performance and if performance seems to be slipping below an acceptable standard then counselling, the

Figure 8.3 A model of the performance management process: the individual employee

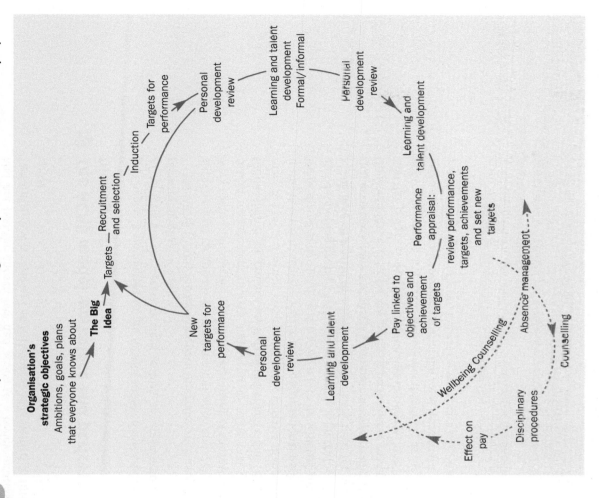

Organisation's strategic objectives
Ambitions, goals, plans that everyone knows about

The Big Idea — Targets — Recruitment and selection

Induction

Targets for performance

Personal development review

Learning and talent development
Formal/informal

Personal development review

Learning and talent development

Performance appraisal: review performance, targets, achievements and set new targets

Pay linked to objectives and achievement of targets

Learning and talent development

Personal development review

New targets for performance

Absence management

Counselling

Wellbeing Counselling

Effect on pay

Disciplinary procedures

absence management system or even the disciplinary system may be used. Even when these processes are used the aim should be to make clear what the required standards are and motivate the individual and team to achieve them. Topics such as learning and talent development, pay systems, discipline and absence management will be dealt with in later chapters of this book, while in this chapter we focus on issues relating to the performance management process and some specific techniques which can contribute to it such as performance appraisal and performance reviews.

Many organisations are linking their performance management system to talent management and according to Angela Baron (2009) some of the best practices appeared to be 'where performance management was acting as a portal to talent management'. In these organisations the term talent management was used in its widest sense, a view endorsed by the authors of this book, so that everyone and not just the chosen few had access to a review process: each staff member's performance was reviewed and they were each helped to find ways to do their job better.

The ACAS model workplace and performance management

In Chapter 1 we referred to the ACAS (2005) model workplace and outlined what ACAS feels are the necessary steps to turn an organisation into an effective high-performing place of work.

The ACAS (2005) model workplace integrates various aspects of HR and emphasises the need for good two-way communication and clear goals that employees can work towards. In essence it demonstrates many of the features of an excellent performance management process and seems to relate well to Armstrong and Baron's (2004) definition, given at the start of this chapter, that stated performance management is a process which 'contributes to the effective management of individuals and teams in order to achieve high levels of organisational performance. As such, it establishes shared understanding about what is to be achieved and an approach to leading and developing people which will ensure it is achieved.'

We have advocated throughout this book the need for policies and procedures so that everyone knows and shares a common understanding of what is supposed to be done and this is clearly a key aspect of performance management. ACAS (2005) says that this is a good start, but that the way things are done is also important. This is an approach we also emphasise throughout this book, as the way organisations manage performance can impact on most of the areas listed in the ACAS (2005) model workplace and consequently can impact on workplace effectiveness.

Pause for thought 8.1

The term performance management is used in a rather different way in a few organisations when they refer to 'performance managing someone out of an organisation' or putting someone on 'performance management'.
Have you heard the terms used like this?
What do you think of this approach to performance management?

Performance management should be about trying to get improvements in performance but, as we showed in Figure 8.3, processes like attendance monitoring or disciplinary procedures are likely to form part of a performance management system. However, organisations that use the term performance management as almost a synonym for disciplining someone have not got the right idea about managing performance and motivating people. Performance management should be about motivating individuals, teams and organisations to make a contribution to the organisation's strategic objectives and should have much more focus on incentives and positive aspects of motivation rather than just focusing on a negative approach to people management as is the case when an organisation thinks that performance management is about 'performance managing someone out of the organisation'. Such a negative approach to performance management is certainly not an approach that we advocate.

The people and performance model

In Chapter 1 we also referred to the research carried out by Professor John Purcell and his team at the School of Management at the University of Bath (Purcell *et al.*, 2003). Their people and performance model also showed the interrelationship of different HR policies. However, while traditional HR policies and procedures were important in this, the other area that they said really made a difference in organisations was 'the way people work together to be productive and flexible enough to meet new challenges'. They found in the organisations they studied that the organisation first had to have strong values and an inclusive culture and, second, have sufficient numbers of skilled line managers to be able to bring the HR policies and practices to life. Both elements fit well with the view of performance management shown in the definition we used earlier from Armstrong and Baron (2004).

Purcell and his team found that in the organisations that were most successful at managing performance, everyone did share common values. There was generally what the researchers called 'a Big Idea' that was meaningful to everyone in the organisation (Purcell *et al.*, 2003). This could be about the importance of customers to the organisation or the pursuit of quality, but in all cases it was an idea that everyone could relate to. Whatever it was, they all shared the idea and then managed the performance of people accordingly.

The people and performance model indicates that it is not just the people management policies and practices that create value to an organisation but that they help form part of the process by creating the building blocks that form the basis of achieving increased performance which Purcell calls ability, motivation and opportunity (AMO) (CIPD, 2007a). This assumes that people have the **ability** to learn new skills and will want to work in organisations where their abilities and skills are recognised and can be developed further. **Motivation** assumes that the organisation will be successful in motivating them to use their abilities in a way that is useful to the organisation in achieving its strategic objectives, while **opportunity** makes the assumption that people will use opportunities to do high-quality work and participate in team activities or problem-solving initiatives if the organisation provides them with opportunities to do this. A successful performance management system, perhaps linked to an inclusive talent management system should certainly help to identify **ability**, **motivate** both individuals and teams and also provide them with **opportunities** to use their skills and abilities.

The role of line managers in performance management

Another important strand in Purcell's effective performance model is line managers. Some traditional appraisal schemes have been accused of being run for the benefit of HR managers or top managers, with many other people in the organisation not really understanding or appreciating what the performance appraisal scheme was trying to achieve. This may have been true of some poorly designed schemes, but is a rather harsh judgement on many excellent appraisal schemes and HR managers and on the contribution they make to their organisations' effectiveness. In order to ensure that performance management does not make the same mistake, there is an increased emphasis on the role of the line manager and on gaining involvement of teams and individuals.

An early definition of performance management taken from Michael Armstrong (1994) defined performance management as 'a process which is designed to improve organisational, team and individual performance and which is owned and driven by line managers.' It is certainly true that line managers now have increased responsibility for many HR areas in relation to managing their staff, but it is disappointing to note that in some organisations they do not always see the necessity for performance management, or consider that it is not a key aspect of their job.

In a CIPD survey in 2005 it was claimed that in only 16 per cent of the organisations sampled was there complete buy-in from line managers, with them becoming actively involved in the performance management process (CIPD, 2005). However, on a more positive note, it was also discovered that line managers in 62 per cent of the organisations surveyed found performance management to be useful, while 22 per cent of the line managers were totally indifferent to the process and 1 per cent were actively hostile.

This reluctance to get involved in performance management may not be entirely the fault of line managers as they may not have been adequately trained, and the relevance of performance management to them and to the organisation's strategic objectives may not have been made clear. In order to make the performance management process as effective as possible it is vital that line managers are trained properly and that they have been trained thoroughly in skills such as coaching (Cunneen, 2006). They have to understand the relevance of performance management to the performance of their team and that it can make a difference to meeting their targets and improving their team performance. It should not be perceived by them to be just an exercise completed once a year where they tick boxes to satisfy the whims of the HR department but as a continuous process involving coaching and feedback which will make a difference to improving performance and developing the talents in their team. If line managers are to use this process to maximum effect to achieve both their team's and the organisation's strategic objectives then top management also have responsibilities to ensure that they clearly demonstrate the importance and relevance of performance management and that they provide adequate resources and training to support this (Cunneen, 2006).

The 2009 survey conducted by the CIPD found mixed views about the roles of line managers; all the participants felt that performance management was an important tool for line managers and a way of them achieving their work objectives but no-one in the survey felt that by enacting performance management it would create better line managers. Rather the view was held that good line managers would also be good at performance management (CIPD, 2009).

Performance appraisal

A good system of performance appraisal is important as part of the performance management process but many organisations that have not yet developed a strategic viewpoint also use performance appraisal on its own. Performance appraisal systems were developed as a tactical approach to developing people before the more strategic idea of performance management had been thought of. Performance management as an approach is widely held to have grown out of performance appraisal, and also to have absorbed some of the newer techniques used in performance appraisal such as emphasis on setting objective standards of performance and competence-based appraisals. However, while most performance management systems do use performance appraisal as a central tactical activity in the good management of employees there are still many other organisations which use performance appraisal as a standalone activity so it is important to consider performance appraisal both as a tool in performance management and as a procedure in its own right.

Performance appraisal is one way of giving employees feedback about their performance at work. According to ACAS (2008):

Appraisals regularly record an assessment of an employee's performance, potential and development needs. The appraisal is an opportunity to take an overall view of work content, loads and volume, to look back on what has been achieved during the reporting period and agree objectives for the next.

This definition clearly shows that the employee does get feedback about their past performance, but indicates that in performance appraisal there is the opportunity to assess or judge various aspects of an employee's work performance by looking back at how they have performed in the past and then by looking forward to agree future objectives or workload.

Fletcher and Williams (1985) went further than this in their definition of appraisal, saying that the assessment of people is not the only thing that we do when we appraise a person's work performance. They feel that there are in fact two conflicting roles involved in appraisal – those of judge and helper. We shall consider each of these facets of appraisal in turn.

First, we all act as judges when we make informal judgements about the way people talk, what they wear and how they behave. These informal judgements may be objective or subjective and we may not even be aware that we are making them. They may not have much effect on people in everyday life, as we don't normally have any right to try to change these things in others, and we don't usually have any power to influence the way people behave. If we start to judge people in a work situation in this informal way with regard, for example, to the way they dress, we are likely to be accused of being too subjective and we might, quite rightly, be accused of treating people unfairly according to our own whims and prejudices. This sort of appraisal is not likely to encourage people to feel motivated about work. In this sense the term 'appraisal' means judging the worth, qualities or value of something, and in a work situation especially it is important that any judgements are fair and are based on objective job-related criteria.

Second, the term 'appraisal' is also used in another way, as Fletcher and Williams (1985) have indicated. When we appraise people in the work situation, we not only judge them but we usually also try to help them to improve aspects of their performance. We may suggest alternative ways of behaving, or suggest training courses or provide developmental opportunities in order to help employees improve their performance and assess their own career developmental needs.

Performance appraisal is therefore about giving feedback to the employee, but also involves the appraiser in being both judge and helper to an individual employee. The performance appraisal interview represents the organisation's provision of a formal opportunity in which to give feedback and be both judge and helper to that employee.

Performance appraisal schemes may be used for a wide range of reasons, some of which may conflict with each other, but the main reasons are likely to include the following:

- to improve current performance
- to provide feedback
- to increase motivation and retention
- to identify potential
- to identify training needs
- to aid career development
- to award salary increases
- to solve job problems
- to let individuals know what is expected of them
- to clarify job objectives
- to provide information about the effectiveness of the selection process
- to aid in career planning and development
- to provide information for human resource planning
- to provide for rewards
- to assess competencies.

Randell *et al.* (1984) suggest that for most employers there are three main uses for appraisal reviews: **performance, potential** and **reward**. That is to say that organisations want to assess an individual's past performance; they may also want to identify their potential for future roles in the organisation and any development necessary to achieve this and they may want to use the appraisal interview as a means of allocating rewards for good or excellent performance. ACAS (2008) agree with this view and say that the three main uses of reviews are a **performance review, a review of potential and development needs** and a **reward review**. All the reasons listed above fall into one of these three categories but there could be conflicts between the various approaches. For example, if the organisation uses performance appraisal as a means of allocating rewards then it is likely that individuals will be much less likely to discuss any developmental needs in case this prevents them getting a bonus. As was shown earlier in this chapter it is becoming increasingly common in organisations to use reviews of potential and development needs as a part of the talent management process. Many organisations try to get too much from one appraisal scheme, and try to use one scheme to fulfil all three purposes. This is unlikely to work, and usually results in the scheme falling into disrepute.

Consequently organisations that use performance appraisal as part of a performance management system will usually conduct the performance appraisal on an annual or biannual basis but will separate these from the personal development reviews which they will organise at various times throughout the year. In this instance the development reviews would be used to discuss development issues while the performance appraisal might be used as part of the process for identifying reward for excellent work.

Personal development review

There may also be more regular separate personal development reviews which in some organisations are referred to as 'one-to-ones' as they provide an opportunity for the line manager to have a one-to-one discussion at regular intervals with individual members of their teams. These are often used alongside performance appraisals, either as standalone tools or as part of the strategic performance management process. Performance appraisal interviews usually happen just once or twice a year but personal development reviews are likely to happen much more frequently than this and to start during the induction period, when the line manager is able to have a one-to-one discussion with the individual team member to identify any gaps in knowledge and skills which need to be developed for them to become an effective team member. Cannell (2007) emphasises the constructive nature of personal developmental reviews and the need to use a variety of techniques to encourage the individual to participate fully and to do most of the talking.

Regular personal development reviews will result in each individual having an individual development plan designed to give detailed goals and provide for activities to enable that individual to achieve their goals. This should start at induction although some aspects of the individual development plan may have been identified as early as the selection stage and then this continues throughout their career. The plan is jointly designed by the manager and the employee, and the manager will provide support and coaching to help the employee to meet their goals. Once again this can form a part of the performance management process.

Objectives or competencies

There are basically two different approaches that can be used by employers when assessing performance. The first is concerned with outputs from the employee: it uses objectives and sets targets for the employee to work towards. The alternative approach is to examine the input that the employee makes to the organisation and determine the level of competence that the employee must achieve in their job.

In organisations where job descriptions based on competence are used, and where staff are used to working towards the achievement of NVQs, the second approach is likely to be favoured. Whichever approach is used there will still be a need to develop a method of assessing the employee's performance using some form of rating scale.

If the first of these approaches (using objectives) is to work well, then clearly the organisation needs to have 'ambitious goals and plans that employees know about and understand' – point 1 of the ACAS (2005) model workplace. They also need 'managers who genuinely listen to and consider their employees' views' – point 3 of the ACAS (2005) model workplace. The management by objectives approach to performance appraisal interviews, discussed later in this chapter, is likely to be preferred in this type of organisation.

If the focus is on the employee's level of competence, then 'people will need to feel valued so they can talk confidently about their work and learn from both successes and failures' – point 6 in the ACAS (2005) model workplace. Competency concerns the behaviour that a worker must have or gain in order to be able to contribute to the achievement of high levels of performance so is about the worker. Competence on the other hand relates to a system of occupational standards with specified levels of achievement so is job related. Hogg (2010) says:

> Although in the 1980s and 1990s HR professionals drew a distinction between 'competencies' and 'competences', now the two terms are often used interchangeably. 'Competency' is more precisely defined as the behaviours that employees must have, or must acquire, to input into a situation in order to achieve high levels of performance, that is a focus on the person, while 'competence' relates to a system of minimum standards or is demonstrated by performance and outputs, so 'competences' focus on the job.

Employees need to be able to operate in a competent way and to possess behavioural competencies that reinforce their technical skills. Competency frameworks have increased in popularity and the CIPD (2007b) survey of learning and development found 60 per cent of organisations in their sample had competency frameworks in place. They also found that the most popular use, by 56 per cent of their sample organisations, was as part of performance reviews and appraisals. When an organisation adopts this approach then competence will be measured and this gives a useful way of comparing actual levels of competence with required levels. This can obviously provide a useful tool for measurement of performance and consequently for the performance management process and it is not surprising that it has grown in popularity.

● Problems

A number of problems may prevent the appraisal schemes from being as effective as they should be as not all organisations follow the ACAS model and some try to create an appraisal scheme that does not fit with the normal culture of their organisation. These problems include:

- the organisation not being clear about the purpose of the appraisal system and consequently trying to use the appraisal scheme to fulfil too many different purposes
- links with pay preventing open discussion of problems or of areas where improvement could be made
- keeping information secret from the employee
- the appraiser attacking the appraisee's character
- being too subjective in judgements
- using appraisal as part of the disciplinary process.

Lack of clarity

We have already shown that most appraisal schemes fall into one of three categories, i.e. they are concerned with performance, potential or reward. An organisation should not attempt to use one appraisal scheme to fulfil all three categories. The particular objectives of an appraisal scheme should be clarified before the scheme is designed in detail, and should have been discussed with employees and other workers, trade unions and managers in order to take account of their views and to gain their commitment to the new appraisal scheme. Everyone should then be clear what the particular scheme is trying to achieve. Any scheme, however good the design, is unlikely to succeed if the managers and the workforce are suspicious of the reasons for its introduction and are opposed to making it work effectively.

While there are good reasons why employers should seek to appraise performance potential or give rewards to good employees, problems can also occur if employers try to achieve too much from their performance appraisal scheme.

It is difficult, if not impossible, to devise a scheme that will appraise successfully all three areas, and there is a grave danger that the performance appraisal scheme will be rejected if it fails to live up to all that is claimed for it. This can easily happen if the scheme is poorly designed or if the managers show a reluctance to impart critical assessments, or if people are not trained properly in the appraisal process.

Linking appraisal with pay

It is quite common for appraisal-related pay to be part of the performance management process and if done well this can be effective and of benefit to both employers and employees. It is generally introduced in order to emphasise a clear link between achieving high standards of performance in jobs and increased pay and is used as a motivational tool (ACAS, 2005). However, there are also problems associated with its introduction: in particular, it is difficult to imagine that a person being appraised is likely to admit to any developmental need, or be willing to accept any help in their performance, if their salary increase depends on a good appraisal. It is therefore recommended that employers should in general try to keep reward considerations separate from the other areas of performance review.

In spite of this advice and research evidence which suggests that performance-related pay (PRP) does not always motivate everyone in a workforce, many employers think that the offer of an incentive or reward is the only way to motivate employees to work harder, and this is often their main reason for introducing performance appraisal. The motivational aspects of pay will be discussed in more detail in Chapter 10, but the important point here is that great care needs to be taken if appraisal systems are linked to pay. It will be especially important to ensure that the criteria being appraised are objective and free of unfair bias, and that there are genuine opportunities for all employees to be rewarded for their efforts. Some employees may be motivated by other things such as increased holiday or more flexible benefits so appraisal-related pay may not motivate them to work harder.

In many organisations financial constraints mean that the number of people who are awarded PRP is severely restricted and there is a serious danger that if the vast majority of the workforce does not feel they have any opportunity to receive a reward, they may feel much more demotivated than they did before the appraisal scheme was introduced. Only the select few who receive the reward will then feel positive about the experience and about the organisation, and even they will not necessarily be motivated to work harder.

When appraisal-related pay is introduced as a part of the performance management system there will be also be other regular development reviews or performance reviews which provide opportunities for discussion of both good and bad performance. These reviews are normally kept separate from the review at which pay is discussed. Consequently they do not provide such an immediate deterrent to discussion of any weaknesses or aspects of poorer performance since their focus should be on past and future performance and the development needs of the individual. However, although this approach does weaken any direct link between pay and performance and learning, it would be foolish to think that it breaks the connection entirely. Employees may still feel confident it will not affect their pay, even if that review is held at a different time of year. On the other hand, they may take the view that discussion of areas of their performance in which they have done less well are worthwhile if this means that they gain access to more learning and development opportunities which may ultimately result in them getting more pay or being more employable.

Keeping information secret from the employee

Appraisal involves, as we have already said, being both a judge and helper for an individual employee. In order that we can help the individual it is also important that they know about the judgements that have been made about them and that they receive feedback about these. Therefore, if people are to be helped to develop, there must be discussion about problem areas, and any judgements made about employees should not be kept secret from them. Obviously the appraisal interview and reports of it do need to be confidential from other employees, but not so confidential that they are a secret from the employee concerned.

Subjectivity or attacks on the appraisee's character

If the person doing the appraising feels insecure about their own performance, there could be a tendency to try to ensure that the employee being appraised doesn't become a threat to them by focusing solely on the aspects of the job that have not been handled well and failing to show recognition for jobs that have been done well. In some cases, subjective judgements may be made because there are no clear criteria on which to appraise the employee, and the appraiser may resort to attacking aspects of the person's character that the person cannot do anything about. In the past many appraisal schemes were based on assessing personality traits that were thought to be important to a particular job, but that in fact were very broad categories that could only be judged subjectively. These included personality traits such as enthusiasm, application, intelligence and resourcefulness.

We imagine that you would not feel very happy with comments about your lack of integrity or poor level of intelligence, and would want to know on what criteria these comments were based.

If appraisal schemes are to be credible to employees, great care must be taken that judgements made are objective and have some basis that can be discussed with the employee. Integrity is likely to mean slightly different things to different people, and judgment of a person's integrity is likely to be fairly subjective. Rather than focusing on subjective topics such as this or on aspects of an individual's personality which they cannot alter, it is better to examine aspects of the job that the person actually does, and make an objective judgement about the person's effectiveness at carrying out each aspect of the job or their success in meeting their objectives.

Appraisers should also concentrate on seeking to help to bring about an improvement in areas of the employee's work where the appraisee can do something to make an improvement. Criticising someone for not being intelligent enough is similar to criticising them for being too short. There is really not much that they can do about it, so it is pointless to judge them on it and impossible to help them to change.

The relationship between appraisal and the disciplinary process

We have already said that appraisal is partly about making judgements about an employee's performance, and that areas where performance is not as effective as it should be need to be discussed. However, this does not mean that disciplinary matters should be saved for several months to be dealt with at the appraisal interview. If a disciplinary offence occurs, then it should be dealt with immediately and not saved for discussion at the time of the appraisal interview. The appraisal interview should be about seeking to motivate employees, not an opportunity to discipline them, although as we shall show later dealing with poor performance should be part of the performance management process.

The role of the line managers in performance appraisal

We have already emphasised the role of the line manager in performance management and traditionally the people who are most likely to be involved at the tactical level in the appraisal process are the person who is to be appraised and their immediate manager. This has the advantage that the managers or supervisors should know their subordinates and should also know about each subordinate's job and the way in which the subordinate carries out their duties. Managers and their subordinates will see each other every day but may be too busy to discuss performance. The performance appraisal interview provides the time for the individual and the manager to sit down together to discuss the individual's progress. This should enable the manager to feel that they are helping the career of one of the staff, and prove to be a motivating experience for the employee, who has the undivided attention of the manager listening to their views and focusing attention on their development.

There can, however, be some disadvantages in having the employee's immediate manager carry out the appraisal, especially if there is a conflict of personalities or if the manager perceives the employee to be a threat and is therefore unwilling to look for positive aspects of the employee's performance. If the appraisal scheme allows a high degree of subjectivity in comments made by the manager, then there is a danger that more will be learnt about the manager's attitudes to work and managing employees than about the employee's performance. Training in performance appraisal techniques is obviously extremely important here.

While it is always important that the line manager is involved in the process of performance management there are others who could be involved in performance appraisal.

ACTIVITY 8.1

The appraisee's immediate supervisor or manager is usually the person most involved in the appraisal process, although in some organisations other people may be involved. Using Table 8.1, write a list of people who you think might be involved in the appraisal process. For each of them, list the advantages and the disadvantages of their involvement.

Table 8.1 People involved in the performance appraisal process

People who may be involved in the appraisal process	Advantages	Disadvantages

Although, as we said earlier, line managers are the most frequent group to be involved in conducting appraisal interviews, they do not always relish this part of their job or see its importance. A list of the others who could be involved in performance appraisal is given in Table 8.2 at the end of this chapter.

The main problem with line manager involvement according to Gillen (2001) is that some managers see appraisal as a low priority for two reasons. It is necessary to understand their viewpoint on this in order to be able to convince them of the relevance of appraisal to them and to their department. According to Gillen (2001), the first reason why it can be difficult to get managers to conduct performance appraisal interviews is because they prefer to spend their time doing things rather than managing things or managing and leading people. Gillen (2001) says that generally most managers went into their jobs not to manage, but to do things, for example to build things, to teach things or to sell things. They did not specifically go into the job to manage either things or people and often consider that these parts of their job are difficult and mean they spend less time on what they enjoy. They therefore tend to put off doing them because they do not see the immediate relevance to them or to their department of initiatives such as performance appraisal.

According to Gillen (2001), the second reason is because managers perceive some specific problems related to appraisal. These will vary from organisation to organisation but are likely to result in line managers saying or feeling some of the following:

1 I've got enough to do without also having to fill in forms for Personnel.
2 The appraisal process is 'divorced' from the realities of my 'business cycle'.
3 Appraisal is inherently unfair.
4 Appraisal is amazingly time-consuming.
5 Giving staff feedback on their performance during an appraisal interview is uncomfortable. (Gillen, 2001)

Some of these statements are undoubtedly true. As we said, it can be difficult to give staff feedback on their performance and sometimes managers struggle to remember their employee's key achievements, particularly those that occurred some months earlier. Appraisal can seem quite time-consuming and may appear to be organised to suit someone else's time schedule.

Some of the other statements are less easy to justify and may result from the line manager's false perception of the situation. If an organisation has established a performance appraisal scheme in the ways we will describe, then it should certainly not be perceived as 'inherently unfair' and managers who feel that the appraisal process is undertaken just to please the personnel or HR department have not had the process properly explained to them.

Whatever the reasons for these negative perceptions of performance appraisal, they do need to be overcome if the scheme is to be successful. Gillen (2001) suggests various ways to erase these misconceptions and to help line managers appreciate the benefits of appraisal. One useful idea he suggests is that line managers should be made aware of the three main elements to their job: doing things, managing things, and managing and leading people, and that they should be involved in a discussion about which of these they enjoy most. After a discussion in which he establishes that performance requirements in a job are generally getting harder and that people do not want to work even longer to achieve them, he then draws a parallel with lifting a heavy load using a lever and explains that this becomes easier if one uses a longer lever. He says that for managers, using performance appraisal and working on the managing and leading element of their job is the equivalent of using a longer lever. It is about working smarter and not harder.

CASE STUDY 8.1 Performance appraisal

Joan Bywell is a busy manager in an insurance company, heading the life insurance division. She has worked with the company for six years and has always enjoyed organising the work to reach targets and implementing new ideas to improve sales and streamline the processing of policies.

The company has now introduced a performance appraisal system so that managers can formally evaluate their staff on a regular basis. Angela Jones, the HR manager, sees this partly as a preliminary step to introducing performance-related pay for administrative staff within the next five years. Angela has devised a form for managers to use to evaluate their staff, and she has distributed these to managers with instructions to complete the evaluation within four weeks and return the forms to the personnel office, to be held on the employees' personal files.

Joan is reluctant to waste valuable managerial time on this process, but she duly fills in the forms for her administrative staff. She decides not to waste more time on endless discussions with her staff, so she gives each employee the completed form and asks them to sign it to confirm they have seen the evaluation and return it to her the next day. She suggests that if they wish to discuss any points, they should make an appointment to speak to her.

George has been with the company for three years. He feels that he works hard and he is hoping he will be considered for a supervisory post when one of the unit supervisors retires next year. George is incensed when he looks at his evaluation and sees that his performance has been graded as 'satisfactory' on a number of criteria such as 'initiative', 'reliability', and 'amount of work completed'. He would have expected a grading of very good or excellent.

George storms into Joan's office and says: 'I know you said we could talk to you if we had any queries about this so-called performance appraisal, but if this is what you think of me, I do not see any point. I think my best plan is to look for a job with a company that will appreciate hard work.'

Joan actually thinks quite highly of George and is perturbed at this turn of events.

Question

Comment on what is wrong with this performance appraisal system and make suggestions for improvement.

Discussion of case study 8.1

This disastrous appraisal nearly ended with the loss of George, a good worker, and is the result of several factors. First, the HR manager Angela Jones has not actually consulted with or involved anyone in the organisation in the design of the appraisal forms or in conducting the appraisal interview and no one has received any training in how to use them. Consequently managers such as Joan are not aware of how important an issue performance appraisal is for motivating her team, identifying talent and improving her team's performance.

Joan is also typical of many of the supervisors described earlier who are very good at the aspects of the job which they see as important, such as achieving targets. However, she does not realise that managing people is an equally important part of her job. If Angela Jones had explained how the performance appraisal process could help Joan achieve her targets and had given her training to this effect then she would have viewed the process in a much more positive light and would have spent time on it.

The performance appraisal form is designed badly so that employees and their supervisors are being asked to rate the individual against criteria which may have nothing to do with their jobs. The amount of work is probably much less important than the quality of the work done and this should be broken down to consider various aspects of the job or to specific objectives or competencies needed. Initiative could be difficult to assess and may not be particularly useful in a job where perhaps there is very limited scope to exercise initiative. Reliability is also a rather vague term as it does not describe the circumstances in which reliability is needed. Angela Jones needs to consult more widely about the criteria that would work on a performance appraisal form and needs to tailor the forms to objectives, job descriptions or competencies required. She then needs to provide training for both managers and subordinates so that everyone is clear about the purpose of the performance appraisal scheme before it is introduced into the organisation. The next section discusses the design of the documentation and Table 8.2 gives an example of documentation using objectives.

Design of documentation

In most appraisal systems it is necessary to have some type of documentation to record what has been agreed. At its simplest this could just be blank sheets of paper for both the appraiser and appraisee, on which they both assess the performance of the appraisee. This provides a means for jutting down ideas and views on performance which can then be used as a basis for discussion at the time of the performance appraisal interview. The disadvantage of this system is that there may be little basis for agreement about the topics to be discussed.

In order to provide for a systematic and consistent approach to performance appraisal, many organisations design an appraisal form. In this case, the manager and the person being appraised both complete a form prior to the appraisal interview. They then exchange forms and at the interview use both the forms as a basis for discussion. This has the advantage of both parties having focused on similar topics and saves time at the interview, as both should have already done quite a bit of preparation for the interview. When designing such a form, there should be clear guidelines explaining what is meant by each section, and the points already discussed in the section on problems must be borne in mind. The criteria to be appraised should not be subjective and should be fair. They should relate to things that employees could

Types of performance appraisal

improve, and there should be opportunities for the employee to see the appraiser's comments and a section in which to respond to those comments. There should also be a right of appeal. The guidelines should indicate what should then happen to the appraisal forms. Where will they be kept? Who will ensure that action is taken on key points?

The actual content of such a form will be influenced by the type of appraisal scheme adopted by the organisation. This will now be discussed.

Management by objectives (MBO)

We have already said that appraisal schemes are most likely to succeed if the criteria to be appraised can be assessed objectively rather than subjectively, and that the appraisal of aspects of a person's personality should be avoided. One way of achieving this is to set clear objectives for the employee to achieve before the next appraisal, and then to focus the discussion at the appraisal interview on the extent to which these objectives have been achieved. An appraisal interview also provides an opportunity to look forward, so the next stage would be to set and agree objectives for the next review period.

One way in which to achieve this would be to look first at the job description and then agree specific objectives for each of the main tasks. This has the additional advantage that the objectives can be linked very clearly to the organisation's strategic goals, so that the individual can see exactly what to do to help the organisation meet its objectives. A sample form for this type of performance appraisal is shown in Figure 8.4.

In this example there is an opportunity to look at past objectives and consider the extent to which they have been achieved, and also a chance to look forward and agree future objectives. Here the appraisee has an opportunity to write comments, as do the manager and countersigning manager. This type of appraisal can also link with overall organisational objectives, and is often used as part of a performance management system, as we shall show later.

Rating scales

This is another form of performance appraisal scheme that seeks to encourage objectivity by focusing on aspects of the employee's job and then indicating by graded statements how successfully the employee has fulfilled each of the main duties listed in their job description. The statements would be linked to the job description with a statement for each category of the job description, indicating levels of performance or level of competence required in that duty, ranging from excellent to poor. The appraiser would discuss the person's performance using these scales during the appraisal interview, and would then tick the statement that they and the appraisee agreed best summed up the appraisee's performance or which matched their level of competence.

Figure 8.4 Sample form for performance appraisal using management by objectives

NAME . . . .   JOB TITLE . . . .

DATE OF APPRAISAL . . . .   DEPARTMENT/SECTION . . . .

JOB DESCRIPTION (To be agreed with employee)

REVIEW PERIOD . . . .

1. Objectives agreed for this last review period. (This should include special tasks, personal training and development.)

2. To what extent have these objectives been achieved?

3. Were there any other major achievements?

4. Were there any obstacles which prevented achievement of agreed objectives?

5. What steps need to be taken to overcome these obstacles?

6. What training, development and education were undertaken during the review period?

NEXT REVIEW PERIOD . . . .

1. What specific objectives have been agreed for the next review period?

2. What training, development and education should be undertaken during the next review period?

3. What follow-up action is needed?

COMMENTS OF APPRAISER

Signed . . . . (Appraiser)

COMMENTS OF APPRAISEE

Signed . . . . (Appraisee)

COMMENTS OF COUNTERSIGNING MANAGER

ACTIVITY 8.2

Do you remember the job description which we gave in Chapter 6? The main duties for this are listed in Figure 8.5. For each of these duties, write a series of statements to indicate the possible degrees of success of someone who is working in this job. It is intended that these statements will form the basic information with which the individual's performance in that job is compared by the appraiser. We have started this for you by suggesting some graded statements for the first row.

Figure 8.5 Job rating

Name of job holder: ....

Job title: Receptionist

Date of appraisal: ....

Main duties	Appraiser's comments	A (Well ahead of standard performance)	B (More than satisfactory, slightly above job requirements)	C (Less than satisfactory, needs slight improvement)	D (Requires constant supervision)
Greet walk-in visitors and ascertain purpose of their visit. Handle or redirect queries as appropriate		Always quick to greet visitors and ascertain purpose of visit, and deals effectively with queries extremely rapidly and effectively so visitors are always highly satisfied	Greets visitors, ascertains purpose of visit, and deals effectively with queries	Normally greets visitors promptly and ascertains purpose of their visit; sometimes slow to redirect queries	Slow to notice walk-in visitors, does not always greet them promptly, and is not always able to deal with queries or redirect them to the appropriate place
Answer phone queries as above					
Answer all initial queries about receipt of payments using the online payment receipts system					

Figure 8.5 Continued

Main duties	Appraiser's comments	A (Well ahead of standard performance)	B (More than satisfactory, slightly above job requirements)	C (Less than satisfactory, needs slight improvement)	D (Requires constant supervision)
Open and sort incoming post by department. Organise delivery of post by assistant receptionist					
Perform clerical tasks assigned by department in agreement with the Office Services Manager					
Supervise assistant receptionists and delegate work as appropriate					
Perform other duties as assigned by the Office Services Manager or other authorised manager					

Comments of appraiser

Signature . . . . (Appraiser)

Comments of appraisee

Signature . . . . (Appraisee)

Comments of countersigning manager

Signature . . . . (Manager)

Discussion of Activity 8.2

This gives a simple way of rating the employee's behaviour in the job that is clear and easy to use, as the appraiser simply ticks the box containing the comment that most nearly reflects the actual performance of the employee. It also means that there is a common standard which all appraisers would use when appraising a person doing that job. In this case, examples of four types of behaviour had to be provided for each aspect of the main duties listed in the job description. This was because many appraisers tend to rate employees as average just to avoid upsetting people or to avoid giving too much praise: by not allowing a middle category, they are encouraged to be more decisive. There may still be a tendency to go for the middle two boxes (and for many employees this will be highly appropriate), but appraisers must be encouraged by training to use the full range of categories if and when this is needed.

In this Activity you were the only person to choose the descriptions for the criteria to be rated, so there could still be some degree of subjectivity involved, as you may have described the performance of each duty in a different way to other people. It would be more usual to involve a team of people to provide the descriptors for each main duty and to get consensus about the descriptors to be used.

Behaviourally anchored rating scales (BARS)

If this appraisal system were to be introduced in a large organisation, it would not rely on just one person's ideas of a suitable range of categories. In the first section of the ratings exercise we have used the following terms as descriptors of the first of the major duties listed in the job description:

- Always quick to greet visitors and ascertain purpose of visit, dealing with queries extremely rapidly and effectively so visitors are always highly satisfied.
- Greets visitors, ascertains purpose of visit and deals effectively with queries.
- Normally greets visitors promptly and ascertains purpose of their visit; sometimes slow to redirect queries.
- Slow to notice walk-in visitors, does not always greet them promptly, and is not always able to deal with queries or redirect them to the appropriate place.

These were purely our own subjective choices, and we had not checked whether or not other people would describe this aspect of the job in the same way. You could find other descriptors that may be more effective than these. We may have chosen terms to describe each level of performance that are different from the way in which other people would describe the same task.

One way to try to get round the subjectivity of having just one person writing the descriptions of behaviour is to use a newer technique, known as behaviourally anchored rating scales. In this case a group of other raters would also be asked to suggest descriptions for a range of behaviour for each aspect of the main duties, so that a wide range of behavioural examples could be collected.

These descriptions are then collated and returned to the sample raters, but this time there is no indication of the scale point for which they were suggested. The sample raters are asked to indicate a scale point from A to D, where A represents excellence and D represents bad work, to which they think each descriptor most aptly relates. The descriptors that are consistently located at the same point of the scale are then used in the final version of the behaviourally anchored scale. This is intended to remove the subjectivity inherent in the simpler rating method and ensure that descriptions used are likely to mean the same thing to most people.

ACTIVITY 8.3

What do you see as the main advantages and disadvantages of this system of behaviourally anchored rating scales? Make a list.

Discussion of Activity 8.3

Compare your list of advantages and disadvantages with the following list.

Advantages

- Objective rating of each of the main duties listed in job description.
- Agreement over suitable descriptors for each category of behaviour.
- Easy to use.
- Useful if lots of people have the same job descriptions so that the amount of time involved in designing the system will be repaid.

Disadvantages

- Time-consuming, as it takes a long time to get agreement on descriptors for each job.
- Only takes account of existing job performance; does not allow for discussion of future potential.

● Behavioural observation scales (BOS)

These form another way of rating performance in a job. These scales are also developed as a result of lengthy procedures, and indicate a number of dimensions of performance with behavioural examples for each. Job analysis is used to identify the key determinants of performance and the performance dimensions are once again related to the job description, but in this case the appraiser is asked to indicate a point on a scale by a numerical value.

An example of such a scale in relation to selected aspects of a lecturer's job is given below. The appraisers simply circle the number that they think relates most closely to the usual behaviour of the appraisee.

ACTIVITY 8.4

You can try this for yourself by selecting a lecturer you know well and assessing them on this scale. Circle the number that most closely relates to the lecturer's normal behaviour.

1 Provides clearly structured lecture that is easy to follow

Almost never   5   4   3   2   1   Almost always

2 Provides up-to-date and interesting material in lectures/tutorials

Almost never   5   4   3   2   1   Almost always

3 Explains to students exactly what is expected of them when they complete written work

Almost never	5	4	3	2	1	Almost always

4 Is willing to give advice and guidance

Almost never	5	4	3	2	1	Almost always

5 Gives detailed and helpful feedback concerning written work that students have completed

Almost never	5	4	3	2	1	Almost always

Discussion of Activity 8.4

We hope that you were fair in your assessment and were not influenced by personality or past grades given to you! In this case you were assessing the lecturer from the position of a student, and you are likely to have a very different view of their work performance to the lecturer's manager or the human resource manager. You may not, however, be able to assess all aspects of the lecturer's job such as their ability to carry out research, or an individual's administrative capabilities, but this exercise is similar to assessment by a person's subordinates which we mentioned earlier. It has the same type of limitations that we discussed then, but it gives you some idea of the way in which different points of view can be important and shows that if this were combined with appraisal from other perspectives, as in a system such as 360-degree appraisal, it could contribute to developing a full picture of a person's effectiveness and provide valuable feedback.

Critical incidents

This involves keeping a record of positive and negative behaviour during a specified period of time. This record of critical incidents is the basis for the appraisal interview although the appraiser would normally be expected to also give feedback on both positive and negative critical incidents as and when they happened. This method does have some benefits as it does not just rely on annual reporting and has the benefit of giving immediate feedback but according to ACAS (2008) the main disadvantage is that it is also very time-consuming.

Narrative report

Using this method the appraiser describes the behaviour of the individual being appraised in their own words in either an essay or report style, as preferred, but without the use of any form for a prompt or for structure. For a narrative report one could start with just a blank sheet of paper as this form of recording is a flexible format which can be adapted to varying circumstances. However, for some appraisers this lack of structure and choice of approach will be too vague and they may have difficulty choosing which aspects of performance to focus on. It also requires the appraiser to have good writing skills and the subjectivity of this format also makes it very difficult to compare levels of performance. There could be accusations of too much subjectivity particularly if there is any link to pay involved.

The appraisal interview

Interviews have already been discussed in some detail in Chapter 7, and the points made there with regard to selection interviews also apply to appraisal interviews. Preparation, privacy and confidentiality, good questioning technique, avoidance of bias, good records and attention to the style of interview will also be important in the appraisal interview.

● Preparation

There is a need, as we explained in Chapter 7, for careful preparation before any interview and employees should be given adequate notice of the date of the appraisal interview to allow them time to prepare. In the appraisal interview this is also likely to mean that care needs to be taken with the layout of the room, so that the person being appraised will not be intimidated by a formal set-up with barriers such as a big desk, and so that they feel comfortable and at ease. There is also a need to avoid interruptions and to ensure that telephone messages are taken elsewhere and that there are no unnecessary distractions.

If the person has been appraised in the past, then the last appraisal record will need to be read to check what objectives, if any, were agreed for the current appraisal period. The individual's job description will also need to be checked and the training and development records examined to discover what training and development has occurred since the last interview. In some cases, if the person who is to be appraised works for several people, it may also be necessary to obtain information from other managers, or in the case of other types of performance appraisal, from subordinates or peers.

As stated earlier it is also useful for both parties in the appraisal to prepare for the meeting, and both the appraiser and appraisee need to have received training so that they know what to expect in order that they can both skilfully handle what is potentially a difficult interaction. A constructive approach used by many organisations is to give both the appraiser and appraisee a form to complete prior to the appraisal interview. In some organisations these are then exchanged, and this has the advantage of focusing the attention of appraiser and appraisee on common issues. In other organisations these forms are simply used as an *aide-mémoire* for the individuals concerned, but if they are exchanged prior to the interview, they can help to clearly identify areas where there is broad agreement so that more time can be allowed to discuss other topics where there are differences of opinion.

● Privacy and confidentiality

We have already indicated that the appraisal is an important way of giving feedback to the employee about their work performance. In the past some organisations did not allow the appraisee to see the records of their appraisal, but we feel that this misses a valuable opportunity for providing feedback from which the employee could learn. On the other hand, the appraisal form and interview have to be kept confidential from other people as there will probably be very personal information on the form, and no one who feels that half the department can hear every word of the conversation is likely to feel willing to discuss their performance openly.

Good questioning technique

The appraisal interview has, as we have already said, much in common with all other types of interviews. Once again the type of questions asked will be important. As this is an opportunity to provide feedback to the employee there will perhaps be slightly more opportunity for the interviewer to do more talking than in some other forms of interview, but this should be treated with caution. It is certainly not the time for the appraiser to do all the talking.

There should be an introductory phase where the interviewer tries to put the person being appraised at ease. It is generally better to follow this with a discussion of the employee's strong points and then try to get information, especially about any areas of perceived weakness, from the employee by asking open questions and teasing out the information. Areas of weakness need to be raised and discussed fully, and open questions are important here. If the interviewer uses closed questions that merely need yes or no answers, they will end up doing most of the talking. Leading questions, which put words in the appraisee's mouth or indicate what the appraiser wants them to say, should also be avoided.

Appraisers should also take great care not to be unduly influenced by a high assessment in one particular area, and should not allow this to cloud their judgement so that they rate all other areas of the employee's performance highly, even though these may not deserve such a high rating. This is known as the 'halo' effect. Similarly, care should be taken to avoid being unduly influenced by one very poor assessment. This is known as the 'horns' effect.

The contingency approach to interviews

While it is fair to say that the style of interview that is generally recommended for appraisal interviewing is a joint problem-solving approach which involves the appraiser and appraisee equally, it is also possible that some other styles of interview may be appropriate in certain circumstances. For example, if the person being appraised is new to the department they may have less to say than someone who has been there longer and so it may be appropriate for the appraiser to do a little more of the talking. If, on the other hand, the person being appraised is very experienced and has worked for the organisation for many years then they may hold many views about their own performance and have clear ideas for improving it. In this case it is possible that the person being appraised might be allowed to do slightly more of the talking. The contingency approach means that the most appropriate style of interview will depend on the circumstances at the time: the approach will be contingent on the circumstances.

The choice of style depends on factors such as the manager's own style, the organisation's culture and the behaviour of the appraisee themselves. In an autocratic organisation where people are not used to having their views considered, there may be a high degree of suspicion if at the time of the appraisal interview the manager suddenly adopts a joint problem-solving approach and actually asks for the views of the employees. This can be a problem for many organisations, because if the organisation normally conducts its affairs in such a way that the employees don't trust the managers to treat them fairly, then it is going to be extremely difficult, if not impossible, for the employees suddenly to start trusting the person who is conducting their appraisal, and to talk in an open and honest way to them. This shows that appraisals should not be used just as an isolated technique to try and motivate the workforce. They need to be an integral part of the way the organisation treats people, and fundamental issues such as the culture of the organisation and its normal style of management also need to be addressed.

Information technology and performance management

Increasingly organisations are using information technology as a part of their performance appraisal or performance management system. This is not just about record-keeping although some organisations do use their intranet site for this and also to explain procedures and for online training for appraiser and appraisee. Some organisations even complete the initial stages of the performance appraisal system online and both appraisee and appraiser can complete online forms and exchange these prior to meeting for a face-to-face interview where they discuss the contents, focusing particularly on differences in their views of performance. In *People Management* there are increasing numbers of IT systems which claim to help with performance appraisal and Google UK lists over one and a half million online references to providers for 360-degree feedback so this is clearly an area where IT is providing a great deal of support (Coomber, 2006).

The opportunity to complete performance appraisal questionnaires online is particularly useful when 360-degree appraisal is used. Getting forms completed using pen and paper from several sources is arduous and collecting and collating the information from a range of sources manually can be very time-consuming. Using online resources has made the use of 360-degree appraisal much easier and may be partially responsible for the increase in its popularity. Online forms can also benefit from being interactive so that the appraisee can even elect to receive feedback on specific aspects of their competence or performance. According to Coomber (2006), other benefits of online collection of appraisal information include improvements in confidentiality and accuracy. It is also much easier and requires much less administration to collate the information from several appraisers into an easily accessible format using graphs and charts.

International issues in performance management and performance appraisal

Performance management and performance appraisal can be difficult to get right but when organisations succeed in this they do create a motivating experience for workers and help to improve performance. In a global organisation operating across many countries and several cultures this is especially difficult to achieve. In some cultures it is difficult to introduce 360-degree appraisal as subordinates may feel reluctant to criticise their immediate manager, because in that culture it is unthinkable to criticise one's superior. In other cultures it may also be difficult for the appraiser to make any comments that would improve the work of someone who was older in years than themselves. Some cultures prefer openness and transparency in the performance management process so individuals know who is responsible for comments about their performance, while in other cultures individuals would be unwilling to comment on performance if they thought the appraisee would know the source of comment.

Organisations have to make choices about the extent to which they take account of different cultures and decide whether to operate different performance management systems in each country or whether they try to get something that will be acceptable to all by adapting the host country's performance management scheme as standard.

One organisation which faced this problem was Kimberley-Clark, probably best known for its Andrex toilet paper, the Andrex puppy and for Kleenex tissues. They operate in 68 countries but did not have a standard approach across all. Their competencies approach was interpreted in differing ways in different countries, resulting in problems when moving staff from one part of the organisation to another, or from one country to another. While their sales and share price were doing badly the performance ratings of their employees still seemed very high as individuals were reluctant to give a below average rating to anyone, even for a below average performance.

In 2003, Tom Falk, the chief executive of Kimberly-Clark, launched a global business plan designed to increase the emphasis on talent management and development of a high-performance culture. The performance management system was a key part of this and in order to get global buy-in from everyone an international project team was appointed representing all regions so that regional and cultural issues were addressed. A system of 360-degree feedback was agreed upon but because of the concerns expressed by workers in some parts of the world, particularly Korea, South America and Asia, it was decided that this feedback had to be anonymous and, while this didn't entirely suit all Western countries, this was the approach adopted. The performance management scheme was web-based but was also translated into the languages of all the countries where the group was based and training was also given in the languages of each country. This meant that each part of the organisation in each country felt increased ownership for the scheme and the amount of effort put into consultation, translation and training seemed to be worthwhile, as in a survey conducted by the company a year after the launch of the new performance management system, 95 per cent of the workforce said that they were confident about its use (Arkin, 2007).

Conclusion

Performance management derives from the human resource management approach as a strategic and integrated approach to the management and development of people and it uses many HR techniques. It emphasises the important role of line managers to take responsibility for the management of the performance of the people in their department. With its emphasis on the need for continuous performance review, performance management also relates clearly to the ideas of continuing talent development and learning. It uses the techniques of performance appraisal but prefers to use the more objective types, such as setting objectives. It does, however, go further than performance appraisal as what is appraised is clearly derived from the strategic plan and both individuals and teams are involved in setting objectives for themselves and in evaluating their success in achieving these objectives.

Line managers play an important part in reviewing the performance of individuals and teams and have responsibility to review progress and development throughout the year, not just at the time of the annual appraisal interview. Both individual and team objectives are clearly derived from the corporate strategic objectives, and everyone is aware that management of performance is the concern of all in the organisation, and not just HR management or the senior management team. Performance management is, above all, a process for sharing an understanding about what needs to be achieved, and then managing and developing people in a way which will facilitate this so that excellent communications, in all directions, are achieved, particularly in global organisations – and employee involvement and engagement are also extremely important.

Improvements in online performance appraisal schemes are helping to increase the use of 360-degree appraisal and can also be particularly useful in international organisations where it may be very time-consuming to collect information from participants who work in different parts of the world. Performance appraisal and performance management are important tools that can contribute not only to an organisation's effectiveness, but they can also help ensure that it becomes a high-performance workplace.

REVIEW QUESTIONS

You will find brief answers to these review questions on pages 492–4.

1 Discuss the reasons for line managers' apparent reluctance to get involved in performance management and suggest ways to convince them of the value of this process to them.

2 What are the main advantages and disadvantages of using 360 degree appraisal?

3 Performance appraisals are intended to motivate employees towards greater productivity and improve communication/relations between managers and their team members. Explain why performance appraisals often fail to achieve this goal, and comment on the skills that managers need to make performance appraisal work.

4 Performance management is described by Armstrong and Baron (2004) as a process which 'contributes to the effective management of individuals and teams in order to achieve high levels of organizational performance.'
   (a) Describe the key stages in the performance management implementation process.
   (b) List the different HR techniques that could be used as part of performance management in relation to the organisation, the team and the individual.

5 Describe three different approaches to performance appraisal and comment critically on the benefits to be gained from these systems.

SELF-CHECK QUESTIONS

Answer the following multiple-choice and short-answer questions. The correct responses are given on page 494 for you to check your understanding of this chapter.

1 Which of the following is stated in this chapter as being least likely to contribute to an organisation becoming an effective workplace?

(a) Policies and procedures that everyone knows about and understands.

(b) Effective health and safety policies and procedures.

(c) Line managers who perceive performance appraisal as totally separate from the realities of their business cycle and their business objectives.

(d) Line managers who perceive performance appraisal as an important aspect of their job that they need to spend time on so they develop their staff and then meet their business objectives.

(e) An organisation with a 'Big Idea' that everyone knows about and understands.

2 Which of the following acronyms is used in Purcell's (2003) People and Performance Model?

(a) AMO

(b) AMP

(c) IMP

(d) AMA

(e) IMO.

3 In this chapter we said that when we appraise someone there are three key, but sometimes contradictory, roles. Which of the following are the three roles to which we referred?

(a) Giving feedback and being friend and helper.

(b) Giving feedback and being judge and source of discipline.

(c) Giving feedback and being judge and helper.

(d) Giving a subjective assessment of performance and being judge and helper.

(e) Giving feedback and being judge and critic.

4 Which of the following is a good reason for organisations to introduce a performance appraisal scheme?

(a) to improve current performance

(b) to provide a check on their staff's integrity

(c) to check on the honesty of their employees

(d) to clarify the employee's contract

(e) to discipline individuals.

5 Appraisal schemes may not be as effective as they should be because of a number of problems. Which of the following is not one of the problems associated with the introduction of performance appraisal schemes?

(a) The organisation is not clear about the purpose of its appraisal scheme.

(b) The performance appraisal scheme is too objective in the judgements made.

(c) Information is kept secret from the employee.

(d) The performance appraisal scheme is too subjective in the judgements made.

(e) Appraisal is used as part of the disciplinary process.

6 Which of the following best describes what is meant by the term 'performance management'?

(a) A process which contributes to the effective management of individuals and teams in order to achieve high levels of organisational performance.

(b) A process which contributes to the effective management of the HR department in order to achieve high levels of departmental performance.

(c) A process which contributes to the effective management of teams in order to achieve high levels of team performance.

(d) A process which contributes to the effective management of individuals in order to achieve high levels of individual performance.

(e) A process which contributes to the effective management of individuals and teams in order to improve the personnel department's performance.

HR IN THE NEWS

FT

FT Report – Digital Business 2007: Tools help staff see the effects of effort

By Sam Hiser

Securing the services of the best available candidates is at the heart of e-recruitment systems. But once the new recruits are on board, technology now plays a big part in helping to monitor, incentivise and manage them.

Performance management software tools are maturing, taking advantage of the internet and replacing custom-grown solutions to help managers more effectively monitor and offer incentives to staff.

Also known as business intelligence (BI) or business performance management (BPM), e-performance management is a growing field.

Oracle, through its Peoplesoft and Hyperion acquisitions, SAP, Cognos and Business Objects are some of the big software providers helping managers collect, organise and massage data coming in from across finance, back office, manufacturing, production, sales and compensation business processes.

A growing list of smaller players, too, provides targeted services in a variety of niches. In the sales performance management (SPM) arena, for example, sales personnel and managers need a clear view of objectives and sales plan rules. They also need real-time visibility on their compensation statements and incentive goal sheets as well as performance comparisons versus prior periods.

A dashboard screen on a desktop, laptop or smartphone allows them to absorb this information by showing up-to-the minute sales and compensation statistics and integrates incentive plan information.

In any sales organisation where the compensation plan drives the business, there is a need for everybody to be connected to central goals and respond quickly.

'You want to turn the business rules into compensation. With a centralised book, you can cascade strategic changes in the call plan,' says Leslie Stretch, senior vice-president of global sales, marketing and on-demand business at Callidus Software. The implications penetrate to the bottom line.

Mr Stretch says integrated software permits incentive compensation to be awarded faster and targeted with precision, while slowness and inaccuracy can demoralise a sales force.

Callidus, for example, is establishing a de facto standard for sales performance it calls the 'true performance index', that a professional can use to monitor the effects of their efforts. They can take this statistic with them – possibly to different employers. For heavily unionised customers, such as telecoms companies, Mr Stretch reports fewer disputes, due partly, he claims, to trust in the Callidus data.

E-performance management tools are making a difference in operations management, too. A UK software and consulting group, eg Solutions, offers straightforward technology and advice which seeks to identify processes and tasks, assign roles, groups, teams and skills, and match desired outcomes with human activity. The business-intelligence gathering mechanism is embedded in the process, which means data input is not segregated from the work itself.

Elizabeth Gooch, eg's chief executive, says: 'It's like driving a car, first in manual and then in automatic.' The key is to make people autonomous optimisers by showing them the results of what they do.

Employees are said to appreciate sharper e-performance management tools and thrive because they feel a greater sense of accomplishment when their efforts are connected with results.

(Financial Times, 7 November 2007, © Sam Hiser. Reproduced with permission.)

Questions

1 What do you think are the main advantages of using performance management software?

2 What in your view are the disadvantages?

Now that you have read this introductory chapter on performance appraisal and performance management, and have completed all the exercises, you may feel ready to progress further. If you would like more opportunities to test your own learning on this subject then you can go to the student website that accompanies this book: www.pearsoned.co.uk/foothook.

WHAT NEXT?

If you feel ready to examine this subject in more depth then there have been several research studies that could help you to further your understanding of how organisations achieve improvements in performance.

A study from the research team at the University of Bath examines case study organisations and how they achieve success when times are difficult:

Hutchinson, S., N. Kinnie, J. Purcell, J. Swart, B. Rayton (2003) *Understanding the People Performance Link: Unlocking the Black Box*, CIPD.

You can also find a free interactive tool on the ACAS website at **www.acas.co.uk** which can help those of you who work in organisations to assess your organisation's performance against the ACAS model workplace.

A similar diagnostic tool is available from the CIPD (2010) at **www.cipd.co.uk** and is called Developing performance management. This can be used to help organisations assess and improve the performance management processes in their organisation.

Read the following longitudinal research study about organisation performance which aims to advance thinking and practice by generating debate and which also seeks to provide some practical advice for organisations.

Miller J. and C. McCartney with contributions from A. Baron, J. McGurk and V. Robinson (2010) *Shaping the future*, CIPD (www.cpd.co.uk/shapingthefuture accessed 12.8.2010).

References

Advisory, Conciliation and Arbitration Service (2005) *The ACAS Model Workplace*, ACAS (www.acas.org.co.uk; accessed 10.8.2010).

Advisory, Conciliation and Arbitration Service (2008) *Employee Appraisal*, ACAS.

Armstrong, M. (1994) *Performance Management*, Kogan Page.

Armstrong, M. and A. Baron (2004) *Managing Performance: Performance Management in Action*, CIPD.

Arkin, A. (2007) From soft to strong, *People Management*, 6 September, Vol. 13, No. 18, 30–33.

Baron, A. (2009) in *Performance Management – Podcast 25*, CIPD.

Cannell, M. (2007) *Performance Management: An Overview*, February, CIPD.

Chartered Institute of Personnel and Development (2005) *Performance Management: Survey Report September 2005*, CIPD.

Chartered Institute of Personnel and Development (2007a) *The People and Performance Link*, May, CIPD.

Chartered Institute of Personnel and Development (2007b) *Learning and Development: Annual Survey Report 2007*, CIPD.

Chartered Institute of Personnel and Development (2009) *Performance Management in Action: Current Trends and Practice*, CIPD.

Chartered Institute of Personnel and Development (2010) *Factsheet: Performance Management an Overview*, CIPD.

Coomber, J. (2006) *360 Feedback*, CIPD.

Cunneen, P. (2006) How to improve performance management, *People Management*, 12 January, Vol. 12, No. 1, 42–43.

Fletcher, C. and R. Williams (1985) *Performance Appraisal and Career Development*, Hutchinson.

Gillen, T. (2001) *Appraisal: Getting Managers' Buy-in*, CIPD (www.cipd.co.uk; accessed 17.9.07).

Hogg, C. (2010) *Competency and Competency Frameworks*, CIPD (www.cipd.co.uk; accessed 10.8.2010).

Purcell, J., N. Rinnie and S. Hutchinson (2003) Open minded, *People Management*, Vol. 9, No. 10, 31–33.

Randell, G.A., P.M.A. Packard, R.L. Shaw and A.J.P. Slater (1984) *Staff Appraisal*, IPM.

Further study

Books

Advisory, Conciliation and Arbitration Service (2008) *Employee Appraisal*, ACAS.

An excellent, clear guide to performance appraisal.

Armstrong, M. and A. Baron (2004) *Managing Performance: Performance Management in Action*, CIPD.

This has become a classic text on the subject of performance management.

Articles

Arkin, A. (2007) From soft to strong, *People Management*, 6 September, Vol. 13, No. 18, 30–33.

An overview of how Kimberly-Clark, a multinational, introduced performance management into its companies across the world.

Cunneen, P. (2006) How to improve performance management, *People Management*, 12 January, Vol. 12, No. 1, 42–3.

A short article that makes suggestions about getting the best from a performance management system.

Fielder, R. (2006) How to unlock discretionary behaviour, *People Management*, 12 October, Vol. 12, No. 20, 44–5.

Another brief article that explains how to energise and motivate staff to work at peak performance.

Table 8.2 People involved in the performance appraisal process

People who may be involved in the appraisal process	Advantages	Disadvantages
The appraisee's manager's immediate manager	Often used as well as the appraisee's manager to check that the manager is being fair. When used as sole appraiser there is the possible advantage of being more objective about employee's work and of not being directly threatened by their success.	Not likely to know the appraisee well and likely to have to obtain information about the individual's performance from their immediate manager.
The HR manager	Often used as a check that the manager is being fair and as a monitor of consistency of approach throughout the organisation. HR managers are sometimes used as sole appraiser for reasons of fairness and consistency and because they are not perceived to be a threat to the manager.	Not likely to know the appraisee well and likely to have to obtain information about the individual's performance from their immediate manager.
Colleagues	This can be especially useful where teamwork is important or in an enterprise with a matrix organisation structure where the individual may report to more than one manager. The main advantage is that colleagues are likely to have a clear idea of how effective the individual is at working with them and the views of several people are likely to provide a balanced perspective.	The colleagues concerned may not know about all aspects of the individual's job. They may be reluctant to express an honest opinion about a colleague, and may be influenced by whether they have a good or poor relationship with that person, or by jealousy or rivalry.
Subordinates	People who work for the individual who is being appraised will certainly have a different view of that individual's abilities and performance and can therefore provide valuable information about the person's performance.	They may be too frightened to express their real opinion if they feel that their manager might hold this against them at some future date. The person being appraised may be reluctant to accept the views of their subordinates.
Self-appraisal	Often used as part of the appraisal process, as in many systems the appraisers and the appraisee complete forms independently of each other and then use them as the basis of discussion. The individual will provide information on different aspects of the individual's performance so that it is possible to compile a total picture of the person's job performance. This may also include those outside the organisation, such as clients or customers who may be able to provide very valuable insights into how an individual is performing.	Some people may find it difficult to analyse their own work performance and may have unrealistic views of how well they have actually done. They may not be willing to admit to weaknesses, although in many cases the opposite is true, and people are more critical of themselves than their manager would be.
360-degree appraisal (not actually a person, but gathers information from all the people mentioned so far)	This form of appraisal gathers information from all the above sources to gain an all-round view of the person's performance. This is extremely thorough and will provide information on different aspects of the individual's performance so that it is possible to compile a total picture of the person's job performance. This may also include those outside the organisation, such as clients or customers who may be able to provide very valuable insights into how an individual is performing.	It can be very time-consuming to collect information from so many people, and may not always be cost-effective. It is also subject to all the disadvantages listed above. If it uses customers or clients it may prove particularly difficult to organise as customers or clients may not wish to spend time participating in questionnaires and cannot be coerced into doing so. Many employers will also be hesitant to use this approach as they may not wish to give their clients or customers any cause to think that they, or any of their employees, might ever provide a less than perfect service or product.

Table 8.2 Continued

People who may be involved in the appraisal process	Advantages	Disadvantages
Assessment centres (not actually a person, so you may not have included assessment centres in this list, but we include them as they form yet another important way of assessing performance)	Individuals undertake a battery of tests to measure: aspects of personality; verbal, numerical and reasoning skills; and ability to lead and work in a team. This provides an all-round view of the person's talents and abilities. Particularly useful when assessing future potential and in the appraisal of potential supervisors or managers.	Expensive and time-consuming to carry out for all employees.

CHAPTER 9

Learning and talent development

Objectives

By the end of this chapter you will be able to:

- explain why learning and talent development is important both to organisations and individuals
- explain the individual's rights to time off for training
- describe a model for achieving strategic learning and talent development
- identify when to use a variety of learning and development techniques
- explain what is meant by experiential learning
- demonstrate the importance of induction training
- outline key issues in international learning and talent development.

Why is learning and talent development important?

Learning and talent development is one of the key aspects of performance management and can help organisations achieve high performance; it is also a key factor in managing and retaining talent even in times of economic uncertainty. Wolff (2009) found that even during the recent recession most employers still recognised the value of learning and talent development, even if they had to work within reduced budgets. However, two-thirds of those surveyed had actually responded to the recession by increasing their efforts to develop skills and talents within their workforce, while at the same time trying to minimise their costs. The CIPD (2010a) also found that in tough economic times more employers were trying to be creative and aimed to develop and retain talent in a cost-effective way.

Most individuals also want to improve their performance in their jobs or learn new skills, perhaps to get a pay increase or promotion or maybe to move to a better job. Learning and talent development can help achieve these aims for individuals too. It can also help attract individuals to an organisation and can then engage their commitment, so that the organisation benefits by keeping their talent within itself; this in turn helps the organisation to achieve its current and future strategic objectives.

Governments too are concerned that their countries are economically viable and that they can provide a good level of services and standards of living for individuals; once again learning and development can play a key role in achieving this. Although there are huge benefits to be gained for organisations, individuals and countries, there has sometimes been reluctance by some employers in the UK to spend money on training or promoting learning and development, so successive governments have started various initiatives such as NVQs, apprenticeships, New Deal or in some areas Flexible New Deal, Train to Gain and Investors in People, all of which aim to encourage employers to improve the skills of their workforce. The Leitch Report in 2006 called for the UK to spend much more money on boosting skills for everyone at every level in order to avoid the UK losing competitiveness because of lack of skills. The Report also called for the creation of a new Commission for Employment and Skills and for employers to have more say in the way skills were developed (Kingston, 2006).

This chapter is about the contribution that learning and talent development can make to organisations and individuals in terms of improving their performance and helping each to achieve their particular objectives. It is also about what organisations and the people in them need to do to ensure that learning and talent development makes this positive contribution to performance. The first part of the chapter will focus on learning and talent development and in the second half of the chapter the focus will shift to consider effective ways of learning.

What do we mean by learning and talent development and how does this differ from training?

The term training was originally used to refer to some specified event designed to improve an individual's performance in a specific aspect of their work. However, as the UK moved from a largely manufacturing economy, where it was appropriate to train people to carry out clearly specified tasks and where a top-down instructor-led approach was suitable, to a much more flexible service and knowledge-based society, good workers became a source of competitive advantage to an organisation and it became more appropriate to focus on individual learning and encouraging people to learn how to learn.

More recently the term learning and talent development has gained in popularity as organisations increasingly recognise that in order to stay competitive they must use, develop and then retain the knowledge and talent of their workers as fully as possible. The focus of their activities has started to switch to learning and talent development as a means of achieving their organisation's strategic objectives. This should be as a part of human resource planning, discussed in more detail in Chapter 2, as it may be necessary to develop talent from within the organisation so future roles can be filled as people retire or leave, or to meet demand for new skills and knowledge because of a change of strategic direction.

According to the CIPD (2010b) the focus on the word talent also implies that whoever is identified as having potential receives appropriate experience and opportunities to develop their skills so they can progress. This could be a very wide definition as it can be argued that everyone has talent and potential and that organisations should seek to maximise this for everyone. In times of scarce resources and limited budgets some organisations use it to identify those who will make the biggest difference to the organisation's performance, either because of their high potential, or because they are in critical roles within the organisation. Focusing on a narrow band of people who are perceived to have talent can be counterproductive as it may, however, build resentment among other workers and may result in higher labour turnover among these groups.

For individuals too, in an increasingly competitive job market, it is also vital that they develop their own talent to keep a competitive edge. The word development also implies something that is ongoing and that progress is made over time. This also fits with the emphasis nowadays on lifelong learning. As people work longer they need to continue to develop to improve their skills, knowledge or competencies and nurture and develop their talent throughout their lives. It appears that many people would like to see their employer offering more opportunities for development such as a training or personal development package and employers who do not provide this could be missing out in attracting staff to their organisation and in retaining staff they already have (Skillsoft 2010, Brockett, 2010).

The concept of individualised learning and talent development implies that this occurs in all sorts of situations, not just in the more traditional, formal training opportunities, although we hope that learning will occur here too. Learning and talent development includes other less formal, more learner-centred approaches to learning such as coaching, mentoring, work shadowing, job swapping and some of these approaches will be discussed later in this chapter. Changes in technology also play a part, enabling the completion of learning and development packages wherever individual workers are in the world, whether at home or at work, as long as they have access to a computer or telephone. Developments with Web 2.0 also mean the sharing of information and learning have become easier.

A move from training to learning and talent development also needs different roles to be adopted by line managers, human resource managers and learning and development specialists who have to become increasingly flexible, often adopting a facilitator role rather than always appearing to be the expert as the traditional trainer might have been. However, although this change in emphasis is undoubtedly occurring, you will still find other terms being used as different organisations will be at different stages in changing the emphasis from training to learning and talent development.

Creating a learning culture

If an organisation is to encourage learning to occur, then it must develop a culture which recognises that people learn in different ways and must provide a range of experiences from which they may learn. As the CIPD (2008) point out it is only learners who can do the learning so the organisation has to be effective in creating a positive environment in which learning can occur and where it can also transfer successfully to the workplace.

Human resource managers and learning and talent development specialists have an important role to play in ensuring that the organisation develops in a way which facilitates the learning that the organisation wants to occur, and that a suitable environment is created in which continuous improvement and talent development is actively encouraged. They themselves need to understand the learning process and the key stages in the provision of learning and development activities to ensure that this happens. Line managers also need to be involved in understanding and encouraging the occurrence of learning, and the organisation should try to minimise barriers and encourage individuals to seek learning opportunities for themselves. The training or learning and talent development opportunities that occur should clearly link with the objectives of the organisation, and its efficiency and effectiveness should be regularly evaluated.

Sometimes organisations aspire to calling themselves a learning organisation. In some ways the term is confusing, since people actually do the learning, but it is good that people have started to see learning within organisations as being of importance. According to Jones and Hendry (1992), the term at its simplest means an organisation where there are 'a lot of people learning' and according to Pedler et al. (1988) it means 'an organisation which facilitates the learning of all its members and continuously transforms itself'. In today's fast-changing world it is necessary for organisations constantly to try to keep ahead of the competition and in order to achieve this increasingly many organisations are creating a coaching culture to facilitate in a cost-efficient way the learning of all in their organisation.

Not all organisations have been as proactive about encouraging learning and development as those that aspire to become learning organisations so governments have also developed many initiatives to encourage organisations to promote learning so that the skills of the country improve. The UK Government has had many such initiatives, as mentioned earlier, and individuals now have a legal right to request time off for training, though this does not necessarily mean that their request will be granted.

The right to request time off for training

While employers may want to focus their resources on just developing talent in certain groups that they identify as having the potential to make a difference to their organisation and its strategic objectives, all employees in organisations with more than 250 employees who have been employed by that organisation for at least 26 weeks have, since April 2010, had the right to request time off for training and this right has been extended to employees in all organisations of whatever size from April 2011. The training requested can lead to a qualification or could be to help the employee develop specific job or work-related skills. Although this is generally taken to mean the right to time off for study or training, according to Green (2010) the potential is much wider and could also include requests for employers to pay for the training, or for adjustments to be made to hours of work to allow for this training. The employer does not have to grant this request but has to seriously consider it.

The employee has to make a formal request in writing, either on paper or by email, and can make one application in every 12-month period. Certain groups such as agency workers, individuals of compulsory school age, or 16- and 17-year-old employees who are already obliged to participate in education or training under the Education and Skills Act 2008 are excluded. However, employees who wish to make a request to study or train must do so in a formal way as laid down by the legislation. According to Frederick (2010) this includes:

● the date of the application;
● a statement that the application is a statutory request in relation to study or training;
● the subject matter of the study or training;
● where and when the study or training will take place;
● who will provide or supervise the training;
● to what qualification (if any) the study or training will lead;
● an explanation as to how the employee thinks that the study or training will improve both his or her effectiveness in the employer's business and the performance of the employer's business;
● whether or not the employee has made a previous application, and if he or she has, the date of that application and how it was submitted.

Some employers may already have a written policy for requests for training and may have a system in place for this. They should ensure that their system at least meets the minimum requirements stated here and if they do not already have a procedure may, in order to standardise this process, choose to design their own application forms which should then incorporate these key points.

While the employee can request training in any area that they think will be of benefit to the organisation there could potentially be conflict if the organisation has chosen to focus on a very narrow group for talent development purposes and to focus their resources just on this group. The employer must give serious consideration to any request but could refuse it. According to Macdonald (2010) they are under a statutory duty to hold a meeting with the employee to discuss a request within 28 days of receiving it. They must also allow the employee to be accompanied at the meeting by a fellow employee and should provide a written response to the request within 14 days. There is also a right of appeal.

The employer can refuse the request but has to justify it on business grounds such as that it would not improve the individual's effectiveness at work or the performance of the business. Other possible business reasons which could be used to justify a refusal to grant time off include the following:

● the cost
● difficulties resulting from this employee's absence for training in meeting demand from customers
● inability to be able to reorganise the work among other staff members
● adverse effect on the quality of a product
● adverse effect on performance or
● changes that are already planned to the structure of the organisation making it difficult to grant this request.

Employees who are refused the right to training can take their case to an employment tribunal though this is based on limited grounds such as if they think the decision to reject their case was based on incorrect information or that the employer did not follow the correct procedure. The employee cannot just complain because they disagree with the business grounds put forward by the employer. If the tribunal finds in their favour, it can order the employer to reconsider the request or award the employee compensation of up to 8 weeks' salary, which in 2011 was capped at £400.00 per week. It is too early to know what effect these new rights will have on organisations' willingness to offer training opportunities to employees, but if employers have adopted a very restricted approach to talent management they could result in some conflict.

The Investors in People award (IIP)

One initiative that has been successful in encouraging many organisations in the UK to become more proactive about learning and development and to link their learning and development initiatives to their organisation's strategic objectives is the Investors in People award which is available to those organisations deemed to have met the standards, giving them the IIP Kitemark of quality.

This initiative aims to improve the quality of British training and talent development practices by setting national standards for good practice and by linking these to the achievement of business goals. From April 2010 the Commission for Employment and Skills became responsible for the strategic ownership of Investors in People in a move which is claimed will strengthen IIP's position, placing it at the centre of their mission to maximise the economic competitiveness of UK organisations (IIP, 2010). Training and development should always be closely linked to the organisation's objectives and the IIP standard encourages people to be trained and developed in ways which exactly suit the organisation's requirements, which should also enable the value of these activities to be clearly demonstrated.

According to the CIPD (2010d) the three key principles of IIP are:

- *Developing strategies to improve the performance of the organisation* – an Investor in People develops effective strategies to improve the performance of the organisation through its people.
- *Taking action to improve the performance of the organisation* – an Investor in People takes effective action to improve the performance of the organisation through its people.
- *Evaluation of the impact on the performance of the organisation* – an Investor in People can demonstrate the impact of its investment in people on the performance of the organisation.

The IIP standards can be expressed simply as Plan, Do, Review. They recognise that all managers, at whatever level, have a vital role to play in the development of their workers. As we said earlier in this chapter, it has often been difficult to get the commitment of line managers to spending time and money on the learning and development of their workers. These standards emphasise this vital role and have had quite an impact in this area. Achieving the IIP award is not the final stage as the organisation then needs to continue to encourage continuous improvement in order to get even better at developing its people and in order to meet the requirements of the standard again in future years. Organisations can achieve higher levels of bronze, silver or gold by providing additional evidence and can also achieve yet another level of recognition if they become 'champions' by publicly profiling their IIP journey.

Learning and talent development strategy

Many organisations have demonstrated commercial benefits from achieving the standards and there are benefits for their workforce too, not only in being part of a thriving organisation but also in improvements in their own training and development. The Investors in People standard provides a framework for organisations to follow to ensure that they utilise key principles when designing learning and development initiatives. However, not all organisations work towards the achievement of these standards and it is still important for those organisations and their managers to take account of certain key issues when designing learning and talent development strategies.

As we explained in Chapter 2 it is important that all HR strategies contribute to the achievement of the overall organisation's strategic objectives; learning and talent development strategies are no exception to this. The CIPD (2010e) say that each organisation needs to identify its own particular strategic direction and ensure that its learning and talent development strategies align with and contribute to the achievement of the organisation's strategic goals. They also need to contribute to the overall performance management in the organisation, to identify learning and training needs (discussed later in this chapter), and establish priorities and pools of talent.

In its 2010 annual survey of learning and talent development the CIPD (2010c) identified the following as being the main learning and talent development strategies being used by organisations. E-learning has become increasingly popular with 62 per cent of the sample surveyed saying they use this method, while 56 per cent of organisations use some form of in-house learning and development, reflecting the trend to be cost-effective. Coaching by line managers is used by 51 per cent of the organisations in this sample.

Designing learning and development

It is not enough just to choose the techniques to be used and hope that these will develop into a programme. It is also important to ensure that any programme contributes to the organisation's strategic objectives and fits with its priorities. When you are designing a learning programme you should have in mind clear objectives for it. What do you want the learners to be able to do and what do you want them to know by the end of the course?

Our approach to the design of learning opportunities is derived and adapted from systematic approaches to training and learning such as the systematic training cycle, which is shown in Figure 9.1. Most recent models of the learning and talent development process, including our own, have used it as a starting point. There are of course many valid criticisms of the systematic training cycle which relate to the fact that its focus is on training rather than individualised learning and that it is more suited to a stable work environment rather than a rapidly changing environment in which the focus has shifted from formal training to more informal approaches to learning. It is also claimed that organisations and learners do not always work through all the stages sequentially and that it is also not clearly linked to the strategic objectives of the organisation. We have tried to address some of these criticisms in our own model

Figure 9.1 The training cycle

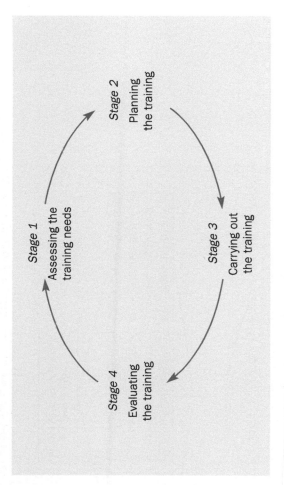

Stage 1
Assessing the
training needs

Stage 2
Planning
the training

Stage 3
Carrying out
the training

Stage 4
Evaluating
the training

for learning and talent development included in Figure 9.2 and each of the stages will now be discussed in more detail.

Assessing learning and talent development needs

It is important to assess what learning and talent development is needed for organisations, teams or departments and individuals. There needs to be an accurate assessment of business and organisational requirements (CIPD, 2010f). This should be done in conjunction with the people or groups concerned and should be aimed at contributing to the organisation's strategic objectives.

While there is much to be gained from both formal training and less formal learning and development opportunities in terms of improved skills and productivity for the workforce, they are nevertheless costly activities, so it is important to provide learning opportunities of the right type for the people or groups who need them. This may in itself present new challenges as different generations of workers have different expectations and preferences for learning approaches. A survey in 2010 by Skillsoft found that people wanted freedom and flexibility in their learning but also learning on demand when needed, so organisations need to think carefully about the methods they use, not just because of their cost but to meet the changing needs of individuals.

This stage of the cycle is referred to as assessing learning and talent development needs and this is frequently done for individuals using the performance appraisal process or personal development review. Learning and talent development needs can be assessed in many ways, but one of the easiest ways is to examine the job that has to be done and the knowledge, skills or competencies that the organisation needs the job holder to have, and then to examine the knowledge, skills and competencies of the person in that job and assess whether there is any gap between the two.

This type of assessment can be completed for a whole organisation, a team or department or for an individual. If there is a gap then a learning and talent development initiative may help the individual, team or indeed the whole organisation to progress to the required standard, but if the gap is caused by some other factor such as poor recruitment, then it may be a waste of money to use learning and talent

Figure 9.2 Model for learning and talent development

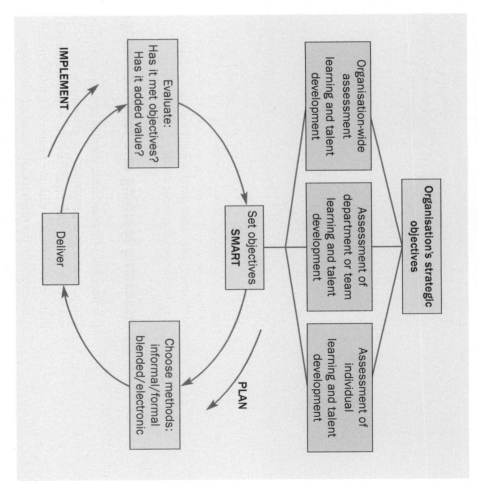

development to try to bridge this gap. However, individuals do not always want the same learning and talent development opportunities as their organisation wants and may want to try to develop their careers by identifying their own gaps in their skills in comparison with the direction in which they wish to develop.

Although no organisation has a limitless budget for learning and development some organisations are able to cope better with the differences between individual learners' aspirations than others. Organisations that are flexible in their approach and that budget for a certain amount of money to be spent on each individual's learning, whether or not it contributes directly to the strategic objectives, are likely to benefit from this approach as they are creating a positive feeling about learning which should result in the individual being more positive about the organisation, resulting in turn in them being successful in learning in other ways that will benefit the organisation. Some organisations are willing to fund specific learning and talent development activities but try to ensure retention of the staff by making it a contractual requirement that the employee pays back the cost of the training and talent development initiative if they leave within a certain specified time such as two years. Some organisations specify a much longer time scale for this, such as the need to stay for five years, and instead of being motivational the employee can feel resentment as they feel tied to the organisation for what, to them, may feel like forever. When employers have spent considerable sums of money on training and talent development opportunities for staff it is easy to see the attraction to them of tying staff into contracts that keep them for a specific period of time to get payback. However, as stated, this can be counter-productive if it causes resentment and is a negative way of using learning and talent development to improve retention. It would be far better to concentrate on the positive motivational aspects of learning and talent development that encourage people to want to work in an organisation and to want to stay working there.

Job analysis needs to be undertaken to establish what is involved in the job. Refer back to Chapter 2 to refresh your memory of the ways in which to carry out this process. The usual result of job analysis is a job description, and a training specifica-tion can be written from this. In many organisations, where employees are encour-aged to work towards National Vocational Qualifications (NVQs), there will already be a national standard for the employee to work towards.

Learning and talent development needs can also be assessed by asking the person or people concerned about their learning and development needs, by using ques-tionnaires, or by an analysis of mistakes (faults analysis). If there are any gaps where they do not meet the standards then there is a possible need for learning and devel-opment to help to close the gaps, and so a need has been identified.

Setting objectives

To do this the person organising the L&TD event or process needs to be clear about what the individual, team or organisation needs to know, or be able to do, or the competencies they need to have acquired after the learning and development has taken place. It is important to establish clear objectives for the learning or develop-ment event since without them there is a danger that the event will become unfo-cused and will not achieve its objectives. It also provides a basis for one way of evaluating the L&TD by establishing whether or not the objectives of the event have been met. 'SMART' objectives are recommended: the acronym can stand for a variety of things but generally refers to the objectives being specific, measurable, achievable, realistic and timely or time-bound.

Planning the learning or development initiative

Once you have decided your objectives for the learning and talent development event, you are then able to plan a programme that uses a variety or blend of tech-niques in order to achieve this aim in the most effective way.

If the learning and talent development is to be effective it cannot be left to chance and a great deal of planning needs to happen first in terms of basic preparation of materials and administration, such as notification to all participants and organisa-tion of the event itself. You need to ensure that everyone is aware in advance of what will be involved in the learning and development event and its timing and location in plenty of time. Letters should have gone to the learners, the people involved in running the event, and the supervisors and managers of those who will be involved so that there is time to arrange cover for their absence from work, if necessary.

Once a learning or talent development need has been identified, there are a num-ber of choices to be made about how it should be met. First, should it be carried out in the organisation (in-house) or by an external organisation such as a college or other training provider? Second, the line manager or learning and development specialist needs to consider which techniques should actually be used. Should formal instructor-led traditional training be used or would the need be met better by less formal individualised learning such as e-learning, coaching, mentoring or the use of learning logs? Once this has been established a specific learning and development programme needs to be identified or designed.

Internal or external learning and talent development

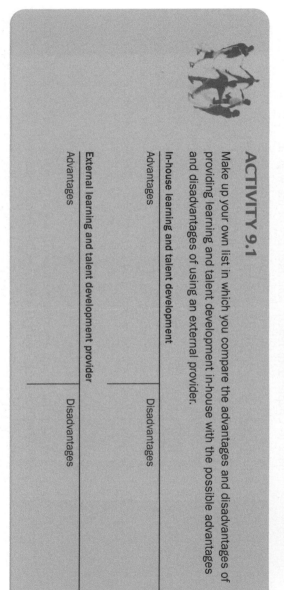

ACTIVITY 9.1

Make up your own list in which you compare the advantages and disadvantages of providing learning and talent development in-house with the possible advantages and disadvantages of using an external provider.

In-house learning and talent development	
Advantages	Disadvantages

External learning and talent development provider	
Advantages	Disadvantages

Discussion of Activity 9.1

Your lists are likely to contain several advantages and disadvantages for both approaches. Among the points you should have considered are the cost and resources available to carry out the initiative. It is likely that in-house learning and talent development will be cheaper and will be tailored perfectly to meet your organisation's needs. However, if the particular need identified is very specialised and is required for only one or two people, or if there is no one with suitable qualifications or experience available to conduct or facilitate the initiative, then it may be better and more cost-effective for them to join a course run by an external provider. However, this depends on the organisation's priorities for learning and talent development. This, although it may not be tailored to meet the organisation's specific needs, will have the advantage of providing a wider experience and opportunities to find out how other organisations do things.

On and off-the-job training

In the past, when people were trained in traditional ways they were often just made to sit next to someone and told to do what they did. This is often referred to as 'sitting by Nellie', and the effectiveness of the training depended on how good Nellie was at her job. If she was good at it, and a naturally good instructor, then it could work well, but there was always a danger that the trainee would learn faults as well as good practice. This was one of the main disadvantages of using 'on-the-job' training. In more recent times the emphasis in a great many organisations has switched back to on-the-job training with the introduction of NVQs. This time, however, the person who does the training and assesses what has been learnt is trained themselves, and there are national standards to work towards, so there should be much greater consistency in approach. This aims to harness the benefits of on-the-job training, in terms of low cost and relevance to the organisation, while ensuring that standards are high and consistent. In this case using on-the-job training could be beneficial, as the training has been planned, there is a trainer who knows how to train, and a qualified person will test whether the individual is competent in that job.

● Learning and talent development techniques

We stated earlier that once the decision has been made about where the learning and development activity is to take place, it is also important to decide on the most appropriate techniques to use. Will formal trainer-centred approaches work best or will more informal learner-centred approaches be better? How much technology should be used? The method used must be chosen to be appropriate for the particular need that has been identified for that person or group and it must fit with the culture and resources of the organisation.

E-learning

As well as the more traditional approaches to learning, trainers and individual learners now have a choice of using e-learning techniques. There is some confusion about what exactly constitutes e-learning but it can include computer-based training and learning, technology based training and learning and web-based training and learning. It may be integrated alongside traditional learning as a support mechanism, or be used separately as part of a distance learning or open learning course. Some university degrees, post-graduate qualifications and training packages are delivered totally by e-learning methods and this makes them easily accessible to people in any part of the world at any time.

One major advantage is that individuals, so long as they have access to the technology, should be able to choose when, where and what they learn and this should increase opportunities for learning. Support can be provided by chat rooms, discussion groups and online tutoring with everyone involved able to respond at a time that is convenient. Alternatively, approaches such as virtual classrooms, social networking sites, audio-visual conferencing and two-way live satellite broadcasts provide immediate feedback so learning and development managers and learners can interact with each other almost as quickly as they would in a more traditional classroom situation.

Some organisations are already embracing the Web 2.0 technologies as a part of their approach to learning and talent development. BT as a technology-based company has embraced the use of social networking as a means of learning and talent development and already spends between 15 and 20 per cent of what would have been classroom based or formal learning and talent development activities on 'providing the capabilities for people to create the content for themselves in the organisation and share it' (CIPD, 2010c). This approach seems in line with the desire of people to learn in more flexible ways and creates new opportunities and ways of learning that could also appeal to those wanting instant access to learning and talent development.

Did you know?

In a survey of workers in the UK, Germany, France and Spain conducted by CEGOS UK, Britain was found to lead in what were regarded as the more innovative approaches to learning with the use of blended learning, mentoring and social media all being stronger than in other European countries.

(Source: Brockett, J., 2010)

With the current concern for environmental issues and our carbon footprints it will be interesting to see whether these approaches will become more popular and replace some of the travel by students and their lecturers. However, it is claimed that many of us spend too long searching for information online with 46 per cent of the respondents in the Skillsoft 2010 survey saying they spent between half an hour and two hours to find information online. If they have an urgent business problem to solve then that could be much too long.

ACTIVITY 9.2

How do you feel about e-learning as an approach to learning? Is it a method you enjoy or is it an approach you dislike?

What about using social networking or social bookmarking sites as a part of your learning?

 del.icio.us Digg Twitter Google Bookmarks Facebook

Do you do this already by sharing documents using methods such as those listed above or by using blogs or tweets? Is it an approach you welcome or dislike?

 You will find the symbols shown above on many HR documents that you find for yourself and on many that we have used if you choose to look at the originals for some of our references. Some Internet sites such as those of the CIPD and ACAS also have facilities for people to share information on blogs or by using other resources such as LinkedIn or Facebook. Check for yourself and evaluate the usefulness of these resources for you.

You can experience some aspects of e-learning for yourself by using the support materials for this book at **www.pearsoned.co.uk/foothook**. Go there now and complete exercise 9.2.

Other learning and talent development techniques

Many other techniques could also be used and we have summarised the suitability of some of these in Table 9.1. Complete the second column for yourself to identify whether in your opinion the particular type of learning and development activity is led more by the learning and development specialist, the learner or equally by both. From your reading in this chapter so far, use the blank spaces in the table to assess the suitability of online discussion groups and audio or video conferencing and the use of podcasts and social networking sites. Spaces have also been left at the end of Table 9.1 for you to add your own suggestions for different training techniques.

Some of these learning and talent development methods are much more participative than others, and it is a good idea to use a variety of techniques to avoid the learner becoming bored and also to give opportunities to practise skills if a skill is being taught. This will also mean that if you are working with a group of people and you utilise a variety of techniques, you are likely to use the preferred learning styles of different individuals at various times. Learning is an active process, and even if it is a list of facts that needs to be learnt, most people learn more effectively when they test themselves, or rewrite information in their own words. This also improves their recall of the information.

Table 9.1 Learning and talent development techniques and their suitability

Training technique	Formal trainer-centred or informal learner-centred approaches	Suitability
Lecture	Formal trainer-centred	This is suitable when a large amount of information needs to be given to a large number of people at the same time. The information can be prepared in advance but a disadvantage is the lack of participation from the audience.
Role play		Here a small group of people have the chance to act as if they were in a real work situation. They have a problem or situation to deal with which would be similar to a situation that they might experience at work. They can practise their responses and receive help and support from the trainer and from the others in the group. This can help in developing awareness of interpersonal skills and can give confidence, as there is an opportunity to practise skills in a protected environment where it does not matter if mistakes are made. There can sometimes be a problem if the role play is not taken seriously or if trainees are too nervous or embarrassed to perform their roles.
Group discussion		This can lead to a free exchange of knowledge, ideas and opinions on a particular subject among the trainees and the trainer with the opportunity to air various viewpoints. It can be useful when there are varying opinions about an issue, or a range of ways in which a situation could be handled. There is a danger that the trainees may wander too far from the subject if it is not handled skilfully by the trainer, and that important points may not be discussed.
Video or film		These can be used to show a real situation and differing ways of handling that situation, or to give information to several people at once. They can show examples of good and bad use of interpersonal skills to a large number of people at once and be used as the basis for a group discussion. They do not demand much involvement from the audience, although the trainer could add to this by use of discussion or questions after each showing.
Project		Normally a task is set by the trainer which will give an individual or group general guidelines to work to, but will also leave a great deal of scope for them to show creativity or initiative. This is a good way of stimulating creativity or initiative but, in order to do so, the project has to be about something that will interest the trainee.
Case study		A case study is a history of some event or situation in which relevant details are supplied for the trainee to get an overall picture of the situation or organisation. Trainees are then asked to diagnose the problems or suggest solutions. A case study provides the opportunity to examine a situation in detail yet be removed from the pressure of the real work situation. This allows for discussion and provides opportunities to exchange ideas and consider different options. Since a case study can limit the number of factors or issues that should be discussed, it may sometimes seem too easy and trainees may not fully appreciate that in the real-life situation there may be other more complex issues to take into account.
Computer-based training		This allows the trainee to work at their own pace through a series of questions or exercises using a computerised training program. The trainees get immediate feedback from the computer program and can cover a range of work in a short space of time, going back over exercises if necessary and learning at a time that is convenient for them. Trainees may be nervous of the technology or may experience difficulties so it is normally useful to have easy access to help or advice at least via a telephone.

Table 9.1 Continued

Training technique	Formal trainer-centred or informal learner-centred approaches	Suitability
Guided reading		A series of recommended reading is provided on a topic, perhaps graded according to difficulty. The trainee is able to work at their own pace through this. Since the reading has been selected by someone else to highlight points on that subject, this can save the trainee time, since they know that the materials will be relevant to the subject. It does not encourage the trainee to research further around the subject or seek materials for themselves.
In-tray exercise		Trainees are given a series of files, memos and letters similar to those that they might have to deal with in a real work situation. They need to decide on the appropriate action to take and the priority for action. This gives an opportunity for trainees to experience the sort of issues that can arise, but it is important that the contents of the in-tray are realistic.
Online discussion groups		
Audio or video conferencing		
Podcasts		
Using social networking approaches such as blogs, tweets, information sharing or Second life		

These points emphasise the importance of providing some opportunities for the learner to practise what they are supposed to be learning, and underline the value for you of completing the exercises as you go through this book so that you continue to learn effectively.

Delivering the required learning or talent development event

Although specialist learning and talent development managers will be trained in learning techniques it is also important that line managers and any other members of staff involved in facilitating or running learning and development events should also be trained appropriately. This is still important if informal learner-centred approaches are being used, since mentors, coaches or group facilitators also need training. Even if the people involved are trained well they will still find that delivering specific learning events will seem different each time as the process also involves interaction with learners who may have different learning styles as well as differing personalities. Some degree of flexibility is therefore necessary to take account of these differences.

Evaluation

This is an extremely important stage in the learning and talent development cycle, and one that is often neglected by organisations. According to Findlay (2004), it is still true to say that 'many learning and development specialists do not evaluate the outcomes of their work – beyond handing out "happy sheets" at the end of courses. These provide feedback on whether the learners have enjoyed a course or other learning interventions but do little to measure its impact.' If no evaluation of learning and development is carried out at all then the organisation does not know whether it has been enjoyed or been successful, or even whether the learning and development objectives have been met, so it may have wasted money and resources on events that were not very effective and which did not help the organisation meet its strategic objectives.

Until recently very little had actually changed in the way training or learning and talent development was evaluated. Donald Kirkpatrick set out the general principles in 1956 in an article 'How to start an objective evaluation of training' (see Findlay, 2004) and, although there have been criticisms of his work, his ideas have lasted well. He basically argued that there should be four levels of evaluation. First, at the end of the learning and development event, the participants should be asked their views on the effectiveness of the learning experience. This could be done by means of a simple questionnaire to the event or course participants and this will at least give clear views as to whether the people concerned liked the learning or developmental experience, what they felt would be useful and what they felt was less useful. Consequently it should yield a great deal of valuable material, which the manager responsible for the design of the learning event should be able to incorporate usefully in the next course.

According to Kirkpatrick's levels of evaluation, the happy sheets equate to level one evaluation. However, this only establishes what the participants say they feel about the course or learning event and it is also important to establish what they have actually learnt so both knowledge and skills also need to be tested. One very effective way to achieve this is to test these both at the start of the learning event and at the end of it. This achieves Kirkpatrick's level two evaluation as it should show how much the person has learnt during the learning and development event.

If the learning is going to have an effect on the department and on the organisation and contribute to its strategic objectives it is also vital to find out what effect the learning and development event has had when the person actually gets back to work. Sometimes people may do well in a learning situation but when they return to their normal work area they revert to their usual behaviour and they seem to forget or not use the learning that has occurred. From the perspective of their line manager and from the organisation's point of view this is a waste so it is important to find out whether transfer of learning to the work situation has occurred. This can be done by questionnaires or with interviews with participants and their line manager a few weeks later, or by a review of the person's work and the effect that the learning or development opportunity has had on them. Kirkpatrick's level three evaluation aims to test whether the learning that has occurred has successfully transferred to the workplace and essentially this level of evaluation aims to measure changes in job behaviour.

Kirkpatrick's fourth level of evaluation relates to whether the learning and development activity has made a difference to the bottom line in an organisation. Has it succeeded in making a difference to the organisation or added value? According to Martin Sloman (2004), 'If you focus your training on the organisation's learning requirements, you won't need to get hung up on assessment.' To achieve this level of evaluation it may be necessary to examine organisational statistics to see, for example, whether sales targets have been met or whether levels of customer satisfaction have improved.

According to Ian Thomson (2004), 'Evaluating training is a way of combining the assessment of the impact of training and development, while raising the profile and influence of HR and training functions.' Therefore it is in the interest of these departments to evaluate at all levels, not only to ensure that the learning objectives have been met, but also to demonstrate to the rest of the organisation that they have been successful in adding value to the organisation by making a difference in key strategic areas.

One of the things that have changed since Kirkpatrick's day is the emphasis that is nowadays placed on the reason for the evaluation. If you understand why you are evaluating something it is easier to select an appropriate method of evaluation. It has been suggested that there are four key reasons why learning and development should be evaluated. These are to:

1 **prove the value of the training** to try to find out whether or not it has worked and achieved what it was supposed to achieve
2 **control the training** to ensure that it is achieving value for money and is fitting with the organisation's priorities and is of a consistent standard
3 **improve the quality of the training** so that standards of administration or of training delivery are improved
4 **reinforce the learning** as a part of the learning process itself (adapted from CIPD 2010g).

Various methods that can be used for evaluation of learning and development or training including the following:

● questionnaires completed at the end of a course by course participants
● interviews of learners asking their opinion of the value of the learning
● calculation of the return on the investment in training
● assessments by tests of what the person has learned or is able to do
● self-review by participants of what they had learned
● discussion with the learner's immediate superior of the improvement in performance
● cost analysis of the learning and development.

Table 9.2

ACTIVITY 9.3

Forms that evaluation can take and those who would find them useful

For each of the main purposes listed in Table 9.2 write next to it which forms of evaluation are likely to be most useful and in the third column write for whom that form of evaluation would be particularly useful.

The purpose of the evaluation	The main forms that the evaluation could take	The people or groups who would benefit most from the evaluation
1 Prove the value of the training		
2 Control the training		
3 Improve the quality of the training		
4 Reinforce or contribute to the learning		

Suggested answers will be found at www.pearsoned.co.uk/foothook.

We have gone through the key principles involved in designing learning and talent development activities but the choices made will depend on the organisation's strategic objectives, what the specific learning and talent development is aiming to achieve, the organisation's culture and the resources and skills available. We shall now examine some of the ways these could be undertaken in one specific form of training called induction.

Induction training

Anyone who leaves one organisation and goes to work in another will appreciate that things are done differently in different organisations, and people sometimes suffer a feeling of culture shock if behaviour that had been acceptable in their previous organisation is not viewed in the same way in the new one. This feeling of culture shock is likely to be even greater if the individual has moved from another country to work or to study. The new person picks up clues from the behaviour of others as to what is acceptable and what is not. Supervisors and managers will be seen to praise certain types of behaviour but will frown on others. At its simplest they are learning about the common view within that organisation of 'the way we do things around here' – the organisation culture.

Although employees will learn a great deal in this informal way, it is also a good idea for organisations to try to ensure that they have the opportunity to learn things that will enable them to perform to their best ability. This will mean that the organisation will need to:

● assess what it thinks people need to learn in order both to do their jobs and to contribute effectively to the organisation's strategic objectives
● plan opportunities to facilitate learning experiences
● evaluate what has worked well, and what has been less successful.

CASE STUDY 9.1 Induction

Read the following story about a student, Ros, who hoped to improve her language skills and earn some money for university by working as a waitress in a hotel in France for the summer. She has just started work as a trainee and is telephoning her mother a few days after her arrival.

Read the story and answer the questions at the end of it.

Ros   Hello, Mum. I got here in the end and I've survived the first day, but it has been quite difficult. I'm not sure how long I will stay.

Mum   Oh dear! What has happened? Was the journey OK? Were you met by someone with a car from the hotel, as they had arranged?

Ros   No, the hotel car didn't turn up. I had to get a taxi and it was miles from the airport, so it cost a fortune. The human resource manager took me to my accommodation, but no one else seemed to be expecting me. I'm living in an apartment with about another eight people, but they were just going out when I arrived and no one had told them that I was also going to be joining them in their accommodation. They were really nice but had trouble finding a bed for me and the only spare bed is in the kitchen and it's broken.

Mum   Well, I expect you felt better when you found out what your job was and got your uniform.

Ros   Well, I'm still not sure what is happening. I got up early yesterday morning, because no one had told me when to start work, but when I got to the office I was told that I was not on duty until today so I'm still not sure what hours I'm actually working. I thought I would only be working for 35 hours a week in France, but some of the others told me that this can be averaged over a few weeks, so it may be more.

I haven't got a uniform yet either, as the only one the HR manager had left was extra large, so was much too big for me. He suggested I wore a black skirt and white blouse until they can get a uniform in a small size for me. I spent the day on the beach with some of the other trainees, so at least that was good, but I had to borrow some clothes for work as the airline has lost my luggage.

Mum   Oh dear! Have you reported it? I hope your luggage will turn up soon. You'll feel a lot more positive when you have your own things.

Ros   Yes, I reported it at the airport and it will be sent here when they find it, but I wonder if I'll still be here by then. Everything is different to what I expected.

The HR manager told me that I would be joining the receptionists rather than the waitresses. Then when I turned up for work again this morning, I was placed in the marketing department. Another girl, who had been working there, has been moved to help at another hotel this week, because the Tour de France is going through the town. Consequently that hotel is full, so a lot of the temporary staff have been moved there to help for the week.

Mum   You should get plenty of opportunities to improve your French working in marketing.

Ros   My boss in marketing is really nice and I have been phoning French and English hotels to check on competitors' prices and I'm going to be helping to do a customer satisfaction survey in both French and English. Mind you, they really need a staff satisfaction survey!

Mum   Well, at least the job sounds interesting.

Ros   Yes, my boss says she wants to keep me in the marketing department, as she has plenty of work for me to do, even when the other trainee returns. The HR manager was talking about me helping to clean chalets next week, so I'm still very confused about the job I'll be doing. I want to come home.

Mum   You're bound to feel unsettled for the first few days, but I'm sure you'll feel better when you get a bit more established and when you have your luggage. Have the meals been good? At least you get your board and lodging provided on top of your wage.

Ros   I hope I'll feel better soon, but today I missed meals so I've only had a baguette.

Mum   Oh dear! Why was that? I thought free meals were part of your payment and in France you would expect them to be good, even for the staff.

Ros   The office staff have breaks at a different time to the people working in the restaurant and the hotel, so there was no food left when I arrived. I'll have to buy something later. I thought I was being paid weekly in cash, as it said in the letter that I was sent. The others say we get paid at the end of the month and that I'll need to set up a French bank account for myself as we get paid by cheque. I hope my euros will last until I get paid. It is proving much more difficult than I thought. All the information I was sent has been wrong.

Questions

1 Comment on what happened.

2 What information should Ros have received before she left England?

3 What information could have been made available on the organisation's intranet site?

4 How could Ros's first few days have been made easier?

ACTIVITY 9.4

Imagine that you are the learning and development manager at the hotel in France where Ros had her summer job.

Design an induction course for Ros and the other students at this hotel.

● What will be your objectives for the induction programme?
● What would you want Ros to know at the end of the programme?
● What do you want her to be able to do by the end of her induction programme?

● Induction

Induction is the process of helping a new employee to settle quickly into their job so that they soon become an efficient and productive employee. It also helps create a favourable image of the organisation in the mind of the new employee, and is therefore also a valuable public relations exercise. Part of the induction process starts at the time of interview, with the information and impression of the organisation that is given at that stage. Any letters or booklets given after this also form an important part of the induction process. Some of the induction may be completed online with materials and tests of knowledge provided on the company intranet site.

New employees need to learn a great deal of information when they join an organisation. This could be learned informally, but this may take a long time and the employee may learn the wrong things. It will be even more important if the person is working in another country or using a second language, and an intervention to help awareness of cross-cultural differences or in language skills may also be needed as part of the induction. New employees are each likely to have their own individual learning needs; establishing what these are during the induction process is important as is starting individual personal development reviews and setting times for individual interviews to review progress regularly.

When new employees actually start work, they will need also to get to know people with whom they will be working, become familiar with their surroundings, learn about their new job and learn about the organisation in which they will be working. Although there is a great deal of information to impart to the new employee, not all of it is needed immediately and in fact there is a danger of overloading the individual with information if it is all given at once. If formal induction courses are run for all new starters then these could be spread over parts of several days, imparting first the most urgent information, such as the geography of the building, canteen arrangements and introductions to supervisors and work colleagues. It may be that the formal courses do not even need to start on the first day, especially if recruitment is sporadic. Small groups of employees may be gathered, perhaps once a month, for the formal induction course, providing of course that their immediate induction needs such as information on safety rules have been adequately covered.

A formal induction course is useful, as several new starters can be given information at the same time. However, the new employees are likely to be starting different jobs in various departments, so that there is still an important role for their line managers to play in their induction, particularly in carrying out personal development reviews and then tailoring individual learning and development initiatives to meet the specific learning and development needs of the individual in that department. A checklist indicating which topics will be covered, when they will be covered and who will cover them is also extremely useful. This can be signed by the employee when they have gone through all the topics and then stored with their training records. It also provides a useful reminder to all of the need to cover these topics.

Table 9.3 gives an indication of the type of things that need to be covered during an induction period. It is useful to indicate who is responsible for dealing with each topic and when it should be covered. A section for the trainee to sign to say that they have completed each topic would also be useful.

Table 9.3   Sample induction checklist

Topic	Person responsible for covering this topic	Day 1	First week	First month
Reception	Human Resource Manager	★		
Documentation and introduction to manager	Human Resource Manager	★		
Hours, clocking on, flexitime, lunch breaks, overtime	Human Resource Manager	★		
Layout of department, outline of function and introduction to staff	Supervisor	★		
Tour of main work areas, staff restaurant, toilets, fire exits	'Buddy' or person delegated by the supervisor to look after and befriend the new starter	★		
Health and safety rules	Supervisor	★		
The organisation – products, services, the organisation's handbook	Learning and Development Officer or on company intranet			★
Rules and procedures – discipline and grievance	Human Resource Manager and on company intranet site		★	
Payment, holiday pay and sickness pay	Human Resource Manager Support materials on intranet system		★	
Communication and consultation	Learning and Development Officer			★
Training and development	Learning and Development Officer			★
Performance appraisal and set-up of personal development plan and reviews	Learning and Development Officer Additional materials on the intranet system			★
Pensions	Learning and Development Officer Additional materials on the intranet system			★
The trade union and trade union-appointed learning representatives	Shop Steward			★

Some of the information will need to be given in a written form, perhaps in a handbook, although increasingly nowadays organisations will keep much of this information also on their intranet system. Although much of this information may also have been given verbally in the formal induction course, it is useful to have a source of reference for things such as who to notify when you are ill. This might not have seemed particularly relevant to a new starter, and indeed may not be needed for a year or two, by which time it may have been largely forgotten unless there is a loose-leaf handbook to refer to or preferably an intranet site where the information is easily accessible and kept up to date.

Since it is important not to give too much information, as the new starter may feel overwhelmed, it is better to spread the information over a period of time and alternate with periods where the person is introduced to their new job and given a chance to settle into this. After all, that is the reason they have joined the organisation. Some organisations may give information on their intranet site prior to the person actually joining the organisation and may test the person's understanding by a quiz. There will still be some things which it is necessary to deliver face-to-face and in some organisations new recruits are asked to arrive later than the rest of the workforce on their first day, so that those who will be involved in their induction can get things organised and deal with any crises that may occur, and then have time to spend on the new recruit.

If the new employee comes from another country, or if the work is in an international organisation where workers come from many different countries, there is also likely to be a need to deal with cross-cultural issues to encourage greater understanding and increase tolerance of different ways of working. The induction period would provide a useful foundation for this and progress could be reviewed during subsequent personal development reviews.

How do people learn?

In a knowledge-based economy, where there is constant change and where people are regularly required to develop new knowledge and skills, perhaps the most useful skill of all is knowing how you and others learn, as well as understanding the key principles involved in designing learning and development programmes.

In this section a range of learning and development and training techniques will be discussed which may also help you to learn more efficiently as well as preparing you to help others to learn.

Henry Ford's statement, above, is becoming even more relevant today, not just so that we all stay young but so that as retirement ages increase we can continue to lead productive and enjoyable lives as we continue to update our skills, knowledge and learning, whether for work purposes or for leisure. According to Age Positive (2007), a team working on strategies and policies to support people making decisions about working and retirement for the Department of Work and Pensions, 'Employees of all ages are benefiting from training and development' and organisations are benefiting too as 'employees of all ages have a variety of skills which make the organisations more effective'.

Factors affecting learning and development

In view of the change of focus to individual learning and talent development a good place to start is to consider your own approach to learning which you can do by completing Activity 9.5.

ACTIVITY 9.5

Make a list of a range of situations where you feel that you have learnt something.

● In each case consider what was your drive, or motivation, to learn.
● Was there a stimulus to increase your drive to learn? What was this?
● Was there any form of reinforcement of your learning? What was this?

Discussion of Activity 9.5

People are motivated to learn by a variety of things, so you may have listed quite a few drives to learn. These may take the form of incentives, encouragement or rewards. Some people may be motivated by the need to do well in an examination or they may perhaps be motivated to learn a new skill because it may provide an improved opportunity for getting a better job or more pay. In other cases the motivation may be the pleasure of learning something new for its own sake or for the respect that other people may feel towards you when you have learnt something impressive. Other people may be motivated to learn by a sense of curiosity or by anxiety or fear of failure and your motivation may change at different stages of your life as you continue with life-long learning.

The tests and exercises in this book and on the associated web pages at **www. pearsoned.co.uk/foothook** should help you to prove to yourself that you are learning. They are one way in which you can show your response to learning.

Learning theories

Psychologists have always been interested in how people learn and there are far too many theories of learning to discuss them all here. Besides, you will undoubtedly study some of these theories of learning in other subjects such as organisational behaviour. However, it is important to consider some of the common issues that occur in these theories as they may give us insights into how we learn and how we can help those in our organisations to learn so that we create high-performing organisations or nations. In particular, drives and motivation and knowledge of results or feedback are important.

The drive and motivation to learn

Behavioural psychologists such as Pavlov and Skinner referred to the instinctive need that led to learning as 'the drive'. In animals this was normally provided by a desire for food, but in people the drive or motivation might be to pass an exam or just to achieve the satisfaction derived from mastering something new. This aspect of their work points to the importance of considering people's motivation to learn. If we can find out what makes people want to learn we should then be able to tailor our instruction better and be more likely to create better performance at work. In Activity 9.5 you identified your own drives and motivation to learn but if you compare them with those of your friends you may find that they are motivated by different factors. Organisations also need to be aware of what will motivate their worker to learn as part of their approach to performance management and need to ensure that other HR policies such as that for reward clearly support their approach.

Behaviourist concepts

Although work with pigeons and dogs may not appear at first sight to be very relevant to learning that occurs within organisations, this work does, in fact, raise a great many important issues, of which those specialising in learning and development should be aware.

Early in the last century Pavlov (1927) trained dogs to salivate when he rang a bell. He noticed that dogs salivated naturally as a reflex response when food was put in front of them. For his experiment he rang a bell every time the dogs were fed; after a time, the dogs would salivate when the bell was rung, whether there was food or not (Figure 9.3). He deduced that the dogs had learnt to salivate by associating the bell with the food, and came to see the learning process as the development of responses

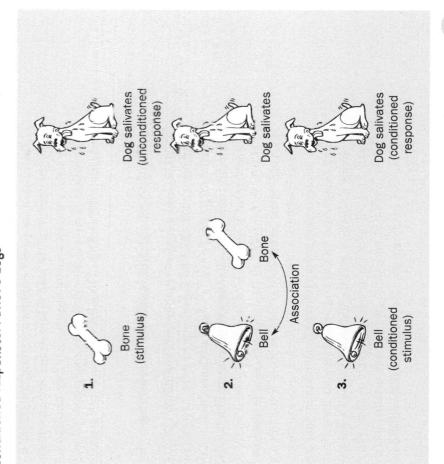

Figure 9.3 Conditioned responses: Pavlov's dogs

to the new stimuli given by the world. He called them conditioned responses, as opposed to the unconditioned or natural responses that came before. His term for the process of learning was 'conditioning'.

Later, Skinner (1953) took the theory further. The limitation of Pavlov's work was that it showed that animals (or people) could learn to apply instinctive responses to new sets of circumstances, but it did not show how totally new responses could be learnt. Skinner in fact succeeded in teaching pigeons to play ping-pong by a process that he called operant conditioning. In this process, the pigeons were watched for any patterns of behaviour that might be useful when playing ping-pong, and whenever they performed they were rewarded with food. Not surprisingly, the birds soon learnt to do certain movements, and they retained their learning better if the reward was repeated regularly, a process Skinner called 'reinforcement'. In human learning, Skinner believed, reinforcement mainly took the form of feedback – information telling the learner whether they are getting the task right.

Skinner believed that all learning took place in this associative manner, and that all complex patterns of behaviour, such as learning ping-pong or learning to speak, could be broken down into small steps that could be taught one by one in a simple fashion. He applied this theory both to training workers and to the education of his own children, and his work is still very influential. It obviously makes sense to break down routine tasks into their component parts, and to provide methodical training to teach complex matters suggests that they can lead to a slow, mechanical set of activities. Many psychologists have challenged Skinner's view, particularly with regard to the learning of complex behaviour such as speech.

On the other hand, you might be wondering whether Skinner's account of the pigeons' learning process was complete. Did insight play no part in their grasp of the rules of the game? In human learning insight often seems to enable people to cut the corners on the road to knowledge, and experience of behaviouristic attempts to cover them. In addition, his emphasis on the visible or objective side of learning led to the practice of setting learning objectives or statements of what a learner had to achieve in terms of action.

Reinforcement and feedback of learning

The behaviourists used reinforcement to indicate a correct behavioural response. The reinforcement could be negative or positive. Rewards such as food for animals or praise for people are positive forms of reinforcement of the desired behaviour, while punishments aim to eliminate incorrect behaviour. Research suggests that positive reinforcement is generally more effective than negative reinforcement in gaining a change in behaviour in the long term, as with negative reinforcement the desired change occurs only as long as there is the threat of punishment. When this threat is withdrawn then behaviour often reverts to the original behaviour.

Reinforcement of your learning could occur by your reading or viewing something and being tested on this and praised by your tutor for your efforts, or by you completing a self-check exercise and giving yourself a pat on the back if you have done well. This will reinforce correct behaviour or show you that you have the right answers, but won't necessarily give you any detailed understanding of what you have done well or of what you did wrong. For that you also need knowledge of results or feedback.

ACTIVITY 9.6

Go to this book's website at www.pearsoned.co.uk/foothook, and complete exercise 9.6 to check and reinforce your own learning in this chapter.

What feedback did you get for this? Was it of use to you? Did this help you to reinforce your own learning?

Knowledge of results or feedback is important if we are to learn effectively. In a training situation this could be by the trainer giving comments on the person's progress, or perhaps by a manager appraising the work of one of their staff as part of the performance management process.

When giving constructive feedback one should start with the positive, and focus first on the behaviour that has been done well before giving feedback about behaviour that has been done less well. Feedback about incorrect behaviour, if given skilfully, is extremely important; it doesn't have to be destructive, and here it is important to focus on specific aspects of behaviour that can be changed. General statements such as 'that was awful' are much too vague to be helpful in changing behaviour. It would be easy for the person receiving the feedback to feel that they are just being criticised unless the person who is giving the feedback also suggests alternative ways of behaving. For example, you might say, 'The fact that you seemed preoccupied with your paperwork when Rosalind walked into the room, and took some time before you greeted her, seemed a very unwelcoming start to an interview. I think that if you had acknowledged her presence immediately and got up and walked towards her to greet her, it would have been a much more welcoming start to the interview, and would have been likely to have made Rosalind feel much more at ease.'

Feedback is a very important part of the learning process. The saying 'Practice makes perfect' could well be modified to 'Practice with appropriate feedback makes perfect', since without the feedback the person could just carry on with the same inappropriate behaviour over and over again.

Experiential learning

Experiential learning, or learning from experience, is particularly useful for learning and development in the workplace situation. It is derived from the work of Kolb *et al.* (1974) in America, and of Honey and Mumford (1992) in Britain. Honey and Mumford's approach to experiential learning can be illustrated by the learning cycle shown in Figure 9.4. Their theory also suggests that different people may have different preferred styles of learning and this is an important factor to consider if we want people to learn effectively.

The learning cycle

People learn in a variety of ways, and over the years may develop certain learning habits which enable them to benefit from certain types of experience more than other types. Students in college and people learning in the workplace are both likely to meet a range of different learning opportunities. Most full-time students nowadays will also work to support themselves to some extent while studying and will themselves have a

Figure 9.4 The learning cycle

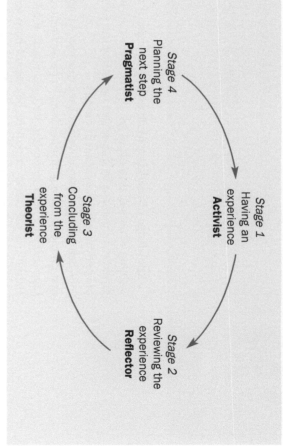

range of work experiences from which they can learn. Some will be mature students who have already worked for a number of years, some will be part-time students combining study with a career, and yet others will be on sandwich course degrees where they have the opportunity of gaining work experience in a placement for a period of time. Knowing about your own learning preferences may help you to understand and you may become more efficient in learning from these experiences.

Stage 1: Having an experience

Most people have plenty of experiences from which they could learn, but age does not necessarily mean that people have learnt more. Some people do not use the experiences that they have. One way of learning is to let experiences come to you (reactive), and the other is to deliberately seek out new experiences (proactive). Anyone who provides learning development opportunities whether as a specialist or a line manager needs to provide suitable experiences from which people can learn (in the form, for example, of case studies, role plays and other simulations), but learners also need to appreciate the need to be proactive and seek for themselves suitable experiences from which to learn. The use of suitable individuals who are willing to act as mentors, or forming a supportive study group of friends, can assist in this process by:

- helping to identify suitable experiences from which to learn
- reviewing with individuals what they have actually done and helping to draw out what they have learnt
- encouraging the individual to be proactive and to seek for themselves suitable learning experiences.

Stage 2: Reviewing the experience

If we are to learn from an experience it is important to review what has happened. Unfortunately we are often too busy to do this, and some people never develop the habit of reflection. The individual should be encouraged to:

- think about what actually happened
- think of other ways in which the situation could have been handled

- make comparisons with what happened in other similar situations
- read about the subject
- compare theory and practice.

Stage 3: Concluding from the experience

There would be little point in reviewing the experiences unless we then drew some conclusions from them. This involves scanning the raw material for lessons to be learned and reaching some conclusions. The individual should be asking:

- What have I learnt from this?
- What could I have done differently?

Stage 4: Planning the next stage

Having reached a conclusion, it is important to try to do things better next time. To be able to do this we need to be able to plan, and this involves translating at least some of the conclusions into a basis for appropriate action next time. The individual should be encouraged to:

- state what they would actually do next time
- draw up a plan of action for handling such a situation again.

The four stages in the process of learning using experiences are mutually dependent. The whole process is summarised in the learning cycle (Figure 9.4).

Learning styles

Honey and Mumford have developed a questionnaire so that individuals can establish their preferred learning style. They developed this approach as a result of their work with managers, as they became concerned to discover why one person will learn from a particular experience but another does not appear to learn anything from the same experience. Further details of their approach are given in the recommended reading. Most people only use one or two learning styles although these are not fixed and can change over time. They say that there are four differing learning styles that clearly link with the four stages of the learning cycle: activists, reflectors, theorists and pragmatists.

Activists

Activists like to get fully involved in whatever is happening. They seek out new experiences and tend to be enthusiastic about new ideas and new techniques. They tend to be open minded and not sceptical, and are often enthusiastic about novelty. They tend to act first and then consider the consequences later. Their days are filled with activity and they often tackle problems by brainstorming.

Reflectors

Reflectors prefer to stand back and observe experiences from different perspectives. The thorough collection and analysis of data are important to them, so they try to avoid reaching definite conclusions for as long as possible. They would rather take a back seat in meetings and discussions and get the drift of the discussion before making their own points. When they act it is as part of a larger picture which includes the past as well as the present and takes into account other people's observations as well as their own.

Theorists

Theorists tend to adapt and integrate observations into complex but logically sound theories. They think problems through in a vertical, step-by-step, logical way. They assimilate disparate facts into coherent theories, and tend to be perfectionists who will not rest easy until things are tidy and fit into a rational scheme. They value rationality and logic.

Pragmatists

Pragmatists are keen to try out new ideas, theories and techniques to see if they work in practice. They positively search for new ideas and take the first opportunities to experiment with applications. They are the type of people who return from a training course full of ideas that they want to try out immediately. They like to get on with things and act quickly and confidently on ideas. They hate long ruminating discussions.

ACTIVITY 9.7

1 Read the description of the four learning styles again or go to **www.campaign-for-learning.org.uk/ourlearning/whatlearner.asp** (accessed 6.8.2010). This site provides some clear explanations about Honey and Mumford's learning styles as well as hints on how to make learning more effective for each style of learner. It also provides lots of useful information about ways to learn more effectively.

2 From the descriptions given, which learning style do you think you use most frequently?

3 Try to discover your learning style. You could do this by testing whether how you think you learn matches an analysis of your learning style by using Honey and Mumford's online questionnaire at **http://www.peterhoney.com/content/LearningStylesQuestionnaire.html** (accessed 6.8.2010). There is a charge for this which at the time of writing was £10.00. Alternatively you could use a shorter online version which claims to provide similar results in a rough and ready learning styles questionnaire: **http://www.brainboxx.co.uk/A2_LEARNSTYLES/pages/learningstyles.htm** (accessed 6.8.2010)

4 Reflect on your findings. Examine the theory by rereading the description of the styles outlined earlier and on these websites.

Discussion of Activity 9.7

You may have discovered that you are equally at home learning in each of these styles. Two per cent of the population use all four styles. The majority of the population – 70 per cent – tend to prefer to use just one or two learning styles. You can use the understanding that you have gained about your learning styles in various ways. You might choose to seek out opportunities to use the learning styles that you generally use less often, and in this way you may become a more rounded learner who is able to make use of a wider range of learning opportunities.

You might, on the other hand, choose to make use of the learning styles that you know you prefer to use, so that if learning opportunities are presented to you in ways that you don't like, you may look for alternative ways to learn about the topic which are more in line with your learning style preferences.

Other approaches to learning styles and methods

There are many different ways of analysing approaches to learning. We have already mentioned the Honey and Mumford learning styles inventory and that of David Kolb *et al.* However, other approaches are used. For example, are you a visual, auditory or kinaesthetic learner? This is sometimes referred to as VAK.

ACTIVITY 9.8

You can check whether you are a visual, auditory or kinaesthetic learner (VAK) at www.businessballs.com/vaklearningstylestest.htm (accessed 6.8.2010).

If you like to visualise, seeing things in colour and using pictures such as mind maps, then you are probably a visual learner. If you prefer to listen to the sounds of things then you are probably an auditory learner, and if you like to move around while learning and link learning with movement then you could be a kinaesthetic learner.

Practical issues relating to individual learning

Whenever we are designing training for individuals or groups, we need to consider learning theory and build into the learning experience as many conditions as we can to ensure effective learning. Not only is it important when learning from experiences for the individual learner to be aware of their preferred learning style, it is also important that the L&TD specialist or the line manager should be aware of differing learning styles and cultural preferences in order to provide a learning experience which will be congruent with the way in which each individual learns best.

Recent approaches to learning and development

Mind mapping techniques

Psychologists are finding out more about the ways in which we think and learn and psychologists now say that our minds work in patterns and that several ideas can be developing at once. The brain then goes through a process of integrating ideas, but this doesn't necessarily happen in a linear order.

Tony Buzan (1982) developed the idea of mind maps to allow people to express themselves freely and encourage creativity, without being necessarily governed by the linear form. Many people, when presenting information in the form of a mind map,

Figure 9.5   Partial mind map of learning and talent development chapter

Learning theories
Behaviourist
Experiential

Systematic
organisation
of L&TD
Assess
Plan
Deliver
Evaluate

LEARNING
AND
TALENT DEVELOPMENT

Value to
the individual   Strategic
the team   objectives
the organisation Performance
                  management

Methods

show a very detailed grasp of the subject which they were not be able to demonstrate in a traditional written form. The mind maps (some examples are used as chapter summaries in this book) start with the central subject, which can be presented pictorially. Lines then lead from this subject to other connected topics. This gives more freedom for ideas to appear without worrying at first about the connections, and it allows for several links to be made between related parts of a topic.

The mind map shown in Figure 9.5 illustrates our view of the key points with which this chapter has been concerned so far. Mind maps encourage creativity, and if they are to be used in a way that helps someone to remember and learn effectively then they should be very visual. The central topic should be written clearly, preferably in capital letters, and underlined. A pictorial representation of that topic is also useful, as it encourages easier recall. Lines should then be drawn from this key word, and the main areas relating to the subject area should be drawn.

Further diagrams or pictures can be useful to make the mind map of the topic memorable. Further lines and words should branch from each of these, and the pattern is then developed. Groups of ideas can be linked by the use of different colours. Links can be made easily, by using arrows or lines, between related topics. Relationships and links with other subjects can also be made and identified at the edges of the mind map.

ACTIVITY 9.9

The mind map in Figure 9.5 is incomplete, since it is being used partway through this chapter. When you have read the rest of this chapter, complete the remainder of the mind map in a way that will make it memorable for you. Draw links with other subjects or topics around the edge of the mind map.

Discussion of Activity 9.9

After reading the whole chapter you may want to include more things that you consider relevant such as e-learning, bite-size learning and blended learning, and international learning and development so you can continue to build your mind map and add further topics to make it relevant to you. In order for it to be useful and memorable you should try to make your mind map as visually attractive as possible.

ACTIVITY 9.10

Consider each of the techniques listed in Table 9.1. Make four new lists as shown below, naming the learning and talent development techniques you think will suit activists, reflectors, theorists and pragmatists. (Some of the techniques may suit more than one style of learning.)

Learning and talent development techniques to suit people who prefer each of the four learning styles

Activist	Reflector	Theorist	Pragmatist

Discussion of Activity 9.10

Your list is likely to include a variety of different learning techniques, some of which we listed earlier and some that you have added for yourselves. We will consider in turn each of the preferred learning styles.

Activist

The techniques that allow activists to participate fully in the learning experience will be the ones that appeal most to them. These could include: role play, group discussion, project work, case studies, computer-based learning and in-tray exercises. The role play is especially likely to appeal to the activist, as it provides plenty of opportunity for them to become involved in a leading role. Activists are likely to be bored by the lack of involvement required from them in techniques such as lectures, videos or films.

Reflector

Reflectors are likely to appreciate learning techniques where they are presented with information that they can then think about, so lectures, films, videos and guided reading are likely to appeal to them. They will probably also appreciate to some extent group discussions and case studies, as long as they do not have to take too active a part and have plenty of time for reflection afterwards. Computer-based training courses, in which they can progress at their own speed and go back to examine again points that they want to look at in more detail, may also prove popular.

Theorist

Theorists welcome opportunities to examine new theories and compare them with other points of view. Lectures and guided reading are likely to appeal most to them as training techniques. Lectures with a fairly academic content are preferred, so that ideas gained can be compared with other ideas and theories. If the guided reading covers a suitable range of material this could also be useful to a theorist, although if the material is not extensive or theoretical enough for them, they are likely to want to delve further into other areas.

Pragmatist

The pragmatist wants to know how things will really work in practice, so they are likely to find training techniques that are close to reality useful. Case studies, role plays and in-tray exercises will appeal to them if they think that they are realistic and of immediate use to them at work.

Bite-sized learning

Some of you may have experienced bite-sized learning for yourselves as the BBC's revision programmes for GCSE use this approach. Octavius Black, managing director of the Mind Gym (2004), says that:

> People often thought that the more time they spent on learning, the better their knowledge would be. In fact, they could learn equally effectively – if not more so – in short bursts. Research shows that we remember and apply much more knowledge when we learn little and often than when we learn lots in one go.

This fits very well with what we said earlier about remembering information. You are likely to be more successful in remembering information if you are frequently spending small amounts of time going over what you have learned.

According to Crofts (2004), one of the most common barriers to learning cited by CIPD members is the amount of time it takes and as workers in the UK work increasingly long hours, bite-sized training certainly fits a need. However, trainers are likely to need to develop different skills to deliver material in a fast-paced way, with exercises taking only a few minutes to complete. This view is supported by a survey of line managers conducted in 2010 where ongoing accessible learning using bite-sized modules on a regular basis and the 'ability to dip into learning' was seen as being one important factor which contributed towards the success of training for busy managers (Wolff, 2010).

However, concerns have also been raised recently about the appropriateness of using bite-sized learning in all circumstances. Woolcock (2010) reported claims that students were sometimes taking A levels in bite-sized chunks and that this was helping them develop short attention spans and was proving inadequate preparation for the more in-depth approach to study needed for university work.

Blended learning

Another type of learning and development that has proved popular is the concept of blended learning. According to Allison Rossett and Felicia Douglas (2004):

> A blend is an integrated strategy for delivering on promises about learning and performance. It involves a planned combination of approaches as varied as coaching by a supervisor, participating in on-line class, self-assessments, and in on-line attendance in workshops and in on-line discussions.

We have already advocated that there should be a mix of learning and development methods to suit the needs of the learners, and blended learning involves planning this into the learning in ways that will suit the needs of particular groups. A blended learning approach is attractive to organisations as it is claimed that it may help to reduce the costs of delivery while at the same time improving the quality of the learning though there is little firm evidence to support this (Hofmann, 2008).

In many instances, online learning forms part of the blend and this may cut down the need for time spent on classroom-based learning, but every organisation has to reach its own blend of learning and development ingredients to suit the needs of the organisation and the participants in the learning and development programme. According to Blain (quoted in *Training and Coaching Today*, 2008), 'the effectiveness of any blended mix hinges on agreeing goals and recognizing the outcomes that the company, individual and the trainer is looking for – with senior management sponsors forming another crucial element'. Blain further advocates that a blend does not have to include technology-based methods but could use any mix of the methods including those currently proving to be most effective with CIPD members, which are in-house development programmes and coaching by line managers (CIPD, 2010c). This approach is in line with the view we have advocated throughout this chapter and shows once again that the blend of approaches to learning must be appropriate to the situation.

Mentors

Rather than just leaving learning experiences to chance, many organisations now use mentors to help individuals to learn. Mentors need to be prepared to guide and suggest suitable learning experiences for their protégé. They may encourage reflection on these learning experiences by asking for reports, and may suggest books to read on the subject. They may also sometimes provide opportunities for the individual to demonstrate what they have learnt by, for example, reviewing a presentation before the learner makes it to the target audience. While their main aim is to encourage individuals to learn, mentors are also likely to learn a great deal themselves by their involvement in this learning experience. In effect, mentors will be encouraging the individual to learn in different ways according to their development needs and to practise using different learning styles and different stages of the learning cycle.

Coaching

Coaches help individuals or groups to perform better, rather like a sports coach. They could be external to an organisation or internal although, according to the CIPD's (2010c) survey of learning and talent development, coaching by line managers is currently the second most popular approach to developing talent with 56 per cent of organisations in the survey reporting using this approach.

According to Sol Davidson (2002), there are three types of coaching: traditional, transitional and transformational:

- Traditional coaching is closely related to training and involves a coach who is an expert in a subject helping to improve the skills and knowledge of an individual or group.

- Transitional coaching is useful where large changes are about to be made in an organisation. Here the coach does not necessarily know all the answers, but will help the group to find successful new ways of working.
- Transformational coaching is targeted at senior management but is aimed at helping the whole organisation move to new ways of working. It could be appropriate when an organisation is faced with a great deal of change.

Pause for thought 9.1

Which of these forms of coaching are most likely to be carried out by internal coaches who are not the person's line manager? Which are most likely to be conducted by line managers and which by external coaches?

Learning logs

Another way in which individuals may be encouraged to learn from their experiences is by the use of a learning log. A learning log is a way of keeping track of a person's development, with emphasis on unstructured, informal activities. This is likely to involve individuals in describing events that they feel are important for their own development process. They would then need to comment on what they had learnt from the experience and how, if a similar situation were to arise again, they would handle that situation. The idea is that because individuals have to write up their learning experiences, they will be likely to do things better in the future. Learning also ceases to be a haphazard process, as it becomes conscious and increasingly learner-centred and puts them in charge of developing their own talent and abilities. This means that the individual will have used several of the stages of the learning cycle.

Keeping a learning log should encourage activists to be more reflective and encourage reflectors/theorists to take action and to do things after reflecting on them. This could be undertaken with a mentor or as a totally self-directed method of gaining insights into your own learning processes. This method is very subjective but tends to encourage an analytical approach to problems. It can also be helpful to get a problem sorted out on paper, with clear targets for how you would handle a similar situation in the future.

Nowadays the pace of change is rapid and people who studied 20 years ago, or even a couple of years ago, may find that their skills and knowledge are outdated. In order to update their members, many professional groups have introduced the concept of continuing professional development (CPD) and they often use learning logs as one way of recording the learning that has occurred and for planning for future learning.

Trade union learning representatives

As part of the shift from training to learning, and in order to promote learning at all levels and within all organisations, the Employment Act 2002 established a new group known as learning representatives. These learning representatives are appointed by trade unions and have several statutory rights. These include the right to time off work in certain circumstances in order to:

- analyse learning and training needs
- provide information or advice relating to any learning or training issues

- organise specific learning or training
- consult with the employer about learning and training issues
- participate themselves in training for their role as a learning representative.

The ACAS (2003) *Code of Practice on Time off for Union Duties and Activities* gives further details of these rights. Union members also have the right to time off to discuss issues or attend learning activities organised by trade union-appointed learning representatives, although they do not have to be paid for this.

Pause for thought 9.2   Compare the role of the union learning representative with what you consider to be the role of the learning and talent development specialists within an organisation. To what extent do the roles differ? To what extent do the roles overlap?

Both the L&TD specialists and the trade union learning representatives are concerned to promote learning so to that extent their roles do overlap but their focus will be different. The specialists, according to Harrison (2009), will be concerned that learning and development adds value to the organisation and to make the link between learning and development and the organisation's strategic objectives. They will be concerned to operate at a strategic level and may take on roles such as promoting L&TD, managing knowledge, or generating income from L&TD activities: there will still be many other L&TD specialists involved in running specific learning and talent development activities and in training managers to do this.

Learning representatives will also be concerned to promote learning but they are operating at a different level as they try to encourage more of the workforce to become involved in learning. As they are a part of the workforce their role is to reach and inform workers who might not normally get involved in learning and development activities to do so: to encourage and discuss options with workers who might have been put off by having to discuss their learning needs with management. If life-long learning is to become a reality then their role should help to kick-start some learning and development activities for all workers.

The learning representatives have a role to play in fostering a positive attitude towards learning and development and increasing motivation to learn. It has also been claimed that large numbers of workers lack basic skills in numeracy and literacy but have successfully hidden this from their employers for many years. In many organisations L&D specialists are now working with learning representatives to reach groups of workers who have not traditionally participated in learning and development and who may have poor basic skills which could be holding back their career progression, so the roles of the L&D specialist and the union learning representative are in many ways complementary to each other.

International differences in learning and development

Cross-cultural issues will be of importance to many HRM or LTD practitioners, particularly if they work in multinational organisations or come to study HRM away from their home country. Therefore, it is important to consider to what extent there is a cultural dimension to learning. Hofstede's (2006) work does enable us to gain some insights into cultural effects on learning and these cultural differences do need to be taken into account when learning or designing learning materials for others.

**Bury College
Woodbury LRC**

Did you know?

A question of how you concentrate and eating while learning divides Europe.

In a survey conducted across Europe less than 20% of respondents in Spain, Italy and France think that eating snacks helps them to concentrate while learning, whereas in Holland that figure rises to 58% while 33% of Germans and British feel a snack and drink aids concentration.

(Source: Skillsoft, 2010)

What do you think about this?

Do you think there are differences between countries in the way people try to concentrate while learning?

Do you snack while learning?

These cultural differences may influence individual learning styles since in countries where it is normal for the learning to be very tutor/trainer-centred and for the learner just to absorb knowledge without questioning, individual learners are less likely to have opportunities to develop an activist or pragmatist approach to their learning. It is likely that trainers will have to adjust their approach for learners who are used to being less participative and hold more formal training sessions than would be necessary in countries and cultures that have moved to being more learner-centred.

E-learning is a popular approach when learning needs to be provided for a multi-national organisation across several countries but once again the appropriateness of this needs to be assessed. Weekes (2009) points out that although in many ways the Internet has helped to shrink the world, one issue that still remains in any learning and talent development provision is to adapt this to local situations and that thinking globally and acting locally is still important in international learning and talent development.

● The roles of learning and talent development specialists in international organisations

However, while there may be differences in styles of learning, according to Sloman (2007), 'It seems that the issues faced by learning, training and talent development professionals are pretty much universal – whether they are in Britain, Bulgaria or further afield.' The CIPD carried out a survey of the changing role of the trainer involving 300 trainers and assembling '50 case studies from 19 different countries, and investigated how trainers in the United States, "old Europe", new emerging Europe, China, India and South Africa saw their roles.' They concluded that 'overall we found more similarities across the world than we thought we would.' There was no single approach that illustrated best practice but lots of approaches were found that showed good practice. Trainers and learning and talent development practitioners were providing that thinking globally and acting locally was effective and were adapting learning approaches to the context of the country they were working in and to the learning styles of the learners in that country. The approaches identified in the CIPD (2007) survey as good practice were:

- showing a clear understanding of the business drivers in their organisation;
- helping their organisation add value and move up the value chain;
- establishing a clear vision and strategy for people development;
- involving others and engaging shareholders in a transparent and open way;
- having both a good overview of what is needed to advance in the long term and also of the short-term priorities;
- using processes and techniques appropriately – without being overcommitted to any one method of delivery;
- applying metrics to demonstrate value; and above all
- understanding the legacy that learners bring with them and adjusting their interventions accordingly.

The factors identified here in an international context by the CIPD survey fit well with our model of the learning and talent development cycle described earlier in this chapter with the emphasis on adding value and contributing to the strategic objectives. It also clearly emphasises the importance of adapting techniques to the learning styles and culture of the people being trained as we discussed earlier.

In the CIPD's 2010 survey the most popular methods for promoting learning and talent development in international organisations are coaching and mentoring with 83 per cent of international organisations mentioning this, followed by on the job training which is used by 74 per cent of the international organisations. This is very similar to the approaches identified in the same survey in non-international organisations where the most effective learning and talent development strategies were first the use of in-house development programmes, used by 56 per cent of the organisations, and secondly the use of coaching by line managers, used in 51 per cent of organisations (CIPD, 2010c). Specific talent management programmes for those identified as having high potential tended to be used by larger organisations and are used across all countries in which they operate.

Conclusion

In this chapter we have provided an introduction to learning and talent development and have emphasised the need for a systematic approach which helps the organisation to achieve its strategic objectives. We have also shown that people learn in a variety of ways and that specialist L&TD managers and line managers will need to adapt the learning experiences they provide to suit individuals and groups. However, while individuals often use only one or two preferred learning styles these are not fixed but will vary over time and will be affected by the culture within an organisation or indeed a country. While the concept of the learning organisation may still be aspirational, organisations wishing to improve learning and develop and retain talent do adopt a wide range of approaches including formal and informal methods. There is an emphasis throughout such organisations on all aspects of learning and talent development and of identifying and agreeing the learning needs with the people concerned. All programmes also emphasise the difference that learning and talent development can make to an organisation by adding value to that organisation and as a powerful means of attracting and retaining talent.

REVIEW QUESTIONS

You will find brief answers to these review questions on page 494.

1 Use the Internet or Government publications to find out more about one of the following topics: Investors in People, apprenticeships, New Deal or flexible New Deal. Using this information, describe how you would persuade a sceptical line manager of the benefits to be gained from introducing the chosen initiative into an organisation of your choice.

2 Interview a manager about their organisation's strategic plans and objectives and try to assess the extent to which learning and talent development in that organisation contributes to the achievement of those strategic plans.

3 Many organisations do not provide an adequate induction programme for new employees. Comment critically on the benefits to be gained from implementing a good induction programme, and outline what should be contained in that programme.

4 Evaluate the relative effectiveness of on-the-job training and off-the-job training.

SELF-CHECK QUESTIONS

Answer the following multiple-choice questions. The correct responses are given on page 494 for you to check your understanding of this chapter.

1 Which of the following is true?

(a) Once individuals have been employed for at least 26 weeks in an organisation they have a legal right to request time off for training.

(b) Individuals who have been employed for at least 26 weeks in an organisation must be granted paid time off for training.

(c) Once individuals have been employed for at least 52 weeks in an organisation they have a legal right to request time off for training.

(d) There is no right of appeal against an employer who does not grant an employee's legal request for training.

2 The illustration in Figure 9.6 shows what happens when Caroline makes a cup of tea. She often chooses to feed the cats at the same time as putting the kettle on. Thus the kettle and the tin of cat food being opened are linked in the cats' minds.

Figure 9.6 Caroline's cats

© Minky 2001

Sometimes she puts the kettle on but she doesn't open a tin of cat food. However, the cats now appear when they hear the sound of the kettle.

(a) What is this effect known as?

(b) According to Pavlov, how should we label the cat food at point 1 in Figure 9.6?

(c) According to Pavlov, what is the link between the kettle and the cat food known as? Label point 2 in Figure 9.6.

(d) According to Pavlov, what should the kettle be labelled as at point 3 in Figure 9.6?

3 When there are very few new recruits to an organisation, should induction be left for several months until there are sufficient to form a group? YES or NO

4 Which of the following is not a coaching technique advocated by Sol Davidson (2002)?

(a) traditional coaching

(b) disciplinary coaching

(c) transitional coaching

(d) transformational coaching

5 Are mentors always training managers? YES or NO

6 Which of the following is true, according to Honey and Mumford?

(a) Learning has occurred when knowledge has been acquired by study.

(b) Learning has occurred when a person knows something that they did not know earlier and can show it, or is able to do something that they were not able to do before.

(c) Learning has occurred when a person knows something that they did not know earlier but can't show it, or is able to do something that they were not able to do before.

(d) Learning is shown by a change in behaviour that occurs just as a result of experience.

7 According to Honey and Mumford, a pragmatist is someone who:

(a) seeks out new experiences and is open-minded, not sceptical, and who is enthusiastic about anything new

(b) integrates and adapts observations into logically sound theories

(c) is keen to try new ideas, theories and techniques to see if they work in practice

(d) collects data in a very thorough way and then analyses it.

8 Which of the following is not one of the stages in the systematic training cycle?

(a) assessing learning and development needs

(b) having an experience

(c) planning the learning and development activities

(d) evaluating the learning and development.

9 Does CPD stand for continuing professional development? YES or NO

10 Which of the following learning and talent development methods, according to the CIPD (2010c), was found to be the most popular in international organisations?

(a) sitting by Nellie

(b) e-learning

(c) traditional off-the-job training

(d) coaching and mentoring.

HR IN THE NEWS

FT Report – Managing employees through the recovery: Eye on the future

By Ian Wylie

FT

Porters, housekeepers and reception staff at the Malmaison hotel chain are used to keeping up with fast-living guests, from pop star Lady Gaga to John Terry and his Chelsea Football Club teammates. But they are not as familiar with the slower pace of 'consolidation' that parent group MWB, which has earned a reputation for rapid growth, has instituted as it put expansion plans on ice for a second year.

Between 2006 and 2009, MWB, which also owns the Hotel du Vin brand, opened 16 hotels across the UK, offering staff a fast-paced working environment with plentiful opportunities to move into new roles or fresh locations. In boom times, staff motivation, development and engagement can almost take care of themselves.

It is a different story since the recession. 'There hasn't been the same breadth of new development opportunities for staff,' admits Sean Wheeler, group director of people at Malmaison. 'It's more of a challenge to maintain motivation and retain the best staff in our business. One year can feel like a long time in the hospitality industry, and we knew that to do nothing could make our top talent feel like their careers were stagnating. We had to ensure they felt like they were continuing to develop their careers.'

In previous downturns, staff training and development budgets were an early target of corporate cutbacks. In this recession, however, the Confederation of British Industry, the employers' body, found evidence that many companies were trying to protect training and staff development budgets, despite cost pressures.

Malmaison, for example, ensured that all staff had an online appraisal to create a personal development and training plan. It set up a wine academy for managers and supervisors, as well as a training programme for kitchen staff.

According to research by Kingston Business School for the Chartered Institute of Personnel and Development (CIPD), a third of employees say their manager never discusses their training or development needs. Yet employee satisfaction surveys suggest the desire for more skills is an important influence on retention and engagement. Most workers recognise that job security now depends on what they bring to the workplace, not their seniority or tenure. They seek learning opportunities and ways to acquire new skills.

'Forward-looking employers have continued to invest for the future in training,' explains Richard Phelps, human resource management leader at PwC, the consultancy. 'The common theme has been a review of which programmes are critical for developing staff, with a focus on improving their content and results, while less essential programmes have been dropped. Organisations have also focused on getting better value from training suppliers by negotiating discounts or deals, while interest in less costly ways of training – e-learning, for example – has grown. There is also an expectation that staff will study for some of their development outside normal work hours.'

Mr Phelps says employers that depend more heavily on the capabilities of their people, such as professional services firms and R&D companies, have shown greater commitment to engaging staff through training. 'Some UK supermarkets are great examples of where brave people-management decisions have paid off to help them secure and develop the next generation of leadership cadre and pick up top performers at all levels from different industries,' he says.

Other examples include DHL Exel Supply Chain, the transport and logistics group, which has continued to deliver its 'Active Leadership' skills development programme for managers. Hewlett-Packard UK, the computer group, runs road shows for staff presented by its managing director in tandem with a leadership training programme.

But while engagement experts accept that training and development encourage greater employee engagement (and vice versa), there is debate over how that link works. 'I subscribe to the view that it is employees' perception of organisational efforts to provide them with training, rather than their actual training experiences, that drives employee commitment,' says Mike Emmott, employee relations adviser at the CIPD. 'In other words, what matters is evidence of the employer caring for the employees and helping them forward their career.'

Training and development provider Maynard Leigh agrees. 'Most employee engagement is based on feelings,' says Stuart Mackenzie, managing director. 'Employees "feel" engaged, and that relies to a large extent on the trust they have in the management's promises. Because the downturn made a lot of promises impossible to deliver, trust has been affected. We have not just been through a financial recession, but through a trust recession as well – and the latter will take longer to fix.'

Training tips in a downturn

'There needs to be a discussion so that training and development reflect the needs of staff as well as the business,' says Sean Wheeler, group director of people at Malmaison hotels.

- Make training employee-led

'There needs to be a discussion so that training and development reflect the needs of staff as well as the business,' says Sean Wheeler, group director of people at Malmaison hotels.

- Tailor training to individuals' needs

'In addition to training from vendors on product launches and initiatives, we also offer in-house training covering everything from time management to negotiation skills as well as desk-side coaching to help with specific needs,' explains Anushka Davies, training and development manager at Softcat, a software company.

- Create a central system for capturing training costs and business impact

'Annual reviews of the purpose of each programme and how the behaviours or skills of staff who have been through the programme positively affect the business are essential,' says Richard Phelps, human resource management leader at PwC, the consultancy.

- Do not assume learning or development has to be long, formal or expensive

'All our staff appreciate our 10-minutes-a-day approach,' says Mr Wheeler. 'We encourage them to take just 10 minutes out of their working day to learn something new – it could be anything from the history of the hotel brand to how we source our coffee or choose our wines.'

- Deliver what you have promised

'It is hugely demotivating to promise employees career development and then not deliver,' says Mr Wheeler.

(*Financial Times*, 22 March 2010, Ian Wylie. Reproduced with permission.)

Questions

1 Why is training so popular in the organisations referred to in this article?

2 What approaches to learning and development did Malmaison use to try to ensure the continued motivation of its staff?

3 What are the advantages and disadvantages of these methods?

4 How did the training methods discussed here contribute to retention and talent management?

WHAT NEXT?

1 ACAS provides some excellent opportunities for you to experience e-learning on its website at www.acas.org.uk (accessed 6.8.2010). It has developed a range of free e-learning resources and you can undertake short e-learning courses and test your understanding of several topics covered in this book, such as discipline and grievance, informing and consulting, and absence management and redundancy.

2 Listen to the following podcasts from the Chartered Institute of Personnel and Development to examine some of the current issues in learning and development at www.cipd.co.uk/podcasts (accessed 6.8.2010):

The value of learning – episode 11. This examines the contribution that learning and development makes to an organisation and links with a key theme of this chapter.

Pushing the boundaries of learning and development – episode 42. This discusses the findings of the Chartered Institute of Personnel and Development's 2010 survey of learning and development issues.

References

Advisory, Conciliation and Arbitration Service (2003) *The Code of Practice on Time Off for Union Duties and Activities,* ACAS (www.acas.org.uk; accessed 31.08.04).

Age Positive (2007) *Training and development,* Department for Work and Pensions (www. agepositive.gov.uk/good_practices/training.asp; accessed 04.04.07).

Black, O. (2004) The future's bite, *People Management,* Vol. 10, No. 8, 25.

Brockett, J. (2010) *UK is Ahead of European Rivals in Innovative Learning Methods,* PM Online, 18.6.2010 (accessed 3.7.2010).

Buzan, T. (1982) *Use Your Head,* BBC.

Chartered Institute of Personnel and Development (2007) *Learning and Development: Annual Survey 2007,* CIPD.

Chartered Institute of Personnel and Development (2008) *Supporting, Accelerating and Directing Learning,* CIPD.

Chartered Institute of Personnel and Development (2010a) *Pushing the Boundaries of Learning and Development: Podcast 42,* CIPD (www.cipd.co.uk; accessed 3.7.2010).

Chartered Institute of Personnel and Development (2010b) *Learning and Talent Development: An Overview,* CIPD.

Chartered Institute of Personnel and Development (2010c) *Learning and Talent Development: Annual Survey Report 2010,* CIPD.

Chartered Institute of Personnel and Development (2010d) *Fact Sheet: Investors in People,* CIPD (www.cipd.co.uk; accessed 4.8.2010).

Chartered Institute of Personnel and Development (2010e) *Fact Sheet: Learning and Talent Development Strategy,* CIPD (www.cipd.co.uk; accessed 4.8.2010).

Chartered Institute of Personnel and Development (2010f) *Fact Sheet: Identifying Learning and Development Needs,* CIPD (www.cipd.co.uk; accessed 4.8.2010).

Chartered Institute of Personnel and Development (2010g) *Evaluating Learning and Development,* CIPD.

Crofts, P. (2004) Support key to success, *People Management,* Vol. 10, No. 11, 55.

Davidson, S. (2002) How to choose the right coach, *People Management,* Vol. 8, No. 10, 54–55.

Findlay, J. (2004) Evaluation is no white elephant, *People Management,* Vol. 10, No. 6, 50.

Frederick, A. (2010) *Topic of the week. Study or Training Requests: Procedures,* 14.6.2010, XpertHR (www.xperthr.co.uk; accessed 5.8.2010).

Green, B. (2010) *Topic of the week. Study or Training Requests: Frequently Asked Questions,* 28.6.2010, XpertHR (www.xperthr.co.uk; accessed 5.8.2010).

Harrison, R. (2009) *Learning and Development,* 5th edition, CIPD.

Hofmann, A. (2008) Developments in blended learning, *Economics and Organisation of Enterprise,* Vol. 1.1, Institute of Organisation and Management in Industry.

Hofstede, G. (2006) *Cultural Dimensions*, www.geert-hofstede_kingsom.shtml (accessed 14.9.07).

Investors in People (2010) *Announcement*, IIP (www.investorsinpeople.co.uk; accessed 3.8.2010).

Jones, A.M. and C. Hendry (1992) *The Learning Organisation: A Review of Literature and Practice*, HRD Partnership.

Kingston, P. (2006) Boost investment to solve skills crisis, Leitch report urges, *The Guardian: Education Guardian*, 5 December (www.guardian.co.uk/eduction accessed 6.8.2010).

Kolb, D., I. Rubin and J.McIntyre (1974) *Organisational Psychology: An Experiential Approach*, 3rd edition, Prentice-Hall.

MacDonald, L. (2010) *Statutory Requests in Relation to Study of Training: Policy on the Right to Make a Request in Relation to Study or Training (Policy)*, 22.3.2010, XpertHR (www.xperthr.co.uk; accessed 5.8.2010).

Megginson, D. and V. Whittaker (2004) *Continuing Professional Development*, CIPD.

Pavlov, I. (1927) *Conditioned Reflexes*, Oxford University Press.

Pedler, M., J. Burgoyne and T. Boydell (1988) *The Learning Company Project*, Training Agency.

Rossett, A. and F. Douglas (2004) The house blend, *People Management*, Vol. 10, No. 8, 36.

Skillsoft (2010) *Rethinking Learning*, HRzone (www.HRzone.co.uk; accessed 11.8.2010).

Skinner, B.F. (1953) *Science and Human Behaviour*, Macmillan.

Sloman, M. (2004) Evaluation and evolution, *People Management*, Vol. 10, No. 14, 50.

Sloman, M. (2007) World standard, *People Management*, 22 March, Vol. 13, No. 6, 38–40.

Thomson, I. (2004) The power and the impact, *People Management*, Vol. 10, No. 8, 15.

Training and Coaching Today (2008) Blended learning: the experts opinions, Issue 1, September, RBI (www.xperthr.co.uk; accessed 8.8.2010).

Weekes, S. (2009) Consider local issues when rolling out e-learning world-wide, *Training and Coaching Today*, Issue 1, 11 February, RBI (www.xperthr.co.uk; accessed 8.8.2010).

Wolff, C. (2009) Managing learning and development in a recession: the 2009 IRS survey, *IRS Employment Review*, 21.9.2009, Issue 929, IRS (www.xperthr.co.uk; accessed 3.8.2010).

Wolff, C. (2010) IRS line manager training survey 2010: How to get results, *IRS Employment Review*, 5.5.2010, IRS (www.xperthr.co.uk; accessed 8.8.2010).

Woolcock, N. (2010) 'Bite-sized' A levels may herald four-year degrees, *The Times*, 1 July.

Further study

Books

Advisory, Conciliation and Arbitration Service (2006) *Recruitment and Induction*, ACAS.

A very useful guide to this subject.

Harrison, R. (2009) *Learning and Development*, 5th edition, CIPD.

An excellent textbook for those who wish to study the subject of learning and development in more depth.

Reid, M., H. Barrington and M. Brown (2004) *Human Resource Development*, 7th edition, CIPD.

Another excellent textbook that covers various aspects of learning and development.

Stewart, J. and C. Rigg (2011) *Learning and Talent Development*, CIPD.

This textbook aims to provide a thorough guide to the whole subject of learning and talent development.

Articles

There are many specialist journals covering the subject of learning and development including the following:

Coaching: An International Journal of Theory, Research and Practice

Development and Learning in Organizations

Human Resource Development International

Human Resource Development Quarterly

Training and Coaching Today

Internet

Apprenticeships (England and Wales)	www.realworkrealpay.info
Apprenticeships (Scotland)	www.scottish-enterprise.com/modernapprenticeships
Chartered Institute of Personnel and Development	www.cipd.co.uk
Department for Children, Schools and Families (formerly the Department for Education and Skills)	www.dfes.gov.uk
The Information Network on Education in Europe	www.eurydice.org
Investors in People UK	www.iipuk.co.uk
Learn Direct	www.learndirect.co.uk
Learn Direct Scotland	www.learndirectscotland.com
The National Academic Recognition Information Centre for the UK	www.naric.org.uk
Qualifications and Curriculum Authority	www.qca.org.uk

CHAPTER **10**

Pay and reward systems

Objectives

By the end of this chapter you will be able to:

● explain the main factors that influence the choice of a particular pay and reward system and the advantages and disadvantages of different types of systems

● explain the importance of developing a pay and reward strategy for an organisation

● explain the process of job evaluation and how to use particular job evaluation systems

● identify current issues relating to equal pay in organisations

● identify issues relating to pay and reward systems in international organisations

● identify potential ethical and environmental issues about pay and reward.

We have indicated in previous chapters that human resource management is concerned that people should work as effectively as possible for the organisation, and that one of the ways in which the organisation attempts to achieve this is by using an appropriate system of pay and reward. The system that is adopted must, as stated in Chapter 2, be in line with and support the key elements of the strategic plan and organisations should develop a pay and reward strategy that suits their particular organisation and the mix of generations of staff within it.

Pay and reward is a key element in performance management and is a vital part of an organisation's HR strategies for the attraction and retention of staff. As we have already discussed in earlier chapters the economic situation and social and demographic changes mean that organisations have to be flexible to respond both to changes in the financial environment and to the expectations of different generations of workers, so the pay and reward system should be reviewed regularly to ensure that it continues to achieve its aims. In the past this has sometimes been an area of HR that was neglected, with some organisations not thinking about the strategic impact of their pay and reward systems or the message they give to employees. The economic situation and scandals over excessive bonuses has helped to focus attention on this area so more HR departments are now starting to think about how to use pay and reward to keep the talent they have, or to attract new talent. In this chapter we shall be examining a variety of payment systems and discussing the philosophies on which they are based as well as the circumstances and the people or groups of workers who may be attracted to and motivated by particular payment systems.

Definitions

Before we proceed, it will be useful to explain and define some of the words we shall use throughout this chapter. According to the CIPD (2010a), 'historically, the aims of reward were to attract, retain and motivate staff. Salaries were what attracted them to an organisation, benefits kept them there, while bonus and incentive schemes motivated them.' However, it is not always so simple and as we discussed in Chapter 9 many young people in Generation Y may also be attracted to an organisation and may stay with it because of the opportunities for learning and talent development that it provides: they may choose to work as volunteers in a not for profit organisation because the organisation's values and corporate and social responsibility policy are in line with their own values. Other perhaps slightly older workers may be attracted to an organisation where there are other benefits such as excellent holidays, better pension provision or opportunities for more flexibility in their working week, while those regarded as knowledge workers may want to achieve success in their chosen area and to achieve recognition for their successes. Since all organisations will have different strategic objectives and will employ different mixes of generations of workers and of part-time and full-time workers, it is important to ensure that the pay and reward strategy chosen helps attract, motivate, engage and retain their workers so that they can achieve their strategic objectives.

Several words are commonly used to refer to the payment made to people at work, and these include the terms 'pay', 'reward', 'wages' and 'salaries'. We shall also explain other terms used in connection with pay and reward systems, such as 'harmonisation' and 'job evaluation' before examining the different types of pay and reward system that are available for an employer to use. We have chosen to call the chapter Pay and Reward so will start with these terms.

Pay is the most straightforward term and normally refers to a monetary award for work done but it can also include monetary payments which do not directly relate to work done such as sickness pay, maternity pay and pension arrangements. Although distinctions between wages and salaries are decreasing as many organisations move towards harmonisation of terms and conditions for different groups of workers, it is also useful to define the differences that do still exist.

Reward is frequently used nowadays to refer to payment systems, especially since many payment systems are strongly motivational to encourage people to work harder and then reward them for their extra effort. The word 'reward' is also useful as it could also apply to either a monetary or non-monetary reward.

We have chosen to use the phrase pay and reward in this chapter since both systems of basic pay and incentivised pay and reward exist today and organisations have to be increasingly flexible in their pay and reward strategies so are likely to use a mixture of approaches. Other terms that are commonly used in pay and reward are discussed next.

Wages refers to weekly pay and may be based on an hourly rate of pay, with possible deductions for lateness or absence, and this hourly rate is often the rate that is referred to in negotiations. Wage-earners are often still paid in cash and are less likely to have benefits such as luncheon vouchers, company cars or expenses. Organisations paying wages have traditionally expected short-term thinking from their employees, and incentives for wage-earners are also usually quick and precise. There has traditionally been less job security for wage-earners than for salaried employees (although this has changed in recent years) and the emphasis is on a short-term relationship with the employing organisation. The peak of wage-earners' earning capacity is comparatively early, perhaps while they are still in their twenties.

Salary refers to monthly pay, and these monthly payments are normally expressed as an annual salary, this being the figure that is normally referred to in negotiations on salary. Those who are salaried normally have their salaries paid directly into a bank or building society and they are also likely to have several fringe benefits, such as company cars, extra payments for additional qualifications, or luncheon vouchers. Some salaried workers get immediate incentives added to their incomes, but traditionally the most widely held incentive was supposed to be a much longer-term consideration, that of good prospects. Salaried employees either are in managerial posts or tend to identify very closely with management, and they perceive themselves to be on a lengthy career progression with the peak of their earning power achieved relatively late in life. In addition, until fairly recently they have expected to have long-term job security.

Harmonisation

There have traditionally been differences in organisations' attitudes towards those paid wages and those paid salaries, but as mentioned earlier, many organisations have tried to get away from the problems that this sometimes causes, and have moved towards a common single status payment system with the harmonisation of terms and conditions of employment for both groups of workers. This means that there is an expectation that all employees can be treated in the same way and will expect the same benefits. In these organisations, everyone is paid a monthly salary rather than a weekly or hourly rate of pay, and everyone gets the same sick pay and redundancy arrangements, works the same hours and eats in the same canteen though in the last few years, according to Egan (2010a), it has become increasingly common for senior executives to move away from this pattern and to have a separate pay and reward structure.

Nowadays there is also much less job security, and career progression for salaried employees as promotion and even job security cannot be regarded as automatic. Many organisations in which salaried jobs were normally secure have removed whole strata of managers and during the recession may not have been replacing people who left or offering opportunities for promotion. The growing trend towards the acquisition of a flexible workforce with increasing numbers of part-timers and contract workers has also led to a blurring of distinctions between the groups, as have the efforts that HR professionals have made during the recent recession to keep workers but perhaps on altered forms of contracts, working fewer hours than before.

The term may also be used to refer to the harmonisation of wages and conditions of employment in different countries. Since 2002, when countries within the euro zone adopted the euro as their common currency, workers in these countries have been able to compare their wages with workers doing a similar job in different countries. This increased level of transparency may result in wages and conditions of employment in different countries becoming increasingly similar, or harmonised.

Pay structures

All but the smallest of organisations have to create some form of pay structure in order to provide a logical way to pay and reward people. According to Egan (2010a), having a payment structure achieves three main aims;

1 It ensures that the pay structure is clearly aligned with the organisation's strategic objectives and rewards behaviours that support those objectives.

2 It provides for an orderly way for pay increases to occur and for career progression to be made clear.

3 It helps ensure that the basis for the pay is fair and that it avoids illegality and unfair gender bias.

There are several ways, or indeed combinations of ways, that can be chosen to form the basis of pay structures but when designing these there are choices that the organisation needs to make about the number and width of the pay grades or pay bands within the structure. Many organisations, particularly in the public sector, have harmonised their entire wage and salary systems of payment into a common pay spine (Egan, 2010a).

Job evaluation

In order to achieve this type of orderly pay system many organisations will use some form of job evaluation. This term will be discussed fully later in this chapter. ACAS (2010a) defines job evaluation in the following way:

Job evaluation is a method of determining on a systematic basis the relative importance of a number of jobs.

As you can see, job evaluation does not actually determine rates of pay that any individual employee should receive, but it can be used as a systematic basis for determining differences in jobs and subsequently the different pay levels for those jobs. As such it seems to us to be an appropriate topic to discuss in this chapter as many organisations use it as the basis for determining their pay structures.

The main influences on payment systems

What the organisation decides to pay staff will depend on many factors, some of which are under the control of the organisation and relate to its strategic plan and some of which are external such as the economy.

ACTIVITY 10.1

We have provided you with a selection of job titles and you have to decide how much to pay these staff. You are to consider who you think ought to be paid the most rather than considering what actually happens in reality.

(a) Put the jobs listed below in order of importance, i.e. with number 1 being the job that you judge should be paid the most.

(b) List the factors that will influence how much you will pay these staff.

Job	
Waiter or waitress	___
Nurse	___
Sales assistant (clothes shop)	___
Car park attendant	___
Office cleaner	___
Accountant	___
Police officer	___
Receptionist	___
Teller (bank)	___
Warehouse supervisor	___
University lecturer	___
Truck driver	___
Secretary	___
Traffic warden	___
Security guard	___
Safety officer (manufacturing company)	___
Warehouse picker	___
Doctor	___
Human resource manager	___
Church minister	___
Fruit picker	___
Ambulance driver (paramedical)	___
Transport manager	___
Computer services officer	___
Lawyer	___
Undertaker	___
Professional football player	___
IT consultant	___

(c) Compare your order with others and try to reach agreement about a list of factors that should be taken into account when you are making these decisions.

Discussion of Activity 10.1

The relative worth of these jobs is likely to vary according to the type of organisation, and your ranking is likely to vary compared with that of your colleagues because you have been highly subjective. You should think about what influenced your choice of each job's worth. Did you have knowledge of some jobs? Did you most value strength, skill, level of responsibility or a caring response, or were you influenced by people you know who do some of these jobs, or by your own career aspirations? There will be many highly subjective influences on your decision.

Many other factors may influence the relative worth of jobs. Your list is likely to include at least some of the following:

- what the organisation can afford to pay
- what other organisations in the area are paying for similar jobs
- national or international rates of pay within the organisation
- legislation and the minimum wage

- trade union or employee demands
- Government initiatives
- the scarcity of particular skills
- the state of the economy
- the introduction of new technology
- the relative worth of jobs as rated by a job evaluation exercise
- the actual performance of the person in the job.

As you can see from this list, an organisation does not have a completely free hand when it decides how to pay someone. Many factors influence the decision of how and what to pay, and we shall discuss these more fully in turn.

What the organisation can afford to pay

Obviously, no organisation can afford to put itself out of business by paying more than it can afford, so this has to be one of the first factors that influence how much an organisation will pay. However, the way organisations view pay and reward has a big effect on what they decide to pay. Some organisations tend to see pay and reward as a cost and therefore try to keep down their costs. This is particularly true in organisations where there is no rigorous method for assessing the return on investment of the pay and reward strategies. In a survey by CIPD (2010b) less than half the respondents (49 per cent) actually knew what their total spend for pay, benefits, financial rewards and national insurance was and most of them are unable to break this down into its constituent parts. Of the 20 per cent who could analyse it and break it down in more detail in public, private and voluntary sectors the total spend on remuneration amounted to two-thirds of organisation income or turnover. The CIPD (2010b) commented that given the economic situation it was extremely surprising that so many employers didn't actually know what they spent on pay and reward and that among those who did, most could not express it as a percentage of their total income. Therefore these employers would not know whether they had to reduce labour costs or increase income in order to maintain or increase profits and they would not be able to work out their return on investment.

A survey by Hay in 2009 found that in a minority of organisations, about 20 per cent, pay is viewed as an investment and then the goal is to 'leverage its value' and ensure that there is a good return on investment in the pay and reward system (IRS Employment Review 2009). These organisations would be much better informed about their total spend on pay and what improvements in profits they wanted to achieve from their investment in pay and reward.

What other organisations in the area are paying for similar jobs

Most organisations will at least take account of the market rates that other organisations are paying. The organisation may refer to published pay surveys or do its own survey of the local area to establish rates that others are paying for similar jobs. The CIPD (2010a) survey of pay trends found that the four most common methods to establish market rates were to:

● use local, national or international pay surveys as appropriate
● review other people's job advertisements
● use national research from specialist organisations such as Incomes Data Services (IDS) or Industrial Relations Services (IRS) or
● use job-evaluated pay databases.

If the organisation can afford to, and if it wants to be able to select the best employees, it may choose to pay slightly more than the going rate. This can cause a spiral of wage increases as other employers retaliate by increasing their wages. When labour is scarce or there is demand for people with a particularly scarce skill this is one way in which many employers will behave.

Even when employing people on a small scale, the rate of payment can have quite an effect locally. Sometimes people from London, or perhaps those moving to or buying second homes in countries such as France or Spain, may have an effect on local wages when they employ a local gardener or cleaner and pay much more than the local rate. Those with second homes will probably be able to afford to pay good wages, particularly if they are used to paying for similar services in a more expensive area such as London. When they pay these same rates to local cleaners they obviously attract good staff, but are then accused by other locals of poaching their cleaners and of setting rates that the locals cannot afford to match. In this situation the second home owners get excellent cleaners but may not make many friends.

National or international rates of pay within the organisation

If the organisation is part of a larger organisation, there may be national or international agreements that will affect what is actually paid, and the human resource manager also needs to assess these rates.

Nowadays as travel to other countries is easier and quicker than in the past, pay rates often have global implications. In recent years poor pay for nurses in Britain, and the subsequent staff shortages, meant hospitals and NHS trusts increasingly had to search further afield for qualified nurses. Many carried out recruitment drives which attracted nurses from countries such as the Philippines to Britain.

What is considered poor pay in one country may seem a fortune to an individual coming from a poorer country. Individually they gain an opportunity to travel and broaden their own experience and may even be able to save money to send home to their families. This may in turn create skills shortages for those countries losing people and consequently some governments have requested that Britain does not carry out recruitment drives in their country.

There may be other ethical and legal issues where companies employ large numbers of low-skill migrant workers who come to this country in search of jobs and better pay than that found in their home country. While they are recruited to fill skills gaps and work in jobs which many UK workers are unwilling to do, in some cases they have been exploited. There have been claims that they are treated badly and are not even paid the legal minimum wage. In 2007 administrators were called into Bomfords, a company which supplied more than 50 per cent of large UK supermarkets with vegetables such as spring onions, beans and peas. According to Felicity Lawrence (2007), 'the company which has a turnover of £150m a year and employs more than 2,000 people at the height of the season – the majority migrants who pick and pack its vegetables – was recruiting its temporary staff through seven agencies. Each of those agencies was found to be breaking the law and had its licence revoked. Some of the Poles employed by one of the agencies were in such fear that the GLA revoked its gangmaster's licence on the spot.' Lawrence (2007) claimed 'Bomford's offered gangmasters an hourly rate for workers that made it all but certain that these gangmasters would be breaking the law.'

The global effects of pay rates are not all in one direction. In the 1960s and 1970s there was talk of a 'brain drain' from Britain and more recently similar problems have arisen as some senior academics and particularly scientists go to America in search of better pay and working conditions and for better research facilities. Multinational organisations also have a range of other issues to consider in relation to achieving equity and fairness in their payment systems and these aspects of international payment will be discussed later in the chapter.

Legislation

All organisations are affected by the law of the country in which they operate, even if they are bringing in migrant workers. In Britain they will also be affected by European Union legislation. The legislation that will have most effect on payment or reward systems is the Equality Act 2010 which harmonises and replaces much of the previous legislation such as the Equal Pay Act 1970, which dealt with differences in pay between men and women, and the other equality legislation that dealt with prohibited forms of discrimination such as race or disability. For example, in the past a person claiming discrimination because they were paid less than someone of a different race would have been dealt with under the Race Relations Act 1976. From October 2010 all claims for equal pay which relate to protected characteristics such as race or disability will be dealt with by the Equality Act 2010 (XpertHR, 2010).

The Employment Rights Act 1996 and the National Minimum Wage Act 1998 are also of importance in setting out rules relating to pay and the minimum wage and these two pieces of legislation will also be discussed in more detail here.

The Equality Act 2010

Equal Pay

According to ACAS (2010b), 'the Act retains the framework that was previously in place' and this means that normally when claiming equal pay it will be necessary to compare the pay of one member of staff with someone of the opposite sex who works for that organisation. However, in some organisations the employees doing a particular job may all be of the same sex and from October 2010 the Equality Act now makes it possible for them to bring a claim. If a claimant can provide evidence that they would have received better pay from that employer if they were a different sex it may be possible for them to bring a claim. However, this may be one area that the Coalition Government may review.

It is also illegal to pay different rates to men and women who do different jobs, but whose jobs have been rated the same under a job evaluation scheme. The whole topic of job evaluation and problems of fairness and equality within job evaluation will be discussed later in this chapter.

Equal value

The concept of equal pay for work of equal value had been established by the 1983 Equal Pay Amendment Regulations and continues in the 2010 Equality Act. This means it is also possible for men and women who are doing totally different jobs and who are paid differently to bring a case against their employer if they feel that their job is of the same value to the organisation as the job done by the higher paid group. The legislation is complex, and most who have brought cases have been supported by their trade union or the Equality and Human Rights Commission. Criteria such as the level of qualifications required, the level of effort or skill involved, and the amount of responsibility and decision making involved in each of the jobs are factors that are likely to be taken into account. In a tribunal hearing of this type, the person of the opposite sex with whom the claimant wishes to compare themselves has in the past had to be identified. As we discussed earlier, under the Equality Act 2010 this problem may be overcome to some extent if the claimant can provide evidence that they would have received better pay from that employer if they were a different sex and it may now be possible for them to bring a claim on this basis.

1 Do you think a real comparator should be used in equal pay or equal value cases or should there be the option of using a hypothetical comparator if there is no suitable comparator of the opposite sex within the organisation?

2 Check the current state of legislation and find out what the Government actually decided on these issues.

Secrecy

One barrier to achieving equal pay in the past was the fact that employees in some organisations did not know what others were paid and were not allowed to discuss their pay as this had been written into their contracts. The Equality Act 2010 has opened up opportunities for discussion as the Act makes it unlawful for an employer to prevent or restrict employees from having a discussion about pay that could be related to protected characteristics though the employer can still insist pay rates are kept confidential from people outside the organisation.

ACTIVITY 10.2

Poppy works full time in a small book shop. There are four shop assistants, two male and another female who are all employed to work the same hours and do the same job. She suffers from depression and has to sometimes have some time off work when this gets particularly bad. One of her colleagues has dropped her pay slip on the floor and when Poppy picks it up and hands it to her she realises she is being paid less than her. She suspects that she is paid less than all the other three full-time members of staff and asks them all how much they are paid. The manager of the shop is very unhappy when he hears of this and asks Poppy to attend a discipli-nary interview in which she is told that this information is confidential.

1   What would be the situation if Poppy found by discussing the rates of pay that the two female members of staff were paid less than the two male members of staff?

2   What is the situation as Poppy definitely is being paid less than the other female member of staff?

3   What are Poppy's rights concerning the issue of discussing the pay of the other staff and relating to the disciplinary action taken against her?

Discussion of Activity 10.2

1   If Poppy discovered that she was being paid less than the two female assis-tants for doing the same job then that would be a straightforward case of direct sex discrimination.

2   If Poppy is paid less than the other female member of staff she may be able to show that this is because of her disability. Disability is one of the protected characteristics referred to in the Equality Act 2010. Poppy can only make an equal pay claim comparing against someone of the opposite sex but she may be able to claim direct discrimination because of her disability. She might be able to bring a claim for combined (dual) discrimination if the men are also paid more than her.

3   When she is disciplined for discussing pay with the other members of staff this is unlawful and she could make a claim for victimisation.

Gender pay reporting 2011–13

The Equality Act 2010 is intended to broaden the scope of previous legislation so that from 2011 public authorities with more than 150 employees will have to produce an-nual statistics relating to gender pay gaps and also to ethnic minority and disability employment rates (CIPD, 2010d). The aim is to provide a transparent pay system so that gender pay gaps can be easily identified and men and women can easily com-pare pay.

Similar requirements for equal pay audits to be compulsory in the private sector will come into effect in 2013 though there is some doubt being expressed at the time of writing as to whether the coalition government will go ahead with these proposals (Soret, 2010). However, the Equality and Human Rights Commission have already published guidelines for voluntary pay reporting and during 2010 they started to monitor the extent to which large organisations are voluntarily monitoring pay and gender pay gaps. They plan to extend the monitoring of voluntary pay reporting to smaller organisations with between 250 and 500 employees in 2011 (CIPD, 2010d).

There are concerns about whether gender pay reporting will in itself be sufficient to solve the pay gap between men and women. If implemented it will provide information so comparisons can be made between the pay of men and women in the same organisation but inequalities start much earlier and may be formed by attitudes in society and the career choices and qualifications chosen at school or university (Cotton, 2009).

Did you know?

One of the causes for the differences in pay is segregation of jobs:

Three-quarters of women work in sectors which are sometimes referred to as the 'five Cs' – cleaning, catering, caring, cashiering and clerical jobs.

(Source: Welfare, S., 2006)

A study of gender equality across Europe has estimated that if full gender equality was achieved it would result in an increase in gross domestic product in Europe of between 15% and 45% and in the UK of potentially a 35% increase in gross domestic product. So there is a clear business case for gender equality in the labour market.

(Source: Wild, S., 2010)

The Employment Rights Act 1996

The Employment Rights Act 1996 is a consolidation Act which consolidates previous legislation relating to employment rights. Under the Employment Rights Act 1996 an employer is not allowed to make deductions from an employee's wages except in the following circumstances:

- When deductions are authorised by law, such as tax or national insurance contributions or orders such as a court order relating to the provision of maintenance.
- When there is a statement in the employee's written contract which specifies that certain deductions may be made from wages and when the worker has already given consent in writing to the deduction, e.g. to pay membership fees for a sports or social club or when deductions are agreed for lateness or poor work.
- Accidental overpayment of wages, or of expenses, even though this is likely to be the fault of the employer.
- When the employee has been absent from work due to strike or other industrial action it is permissible for the employer to deduct money from the employee's wages.
- In retail organisations, employers may also deduct money from wages to make good any cash deficiency in the till or any shortfall in stock. This deduction should not exceed 10 per cent of the wages due to the employee concerned on a particular day and the deduction must also be made within 12 months from the date that the discrepancy or shortfall in stock was discovered.

The National Minimum Wage Act 1998

The National Minimum Wage Act 1998 established a single national minimum rate with no variation for regions, jobs, size of organisation or industrial sector. Differences in the minimum wage rate will be allowed, however, based on age and this has not changed in spite of the changes to the legislation relating to age. The national minimum wage provides a degree of protection for some of the lowest paid groups of workers as it applies not just to full- and part-time employees but also to workers paid by piecework, to homeworkers, agency workers, commission workers and casual workers. So the migrant workers involved in fruit picking who were discussed earlier in the chapter are among those who should be covered by it. Although the minimum wage legislation does apply to all employers regardless of their size, the type of business or the region in which they are based, there are still certain groups who are exempt from its provisions. The main groups which do not qualify for the minimum wage are:

● The self-employed
● Volunteers
● Students working as part of their undergraduate or postgraduate degree programme
● Workers on specified training schemes
● Residents of some religious communities
● Prisoners
● The armed forces.

From 1 October 2010 the adult standard national minimum wage rate for workers aged 21 and over is £5.93 per hour while the rate for workers aged 18–20 inclusive is £4.92 per hour. The youth rate for 16- and 17-year-old workers is £3.64 per hour. For the first time there is also an apprentice rate which is £2.50 per hour for those apprentices who are under 19 or who are aged 19 or over but are in the first year of their apprenticeship (CIPD, 2010c).

These rates are usually updated each year. Employers have to keep records for national minimum wage purposes and employees should have access to these records with a right to complain to an employment tribunal if the employer fails to give them the required access to the records.

● Trade union and employee demands

It is important to consider the views of both trade unions and employees in general, and any payment system that an organisation may design needs to be introduced after full discussion and consultation with employees and trade unions. The most effective payment systems will have been selected to meet the needs of both the organisation and the workforce, will have the commitment of all groups and will have been developed, introduced and updated with the participation of employee representatives, whether or not they are members of a trade union. In 2010 the Nationwide Building Society showed how to achieve this and won a CIPD People Management Award for their innovative review of their pay and bonus system which staff helped to design. Nationwide's previous scheme had become outdated and focused too much on volume instead of value, was not very cost-effective and did not differentiate sufficiently clearly between high and low performers. Changes needed trade union support as they would form a part of the employees' contracts. Nationwide talked fully with everyone so all generations of workers were consulted, listened to what employees said they wanted, and gained full union support. In 2009 Nationwide launched their new total reward package which succeeded in increasing sales performance by 184 per cent of the target in the first quarter and which received excellent feedback from employees. This organisation also clearly had tools in place to measure the return on investment of its reward strategy (*People Management*, 2010a, p. 12).

Did you know?

'Forty years after the Equal Pay Act women are still on average paid 20.2% less per hour than men (combining full-time and part-time earnings.)'

(Source: Equality and Human Rights Commission, 2010)

Government initiatives

The Government can have an effect on the supply of labour as it introduces various training initiatives for adults or young people who are facing unemployment. This should have the effect of providing people with relevant skills that employers need, but it also has an effect on wage expectations, since if people are used to receiving a very low training allowance they are likely to feel pleased if they get a job that pays more than this, even if it is still a comparatively low wage.

The scarcity of particular skills

Even in years where there has been high unemployment, there has also been a scarcity in some industries of particular types of skilled workers. This may be due to failure in the past to train people adequately, but it appears that there is often a mismatch between the skills that employers require and the skills that those who are without jobs can offer. In a situation such as this, the relatively small number of people who do have the necessary skills can command high wages or salaries and may move from one organisation to another as different employers try to outbid each other for their scarce skills.

The state of the economy

We have already mentioned that the availability of labour and the scarcity of particular skills will have an effect on the wages paid. Other economic factors such as inflation will also have an effect, as in times of high inflation there will be increasing pressure from workers to increase salaries to keep pace with, or get ahead of, inflation. In the recent economic downturn in 2009 the private sector suffered most but with Government cuts planned across most areas of the public sector in 2010 and 2011 the situation is likely to be more difficult for workers in that area. However, in spite of this the CIPD (2010b) found that most public sector workers were expecting a pay increase in 2010.

New technology

The relative pay levels of people in different jobs can change over time, for example, when new skills have to be learnt with the introduction of new technology, so that a particular group of workers change from being of low skill level to needing a high level of technical expertise. This change in skill level is likely to be reflected in a demand for higher wages.

The relative worth of each job as rated by a job evaluation exercise

Job evaluation is a way of rating the value to the organisation of the jobs that people do. It does not in itself decide what pay should be awarded to each job, but it is a systematic way of comparing different jobs so that this can be used as the basis for forming a payment system. The various ways in which job evaluation can be carried out and the different types of scheme will be discussed later in this chapter.

The performance of the individual employee in the job

In many organisations it will also be important to assess the effectiveness of the person doing the job. Whether this happens will depend on the type of payment system used and the organisation's views on collectivism or individualism with regard to payments. Organisations that favour collectivism will want to minimise differences in pay between employees as this may avoid costly or time-wasting disputes, while other organisations will want to pay everyone individual rates as far as possible in order to reward each person for their efforts, and these two perspectives will result in a variety of differing types of payment system.

It is clear that the last two factors are of great importance to payment systems, so we shall now go on to discuss each in detail.

Job evaluation schemes

Very few organisations will pay all the people who work for them exactly the same regardless of the job they do or how well they do that job. Organisations do have to have regard to equality legislation and create a fair and transparent system for pay and reward, so most organisations seek to find ways to compare the worth of different jobs to the organisation, as well as a person's performance in each job. We considered in the previous chapter the ways in which individual performance may be assessed, but here we shall concentrate on ways of comparing the relative worth of different jobs. If organisations were to base decisions about the relative worth of different jobs on managerial whims, they would be accused, quite rightly, of being unfair. That is why many organisations use a system for assessing the worth of different jobs based on job evaluation.

Job evaluation does not determine the correct payment level for a job, but rather provides a possible ranking of a job relative to other jobs. This has the merit of being systematic and of appearing objective, although in reality there is normally some degree of subjectivity in all job evaluation schemes. There are normally three stages involved when an organisation is deciding how much to pay for each job:

● evaluate the jobs in the organisation and get a ranking for them
● decide which jobs are similar in terms of the job evaluation exercise and group them together
● decide what pay to attach to these jobs, partially on the basis of market value.

There are a variety of job evaluation schemes in existence, and discussion of these could occupy a full chapter in its own right. We shall seek to give a brief outline of some of the more commonly used types of job evaluation scheme. They can be divided into non-analytical and analytical schemes, and we shall consider each of these groups in turn.

Non-analytical schemes or analytical schemes

Non-analytical job evaluation schemes compare whole jobs rather than analysing the components of each job and assessing them factor by factor. There are three main types of non-analytical scheme:

● whole job ranking
● paired comparisons
● job classification.

Analytical schemes break the jobs down and try to compare skills or competencies needed in each job. The main analytical schemes are:

● points rating
● proprietary schemes.

In order to understand the basics of each of these approaches, you should read the following case study and complete Activities 10.3, 10.4, 10.5 and 10.6.

CASE STUDY 10.1 Job evaluation

The Hookworth Department Store is concerned that its payment system does not accurately reflect the true value of different jobs to the organisation. The management is trying to decide on a form of job evaluation to use as part of a review of the jobs for the whole organisation. They have provided you with three job descriptions to use as a way of identifying the most suitable form of job evaluation to use. You need to consider the job descriptions provided and imagine that you have to evaluate the jobs as part of a job evaluation exercise which will ultimately be used as the basis of the organisation's payment system. You are being asked to evaluate only three jobs, whereas in reality there would be far more jobs than this in a full job evaluation exercise in most organisations.

Read the following three job descriptions and complete Activities 10.3, 10.4 and 10.5. When you have completed these you should be in a good position to decide on an appropriate form of job evaluation to adapt for the whole organisation as requested in Activity 10.6.

Job description A

Job title:	**Office Receptionist**
Reports to:	Office Services Manager
Responsible for:	Assistant Receptionists (2)
Purpose of post:	To ensure that visitors to the company are received in a welcoming fashion, answer routine queries and ensure that all other queries are handled expeditiously by the appropriate staff member. To ensure that all telephone queries are handled in the same manner.
	As the first point of contact for the company, the receptionist must maintain high standards of customer care.
Contacts:	All customers and other visitors, to deal with initial and routine queries. All members of staff, to pass on queries as appropriate.

Major duties:

- Greet walk-in visitors and ascertain purpose of their visit. Handle or redirect queries as appropriate.
- Answer phone queries as appropriate.
- Answer all initial queries about receipt of payments using the online payment receipts system.
- Open and sort incoming post by department. Organise delivery of post by assistant receptionists.
- Perform clerical tasks assigned by departments in agreement with the Office Services Manager.
- Supervise assistant receptionists and delegate work as appropriate.
- Perform other duties as assigned by the Office Services Manager or other authorised manager.

Job description B

Job title:	**Human Resource Assistant**
Reports to:	Human Resource Manager
Responsible for:	No one
Purpose of post:	To provide a day-to-day advisory service for the managers in the company on matters of human resource management policy and procedures, and to monitor and implement procedures.
Contacts:	Managers from head office and throughout the branches. Employees, to deal with initial and routine queries. Prospective employees, to deal with initial enquiries regarding job vacancies. Outside organisations such as employment agencies, training organisations and newspapers.

Major duties:

- Greet visitors and ascertain purpose of their visit. Handle or redirect queries as appropriate.
- Answer phone queries as above.
- Answer all initial queries about applications for employment.
- Pass all rejected applications to typist for standard rejection letters and check and sign these letters.
- Monitor application for employment forms submitted by line managers on behalf of candidates selected by them.
- Agree salary details, in accordance with company pay scales, with line manager.
- Enter agreed salary, contract, job title and joining details on successful applications and pass to typist for documentation.
- Sign joining documentation on behalf of the company.
- Advise line managers on the interpretation of the organisation's human resource policies and procedures.
- Advise line managers on the interpretation and implementation of the organisation's sickness pay and pension schemes.
- Advise line managers on the interpretation of relevant employment legislation.
- Advise line managers on employees' salary entitlements.

- Ensure that the human resource management records are kept up to date on the computerised information system, and that there is no unauthorised access to these and any manually produced records.
- Provide up-to-date reports or data for use by managers.

Job description C

Job title:	**Sales Assistant**
Reports to:	Buyer of China Department
Responsible for:	No one
Purpose of post:	To sell china goods and assist customers with their purchases and with any queries or problems that they might have.
Contacts:	All customers and other visitors to make sales of china and deal with routine queries.

Major duties:

- Sell china goods to customers.
- Provide expert advice about the various products on sale.
- Provide a high standard of service and customer care.
- Unpack with care valuable merchandise and pack customers' purchases carefully, including packing them for export.
- Display products attractively to encourage sales and promote certain special offers.
- Perform clerical duties associated with the work of the department, e.g. completion of orders, forms for returns or breakages.
- Handle accurately and honestly cash and credit transactions.
- Total cash and credit transactions and deliver money to Cash Control Office.

Non-analytical job evaluation schemes

The first two activities ask you to consider the non-analytical approach to job evaluation.

Whole job ranking

ACTIVITY 10.3

(a) Consider each of the three job descriptions given in case study 10.1 and decide which job you feel is worth most to the organisation, which is the next in value and which is of least value to the organisation. Rank the jobs in order with the job you feel is worth most to the organisation being ranked as number 1.

1 _____

2 _____

3 _____

(b) What are the advantages and disadvantages of this approach which is known as whole job ranking?

Discussion of Activity 10.3

This is the simplest form of job evaluation exercise and we have ranked the three jobs in the following order: 1. Human Resource Assistant 2. Sales Assistant in China Department; 3. Receptionist. You may have reached a different rank order to us or to other students. This is because this is a very subjective way of ranking the jobs, and the criteria we took into account may be different to those that you have used. There is nothing in this method to indicate what criteria have been chosen. We have asked you to make decisions about only three jobs, and it would be more difficult to use the whole job ranking system in a large organisation where there were many different jobs to rank. In that case, the jobs would probably have to be grouped into categories first for ease of comparison and so that the appropriate criteria were used, e.g. for clerical jobs, as it could be a problem to identify suitable criteria if the jobs were very dissimilar.

We could make this system slightly more objective by agreeing the criteria to be considered in advance of the exercise, but even this would not help us to identify the extent of difference in the value of the different jobs to the organisation, so we would still have difficulty deciding how much more to pay the job that was ranked first compared to the job that was ranked second. In reality, job evaluation schemes should not depend on the subjective judgements of just one person. It would be better to involve more people in an exercise such as this and then get a consensus view from this job evaluation panel about the ranking of each job.

Advantages of whole job ranking

● simple
● cheap to operate
● easy to understand.

Disadvantages of whole job ranking

● subjective
● no analysis of jobs to explain reason for ranked order
● difficult to use with large number of jobs.

Paired comparisons

ACTIVITY 10.4

(a) Refer to the three job descriptions given in case study 10.1, but this time compare pairs of jobs and decide which you feel is worth more to the organisation, so that each job is compared with the other jobs in turn. Use the following points system to work through this exercise.

● If you feel that a job is worth more than the job it is being compared with, give it 2 points.
● If you feel it is worth the same as the job it is compared with, give them both 1 point.
● If you feel it is worth less than the other job, give it zero points.

Enter the values that you give each job in the chart overleaf, and then add the scores for each job. The job with the highest value will be the one that you decide to pay the most, followed by the job with the next highest value and the job with the lowest value.

We'll start by examining Job A, the job of the receptionist, and will compare our view of its value to the organisation with the value of the other two jobs to the organisation. Place all your scores for Job A in the vertical column below the heading Job A so that at the end of the exercise you can add up all the points for this job.

For example, if you think that Job A, the office receptionist's job, is of more value to the organisation than Job B, the Human Resources Assistant's job, then on the chart below you should write '2' in the vertical column below Job A and on the horizontal line next to Job B.

Now compare Job A with Job C and, for example, if you decide that Job A is perhaps of less value to the organisation than Job C, you should write 'O' in the next space down in column A, on the horizontal line next to Job C. Then add the total points in this column to gain a total score for Job A. Now complete this exercise for yourself and add up the total score in each column for each of the jobs in turn.

	JOB A	JOB B	JOB C
JOB A	No score in this section as Job A cannot be compared with itself		
JOB B		No score in this section as Job B cannot be compared with itself	
JOB C			No score in this section as Job C cannot be compared with itself
TOTAL SCORES FOR EACH JOB			

Total points for each job A =   B =   C =

1st job _____

2nd job _____

3rd job _____

(b) Did you rank the jobs in the same order as before? What are the advantages and disadvantages of this approach?

Discussion of Activity 10.4

This is also a simple method of job evaluation, but it is slightly more systematic than whole job ranking. It still does not analyse particular jobs in detail and, although the numerical values attached to each job create an impression of objectivity, this is really not the case as again there is nothing to indicate what the criteria used might be. A large number of calculations may need to be made – for an organisation that intends to analyse 50 or more jobs, 1,225 calculations would need to be made. There are, however, computerised systems that work on this basis and solve this particular problem. Once again, an improvement to this approach would be to involve a job evaluation panel, drawn from various sections of the workforce, and then try to get agreement about the rating of various jobs.

351

Advantages of paired comparisons

- simple
- easy to understand
- slightly more systematic than whole job ranking
- it is easy to fit new jobs into this system.

Disadvantages of paired comparisons

- subjective
- no analysis of jobs to explain reason for ranked order
- the need for an enormous number of calculations if it is to be used with a large number of jobs.

Job classification

The exercises you have just completed indicate in a very simple way the main stages and the main problems with two forms of non-analytical job evaluation. The third non-analytical form of job evaluation is known as job classification. It is similar to job ranking but uses a different approach. In this case the number of groups of jobs, or pay grades, is decided first and a general job description is then produced for all the jobs in each of these groups. An individual job that is considered to typify this group of jobs is then used as a benchmark. Each job is compared with the bench-mark jobs and the general job description, and placed in an appropriate grade.

Advantages of job classification

- simple to operate
- easy to understand
- it is easy to fit new jobs into job classification structure.

Disadvantages of job classification

- difficult to use with a wide range of jobs
- not analytical.

Analytical methods of job evaluation

Now consider an approach to job evaluation which is described as analytical by com-pleting Activity 10.5.

Points rating

ACTIVITY 10.5

In this approach you will work with a job evaluation committee who have specified that the following criteria should be used in evaluating jobs:

- skill
- responsibility for people, e.g. in a job caring for children
- responsibility for equipment and materials

- responsibility for other employees
- mental effort
- physical effort
- working conditions.

Rate the three jobs, as described in their job descriptions in case study 10.1, according to these criteria. You can give up to 10 points for each of these factors for each job:

10 exceptional
7–9 high
4–6 medium
1–3 low
0 negligible

Then add the total scores for Job A, Job B and Job C.

For example, if you feel that a medium level of skill is required by an Office Receptionist as described in job description A you will give that job between 4 and 6 points in that category. If you feel that Job B, the Human Resource Assistant, shows a high level of responsibility for people, you will give it between 7 and 9 points. Remember that in job evaluation it is the job you are evaluating, not the person, so you do not need to know how effective a person actually is in that job.

Discussion of Activity 10.5

The points rating approach is probably the most commonly used type of job evaluation scheme, and is regarded as analytical because instead of comparing whole jobs, the jobs are broken down into a number of factors such as skills, responsibility, physical requirements, mental requirements and working conditions. Each of the factors is awarded points based on a predetermined scale, and the total points determine the position of that job in the rank order. A weighting is often attached to the particular importance of each attribute to the organisation.

Although this scheme is analytical, there is, as we said earlier, an element of subjectivity in all job evaluation schemes, as subjective decisions are made about which factors will be weighted most highly to show their importance to the organisation. Care should be taken to avoid sex bias in the choice of factors for high weighting. Many older schemes based on this system were biased against women as characteristics such as physical strength, normally associated more with male employees, were given higher weighting than factors such as dexterity, which is more often associated with women.

Points rating schemes are easy to understand and are more objective than the non-analytical schemes. Because they are analytical, they can be used to explain the extent of differences between jobs and hence to justify subsequent differences in pay. They can, however, be time-consuming and costly to develop as a panel of people is likely to be involved.

Proprietary schemes

Faced with the time and costs involved in designing and validating their own job evaluation scheme and checking that it is free of unfair bias, many organisations decide to buy a proprietary scheme or employ a consultant to design a scheme specifically for them. A scheme designed specifically for one organisation is obviously a good idea and is likely to have a great deal of credibility with the workforce, but buying a proprietary scheme has the additional advantage of giving access to extensive comparative data on job markets and rates of pay which designers of proprietary schemes also collect. This can provide much more comprehensive data on which to base decisions about payment levels to relate to jobs than any one organisation could collect.

ACTIVITY 10.6

Compare your evaluation of the three jobs using this points rating method with your earlier evaluations of the same jobs completed using the whole job ranking method and then the paired comparison method.

Were your rankings of the jobs the same or different in all three cases? Why was this? Which of these methods would you recommend to the senior management at the Hookworth Department Store for use in their full job evaluation for the whole store? Why was this?

Discussion of Activity 10.6

Having completed activities to establish the ways that two non-analytical approaches to job evaluation work, and Activity 10.5 to see how one analytical scheme, the points rating method, works, you should now be in a position to make a recommendation to the management of the Hookworth Department Store as to the most suitable form of job evaluation for them to use.

Since only the analytical forms of job evaluation would stand up to examination in an equal pay case at an employment tribunal we hope that you have selected the points rating method, or a proprietary scheme based on a system of points rating, to recommend to the management of the Hookworth Department Store.

Different types of payment system

There are, as we have shown, many factors that affect what the organisation pays its workforce, but whatever payment system is chosen will give a different message to the workforce about the issues and values that the organisation feels are important. It is important that the message given is appropriate to support the strategic objectives of the organisation. In this section we shall consider some of the different payment systems that the organisation might choose. There are many variations in systems of payment; some of the more common types will be considered here.

- time rates
- individual payment by results (piecework)
- group incentives

- profit sharing
- performance-related pay or merit rating
- non-monetary awards
- cafeteria-style payments or flexible pay
- total reward.

● Time rates

This is the simplest of all payment systems: as the name implies, people are paid according to the time they spend at work. This may be based on an hourly rate, a weekly rate or an annual salary. In spite of all the talk of incentive schemes and movement towards a human resource management approach with performance-related pay systems, this is still an extremely popular way for many organisations to pay people. This is largely because it is a simple system that is easy to understand and does not result in a great many disputes. On the other hand, organisations that have moved away from this system of payment have done so because it provides little incentive to improve productivity or efficiency.

As we said earlier, each employer needs to establish what motivates their employees. If it is a really interesting job then the employees may be motivated primarily by the satisfaction gained from the job itself. If the employer wants an organisation where everyone works together then they will be concerned to provide a reasonably competitive level of pay for all employees and won't want to pay bonuses or divide the workforce by performance-related pay systems, so that time rates and harmonisation of terms and conditions of employment are likely to appeal to them. The basic rate paid must be sufficiently high that it is adequate for most people's needs. If the rate of pay falls behind this level then the workforce are likely to be demotivated.

Pause for thought 10.2 What do you think about this philosophy? Does it link with anything you have studied on other modules about motivation theory?

The idea that pay is necessary at a certain level to provide for an employee's basic needs, but that to increase pay beyond this is not likely to result in increased performance at work, links very clearly with the work of another motivation theorist, Frederick Herzberg (1966), whose ideas you may have studied, and with his motivation/hygiene theories. Herzberg said that certain things, such as pay and good conditions at work, which he referred to as hygiene factors, were necessary to prevent employees from becoming dissatisfied with work, but that an improvement in these things would not necessarily motivate employees to work harder although it would remove the dissatisfaction. He said that these were the sort of things that people moan about, but that when the dissatisfaction had been removed and the pay or working conditions improved, these people would still not be actually motivated to work harder. The motivators, according to Herzberg, were factors such as making the job more interesting or giving the employee more responsibility.

Payments on time rates, as we have said, don't normally vary from week to week and people are paid for going to work, regardless of how hard they actually work when they are there. In the next Activity we would like you to consider a particular example of a time rate payment system, where there are some variations in the payments people receive.

ACTIVITY 10.7

Imagine that you are a branch manager in a large building society. You are talking to one of your staff, a graduate who is regarded as being bright and a hard worker and who should have an excellent future with the organisation. You ask how things are going and are rather dismayed when she replies, 'OK, but I'm getting a bit disillusioned. I seem to work hard and yet it will take me at least six years to get to the top of the pay scale. Most people around here seem to be at or near to the top of the pay scale already and they seem to take life easy and don't work nearly as hard as I do. I'm thinking seriously about looking for another job.'

1 What is this type of pay scale supposed to achieve for the organisation?
2 What are the advantages and disadvantages of this type of payment system?
3 How does this payment system relate to what you know about motivation theory?

Discussion of Activity 10.7

1 An incremental pay scale is a form of time rate payment system, as people are still paid for the time that they spend at work regardless of the amount of effort they put into their work. In this case they are also paid an extra amount or increment for each year that they work for the employer. This is supposed to encourage employees to stay with the same employer for a long period of time, and so result in a stable workforce. There is also an implication that people will become more knowledgeable and effective in their job as they work for more years and gain more experience. This is not necessarily true, and although some people do learn from experience and will become more valuable employees the longer they are employed, you may be able to think of people that you know who have done the same job for years and who seem to have stopped learning from experience, and who do not appear to be any more effective in their job than they were on the day they started. Care needs to be taken with this type of payment scheme to ensure that it meets the requirements of the Equality Act 2010.

2 *Advantages of incremental payment schemes:*

● simple
● easy to calculate wages
● rewards experience
● leads to a stable workforce.

Disadvantages of incremental payment schemes:

● no incentive to work harder
● slow progress for high fliers
● needs to be used with great care to avoid accusations of age discrimination
● no incentive at top of the scale.

3 This approach tends, like other forms of time rates, to reflect a collectivist view that everyone should be treated the same and that to pay people differently would be divisive. With incremental pay scales such as this, differences that are taken into account are usually about non-contentious things such as length of service. Everyone can see that people are treated fairly and that they will get the same treatment. This approach tends to be favoured in relatively large,

impersonal, bureaucratic organisations, which place emphasis in determining pay on the jobs rather than the people. This form of payment system will also work best where the pace of change is slow and where there is little scope for individual initiative. An incremental pay system doesn't tend to work well in a fast-moving organisation where it is likely to stifle initiative and innovation.

We shall now examine a group of payment systems that reflect a more individualised approach, where individuals are rewarded for their contribution. We shall consider both individual payment by results and performance-related pay. Though these are very different approaches it is important that whatever approach to incentives is chosen is relevant to the workers, is measurable and fair and open to all. Incentive schemes can inadvertently have the effect of demotivating staff if they are not communicated clearly to all and if the targets are unrealistic or the process lacks clarity so it is not understood. Employees need to know what is expected of them to get the reward, how it will be measured and what the reward for their effort will be (Goss, 2010).

Individual payment by results (piecework)

This approach, based on individualism, reflects the view that since some people work harder than others they should be paid different amounts to reflect the differences in effort that they have made. In this system the amount that people are paid depends on how much they produce, so there are very clear criteria and a strong link between earnings and effort. This system is most common in types of manufacturing environment where it is easy to identify the products that each individual has made, or to identify clearly an individual's contribution to a manufactured product.

The main advantages to the employer of payment by results can be summarised as follows:

- there is a strong incentive to increase effort, as there is a very clear link with earnings
- if an increased number of tasks are completed in the same amount of time, using the same equipment, the costs per unit of output will be lower.

Like all payment systems, there are disadvantages as well as advantages. *The main disadvantages are that:*

- it can be expensive to install and maintain
- it can result in many disagreements about standards or levels of production
- production may increase at the expense of quality
- the emphasis on personal performance can cause friction between employees.

This payment system is expensive to install and maintain, as there needs to be a fair system for assessing the norm for levels of production so that production over and above this level can be paid. Work study engineers are often employed to find the most efficient method of carrying out a task, and managers and trade union officials may spend a great deal of time timing different stages in the production process. There is an emphasis in the payment by results system on providing an incentive, but also on control and measurement. Even with controls in place there can be problems, as Activity 10.8 shows.

ACTIVITY 10.8

Imagine that you are the human resource manager in a knitwear manufacturing company. You are about to negotiate with the trade union on the current round of pay talks. The sewing machinists are paid on a piecework system but there is a great deal of absenteeism, particularly on Fridays. It seems to you that many workers increase their levels of production on the other days of the week so that they can have Fridays off. The company wants to ensure regular high levels of production on every day of the week in order to meet its full order books.

1 What is the underlying message that a piecework system, such as this one, intends to give to the employees?

2 Why is this system not working as well as the organisation wants?

3 How does the situation within this organisation link with motivation theories?

Discussion of Activity 10.8

1 The underlying message that a piecework system is intended to give is that a person will be rewarded for working hard, and the more they produce, the more they will be paid.

2 The system is not working as well as management had hoped because management have assumed that the workforce are only motivated to work harder for money, and that they will continue to work harder and harder for more and more money. Remember the factors that Herzberg (1966), for example, suggested as motivating factors.

3 This situation relates to the view that people may be motivated by a variety of things. In this case the workers wanted a high level of income, but they also wanted some time to relax and spend that income. Some people may be motivated by the opportunity of earning more money, especially if they are saving for some large expenditure. However, not everyone will attach the same degree of importance to financial rewards all the time, and the organisation needs to find out what its employees will value. The employees here seem to be sending a message that leisure is something they value, but other people might be motivated by promotion, a company car, increased responsibility or the increased respect of colleagues.

Individual payment by results is not always particularly appropriate, as we have seen in Activity 10.8. This payment system is most appropriate where:

● it is possible to measure work
● it is easy to attribute it to individuals
● the pace of work is under the employee's control
● management can provide a steady flow of work for the employee to do
● the work is not subject to constant changes in method, materials or equipment.

There are a variety of payment by results schemes. These include:

● group incentives
● individual time saving
● measured day work.

● Group incentives

These are based on the same principles as the individual payment by results system, but are used when the individualistic approach is not wanted by the organisation. For example, in order to try to encourage teamworking or to take into account support workers who contribute to overall output, but whose contribution may be difficult to assess, some organisations introduce a system of group payment by results. The form of incentive or reward chosen should reinforce behaviour that results in effective teamwork and this also needs to fit with the culture and structure of the organisation. According to the CIPD (2010e) 'hierarchical structures are inappropriate for teamworking. It is difficult to foster team spirit if individuals are focusing on promotion.'

The size of the group may vary from small teams or work units to the whole plant or enterprise. All types of reward or incentive can work with teams and the most usual include team pay or bonuses through to non-financial rewards such as recognition or increased responsibility for the team.

ACTIVITY 10.9

Make a list of the advantages and disadvantages of plant- and enterprise-wide payment by results schemes.

Discussion of Activity 10.9

You may have suggested some of the following advantages and disadvantages.

Advantages

- Employees see how they contribute to the whole organisation's effectiveness.
- Employees are usually encouraged to find ways to improve performance and productivity.
- Employees become interested in how the organisation is managed.
- It is cheaper to install plant- or enterprise-wide payment by results schemes than individual payment by results schemes.
- There is usually a need to discuss financial information with employee representatives and this can result in an improved understanding of how the organisation is run.

Disadvantages

- There is a weaker link in employees' minds between the bonus and the level of their effort, so it may not be a strong incentive.
- Schemes can be difficult to understand.
- Bonus payments could be affected by factors such as inflation which the workforce can do nothing about.

● Measured day work

Measured day work is another individualised payment scheme. In this case pay rates are agreed at a higher rate than would normally have been paid for a time worker doing the same job, but there is an agreement that the workers will work at a specified level of performance. These levels of performance are agreed using work study techniques and then management carefully monitors the actual level of performance. A further variation of this is the stepped measured day work system, where a number of levels of performance are specified and workers can choose at which level to work. If their work improves they can progress to higher levels and increased pay. These systems have the advantage that the employees' pay will not fluctuate wildly on a daily or weekly basis, and so they provide for stability, but they do not allow individual workers as much flexibility as to how hard they want to work each day.

Profit sharing

This is a form of payment scheme where the focus is on the group rather than the individual. Employees all receive a bonus, and its size depends on the profits made by the organisation that year. Once again there is little direct incentive for individuals to work harder, as it is difficult to see how their contribution actually relates to the profit made, but many profit-sharing schemes encourage employees to get involved with how the scheme is run. Sometimes, bonus payments are made in shares rather than cash. This is also intended to give employees an interest in the enterprise, but can result in a risk to both shares and job if the organisation does not do as well in the future. It is difficult to see this as a strong motivational force.

Performance-related pay or merit rating

Performance-related pay, which is sometimes referred to as merit rating, is also a way of linking an individual's pay progression to their level of performance or to a rating of competence. It is once again an individualistic approach which favours rewarding people differently according to level of performance or competence, and it aims to motivate all employees and give clear indications of what the organisation expects from employees. Performance-related pay differs from payment by results as it doesn't relate just to the quantity of a product that is produced, and may apply to workers even where there is no end product to measure.

Initially, performance-related pay was used as a motivational tool primarily for non-manual employees, but in the 1980s it was extended to shop floor workers and has been discussed and used as a tool in some parts of the health service and in education. Increasingly some organisations have become aware of limitations to PRP as it did not always deliver the results expected or may have had unintended consequences as it encouraged employees to focus on their own results rather than working as a team.

Performance-related pay is often regarded as a key feature of performance management, as outlined in the previous chapter, and although some performance management schemes do not operate performance-related pay, most do use it. While the motivational theorists cast doubt on the value of money as a motivator, many managers instinctively feel that money will motivate employees. Some organisations, even if they do not feel that it will have a strong motivational effect, introduce performance-related pay as a way of being fair and rewarding high performers' past performance, and so argue that equity is the rationale for the introduction of such a scheme. The fact that performance is considered at all can also have positive effects, in that it helps to create a culture in which performance is valued and recognition of good performance can be a reward in itself. According to Egan (2010b), 60 per cent of private sector workers but only 36 per cent of public sector workers would like their pay to reflect their performance, once again showing how important it is for employers to find out what motivates their particular workforce. If a performance-related pay system is to be perceived to be fair it is important to emphasise that performance-related pay needs to be based on what can be seen to be a fair and just system of allocation, with clear, objective criteria being used.

In some organisations wider definitions of performance are now being used and the focus is moving towards assessing an employee's contribution or input to the organisation rather than just their output. This is much broader than measuring their performance simply in terms of what they have achieved. Some of their achievement, or lack of achievement, may be because of external factors outside their control such as a change in the economy, or a competitor going out of business, but their contribution to helping to achieve departmental or organisational objectives is under their control more (Egan, 2010b).

ACTIVITY 10.10

Imagine that you work in an organisation where performance-related pay has recently been introduced. You are appraising one of your subordinates, a man in his fifties who has been with the organisation for about 15 years. You have discussed most of the rating criteria, which have all been satisfactory. You say, 'Your work has been good but are there any areas where you feel there could be improvements?' He replies, 'I'm happy in the job but I don't really see much point in working a great deal harder. The mortgage is paid off now, the children have finished their education and if I earn more money I will only have to pay more tax on it. I want to take life a bit easier now and spend more time at home or away in the caravan. I don't always want to be taking work home with me.'

1 What are the advantages and disadvantages of performance-related pay?
2 How does the situation here link with what you know about theories of motivation?
3 Suggest alternative ways of motivating this employee to work to his full potential.

Discussion of Activity 10.10

1 *Advantages* of performance-related pay:
   ● Rewards the individual by linking systematic assessment of their performance to their level of pay or to a bonus.
   ● The factors taken into account may be weighted to reflect their relative importance to the organisation.
   ● It can be used where an incentive is needed but the actual work rate is difficult to measure.
   ● It can reward factors not easily taken into account in other payment systems.
   Disadvantages of performance-related pay:
   ● There may be disagreements about the performance factors to be assessed, and if great care is not taken in the choice of the factors there may be claims that they are too subjective or even of sex bias.
   ● Bonus payments may be too infrequent to provide a direct incentive.

2 This is another example of the view that individuals will be motivated by different things and that we value different things. This would link with Maslow's (1954) hierarchy of needs mentioned in Chapter 11 on health, safety and wellbeing.

3 The situation described reflects the view that there needs to be a range of different forms of incentive so that individuals can choose what will motivate them. In this case the employee might well be motivated if he was offered the opportunity to work for increased holidays.

Performance-related pay can be paid in several ways, and may even involve non-financial rewards. The most commonly used financial rewards are:

● salary increases within the normal salary scale
● salary increases above the maximum point of the normal pay scale
● where each employee is paid on an individual fixed rate, with good performers getting something above the normal rate
● lump sum payments that are not included in salary.

Salary increases within the normal salary scale

This is a commonly used form of performance-related pay, and gives a clear message that although there is a fixed scale for the job and everyone's pay depends on performance, exceptional performers can progress through this scale more rapidly than others.

Salary increases above the maximum point of the normal pay scale

This is sometimes used when the organisation wants to maintain its existing incremental pay scales but also wants to reward excellent performance. In this case high performers benefit as everyone else progresses along the normal scale until they reach the maximum, but it is of no benefit to average employees who have reached the top of the scale because of the length of their employment.

Each employee is paid on an individual fixed rate, with good performers getting something above the normal rate

In this case the individual is paid on a particular rate, but there is no automatic annual salary increase. The organisation budgets for a percentage increase each year, but then allocates this money according to assessments of employee performance, with excellent performers receiving most, good performers getting some allocation of award and poor performers receiving nothing at all. This gives a very clear message to all concerned, and may result in those who are assessed as being poor performers leaving the organisation.

Bonus payments that are not included in salary

Bonus payments and cash incentives are forms of payment that are not incorporated into an employee's salary. Incentives are used to influence future employee performance and to encourage the employee to meet predetermined targets. Bonuses can be used in the same way or could be *ad hoc* one-off rewards given retrospectively for work that has been done well. Both are intended to help attract and retain talented workers, to motivate and ensure they are engaged with the organisation with the intention that this will ultimately lead to an enhancement of the performance of the organisation.

Traditionally bonuses and cash incentives were used as a motivational tool for manual workers to use alongside basic pay or as an addition to a piece work system. More recently it has become normal to use this approach for managers and non-manual workers and according to the CIPD (2009a) this forms a part of a 'new pay' philosophy in which the guaranteed basic pay forms a small proportion of the over-all reward package, with the aim that the bonuses will be linked clearly to improved performance which in turn links very clearly to achieving the organisation's strategic objectives. There is less security of income for managers and therefore more incentive for them to work harder to be successful and this is ongoing as bonuses constantly have to be re-earned during each financial period.

Organisations are also attracted to the idea of bonuses as it means that they have less to pay in terms of some of the add-on costs to salary such as employer's pension contributions. They may also provide a way for differentiating the level of pay between workers with high or low levels of performance and as a way of having some flexibility related to the organisation's overall financial position: bonuses could be set at a higher level if the organisation is in good financial shape but could be reduced or stopped when the financial situation is less favourable.

Bonuses have become very controversial after revelations of the huge sums that city bankers or executives received in bonuses, sometimes even when they did not meet their targets! This has resulted in a huge amount of discussion about bonuses and their usefulness. Many employers, including those in the world of finance, argue that a lump sum payment has more impact than if the same amount were included in normal salary and this is used as a way of attracting people to these organisations and also as a way of retaining them, since they will want to stay until their bonus has been paid. Bonuses do draw attention to the organisation's policy for rewarding ex-cellence, especially if the opportunity is used for a special presentation ceremony, but in many organisations it seems to be expected that there will be a bonus even if tar-gets have not been achieved. According to the CIPD (2010b) many of the organisa-tions they surveyed planned to review and modify bonus schemes in 2010 to ensure that 'they align to the organisation's objectives'.

Mathews raises questions about the role of HR in relation to what she calls 'fat-cat failures'. They are the 'group of former MPs, directors and sporting figures who have successfully turned logic on its head by attracting enormous rewards for being no good at their jobs' (Mathews, 2008). When organisations want to attract someone who in their opinion has some rare talent, they often do not consider that the person may not perform as well for them as they have done in their previous role. They tend to be so focused on getting that person to work for them that they create a fantastic package of pay, reward and benefits with-out giving sufficient thought to what will happen if the indi-vidual does not perform at expected level. Mathews emphasises the point that HR managers need to have more input into identifying performance criteria and play a role in ensuring exit packages take into account the possibility of failure.

Non-monetary awards

As shown in Activity 10.10, people may be motivated by a range of different factors and may not always be motivated by being paid more money directly in their pay, especially if they lose a great deal in tax. Although we are all pleased to get more money, there is no public recognition of a job well done in that approach. This view is recognised in many organisations, which now seek to provide both monetary and non-monetary awards. Some of the non-financial awards we have selected will also have a monetary value. We have included them as non-monetary awards as the fact of an award being special, in recognition of a job well done or special effort made, may have a motivating effect larger than purely monetary value. Saying 'thank you' is a much overlooked form of non-monetary award in many organisations.

Some organisations are very original with the types of awards of offer. Sky TV achieved a profit of £780 million for the year up to June 2009 and thanked its staff for their efforts during the recession by staging a two-day music and entertainment festival for 20,000 staff and their friends and family. They asked their staff what forms of rewards they would like for an employee reward day and organised two music festivals, one in London and one in Edinburgh, as a result. Other individual rewards which proved extremely popular were the opportunity to stand on a replica of the empty Trafalgar Square plinth. Dev Ravel, the director of reward at Sky, is quoted as saying, 'Skyfest is designed to be great entertainment and to enhance our employee reward package' (Rewards and Benefits Today, 2009).

In spite of the ingenuity used at Sky TV the most commonly used non-financial rewards are:

- commendation
- overseas travel
- gifts
- gift vouchers
- green/environmental rewards.

Commendation

The opportunity to commend someone for the efforts that they have made can be extremely important as a way of rewarding and motivating them, whether this is done through the normal performance appraisal interview or at a public ceremony at which a letter or certificate of commendation is presented. The latter situation, with the attendant publicity, will serve as a reinforcement of the values that the organisation wishes to encourage and may also motivate others to improve their work performance.

Overseas travel

This type of reward used to be used primarily to reward sales staff for improvements in sales, but in recent years it has become an incentive on offer to many other individuals. Sometimes overseas travel is used as an incentive for team effort, with the whole team being rewarded with a trip abroad.

This type of reward can be in the form of overseas holidays or the opportunity to attend a high-profile training course held at an exotic destination.

Gifts

Other gifts awarded to people who have made significant improvements in their performance include consumer items such as cameras, household luxuries or jewellery. Once again there is the problem of choosing an appropriate range of gifts, as individuals are not likely to be motivated by the opportunity to acquire a new microwave oven, for example, if they already own one.

Gift vouchers

Gift vouchers are perhaps the most flexible form of incentive payment and are also very popular with individuals, as they offer real choice. Many high street stores promote the use of their gift vouchers to organisations that are thinking of establishing this type of scheme.

Green/environmental rewards

This is a new type of award which recognises workers' concerns about environmental issues or about individuals' carbon footprints and which aims to provide rewards which address in a positive way their environmental concerns. Clive Wright (2007) said at a recent CIPD meeting that the forms these awards could take included the following:

company discounts for solar panels or wind turbines; home efficiency consultancy as another option in a flexible benefits programme; extra volunteer days for green projects . . . discounts or preferential loans for public transport or access to discounts on recycled products.

Pause for thought 10.3 What do you feel about green awards as a motivational tool? Which potential green or environmental reward would motivate you to work harder?

Cafeteria-style payments or flexible pay

An even more flexible approach to pay is sometimes referred to as the 'cafeteria approach' or 'flex pay', because employees can choose their own preferred reward or combination of rewards. It gives an opportunity for employers to find a pay package that will suit a diverse range of staff, whether male or female, full time or part time, and who come from a wide age range. This can prove attractive for recruiting and retaining labour. In the cafeteria approach the workforce are told what rewards or benefits they can choose from each year. This could mean that they select from gift vouchers, gifts or holidays or they may prefer to choose from other benefits such as improved healthcare options, health or life insurance, an improved pension scheme, longer holidays or even additional cash. Companies that have introduced flexible schemes such as this have done so not to cut costs but to tailor their benefits to the needs of their workforce, and they have found that younger staff prefer cash or a second car, older staff often prefer to improve their pensions or health cover, while staff with young families may prefer longer holidays.

In order for a flexible system to work there has to be an excellent system established for administration, and improvements in computer technology help here.

There must also be an appropriate culture within the organisation and excellent communication with members of the workforce and their representatives. Not all organisations have moved towards a complete menu of options: some have felt that staff might be confused by too much choice and have gone for schemes that offer core benefits to all staff with some additional choice over certain options.

Total reward

Total reward, like that of flexible pay, recognises that pay is not the only motivating force for people but it goes even further to include other aspects of employment in the total reward package. Total reward is a newer concept than flexible pay that some organisations are developing. The CIPD (2010b) found in their annual reward management survey 'that a total reward approach has been adopted by one third of the sample, while a further two in ten plan to take this approach in 2010.' Total reward schemes normally do offer flexible pay and benefits but also include aspects of work such as career and personal development, flexitime, a challenging job at work, opportunities for individual growth and development and recognition for achievements. Sometimes they even allow for individual preferences for type of office layout, space and equipment as well as for administrative support. Total reward schemes aim to align employers' HR and business strategies with employees' needs in order to ultimately achieve improved performance. According to the CIPD (2009b) total reward 'goes beyond standard remuneration by embracing the company culture, and is aimed at giving all employees a voice in the operation, with the employer in return receiving an engaged workforce performance'.

Many organisations are having to rethink their reward strategies as a result of the economic situation and changing demographics. According to CIPD (2009b), 'both new and old-economy companies are currently having to rethink their reward strategies.' There are no longer jobs for life in the old, more traditional style of organisations and newer organisations, who may not have had such good job security anyway, can in some cases no longer afford large financial rewards and stock options. The increasingly diverse workforce also demand different benefits so some organisations are adopting a total reward approach in order to attract and retain workers. In the 2010 reward survey (CIPD, 2010b) the four key reward priorities for 2010 were found to be:

- making certain that the total reward strategy is aligned closely with the organisation's strategic objectives
- ensuring the package is competitive in comparison with other organisations
- minimising costs
- ensuring that the total reward strategy achieves the engagement of employees.

These organisations clearly do understand that pay and reward does contribute to achieving the organisation's strategic objectives. While they are still nervous and keen to minimise costs they are also aware that total reward is a strategy for improving employee engagement and for keeping the talent that they already have in their organisations.

Reward strategy

We have shown some of the influences on the way that pay is determined within an organisation and the messages that each payment system gives to workers. Because the payment system is important for motivating and giving clear messages about what is considered by the organisation to be important, it should be related to the organisation's strategic objectives. This has not always happened and although some organisations are clearly using pay and reward as a strategic tool to attract and retain talent, many other organisations have not yet adopted this approach. In 2007 the CIPD (2007a) annual reward survey results showed that only 35 per cent of respondents reported having a reward strategy while another 40 per cent said that they intended to create one in 2007. By 2010 the position remains virtually the same or a little worse and, according to the CIPD (2010b), just over a third of respondents have a reward strategy in place and a further 30 per cent intend to create one in 2010. It is very disappointing that the number reporting they had reward strategies in place remains virtually unchanged and in itself seems a relatively low number for such an important issue. The number of organisations who say they plan to implement reward strategies the following year has declined slightly and it is clear some employers have good intentions but do not always follow them up.

In a CIPD podcast about reward (2007b) Charles Cotton says, 'Our research still shows that most organisations are kind of adopting a tactical approach to reward. It tends to be knee-jerk, short-term, reactive, rather than actually going out there and saying, well actually, what as an organisation do we need or want to achieve to be successful? What do we need from our employees in terms of values, attitudes and behaviours to be successful and, actually, how are we then going to reward and recognise them for when they actually show and exhibit those values?' As we have shown there are some excellent examples of employers who are adopting a more strategic approach to pay and reward but based on the statistics many organisations are not doing this yet.

Pause for thought 10.4 Consider the quotation from Charles Cotton taken from the CIPD (2007b) podcast. Which of the views expressed here is most typical of the performance management approach to managing people?

International issues in managing pay

Anyone who is concerned with HR in a multinational organisation will appreciate the added complexities of establishing a fair and equitable payment system which operates successfully across many countries. Some of the factors that determine payment systems will be the same as those we have discussed earlier in this chapter when determining pay rates in organisations in the UK but added to these will be issues such as fluctuating currency exchange rates and varying costs of living. There may also be additional payments relating to the need to provide for security and safety for the workforce and to pay people at a substantially higher rate if they are working in a dangerous area. Issues relating to family, accommodation, schooling, healthcare and regular flights home may also form part of an international payment package.

The euro

Although Britain has no commitment at present to join the single European currency and has to hold a referendum before any decision is made, the fact that other European countries are using the euro does have an impact. UK organisations need to consider the strategic implications as there is increased competition and greater transparency on pricing and easier comparison of wages and benefits between those countries within the euro zone. The introduction of the euro in these countries brings both opportunities and threats which organisations should examine.

Wages and pensions departments have had to review their practices if their workforce covers several European countries. Data relating to pay in those countries using the euro are easier to compare but historical data on pay may also need to be converted to ease comparisons. For expats working abroad, life is easier if both their home country and host country are in the euro zone, as there will be no exchange rate fluctuations to alter the value of their salaries.

The adoption of the single currency was supposed to result in increasing levels of movement of workers between countries within the euro zone as people find it easier to compare wages and conditions. This is also a help for trade unions when negotiating pay deals for workers in several countries and can lead to a greater harmonisation of not only wages but also terms and conditions. Pension plans, share option schemes and profit-related pay schemes are also affected. However, the fact that Britain has not adopted the single currency does not seem to have deterred many European workers from seeking jobs in Britain. While in some areas of France jobs for French graduates continue to be difficult to find there is a thriving community of French graduates living and working in London and in many other large British cities. Having a good command of the language, a high degree of education and desirable skills and competencies means that these workers are able to take up opportunities in Britain which may not be available to them at the moment in France.

HR departments have a very important role to play in examining the strategic implications of the euro for their organisation and may need to develop, in some cases, into a Europe-wide function. In multinational organisations, particularly where some of the workforce work in euros but others are outside the zone, communications and training will be particularly important. The HR department may also need to review their organisation's payment systems, pensions scheme, expatriate programmes and procedures for union negotiations and consider the cultural implications of the single currency and possible need for harmonisation of pay and conditions. They will also be involved in any practical issues relating to actual payments to some workers in euros.

● Ethical issues

Low paid foreign workers

When considering what to pay people there are many ethical issues to consider in terms of what society values and is willing to pay people in differing jobs and professions. While the law does provide some guidance to employers in terms of equal pay or ensuring the minimum wage is paid there are still some groups such as migrant workers who, as we have seen, are sometimes exploited by unscrupulous employers and who have not even received this minimum level of protection and other groups such as bankers or senior executives who seem to be able to pay themselves huge bonuses whether or not they have achieved their targets.

While people in the UK continue to expect clothes and food at cheap prices this is often also achieved at the expense of overseas workers who may be working long hours in poor conditions for less than a living wage. According to McVeigh (2007a), 'Charities campaigning for workers' rights accuse retailers of maximizing profits in demanding rock bottom prices from suppliers in the developing world.' As a result of allegations in the *Guardian* newspaper about the exploitation of workers in Bangladesh, MPs called for action to protect overseas workers. 'Lynne Featherstone, who at that time was the Liberal Democrat international spokeswoman, said legislation should guarantee that pay and conditions of overseas workers met international standards: "It's obscene that [UK shoppers] can earn more through their club card points than the people who produce the goods they are buying"' (McVeigh, 2007b).

Some countries are developing rapidly and becoming sufficiently powerful that they can put pressure on foreign firms. For example in China the communist party called on employers to raise salaries and improve the training of workers after some foreign firms including Honda, Toyota and Hyundai were hit by strikes. The premier Wen Jiabo was quoted as saying 'that the era of low cost labour in China was coming to an end and that firms should improve skills, boost spending power and provide fair conditions for migrant workers' (*People Management*, 2010b). These are the same types of things that workers in the UK also appreciate.

Pause for thought 10.6 What do you think? Should there be stronger legislation in place to protect overseas workers? Would you be willing to pay more for goods you buy if it meant that overseas workers received a living wage?

Bonus culture

After the global banking crisis there is also the question of whether or not a bonus culture was partly to blame as it drove individuals to operate in ways that achieved their own short-term targets and those of the organisation, for example by selling more mortgages. But this emphasis on a short-term fix may have had an impact on financial stability worldwide as often mortgages or other products were sold to people who would not be able to repay them. According to the Financial Services Authority, quoted by CIPD (2009a), 'Although it is difficult to prove a causal link, there is widespread consensus that remuneration packages may have been a contributory factor to the global crisis.'

There are also the ethical questions of whether it is right to pay bonuses at all to people who have not earned them or in organisations that have not made a profit, and also the questions of exactly how much difference there should be between the salaries of the workforce and their directors who may receive huge bonuses. Levels of inequality appeared to be growing with the bonus culture and the whole issue of creating what is a fair and equitable system of reward is one that is going to be discussed a great deal in the future.

Pause for thought 10.7 What do you think? Should directors, bankers or top sports people have limits set on their pay?

Should they be rewarded for failure?

In your view how much difference should there be between the pay of directors in an organisation and their workforce?

What would you base their bonus payments on?

Conclusion

We have examined some of the types of payment systems that are available to employers and related them briefly to what they are supposed to achieve for the organisation. No scheme is perfect for all organisations, and all schemes have advantages and disadvantages. Each scheme gives a clear message about the values of the organisation and should be a reflection of its mission statement. The choice of payment scheme will depend on the wishes of the workforce as well as the culture of the organisation, and these should be taken into account before any scheme is introduced. The workforce should be involved in discussion, design, implementation and review of whatever payment scheme is introduced. With the increasingly diverse workforce at the start of the twenty-first century, and moves towards a flexible workforce, many organisations have introduced flexible approaches to the pay and benefits that they provide for employees, using their payment systems as one mechanism for achieving their strategic goals whether these are national or international.

Particular care should be taken to ensure that the basis for the chosen payment system is transparent and understood by the workforce; full consultation with the workforce has occurred; and the selected pay system does not lead to unfair discrimination based on gender. This is still as necessary today as it was more than 40 years ago when the Equal Pay Act 1970 was first introduced. All organisations should ensure that they are rewarding and motivating all members of their workforce, regardless of their sex, in a fair way. A modern workforce has to be based on fair reward. The voluntary gender-pay audits which are being conducted by the Equality and Human Rights Commission should help provide data for starting to address the gender pay gap. However, employers should be regularly reviewing their pay systems not only to ensure there is no unfair bias but also to ensure that their pay and reward strategies achieve what they were supposed to achieve, and that they continue to attract, motivate, engage and retain staff and, ultimately, that they contribute to the achievement of the organisation's strategic objectives.

REVIEW QUESTIONS

You will find brief answers to these review questions on pages 495–6.

1 The minimum wage alters each year. Find out how much the minimum wage actually is at the present time. How much is the rate for adults aged 21 or over?

How much is the rate for those aged 18–20?

What are the rates being paid to those who are on Government training schemes such as apprenticeships?

2 Interview managers or employees from three organisations of your choice from different industrial sectors to establish what effect, if any, the introduction of the national minimum wage has had on that organisation/industrial sector.

3 Explain the process of job evaluation and comment on how a points rating job evaluation scheme can contribute to perceptions of fairness from the point of view of employees.

4 Fairness in pay is an objective of both employers and employees. Describe briefly the issues that need to be considered with reference to fairness, and evaluate critically the approaches that employers could adopt to achieve fairness.

5 Imagine that you are a consultant employed to select a job evaluation scheme for an organisation that employs 500 employees in a large range of clerical jobs. Write a report to the human resource manager in which you outline the advantages and disadvantages of the various types of job evaluation scheme and recommend what you consider to be a suitable job evaluation scheme for this organisation.

SELF-CHECK QUESTIONS

Answer the following short-answer questions. The correct responses are given on page 496 for you to check your understanding of this chapter.

1 Does harmonisation of wages and conditions of employment mean that managers and other employees and workers in the same organisation in different countries get different payment systems and conditions of employment to each other? YES or NO

2 Does job evaluation determine the amount of pay for a person doing a particular job? YES or NO

3 Are the following all types of non-analytical job evaluation schemes: whole job ranking, paired comparisons, points rating? YES or NO

4 Are all of the following advantages of the whole job ranking method of job evaluation: it is simple, cheap to operate and easy to understand? YES or NO

5 Is the points rating system of job evaluation an analytical method of job evaluation? YES or NO

6 Does job evaluation take account of the individual's performance in the job? YES or NO

7 Does an incremental pay scheme provide an incentive for people to work harder? YES or NO

8 Does a payment system based on time rates reflect an individualistic approach to the way people are paid? YES or NO

9 Is piecework another name for individual payment by results? YES or NO

10 Is performance-related pay a way of linking an individual's pay progression to their length of employment with the organisation? YES or NO

WHAT NEXT?

1 This chapter aimed to introduce you to the topic of payment systems and by this stage you should be able to meet the objectives stated at the beginning. You may now want to go further with the subject and the resources listed in the references and further study sections will help you to do this. There are lots more activities for you to check your understanding of Chapter 10 on our student website at **www.pearsoned.co.uk/foothook.**

2 Go to **www.cipd.uk/podcasts** and listen to or print the transcript for Reward – episode 5. This explores differing views of the ways organisations are tackling payment systems and also discusses the benefits of additional pay as a motivational tool compared with other forms of benefits. Which of the views expressed in this podcast do you agree with?

3 Go to **www.cipd.co.uk/podcasts** and listen to or print the transcript for podcast 34 – Executive remuneration and podcast 41 – Creating a competitive reward approach. Podcast 34 discusses some of the ways that HR should influence executive pay and sets out the CIPD's views on how to create a fairer system. What do you think of this approach? How influential should the HR department be in this area?

Podcast 41 has HR managers from different organisations discussing how they try to motivate their workforces in ways that align with their organisations' strategic objectives. Which methods do you think are likely to be most successful?

HR IN THE NEWS

FT Report – Bonuses may be the back door to a widening pay gap

FT

By Tony Jackson

Some two-thirds of senior UK civil servants, the new UK chancellor George Osborne said last week, received a performance bonus last year. He finds that odd, and so might most of us. Indeed, we might suspect it is essentially a back door to wage inflation.

But as so often, the public sector is taking its cue from business. The bonus system has many advantages in principle. But in the corporate sector, it risks degenerating into a means of widening the gap between top earners and the rest.

Let us recall that originally the system aimed not to enrich individuals but to protect employers. Their problem: that while the economic cycle goes up and down, wages only go up. It was not always so. In the two-year slump of the early 1920s, UK wages fell 30 per cent. But in both the UK and US, average wages have not fallen in any year since the Great Depression.

Bonuses, by contrast, are in principle variable. They were adopted early by the stockbroking industry, which is used to the whipsaw of bull and bear markets. As recently as the 1960s, it was not uncommon for London brokers to pay no salary at all. The partners simply reckoned up the surplus at the end of the year and divided it among the staff.

In a much modified form, the principle crept into British boardrooms in the 1980s. And in the past decade it has run amok.

Take the UK retailer Marks and Spencer. In 2000, executive directors – including the boss – were entitled to a maximum bonus of 30 per cent of salary if they beat the targets set for them.

By 2005 that ceiling had risen to 150 per cent and is now 250 per cent. In addition, directors now receive a 60 per cent bonus for merely meeting their targets.

As a result, the proportion of pay accounted for by basic salary has been tumbling. On M&S's own figures, a director performing on target now gets 36 per cent of compensation from salary, compared with 100 per cent 10 years ago.

Quite right too, some would say. The more variable pay is, the more it is in line with the interests of the shareholders. There are two snags to that.

The first is that the median base salary for FTSE 100 chief executives has risen faster since 2000 than for the workforce overall – by 49 per cent versus 40 per cent. For M&S, the figure is 74 per cent.

The second is that bonuses are not always as variable as they look. It is to the credit of M&S, which has performed pretty dismally of late, that last year only one executive director received a bonus at all. But, for every M&S there is a Royal Dutch Shell, which last year paid bonuses despite missing targets.

And in investment banking, bonuses were paid out in 2008 despite enormous losses. This would have been incomprehensible to an earlier generation of bankers. How can you share out profits when there are none?

This kind of ossification, whereby bonuses become a fixed entitlement as wages did before, need not surprise us.

Professor David Marsden, an employment specialist at the London School of Economics, points out that if you deny a subordinate a bonus, you create a headache for yourself in motivating that employee for the next year. But the insidious bit – as the civil servant example confirms – is that big bonuses are mainly confined to high earners. The widening pay gap is a social worry already. Bonuses are becoming a machine for worsening it.

Financial Times, 24/05/2010 (Tony Jackson), Reproduced with permission, © The Financial Times Ltd.

Questions

1 Do you think that chief executives should still receive an enormous bonus even if the organisation that they have led has performed badly? List the arguments for and against this.

2 To what extent do you think that the bonus culture is increasing the gap between rich and poor?

References

Advisory, Conciliation and Arbitration Service (2010a) *Advisory Booklet – Job Evaluation: Considerations and Risks*, ACAS, (available at www.acas.org.uk; accessed 24.8.10).

Advisory, Conciliation and Arbitration Service (2010b) *The Equality Act – What's New for Employers*, ACAS (available at www.acas.org.uk; accessed 24.8.10).

Chartered Institute of Personnel and Development (2007a) *Total Reward*, CIPD (www.cipd.co.uk; accessed 26.08.2010).

Chartered Institute of Personnel and Development (2007b) *Podcast: Reward – episode 5*, CIPD, 06.03.2007 (www.cipd.co.uk; accessed 29.08.07).

Chartered Institute of Personnel and Development (2009a) *Bonuses and Cash Incentives*, CIPD, (www.cipd.co.uk; accessed 28.08.10).

Chartered Institute of Personnel and Development (2009b) *Total Reward*, CIPD, (www.cipd.co.uk; accessed 25.08.10).

Chartered Institute of Personnel and Development (2010a) *Pay and Reward: An Overview*, CIPD, (www.cipd.co.uk; accessed 25.08.10).

Chartered Institute of Personnel and Development (2010b) *Annual Survey Report 2010: Reward Management*, CIPD, (www.cipd.co.uk; accessed 25.08.10).

Chartered Institute of Personnel and Development (2010c) *National Minimum Wage*, CIPD, (www.cipd.co.uk; accessed 25.08.10).

Further study

Books

ACAS Advisory Booklets, particularly those on the Equality Act 2010, payment systems, job evaluation and appraisal-related pay are useful sources of information.

There are several publications about the Equality Act 2010. Some aim to give guidance to employers while in others the focus is on the employee. The following are particularly useful:

Equality and Human Rights Commission (2010) *What Equality Law Means for You as an Employee: Pay and Benefits*, Equality and Human Rights Commission.

Chartered Institute of Personnel and Development (2010d) *Discrimination*, CIPD, (www.cipd. co.uk; accessed 26.08.10).

Chartered Institute of Personnel and Development (2010e) *Team Reward*, CIPD, (www.cipd.co. uk; accessed 27.08.10).

Cotton, C. (2009) *Press Release: Gender Pay Reporting 'No Magic Bullet' to Solve the Pay Gap, warns CIPD*, CIPD, 27 April (www.cipd.co.uk; accessed 26.8.2010).

Egan, J. (2010a) *Factsheet: Pay Structures*, CIPD (www.cipd.co.uk; accessed 25.08.10).

Egan, J. (2010b) *Factsheet: Performance-related Pay*, CIPD (www.cipd.co.uk; accessed 25.08.10).

Equal Opportunities Commission Hong Kong (2003) Eliminating discrimination: systems and policy reviews, equal pay for work of equal value, *Equal Opportunities Commission Hong Kong Annual Report 2001–2*, HKEOC (www.eoc.org.hk//EOC/GraphicsFolder/Inforcenter/ Annual/default.aspx?year=2001; accessed 24.6.04).

Equality and Human Rights Commission (2010) *Voluntary Measures Proposed for Publishing Pay Gaps*, Equality and Human Rights Commission, 19 January (www.equalityhumanrights. com; accessed 27 August 2010).

Goss, F. (2010) How to set up incentive programmes, *People Management*, 12 August, 33.

Guardian (2010) *Factfile UK Sport, Fact File UK Part Four: Education, Sport and Culture*, 27 April, 18.

Health and Safety Executive (2007) *The Gangmaster's Licensing Authority*, HSE (www.hse.gov. uk/agriculture; accessed 08.08.07).

Herzberg, F. (1966) *Work and the Nature of Man*, Staples Press.

IRS Employment Review (2009) Hay survey assesses future of reward strategies, *IRS*, Issue 928, 21 August (www.xperthr.co.uk; accessed 25.8.2010).

Jackson, T. (2010) Bonuses may be the back door to a widening pay gap, *The Financial Times*, 24 May (www.ft.com; accessed 25.8.2010).

Lawrence, F. (2007) The miracle of cheap fresh food depends on illegality, *The Guardian*, 17 July, 28.

Maslow, A. (1954) *Motivation and Personality*, Harper & Row.

Mathews, V. (2008) Executive pay: fat-cat failures, *Personnel Today*, 2 January (www.xperthr.co.uk; accessed 28.8.2010).

McGregor, D. (1960) *The Human Side of Enterprise*, McGraw-Hill.

McVeigh, K. (2007a) Asda, Primark and Tesco are accused over clothing factories, *The Guardian*, 16 July, 1.

McVeigh, K. (2007b) MPs want UK to pay living wage to overseas staff, *The Guardian*, 17 July, 9.

Oakeshott, I. (2010) Pakistan needs your bonus, says the minister, *The Guardian*, 22 August, 12.

People Management (2010a) The CIPD People Management Awards, 12 August, 15.

People Management (2010b) Pressure's on for foreign firms in China, 1 July, 8.

Rewards and Benefits Today (2009) Sky reward scheme uses arts festival to help celebrate success, Issue 1, 1 September (www.xperthr.co.uk; accessed 25.8.2009).

Soret, N. (2010) *Factsheet: Equality Act 2010*, CIPD (www.cipd.co.uk; accessed 26.8.2010).

Welfare, S. (2006) Equal pay at a crossroads, *IRS Employment Review*, Issue 843, 24 March (www.xperthr.co.uk; accessed 08.08.07).

Wild, S. (2010) *Equal Pay Where Next? The Business Case for Equal Pay: How the Business Case for Equal Pay Plays Out in Practice and What Can Be Done to Strengthen It*, May, Equality and Human Rights Commission, 2.

Wright, C. (2007) Letter from the chair, *Reward Review*, CIPD, Spring/Summer 2007.

XpertHR (2010) *Employment Law Reference Manual*, XpertHR (www.xperthr.co.uk; accessed 29.8.2010).

Equality and Human Rights Commission (2010) *What Equality Law Means for You as an Employer: Pay and Benefits*, Equality and Human Rights Commission.

Government Equalities Office (2010) *Equality Act 2010; What Do I Need to Know? A Summary Guide to Your Rights*, Crown copyright.

Perkins, S. and G. White (2008) *Employee Reward*, CIPD.

This gives a thorough coverage of all aspects of reward in a very accessible way and is ideal for those wanting to study reward in more depth.

Articles

Goss, F (2010) How to set up incentive programmes, *People Management*, 12 August, 33.

Internet

The Advisory, Conciliation and Arbitration Service   **www.acas.org.uk**
This site has guidance on various aspects of pay and texts of leaflets that can be downloaded directly or ordered.

Department for Business, Innovation and Skills   **www.bis.gov.uk**
Up-to-date information about the minimum wage at this site.

Incomes Data Services (IDS)   **www.incomesdata.co.uk**
Abstracts from articles in the section on pay and labour market data.

CHAPTER 11

Health, safety and wellbeing

Objectives

By the end of this chapter you will be able to:

● explain what is meant by the terms 'safety', 'hazard', 'risk', 'wellbeing' and 'health'

● explain the key points in the main legislation relating to health, safety and wellbeing at work

● explain the reasons for managing employee health, safety and wellbeing

● explain the role of various people and groups in health and safety and wellbeing at work

● describe the Health and Safety Executive's approach to stress management

● explain the main health and safety issues in an international context.

In Chapter 1 we traced the history of people management and considered several approaches to what at that time was referred to as welfare. Some people who adopted the 'hard' human resource management approach tried originally to distance themselves from all these welfare approaches, as they felt that they showed a lack of business awareness. However, reducing accidents and improving occupational ill-health is extremely important for organisations today and many are taking an increasing interest in areas such as managing absenteeism. Health and safety are also coming under Government scrutiny as they want to improve the productivity of the workforce and remove unnecessary bureaucracy. The changing demographics of an ageing workforce combined with what is claimed to be a growing obesity problem in the UK are also likely to mean that the country has a new imperative for employers to become more involved in health if organisations want to be effective and productive. Paton (2010) quotes from a 2010 survey by BUPA which said that 'government, the NHS, private providers and OH (Occupational Health) providers are all going to have their work cut out in dealing with an ageing, sicker working population, while firms with the healthiest (and therefore least absent) and most engaged workforce will be the ones best placed to thrive in an increasingly competitive global environment.'

Not everyone takes such a negative view. ACAS (2010a) emphasise the fact that work is good for people's health but stress the value of a good work–life balance.

This is particularly important if we are to benefit from people working longer as will be necessary with an ageing population and no compulsory retirement age. ACAS (2010a) indicate that the growing awareness of a good work–life balance has made people increasingly conscious of the relationship between our mental and physical health and the job we do, so it is no longer sufficient for employers to just comply with legislation. There is clearly a strong case to be made for organisations to pay more attention to the health, safety and wellbeing of their workforces and to see this as another aspect of their approach to performance management.

Many organisations do realise the importance to their success of a healthy and productive workforce and are already seeking to adopt a more proactive approach. As the economy gradually recovers more employers are focusing on aspects of HR where they can get improvements in employee engagement, which will in turn help them retain talent. Strategies to improve safety and improve health are attractive ways to achieve this and should form a part of the organisation's approach to performance management. As we explained in Chapter 8, performance management in some organisations is being integrated with a wider range of HR processes than was traditionally the case and now involves processes designed to promote wellbeing, engagement and development of potential. Clearly issues relating to health, safety and wellbeing can contribute to this and as these approaches are not necessarily costly they may be particularly attractive to organisations trying to keep their budgets under tight control. Investors in People (IIP), which is perhaps better known for its business tool linking training to the strategic objectives of the organisation (discussed in Chapter 9), have developed a new standard for health and wellbeing. IIP (2010) claims increasing evidence of a direct relationship between developing effective health and wellbeing programmes and increased productivity and that there is an excellent return on investment from these programmes.

In this chapter we shall first examine what the terminology means before discussing the law relating to safety and the roles of those involved. Later we shall discuss the changing emphasis on health and wellbeing in more detail.

Did you know?

The positive effects of work are beneficial not only for employers but employees too and can contribute to their sense of happiness and wellbeing. According to ACAS (2010a), 'work can have a positive impact on our health and wellbeing. Healthy and well-motivated employees can have an equally positive impact on the productivity and effectiveness of a business.'

This seems to be true in some other cultures and there is evidence that work can also contribute to our sense of happiness. In the annual happiness survey carried out in Hong Kong in 2009 those who loved their jobs were happiest, followed by those who loved food and cooking, though when analysed by occupation those who were retired were listed as the happiest of all!

(Source: Chiu, 2009)

Definitions

Safety

We define safety as absence from danger and avoidance of injury.

According to this definition, we should expect employers to do everything in their power to keep employees away from danger and free of injury while at work. This does not sound like a great deal to expect from an employer, but there is often a conflict in the employer's mind between increased production, which sometimes may involve some risk taking, and the necessity to keep employees safe and uninjured, which may cost money. Legislation has developed over a number of years to protect workers, and was initially designed to protect those who were weak and particularly vulnerable to exploitation from any employers who, tempted by the lure of increased production, might put their employees at risk of injury. Nowadays, with increasingly flexible patterns of work being available, many employees may work from home or even from their car, for all or part of their working week, so employers will also have to consider the health and safety issues arising from this.

Hazard

A hazard is something that could cause harm to someone. Employers who are being proactive about health and safety therefore have to try to identify potential hazards before they actually do cause any harm. Stranks (2007a) says that a hazard can further be defined in three areas, as follows:

- exposure to harm
- something with the potential to do harm – this can include substances or machines, methods of work and other aspects of work organisation
- the result of departure from the normal situation, which has the potential to cause death, injury, damage or loss.

Risk

The term risk relates to the chances of the hazard actually resulting in harm being done to someone. Once the employer has identified a potential hazard then they have to estimate the chances or risk of someone being harmed by it.

We shall discuss the idea of risk assessment later in this chapter. The emphasis in health and safety today is on the prevention of accidents if possible by eliminating anything that could be a hazard and by predicting the level of risk in various situations. It is not, of course, always possible to eliminate all hazards or minimise all risks in a workplace, but employers are expected to predict potentially dangerous situations and then do something about them to ensure they become less dangerous. The emphasis in modern health and safety is to encourage those who own, manage or work in organisations to take responsibility for health and safety in them. For this to happen, both the workforce and safety representatives also need to be involved, risks need to be assessed and action needs to be taken to reduce these where possible. This is, however, currently a subject of debate as some feel that the UK has become too risk averse, to the extent that this stifles initiative and this will be discussed later in the chapter.

Wellbeing

According to Michaelson *et al.* (2009) 'personal wellbeing describes people's experiences of their positive and negative emotions, satisfaction, vitality, resilience, self esteem and sense of purpose and meaning. Social well-being is made up of two components, supportive relationships and trust and belonging both of which are critical elements of overall well-being.' The forerunners of HR managers were concerned with employee welfare and much of the legislation about health and safety also uses the term welfare. We have chosen to use the term wellbeing instead of welfare as nowadays welfare has a slightly negative connotation and suggests some degree of dependency. Wellbeing clearly includes dealing with what might be regarded as welfare issues but looks at all aspects of a person's wellbeing and does not focus just on the negative aspects. It also has a more positive feel as the individual also has responsibilities for their own wellbeing so should be working in partnership with others on this.

According to Tehrani et al. (2007) people have mental and physical needs for social support, safety and health, and also need to feel that they are not overwhelmed by events and can cope with life. These are all aspects of wellbeing and as a large part of our lives is spent at work it is natural to expect employers to play a part in employees' wellbeing. In the past many employers merely reacted to issues about health and safety and welfare without appreciating the benefits that adopting a more proactive approach could bring them. Many still operate in this way. However, some more progressive employers are adopting a much more proactive approach to health, safety and wellbeing to prevent problems arising in the first place.

Health

Here the concern is for good health. We define good health as being physically and mentally well with body and mind in excellent working order.

This goes further than safety in that the employer is no longer just expected not to do anything to injure their employees, but should seek to promote activities that encourage the good health of the employees. We shall return to a discussion of health promotion activities later in this chapter.

Safety

According to the Health and Safety Executive's (HSE's) Health and Safety Executive Statistics (HSE, 2010a) the provisional figures for 2009–10 show there were 151 workers fatally injured at work during this period, which is 31 per cent lower than the average for the previous five years and is also one of the lowest rates for fatal injuries in Europe. At the time of writing the latest figures available for accidents requiring absences of three or more days from work were for 2008–9. These showed an estimated 246,000 non-fatal reportable injuries. Overall there was a loss of 29.3 million working days and of these 24.6 million were due to work-related illness (HSE, 2010b). There is a downward trend both in the number of accidents requiring three or more days off work and in work-related illness but these still amount to a significant loss of work and increased costs to employers (HSE, 2010b). It is claimed that over 40 million potential workdays are lost to business each year and it is estimated that this costs British employers somewhere between £3.3 and £6.5 billion each year (HSE, 2010c).

ACTIVITY 11.1

Sometimes employers are reluctant to spend money on safety improvements as they don't feel this is justified. There are, however, costs associated with accidents. What are the possible costs to an individual employer of accidents at work?

Discussion of Activity 11.1

Obviously, depending on the severity of the injury, there are costs to the injured person in terms of pain and suffering, and possible loss of earnings. There are also costs to the employer, and your list is likely to include at least some of the following:

- cost of lost time and production due to absence caused by injury
- cost of lost time and production due to dealing with the injury
- cost of replacement worker or of training the replacement
- cost of replacing broken machinery or unsafe machinery or equipment
- cost of compensation to injured employee
- higher insurance premiums if the organisation's accident record is not good
- cost involved in carrying out a full investigation into the causes of the accident
- cost of paying fines or even facing imprisonment if the employer was to blame for the accident
- cost of poor morale within the workforce
- cost of people not being willing to work for the organisation because of its poor reputation for safety.

You may have found some other costs involved in accidents as well. Employers should be aware of the hidden costs of accidents; if they carried out a cost–benefit analysis they would probably be amazed at how much accidents were costing them and be more prepared to spend money on accident prevention. In their studies of accidents, the Health and Safety Executive (1995) identified one organisation where the costs of accidents amounted to as much as 37 per cent of profits. This organisation did not have a particularly bad record on health and safety, nor had it suffered any major disasters, fatalities or prosecutions.

We believe that health and safety is an important area of concern for all HRM practitioners, since it is in the organisation's interest to pursue any initiatives that will provide benefits and services which the employees will want and value but that will also fit with the strategic needs of the organisation by enhancing levels of employee performance.

Employers can check for themselves the actual costs both of accidents and work-related incidents in their organisations by using the accident and incident calculators provided by the Health and Safety Executive. They allow employers the choice of two different ways to calculate the annual costs of accidents in their organisation and also of using an interactive tool to calculate costs of other work-related incidents. Now there is really no excuse for employer ignorance of the cost of accidents or work-related incidents in their organisations.

If you would like to see how easy it is for employers to calculate the costs of accidents and work-based incidents by examining these tools for yourself, go to **www.hse.gov.uk/costs/accidentcost_calc/accident_costs_intro.asp** (accessed 6.9.2010).

Legislation

Did you know?

The Corporate Manslaughter and Corporate Homicide Act 2007 came into effect on 6 April 2008 across the UK. The Act set out a new offence for convicting an organisation where a gross failure in the way activities were managed results in a person's death.

The offence does not require organisations to comply with new regulatory standards. But the Act means that those who disregard the safety of others at work, with fatal consequences, are more vulnerable to very serious criminal charges. Courts will look at management systems and practices across the organisation, providing a more effective means for prosecuting the worst corporate failures to manage health and safety properly.

(Source: Ministry of Justice, 2008)

Much of the early development of legislation to protect employees at work was closely linked to the historical development of people management. The more enlightened employers were concerned to improve working conditions for their employees and appointed industrial welfare workers to help with this. Less enlightened employers were compelled to pay some attention to the protection of selected groups of employees, and as early as 1840 legislation designed to limit the hours that children worked was passed. In more recent times several new Acts have been passed and regulations issued to protect employees.

The Health and Safety at Work Act 1974 (HASAWA)

In Great Britain the foundation for the system of regulating health and safety at work was introduced by the Health and Safety at Work Act 1974. Although this was a long time ago, HASAWA is still very important today and forms the foundation for much of the later legislation. According to Hackitt (2010), one of the fundamental principles underpinning the Health and Safety at Work Act that still applies today is that 'those who create risk are best placed to manage it'. This means that those who create risks have duties to protect both workers and the public from their actions so that those who are the main risk creators are also the main duty holders in law. According to XpertHR (2010a) the main duty holders are likely to be employers and the self-employed but could also include employees, designers, manufacturers, importers, suppliers and those in charge of premises. In this chapter we shall focus principally on the duty holders who are employers and employees.

Before HASAWA, the legislation that could be used to protect employees at work was patchy and applied to vulnerable groups such as women or children, or to particular industries where there were thought to be high risks. The vast majority of the working population before 1974 were not actually protected by any health or safety legislation. The Health and Safety at Work Act 1974 set up some new bodies such as the Health and Safety Commission (HSC), the Health and Safety Executive (HSE) and reinforced the power of others such as local authorities. In 2008 HSC and HSE merged to form one single body called the Health and Safety Executive (HSE) and this is now the organisation responsible for the promotion of health and safety at work in Great Britain (Hackitt, 2010a). It does continue to work closely with local authorities and the roles of the Health and Safety Executive and the local authorities will be discussed later in the chapter.

HASAWA was the first piece of legislation designed to protect everyone at work, and also to protect others who were not at work, such as customers or even passers-by. It is estimated that it brought an extra 3 million people under the scope of protective safety legislation for the first time.

The main aim of the Act was to provide a comprehensive system of law which would raise standards of safety and health for all persons at work and also protect members of the public who might be affected by their actions.

More than 36 years after the Health and Safety at Work Act 1974 became law it still forms the foundation of health and safety legislation in the UK, so it is important to understand some of the fundamental principles that underpin this important piece of legislation.

ACTIVITY 11.2

Both employers and employees have responsibilities under HASAWA. List what you would expect to be the duties of employers and employees with regard to health and safety.

Duties of employers	Duties of employees

Compare your lists with the following duties summarised from the Health and Safety at Work Act 1974.

Discussion of Activity 11.2

Your list probably included some indication that employers were to take responsibility for having a safe workplace with safe equipment that would not injure anyone, and you also probably thought that employees too should take care not to harm anyone at work. There are no specific rules about lighting or temperature in the way that there are in some other Acts. Instead the Act is trying to involve people and make everyone take some responsibility for their actions. This approach is therefore moving towards a human resource management approach, and health and safety is not just in the domain of the human resource specialist but is shared with others. Sometimes the human resource specialist does have some aspects of health and safety included in their job description, and they may, for example, be expected to chair the safety committee if there is one.

The responsibilities of employers under the Health and Safety at Work Act

Employers have a basic duty of care to their employees to ensure their health, safety and welfare. As well as this rather general duty, they have five other duties. These are:

- to ensure that the workplace itself is safe; that equipment has been maintained correctly and work is safely organised
- that accidents do not occur because of incorrect handling, storage or transportation within the workplace
- that there is training, supervision and information relating to health and safety
- that the workplace itself is maintained adequately and that there are safe ways to get into and out of the buildings
- that provisions for wellbeing are adequate.

All of these duties are expressed in quite general terms and there is nothing in the Act to specify, for example, how much training or information should be given. The words 'so far as is reasonably practicable' are used frequently within HASAWA. The exact meaning of this phrase will be discussed later in this chapter. The employer also has a further specific duty to produce a safety policy statement and we shall also discuss later in the chapter what this involves.

As we said earlier, HASAWA was designed to gain involvement in health and safety from as many sources as possible, so the responsibility was not just one way. Employees also have responsibilities.

The responsibilities of employees under the Health and Safety at Work Act

As you might expect, there are fewer responsibilities for the employees than for the employers. They have three main areas of responsibility under HASAWA in relation to health and safety. These are:

- to take responsibility for their own health and safety, and for any health and safety problems which might be caused to colleagues by their actions or in some cases their failure to act
- not to recklessly interfere with or misuse any machinery, equipment or processes
- to cooperate with employers about health and safety initiatives.

Although they may not seem very onerous responsibilities, they are important since employees who do not follow these guidelines could be disciplined or even face prosecution themselves if an accident occurred for which they were responsible. They should cooperate about health and safety issues, such as wearing protective clothing, if the employer provides it. Since they must take responsibility for their own health and safety and that of others, they must also not do anything to interfere with safety guards, as this could result in injuries to themselves or to other people.

Pause for thought 11.1 The phrase 'as far as is reasonably practicable' is used several times in HASAWA. What factors do you think should be considered in determining whether or not something is 'reasonably practicable'?

This phrase means that circumstances, risks and cost need to be considered when an employer is endeavouring to make the workplace safe for employees. It would be very difficult to make anywhere completely safe and eliminate all accidents. Accidents are by definition something that you cannot predict; nevertheless, many situations do occur where it is possible to predict that someone could be injured if improvements are not made, and employers should try to anticipate the likelihood of these types of accident and take steps to prevent them from occurring. 'Reasonably practicable' means that a calculation must be made in which the risk is compared with the sacrifices, cost and level of effort needed to avert that risk. If there is a very slim chance that a comparatively minor accident might occur, but this chance could be eliminated by spending thousands of pounds on new equipment and also by disrupting the workforce, it might not be considered to be reasonably practicable to do so. If, however, the risk was of a serious injury or possibly death, then it would be reasonable to take every step and spend any amount of money to eliminate this risk. The term 'as far as is reasonably practicable' therefore means that the employer should do as much as they can to try to eliminate risks but that they need to review the balance between the risk and the amount of effort required to eliminate that risk.

Control of Substances Hazardous to Health Regulations (COSHH) 1988

This is another far-reaching piece of legislation comprising 19 regulations and 4 approved codes of practice which came into effect on 1 October 1989 and which have subsequently been revised in 1999, 2002 and 2003. Apart from some minor changes to tidy up the 1999 regulations, as these amendments relate to fairly specialised areas they do not alter the main thrust of this legislation and are too detailed to include in an introductory HRM textbook.

COSHH is designed to protect anyone who works with substances that could be hazardous to health. The regulations apply to all workplaces and include all substances with the exception of asbestos, lead, materials that produce ionising radiation and substances underground, which all have their own separate legislation. The legislation basically applies to any other substances that can cause harm by being inhaled, ingested, coming into contact with the skin, or being injected or introduced into the body, so they do cover a very wide range of substances.

COSHH regulations require all employers to carry out an assessment of risks to their employees from substances that are identified in the workplace as being potentially hazardous to either their employees or others who might be affected. Any risks that are identified must then be controlled. This emphasis on assessing risk and then doing something about it is a very different approach to that of HASAWA.

While it would be easy to assume that these regulations would not have much effect on ordinary workplaces, this is not in fact the case, as many of the substances identified as potentially hazardous will be found in any workplace – e.g. fluid for photocopiers or cleaning products – so in reality all workplaces are affected. The main areas that employers should focus on are:

- assessing the risk of substances used and identifying the required precautions
- introducing appropriate measures to control or prevent the risk
- ensuring the correct use of the control measures, and that equipment is regularly maintained
- conducting health surveillance to monitor health of employees where there is a known identifiable risk
- informing and training employees about risks that may arise from their work, and informing them of the necessary precautions to take.

The Framework Directive

The European Union Framework Directive has broad objectives which were implemented in EU member states by 31 December 1992. This established in general terms the European Commission's approach to health and safety. The main objectives of the directive were to introduce measures to encourage improvements in safety and health of workers at work. In order to do this it contains general principles concerning the prevention of occupational risks, the protection of health and safety, the elimination of risk and accident factors, as well as informing, consultation and providing balanced participation in accordance with national laws.

The British response to the EU directive was made in the Management of Health and Safety at Work Regulations 1992, which were accompanied by an approved Code of Practice which came into effect on 1 January 1993. Five further sets of regulations were also implemented in Britain on 1 January 1993 and all these have become known as the 'six-pack'. The 'six-pack' comprised:

- Management of Health and Safety at Work Regulations 1992
- Workplace (Health, Safety and Welfare) Regulations 1992
- Provision and Use of Work Equipment Regulations 1992
- Personal Protective Equipment at Work Regulations 1992
- Health and Safety (Display Screen Equipment) Regulations 1992
- Manual Handling Operations Regulations 1992.

Legislation becomes out of date and does not always meet the requirements of modern organisations, so amendments are often necessary. All of the original 'six-pack' regulations have been amended and updated so the new dates and any significant changes will be included with the regulations as they are discussed. The Provision and Use of Work Equipment was amended in 1998 and the Management of Health and Safety at Work Regulations in 1999. The remaining four regulations were also amended later under the Health and Safety (Miscellaneous Amendments) Regulations 2002.

The Management of Health and Safety at Work Regulations 1999 (MHSWR)

This is the law in the UK that implemented the Framework Directive. The HASAWA covered some parts of the directive but there were also new things that employers needed to do, such as carrying out certain detailed procedures, assessing risks, implementing certain safety measures and communicating with staff on health and safety. According to Stranks (2007a), 'these regulations do not stand alone – all other modern health and safety legislation such as the Workplace (Health, Safety and Welfare) Regulations 1992 and the Provision and Use of Work Equipment Regulations 1998, must be read in conjunction with the general duties under the MHSWR.' This is therefore a very important piece of legislation which has the following key features.

It states that employers shall:

- carry out assessment of health and safety risks to both employees and the public (this may be done in writing or on computer)
- monitor and review protective and preventive measures
- appoint a competent person or persons to be responsible for protective and preventive measures
- establish emergency procedures
- give comprehensible and relevant information and training to employees (the training can be provided by a suitable training provider other than the employer)
- cooperate with any other employers who may share the same work site.

Also, employees shall:

- use equipment in the way in which they have been trained to use it
- report any dangerous situations or any problem areas that they spot in the arrangements that the employer has made for health and safety.

These regulations are intended for use in cases of criminal action against an employer, and may not be used in any civil cases as evidence of negligence.

Pause for thought 11.2

To what extent do you feel that the Management of Health and Safety at Work Regulations 1999 differ from the HASAWA 1974?

These regulations are more forceful than HASAWA and specify that employers 'shall' do certain things, whereas HASAWA only expected employers to carry out its provisions 'so far as it is reasonably practicable' to do so.

The new regulations also mean that employers have a legal duty to predict what could go wrong, before it actually happens, and to take preventive action to avoid it happening. They must record the preventive action that they have taken. This is referred to as risk assessment and is the same principle as under COSHH, but it is now applied more widely. This will be discussed more fully later in the chapter.

The new regulations require employers to be proactive and actively manage activities aimed at protecting the health and safety of their employees. This is more in line than previous legislative measures with the human resource approach of being proactive and actively managing human resources.

Workplace (Health, Safety and Welfare) Regulations 1992, amended by the Health and Safety (Miscellaneous Amendments) Regulations 2002

This law is intended to rationalise older pieces of legislation and provide clearer ruling as to exactly what facilities the employer should provide for the employee. As stated earlier it is important that it is read in conjunction with the Management of Health and Safety at Work Regulations (MHSWR) 1999.

Employers shall:

- provide a good working environment with appropriate temperature, ventilation and level of lighting
- carry out maintenance and be responsible for keeping the workplace clean.

The 2002 amendments include further guidance for employers about achieving this, primarily in relation to rest rooms and rest areas. The amendments specify that there should be sufficient seats (with backs) and tables for the number of people likely to use them at any one time.

The 2002 amendment regulations state that employers must ensure they meet the needs of any disabled workers by also providing suitable rest areas for them. Other equipment and facilities, such as workstations, passageways, doors, and washroom facilities, should also be designed to meet the specific needs of disabled workers.

Provision and Use of Work Equipment Regulations 1998, amended by the Health and Safety (Miscellaneous Amendments) Regulations 2002

This law aims to bring together many older laws governing equipment used at work. Employers shall:

● consider when they purchase new equipment the working condition of the equipment and risks that it may pose to employees

● ensure the provision of appropriate levels of lighting and warnings about the safe use of the equipment

● ensure that the equipment is suitable for the use to which it will be put

● provide adequate information and training

● provide adequate protection from any potentially dangerous parts of the equipment or machinery.

Personal Protective Equipment at Work Regulations 1992, amended by the Health and Safety (Miscellaneous Amendments) Regulations 2002

These regulations replace part of more than 20 old pieces of legislation which were concerned with provision of protective equipment for employees. They aim to ensure suitable provision of protective equipment such as head protection, high visibility clothing or safety harnesses. Employers must ensure the equipment is appropriate for the likely type of risks, the specific working conditions in the workplace and the duration for which it is likely to be worn. In addition, they should consider the ergonomic requirements of the job, state of health of the person employed and any particular characteristics of their workstation that might affect the use of the personal protective equipment. Particular attention should also be paid to ensuring that the equipment provided is hygienic and compatible with any additional personal protective equipment that the worker may need to wear simultaneously.

Employers shall:

● ensure that equipment used is suitable for the job to be done

● adequately maintain, clean and replace equipment as necessary

● store it safely when it is not in use

● ensure correct use of the equipment

● inform and train employees in the correct use of the equipment.

Health and Safety (Display Screen Equipment) Regulations 1992, amended by the Health and Safety (Miscellaneous Amendments) Regulations 2002

This law implements the EU's Visual Display Unit Directive and specifies minimum levels of health and safety for people who spend a large part of their time at work working in front of computer screens or who are about to become employed in that capacity. It is primarily aimed at the prevention of damage to their upper limbs, and to prevent eye strain, fatigue and stress.

Employers shall:

- assess the risks and reduce any that are found
- ensure that workstations meet at least the minimum requirements
- ensure that the work is planned to include breaks and changes of activity
- arrange for employees to have their eyes tested regularly at time limits designated by the optician appointed by the employer and provide spectacles if necessary
- provide appropriate training for users or those about to become users of visual display units.

Eyesight tests should be completed as soon as possible after any request, or in the case of someone who is about to start work, before they become a computer user.

Manual Handling Operations Regulations 1992, amended by the Health and Safety (Miscellaneous Amendments) Regulations 2002

This aims to reduce the levels of injury and ill-health associated with manual handling of loads at work.

Employers shall:

- ensure, as far as is practicable, that employees do not need to use risky techniques when handling loads
- assess whether any risks are inherent in the manual handling that has to be done
- take necessary steps to reduce risks by introducing mechanical help, ensuring loads are lighter and assessing the capabilities of the individual
- ensure the provision of information to all employees
- if employees sometimes work on another employer's premises, liaise closely with the other employer.

When trying to determine whether each specific manual handling activity involves any risk, employers should pay particular attention to the following:

- the physical suitability of the employee for safely completing the particular form of manual handling required
- what the person is wearing and its suitability for the job
- the amount of knowledge and training that the person has received
- the results of any risk assessments that have already been completed that relate to the job
- whether the employee has been identified as being one of a group of employees who are particularly at risk
- the results of any health surveillance that has been undertaken.

This legislation is far reaching in its scope although its effects will vary from one organisation to another, depending on the nature of the work undertaken.

Reporting of Injuries, Diseases and Dangerous Occurrences Regulations (RIDDOR) 1995

RIDDOR requires employers to report certain work-related accidents, diseases and dangerous occurrences to the enforcing authorities so that they can identify risks and investigate serious accidents. The following briefly describes some of the circumstances in which reporting should occur:

● The death or major injury of an employee, or of a self-employed person working in the organisation, or of a member of the public must all be reported to the enforcing authorities immediately and this must be followed within 10 days by a completed accident report. Reportable major injuries include fractures, amputation, dislocation, loss of sight.

● If an employee or self-employed person working on your premises suffers an accident or injury which requires that person to be absent from work for at least three days, then a completed accident form must be sent to the enforcing authorities.

● Some work-related diseases, such as occupational dermatitis, skin cancer or occupational asthma have also to be reported on a disease report form to the enforcing authority, as do infections such as hepatitis, tetanus or tuberculosis.

● There may be instances where something occurs which does not actually result in a reportable injury but which could have done. For example, the collapse of a lift or an explosion in a closed vessel are likely to constitute a dangerous occurrence, even if no one is injured. Any dangerous occurrence has to be reported immediately by telephone to the enforcing authorities. An accident report form should also be completed within 10 days of the dangerous occurrence. (Details of where to find more information are given in 'Further study' at the end of the chapter.)

The enforcing authority will be the environmental health department of the local authority if the type of the business is an office, retail or wholesale, warehousing, hotel or catering, sports or leisure, a residential home or place of worship. Accidents or dangerous occurrences which happen in any other type of business will need to be reported to the area office of the Health and Safety Executive. Nowadays accidents and dangerous occurrences can even be reported using the Internet. Have a look at the websites at the end of this chapter for more details of how to do this.

The Working Time Regulations 1998

We discussed the Working Time Regulations 1998 briefly in Chapter 4, but have also included them here, since the hours people work can have a big impact on their health, wellbeing and safety in the workplace though other factors such as liking their job and the amount of support they get from colleagues can mitigate against some of these negative effects (CIPD, 2010a).

It has often been claimed that the UK is the 'long hours capital' of Europe and that working such long hours adversely affects workers' health. In some organisations there is a culture of 'presenteeism', where people are expected to arrive early for work and leave late, forgoing home and social life. While some workers thrive in a long hours culture and live to work, such a culture is likely to hide a great deal of inefficiency and result in increased levels of stress and ill-health for many other workers. These regulations attempt to control the hours worked and control the way the hours are organised. They also establish minimum holiday levels for employees in the UK, although it is frequently claimed that a large number of UK employees actually fail to take all the holiday they are entitled to, either because they are too busy or are too frightened to be away from work for their whole holiday entitlement.

Did you know?

Death from overwork is so common in Japan that they even have a special word for it, *Karoshi*. The first documented case of Karoshi occurred in Japan in 1969 but there have been many cases since. In Japan the spouses of those who have died from Karoshi have won claims for compensation from the companies concerned and each year between 20 and 60 claims for compensation are brought. This is still probably a gross underestimate of the real number of cases of Karoshi in Japan.

(Source: Nishiyama and Johnson, 1977)

The recession in 2008 and 2009 caused the percentage of people working more than 45 hours per week in the UK to fall from 20.4 per cent to 19.3 per cent. Philpott (2010) says that this may have been just temporary as there are now some indications that the total number of hours worked each week have been increasing since mid-2009, but the numbers of people working between 18 and 30 hours per week have also increased. He claims it would be more appropriate to talk not of a long hours culture, but of a mixed hours culture as while it is true that one in five workers do work more than 45 hours per week there are also a similar number of people working between 16 and 30 hours per week.

Although the 48-hour working week means workers in the UK still work much longer hours than their counterparts in France, it is nevertheless considerably better than the expectation in countries such as Japan. In Japan it has been documented that many workers regularly work for over 100 hours per week, for many weeks, or even years at a time and that this frequently leads, not surprisingly, to ill-health or even death. Since we work increasingly in a global economy, where people are constantly accessible via mobile phones or email, these long-hour work practices are spreading to the USA and the UK.

From 2009 statutory holiday entitlement is 5.6 weeks. This right applies to all workers and not just employees. (The distinction between workers and employees will be discussed in Chapter 12.) Having rights to holiday is not of much use if workers do not take them and employers should take steps to make sure that workers use their holiday entitlement. They should discourage a culture of presenteeism and regard this as good management practice and as a way of contributing to the prevention of ill health.

● Legislation about smoking

Four related pieces of legislation have been introduced in Scotland, Wales, Northern Ireland and England prohibiting smoking in public places, including workplaces, and similar legislation has been introduced throughout the rest of Europe.

The Smoking, Health and Social Care (Scotland) Act 2005 was the first to come into effect and resulted in a ban on smoking in public places, including workplaces from March 2006. A similar ban on smoking in public places came into effect in Wales from 2 April 2007, in Northern Ireland from 30 April 2007 and in England from 1 July 2007. These related pieces of legislation are designed to protect workers who may previously have been affected by passive smoking and also to promote positive health improvements by encouraging smokers to stop.

● The Corporate Manslaughter and Corporate Homicide Act 2007

The Corporate Manslaughter and Corporate Homicide Act 2007 made corporate manslaughter a criminal offence from April 2008. This has also increased the interest in health safety and wellbeing as companies found guilty could face an unlimited fine if they are found to have caused death through gross negligence or failures in their safety systems. People working for some organisations such as Crown bodies, previously exempt from prosecution, are now covered by this legislation. While this is to be welcomed, Richard Jones (2007) argues that it does not go far enough and that there are still too many exemptions. He goes on to say that 'HR needs to actively engage workers in helping keep workplaces safe, and should regularly consult them on health and safety issues.' Safety should certainly be of concern to all managers including HR managers and line managers.

Most of the legislation discussed here, with the exception of the anti-smoking legislation, has focused primarily on safety although clearly health and wellbeing are also closely linked to this.

The people and organisations involved in health, safety and wellbeing

We have already discussed at length the roles of employers and employees but there are other health, safety and wellbeing roles currently undertaken by the Health and Safety Executive and local authorities. What do these organisations actually do? How are they organised?

In 1999 John Prescott, who was the Deputy Prime Minister at that time, announced a new impetus for health and safety called Revitalising Health and Safety. He said that the Health and Safety at Work Act 1974 had done its job as evidenced by the fact that the 'number of deaths at work today is a quarter of the 1971 level'. However, he wanted a strategic appraisal of the health and safety framework in order to build on the work of the previous 25 years and to establish a new agenda for the first 25 years of the new century (Prescott, 2000). As a part of the Revitalising Health and Safety impetus, targets were set from 2000 onwards which were to be achieved by 2010. These targets were to reduce the number of days lost due to work-related injuries per 100,000 workers by 30 per cent, to reduce the incidence of work-related ill health by 20 per cent and to reduce the numbers of fatalities at work by 10 per cent. The assessment of whether or not these targets have been achieved will start in autumn 2010 but will only be completed by autumn 2011.

Pause for thought 11.3 To what extent do you think that targets are useful in health, safety and wellbeing? Go to www.hse.gov.uk and check for yourself whether or not these targets have been met. What more can organisations do to become healthy and safe workplaces?

Another concern was to simplify and streamline the number of organisations involved in Health and Safety. The merger of the Health and Safety Commission and the Health and Safety Executive in 2008 was a direct response to that concern but the Conservative–Liberal Democrat Coalition Government subsequently announced further plans to streamline health and asked Lord Young of Graffham, a former cabinet minister, to review health and safety legislation (Woolf and Dowling, 2010).

The Health and Safety Executive (HSE)

The HSE is responsible for promoting better health and safety at work within Great Britain. Its mission is:

The prevention of death, injury and ill-health to those at work and those affected by work activities (HSE, 2010d).

It consists of policy advisers, inspectors and experts in medicine, science and technology. They are responsible for making provision for enforcing the legislation, for dealing with daily administration and conducting research and for identifying any new risks or hazards that emerge with changes to technology or work practices.

In June 2009 HSE launched a new strategy *The Health and Safety of Great Britain: Be Part of the Solution* and one of its key features is that it sets out to involve all stakeholders in health and safety. Hackitt (2010b) emphasises the fact that while HSE and their local authority partners lead and coordinate health and safety, the success of the strategy relies on everyone playing a part and not just leaving it to these groups. This is particularly important as the UK economic situation improves as traditionally any improvement to the economy has also resulted in an increase in work-related accidents and ill-health.

Alongside local authorities HSE is also an independent regulator for health and safety and their main role is to assist others in preventing work-related accidents and ill-health. Its inspectors can achieve this by conducting workplace inspections and by other more proactive measures such as getting stakeholders involved and providing guidance by giving information and advice.

Local authorities (LA)

Local authorities also have responsibility for enforcement of health and safety in approximately 194,000 workplaces. Under HASAWA, the Secretary of State for Work and Pensions (DWP) can make regulations for local authorities to take on responsibility for certain activities and to ensure that there is no duplication of effort between them and the Health and Safety Executive. The local authority inspectors, normally known as environmental health officers, are responsible for health and safety mainly in the services sector, while the HSE tends to concentrate on the more hazard-prone industries. There is a liaison committee which ensures consistency of approach between the HSE and local authorities. The HSE publishes a wide range of material each year explaining its role and the practical implications of legislation. The Health and Safety Executive can provide guidance, approved codes of practice and regulations.

The Gangmasters Licensing Authority (GLA)

Not all workers are lucky enough to work in well-organised and regulated workplaces even in the UK. The death of 18 Chinese cockle pickers in Morecambe Bay, Lancashire,

The people and organisations involved in health, safety and wellbeing

in 2004 drew attention to the world of unscrupulous operators who employ migrant workers, sometimes illegally, to work in low-skilled jobs. The Gangmasters Licensing Authority was formed to license genuine workforce organisers and providers of migrant workers and has the power to revoke licences where poor practice has occurred. Initially legislation targeted the agricultural sector where gangmasters and migrant workers primarily worked. However, it is claimed by MPs and trade unions that 'legislation to regulate gangmasters in the agricultural sector could be pushing unscrupulous operators into providing workers for care homes instead' (CIPD, 2007). The Labour MP Jim Sheridan who was responsible for legislation creating the GLA has been pushing for a new bill to extend the GLA's remit could be rolled out universally sector by sector. There are really important health and safety issues here. We don't want workers to be abused or intimidated, but we don't want them in skilled jobs either if they are not qualified' (CIPD, 2007).

The world of work has changed dramatically over the years and there is now a much more diverse workforce working in increasingly flexible ways. These new aims are intended to address this. New health and safety issues arise as people work from home, or while on the move, and the risks to their health and safety also need to be assessed. There are also fewer large employers and more small ones.

● The enforcing authorities

We shall now discuss how the current inspection of workplaces and investigation of accidents is shared between HSE inspectors and local authority enforcement officers. Basically the HSE inspectors cover work conducted primarily in factories, building sites, mines, fairgrounds, quarries, railways, chemical plants, offshore and nuclear installations, some warehouses, most offices, hotels, catering, consumer services, sports and leisure activities and places of worship. Both have similar powers of enforcement. These include a right to:

- enter employers' premises
- carry out inspections/investigations
- take equipment or materials on to premises
- take measurements, photographs or recordings
- carry out tests on articles or substances
- examine books and documents
- issue improvement notices
- issue prohibition notices
- issue a Crown notice.

The last three points are very important and we shall consider each in turn. However, sometimes when an enforcing inspector finds a breach of the law which is relatively minor they may feel that improvement notices and prohibition notices are not appropriate.

Informal methods

In the case of a minor breach in legislation the inspector may choose to use informal methods and may simply give the employer or contractor advice about what they should do to comply with the law, and explain the reasons.

Improvement notices

If the inspector feels that an organisation is contravening one of the relevant provisions of legislation then they can issue an improvement notice which will specify that improvements must be made within a specified time limit to bring the equipment or process up to the required standard of safety.

Prohibition notices

If when the inspector visits they feel that there is serious danger or risk of injury to employees, they can issue a prohibition notice which will stop work activity immediately until the risk has been dealt with. In some circumstances a deferred prohibition order may be issued: this would occur, for example, if it would be difficult to stop a process in mid-cycle or if there was no immediate risk of injury.

Crown notices

This is a type of notice which HSE can issue to a Crown organisation such as a government department or the Prison Service. It would be issued under the same sort of circumstances that would merit a prohibition notice or improvement notice for other organisations.

The Health and Safety Commission's Enforcement Policy Statement (2008) states the approach which both the Health and Safety Executive and local authorities should take in relation to law enforcement. The overall aims of the HSC are to protect the health, safety and wellbeing of employees and to safeguard others such as members of the public who may be exposed to risk from the workplace or activity.

Normally in England and Wales most prosecutions would go to a magistrates' court but more serious cases are referred to the Crown Courts. Under the Scottish judicial system the majority of cases go to a sheriff court or before a jury. Organisations and individuals can face prosecution, and prison sentences and unlimited fines can also be given by the Crown Courts.

Any accidents at work that result in death are treated as manslaughter. The police are involved in these cases and have overall responsibility for them. However, there had been general dissatisfaction that the system was not tough enough and that employers were on occasions shirking their responsibilities with regard to health and safety and frequently escaping prosecution even when an employee had died as a result of the company's actions or inactions. The Corporate Manslaughter and Corporate Homicide Act (2007), mentioned earlier, is intended to create a criminal offence of corporate manslaughter for the first time. According to Baker (2007), 'The law is likely to lead to more prosecutions for deaths resulting from an organisation's acts or omissions, and may lead to higher fines. It will certainly lead to greater scrutiny by the courts of the way in which companies organise themselves internally in terms of health and safety.' This should make it easier to examine the conduct of senior managers, and a company can be found guilty of corporate manslaughter if it can be proved that the way they managed and organised their activities led to a death and that this amounted to a gross breach of its duty of care to the employee.

In 2008 the HSE (HSE, 2008) revised its Enforcement Policy Statement to reflect the merger between HSC and HSE and it restated the criteria for whether or not particular incidents or complaints should be investigated. This Policy Statement stresses five main things:

1 *The principle of proportionality.* This means that the severity of the action taken should be in proportion to the level of risk and the seriousness of the breach of law.

2 *Targeting.* The people/organisations who cause the most serious risks or who have failed to control hazards in the workplace adequately should be the ones to be targeted by the inspectors.

3 *Consistency.* For people to have faith in the system and the inspectors they need to feel that they will be treated in a consistently fair way. This does not mean identical treatment for duty holders but involves taking a similar approach when the circumstances seem similar and consequently achieving similar ends.

4 *Transparency.* Every action taken should be clear, with explanations given for any action that is taken so that duty holders know what is expected form them in relation to health, safety and wellbeing.

5 *Accountability.* The enforcing authorities must be held accountable for their actions and so must have policies and standards to be assessed against. They also need to have clear ways for people to make comments or complaints and for dealing with these (HSE, 2008).

Prosecution

If the case is very serious then the inspector may also need to initiate a prosecution. Any decision about whether or not to prosecute will be taken after considering the HSE's Enforcement Policy Statement.

Safety representatives

As we said earlier, there is a duty for employers to consult with and involve safety representatives in the workplace. In October 1978 the Safety Representatives and Safety Committees Regulations came into effect. These regulations form part of the Health and Safety at Work Act, and within a year over 100,000 safety representatives were in post. The regulations provide that any recognised trade union can appoint safety representatives, and they recommend that in general the people who are appointed should have worked for that employer for at least two years so that they have a reasonable range of experience from which to draw. In some trade unions the shop stewards take on the role of safety representatives, while in others the safety representative is a separate post. The people to fill these positions are, however, selected by the trade union, not by the management. Organisations where there are no recognised trade unions can still appoint safety representatives, and they are normally elected by the workforce. As more employers start to appreciate that there are benefits for the business and a clear return on investment to be gained from focussing attention on health, safety and wellbeing, this role could become even more important.

The safety representative's main function is to represent the employee in consultation with the employer on issues relating to health and safety in the workplace, and they can investigate hazards or potential hazards as well as carrying out inspections of the workplace. They are entitled to paid time off to perform their duties and for training to enable them to carry out their duties effectively, and they may also require some facilities such as the use of a telephone, a filing cabinet and a room to conduct interviews. If two or more safety representatives make a written request to management for a safety committee to be established, then the employer is legally obliged to fulfil that request.

The Management of Health and Safety at Work Regulations 1992 (MHSWR) as amended in 1999 add to the Safety Representatives and Safety Committees Regulations 1977 and specify that every employer shall consult safety representatives in good time with regard to:

● the introduction of any measure at the workplace which may substantially affect health or safety of the workforce

● arrangements for appointing or nominating a 'competent person' who is able to assist the employer to carry out risk assessment exercises and help them in carrying out duties in relation to health and safety

● the health and safety information that the employer is supposed to provide to employees

● the planning and organisation of health and safety training

● the health and safety consequences of the introduction of new technology at work.

There are, as you can see, a wide range of duties performed by safety representatives. Safety representatives usually receive excellent training from trades unions for this demanding role and those who take on these roles can also choose to take the training further and use it as part of a professional qualification in health and safety.

Safety officer or safety adviser

None of the legislation actually specifies the need for a safety officer but, as the law has grown in complexity, many organisations have felt that it is necessary to appoint a person to specialise in this area of work. This is a management appointment and must not be confused with the trade union/employee-appointed safety representative. Safety officers are sometimes appointed to advise senior management without being part of any other department and report directly to the board, but in many organisations they form part of the human resource management department. Smaller organisations may not wish to appoint a full-time safety officer and may instead call on the expertise provided by independent consultants to act as safety advisers. It is important that anyone appointed as safety officer or safety adviser has the status and level of competence to provide authoritative advice to management and the workforce on aspects of health and safety.

A competent person

This has a specific meaning in terms of health and safety as the Framework Directive (Article 7), which is discussed later, says that employers must designate 'a competent

The people and organisations involved in health, safety and wellbeing

person' who has practical and theoretical knowledge of particular equipment and who is able to identify any problems that may occur with it. The provision of this directive is reflected in Regulation 6 of the Management of Health and Safety at Work Regulations 1992 and clearly refers to a management nominee, although not necessarily to the safety officer but to someone who because of their knowledge and experience of particular machinery, plant or equipment is able to identify problems or defects in it. That person needs to be competent not just to do the job but to carry out risk assessment for health and safety for employees and the public, and must monitor and review protective and preventive measures. A safety officer may fulfil this role but is not likely to be the only designated competent person, as they are unlikely to have the required level of knowledge or experience for all machinery.

Safety committees

Safety committees have to be established, as we said earlier, if two or more safety representatives request the organisation to do so, but many organisations do not wait for this request, and it is good practice to set up a safety committee in any case. The main objective of a safety committee is to promote cooperation between employers and employees in instigating, developing and carrying out measures to ensure the health and safety at work of employees. In organisations seeking to improve health, safety and wellbeing this provides a useful way of gaining increased employee engagement. Safety committees are likely to provide some or all of the following functions:

- study figures and trends for accidents and notifiable diseases
- examine safety audit reports
- consider reports and factual information provided by inspectors
- consider the reports of safety representatives
- assist in development of safety rules and safe systems of work
- monitor the effectiveness of safety training in the workplace
- monitor the effectiveness of the safety and health communication in the workplace
- encourage publicity for health and safety programmes in the workplace
- provide a link with the appropriate inspectorates.

Membership of the health and safety committee

The membership of the committee should be agreed between management and the employees. The committee should normally include equal numbers of people from management and the workforce and should have representation from different areas of the workforce and different grades of management. People such as the organisation's doctor, nurse or safety officer should also be invited to attend as *ex officio* members. It is a good idea for the person who chairs the committee to have sufficient status within the organisation that they can authorise money to be spent on necessary aspects of health and safety without having to refer all such decisions to higher authority. A senior member of the management team would fulfil this role well, although in many organisations the chair of the safety committee may also alternate between management and the workforce.

Health and safety arrangements

Safety policy statement

You will remember that under HASAWA one of the duties of an employer is to provide a safety policy statement to show each person's responsibilities and the arrangements they have made to carry out the policy. The safety policy applies to all organisations that employ more than five employees. This is supposed to be a document that can be used to show in a practical way how the arrangements for health and safety are to be carried out in the workplace, and it should be designed to have a genuine effect on health and safety working practices. This means that it should be clearly written and should be easily available to any employee, and a copy should preferably be given to each employee. It does not mean that it is a secret document, as some organisations in our experience seem to think, kept locked in a filing cabinet well away from the gaze of employees. In order to encourage awareness of health and safety and produce an effective safety policy document, it is also advisable that a range of people, including workforce representatives, should be involved in its design and that key decision makers have been involved fully in these discussions. In some organisations a person will be chosen to champion the policy and targets for improvements in specific areas of health and safety may also be set. Arrangements should also be made to review the health and safety policy regularly, at least annually, since what is important is whether the policy is having an effect on health and safety in the workplace, rather than how well written it is.

The HSE has examples of policies for health and safety and risk assessment on their website (**www.hse.gov.uk**) and while individual organisations are recommended to design their own policies to suit their organisations the model health and safety policy arranges issues in columns under three headings. These are:

● Statement of general policy
● Responsibility for health and safety
● Actions/arrangements made for health and safety.

Statement of general policy

The safety policy should show management's approach to health and safety and should indicate what management plan to do in relation to different aspects of health and safety such as the prevention of accidents, training for health and safety or the ways for engaging with the workforce about health and safety.

Responsibility for health and safety

The second column should indicate who is actually responsible for each of the specific tasks. The safety policy is basically concerned with people, their duties and their accountability. It could also include a management chart showing the chain of command in respect of health and safety, with a clear statement that the ultimate responsibility for health and safety rests with the board or chief executive or equivalent. The safety policy document should carry at the end the signature of the person with the ultimate responsibility for health and safety at work. There should be a clearly defined role for the safety adviser, if such a position exists, and clear explanation of their relationship to senior management and line management. This part of the document should also indicate the role of those appointed as 'competent persons' to assist the employer in implementing the safety policy.

The action/practical arrangements

This section should establish systems and procedures and the practical arrangements for their implementation. It should also show the system for monitoring safety and for publishing results. The section of the safety policy covering arrangements should be a practical section that is regularly reviewed and updated.

Some of the topics that could be included under the arrangements for managing health and safety are listed below.

- Any specific health and safety risks that arise from the organisation's work activities
- Arrangements for consultation with employees
- Arrangements to ensure that plant and equipment are safe to use
- Arrangements for organising the safe handling and use of substances
- Systems for the provision of information, instruction and supervision
- Ways of ensuring competency for tasks and training
- Methods for dealing with accidents, first aid and work-related ill-health
- Methods to be used for monitoring all aspects of health and safety
- The arrangements that have been made for emergency procedures such as for fire and evacuation
- Details of any specific key areas of risk for jobs in that organisation.

Specific health and safety risks arising from an organisation's work activities

This means that the arrangements for carrying out risk assessments, the results of the risk assessments and the actions taken will all need to be shown, although the findings and resulting actions will need to be shown in a separate document. The HSE's template for a health and safety policy also gives a template for conducting risk assessments and HSE (2010f) suggest both should be prepared at the same time. Risk assessments will be discussed in more detail later in the chapter.

Consultation with employees

We have already discussed the fact that if there is a recognised trade union which has appointed safety representatives then by law they must be consulted about any changes likely to affect the health and safety of their members. If there is not a recognised trade union then the employers must consult their employees directly or through a works council.

Safe plant and equipment

This requirement is taken directly from HASAWA and means that employers must keep vehicles, machinery and equipment in good working order. In the safety policy, the names of people responsible for this should be stated, as should arrangements to deal with problems. Those responsible for checking that new machinery and equipment meets the required standards should also be listed here. Records of maintenance and service history of vehicles should be kept, perhaps separately in a log book.

Safe handling and use of substances

This section relates to those responsible for identifying substances that need a COSHH assessment. Once again the names of people with responsibilities should be listed here. This includes the names of those carrying out the assessments, those responsible for ensuring that any actions needed are taken, those who have to tell employees about the results of the assessments as well as the names of those people who have responsibility for checking the safety of new substances prior to purchase. There should also be an indication as to the frequency of assessments.

Information, instruction and supervision

This should show where health and safety law posters are displayed or where leaflets relating to health and safety are kept. It should also detail where health and safety advice can be obtained and the names of those responsible for supervising the work of trainees or young employees.

Competency for tasks and training

The names of people who provide induction training and job-specific training should be listed here. Some jobs may pose particular risks, for example the risk of back injury to workers involved in the manual handling of heavy or awkwardly shaped goods. Both the jobs and the training needed should also be identified. Training records should be kept for all health and safety training as well as other training and the safety policy should indicate where the records are stored and by whom.

Accidents, first aid and work-related ill-health

In this section any health surveillance required for certain jobs, such as work with flour, asbestos or some chemicals, needs to be identified. This should mean any problems in a worker's health caused by the job will be identified at an early stage so that action can be taken to prevent their health becoming worse. It shows who is responsible for health surveillance and where records are kept.

The locations of first aid boxes need to be shown and first aiders should be listed. Records of all accidents, however trivial, and instances of work-related ill-health should be recorded in the accident book and the location of this book should also be given in the health and safety policy.

Monitoring

It is very important that the policy is used and that good practices are checked regularly. Those who have responsibility for checking that working conditions are safe and that safe practices are being followed should be listed here, as should those who are responsible for carrying out investigations of accidents or investigating work-related causes of sickness absence.

Emergency procedures – fire and evacuation

Obviously it is important that there are adequate safety procedures in place in case there is a need to evacuate the building in an emergency. In this section it is important to state who checks the escape routes and the frequency of these checks. Safety equipment such as fire extinguishers have to be maintained and checked, alarms need to be tested, emergency evacuation drills need to be carried out and records of these must be kept.

Key areas of risk

These will vary depending on the organisation and the type of work undertaken, but might include risks relating to particularly dangerous substances such as asbestos, or to stress or potential violence to staff from members of the public. Each organisation will need to carry out its own risk assessments relating to the areas of risk which are identified.

People need to be aware of their responsibilities as, if something goes wrong and a serious accident occurs, the relevant enforcement officers will want to know who was responsible. These enforcement officers would carry out a full investigation and would also want to examine the safety policy document. If a supervisor did not know that they were responsible for checking that a protective guard was in place, then the employer would have to be able to prove that they had informed the supervisor of their responsibilities and had also trained them adequately in the fulfilment of these responsibilities. Many tasks will of course be delegated to different levels of management and employees do, as we have seen, have some responsibility for their own actions. Senior management cannot, however, abdicate their ultimate responsibility for overall safety within the organisation, and must try to ensure the health and safety of their employees and others affected by their employees' actions. Those who carry the ultimate responsibility for this, such as the board of directors, could face prosecution and possibly a large fine or even a spell in prison for individual directors if their organisation is found to be at fault. Similarly, others with specific responsibilities such as safety officers, human resource managers, line managers or training officers could be charged and convicted of an offence.

First consider the following case study and identify the health, safety and wellbeing issues that you think occur here, then complete Activity 11.3.

CASE STUDY 11.1 Health and safety

The Sheffley Company employs nearly 330 employees and specialises in the production of steel castings. The organisation has a director, Mr Jones, whose great-grandfather founded the business. There is a new production manager, Mr Tandy, an import and export manager, Ms Jeffries; and an administration manager, Mrs Groves. Mr Tandy has eight line managers reporting to him, who have a total of 280 employees working for them. Mrs Groves has a payroll manager, a canteen manager and a personnel officer reporting to her and Ms Jeffries runs the purchasing, goods inward and goods outward departments, and the warehouse and export sections.

The work involved in the production of steel castings is hazardous and the company has not had a good record with regard to health and safety. It is not only in the production areas that there have been problems – the offices also have suffered rather a large number of accidents which have required employees to have more than three days off work to recover. The office staff are expected to regularly work long hours and work whatever hours are necessary to complete the job. Several are absent with serious long-term illnesses including the payroll manager and of course this puts additional pressure on those who remain. Mrs Groves is beginning to show signs of the strain from doing her own job and that of the absent payroll officer and is suffering from regular headaches and feelings of anxiety.

The new production manager decides that something must be done about the record on health, safety and wellbeing. He decides a punitive approach will work best and in the weekly meeting with the production supervisors he informs them that from next week any employee who does not wear the protective equipment provided will be dismissed. The safety equipment comprises safety boots, safety goggles and overalls.

During the lead-up to the introduction of the safety equipment, notices are put up to explain the disciplinary penalty for non-compliance with the regulation, but information about the use and location of some of the equipment is not provided. Neither the safety representatives nor the safety committee have the opportunity to inspect the new protective equipment or to advise employees on its suitability.

The employees prove to be reluctant to wear the protective goggles which, they complain, pinch their skin and impair their vision. The production manager realises that the enforcement of safety is going to be problematic, and at the next week's meeting informs the supervisors that they do not have to be too rigid in their enforcement of the rules.

Two serious accidents occur just a month later in the production area and a further serious accident occurs in the offices. In the first incident molten metal splashes onto the foot of an employee, causing serious burns. In a separate accident a few days later an employee slips, splashing molten metal close to his eyes. Luckily his sight is saved, but he suffers severe burns and scarring. The accident record in the offices is also unsatisfactory, and one employee is injured when chemicals used in the photocopier spill on her leg, causing a severe itchy rash to develop. She has been having problems at home but has felt she must keep working although her mind has not been on her work all the time. Other employees in the wages office complain of backaches and headaches which they say are caused by poor lighting, uncomfortable chairs and badly adjusted screens on their visual display units.

You should be able to identify some of the many issues raised here about health, safety and the wellbeing of the employees such as the exact nature of the employer and employee responsibilities. The employer in this case, and indeed anyone involved in this area of work, also needs to comply with legislation, so, based on your reading of the chapter so far, you should also be able to identify the key legislation infringed by both the employer and the employees. A full discussion of this case study can be found if you go to our website at **www.pearsoned.co.uk/foothook**.

ACTIVITY 11.3

Design a safety policy statement for Sheffley Company. Remember that this should be a practical document that can be used by people in the organisation. Use the sections and main headings that we have given earlier (see pages 399–401).

Risk assessment

The idea of assessing and controlling risks was introduced to Britain with the Control of Substances Hazardous to Health Regulations 1988, when employers had to assess the risk of harm to people from certain substances being used at work. This was developed further in the 'six-pack' regulations in 1992. The 1992 Code of Practice for the Management of Health and Safety at Work made it a legal duty for employers to assess and record health and safety risks, and to appoint a 'competent person', i.e. a person who has been suitably trained, and who is allowed adequate time and facilities, to perform this role and assist in this and other safety tasks.

Every organisation has to carry out its own risk assessment, and strategies for this should be devised by management after consultation with all interested groups in the workforce.

According to the HSE in the booklet *Five Steps to Risk Assessment* (HSE 2006), the five main steps involved in assessing risks and hazards in the workplace are:

1 Identify the hazards.
2 Decide who might be harmed and how.
3 Evaluate the risks and decide on precautions.
4 Record your findings and implement them.
5 Review your assessment and update if necessary.

Assessments do not have to be carried out by health and safety experts and small organisations may choose to undertake the initial assessment of risk by themselves; alternatively, they may prefer to employ a consultant.

Steps 1 and 2 Identify the hazards and decide who may be harmed by them

Most organisations should be able to carry out the first two steps quite easily and identify sources of risk and then identify those who may be harmed by the risks. Many of the risks will probably be well known to you already such as the risk of slipping in areas where the floor may sometimes be wet, but sometimes even obvious hazards such as this are ignored. Identifying hazards involves looking and talking to people in the area being assessed. It also involves identifying which groups of workers are likely to suffer harm and the type of injury that they are likely to suffer.

Step 3 Evaluate the risks and decide on precautions

Once you have identified the hazards and those likely to be affected by them then you must do something about them. Remember under the Health and Safety at Work Act 1974 you have to do everything that is 'reasonably practicable' to protect people from harm.

Pause for thought 11.4

If the floor is sometimes wet due to cleaning or spillages, what could you do as a precaution?

It is best to try to get rid of the risk if it is possible but if not then ways to minimise the risk should be tried. What could you do to prevent accidents in the case of a wet floor that was slippery in your college/university or workplace?

Your answers should follow the following order if possible. Complete them in the grid below.

Order for trying to control risks	Your response to each of these where there is a wet and slippery floor
1 Try to find a way of doing the job that carries less risk	
2 Ensure people don't come into contact with the hazard	
3 Minimise exposure to the hazard	
4 Issue personal protective clothing	
5 Provide adequate facilities to deal properly with people who have suffered in some way because they come into contact with the problem	

Go to www.pearsoned.uk/foothook now to check your answers to this exercise.

Step 4 Record your findings and implement them

Small organisations with five employees or fewer do not have to record their findings but it would be good practice to do so anyway. Workers need to know what is happening as far as minimising risks is concerned and it also helps to involve them more in health and safety. According to the HSE (2006) employers need to show that:

● a proper check was made;
● you asked who might be affected;
● you dealt with all significant hazards, taking into account the number of people who could be involved;
● the precautions are reasonable, and the remaining risk low; and
● you involved your staff or their representatives in the process.

Although it would be excellent if you could tackle all hazards immediately this will probably not be practicable so you need to plan an order of priority. Which are the most dangerous hazards? Which are quick and easy to solve? Are there any temporary solutions that could be used while a longer term solution is being organised? How will you monitor your solutions are working? Who is due to take action on each point and by when?

Step 5 Review your risk assessment and update if necessary

All workplaces are subject to constant change so something that works well at first may, due to changing circumstances or work patterns, no longer be so effective. Therefore the risk assessment needs to be monitored on a regular basis. For some organisations where there is a great deal of change this may involve reviewing risk assessments on a monthly or perhaps even weekly basis, while for other organisations an annual review may be more appropriate unless some unexpected change makes it more urgent to review risks.

Pause for thought 11.5 Do you think there is too much emphasis on risk assessment, or not enough?

Michael Gove, the education secretary, believes parents are often frustrated by the lack of adventure in education in schools as activities have been restricted because of health and safety concerns and he says that this will be tackled by Government.

Garath Malone's TV series about the education of boys where he attempts to improve the literacy skills of boys by getting them to do more adventurous and often more dangerous things seems in tune with Gove's views. Blogging teachers responded to the programme by saying it was unreal as they would have to complete mountains of paperwork and face tons of red tape in conducting risk assessments to submit to local authorities before any such activities would be possible. It seems Michael Gove intends to change the health and safety laws to lessen the amount of risk assessment that schools have to do and also wants to change the compensation culture so it becomes more difficult to sue if accidents occur (Millard, 2010).

What do you think? Should there be more opportunities for adventure combined with less risk assessment in schools?

Should it be more difficult for parents of a child injured in an accident at a school to sue?

Wellbeing

One of the earliest roles for HR specialists included that of the welfare officer (Fowler, 1994). The focus of this role was on the wellbeing of employees and it sometimes meant taking a paternalistic viewpoint, i.e. adopting a moral stance and telling people what was best for them. The modern HR function has changed and become more complex, adopting a more strategic and integrated approach to human resource management, a theme taken up in a number of chapters. Individual wellbeing, however, is still a factor which has an obvious impact on employees' ability to function at high levels and add value to their organisation. Employees who cannot concentrate at work or who may even stay away from work because of physical or psychological health problems obviously cannot contribute to their full potential, which has a negative impact on the goal of high-performance working (Incomes Data Services, 2002). In this context, the Engineering Employers' Federation (EEF, 2001) identifies effective stress management as 'a key part of a positive, proactive human resources policy'.

The Health and Safety Executive (HSE) has also been focusing on ways to draw all employers' attention to the benefits to be gained from a more proactive approach. The Revitalising Health and Safety initiatives were started because organisations are operating more and more in new ways with increasingly flexible methods of working. This has been followed by a new strategy called *The Health and Safety of Great Britain: Be Part of the Solution*. The HSE has been consulting and working with employers to demonstrate the business case for improved health and safety measures and for the need to involve everyone in this.

● The role of the employer in employee wellbeing

One area of debate on the subject of wellbeing is whether this is a personal and private matter. We have already said that there is a business case for employer involvement in the health and safety of their workforce but should an employer also have a right to enquire into other aspects of the wellbeing of employees that involve their private lives? If so, how far should this go?

Go to our website at **www.pearsoned.co.uk/foothook** for further discussion and to check your arguments with ours.

If an employee's personal problems result in falling standards at work, or even in an event that could be construed as misconduct, this could result in formal disciplinary action. On the whole, managers prefer to handle such issues in an informal manner to preserve good working relationships, and regard formal discipline as an action to be taken if the informal approach fails. This approach is encouraged by the ACAS guidelines on discipline (2009). You will find a fuller discussion of this in Chapter 12. It should suffice to make the point here that the proper use of counselling may obviate the need to embark on formal disciplinary action. According to the Inland Revenue Service (2007) at least one in five employers do provide employee assistance programmes (EAPs) though most are actually funded by the employer and are provided on their behalf by external suppliers. Typically about 10 per cent of the workforce use the EAP in any year but the popularity of EAPs has increased with employers after a legal case in 2002, when it was argued that just having an EAP provided sufficient defence for an employer against stress compensation claims. This was subsequently modified in a 2007 case so that it is not now possible just to rely on this as a defence in stress management cases. Typically the EAP service provided involves help with counselling, often by providing access to telephone helplines and to specialist advisers. Since corporate manslaughter is now a criminal offence employers should certainly be diligent in their responsibilities regarding any health, safety or wellbeing issues that could result in death and should of course take their responsibilities for all health, safety and wellbeing issues equally seriously.

Finally, we can justify an employer's interest in the wellbeing of employees with reference to the basic need to develop good working relationships, on the part of individual employees, individual managers, and from a corporate point of view. Abraham Maslow (1954) was one of the first writers to describe motivation in terms of human needs, and these concepts have often been applied to the workplace. One of the needs that Maslow identified is the social need for relationships, and indeed the importance of relationships has been reinforced by the inclusion of this factor in the HSE's list of aspects of stress management. A number of surveys on motivation have identified the importance of good relationships at work, and specifically the relationship between supervisor and subordinate. It is not inappropriate to care about the people we work with. Much has also been written about corporate image, and many employers wish to be recognised as 'good employers', especially since corporate image can affect an organisation's ability to attract and retain good employees and can therefore have a major impact on the success of the organisation.

The reasons for employers to be involved with employees' problems can be summarised as follows:

● to address problems with productivity, standards of work, attendance and turnover
● to meet legal obligations to ensure the health, safety and wellbeing of employees
● to avoid the development of disciplinary problems
● to maintain good employee relations
● to improve performance as a part of the performance management process.

Types of problem and their sources

There can be an infinite range of personal problems faced by workers which could affect their work. Many will arise from sources outside the organisation, such as family breakdown, alcoholism, drug abuse, care duties or bereavement, while others might be the result of bullying, working conditions, excessive workload or some form of discrimination in the workplace. The HR department needs to be clear about each of these issues and have policies and procedures in place to deal with issues such as alcoholism or drug abuse and should certainly also have effective policies to prevent unfair discrimination or bullying within work. It is not within the scope of this textbook to deal with all these specific issues but one area which has caused a lot of concern recently is the area of stress, which we shall focus on next. As you saw in the case of *Walker v. Northumberland County Council*, there can be serious repercussions for both the employee and the organisation if an employer fails to deal with stress in an appropriate way.

Stress and stress management

Stress is one major area of concern, and can be regarded as an umbrella term for a range of problems. Stress is manifested when people are dealing with so many pressures that their normal behaviour patterns become affected. Hans Selye (1956 and 1974), a noted writer on stress, used the terms 'eustress' and 'distress' to explain that stress is not always a negative concept. Sometimes people are stimulated by having to deal with a number of issues; this can be exciting and motivating. When it becomes too much and one cannot cope and at the same time continue to behave within the range of one's normal behaviour patterns, this is what Selye refers to as distress. This is what we normally mean when we refer to stress these days (Le Fevre et al., 2003).

What are the causes of stress? There are a wide range of factors that cause stress both in personal relationships and in work relationships (see Figure 11.1); these factors are referred to as stressors. Holmes and Rahe (1967) identified a number of life events as being sources of stress. Ranked at number one as a source of stress was the

Figure 11.1   Some causes of stress

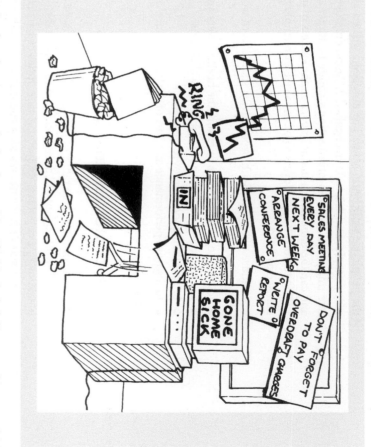

death of one's spouse, and other factors identified included divorce, taking on a high mortgage and taking a holiday.

It is also recognised that circumstances at work such as poor relationships, especially with one's manager or supervisor, and overwork or underemployment can contribute to stress. The case of John Walker mentioned earlier is an example of too high a workload combined with the demanding nature of the work contributing to stress.

The symptoms of stress include the behavioural changes we previously identified that might alert you to the fact that a colleague is under pressure. If not dealt with, the end result can be physical or mental illness leading to mental breakdown.

The Health and Safety Executive (HSE) has played a major role in the development of guidelines for employers on various aspects of stress management. The duty of care addressed in the Health and Safety at Work Act 1974 applies to employees' physical and mental wellbeing, and since these can be affected by stress caused by workplace factors, the duty of care constitutes an obvious legal obligation to pay attention to stress management. The Management of Health and Safety at Work Regulations 1999 also impose a duty on employers to conduct a risk audit on potential hazards in the workplace, which also applies in this area as the effects of stress can be regarded as a hazard.

Organisations can use these standards to measure their achievements in terms of stress management. The stress management standards are not legally enforceable on organisations, but the HSE may use them as evidence that an organisation is not fulfilling its duty with regard to stress management. The HSE has already issued an improvement order against one organisation for failing to manage stress adequately: West Dorset Hospitals NHS Trust in 2003 (reported by Hayden-Smith and Simms, 2003), though Incomes Data Services (2004) report that the Trust has since remedied the situation with suitable interventions.

The standards address six areas of work that should be audited. These are laid out with a brief description of what each entails in Table 11.1. The basic idea is to ascertain what percentages of staff feel that they are able to cope with any work situations in these six areas. According to the International Stress Management Association (2004), 'the target is for all organisations to match the performance of the top 20% of employers that are successfully minimising work-related stress.' Organisations must also be able to show that they have systems in place locally to respond to any individual concerns and should be carrying out risk assessments for stress. As Quinn (2004) points out, the identification of stress factors through such an audit makes the eventuality of stress foreseeable, so employers would be obligated to take some action in such an instance.

Did you know?

According to the Health and Safety Executive (2009a):

- The cost to society of work-related stress is about £4 billion per annum.
- In 2007–8, 13.5 million working days were lost because of stress.

(*Source:* HSE, 2009a)

Table 11.1 HSE stress management standards

Area of work	The standard	Desirable outcomes that organisations should be working towards
Demands This is about demands caused by the workload, work pattern or the work environment.	Employees should be able to indicate that they can cope with the demands of their job. There should also be systems in place to help deal with any concerns of individuals.	The organisation should ensure hours of work are reasonable and that demands made on the workers are not excessive and that their abilities and skills are matched appropriately to their job. There should be a matching of people's skills to their jobs. There should be systems set up to address concerns that workers may have so that these can be resolved.
Control This is about how much influence an individual has about their job.	Employees should be able to indicate that they get a say in the way they do their work. There should also be systems in place to respond to individual concerns.	Individuals should have control over their pace of work wherever possible. They should get opportunities and be encouraged to use their skills and initiative in their work. They should be encouraged to develop new skills so they can undertake new or more challenging work. The employees should also have a say about when breaks should be taken and be consulted about their work patterns and breaks.
Support This concerns the support mechanisms, or lack of them, from colleagues, line managers, and others such as HR staff. It is also about levels of employee awareness about support.	Employees should be able to indicate that they receive adequate support and information from colleagues and superiors. There should also be evidence of systems in place to adequately address employee concerns.	There should be policies and procedures in place to adequately support staff and there should also be systems in place to enable and encourage managers to support staff. Since support is also sometimes provided by colleagues there should be systems in place to encourage employees to support others. Employees should know about available support and also how to access resources necessary to do their job. They should also get regular and constructive feedback.

Table 11.1 Continued

Area of work	The standard	Desirable outcomes that organisations should be working towards
Relationships This is about encouraging positive behaviour so that conflict is avoided and about creating ways to deal with unacceptable behaviour.	Employees should be able to indicate that they are not subjected to unacceptable behaviour at work such as bullying or harassment and that there are systems in place to deal with these issues.	The organisation should promote positive behaviour to ensure fairness and avoid conflict and employees share information about their work. The organisation should have policies in place to prevent or resolve unacceptable behaviour and employees should be encouraged to report unacceptable behaviour.
Role This concerns the extent to which people understand their role and whether the organisation ensures the individual does not have conflicting roles.	Employees should be able to indicate that they understand their role and responsibilities and there should be systems in place to address individual concerns.	The organisation should provide information about the employees' roles and should try to ensure as far as possible that the different requirements it places on employees are compatible and clear and that the individual understands them. If they have concerns about role conflict or about their role then they should be able to raise them.
Change How much change are employees expected to cope with, and how well prepared are they when they do have to deal with change? Are the arrangements for information sharing and consultation adequate?	Employees should be able to show that the organisation engages with them frequently when undergoing organisational change and that there are systems in place to respond to any concerns they may have.	The organisation should be consulting adequately and providing opportunities for individuals to contribute to and influence the changes. This information needs to be timely and sufficient for employees to understand the reasons for the changes and the likely impact on their jobs. Employees also need to be aware of the timetable for changes and have suitable access to support during the change period.

(*Source:* Adapted from HSE (n.d.), *What are the Management Standards?*)

Pause for thought 11.7 Consider any organisation in which you have worked. To what extent do you think that organisation has considered each of the stress management standards?

What is your evidence for this?

How does this compare with the views of others in your class about organisations in which they have worked? Did job roles seem clear and unambiguous? Were you made aware of structures to support you?

As you can see from these standards there are a great many implications for HR departments to ensure that they have not only policies in place but also that they have designed jobs well to ensure there is no role incompatibility or work overload, that individuals understand their roles through induction and subsequent training and that there are support systems in place for those who may be experiencing problems. Management also need training to ensure they respond in an appropriate way to those suffering from stress. This means that they need to recognise that just increasing workloads and hoping that the person can cope is not a satisfactory way to manage but that there is a need for proper analyses of the job and the workload, and to match these to the person's capabilities.

An additional factor to do with employer obligations is that employment tribunals hearing cases of unfair dismissal would expect employers to have conducted a full investigation of the circumstances surrounding an incident of alleged misconduct or incompetence. The investigation should have shown whether this may have arisen as a result of personal problems or stress, particularly in the case of a person who previously had a good work record. Employers would be expected to take any such extenuating circumstances into consideration. You can read more about this in Chapter 13. The point about legal obligations could be summarised in the statement that employers have a duty of care.

Organisational policy and procedures

Policy statements and procedures provide guidelines for all employees. They let managers know how to handle problems, and inform everyone about the help, assistance and support they can expect to receive including the things in the stress management standards. There is a dual role for policies as far as situations requiring counselling are concerned. First, there is a need for policies relating directly to the provision of counselling and, second, an organisation should have policies dealing with workplace behaviour or events that have been identified as causing distress. For instance, in a *Guardian* Careers Section article, Professor Cary Cooper was quoted as saying that bullying probably accounted for a third to a half of all stress related illness (Venning, 1995).

Policies on bullying and sexual/racial harassment can help to eliminate these unwanted behaviours and promote a less stressful working environment. Many organisations such as banks and retail outlets, where staff handle cash and at the same time have direct contact with the public, have recognised that specialised counselling is necessary to deal with the trauma their employees can suffer after an episode involving violence or a threat of violence. This is true when they have either been directly threatened or witnessed an incident. Employers will obviously have to decide which issues are most important for their organisations, and this may involve surveying employees to discover which issues are of concern to them, and which solutions the employees would most like to take advantage of. The package of wellbeing policies, procedures and benefits an employer offers to employees is often referred to as an 'employee assistance programme'.

Policies should also address the following issues:

- who will be involved in providing counselling, and what are the parameters of their roles
- what type of services will be offered
- issues of confidentiality, (Seenan, 2004)

Did you know?

Some occupational groups and industry groups are more prone to stress than others. According to the HSE, groups that suffer particularly high levels of stress include teachers and nurses, housing and welfare officers, customer service workers and some professional and managerial groups, particularly those in the public sector.

(Source: HSE, 2009b)

Health promotion

So far, we have focused primarily on approaches to safety and wellbeing in response to legal requirements and as a way for employers to ensure that they motivate their workers. Recent legislation encourages employers to be proactive about safety and to carry out risk assessments and then take action to reduce or eliminate risks identified. The introduction of the 'fit note' to replace the 'sick note' has changed the focus to one where employees do not have to be 100 per cent fit to return to work but could be fit to do some work. According to Woollen (2010) the previous situation was very restrictive, with GPs only having two choices with the patient either being fit for work or not. The Government's intention appears to be to get employers and employees talking to each other after taking advice from the GP and that the employee could return to do some work before being fully fit. The 'fit note' also aims to make it easier to have a quicker return to work as in the past many employers have not allowed a worker to return until the end of their sick note and since this is often based on an estimate by the GP of the length of time needed for a particular illness, many days which could have been worked productively may have been lost. ACAS (2010b) also feel that since sick work can be good for health it is better to get people back to work as soon as possible. With a 'fit note' a GP can now indicate that a person 'may be fit for work'. If they choose to say this then they have to indicate one of the following options:

- phased return to work
- amended duties
- altered hours
- workplace adaptations.

Clearly if one of these options is chosen then there should be a discussion with the worker before they return to work (CIPD, 2010b).

Many good employers not only promote measures to promote improvements in safety and wellbeing but also encourage developments to ensure good health among their workforces.

The high cost of absenteeism is a strong financial reason for both individual organisations and the Government to take measures to promote and improve health. According to Griffiths (2009) the current UK recommendation is for moderately intense levels of physical activity for at least 30 minutes every day and the introduction of opportunities for exercise to the workplace could help to alleviate stress, musculoskeletal problems and some common mental health problems. Many people will lapse their membership of gyms after a short period of time because of other pressures in their lives so suggestions to incorporate exercise into work where people may be already spending between 40 and 85 hours a week could be useful. One innovative solution trialled with nurses and office workers was the introduction of a walking work station and though this might not be attractive to everyone, users reported improvements in energy and relief from back pain (Griffiths, 2009).

Many employers already provide some preventative measures such as health screening services and membership of private health insurance schemes for their managers, and some are extending this provision to the workforce as a whole. Increasingly, organisations are actively trying to promote a healthier lifestyle among their employees. Among the measures that have been tried are:

- help for smokers to quit, with support/self-help groups and psychologists giving advice and support

- a healthy diet, with a wider choice of health foods on the menu at work
- supply of free fruit at work
- membership of a health club or purchase of multi-gym exercise equipment for employees to use to get fitter and as a way of tackling obesity
- online assessments of health or lifestyle screening with advice available for lifestyle changes
- stress management programmes
- policies and education programmes on HIV/Aids
- policies and education on substance abuse.

In organisations where these programmes have been made available to all the workforce on a long-term basis, there have been benefits to employees' health, with weight reduction and improvements in blood cholesterol and blood pressure levels, and also improvements in absenteeism rates. It is claimed that the cost of the introduction of this type of programme is more than offset by the savings from lower rates of absenteeism. The CIPD (2006) stated that 'a survey of 97 organisations showed that employees who were participating in "wellness" programmes each incurred between £1,335 and £2,910 less per year in healthcare and absenteeism costs than colleagues who were not participating'.

ACAS (2010a) say that an unhealthy workplace where there are high levels of absence is usually synonymous with poor management and aspects of poor management may include a bullying culture, low productivity and unreasonable work demands being made on the employees. In their opinion, to get employees motivated to go that extra mile there need to be both effective policies and a high level of trust between management and the workforce, with involvement of workers in decisions and open communications. Line managers are also important in ensuring a healthy workplace and they need to be well trained and confident. (Refer back to discussion of the ACAS model workplace in Chapter 1.)

Absence management

While prevention is always better than cure one of the areas that many HR departments are also becoming increasingly interested in, and which can be used in a complementary way to a wellness programme, is absence management. Westminster City Council 'introduced improved absence management procedures which have reduced its absence rate by more than two days per person per annum and saved it £800,000 annually' (Inland Revenue Service, 2007b). They achieved this by using a mixture of approaches such as the introduction of an employee assistance programme and a new absence management programme which involved return to work interviews and earlier and more positive use of the occupational health department and trigger points. This meant that 'once an employee had more than seven cumulative days' sickness absence in any rolling period, then an enhanced sickness management procedure kicks in. And if sickness absence exceeds 20 days in any one episode, then long-term sickness management procedure applies. Further, when more than eight days of sickness have been recorded over the rolling 365-day period the employee's manager will refer the employee to the council's in-house occupational health service.'

Failure to take steps to reduce risks in the workplace is likely in the future to lead to higher insurance payments for organisations as insurance companies start to link premiums to the way that organisations manage risks of accidents and ill-health. Smokers generally suffer worse health than non-smokers and the charity Action on

Smoking and Health (ASH) claims that 34 million working days are lost in Britain each year, just because of smoking. Some employers are becoming more proactive about their employees' health and are introducing measures such as bonuses to encourage smokers to quit. These can, however, prove controversial as non-smokers may then also want to benefit from bonuses.

International issues in health and safety

Although British health and safety legislation does not apply to workers based outside Britain, employers still have a duty of care towards their employees, no matter where they work. Employees who operate in a global scene need additional knowledge relating to the particular country in which they are working, and this also applies to health and safety. The HR departments in those organisations need to check on health and safety legislation in the countries concerned, and should also carry out a risk assessment of not only the job but also the country, and should evaluate the employee's health. This would help ensure, for example, that they are not sending an asthmatic employee into a very dusty desert environment that would probably make the employee's health worse.

There are also social and ethical responsibilities that large organisations need to take into account when some of their products such as clothing or food is being produced in third world countries for them. Although they produce goods at cheap prices for those in the developed world, this is often at the expense of the workers in that country, by paying people poorly and by allowing them to work in poor health or safety conditions that would not be tolerated in the UK.

Even within Europe we have seen that individual countries can interpret European directives in different ways so the actual health and safety legislation in countries may vary. Attitudes to safety can be different and vary from one culture to another. In cultures where people tend to sue for damages, such as America, people are used to having lots of rules even when they are relaxing, away from work, so on beaches they only swim in the designated areas and obey the lifeguards. In the Greek islands, tourists would seek their own sheltered cove and swim from their own secluded beach so would have to take more responsibility for their own safety. Such differences in cultural expectations do shape attitudes to health and safety, so it is important to take into account the culture of the country and consider this in relation to health and safety. When Disney first opened in Paris some of the instructions on rides such as the requirement 'to exit the ride using your left foot first' jarred a little with Europeans who were used to making such decisions for themselves!

Some employees are sent to work in countries which may be regarded as high risk and where dangers such as kidnapping could occur. Staff need to be briefed as to precautions to take in these countries, as do the local staff, who may actually be more at risk than the expat staff, who probably live in a secure compound and have a driver to transport them safely. Some groups such as humanitarian aid workers are also likely to be at risk, since the nature of their jobs ensure that they are likely to be working in high-risk areas. However, they should still not be exposed to unnecessary risks.

HR departments who have staff working in potentially high-risk countries should carry out risk assessments, relating both to the dangers to health and to potential threats to safety, and should devise suitable emergency plans which can be put in place quickly. They should also devise suitable training programmes, perhaps drawing on local knowledge and expertise, for people undertaking these jobs. The workforce could even be involved in analysing the hazards and designing their own security plans for the compounds in which they live. Training in potential high-risk countries is likely to cover specific issues such as personal safety, office security, compound security, threats to convoys, risk analysis, first aid and emergency evacuation plans.

If this is done the workers are likely to feel and be safer and since health and safety will be perceived as being important, it is likely that they will take more care themselves. Measures such as these can do a great deal to eliminate unnecessary risks, although it is impossible to eliminate all risks completely.

Conclusion

We said at the beginning of this chapter that it is not enough for employers just to be concerned about preventing accidents in order to comply with legislation, although that in itself is a good start. We have shown in this chapter that there has been a change of approach from mere compliance with minimum legal requirements in the legislation prior to HASAWA to the encouragement of increased involvement of all, and nowadays to seeing a business case as well. In difficult economic circumstances many organisations find their profit margins are extremely tight and improving health, safety and wellbeing is one way to give their organisation a cost-effective competitive edge.

This approach to health and safety links with the overall business objectives of maximising efficiency and effectiveness by improving morale and reducing costs, and also allows for some scope for individuality and flexibility in how this is to be achieved. It is the approach to health and safety that we would advocate, and it is a very different approach to the purely legalistic one of just being concerned with not breaking the law. This approach to health and safety involves the following features:

- The need to create a culture in which health, safety and wellbeing are seen to be important to the organisation. The safety policy statement will contribute to this if it is effectively written, known about and acted upon. The legal requirements must be complied with and risk assessments undertaken, as well as information about health and safety gathered and a cost–benefit analysis carried out. If there is to be a culture of health and safety awareness, there also need to be campaigns and publicity, and involvement of top management, individuals and teams. There needs to be regular communication and discussion of health and safety and the contribution that improvements will make to the organisation's overall effectiveness, so that all members of the organisation realise that health and safety are important to the way it operates.

- Commitment from the top to the achievement of progressively higher standards as expressed in the mission statement and safety policy. Top management must not only sign the policy documents but also set a good example in relation to health and safety, and emphasise that it is an area of importance to them and to the future of the organisation by showing their interest and by setting up new systems and monitoring the effectiveness of these systems.

- Commitment throughout the organisation, with all parties clear about their own responsibilities for health and safety, the targets they have to meet and the contribution these make to the organisation's objectives. This should be considered as an aspect of performance management, as individuals and teams would be encouraged to take responsibility for their own actions and to agree and work towards targets when making improvements.

- Managers to demonstrate by their example their commitment to the importance of a safer and healthier work environment. They should also find ways to motivate everyone to make a contribution to health and safety improvements. Prizes and awards to individuals and teams can have an important effect.

- Policies and procedures designed to take account of the importance of a safer and healthier environment. There should also be effective systems to monitor their effectiveness.

- Policies to be backed by adequate resources for equipment and training. Provision of good health and safety costs money but the cost of not providing these can be higher, as any cost–benefit analysis is likely to prove.

- The setting of realistic and attainable targets for everyone in the organisation.

- Encouragement of all to take responsibility for their own actions and involvement of all in health and safety.

Our approach seems to be in line with both ACAS and Investors in People (IIP) in stressing the importance of good management to heath, safety and wellbeing. IIP (2010) say 'Investors in People has learnt that the key determinant of people's well being is how well they are managed and supported. The role that line managers and teams play in providing support to employees, particularly in today's changing climate, is therefore extremely important' Essentially it is all about good management and ensuring that health, safety and wellbeing are perceived to be an important aspect of performance management and should support the organisation's strategic objectives. In turn this should lead to better performance and provide an excellent return on investment.

REVIEW QUESTIONS

1 Interview people (friends, family or work colleagues from a range of organisations) about their own responsibilities in relation to health and safety and then about their perceptions of other people's roles in their particular organisation. Try to establish how the roles relating to health and safety differ for managers, other employees, human resource managers, safety officers, safety representatives and someone designated to be a 'competent person'. Are these roles the same in different types of organisation? How do they compare with what we said earlier in the chapter about these roles? Is health and safety perceived to be an important part of performance management?

2 Obtain a copy of the safety policy for either your college or your workplace.
   (a) Use this to identify the roles of various people in the organisation in relation to health and safety.
   (b) Use the safety policy to assess whether health and safety are linked to the organisation's strategic objectives.

3 Design a checklist for carrying out a safety inspection in the workplace. Use your checklist to actually carry out an inspection of a designated area either at work or in your college. Write a report about your findings for the safety officer.

4 Write a short report in which you assess the impact of one piece of health and safety legislation on an organisation of your choice.

5 Prepare arguments and then debate the following statements in two teams. Try to persuade the members of the other team to your point of view.

   TEAM A: There is much too much legislation regarding health and safety at work and this is unnecessary as it is in the employers' interests to look after their employees. Legislation merely hinders employers in their ability to run their businesses effectively.

   TEAM B: Legislation is necessary to control employers who would otherwise ignore health and safety issues at the expense of their employees' health, safety and wellbeing.

SELF-CHECK QUESTIONS

Answer the following multiple-choice and short-answer questions. The correct responses are given on pages 496–97 for you to check your understanding of this chapter.

1 Which of the following was the first piece of legislation designed to protect every one at work, and also to protect others who were not at work, such as customers or passers-by?
   (a) the Factories Act 1961
   (b) the Offices, Shops and Railways Premises Act 1963
   (c) the Fire Precautions Act 1971
   (d) the Health and Safety at Work Act 1974
   (e) the Control of Substances Hazardous to Health Regulations 1988.

But most interesting is the recommendation that social performance should be made a key factor in setting the remuneration of managers.

Danone, whose head of human resources sat on the Lachmann commission, already does this. But few others do.

The report also underlines the fact that the health and wellbeing of the workforce is first and foremost the responsibility of managers, and cannot be outsourced to external advisers as many French companies appear to be doing.

The question now is how to define social performance.

The French report suggests the issue needs to be treated extremely seriously. It suggests the issue is so serious that the board of a company and not just its top management must make it a priority, as much so as delivering profits and dividends to its shareholders.

Financial Times, FT.com, 19/02/2010 (Paul Betts), Reproduced with permission. © The Financial Times Ltd.

Questions

1 To what extent do you think the organisations mentioned here would benefit from using the Health and Safety Executive's stress management standards as a part of their stress policies?

2 In your opinion do you think that measures of social performance should be considered when deciding managers pay? If so, what measures should be used?

3 Do you think that measures of health, safety and wellbeing should be included as a part of the balanced scorecard approach in organisations?

4 To what extent do you think measures of a country's wellbeing should be included when comparing the performance of countries? Should there be something like the balanced scorecard, discussed in Chapter 1, as a gauge of countries' success and prosperity with measures such as a happiness index or metrics about wellbeing being used alongside economic measures?

WHAT NEXT?

Research conducted by Aberdeen University on 13 offshore oil installations applies the balanced scorecard to occupational health. The article also discusses the results of interviews with UK and Norwegian managers on health and safety performance indicators and the reasons for including occupational health and safety as one measure of performance within the balanced scorecard. What do you think about the idea that measures of occupational health should be included in an assessment of an organisation's performance?

Mearns, K. and J.I. Havold (2003) Occupational health and safety and the balanced scorecard, *The TQM Magazine*, Vol. 15, No. 6, 408–423.

References

Advisory, Conciliation and Arbitration Service (2009) *Discipline and Grievances at Work: The ACAS Guide*, ACAS.

Advisory, Conciliation and Arbitration Service (2010a) Health, work and wellbeing, ACAS, 2.

Advisory, Conciliation and Arbitration Service (2010b) Statement of fitness for work or 'fit note', ACAS (www.acas.co.uk; accessed 13.9.2010).

Baker, J. (2007) Net closes on corporate killing, *People Management*, Vol. 13, No. 5, 8 March, 22.

Cacanas, Z. (2004) *The Guardian*, 24 July.

Chartered Institute of Personnel and Development (2006) *Occupational Health and Organisational Effectiveness*, CIPD (available at www.cipd.co.uk; accessed 10.09.07).

Chartered Institute of Personnel and Development (2007) *Gangmaster Legislation Should be Extended*, CIPD, 31 July (www.cipd.co.uk/news/_articles/gangmasterlegislationshould beextended.htm; accessed 10.09.07).

Chartered Institute of Personnel and Development (2009) *Annual Survey Report 2009: Absence Management*, CIPD (www.cipd.co.uk; accessed 10.9.2010).

Chartered Institute of Personnel and Development (2010a) *Factsheet: Working Hours and Time Off Work*, CIPD (www.cipd.co.uk; accessed 11.9.2010).

Chartered Institute of Personnel and Development (2010b) *Factsheet: Absence Measurement and Management*, CIPD (www.cipd.co.uk; accessed 10.9.2010).

Chiu, A, (2009) Food, job best foundations for success in pursuit of happiness, *South China Morning Post*, 8 December.

Engineering Employers' Federation (2001) *Managing Stress at Work*, EEF.

Fowler, A. (1994) Personnel's model army, *Personnel Management*, September, 34–3.

Griffiths, L. (2009) Addressing obesity in the workplace, *Occupational Health*, RBI, Issue 1, 1 February (www.xperthr.co.uk; accessed 6.9.2010).

Hackitt, J. (2010a) Foreword. *The Health and Safety of Britain: Be Part of the Solution*, HSE (www.hse.gov.uk; accessed 8.9.2010).

Hackitt, J. (2010b) Foreword. *The Health and Safety Business Plan 2010–11*, HSE. (www.hse. gov.uk; accessed 8.9.2010).

Hammond, D. (2001) Dangerous liaisons, *People Management*, 30 May, 26–7. (www. peoplemanagement.co.uk/pm/articles/2001/05/674.htm)

Hayden-Smith, J. and R. Simms (2003) Pressure points, *People Management*, 25 September, 17.

Health and Safety Executive (n.d.) *What are the Management Standards?* (available at www. hse.gov.uk/stress/standards/index.htm; accessed 17.09.2010).

Health and Safety Executive (1995) *Be Safe: Save Money. The Costs of Accidents: A Guide for Small Firms*, HSE Books, 4.

Health and Safety Executive (2006) *Five Steps to Risk Assessment*, HSE, INDG 163 rev. 2 (available at www.hse.gov.uk; accessed 8.09.2010).

Health and Safety Executive (2008) *HSE Enforcement Policy Statement – Updated*, HSE (www. hse.gov.uk; accessed 10.9.2010).

Health and Safety Executive (2009a) *How to Tackle Work-related Stress*, HSE (www.hse.gov.uk; accessed 6.8.2010).

Health and Safety Executive (2009b) *Statistics: Stress-related and Psychological Disorders*, HSE (available at www.hse.gov.uk; accessed 17.9.2010).

Health and Safety Executive (2010a), *Health and Safety Executive Statistics: Fatal Injury Statistics*, HSE (www.hse.gov.uk; accessed 6.8.2010).

Health and Safety Executive (2010b) *Self-reported Work-related Illness and Workplace Injuries in 2008–09: Results from the Labour Force Survey*, HSE (www.hse.gov.uk; accessed 7.8.2010).

Health and Safety Executive (2010c) *HSE Revitalising Health and Safety*, HSE (www.hse.gov. uk; accessed 7.8.2010).

Health and Safety Executive (2010d) *The Health and Safety Executive Business Plan 2010/11*, HSE (www.hse.gov.uk; accessed 7.8.2010).

Health and Safety Executive (2010e) *2010 Myths*, HSE (www.hse.gov.uk; accessed 7.9.2010).

Health and Safety Executive (2010f) *Example Health and Safety Policy*, HSE (www.hse.gove.uk; accessed 11.9.2010).

Holmes, T.H. and R.H. Rahe (1967) The social readjustment rating scale, *Journal of Psychosomatic Research*, August, 216.

Incomes Data Services (2002) *IDS Studies Plus: Employee Assistance Programmes*, IDS.

Incomes Data Services (2004) *IDS HR Studies 775: Managing Stress*, IDS.

Inland Revenue Service Employment Review (2007a) *Employee Assistance Programmes: The IRS Report*, IRS 874, 4 June.

Inland Revenue Service Employment Review (2007b) *Westminster City Council's Successful Absence Management Procedure*, IRS 877, 18 July.

International Stress Management Association UK (2004) *Working Together to Reduce Stress at Work*, International Stress Management Association UK.

Investors in People (2010) *Why Should You be Improving Health and Wellbeing?* IIP (www.iip.co. uk; accessed 11.9.2010).

Jones, R. (2007) Manslaughter Act doesn't go far enough, *Personnel Today*, 6 March.

Le Fevre, M., J. Matheny and G.S. Kolt (2003) Eustress, distress, and interpretation in occupational stress, *Journal of Managerial Psychology*, Vol. 18, No. 7, 726–744.

Maslow, A. (1954) *Motivation and Personality*, 2nd edition, Harper & Row.

Further study

Books

Michaelson, J., S.Abdallah, N.Steur, S.Thompson and N.Marks (2009) *National Accounts of Well-being*, The New Economics Foundation (www.neweconomics.org/publications/national-accounts-well-being; accessed 16.9.2010).

Midgley, S. (1997) Pressure points, *People Management*, 10 July, 36–39.

Millard, R. (2010) Gareth Malone's lesson in how to teach boys, *The Sunday Times*, 12 September, 16.

Ministry of Justice (2007) Justice for corporate deaths: Royal assent for corporate Manslaughter and Corporate Homicide Act, Ministry of Justice (www.justice.gov.uk/news/newsrelease260707b.htm; accessed 12.09.07).

Nishiyama, K. and J. Johnson (1997) *Karoshi – Death from Overwork: Occupational Health Consequences of the Japanese Production Management*, 6th Draft for International Journal of Health Services, 4 February (available at www.workhealth.org/whatsnew/lpkarosh.html; accessed 17.09.2010).

Paton, N. (2010) Future challenges in workplace health, *Occupational Health*, 1 August (www.xperthr.co.uk; accessed 6.9.2010).

Philpott, J. (2010) *Work Audit: Working Hours in the Recession*, CIPD, 1–2.

Quinn, J. (2004) Dodging the draft, *People Management*, 30 June, 17.

Seenan, G. (2004) No frills – and no travelling toilet class, *The Guardian*, 24 July.

Selye, H. (1956) *The Stress of Life*, McGraw-Hill.

Selye, H. (1974) *Stress without Distress*, Lippincott.

Stranks, J. (2007a) *The Health and Safety Handbook: A Practical Guide to Health and Safety Law, Management Policies and Procedures*, Kogan Page.

Tehrani, N., S.Humpage, B.Wilmott and I. Haslam (2007) *Change Agenda: What's Happening with Well-being at Work?* CIPD, 3.

Venning, N. (1995) Taking the bull by the horns, *Guardian Careers Section*, 15 April, 2–3.

Woolf, M. and K. Dowling (2010) Gove's new curriculum, *The Sunday Times*, 12 September, 1.

Woollen, R. (2010) The fit note – friend or foe, *Managing People*, 1 April.

XpertHR (2010a) *Employment Law Reference Manual, Health and Safety*, XpertHR (www.xperthr.co.uk; accessed 10.9.2010).

XpertHR (2010b) *Outlook Video: Equality Act–Disability*, XpertHR (www.xperthr.co.uk; accessed 11.9.2010).

Articles

Advisory, Conciliation and Arbitration Service (2010) *Health, Work and Wellbeing*, ACAS.

This booklet focuses on measures that employers can take to help promote good health in their workforce and also discusses the importance of work for keeping people healthy.

Stranks, J. (2007b) *Health and Safety at Work: An Essential Guide for Managers*, revised 8th edition, Kogan Page.

This is available as an electronic book and as the name implies gives clear practical guidance for managers.

Internet

Control Risks Group   www.crg.com

The Health and Safety Executive   www.hse.gov.uk

HSE publications exist on a wide range of topics, too numerous to include here, from general books to detailed explanations of legislation. Some of its leaflets are also available on the web page listed at the end of this chapter.

RIDDOR   www.riddor.gov.uk

The site gives information about RIDDOR and has forms which can be downloaded to report accidents and dangerous occurrences, or these can now be reported directly online.

XpertHR   www.xperthr.co.uk

An excellent source of articles from various publications.

CHAPTER 12

Discipline and grievance

Objectives

By the end of this chapter you will be able to:

● understand the meaning of the terms 'discipline' and 'grievance'

● understand the role of human resource managers and line managers in discipline and grievance handling

● explain the importance of the ACAS Code of Practice on disciplinary and grievance procedures (2009)

● describe the main features of a disciplinary procedure and of a grievance procedure

● design a simple disciplinary and grievance procedure.

In any organisation, however good the management and however highly motivated the workforce, there will be occasions when problems or difficulties occur between management and employees. In order that employees are able to work to their optimum performance and that these problems do not turn into even bigger issues, suitable ways of dealing with them need to be devised before they occur. If the problem has arisen from something that management has done, this may result in the employee concerned having a grievance. If, however, it is a problem arising from the behaviour or attitude of an employee, then disciplinary action may be called for.

Human resource managers are concerned to get the best out of people, and although the human resource approach tends towards a dislike of rules and procedures, in favour of a more individualised approach, there are times when this is not possible because of the need to comply with legislation or codes of practice. This is the case where discipline and grievance are concerned. While discipline and grievances are individual issues, it would be unfair to treat each case in a totally different way, and to do so might result in a claim for unfair dismissal against the organisation, or dissatisfaction among the workforce. Human resource managers need to consider these issues and design suitable procedures in order to enhance both the performance management process within the organisation and to enable employees to contribute fully to the strategic objectives of the organisation.

The role of the human resource manager and the line manager

Discipline and grievances are sensitive issues requiring skilful handling, and in many organisations they have traditionally been an area that has been left to human resource managers. This has been partly due to the fact that the human resource managers were likely to be trained in skilful handling of sensitive interpersonal issues, but also many managers and supervisors were often unwilling to tackle something that might result in their unpopularity and cause difficulties in maintaining a suitable relationship with someone they had to work with on a daily basis. This attitude has changed considerably in recent years, as more and more of the human resource function has been devolved to line management; line managers in many organisations are nowadays expected to handle any discipline or grievance situations that arise in their section, at least in the early stages. Human resource managers still have several important roles to play, however:

● in devising the procedures
● in providing specialist advice
● in ensuring that everyone is aware of the procedures and acts consistently
● in ensuring that line managers are suitably trained
● in monitoring the effectiveness of the procedures.

Discipline: introduction and definitions

The *Shorter Oxford English Dictionary* defines discipline in the following ways: "To subject to discipline; in earlier use, to educate or train; later, to bring under control.' The term 'discipline', as we can see from this definition, can be used in various ways. It can refer to self-discipline, where an individual as a result of practice and training works in an ordered, self-controlled way, or is trained by others to work in a certain way, or it can be used to refer to the need to discipline someone by pointing out to them the error of their ways or by punishing them for mistakes that they have made. Human resource managers are concerned to motivate people to ensure they reach their maximum potential, and the adoption of a punitive approach is unlikely to facilitate much motivation.

Students dealing with case studies about disciplinary situations often tend to respond initially by enjoying the power to punish and often want to dismiss the alleged offenders. Sometimes new, inexperienced managers may adopt the same approach. In reality this approach is likely to prove counterproductive, as valuable staff who have been costly to recruit and train would be lost, and the motivation of everyone concerned would be low. Handling a disciplinary situation in an unfair way may result in the employee being dismissed, but this might also result in a case for unfair dismissal being brought against the organisation. This could be expensive if the organisation lost, and in any case would be expensive in terms of:

● the time needed to prepare for the tribunal
● the time lost
● disruption caused as witnesses are called
● the bad publicity for the organisation itself
● employee retention
● the poor employee relations likely to ensue because of unfair handling of a disciplinary situation.

In order to try to minimise these problems and to encourage employers to handle disciplinary offences in a fair and reasonable manner, the Advisory, Conciliation and Arbitration Service (ACAS) has published codes of practice since 1977 and their latest, *Code of Practice 1: Disciplinary and Grievance Procedures*, came into effect on 6 April 2009.

Disciplinary procedures and practices

The ACAS Code of Practice on Disciplinary and Grievance Procedures

This aims to help all who may be concerned with this topic by providing practical advice about handling disciplinary and grievance procedures. A code of practice has an interesting status in law. An employer cannot have an unfair dismissal case brought against it in an employment tribunal just because it has not carried out a procedure as stated in the code of practice, but it would ignore the code of practice at its peril, as failure to comply with it is likely to be used as part of the evidence against it in an unfair dismissal case. It is also possible for the employment tribunal to increase or decrease an award by up to 25 per cent if one of the parties has not taken account of this code and consequently there is a strong financial incentive to get things right.

In the code, ACAS clearly states that although disciplinary rules are likely to be mainly designed by management, other groups such as trade unions, line managers, workers and employees should also have a part to play in formulating them. ACAS emphasises the fact that the main reason for having disciplinary rules is to promote fairness and set standards of conduct, and to provide a fair and consistent method of dealing with alleged offences. According to ACAS, one of the main reasons for having procedures is to ensure there are orderly employment relations so that everyone knows what is expected of them. If the rules have been designed solely by management without the involvement of other interested parties, employees and workers may be more cynical about management's motives and individuals may feel that when they are disciplined it is because of victimisation, or because their supervisor dislikes them. In order for the disciplinary procedure to be credible to employees and other workers, it is clearly in management's interests to involve them in its design. Good employers will certainly appreciate this need.

Other employers, however, may merely be motivated in their provision of a disciplinary procedure by the need to comply with the legislation. The Employment Rights Act 1996 requires employers to provide employees with a copy of their disciplinary procedure within two months of the commencement of their employment or provide access for the workers to an accessible document which gives appropriate information. This could be done in their letter of engagement, in their contract, or with the written statement of terms and conditions of employment. Following strict procedures may be more difficult for smaller employers, but at the very least ACAS (2009a) recommend that they should put the disciplinary procedure on a notice board. Employment tribunals will take into account the size of the organisation and the administrative resources that are available to the organisation when they consider cases. It is good practice to go through the procedure with all new employees and ensure that they understand it. It is vital that all employers, regardless of their size, do follow the ACAS Code of Practice on Disciplinary and Grievance Procedures.

These factors should prove sufficient to motivate the employer to provide a disciplinary procedure but, if not, in the last resort some employers may be motivated by the fact that they may need evidence that they have acted fairly and followed a fair procedure in the event of an alleged unfair dismissal claim before an employment tribunal. For whatever reason, it is obviously important to adopt a clear disciplinary procedure so that both the employer and the workforce know what standards of conduct are expected and what may happen if these standards are not achieved.

'Worker' applies to all workers whether they are employed on a contract of employment or not. As such it is a much broader term than 'employee' since it could apply also to workers who were employed by an agency or who worked as volunteers in a charity. In the ACAS *Code of Practice on Disciplinary and Grievance Procedures* (2009a) both these words are used. Some of the provisions in this Code of Practice just refer to employees while others, in particular the right to be accompanied at disciplinary and grievance hearings, have a wider meaning and apply to all workers.

The importance of fairness in a disciplinary procedure

The ACAS *Code of Practice* (2009a) emphasises that it is important to have a fair procedure. According to ACAS (2009a), in order to be fair a good disciplinary procedure should allow for the following features:

- issues should be resolved promptly
- issues should be handled consistently
- thorough investigations should be conducted
- employees should be informed of the facts of the case against them and should have opportunities to state their side of the case
- employees should have the right to be accompanied at any formal meeting about discipline or grievances
- there should be clear rights of appeal.

As an employment tribunal clearly has to take these factors into account and since employers could find any awards made against them increased by 25 per cent, it is clearly important that they incorporate these points into any disciplinary procedure that they design and that they pay attention to complying with these points when disciplining any individual. Issues such as bullying, whistle-blowing or harassment might need to form part of a separate procedure. ACAS (2009a) also recommend that independent third parties could be used as mediators at each stage of the proceedings in either cases of discipline or grievance.

ACAS give further good practice advice about how to handle disciplinary situations in their booklet *Discipline and Grievances at Work: The ACAS Guide* (ACAS, 2009b). This provides practical guidance and is important in helping to clarify what is meant and also suggesting ways to achieve it. It explains some of the features of a disciplinary procedure and these are discussed next. However, it is important to note that though this provides an excellent guide to good practice employment, tribunals do not have to take into account what is said in the guide in the way that they must for the actual *Code of Practice* itself.

Features of a disciplinary procedure

ACAS (2009b) lists the following as being good features which should be contained in a disciplinary procedure. According to ACAS, good disciplinary procedures should:

- be in writing;
- be non-discriminatory;
- provide for matters to be dealt with speedily;
- allow for information to be kept confidential;
- tell employees what disciplinary actions might be taken;
- say what levels of management have the authority to take the various forms of disciplinary action;
- require employees to be informed of complaints against them and of supporting evidence, before a disciplinary hearing;
- give employees a chance to state their case before management reaches a decision
- provide employees with the right to be accompanied;
- provide that no employee is dismissed for a first breach of discipline, except for gross misconduct;
- require management to investigate fully before any disciplinary action is taken;
- ensure that employees are given an explanation for any sanction and allow employees to appeal against a decision;
- apply to all employees, irrespective of their length of service, status or say if there are different rules for different groups. (*Discipline and Grievances at Work: The ACAS Guide*, ACAS, 2009b.)

It may seem obvious that rules should be in writing, that any disciplinary cases should be kept confidential, and that disciplinary issues should be dealt with quickly. If they are not written down people will remember the rules differently, and varying approaches to discipline will occur. This becomes an even greater problem if there is a long time lapse before an investigation occurs as witnesses can forget what has actually occurred. Many organisations nowadays will put disciplinary rules on their intranet sites as well as in their organisational handbooks, and will often give guidance about time limits for investigations.

The rules should not discriminate against or disadvantage any specific group. Since the management must ensure that these rules are available to everyone, the rules may also need to be translated into other languages where English is not the first language of some of the workers.

The disciplinary rules should also be explained orally for new workers during the induction period. This will be of help to those with a disability such as a visual impairment, who may also require a large print, Braille or an audio version of the procedure, but will also ensure any workers who are unable to read will know of the rules and will avoid the risk of them experiencing inadvertent discrimination. Employees may otherwise be uncertain as to what they may and may not do.

Clarity is also important for supervisors and managers so it is necessary that the rules specify who can take disciplinary action. If this does not happen supervisors and managers may adopt different approaches to discipline between different departments, with some supervisors unsure of what action they have the power to take.

Although there is a need for consistency in order to be non-discriminatory, in some rare cases it may be legitimate to have different rules for different departments. Employees do need to be aware of the rules that apply to them and what the disciplinary action is likely to involve, and their managers also need to be fully aware of these rules. A catering department is likely to have additional rules about hygiene that are not likely to be as relevant to a transport department. So the rules should specify to whom they apply.

It is necessary that employees know what misdemeanours are regarded as serious by management. In order to be fair, the worker should be informed of the case against them and should be able to see the evidence against them before the disciplinary hearing. They must have an opportunity to state their case prior to any decision being made, and have the right for a trade union official or a friend to accompany them.

Workers can make genuine mistakes, and as we have already shown it is extremely expensive to recruit and train staff, so as we have said earlier, retention is an important area for organisations to consider. On these grounds alone it pays to be fair to workers and to avoid dismissing them wherever possible. In order to give workers a fair chance it is important not to dismiss anyone for a first breach of discipline, unless it is a case of gross misconduct. This ensures that the individual has a chance to learn from their mistake.

Management may also occasionally make mistakes, and the worker may not have committed a disciplinary offence at all. To prevent someone being disciplined for something they did not do, it is important to ensure that no disciplinary action is taken before a full investigation into the alleged offence has been carried out.

If workers are to learn from their mistakes, then they need to be very clear about what they did wrong, how to do it right and also to have a clear explanation of any sanctions imposed. It is still possible that, in spite of all these precautions, occasionally management may make a mistake in disciplining a person. In order to remedy this and to ensure that people don't feel that they are being disciplined just because their supervisor doesn't like them, it is important to have an appeal procedure that is made known to them.

It is also vital to follow the requirements of natural justice, so employees should be given the chance to talk with someone who has not been, and will not be, involved at all in this issue. They should then be informed of allegations and the evidence against them prior to any meeting. Opportunities for them to challenge the allegations before decisions are reached should also be ensured and, as already mentioned, there should be a right of appeal. Moreover, these rules should apply to all employees regardless of length of employment or position in the hierarchy.

Disciplinary offences

It would be impossible to fully itemise the range of behaviour that might result in disciplinary action. Nowadays many employers find a great deal of their time is spent dealing with disciplinary cases involving the misuse of social networking sites or email abuse. This could involve workers accessing these sites or using their personal email at times when they are not supposed to but also frequently involves staff posting inappropriate comments relating to work or the organisation on these sites.

Other common offences are issues about absenteeism, timekeeping or poor performance at work. There may also be concern about a range of issues including failure to obey organisation rules, such as rules about health and safety, theft, sexism, racism, problems arising from fighting or threatening behaviour, and alcohol or drug abuse. Most employers divide offences into two categories depending on the seriousness with which they are viewed within that organisation. They list issues that they regard as disciplinary offences, and then itemise as gross misconduct further offences that they consider to be more serious. These offences may be handled in different ways, depending on the seriousness with which the organisation regards them.

Did you know?

In China an online game called Happy Farm involved participants in cultivating vegetables but some took a short cut by stealing vegetables from others. Such was the craze for this game that many employees spent time at work playing this game and subsequently some faced disciplinary action from their bosses though sometimes their bosses ended up joining in. Maggie Zhang, a secretary in Shenzhen is quoted in the *South China Morning Post* as saying, 'My Hong Kong boss warned me several times to stop playing. But . . . he ended up joining the game and is always stealing my vegetables.'

However, not all employers were so sympathetic and '19 government officials in Hunan province were given a verbal warning after being caught stealing vegetables during working hours.'

(*Source*: He, H., 2009, *South China Morning Post*, 12 December)

Pause for thought 12.2

Consider any organisation that you know reasonably well, perhaps one where you have worked yourself.

1 What disciplinary rules did the organisation have?
2 How were these disciplinary rules made known to you?
3 What were considered to be disciplinary offences?
4 Were there any offences that were regarded as particularly serious in this organisation and that constituted gross misconduct? List these.
5 Compare your list with the list made by someone who has experience in a different organisation. Can you find reasons for the differences and similarities?

It is probable that there were disciplinary rules in most organisations and that these were made known to you by you being given or shown a copy of them as part of your induction to your new job. Most organisations will have a list of offences that might constitute gross misconduct. When you compare your list with that of a friend who has worked in a different organisation, you will probably have listed many of the same offences as ones that constituted gross misconduct. Theft, dishonesty and verbal or physical abuse are likely to be regarded as serious in most organisations. It is also probable that there will then be some variation in your lists as to what else constitutes an offence, depending on the attitudes in that particular organisation and the nature of the work done there.

Organisations involved in food preparation may be particularly concerned with hygiene, and may list offences concerning lack of personal hygiene as ones that could constitute gross misconduct. Organisations such as banks or building societies, where there is a need for a high degree of security, may be very concerned with email abuse and have extremely strict rules about what is acceptable for workers to both send and receive. Other organisations, such as universities, may be much more concerned with freedom of information so may have very different rules. Offences also change with time, fashion and new technology. Many organisations now have specific policies regarding both email and appropriate use of the Internet at work and some have also had to introduce policies to control the use of mobile phones at work.

Pause for thought 12.3 Tim Hancock has worked for your organisation for nearly a year. He has in general been a good employee, but you have noticed that recently he has started to arrive about 10 minutes late for work each morning. You are his supervisor. Describe the action you would take.

The way in which you, as Tim's supervisor, choose to deal with this situation depends on a number of factors. First, there is your own attitude to this issue, but more importantly there is also the attitude of the organisation to issues of poor timekeeping to consider. You may have personal views about this but you need to act in a way that is consistent with those of the organisation. Personally you may not feel too concerned about this issue as long as the work gets done, or you may take the view that it is a form of dishonesty when an employee steals time from an employer. In some organisations this may not be viewed as a problem at all. Employees may have the opportunity to create their own flexitime system without management worrying unduly about this. However, the views of the organisation will be expressed in its disciplinary procedure, and it is likely that poor timekeeping will be an area of concern. If that is the case, you, as Tim's manager, have to do something about Tim's lateness. It is not as yet a particularly serious offence, but it has the potential to become more serious if left unchecked. There may of course be a perfectly good reason why Tim has suddenly started to arrive slightly late for work. The first thing that needs to be done is for you to have a chat with Tim about it and try to find out the reason for this change in behaviour. This can be informal. It gives Tim the opportunity to explain, and also lets him know that you are aware of his lateness and are concerned about it. If he has a good reason then you will have to consider your reaction. If there is illness at home, this is likely to be a temporary situation, and you may reach an arrangement with Tim about his time of arrival for a limited period of time which can be reviewed at a later date. If the problem is related to a change in a public transport timetable, you may have to consider whether you can be flexible or not.

Pause for thought 12.4 Jasmine has worked for your organisation for nearly five years. Her work has always been good, but recently you have received many complaints from customers about the goods that they have ordered being late or not being received at all. You check through the records and find that all these delays can be traced back to orders that Jasmine has dealt with. You are Jasmine's manager. How will you deal with this situation?

As Jasmine's manager you will have to take some action about her poor quality of work since it is causing problems to customers, and there have been complaints. However, you know that Jasmine has always been a good worker so you need to talk to her about the problem and try to find out what the cause is. Once again, you need to have an informal chat with her to find out the cause of the problem and then decide on the action to take. You may find that there is a perfectly good reason, such as a problem relating to home life, for the change in the standard of her work. If this is the case then a counselling interview is likely to be most appropriate. If, however, there doesn't appear to be a clear reason, an informal discussion which lets Jasmine know of your concerns and reaches agreement about expected improvements should suffice.

● The disciplinary procedure

This will be set out in writing and needs to fulfil the criteria already discussed as essential features of a disciplinary procedure. The most important areas to be included in the procedure relate to the ways in which disciplinary issues should be handled and recorded, and you will have seen in the discussions of the previous exercises that informal chats were one of the first procedures that the manager should consider. The types of action that could be used are listed below and will be discussed next.

1 informal actions
2 formal actions
3 inform the worker of the result
4 the appeals procedure
5 the nature of gross misconduct
6 records.

1 Informal action

Informal action is normally the most appropriate way of dealing with alleged minor misconduct or unsatisfactory performance. This may just involve the supervisor or manager having a quiet word with the individual and can be a quick and easy way of sorting out a problem. This type of informal action was exactly what we recommended in both the situations in the 'Pause for thought' exercises 12.3 and 12.4 which you examined earlier in this chapter. However, if this doesn't work, or if the alleged offence is regarded as being rather more serious in nature, then it is time for the employer to show their dissatisfaction and to take some formal action.

Pause for thought 12.5 Consider once again Pause for thought 12.3. If after the informal chat or chats there was still no improvement in Tim's timekeeping, his manager would be likely to start the formal disciplinary process.

2 Formal action
Investigation

Once the informal action has been taken, if the misconduct reoccurs or the unsatisfactory performance fails to improve, it may be necessary for the employer to try a more formalised approach. The organisation needs to carry out a full investigation before this is decided upon. According to Kaye (2007), the Employment Appeal Tribunal has given guidance that indicates that 'employers should carry out an investigation, even if the employee is arrested and charged with a criminal offence. It may not be practical to wait for the outcome of criminal proceedings, because these may take several months.' A thorough investigation is important.

While workers have rights to be accompanied at disciplinary meetings, Cole (2007) says that we should 'Remember the right to be accompanied does not apply to a genuine investigatory/fact-finding meeting.' Therefore, it should be made clear exactly what the nature of the meeting is going to be and it should not be allowed to drift into a disciplinary hearing as at that stage the worker would have other rights such as the right to be accompanied. The investigatory meetings and potential disciplinary meetings should be kept separate. On this subject Cole (2007) says, 'Halt an investigatory meeting if it looks like turning into a disciplinary meeting and start formal disciplinary procedures.'

If after conducting a thorough investigation it appears that there may have been misconduct then the next stages should involve a letter, a meeting and possibly an appeal. The actual procedure may vary depending on whether the potential disciplinary action involves misconduct or capability, but both will be similar.

Letter

After a thorough investigation has been conducted the first stage in the formal process is to inform the employee of the alleged misconduct in writing to ensure that the individual realises that there actually still is a problem. This letter should explain the nature of the alleged misconduct and the reasons that this is not acceptable within the organisation. The letter must also inform the individual of the basis of the complaint against them and should also invite them to a meeting and inform them of their right to be accompanied at this meeting. Copies of documents such as witness statements that will be used at that meeting should be given to them.

Meeting

Setting up the meeting

The date, time and place of the meeting should, if possible, be agreed with the individual concerned and should also be timed to allow them sufficient time to prepare adequately for this meeting. The meeting should be held somewhere private where there will not be any interruptions.

At this meeting the employer should first explain the complaint and go through the evidence. Then the individual should go through their case and answer any allegations that have been made against them. They can also ask questions, call witnesses, present evidence and raise any points about witness information.

If there is a problem in holding this meeting at the agreed time due to a legitimate reason, e.g. employee illness or unavailability of their chosen companion on that date, then the employer can arrange another date. This should normally be within five working days but this can be extended by mutual agreement. However, if the individual simply fails to attend the meeting, without giving any good reason, then the employer could hold the meeting and even reach a decision in their absence.

3 Inform the worker of the result

After the meeting a decision should be made about whether disciplinary action is justified

(a) If it is decided that disciplinary action is not justified, or if no further action needs to be taken, the employer must notify the individual in writing of this fact so they no longer worry.

(b) If, however, disciplinary action is decided upon then the employer has to decide the form of the action, taking into account the individual's explanations, their past employment record, and any actions that have been taken in similar cases in the past, and whether the proposed disciplinary action is reasonable in the circumstances. The employee must then be notified of the decision.

Types of formal action that could be taken

Slightly different forms of action may be appropriate for cases of misconduct or for those involving unsatisfactory performance but basically after conducting a full investigation the steps are as follows.

The first forms of formal action in a case of alleged *misconduct* could include the following:

- *A first written warning* stating the nature of the misconduct and stating what change in behaviour is required.
- The individual being told that this is part of a formal disciplinary process and the consequences if they fail to change their behaviour.
- The likely consequences, such as a final written warning, which could ultimately lead to their dismissal or some other sanction, but that this would only happen after they had been given the chance to present their case at another formally convened meeting.

The first forms of formal action in a case of alleged *unsatisfactory performance* may be slightly different but could include *a first written improvement note* being given to any individual who is performing in an unsatisfactory way which states:

- the nature of the performance problem
- the required improvement
- the timescale within which the improvement should occur
- a review date and
- the support, if any, that the employer will provide to help the individual to reach the required level of performance
- notification that failure to improve, if this is what has been decided upon, could result in a final written warning and ultimately dismissal.

Final written warnings

When the requisite improvement in either performance or behaviour has not been made within the stated timescale, or if the alleged offence is sufficiently serious, the employee should normally be issued with a written warning. Once again, before this stage of the process they should be given the opportunity to present their case at a meeting.

Any final written warning that is issued should once again make the following clear to the individual:

- the grounds for the complaint
- that failure to make the required improvement within a specified time may result in dismissal or another penalty
- that there is a right of appeal.

Final written warnings should be disregarded once the specified time limit has elapsed if the required improvement has been made. ACAS provide an excellent set of sample letters to be used in various circumstances. These can be accessed at **www.acas.org.uk**.

Dismissal or other penalty

The subject of dismissal will be considered in more detail in the next chapter. However, we shall mention it briefly here as it is sometimes the final stage in the disciplinary process. Any decision to dismiss must be taken by a manager who has the necessary authority. The employee must be told as soon as possible of the decision to dismiss them, the reasons for the dismissal, the date on which their employment contract will end and their notice period and right of appeal.

Some organisations may choose to use alternative forms of sanction against the individual rather than dismissal. These could include demotion to another job, loss of seniority or pay, or a disciplinary transfer. These types of sanction may only be used if the employee's contract specifies these as alternatives or if agreement is reached with the individual concerned to allow them to be used.

4 The appeals procedure

The last section of the formal disciplinary procedure should indicate what the employee should do if they are not happy with the action taken against them. There should be a clear appeals procedure, with time limits for the submission of appeals stated. There should be the opportunity for a meeting to discuss the appeal and the person once again has the right to choose to be accompanied at this meeting. The appeal should be heard by a senior manager who has not been involved in the original disciplinary meeting. Again the employer must inform the employee about the final appeal decision. Even in a small organisation it is good practice for a different manger, who has not been involved in the case, to hear the appeal.

5 The nature of gross misconduct

As we said earlier, organisations will have different ideas as to what constitutes gross misconduct. The employee should be given some indication of this also in the disciplinary procedure. It is impossible to design a list that covers all possibilities, but the organisation should list some of them. For example, the procedure may say that the following constitute gross misconduct and if any employee, after a full investigation, is found guilty of any of these offences they will be dismissed, even for a first offence:

- theft
- deliberate damage to the organisation's property
- fraud
- incapacity to work because of the influence of illegal drugs or alcohol
- physical assault
- sexual harassment
- racial harassment
- serious infringement of health and safety rules.

These are examples of offences that normally constitute gross misconduct, but it is not an exhaustive list and other serious offences may also constitute gross misconduct and merit dismissal.

It is also a good idea to state the organisation's position on criminal offences committed outside employment. There should be a statement in the disciplinary procedure indicating that a criminal offence which occurs outside employment may be considered as gross misconduct and may result in dismissal. The word 'may' should be stressed here, as this is not an automatic reason for dismissal. The main considerations should be the nature of the offence and the type of work that the employee normally does, and whether the offence makes the employee unsuitable for their job.

In these cases, the employee concerned will normally be suspended from work on full pay while a full investigation is being carried out. Suspension on full pay does not imply any guilt.

6 Records

It is extremely important that accurate records of the proceedings are kept. According to the CIPD (2010a), 'All records should be kept meticulously, as this will be vital should a case be pursued at an employment tribunal. The type of records that should be kept by employers are minutes of meetings, email, attendance notes, notes of telephone calls, copies of correspondence etc.' While it is important to keep accurate records should the case become one of alleged unfair dismissal, it is also important at all stages of the disciplinary process to have an accurate record of what has happened so that the organisation is aware of the stage in the proceedings which has been reached.

All warning letters should also state that the warning will be recorded on the employee's file for a set period of time. The period of time will vary between organisations. It may perhaps be three months for a written warning and six months for a final written warning. Once that period of time has elapsed, if the worker's conduct or performance has improved to the employer's satisfaction, the letter and note of the offence should be removed from that person's record. If they later commit the same or a different breach of disciplinary procedure, then the procedure must be started again. So if the employee who has been given a warning for an infringement concerning timekeeping then commits a different infringement, for example, by carrying out poor quality work, the employer should not go to the next stage of the disciplinary procedure but should start with an informal talk and issue a separate warning if that proves necessary.

If the employer ignored the fact that the warning was out of date or was about a different type of disciplinary offence, then it could hardly expect to win its case if it eventually dismissed the worker and they later decided to go to an employment tribunal to claim unfair dismissal. Such actions would be regarded as procedurally incorrect.

If records of warnings were kept on a worker's file indefinitely, then this could prejudice the person reading the file at a later date against this employee. The employee may well have changed over the years and so an unfair impression of this person would be given. The employee has the right, under the Data Protection Act 1998, to check their records to ensure that erroneous or out-of-date information is not being held and possibly used against them. Refer to the section on data protection in Chapter 4 for more information.

Cases that may pose particular problems

The ACAS *Code of Practice* (2009a) also advises that certain situations may require special consideration. They list as particularly difficult cases:

- trade union officials
- criminal charges or convictions outside employment.

The ACAS guide (2009b) adds to these another situation that may require special consideration:

- employees to whom the full procedure is not immediately available.

The mini case studies in Activities 12.1 and 12.2 serve to illustrate some of these areas of concern. How would you handle each of these cases?

ACTIVITY 12.1

Jane has been employed by your organisation for 10 years. She works as the assistant manager in the wages office and has always been an excellent worker. You hear, on the grapevine, that she has been accused of stealing £100 from the funds of the local youth club, where she acts as treasurer.

Imagine that you are the manager of the wages office. What will you do when:

1 You first hear the rumours?
2 She is subsequently convicted but given a conditional discharge for this offence?

Discussion of Activity 12.1

1 This is perhaps one of the most difficult situations for a manager to deal with. If the offence had happened at work it would have been a clear case of theft from work and, after going through an investigation and the disciplinary procedure, may have been considered gross misconduct with the possibility of dismissal. As it is, should the manager consider this to be a disciplinary issue or not? ACAS (2009b) says that being charged with a criminal offence, and even being convicted of one, does not necessarily warrant disciplinary action being taken. Even if the employee is convicted of the offence and is absent from work because they are being remanded in custody, there is no automatic reason for disciplinary action or dismissal.

Initially when you, the manager, hear of the alleged theft from youth club funds you will need to establish the facts of the case as best you can. You are likely to need to talk to Jane as part of this process. The main question that you as an employer must decide is whether the matter is sufficiently serious to warrant starting the disciplinary procedure. The main consideration should be whether the offence, or the alleged offence, makes the employee unsuitable for the type of work they are currently doing. You then have three options:

(a) You could do nothing, if you are satisfied with Jane's explanation and decide that the matter is not sufficiently serious to be taken further within the disciplinary procedure.

(b) You might consider suspending Jane on full pay pending the result of the court case. This would remove her from the situation at work where there would be gossip and rumours, and would also ensure that if anything went missing from work she would not be automatically accused. In many ways this is an attractive option, but the manager would need to be aware that the organisation may be paying Jane for several months before her case is heard.

(c) You could consider moving her to another section where she would not deal with cash handling, although of course many wages offices do not necessarily deal with money anyway. This would have the same advantages as in (b), but Jane would be earning her wages. She still might be accused, however, every time anything went missing. You may of course not have any other suitable post to which she could transfer, and depending on her contract you may need her agreement to the transfer.

2 When Jane is found guilty, then there are once again a variety of appropriate responses. The main guidance is given in the ACAS Code of Practice (2009a), which states that offences which occur away from the workplace should not be treated as automatic reasons for dismissal. It goes on to say that the most important factor

Disciplinary procedures and practices

will be whether the nature of the offence makes the employee unsuitable for their particular job. The *Code of Practice* on disciplinary and grievance procedure would still need to be followed. She should be written to and called to an interview with representation if she requires it. A decision then needs to be made. The right of appeal should also be explained.

In the case of Jane, it would be possible to say that since she was found guilty of theft, this would affect people's view of her in a position of trust and so she may be dismissed for gross misconduct. Most disciplinary procedures follow ACAS's guidelines and include a section which states that offences which occur outside work may constitute gross misconduct. Dismissal should not be automatic, however. Other options are available and it depends on the circumstances.

This case study, concerning potential disciplinary offences that occur away from the place of work, helps to illustrate one of the more difficult cases that may arise and shows how useful it is to refer to the ACAS *Code of Practice on Disciplinary and Grievance Procedures* (2009a) for guidance in this area.

ACTIVITY 12.2

Paul has worked for Shepley Computers for four years, and for the past six months has worked on the night shift. He has a blemish-free record and is a highly regarded member of the workforce. One hot night in summer he leaves work after signing in at nine o'clock and goes to the pub. He returns to work under the influence of alcohol, and his supervisor, who has noticed his absence, tells him that he is suspended and must go home immediately. Paul becomes abusive and threatens to punch his supervisor. He takes his supervisor by the shoulders and shakes him while all the time threatening to punch him. His supervisor tells him that he is dismissed and should collect all his money and documents at the end of the week.

1 Do you feel that Paul's supervisor acted correctly in this case?
2 If not, how would you have handled this situation?

Discussion of Activity 12.2

1 Offences that occur when the human resources department is not available to give advice, as in this case, need particular attention. Paul's supervisor, who works on the night shift, would not be likely to have the human resource manager to turn to for advice when a potential disciplinary situation like this suddenly occurs, so he needs to be well trained to know how to handle a situation such as this. He needs to be very clear in his own mind exactly what powers are available to him. In this case the supervisor initially acted well in suspending the employee. Paul was drunk and abusive and was behaving in a threatening manner towards him. Suspension with pay is a useful technique when there needs to be an opportunity to calm the situation or when time is needed to complete an investigation into whether or not an offence has occurred. He then acted rather rashly in telling Paul that he had been dismissed. No one should be dismissed unless a proper investigation has been carried out. Taking away someone's livelihood is a serious matter which could result in an employment tribunal case for unfair dismissal being brought against the organisation. Even though some of Paul's actions, such as being drunk

at work and acting in an abusive and threatening manner, could clearly be classified as gross misconduct, there still needs to be a full investigation with an opportunity for Paul and his superior to state their cases and for union representation, before a disciplinary decision is reached, so clearly Paul's supervisor has not acted in a correct manner.

2 Clearly in this situation the ACAS Code of Practice was not followed, so your answer about how you would have handled the situation should have followed this:

(a) Suspend Paul on pay.

(b) Investigate.

(c) Write a letter to inform Paul of the concerns and give him the opportunity to be represented by a colleague or trade union official.

(d) Hold a meeting with Paul and his representative.

(e) Make a decision and advise Paul of his right to appeal.

Absence control

Absences are often another area of particular concern to employers. Here what is important is to find out exactly what the reasons are for the absence. In many organisations an absence control procedure is used, and this may result in the disciplinary procedure being used less frequently. Absence control systems usually require the employee to telephone the supervisor on the first day of absence, and the supervisor will go through a checklist of points with them. If the supervisor is not available there will be a second or a third designated person with whom the absent person will have to speak. An interview will be held with the supervisor or other designated person when the absentee returns to work.

There will also be a system of visits for people who are absent on a long-term basis to ensure that the organisation stays up to date with their current situation and knows when to expect them to return to work. Supervisors and managers will be aware of the level of absenteeism in their sections and will encourage good attendance.

The aim of an absence control procedure is to minimise the need for the use of the disciplinary procedure, by creating a culture in which everyone is aware of the importance of good attendance and of their value to the organisation. The danger is that some employees may feel pressurised into returning to work before they are really fit, and this may prove to be counterproductive, resulting in their needing more time off later to recover fully.

If there is not a good reason for the absence then this is likely to be an issue considered to be misconduct. If a person has a record of short-term absences without suitable explanations or adequate medical evidence, then they can be dealt with under the organisation's normal disciplinary procedure. There is usually a specified level of absence, e.g. 10 days in three months, after which more formal controls will be introduced, leading to counselling or disciplinary action as appropriate.

Disciplinary procedures and ill-health

If employees are away on a long-term absence due to a genuine illness then the situation needs to be dealt with in an entirely different way. You cannot warn someone that there must be an improvement in their attendance if you know that this is impossible because of the nature of their illness. Instead, regular contact needs to be maintained with such employees to establish the likelihood of their return, and medical evidence needs to be sought. A company doctor's advice may be needed. In the end it may be that the person is unable to return to work in the foreseeable future, and it may be necessary to consider whether there are any other suitable jobs that they may be able to undertake, or whether their employment needs to be terminated. Other factors, such as whether they have exhausted the organisation's sickness pay scheme, the age of the person, whether the illness is as a result of a disability as defined by the Equality Act 2010, and whether they could take early retirement under the organisation's pension scheme, will need to be considered here in order to find the best solution for both the employee and the organisation. There is also likely to be a need for employee counselling and advice, and this process, if handled with the sensitivity it deserves, is likely to be extremely lengthy.

Disciplinary hearings

The actual disciplinary hearing is similar in many ways to the interviews discussed in Chapter 7. The manager who is conducting the hearing will need to prepare thoroughly, have the relevant information to hand and arrange for a quiet room with no disturbances and with an appropriate layout in which to hold the hearing. The disciplinary hearing should be conducted in a systematic and fair way in order to ensure that all the relevant information is considered. The manager chairing it should explain clearly the purpose, who is present and why they are there, and the sequence.

Although there are many similarities between disciplinary hearings and interviews, and one would expect them to be conducted in a similar way, there are some specific legal definitions that apply to disciplinary hearings. It is important to consider these as there is a legal right for workers to be accompanied at a disciplinary hearing and this is not something that would normally apply at most other hearings, with the exception of the grievance hearing which will be discussed later in this chapter.

Disciplinary hearings are defined as all meetings where either disciplinary action or some other action could be taken against a worker. This includes any meeting that might result in actions such as a warning, final written warning, suspension without pay, demotion or dismissal being taken against the worker. It also applies to meetings to confirm warnings or other disciplinary action and to appeal hearings, even if they are held after the worker has left the employment concerned.

The right to be accompanied at a disciplinary interview

The Employment Relations Act 1999 gave workers the right to request a companion to accompany them at disciplinary or grievance hearings. This can be a fellow worker or a trade union official or even, in certain circumstances, a lay trade union official. The companion can address the hearing and advise workers, but is not supposed to answer questions on behalf of the worker. It is in order for a worker to request an alternative date for a hearing if the companion of their choice is unavailable on the designated date for the hearing.

The ACAS *Code of Practice on Disciplinary and Grievance Procedures* (2009a) and the *ACAS Guide* to this (2009b) give practical guidance about workers being accompanied at disciplinary hearings. They explain that as well as the rights to be accompanied already mentioned, some workers may have other additional rights to be accompanied by different people specified in their contracts of employment. Employers should also consider sympathetically any specific needs raised by disabled workers or by a disabled companion.

Trade unions are supposed to ensure that there are suitable training and refresher courses for all their officials, so that they can confidently take on the role of companion if requested. However, ACAS explain that although workers can request a trade union official or a fellow worker to accompany them at any disciplinary hearing, the person selected for this role does not have to agree to do this and should not be pressurised to take on the role if they do not want to do it.

Before the hearing the worker should inform the employer of the name of their companion so that the companion can also be involved in discussions about choosing a convenient date and time for the hearing. The companion may carry out the following roles:

- stating the worker's case for them
- summarising the worker's case
- responding on behalf of the worker to any views expressed at the hearing
- discussing points with the worker during the hearing
- asking witnesses questions.

However, the role of the companion will depend on what the worker wants them to do and the worker may choose not to allow them to do some of these things.

If an employer fails to comply with a reasonable request for a worker to be accompanied at a disciplinary hearing the worker may complain about this to an employment tribunal. If the worker's companion cannot attend the hearing on a specific date and the employer fails to rearrange a hearing to take account of this then this can also be the cause for a complaint to an employment tribunal. Two weeks' pay can be awarded by a tribunal in these cases and this could be increased if the tribunal also decides that the worker has been unfairly dismissed.

Grievance: introduction and definitions

ACAS (2009a) defines grievances as 'concerns, problems or complaints that employees raise with their managers.' We shall use the term 'grievance' in this way as a form of dissatisfaction about which the employee feels sufficiently strongly that they formally raise the issue with their management representative or shop steward. Sometimes it can be difficult for an employer to differentiate between what may appear to be minor concerns and grumbles, and grievances. The CIPD (2010b) says that 'any communication which contains a problem or complaint that the employees raise with their employer should potentially be treated as a grievance.' If there is any doubt about whether the issue is a true grievance then the employer is advised to ask the employee or worker directly. Since grievances can be raised in many different ways including letters, emails, memos, resignation letters or more formally by a worker's solicitor and since some of these may just appear to be expressing a general dissatisfaction, case law shows that it is wise for the employer to make this check.

The ACAS *Code of Practice on Disciplinary and Grievance Procedures* (2009a) provides guidance on grievance handling. Grievances may arise for a multitude of reasons. An employee may become dissatisfied with their hours of work or working conditions, they may feel a supervisor shows unfair favouritism to others, or may feel dissatisfaction about pay or sexual harassment. Some grievances may appear trivial and others, such as alleged sexual harassment, may be very serious, but to the employee concerned they will all have been serious enough to raise formally. A survey of 147 organisations by the IRS Employment Review (2007) found that among this sample 'the most common cause of grievances were breakdowns in relationships between colleagues or between employees and their line managers.'

Anyone in an organisation could have a grievance, even a member of management. Some grievances may become a collective issue, with negotiations between management and a trade union arising over an issue such as a collective grievance about pay or working conditions. This chapter will focus solely on grievance as an individual issue.

Grievance procedures and practices

Reasons for having a grievance procedure

Employees need to know how they can raise a grievance and seek redress for any grievance that they might have. They need to feel confident that their grievance will be treated in a fair way and that they will get to know the result of raising this grievance within a short period of time. It is also important to settle the grievance quickly, to prevent it becoming a larger grievance that involves more people and takes longer to resolve.

If there were no procedure for raising and resolving grievances, it would be likely that employees would grumble to colleagues, and not only their work but the work of the department would be liable to suffer as a result. Therefore the main aim of the grievance procedure is to settle disputes fairly and as near to the source of grievance as possible. If there were a grievance over an issue such as safety or harassment, failure to provide a mechanism to deal with the grievance could result in serious repercussions, with perhaps accidents or a sexual or racial harassment case occurring. A grievance procedure in effect provides a safety mechanism to prevent issues from getting out of control. It also ensures that management have a channel to hear about issues that may be worrying their staff.

Discipline versus grievance

Disciplinary action is, as we have seen, normally initiated by management to express dissatisfaction with, and bring about changes in, employee behaviour; grievance, on the other hand, is normally initiated by employees for similar reasons, but in respect of management's, or perhaps co-workers', behaviour. There is a need for fairness and justice in both procedures although they are initiated by different parties. Because of this it is sometimes claimed that they are the opposites of each other, and should be viewed as complementary processes in industrial justice.

Pause for thought 12.6 Consider what you have just learned about grievance and discipline. In what ways do you consider discipline and grievance to be opposites? Are there any facts which make you think that they are not truly opposites?

As we have shown, discipline and grievance are both concerned with fairness and justice. They differ in that the people who initiate the action in each case differ. The management initiates disciplinary action against employees, and employees initiate grievances mainly against their supervisors and managers. In this way they may be considered to be opposite faces of industrial justice. However, this disregards the balance of power in these cases. To consider them to be true opposites would entail the assumption that when an employee initiates a grievance they have the same amount of power as management, which is clearly not the case. An employee who has a grievance will not be able to insist that action is taken against the person who has caused the grievance, and will have to rely on management's willingness to take action.

The informal grievance procedure

The Labour Research Department (1995) conducted a survey of the grievance procedures of 85 organisations. It found that the majority of complaints are resolved in an informal way, making it unnecessary to raise them as a formal grievance. Informal grievance procedures seem to be just as important in organisations as informal disciplinary procedures. However, a small number of complaints will not be resolved informally, and for these it is necessary to have a grievance procedure.

These findings are supported by Cully et al. (1999) in their study of Britain at Work as depicted by the 1998 Workplace Employee Relations Survey. This showed that while 91 per cent of employees had access to grievance procedures in the organisations which were surveyed, in only 30 per cent of the organisations had the formal grievance procedure actually been used during that year. According to Cully et al. (1999), 'One reason for this might be that employees had nothing to complain about. Another might be that the procedure is not a particularly effective mechanism for resolving problems.'

We have already outlined the reasons for having a formal grievance procedure, and in the next section will consider the form that the grievance procedure should take and the main points to be considered when designing a grievance procedure, before considering the way in which the grievance interview should be handled.

The formal grievance procedure

Sometimes it proves to be impossible to settle grievances in an informal manner, so in order that both workers and managers are clear about how to handle grievances and to ensure grievances are resolved quickly and fairly, a grievance procedure should be designed and issued to all employees and other workers. It is a good idea, once again, to involve various groups in the design of a procedure to suit a particular organisation and to ensure that everyone in the organisation understands the rules, where they can be located and how to use them.

The key features in the formal grievance procedure

The Labour Research Department (1995) found that 80 per cent of the grievance procedures that it reviewed had between three and six stages after the informal stage. ACAS (2009a) indicate that so many stages should not be necessary for most organisations and that for smaller organisations the formal grievance procedure is likely to comprise just two stages. After the grievance has been dealt with and a meeting held there is a right of appeal, which should be to a more senior manager, or if this is not possible to a different manager who has not previously been involved in the grievance. In most organisations it should be possible to achieve at least this two-stage procedure. However, where there is only one stage, for instance in an extremely small organisation, perhaps where there is only a single owner/manager, it is particularly important that the person dealing with the grievance deals with the grievance in as impartial a way as possible. In larger organisations ACAS (2009b) say a further appeal to a higher level of management such as a director may be appropriate. We do not feel that there is any advantage in having more levels than three in the procedure, even if there are more levels in the management hierarchy. We would suggest that three main levels should prove adequate for most organisations.

Outlined below are the possible main stages in the formal grievance procedure.

Stage 1
Inform the employer in writing of the grievance

The worker should raise the grievance in writing, with the immediate supervisor, who will reply within a specified time, e.g. five working days. If the grievance is about the supervisor, there needs to be an opportunity to bypass this stage and to raise the grievance with a manager at the next highest level.

Hold a meeting

Once the formal grievance has been raised there should then be a meeting at which the grievance is discussed and then the manager should set out their decision with reasons for it. The manager should of course take time to prepare adequately for this meeting but should still respond quickly and arrange for the meeting within a reasonable timeframe, such as five working days. The manager may need to check earlier records to establish whether any similar grievances have been raised and there may need to be special arrangements made in some circumstances. If English is not the first language of the person raising the grievance, it may be necessary to provide an interpreter. Alternatively, if the person raising the grievance, or their companion, is disabled it may be necessary to make some reasonable adjustments to the room layout.

The manager is in control of this meeting and should ensure that it is conducted in a calm, fair and orderly manner with normal courtesies such as introductions being adhered to if this is necessary. Many of the features of a grievance meeting are the same as for other types of interview, though ACAS (2009b) advise that this type of meeting does differ from a disciplinary interview as it is more likely to result in an amicable solution.

There is a need for a quiet, private room arranged to facilitate ease of communication. The employee or their companion is likely to do most of the talking, since they are raising the grievance. There may be a need to call witnesses, and after hearing all the evidence from both sides the manager should adjourn before reaching a decision. The manager must ensure a fair hearing and that everyone concerned is aware of the purpose of the meeting, who is to be called as witnesses, the time limits within which a decision will be reached, and the way in which the decision will be announced to the employee or worker concerned. ACAS (2009b) also suggest that consideration should be given to having someone not directly involved in the case to taking notes and acting as a witness of the proceedings. The manager will also need to finish by summing up the key points and may need to adjourn the meeting before reaching a decision.

If there is not a swift and fair resolution of grievances, the grievances may tend to build up and the work of the section is likely to suffer. At worst this could ultimately result in a high labour turnover or a high level of absenteeism as people remove themselves from a situation where they feel unhappy, or it might escalate into an industrial dispute.

Some organisations may, in addition to these procedures, decide to have a whistle-blowing procedure. This will then provide additional protection for workers who raise grievances about issues that involve some form of wrongdoing within the organisation, e.g. workplace hazards or fraud.

Ensure the worker is informed of their right to be accompanied

The worker has, depending on the nature of the grievance, a statutory right to be accompanied at a grievance hearing and the manager should make them aware of this right. The statutory right applies if the grievance relates to something that concerns the performance of 'the duty of the employer in relation to a worker'. For example, this could apply in relation to a grievance raised about equal pay, because the employer has a clear duty to provide equal pay to all workers. Ultimately it will be the employment tribunals that will decide in which cases the worker should have been given the right to be accompanied at the grievance hearing, so it would be good practice to allow any worker raising a grievance to be accompanied, if they request it.

Decide on appropriate action

The manager has to decide what action is appropriate in the circumstances of the case and they should ensure that the worker knows the timeframe in which a decision will be reached and of their right of appeal if they are not happy with the decision.

Stage 2
Appeal

If it has not been resolved, the individual should request in writing an interview with a more senior manager. This manager should then arrange to hear the grievance within a specified time period, e.g. within five working days. The worker should once again be informed of their statutory right to be accompanied and a date set for them to present their case at a meeting. The manager should make a decision about the grievance within a specified time period and the worker should be informed of this. If there is likely to be a delay in reaching a decision then the worker should also be given a clear reason for this and told when they can expect a decision.

Stage 3

As stated earlier, in a larger organisation there may be a further stage to the grievance procedure. If it has not been resolved at stage 2, the individual should raise the grievance with the general manager or director or the next most senior person. Once again, the worker should be told of their statutory rights to be accompanied at a hearing at which they present their case. As in the earlier stages, an indication about the time it will take to reach a decision should be given to the worker, as should explanations about any unavoidable delay.

Time limits

You will have noted that fairly strict time limits were specified in the section on stages in the procedure. If there is not a satisfactory response to the grievance within a specified time limit, then the employee should be able to raise the grievance with the supervisor's immediate management. There should be a clear time limit for each stage of the grievance procedure, as without this there is a danger that, although a manager or supervisor may have good intentions to deal with a grievance, it will nevertheless be overlooked.

Representation

At each stage in the formal grievance procedure the worker should be informed of their statutory right to be accompanied by a companion who is another employee or who is a trade union representative. This right, once again, applies to all workers and not just employees, so agency workers, home workers, the self-employed or those doing voluntary work could all raise grievances and have the right to be accompanied. As we said earlier in this chapter, the right applies specifically when there is a requirement to attend a grievance hearing which relates to legal or contractual commitments such as grievances relating to grading or promotion, if they arise out of a contract. Some other grievances may not relate to contractual or legal matters but it may be safer for employers to allow workers to be accompanied rather than finding themselves testing the interpretation of the law at an employment tribunal.

Exceptional circumstances and special considerations

In exceptional circumstances it may not be practicable to raise the grievance with the immediate manager. This may be because the grievance is caused by the manager or because the manager will not be available, perhaps because of illness, to deal with the grievance with the urgency that it deserves. In those exceptional circumstances the grievance may be taken to the next level of supervision.

Some organisations may also want to establish special additional procedures to deal with specific types of grievances relating, for example, to discrimination, harassment or bullying and may design policies specific to these issues. The organisation may feel the need to have separate procedures as these are all very difficult areas that may need extra-sensitive handling.

Records

Records of grievances raised and the responses made to them should be kept. They should, in accordance with the Data Protection Act 1998, be kept confidential but certain information or data should normally be available to the individual concerned on request.

Shazia, as the shop steward, is entitled to reasonable time off to carry out her trade union duties, so it is in order for her to request time off. However, as we said earlier, a grievance should be settled as near to the source of the problem as possible. You need to remind Shazia, who as a shop steward should certainly be aware of this, that if she has a grievance herself, or if she is acting on behalf of one of your department, then you are the person with whom the grievance should first be raised. You should point out that if you cannot deal with this satisfactorily within the specified time period then of course she may then raise the grievance, in line with the grievance procedure, with the general manager.

Although there is a need for grievances to be settled as near to the source of grievance as possible, this becomes difficult if the grievance is about the manager or supervisor concerned, so if the grievance is about you as the supervisor, Shazia may be unwilling to discuss it with you. Nevertheless, if it is about you, you will need to know about it sooner or later, so at least you should try to ascertain the nature of the grievance before allowing it to go further.

Mediation

ACAS (2009a) recommend mediation at any stage in both discipline and grievance procedures and some organisations' disciplinary and grievance procedures formally include this as a stage in both processes. It is likely to work best in a grievance situation involving relationships where there is perhaps a less formal environment and neutrality from a third party would enable both sides to explore issues in a calm way. Mediation involves someone who has not been involved in the disciplinary or grievance issue, an independent third party, helping the two parties to the dispute to reach a voluntary agreement. Mediators are not supposed to make judgments or say what should happen but help the parties to reach agreement.

Lind (2009) states that mediation is not an actual part of the legal process but that mediators can be useful as 'completely neutral, they help identify areas of common interest, but the parties reach their own solutions.' Both parties have to agree to mediation and any solution is binding on both parties. Since tribunals now have discretionary powers to increase or decrease awards by up to 25 per cent for either party failing to follow the ACAS *Code of Practice*, it could increase the role of mediation as it is one way to show that all steps have been tried when attempting to resolve differences in either a disciplinary or grievance situation.

Conclusion

We have shown in this chapter the meaning and the importance of grievance and disciplinary procedures to the organisation and the increasing role that mediation can play in each of these. Both specialist human resource managers and line managers have an extremely important role to play in the design of procedures that are fair to all; it is also vital that cases of grievance or discipline are dealt with in accordance with the organisation's procedures. Knowledge and understanding of the ACAS *Code of Practice 1* (2009a), and *Discipline and Grievances at Work: The ACAS Guide* (2009b) are both valuable aids to help ensure that fair procedures are designed and that disciplinary and grievance interviews are handled well. Good procedures and clear policies for dealing with both discipline and grievance issues should result in fewer instances of these types of problems for the organisation. Any issues that do arise are dealt with in a fair way that everyone understands. Organisations should at the design stage involve representatives from different levels and types of work to ensure policies and procedures really do meet the requirements of both the organisation and the workers. The chosen form of their policies and procedures should also be guided by advice in the ACAS *Code of Practice* (2009a) and include the statutory right to be accompanied for workers at both discipline and grievance hearings. Organisations must also be clear about whether they are interpreting the right to be accompanied in its strict legal sense at specific types of discipline or grievance hearings, or whether they are extending this right to workers in any discipline or grievance situation. In the next chapter we examine the consequences of getting a disciplinary case wrong, and discuss unfair dismissal and redundancy.

The mind maps shown in Figures 12.1 and 12.2 summarise the key points covered in this chapter. When you have examined these, test your understanding of the chapter with the review questions and self-check questions.

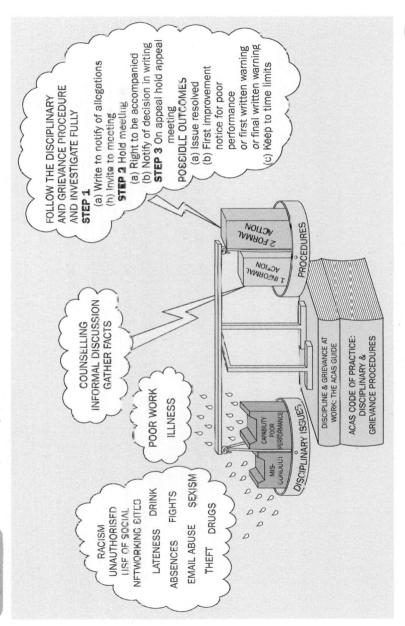

Figure 12.1 Mind map: discipline

447

Figure 12.2 Mind map: grievance

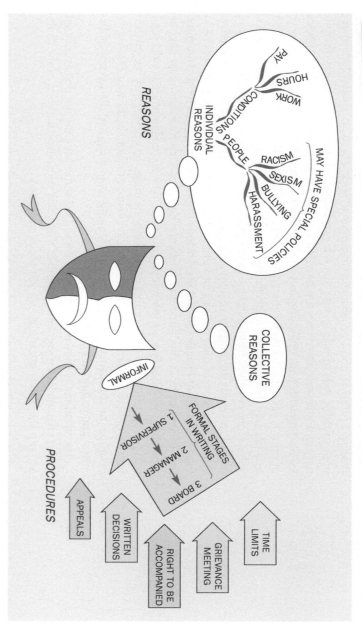

REASONS

MAY HAVE SPECIAL POLICIES

PAY
HOURS
WORK CONDITIONS
INDIVIDUAL REASONS
PEOPLE
RACISM
SEXISM
BULLYING
HARASSMENT

COLLECTIVE REASONS

INFORMAL

FORMAL STAGES IN WRITING
1 SUPERVISOR
2 MANAGER
3 BOARD

PROCEDURES

APPEALS

WRITTEN DECISIONS

RIGHT TO BE ACCOMPANIED

GRIEVANCE MEETING

TIME LIMITS

REVIEW QUESTIONS

Brief answers to review questions are provided on page 497.

1 Interview both a line manager and an HR manager and try to establish what roles they play in relation to grievance and discipline handling in the workplace. How do your findings compare with what we have said in this chapter?

2 Obtain a copy of an organisation's discipline and grievance procedure and compare it with how we have described these processes. Identify and comment on the similarities and differences.

3 Obtain a copy of the ACAS *Code of Practice 1: Disciplinary and Grievance Procedures* (2009a). Use this, and our suggestions in this chapter, to rewrite or modify either of the procedures you used for question 2, if you find that this is necessary.

4 You have joined an organisation which has expanded recently and now has 100 employees. This organisation started as a small undertaking with only 18 employees and has never had a formal grievance procedure. Write a report for the general manager outlining why it is important to have a formal grievance procedure and suggesting what the procedure should contain.

SELF-CHECK QUESTIONS

Answer the following multiple-choice questions. The correct responses are given on page 497 for you to check your understanding of this chapter.

1 According to ACAS, disciplinary procedures should be designed to:
   (a) provide a fair way to gather evidence against the offender
   (b) ensure that someone is caught for the offence
   (c) promote fairness and set standards of conduct
   (d) point out the mistake that has been made
   (e) provide fair methods of punishing the offender.

2 According to ACAS (2009b), a grievance is:
   (a) any communication that the employee has with their manager
   (b) concerns, problems or complaints that employees raise with their employer
   (c) a dissatisfaction expressed to colleagues
   (d) concerns, problems or complaints which have not been raised by the employee with their employer
   (e) anything that disturbs an employee though they are too embarrassed to discuss it with their manager.

3 Which of the following is **not** listed in the ACAS *Code of Practice* as a feature that a fair disciplinary procedure should possess?
   (a) Issues should be dealt with promptly.
   (b) Issues should be handled consistently.
   (c) The facts of the case against the employee should be kept secret until the disciplinary hearing.
   (d) The employee should have the right to be accompanied at any formal meeting about discipline or grievance.
   (e) There should be clear rights of appeal.

4 The ACAS *Code of Practice* (2009a) states which of the following?
   (a) That only employees have the right to be accompanied at disciplinary hearings.
   (b) That only employees have the right to be accompanied at grievance hearings.
   (c) That workers have the right to be accompanied, in certain circumstances, at formal disciplinary or formal grievance hearings.
   (d) That workers have the right to be accompanied, in certain circumstances, at informal discussions or counselling relating to discipline.
   (e) That workers have the right to be accompanied, in certain circumstances, at informal discussions relating to grievances they raise.

5 Which of the following should happen once the time limit for a written warning has elapsed?
   (a) the warning should still be kept on the employee's personal record file
   (b) the warning should be removed from the employee's personal record file and placed in a central file in which records of all disciplinary offences are kept
   (c) the warning should be removed from the employee's personal record file only if the data are stored on computer
   (d) the warning should be removed completely from the employee's personal record file
   (e) the warning should be removed from the employee's personal record file after a further three months has elapsed.

6 According to ACAS (2009b), if a serious criminal offence occurs outside employment:

(a) this is automatically considered to be gross misconduct and dismissal is justifiable

(b) this is automatically considered to be gross misconduct and dismissal may be justifiable

(c) this should not be treated as an automatic reason for dismissal – the main consideration should be whether or not the offence makes the employee unsuitable for their type of work

(d) this should not be treated as an automatic reason for dismissal – the main consideration is whether you think that the employee is likely to commit the offence again

(e) this should not be treated as an automatic reason for dismissal – the main consideration should be the length of service the employee has had with your organisation.

7 The recommended first stage in a grievance procedure is:

(a) to raise the grievance with the top management immediately

(b) to grumble to your colleagues about your grievance

(c) to raise the grievance with your supervisor's manager

(d) to raise the grievance with the area manager

(e) to raise the grievance with your immediate supervisor.

8 Which of the following is TRUE?

(a) An employment tribunal has the power to increase or decrease awards against employers or employees by 10 per cent.

(b) An employment tribunal has the power to increase or decrease awards against employers or employees by 25 per cent.

(c) Only large organisations with over 500 employees need to have a formal disciplinary procedure.

(d) Workers who are not employees of the organisation never have the right to be accompanied by a trade union official or colleague at a disciplinary hearing.

(e) Workers who are not employees of the organisation never have the right to be accompanied by a trade union official or colleague at a grievance hearing.

9 Nowadays the role of human resource managers in handling discipline and grievance situations is:

(a) always purely advisory

(b) non-existent, as line managers deal with these topics

(c) purely to check on line managers and ensure they handle things correctly

(d) only to design the procedures themselves

(e) a mixture of things, including advice and guidance.

10 The initials ACAS stand for:

(a) Advisory, Counselling and Aid Service

(b) Aid, Counselling and Arbitration Service

(c) Aid, Conciliation and Arbitration Service

(d) Advice, Conciliation and Arbitration Service

(e) Advisory, Conciliation and Arbitration Service.

FT Report – Recruitment: Social networking and workplace discipline

By Richard Donkin

About six years ago I embarked with two collaborators on a book about the importance of networks in the future of work. I wrote an introduction and a chapter, then waited . . . and waited.

The collaboration died; a pity because we had some good material, including stories about early communications networks in Roman times, the road networks of the Incas and various intelligence networks, both ancient and modern.

The time seemed right. The initial internet-inspired investment euphoria had disappeared and there was not much sign of what would come to be known as Web 2.0 technology or any discussion of long-tail distribution graphs that were still confined to statistics textbooks.

Interest in networks was spreading, however, as work-related networking groups such as First Tuesday began to grow in popularity and books such as Malcolm Gladwell's *The Tipping Point* were beginning to investigate the workings of networks. The internet had stimulated a thirst for sharing information very similar to that during the Enlightenment when thinkers and scientists exchanged letters through European academies and societies.

I can trace my interest in networks back to a column in 1998 inspired by a meeting with Karen Stephenson, an anthropologist, who specialised in studying the social dynamics of communications and how they applied in the workplace.

She was fascinated by the way information was distributed among groups of people on what she called 'invisible lines of trust'. The most interesting people in these lines of communication she described as 'pulse-takers', what Gladwell called 'mavens'.

Mavens are the people in offices or pubs who seem to know everything. They are the ones with their ears to the ground. They are not usually the bosses (who might well know things but are bound by confidentiality obligations).

Mavens do not know all the answers, but they know where to find snippets of information and where they can go to test their theories. Sometimes their 'news' is no more than an educated guess but, for those who rely on them, they become a trusted source. People not only seek information from them but also pass on to them their own titbits.

I had seen the way this worked in a newsroom that had also benefited from an early electronic message system that allowed the creation of special-interest 'user groups'. In this way, long before the email, or social networking websites, journalists had been exchanging vital screen-based messages such as: 'Fancy a pint?'

So there is nothing really very new about social networking. Nor is there anything new in the fears that this kind of thing can be disruptive to the working environment. In the 1930s typing pool supervisors were constantly complaining about what they regarded as distracting levels of gossip among their workers.

Today the complaint is levelled at internet-based social networking. The worry is well founded. Various studies have been published recently arguing that internet-based social networking in offices is wasting business time. Whether or not you subscribe to the dodgy statistics presented in these studies, it's difficult to deny there must be a significant cost to business in lost hours.

A recruitment company head told me a week ago he had banned access to the Facebook website in his office. 'I noticed that the people who seemed to be on there all the time were the ones that were the least productive. The most productive people didn't go there much in work time,' he said.

In this respect I would say there are three categories of office workers: those who just get on with their work and don't take much interest in internet-based exchanges. Those who enjoy looking in to their web pages during breaks and slack periods and, finally, those who become addicted to the technology and can't help popping on to these sites at every possible opportunity.

The first two are not a great problem for managers. It is the third – usually people who find little intrinsic stimulation in office work – that poses the biggest problem. But this group has always existed. It exists in school classrooms, offices and on factory floors.

Ironically it's among such groups that you can sometimes find entrepreneurs, artists and dreamers. But that doesn't help when work consists of repetitive administrative tasks.

I'm not seeking to disparage this kind of work, or to defend the fickleness of dreamers. There are individuals, however, who simply do not thrive in routines. Perhaps they should be sifted out by those who recruit for routine work. But the workplace would be pretty dull without them.

Depriving easily-distracted individuals of external stimulation may be the only way to suppress their mercurial instincts long enough to focus their talents on the job in hand. But it cannot be a long-term solution. First, many people are learning to bypass attempts to block access to certain sites. My schoolboy son was explaining to me this weekend how he achieves this in his classroom. I didn't know whether to be angry or proud.

Second, social networking is a phenomenon that is not going away. As the initial excitement dies, its use will become routine. I noticed this week that newspaper accounts reporting the deaths of four firefighters, at the Atherston warehouse fire in Warwickshire, had drawn biographical details from Facebook entries. Photographs of the dead were being compiled on a Facebook group and friends were visiting the site of one of the firemen to pay condolences. Socially this is comparable with the in-memoriam columns in newspapers. Disseminating information in this way is important: the full disaster of the battle of the Somme in 1916 was not revealed by the government of the day but in the long columns of deaths recorded publicly by families in British newspapers.

Here is the real issue of social networking for business. Its potency has taken companies by surprise. Many bosses, initially dismissive of these sites, now feel threatened, partly because they worry their workplaces are being undermined and partly because they feel they must exclude themselves for fear that their presence in a network will be unwelcome. Not unreasonably they feel they must preserve distance from staff they may discipline, promote or make redundant.

Just as any social arena – the home, the workplace, the street – becomes a stage for human interaction, so does the internet network. Yes, there are threats but there are opportunities too. We all need to learn how to use this thing sensibly. Education and debate may prove a more positive route than censure.

(Financial Times, 8 November 2007. Reproduced with permission.)

Questions

1 Do you think that employers are justified in banning the use of social networking sites and treating their use during working time as a disciplinary offence?

2 How useful are social networking sites for sharing work-related information?

3 List the advantages and disadvantages of including social networking sites as part of a disciplinary procedure.

WHAT NEXT?

Find some good examples of disciplinary and grievance letters and forms by going to the ACAS website: **www.acas.co.uk/index.aspx?articleid=1439.**

You can also view a video showing how mediation might work at **www.acas.co.uk/index.aspx?articleid=2835.**

Still on the ACAS website, test your knowledge and understanding of discipline and grievance issues by taking its online course. This is designed for managers but if you have studied this chapter and answered the questions as you have gone through it you should have a good basis for developing your knowledge and understanding further by using these online materials: **www.acas.org.uk/index.aspx?articleid=2113.**

References

Advisory, Conciliation and Arbitration Service (2009a) *Code of Practice 1: Disciplinary and Grievance Procedures*, ACAS.

Advisory, Conciliation and Arbitration Service (2009b) *Discipline and Grievances at Work: The ACAS Guide*, ACAS.

Chartered Institute of Personnel and Development (2010a) *Discipline and Grievances at Work: Fact Sheet*, CIPD (www.cipd.co.uk/subjects/emplaw/discipline/disciplingrievprocs.htm?; accessed 6.5.10).

Chartered Institute of Personnel and Development (2010b) *Discipline and Grievance Procedures: Member Resource*, CIPD (accessed 01/04/2010).

Cole, K. (2007) Look beneath the labels, *People Management*, 25 January.

Cully, M., S. Woodland, A. O'Reilly and G. Dix (1999) *Britain at Work as Depicted by the 1998 Workplace Employee Relations Survey*, Routledge.

He, H. (2009) Stealing cyber veggies thrives in a lonely world, *South China Morning Post*, 12 December.

IRS Employment Review (2007) Survey: dispute resolution, disciplinaries and grievances 2007, IRS, 879, 20 August.

Kaye, M. (2007) Unspoken disciplinary requirements, *People Management*, 25 January.

Labour Research Department (1995) *Bargaining. Report 149*, Labour Research Department, April.

Lind, M. (2009) Where does mediation fit into dispute resolution? *People Management*, 23 April.

Further study

Books

Advisory, Conciliation and Arbitration Service (2009b) *Discipline and Grievances at Work: The ACAS Guide*, ACAS.

This gives practical guidance about the ACAS *Code of Practice 1: Disciplinary and Grievance Procedures*.

Internet

The Advisory, Conciliation and Arbitration Service   www.acas.org.uk
Another source of information for ACAS publications, some of which are published in full on this site.

The Department for Business, Innovation and Skills   www.bis.gov.uk
Many useful publications, discussion documents and some pieces of legislation can be found on this site.

The TUC   www.tuc.org.uk
This gives the TUC's views on many current issues and new legislation.

453

CHAPTER 13

Dismissal, redundancy and outplacement

Objectives

By the end of this chapter you will be able to:

● explain what is meant by the term 'fair dismissal'

● explain what is meant by 'redundancy'

● define the term 'outplacement'

● describe the services that an outplacement consultancy may provide.

I n Chapter 12 we explained that there may be occasions when not everything in the relationship between employer and worker goes smoothly: the employee or worker may be dissatisfied with the employer and raise a grievance, or the employer may have to use a disciplinary procedure against an individual who is proving to be unsatisfactory. Human resource managers want to get the best from the people they employ: people are, as we have shown, very expensive to recruit and train, and HRM specialists will not wish to waste these resources. However, there will be occasions when it becomes inevitable that the organisation will have to end the employment of one or more employees, and line managers as well as human resource specialists will need to know something about this process.

This chapter will examine ways in which employment may be ended fairly. We shall then consider one particular type of dismissal – redundancy – and examine ways in which the effects of redundancy may be lessened by the provision of an outplacement service. Redundancy is usually inevitable in an economic downturn and while in the public sector there have been job cuts resulting in redundancies, the effects on the private sector, or on parts of it, have not been as great as perhaps might have been expected, as employers have often adopted other measures such as reducing hours or wages or adopting more flexible work practices that have minimised the need for redundancies. Nevertheless this topic is of great importance in the current economic climate.

The chapter presents general guidance only, and is intended to provide not a complete or authoritative guide to employment law, but rather an appreciation of general principles with which students of HRM should be familiar and which they may use to guide them in dealing with people who are dismissed from an organisation.

It is important for a number of reasons that any dismissal should be fair. The workforce will be better able to trust and work effectively for a management that operates fair procedures and the reputation of the organisation in general will also benefit from this.

Fairness is both a moral and a legal issue, and sometimes organisations that have tried very hard to be fair in their procedures and practices will still be found in the eyes of the law to have acted unfairly. This may be because individual managers or supervisors have made errors in the way they handled an issue, or failed to document their actions adequately, or because of some legal technicality. HRM practitioners, therefore, need to be aware of the importance of legislation and must endeavour to have systems, procedures and training in place so that everyone involved in the dismissal process acts in a fair way. They also need to know where to find detailed guidance, as they cannot know in minute detail every aspect of the law: there are many specialist texts that can help with this. Although the HRM practitioner needs to be sufficiently aware of legislation and the need for fair procedures to be able to deal with issues that arise on a day-to-day basis, it may be that, faced with an unusual problem, they will also need the advice of the organisation's solicitor.

Legislation changes constantly, which means that you should be aware of general principles with regard to dismissal but you should always be prepared to check for the most recent legislation and the most recent interpretation of it, and not just rely on notes that you made years earlier. Textbooks become out of date, and you should always look for the most recent edition to guide you, although even this may not be enough to take account of the latest changes in law. We have also listed some useful sources of information at the end of the chapter.

People leave organisations for a host of reasons, and of course not all who leave are dismissed. Resignations and retirements do not normally cause any legal problems to the organisation, but employers need to take great care in the case of dismissals that they abide by the law, and ensure not only that they dismiss for a potentially fair reason, but that the way they handle the dismissal and the whole dismissal process is also fair. As we said in Chapter 12, this means that employers who are dismissing someone must also take into account the ACAS Code of Practice on disciplinary and grievance procedures.

Organisations, in particular, which employ people abroad need also to ensure that they are fully aware of the legislation which applies within the countries in which they operate.

Dismissal

Usually both employers and employees understand when a dismissal has occurred as it results in a person's employment being ended. That person may have to work their notice period or the employer may prefer to pay them for this time, but terminate their employment immediately. This is often referred to as payment in lieu of notice. In circumstances where the dismissal has occurred because of the employee's gross misconduct, the employee is not entitled to any notice or payment in lieu of notice. There are, however, other circumstances in which dismissal may occur which may be less well known, such as the non-renewal of a fixed-term contract or constructive dismissal. We shall consider each of these in turn.

Fixed-term contract

This sounds straightforward enough, and occurs when there is a fixed-term contract for a particular period of employment. If the contract is not renewed, this technically counts as a dismissal although it is normally expected by both the employer and the employee. Sometimes in the past, organisations insisted that individuals whom they employed on fixed-term contracts gave up their rights to claim unfair dismissal by making them sign a waiver clause at the start of their employment. Waiver clauses in fixed-term contracts were abolished under the Employment Relations Act 1999 so an individual can no longer be made to sign away their right to claim for unfair dismissal.

Constructive dismissal

The second definition given here is a little more complicated, and is known as constructive dismissal. It is often hard to prove that the dismissal was unfair, as the person has normally resigned and given some other reason for leaving. It is later, when they realise that the resignation was because of the employer's conduct that they might decide to bring a case of constructive dismissal. For a case to succeed, the employer normally has to have done something so seriously wrong that the employee was justified in feeling that they could no longer work in that workplace, as the employer's action would be regarded as a significant breach of the employment contract. The person claiming constructive dismissal must also have raised the grievance formally in writing and tried to get satisfaction from the grievance procedure before handing in their notice. A possible example is an employer who bullied the employee so that their life was a total misery and the person felt obliged to leave. In this type of case the employer would not have followed the statutory discipline, dismissal and grievance procedure since they did not actually dismiss the employee. However, the employee must have followed the statutory grievance procedure before presenting a claim for constructive unfair dismissal.

Pause for thought 13.1   We said earlier that dismissal should be for a potentially fair reason and that a fair dismissal procedure should also be followed. What do you consider to be potentially fair reasons for dismissal?

Potentially fair reasons for dismissal

You have probably listed offences such as theft, poor attendance, assault, fraud, being under the influence of drugs or alcohol, sexual harassment or racial harassment, or perhaps a serious breach of a safety rule. If you refer back to Chapter 12, you will see that these are all examples of misconduct or of gross misconduct, although poor attendance, if it is due to ill-health, may be an example of lack of capability.

There are four other potentially valid reasons for dismissal besides misconduct and lack of capability, and each of these covers a wide range of situations. For a dismissal to be fair, an employer must first be able to prove it was for one of these reasons:

- conduct
- capability
- a statutory requirement
- some other substantial reason
- redundancy

- retirement. (This will no longer be a potentially fair reason for dismissal after October 2011 when the default retirement age will be abolished. There are transitional retirement arrangements in place between April 2011 and October 2011 (CIPD, 2010a).)

The need to act reasonably

Do you think that if an employee is guilty, for example, of misconduct or proves incapable of doing the job, this means that if the employer dismisses them it will automatically be fair? In Chapter 12 we said that it was important for an organisation to have a fair disciplinary procedure modelled on the ACAS *Code of Practice* on disciplinary and grievance procedures. It is important, if an organisation is considering dismissing someone, that it not only has potentially fair grounds for dismissing them (i.e. it is dismissing them for one of the reasons listed earlier), but it also acts fairly in the way that it carries out this dismissal. The organisation needs to have a fair procedure for handling dismissals and should have followed its own procedure in a fair way. This also means, as we have already said, that the employer must have complied with their own disciplinary and grievance procedures. This is what we mean by the condition that the dismissal also has to be actually fair. An employer should strive to be fair but may still face a claim for unfair dismissal, as dismissed employees may have a different perception of whether their treatment was fair.

Employment tribunals examine dismissal cases from two points of view. One is whether employers have acted reasonably in treating the grounds as sufficient reason to justify dismissal. The other is that they must satisfy the tribunal that they acted reasonably in the dismissal procedure. If an employee brings a claim for unfair dismissal, the tribunal will have to make a judgement about what happened after considering evidence from both parties; consequently it is important for employers to follow their own procedure and have clear records and documentary evidence.

ACTIVITY 13.1

Susan has been employed by your organisation for three years as a clerical assistant. During the past year there have been many problems with poor attendance and timekeeping. Susan's manager has tried to establish whether there is a problem underlying this poor attendance and timekeeping, but has found no clear explanation. Susan has been counselled about this situation and has gone through the disciplinary procedure. She was written to and invited to attend two disciplinary interviews to discuss her poor attendance and timekeeping and she has been issued in the presence of her trade union representative with a written warning after the first meeting and a final written warning after the second meeting. The organisation has followed its own disciplinary procedure. The final written warning was issued only three weeks ago, and yet since then Susan has already had one day absent from work and has been late twice. She has not provided any good explanation for this, but simply says that she overslept and then did not feel like coming to work.

Do you think that the employer has potentially fair reasons for dismissing Susan? Give reasons for your answer. Which category of dismissal would this fall into?

If the employer does decide to dismiss Susan, do you think that it is being fair in the way that it is handling this dismissal?

Discussion of Activity 13.1

From the evidence given, this case looks to be a potentially fair dismissal on the grounds of misconduct, as Susan does appear to have behaved badly and the employer does appear to have a valid reason for dismissal. In this case, the management appears to have a disciplinary procedure which they followed and seem, from the evidence given here, to have acted reasonably and fairly. A case such as this would probably not go to an employment tribunal, but there may be other circumstances not given here that might lead Susan to feel her dismissal was unfair and to pursue a tribunal case.

● Conduct

Conduct is the most common reason for dismissal and results in the most claims of unfair dismissal at employment tribunals. Both serious acts of misconduct, such as gross misconduct, and more minor but frequently repeated acts of misconduct result in dismissals that fall into this category. In Activity 13.1 Susan's dismissal was for a series of minor but repeated lapses in her conduct.

● Capability

Lack of capability could arise for several reasons. According to the CIPD (2007), capability issues normally fall into one of the following three categories:

● qualifications – defined as 'any degree, diploma or other academic, technical or professional qualification relevant to the position' held by the employee

● incompetence or poor performance – occurs where, usually through no fault of their own, the employee is simply incapable of delivering work to the required standard. For example, a person who works in a dog kennels who frequently forgets to lock the kennels and feed the animals. (Obviously great care must be taken to ensure that the incompetence is not related to a disability.)

● illness – for example, where an employee's illness makes it impossible for them to perform their duties.

The first of these categories is reasonably straightforward and would cover situations where the employee did not have the qualifications that they claimed to possess. Lack of qualification is a potentially fair reason for dismissal. Although good selection procedures should mean that people who do not have the desired qualifications are not employed, there are many well-publicised examples of people who have lied about their qualifications and who have worked for an organisation for a number of years before being found out and dismissed. There have even been cases of doctors who have practised for many years without people realising that they did not have any medical qualification. In a case such as this there would be a potentially fair reason for dismissal.

In the second situation the employee simply may not be able to do the job, however hard they try. Some people may prove to be incapable of doing the job required because they lack the required level of skill or ability. This could be a reflection on the organisation's selection techniques or training, but if training and opportunities to improve have been given, it may be necessary to dismiss the person if they still prove to be incapable.

Problems relating to absenteeism, particularly relating to long-term illness, can be more difficult. We discussed some of the problems in the last chapter, and clearly not all absenteeism would fall into the category of misconduct as Susan's behaviour did. Many absentees are genuinely ill but the organisation, as we said in Chapter 12, may reluctantly, having exhausted all its procedures, have to consider whether or not to dismiss. This needs to be handled in a totally different way to a misconduct dismissal, and such a dismissal would be on the grounds of the person not being capable of doing the job. The employer needs to show that it believed in the employee's lack of capability and had made reasonable enquiries about these.

Particular attention, however, should be paid to the requirements of the Equality Act 2010, before making any decision to dismiss on ill-health grounds. If many of the absences are directly attributable to a disability the employer may have to discount these from their calculations when considering whether or not the employee's attendance record is satisfactory. This was the case in *Cox v. The Post Office* (IT/1301162/97) where it was decided that the Post Office should have discounted Cox's absences due to asthma, since this is classed as a disability, from the figures for his attendance which they had used to justify his dismissal.

It is also important to note that if the illness itself leads to a disability the employer should first try to establish whether reasonable adjustments could be made to enable them to keep their job, before considering dismissal. According to Gill Sage, an employment law specialist, 'No decision to terminate an employee's contract on the grounds of ill-health or to subject someone to any other detriment should now be taken solely on the basis of absence from the workplace' (Sage, 1998, p. 24).

A statutory requirement

This is a rarer reason for dismissal, which deals with the situation where the employer would be breaking the law if it continued to employ that person. Possible examples of this would be employing a person who did not have a work permit, or employing a person who was legally too young to work full time in that particular work environment, the results of police checks on people working with children or vulnerable adults, or possibly employing a driver who had lost their licence and was disqualified from driving.

Some other substantial reason

This category is to cover eventualities not listed already, where there is a genuinely fair reason for dismissal that does not fit neatly into any of the listed categories. One example of this is where the contract is only temporary and is not renewed. Legally the person has not been dismissed because of their misconduct or because of lack of qualification, or even because of some legal requirement, so this form of dismissal would fall into the category of some other substantial reason.

Redundancy

Many employers dislike discussing redundancies and invent other names for this type of dismissal. They refer to it as 'downsizing' or 'delayering', or even as being 'forced to let someone go'. It is certainly a very unpleasant form of dismissal for all concerned, as the person involved is not normally being dismissed because of anything that they have done wrong but as a result of the organisation's need to streamline its operations or cut back in some areas because of an unforeseen crisis, or perhaps through poor human resource planning. Many organisations are striving to be increasingly flexible in their deployment of people and often employ temporary or agency staff, with the result that redundancy affects more and more people in an increasingly wide range of jobs as these organisations move from traditional employment patterns to new ones.

Redundancy can occur because of three main circumstances:

- the whole business closes
- part of the business or a particular workplace closes
- there is less need for a particular type of work, which results in some employees being surplus to requirements.

We shall return to the topic of redundancy later in this chapter.

Retirement

From 1 October 2006, as a result of the Employment Equality (Age) Regulations 2006, until April 2011 it was possible for employers to fairly dismiss a person when they reached 65 as part of a planned retirement provided they notified them in writing of their intention to do this at least six months prior to the date of retirement. However, the Government will abolish the default retirement age of 65 and employers will not be able to issue any new notifications of forced retirement after 6 April 2011 though during this transitional period any forced retirements that have already been started can continue to completion. In order for this to be fair the notice of the retirement has to have been issued by the employer prior to April 2011, the date of the retirement itself must take place before 1 October 2011 and all the requirements of the statutory retirement procedures must be met (Simpson, 2010).

After 1 October 2011 it will still be possible for an employer to set a compulsory retirement age but they will have to be able to justify it objectively and this may prove difficult for many organisations. Employers will also be able to decide on a case by case basis to retire an individual but must once again provide objective reasons. The reasons will be important and will need to be for one of the five remaining potentially fair reasons for dismissal mentioned earlier in the chapter, i.e. capability, conduct, redundancy, illegality or some other substantial reason.

In order to provide an objective justification for continuing to operate a compulsory retirement age the employer will have to be able to show that it is a proportionate means of achieving a legitimate aim. According to Simpson (2010) in this case proportionate means that

what the employer is doing is actually achieving its aim;

the discriminatory effect should be significantly outweighed by the importance and benefits of the legitimate aim; and

the employer should have no reasonable alternative to the action it is taking.

The legitimacy of the aim is also important and cannot be about trying to save money by getting rid of older, more expensive workers. Potential legitimate aims could include some economic factors relating to the efficiency of the business, or could be concerned with issues of health, safety and wellbeing of particular groups or the training requirements of the job. It will be interesting to see how these new rules are interpreted as case law develops but the article at the end of this chapter relating to the situation in the US gives some ideas of potential problems that might occur.

● Who can bring a case for unfair dismissal

It is obviously important that all dismissals should be fair, but the law normally provides the opportunity for only some employees (those who have one year of service), to bring a case claiming unfair dismissal before an employment tribunal, though for some forms of dismissal categorised as automatically unfair there is no service requirement at all: this will be discussed later. If you remember our discussion of equal opportunities issues in Chapter 5, you will recall that there was no mention of a qualification period for cases of sex discrimination, racial discrimination or discrimination on grounds of disability. This is because many cases of discrimination occur before people are actually employed at all. However, for most cases of unfair dismissal to be brought before a tribunal, employees do have to have been employed for a certain length of time, although the actual length of employment required has varied over the years. This means that some unscrupulous employers may be tempted to treat people who do not have sufficient length of service with them in an unfair way, as they know that a case for unfair dismissal cannot be brought against them. Clearly this is not good practice and employers should treat all workers in a fair way.

Did you know?

Between 1 April 2008 and 31 March 2009 there were 55,000 claims to employment tribunals made for unfair dismissal. Of these 31,534 (57%) went to ACAS for conciliation and 16,282 (61%) were settled before reaching the tribunal and a further 8,131 (26%) were withdrawn. Only 7,121 (13%) got to an employment tribunal.

(*Source*: Advisory, Conciliation and Arbitration Service (ACAS), 2009)

● How to bring a case for unfair dismissal

Any employee with the required one year of service who feels that they were dismissed unfairly can complete an application for the case to be decided by an employment tribunal. Forms are easy to obtain and available from Job Centres, Law Centres or Citizens Advice Bureaux, or the process can be started by applying online at **www.employmenttribunals.gov.uk**. The tribunal system was overhauled in October 2004 and one result of this is that a new user-friendly application form (ET1) was introduced from April 2005. Once the claimant has completed their application it should be sent to the relevant employment tribunal office or it can now be completed online.

For acceptance of unfair dismissal cases, and most other types of case, there is usually a time limit of three months from the date the employment ended. Employment tribunals do not usually accept cases outside the relevant time limit, but this does depend on the reason for the delay and in some exceptional circumstances late cases may still be considered. Tribunals will not consider claims unless they are assured that the organisation's grievance procedure has been exhausted.

The application form is allocated a case number by the tribunal office and a copy is sent to the respondent within five days of the tribunal receiving the application. (The respondent is the person the case is brought against. In most cases it will be the employer.) The respondent will be sent a response form (ET3) which they are asked to complete, indicating whether they agree with or are resisting the claim against them. They must complete this form within 28 days in order to be allowed to answer the claim against them. Usually copies of both forms are also sent to ACAS, the Advisory, Conciliation and Arbitration Service.

Conciliation

ACAS has been using conciliation for several years but the concept of a conciliation period was changed in October 2004 to encourage employees and employers to try to reach a settlement at an earlier stage. Conciliation by ACAS will normally be concentrated into a short, fixed period of between 7 and 13 weeks, depending on the nature of the claim, and once this time has ended ACAS is no longer able to be involved. In its role as conciliator, ACAS may repeat information provided by one side to the other side to try to bring about a settlement, but this information is not normally repeated at the tribunal itself, unless all parties give their permission.

From April 2009 it has not even been necessary for the employment tribunal process to have started for ACAS to get involved. Since this date ACAS has offered a proactive form of conciliation in individual disputes before a claim has even been made to an employment tribunal. This is referred to as Pre-Claim Conciliation (PCC). Between April 2009 and February 2010, the ACAS helpline had received 8,304 pre-claim conciliation applications.

Ed Sweeney (2010), chair of ACAS, commented to PM online that 'This data indicates that workers and employers are increasingly taking steps to avoid employment tribunals. The current economic climate has created difficult workplace challenges for managers, HR professionals and employees. The earlier issues can be resolved the more likely people are to stay in employment'.

Pre-Claim Conciliation looks set to prove very popular and does not stop the case going to an employment tribunal if a satisfactory settlement has not been achieved. In most cases the tribunal does not know about any of the correspondence between the parties and ACAS, so the tribunal will review the case on the evidence presented to it in writing and by witnesses at the tribunal hearing.

Arbitration

The Employment Rights (Dispute Resolution) Act 1998 gave ACAS the powers to draw up an arbitration scheme for simpler cases of unfair dismissal which don't involve complex law and for claims about flexible working. This was introduced into England and Wales in 2001 and in Scotland in 2004. In the case of alleged unfair dismissal this provides an alternative way to resolve unfair dismissal disputes, in which the ACAS arbitration service operates as a voluntary alternative to employment tribunal hearings. People who choose this option have to agree to accept the decision of the arbitrator, who is able to make exactly the same awards as an employment tribunal. 'In submitting their dispute to arbitration the parties are accepting that the arbitrator's decision is final and binding. They are also agreeing to do everything necessary for the arbitration process to proceed smoothly' ACAS (n.d.).

The aims of this scheme are to cut the number of expensive tribunal cases and to create a quicker and simpler system that is free of much legal jargon. However, this has not proved to be a very popular alternative to employment tribunals and according to ACAS (2009) 'to date, ACAS has accepted 61 cases for resolution under the scheme across England, Scotland and Wales'. ACAS (2009) also commented that 'where dismissals have been found to be unfair, remedies have been broadly consistent with the range of amounts awarded at employment tribunals.'

Employment tribunals

The tribunal itself normally comprises three people: the chair, who has to be legally qualified and have worked as either a solicitor or a barrister for at least seven years, and two wing members. One of the wing members will be chosen from a list of names submitted by employers' organisations and the other will be chosen from a similar list submitted by workers' organisations. All are there because of their knowledge and experience, in their different ways, of employment issues and work-related problems and their aim is to ensure a fair hearing for all concerned. They will probably ask questions to clarify any points they are unsure of during the course of the tribunal hearing.

ACTIVITY 13.2

Find out from www.acas.org.uk how many cases of alleged unfair dismissal have been brought during the last year.

(a) How many of these cases have been heard at employment tribunals?

(b) How many of these cases have been taken to ACAS voluntary arbitration?

(c) What was the success rate in each category?

(d) How many cases involved pre-claim conciliation?

(e) How many involved arbitration?

Automatically fair reasons for dismissal

There are a very small number of situations in which dismissal is likely to be viewed as automatically fair. These include situations where the reason or main reason for the dismissal involved the employee:

● in problems of national security

● taking part in an unofficial strike or some other type of unofficial action (this does not apply in all circumstances)

● taking part in an official strike or some other form of official action and where all the relevant employees who participated in the same action were also dismissed and not re-employed during the next three months.

National security is obviously a serious concern, so someone who endangered national security, perhaps by selling secrets, would obviously come into this category. Taking part in unofficial strikes and even official strikes can also be a very risky undertaking for the employee, even though these actions do not seem to be in quite the same category as endangering national security.

Automatically unfair reasons for dismissal

Some reasons for dismissal are likely to be automatically unfair, and in these cases an employment tribunal does not need to go through the process of establishing whether there was a fair reason for the dismissal before it assesses whether or not the employer acted reasonably. These include dismissal related to discrimination on grounds of sex, race, disability or a spent conviction, as these areas were originally covered by the Sex Discrimination Act 1975, the Race Relations Act 1976 or the Disability Discrimination Act 1995, which have been superseded by the Equality Act 2010. In all of these there is no requirement for a length of service qualification for bringing a claim before an employment tribunal. Similarly, it is also automatically unfair to use any of these as the basis for selection for redundancy.

Some other examples of automatically unfair dismissal are given next but this is not an exhaustive list:

● trade union-related dismissals

● dismissal on maternity- or pregnancy-related grounds

● dismissal for taking, or proposing to take, some action on health and safety grounds

● dismissal for having sought in good faith to exercise a statutory employment right

● dismissal of a shop worker or betting shop worker for refusing, or proposing to refuse, to do shop work on Sundays

● acting or offering to act as a representative for consultation about redundancy, business transfer or occupational pension trusteeship matters

● dismissal of the employee because they try to make the employer pay them the minimum wage.

In cases where there are automatically unfair reasons for dismissal, the employment tribunal does not have to go through the two-stage process, first establishing that there was a fair reason for the dismissal, then investigating whether the employer acted reasonably. In these cases the employment tribunal has to find the dismissal fair or unfair solely with regard to the reasonableness of the actions of the employer and the reason for the dismissal.

Trade union-related dismissals

It is an automatically unfair reason for dismissal if the dismissal is for trade union membership or activities. This will apply whether the employee is dismissed because of expressing their intention to join a trade union or not to join a trade union, or for their actual membership or non-membership of a trade union. It also applies if someone is dismissed just because of their trade union activities, such as handing out leaflets or going to a trade union meeting.

Dismissal on maternity- or pregnancy-related grounds

The law relating to pregnancy is complex but it obviously does not make very good business sense to dismiss someone in whom an organisation has invested time and training just because she is pregnant. This is another automatically unfair reason for dismissal. An unfair dismissal of this type could also prove to be potentially very expensive for an employer as many claims of this type are also brought under sex discrimination legislation and there is no upper limit set on the amount of compensation that the woman could claim.

Dismissal on health and safety grounds

Once again the dismissal will be automatically unfair if the employer dismisses the employee or selects them for redundancy because they tried to bring health and safety issues to the attention of the employer. It would also be an automatically unfair dismissal if it was because the employee carried out or even just tried to carry out designated duties relating to health and safety or prevention of accidents at work, or because of their activities as a safety representative or on a safety committee.

Dismissal for wishing to exercise a statutory employment right

The dismissal will be automatically unfair if it occurs as a result of the employee bringing proceedings against the employer or alleging that an employer has infringed a statutory employment right such as a right to a minimum period of notice or the right of a trade union official for paid time off to carry out duties.

Dismissal of a shop worker for refusing to work on Sundays

Shop workers or betting office workers who are dismissed for refusal to work on a Sunday are also able to claim this as an automatically unfair reason for dismissal. When Sunday trading was introduced, some workers feared that they would be dismissed if they were unwilling to work on a Sunday so this is designed to afford them some protection.

Dismissal of a person because of their actions as a representative of the workforce for consultation about redundancy, business transfer or occupational pension trusteeship matters

Another automatically unfair reason for dismissal occurs if the employer dismisses a person who was acting on behalf of the workforce, or who is proposing to act as their representative in connection with negotiations about redundancy or business transfer or occupational pension trusteeship. This is to prevent unscrupulous employers from effectively 'shooting the messenger' by dismissing unfairly those who try to help or act on behalf of the employees.

Dismissal of the employee because they try to make the employer pay the minimum wage

In this instance the employee may have been trying to ensure that the employer pays the minimum wage to themselves or to other employees. If they have not been paid the minimum wage it is against the law, and if the employee who raises this issue is dismissed because they have raised it, then it will be an automatically unfair dismissal.

Wrongful dismissal

Wrongful dismissal is based on contract law and relates to instances when the employer has broken the contract. One of the most common examples of breach of contract is when the employee is dismissed without notice in circumstances where this is clearly not deserved because of any wrongdoing on the part of the employee, or where the employee is dismissed but with the incorrect period of notice. Unlike claims of unfair dismissal, there is no qualifying length of service required for eligibility to bring a case of wrongful dismissal. According to the CIPD (2010b), 'the most common example of a wrongful dismissal is failure to give the employee the correct length of contractual notice or statutory notice.'

Compensation for unfair dismissal

If a former employee wins their case for unfair dismissal at an employment tribunal the compensation awarded may take several forms.

Reinstatement

In this case the employment tribunal or ACAS arbitrator says that the employer must give the former employee their old job back on exactly the same terms and conditions as before and pay compensation for any loss of wages while not employed. Failure on the part of the employer to comply with this order is likely to result in additional financial awards, known as an additional or special award, being made to the employee.

Re-engagement

This means that the employment tribunal or ACAS arbitrator states that the employer must re-employ their former employee but it may be in a different job or on different terms and conditions of employment. For example, it may not be possible to give them back their old job as the vacancy may already have been filled by a new employee.

Compensation

This means financial compensation and is divided into the basic award and the compensatory award. The basic award is calculated in the same way as the statutory redundancy payment which is discussed later in this chapter. It is calculated by taking into account the age, number of years in that employer's service and amount of the average weekly wage. At February 2011 the weekly wage included in the calculation is subject to a weekly maximum of £400 per week and the maximum basic award that can be awarded is £12,000. There is guidance about the various awards at Business Link and there are various sites that publish easy tables for calculating these figures but these amounts are index-linked and change most years in February. One site that gives opportunities to check potential awards in various situations is **www.jobrights.co.uk**.

In some circumstances there may be deductions taken from the amount awarded by the employment tribunal – for example, if the employment tribunal feels that the employee partially contributed to their own dismissal or if the employer offered to reinstate the employee and they refused unreasonably.

A compensatory award may also be made and this is to take account of factors such as loss of earnings, loss of pension rights or loss of benefits, such as company car or house. The maximum compensatory award in 2011 was £68,400. There are unlimited awards made, as mentioned earlier, in cases of dismissal related to sex, race or disability discrimination. An additional award may also be made if the dismissal was for trade unionism.

Redundancy

We discussed earlier the fact that redundancy can be a potentially fair reason for dismissal. However, great care must be taken in the selection of those who are to be made redundant, and a large number of employment tribunal cases are brought each year where employees feel that they have been unfairly selected for redundancy.

Any organisation should first choose to take various steps to try to preclude or minimise the need for redundancies. Good human resource planning should help to minimise this need, but however effective the human resource planning, there may still be a need for redundancies because of other problems, such as the unexpected loss of a large order or the failure of the business of a large debtor. 'In a survey of 116 employers conducted for IRS Employment Review in the year up to March 2009, 84.5% of the employers . . . have made redundancies during the past three years. Most of this group (92%) have also had other experiences of job losses, having reduced their headcounts within the past year' (Murphy, 2009). Clearly in the current economic situation this is an important issue which needs to be handled correctly.

Consultation

Consultation is a very important stage in redundancies, both for legal reasons and in order to maintain morale. Morale is always likely to be low when there is a threat of redundancy, but rumour and uncertainty are only likely to make it worse. The law on redundancy in Britain is mainly derived from the Trade Union and Labour Relations (Consolidation) Act 1992, the Collective Redundancies and Transfer of Undertakings

(Protection of Employment) Regulations 1995 and the Collective Redundancies and Transfer of Undertakings (Protection of Employment) (Amendment) Regulations 1999. This means that:

- If 20 or more employees at one establishment are to be made redundant, within a period of 90 days, consultation should start at least 30 days before the first dismissal.

- If 100 or more employees at one establishment are to be made redundant, within a period of 90 days, this consultation should start at least 90 days before the first dismissal is to occur.

In practice, in Britain, consultation frequently occurs at the same time as the notification of redundancies so that the redundant employees are often already working their notice when the consultation is supposed to be taking place. This has the effect of making it rather more difficult to achieve much by consultation in terms of avoiding dismissals or reducing the numbers since those to be made redundant have already been selected.

Groups to be consulted in collective redundancies

The following rules apply to those who should be consulted in collective redundancy situations. In this instance the definition of redundancy is slightly different to the one we used earlier for redundancy pay. Here it relates to a situation where an employer proposes to dismiss at least 20 employees at one establishment within a 90-day period. The dismissal is unrelated to the quality of work of the individual concerned as it could be due to the need for fewer employees to do a particular task or because of reorganisation or reallocation of work:

Under the 1999 regulations,

- If there is a recognised independent trade union within the organisation, then the consultation must be with them.

- If there is no trade union recognition agreement in place then the employer has a choice and may consult either with a trade union or with employee representatives.

- Representatives of all employees affected should be consulted and not just those who are likely to be made redundant.

- Any organisation that has been obliged collectively to consult must also notify the Department for Business, Innovation and Skills (BIS)

- If those employees who are likely to be affected by the redundancies are not in a trade union, and there are no other suitable representatives for employees already in place in the organisation, then the employees must be given the opportunity to elect representatives. The employer should make arrangements to ensure the fairness of these elections and must also comply with the election rules set out by BERR (now BIS).

- If the employees fail to elect representatives after being given opportunities to do so, then the employer will have to give the information direct to all relevant employees in order to fulfil its legal obligation to consult.

The information needed for consultation

The employee representatives will need sufficient information from the employer about its proposals to be able to participate fully in a meaningful way in the consultations. Certain information must be given to them in writing. This must be handed individually to each of them, sent by post to an address they have given the employer or, in the case of consultation with a trade union, sent to its head office.

The employer must provide the following information:

- the reasons for the proposed redundancies
- the numbers and types of jobs that are likely to be affected by the proposals
- the anticipated total number of employees who are likely to be affected in each job at the organisation
- the proposed selection methods for those to be made redundant
- the proposed method of actually dismissing people and the anticipated period over which dismissals will take place
- the proposed methods of calculating redundancy pay.

Worker consultation in Britain and in other European countries

The penalties for not consulting adequately may result in a fine for not notifying the Department for Business, Innovation and Skills (BIS). The trade union representatives, employees' representatives or the employees themselves can apply to an employment tribunal which can make a protective award of up to 13 weeks' pay for each employee. Employers can, in their defence, claim that there were special circumstances which made it impossible to comply with the legislation and in many cases the consultation seems to amount to announcing the redundancies. The 1995 and 1999 regulations are the UK's response to a European ruling in 1994 from the European Court of Justice. However, the Government was not willing to sign up to a European Directive for Information and Consultation Rights. In spite of the fact that the British Government refused to sign this Directive, which would have given greater rights to consultation for the British worker, it still claimed to be furious about the lack of consultation from Corus, the steel producer giant, when the company announced redundancies in 2000.

In spite of the British Government's initial refusal to sign these documents, it did eventually agree and the possible implications of the Information and Consultation Directive 2002 will be discussed later in this chapter.

The rules regarding redundancy in the other European countries do not appear at first sight to be very different to those of the UK, but the duty to consult starts sooner in France, Germany and Spain and usually applies when smaller numbers of employees are involved. Also, the duty to consult cannot be undertaken retrospectively in those countries, so the consultation has to occur before those selected for redundancy are told of the decision. It is often claimed that the laxer laws relating to redundancy in the UK make us the easiest European country in which to make staff redundant.

Marks & Spencer found, to its cost, that expectations of the way redundancy should be handled are different in the rest of Europe, when in March 2001 it announced it was closing all its stores abroad. It probably felt it had consulted sufficiently, and possibly this would be true if British standards applied. However, it was undoubtedly surprised by the way its staff in France reacted with instant walk-outs in protest, TV and radio interviews with tearful staff and pictures in newspapers in France and Britain which depicted window displays in their Nice store in which a coffin appeared draped in black with mannequins dressed in mourning and bound in chains. Support from the Prime Minister, Lionel Jospin, followed and the Government in France supported the trade unions in court action against Marks & Spencer relating to lack of consultation, and Marks & Spencer was effectively stopped from making the redundancies, at least for a time.

In France, employers are obliged by law to establish a workers' council and the council must be consulted throughout any redundancy process with a view to finding suitable alternatives to the redundancies, rather than, as so often happens in Britain, the consultation process starting as the employees are given their notice. Moreover, in France, each individual employee must be spoken to personally before any public announcements are made and plans for training individuals should also be established. Decisions on redundancies should not be sent by fax or email, as was alleged to have happened to Marks & Spencer's French employees. Trade unions in France can apply to the courts to stop redundancies from occurring, as happened in this case. John Monks, TUC General Secretary, said of the Marks & Spencer case, 'This welcome decision underlines the better protection available to workers across the Channel – French workers have shown they will not put up with such high-handed behaviour.'

It may be the fashion in Britain to announce job losses to the media whenever a company needs a short term boost to its share price. But as this decision shows, in France employers need to act responsibly, taking into account the needs of their workforce as well as their shareholders. This shows why people at work in the UK need European proposals for wider information and consultation rights to become law as soon as possible.

(Monks, 2001)

As well as an order by the courts to prevent redundancies from taking place, there are also other penalties available in France for non-compliance with the law. This could, in theory at least, be prison for the directors of a company, although in reality this has never occurred. There is also a requirement in France, Germany and Spain for a social compensation plan and, according to the European Industrial Relations Observatory (2001), this is common in most other European countries as a way of promoting redeployment and negotiating termination of employment through early retirement, redeployment and voluntary redundancy. According to the EIRO, 'The tangible outcome of redundancy negotiation tends to be:

- a reduction in the planned number of redundancies, the withdrawal of announced redundancies or the provision of employment guarantees
- the guaranteed safeguarding of wage and working conditions by the new employer
- a commitment to avoid compulsory redundancies.' (European Industrial Relations Observatory, online, February 2001.)

The EU Information and Consultation Directive 2002 can also apply to redundancy consultation. The Directive established, as we said in Chapter 3, a very general framework for information and consultation and since 2008 has applied to all organisations, even small businesses.

From the appropriate times, according to the size of the organisation concerned, it will be necessary for organisations to negotiate voluntary agreements about consultation and information with workers and whatever is agreed will need to be put in writing. The types of issue to be addressed should include information about the probable activities of the organisation and its financial situation, the employment situation within the organisation, especially where there is any likely threat to employment, such as in a redundancy situation. However, there should be information and consultation about any potential changes to the work situation, even if these do not go as far as actual redundancies.

Steps to preclude the need for redundancies

While good employers should always be looking to the future and planning their manpower needs to suit their strategic objectives, there can also be changing economic situations caused by situations such as global events that are outside the employer's control and not easy to predict. Employers do need to be flexible and so have to develop a range of strategies to avoid or limit redundancies.

Even before the Information and Consultation Regulations 2004 came into effect, organisations in the UK were supposed to consult in order to prevent or minimise the need for redundancies. It is foolish to contemplate making good employees redundant if a simpler solution is feasible, so a calm, objective review of the situation is called for and a consideration of all possible alternatives. The consultation must be undertaken with a view to reaching agreement with the appropriate representatives and should include the following:

- the actual numbers and job categories likely to be affected
- the reasons for the redundancies
- the criteria for selection
- the dismissal procedures and timescales during which the redundancies will occur
- the basis for the calculation of compensation if it is different from the statutory minimum.

According to the CIPD (2010c), consultation should also include:

- why and how the individuals have been selected
- possible ways of avoiding redundancy
- possible alternative work.

This sounds reasonable but, as stated earlier, there have been many occasions in the UK where consultation has only started after the redundancy period has been announced so although it is possible that dismissals may still be avoided, it seems less likely. Some bad employers also prefer to face the financial penalties rather than go through the process in the way in which it was intended.

The steps which can be taken to avoid redundancies will depend to some extent on the timescale available. Some employers are keen to look after their employees and to part company with them on as good terms as possible. Employers are supposed to consider alternatives to compulsory redundancy and, according to the CIPD (2010c), 'Organisations should always try to avoid redundancies. Ways of doing this include:

- natural wastage
- recruitment freeze
- stopping or reducing overtime
- offer early retirement to volunteers (subject to age discrimination issues)
- retraining or redeployment
- offering existing employees sabbaticals and secondments.

- pay freezes
- short-time working
- pay cuts in return for taking time off work
- "alternatives to redundancy" (ATR) schemes in which employees do not work for the employer for a specified period, and are free to seek new work whilst receiving an ATR allowance.'

The methods chosen will depend on the particular circumstances within the organisation. Natural wastage may work well if two organisations are combining and if there is sufficient time to allow for natural wastage to occur, but is unlikely to be the best solution if the organisation needs to reduce staff immediately and most solutions also carry some costs to the organisation. Some of the options aimed at reducing the need for redundancy might not be possible for all employers as they could involve breaking their employees' contracts, so care must be taken to discuss and consult widely before seeking to implement some of these steps.

Many organisations do already engage in meaningful negotiation with their employees and do take steps to minimise the need for redundancies. Some go much further and provide outplacement services and these will be discussed later.

Selection for redundancy

If the consultations or measures chosen as a result of them fail to work, the employer needs to decide how to select and implement the redundancies. Ideally there should be an agreed procedure for handling redundancies but if not, then criteria which are fair need to be chosen and the pool of workers from among whom the redundancies are to occur also needs to be identified.

Selection criteria for redundancy

Employers need to choose criteria for selection carefully.

CASE STUDY 13.1 Redundancy

Read the following case study and answer the questions that follow.

The Spartan Insurance Company has decided that it is overstaffed and that it must cut back on its office staff. The departmental manager for administration recommends that the post room and print room, which between them employ seven staff, should be amalgamated into one section. This will eliminate the need for three members of staff.

The post room is run by Mr Arshad Mohammed, who is aged 34, is extremely efficient and has been with the organisation for three years. There are three other members of staff in this section – Mrs Sarah Sergeant, Ms Sandra Smythe and Mr Terry Gibbs. Mrs Sarah Sergeant, a widow aged 55, has worked for Spartan Insurance for 20 years. She has always been an extremely reliable employee, but since the death of her husband 18 months ago she has suffered greatly from ill-health and has had a series of illnesses linked to depression.

Ms Sandra Smythe is a fairly recent recruit to the organisation. She is aged 25 and has been employed for six months. She has settled into the job well and is very efficient in everything she has to do, but is the first to admit that she still has a great deal to learn.

The most junior member of staff in this section is Terry Gibbs. He is only 20 and joined Spartan Insurance Company straight from school. He has been employed by the company for two years and seemed to have a few problems making the transition from school to work; Mr Mohammed has spoken to him informally once or twice about his attitude to work. More recently Mr Mohammed has had to warn him about his timekeeping, and he received a written warning about this. The written warning is still current and does not expire for a further month, but Terry has taken this warning extremely seriously and there has been a noticeable improvement in both his attitude and his timekeeping.

The print room has three staff – Mr George Brownlow, Mrs Rashida Ali and Ms Sally Wilson. Mr Brownlow, aged 44, is the supervisor of this section but in reality he does not actually perform any supervisory duties. Neither is he qualified to service any of the machines. He spends most of his time grumbling about the company and telling the other staff to get on with their work. He has been employed by the organisation for 10 years and it is generally thought that he was moved to his present job where he would be out of everyone's way, because of his generally uncooperative nature. It is believed that this situation was allowed to develop because he was a close personal friend of a former branch manager. This manager has long since left the organisation but Mr Brownlow is always clever enough not to do anything to warrant dismissal, and has not even received any warnings about his work. He is also a prominent local councillor and spends quite a bit of time attending council meetings.

Luckily for Mr Brownlow there are two very efficient employees who cover for his inefficiency and who do most of the work. Mrs Ali is 35 and has worked for Spartan Insurance for four years. She knows almost everything that there is to know about the machines and in effect runs the section. Sally Wilson is also extremely efficient; she is 17 years old and has been employed for a year, having started last summer straight from school.

Questions

1 What criteria would you propose for selection for redundancy here?
2 Which employees would you select for redundancy?

Discussion of Case Study 13.1

You might have chosen criteria based on length of employment or factors such as level of competence or attendance and timekeeping.

If you chose to use the last in first out principle then you would make the following people redundant: Ms Sandra Smythe (employed for 6 months), Mr Terry Gibbs (employed for 2 years) and Ms Sally Wilson (employed for 1 year). LIFO (last in first out) has often been the preferred choice by trade unions and it seems an objective method of selection, with those who have the shortest length of employment with the organisation being chosen for redundancy. This method also has the advantage of being easy to use and understand as well as being less costly in terms of redundancy pay. It may, however, as in this case, mean that those who are selected for redundancy are those who, although they have the shortest length of service, may be keen, enthusiastic employees who will have much to offer the organisation in the future. This might result in a stagnating, ageing workforce who lack the skills and versatility required for future business success. From an employer's point of view it is not a very satisfactory way of selecting redundant employees. Care also needs to be taken with this approach to avoid accusations of age discrimination as it is quite likely in many organisations that the last to join may also be the youngest. However, last in first out can still be used as a selection method but only if it is used as a part of a range of criteria – and even then it should be used with caution.

If you chose criteria such as timekeeping and level of efficiency you are likely to have proposed the selection of Mr Brownlow, Mr Terry Gibbs and Mrs Sergeant.

Employers often choose to use other criteria so that they can retain efficient employees while making redundant others who may not have given such good service, even though they have been employed for a much longer period of time. Caution also has to be exercised in this case to ensure that the criteria chosen are objective and fair. Just saying that someone has, for example, 'a poor attitude to work' is not likely to prove adequate grounds for selection for redundancy, as this is rather vague and subjective. More objective criteria need to be used, and the ability to do this depends on whether the organisation has effective records of employee capability and competence. You would need to break job performance down into several areas such as level of skill, knowledge, experience, flexibility, productivity, appraisal records. If you selected Mr Brownlow for redundancy, you would need to have clear evidence about levels of efficiency and output. If, on the other hand, you chose Terry Gibbs for redundancy because of his poor attendance record, you would have to ensure that there are clear records for absence and that the pattern of absenteeism does not appear high because of an uncharacteristic level of ill-health just prior to the redundancy period. Criteria such as disciplinary warnings also need careful checks to ensure that they are still 'live'.

Some criteria may also make the redundancies potentially unlawful if, for example, they apply disproportionately to one sex, one ethnic group, one age group or to employees with disabilities. Whatever the selection criteria used, employers should take care to ensure that the criteria are neither directly nor indirectly discriminatory. Selection of part-time rather than full-time employees may, for instance, constitute indirect sex discrimination if the majority of part-time employees are women and the majority of full-time employees are men.

According to the CIPD (2010c), 'where there is a choice between employees, selection must be based on objective criteria which may include:

● length of service
● attendance records
● disciplinary records
● skills, competencies and qualifications
● work experience
● performance records.

Tribunals generally look favourably on selection procedures based on a points system. However, the fairness may be suspect if only one person has made the selection and care should also be taken to avoid factors which may be discriminatory such that 'selecting part-timers in preference to full-timers could be discriminatory if a high proportion of women are affected' (CIPD, 2010c).

Rights of redundant employees

Consultation with individual employees

Employers should also consult with each individual employee who is to be affected by the redundancies, even if there has also been consultation with the unions or with employee representatives. This consultation should:

- explain why the redundancies are needed
- explain why the particular employee has been selected
- show any relevant documentation
- explain why no suitable alternative work is currently available
- explain any requirements during the notice period such as whether normal working or part-time working is required, whether payment will be made in lieu of notice, and explain what time off is allowed to seek alternative work or for training.

Suitable alternative employment

The employer should offer a suitable alternative job if there is one, rather than making the employee redundant. If the employee's job title is broad, there may be sufficient flexibility to make an offer easily. If this is not the case, the employer should not automatically assume that any alternative employment that involved less pay or status would necessarily be unsuitable to the employee; it should still be discussed. The employees should, however, be given sufficient information about any alternative job so that they can realistically reach a decision, and they should also be offered the chance of a trial period. This should be of four weeks' duration, and will give both the employer and the employee the chance to assess the job's suitability. It should start as the old contract finishes. If a longer trial period is required because of the need for retraining, this should be agreed in writing before the date of commencement of the trial period. If either party finds the new job to be unsuitable during this period then the redundancy situation will still apply, and the redundant employee will still be entitled to their redundancy pay.

If the offer of suitable alternative employment is refused by the employee, then the employer has the option of withholding redundancy pay. Any claim to an employment tribunal will have to assess the suitability of the offer and the reasonableness of the refusal.

Right to time off for job searching or retraining

Employees who have worked for two years for the employer and are about to be made redundant have a statutory entitlement to a reasonable amount of time off from work to look for other jobs or to retrain in order to be able to improve their employment prospects. Any employee who is not allowed a reasonable amount of time off for these purposes can make a complaint to an employment tribunal.

Redundancy pay

Employers are expected to compensate any employee who has been made redundant, and who has worked for them for at least two years in continuous employment by paying them an amount of redundancy pay. The actual amount that the employee may be entitled to if they are redundant is calculated according to age, length of service and weekly pay. There is an upper earnings limit for the amount of weekly pay that may be included in this calculation, and this amount alters each year. Currently the limit on the weekly rate is £400 (2011). Redundancy pay is tax free and does not affect the right to unemployment benefit. Furthermore, the amount that the employee receives is not affected even if they start another job immediately. Although redundancy pay has been exempt from the Equality Act 2010, there have been some alterations to the upper and lower limits. The calculation of redundancy is based on the actual age of the employee at the date of dismissal, and takes account of each year of service in the appropriate age band as follows:

● for each complete year of employment in which the employee was below the age of 22, half a week's pay
● for each complete year of employment in which the employee was aged 22 or over but was below the age of 41, one week's pay
● for each complete year of employment in which the employee was aged 41 or over, one and a half weeks' pay.

(Source: Jobs and Money, p. 24, The Guardian, 14 April 2001)

Did you know?

Even after the Equality Act 2010 one area where it remains legal to pay different rates because of age is in redundancy. The reason redundancy pay increases with age is to compensate, to some extent, for the increased difficulty that older workers may experience when faced with finding a new job. A survey carried out by the Career Management Association on its website found that people made redundant up to the age of 44 remained out of work for an average of 2.8 months. Those aged 45 or over had an average period of unemployment of 18.7 months.

ACTIVITY 13.3

Consider once again Case study 13.1 and the above information about the rates of pay of the individuals concerned. In order to simplify the calculation, imagine that each of the people concerned has worked for a whole number of years for the organisation.

Mr Brownlow: £450 per week
Mr Mohammed: £400 per week
Mrs Sergeant: £300 per week
Ms Smythe: £250 per week
Mr Gibbs: £200 per week
Mrs Ali: £250 per week
Ms Wilson: £200 per week

How much redundancy pay would each employee be entitled to?

Discussion of Activity 13.3

Mr Brownlow has worked for the organisation for 10 years and is aged 44. He has worked for 3 complete years since age 41, so is entitled to $3 \times 1\frac{1}{2}$ weeks' pay for that period of time. He has also worked for 7 years between ages 22 and 40, so is entitled to 7×1 weeks' pay.

Therefore Mr Brownlow would be entitled to $11\frac{1}{2}$ weeks' redundancy pay if he were selected for redundancy. His weekly earnings are above the maximum allowed in this calculation, so he would actually be entitled to $11\frac{1}{2} \times £400 = £4,600$.

Mr Mohammed has worked for the organisation for only 3 years and he is aged 34. He would therefore be entitled to 3×1 week's pay. His weekly pay is £400 which is the limit of the maximum entitlement so he would get the full amount of this included in the calculation. Thus he would receive $3 \times £400 = £1,200$.

Mrs Sergeant has worked for the organisation for 20 years and is aged 55. She has worked 14 years since the age of 41 and would be entitled to $14 \times 1\frac{1}{2}$ weeks' pay = 21 weeks' pay. She worked for a further 6 years before she was 41 and would be entitled to 6×1 weeks' pay = 6 weeks' pay.

The total number of weeks of redundancy pay she is due is therefore 27. Her weekly wage is £300 which is below the maximum entitlement. She would be entitled to $27 \times £300 = £8,100$.

Mr Gibbs is aged 20 and has worked for the organisation for 2 years. Since he is still under 22 he will only be entitled to $2 \times \frac{1}{2}$ weeks' redundancy pay = 1 week's redundancy pay. His weekly wage is £200 and so he would be entitled only to £200 in redundancy pay.

Sally Wilson and Sandra Smythe would not be entitled to any redundancy pay as they have not worked for the required qualification period of two years.

Tables are provided by Business Link so their guide to redundancy payments can be used to make this calculation easier. This can be found at **www.businesslink.gov.uk**.

More favourable redundancy schemes

You will have noticed that the statutory levels for redundancy pay are not very high, especially if the person concerned is young, or has not been employed by the employer for very long. This seems to contradict the huge amounts of redundancy pay that some people are rumoured to receive. This is because some employers have decided to make a more generous provision than is required by law. They may do this in some of the following ways:

- calculating entitlements based on actual pay rather than applying the upper earnings limit
- reducing the length of qualifying period necessary to receive redundancy pay from, for example, two years to one
- adding amounts to the statutory scheme
- making a more generous calculation such as two or three weeks' pay for each year of service.

Outplacement

Employers may also be concerned to help their employees in other ways through this difficult period, and may provide an outplacement service. This is the international name given to the process that many employers use to assist redundant employees. Outplacement can be defined as the process whereby the employer actively helps the employee to come to terms with the redundancy and assists them in the process of finding a new job or developing a new career. It is a type of aftercare service for employees who are facing redundancy, though it is by no means standard practice for all employers to provide such a service. It has been defined by Alan Jones (1994) as 'the provision of support to candidates during the transitional phase between involuntary/voluntary job loss and resettlement'. This is a useful definition as, although much of outplacement is concerned with job search skills and the finding of a new job or career, there are other avenues to explore such as further training or part-time or voluntary work, or perhaps self-employment. This definition also states that support is provided to the candidate, and this makes it clear that the responsibility for the resettlement process still rests with the candidate themselves but that help and active support will be given by the outplacement provider.

The CIPD (2003) adopts a similar approach and defines outplacement as:

Activities designed to enable individuals to develop awareness of their capacities, potential, skills and limitations, to help them to pursue the career opportunities open to them and to manage the transition through a career change or into re-employment following the loss of a job.

Once again the emphasis is on helping the individual during a difficult period but in many ways the fact that the employer provides an outplacement service also gives a very strong message to those who are still employed that they are working for a caring employer even though times may be hard. This is important as managing to keep morale high among the remaining employees can be a very difficult issue during a redundancy period.

While outplacement is generally provided by or for employers not all organisations provide this service and on occasions individuals whose organisation has not provided this facility may buy this provision for themselves. Research conducted by the careers advice service in 2010 found that 'nearly one in three jobseekers said HR handled their redundancy poorly.' This survey had involved more than 1,000 jobseekers and it revealed a 'deep dissatisfaction with HR' (PM online, 2010). Clearly in many cases workers facing redundancy perceive a need for more help from HR and for some form of outplacement service.

The benefits of providing an outplacement service

However, there are many human resource managers who, when faced with making employees redundant, do realise that it is important for the organisation to handle this difficult process as smoothly as possible, both for the sake of the individuals concerned and for the morale of the remaining employees, and in order to maintain or even enhance the good reputation of the organisation. In particular, the benefits to the organisation are likely to include:

- improved morale for remaining employees
- key staff are more likely to remain with the organisation if they see that other employees are treated well even in a redundancy situation
- good public relations with the local community will be less likely to be affected by the redundancies if they have been handled well
- there may be fewer problems with objections from trade unions if a good outplacement service is provided.

Individuals vary in the effect that redundancy has on them. For a few people it may provide a welcome opportunity to change direction in their careers, while others who have worked for a long time for an organisation may find redundancy a very traumatic experience with which they need help.

The outplacement process normally consists of provision of the following services:

● Counselling about the feelings brought about by the redundancy itself. This may sometimes involve also counselling the partner of the person who has been made redundant.
● Counselling about career or other options.
● Provision of facilities for conducting a job search.
● Provision of facilities for writing letters of application or curriculum vitae.
● Help with writing curriculum vitae and applications for jobs.
● Psychological tests to assist in career choice.
● Opportunities for practising interview skills.
● Possible direct contact with prospective employers.
● There may be provision of facilities in which interviews can be conducted.

According to Wise (2009) it is also good practice for employers to continue to provide support even after the date of termination of employment and she suggests 'maintaining contact with redundant employees via email, letter or telephone, to communicate any suitable re-employment or networking opportunities and to encourage redundant employees to continue meeting with each other or retained staff for social support and information sharing'. This means that the employer should commit to a long-term form of assistance for their former employees.

An outplacement service can be provided either 'in-house', by the human resource department, or by external consultants.

ACTIVITY 13.4

List the advantages and the disadvantages of the provision of an in-house outplacement service and compare these with the advantages and disadvantages of external provision of an outplacement service.

Provision of in-house outplacement service

Advantages	Disadvantages

Provision of external outplacement service

Advantages	Disadvantages

Discussion of Activity 13.4

Your list probably indicates that provision of an internal outplacement service is likely to be cheaper than using a consultancy. Since many redundancies occur as part of a cost-cutting exercise, employers will be loath to spend additional money and cost may be a major concern. However, an organisation may not have sufficient facilities or levels of expertise to provide the standard of service that is required. Not only that, but it may be difficult, or even impossible, for redundant employees who have recently been told of their redundancy by their line manager or by the human resource manager to be helped by counselling from the same manager or any other manager within the organisation. Even identifying managers or others with suitable expertise may be a problem.

On the other hand, there may also be problems in finding a suitable consultancy with a high degree of expertise in this area. Anyone can establish themselves in business as an outplacement consultant, and they do not necessarily have to have any qualifications. This has been a cause for concern in recent years, with some people being charged high fees for an inadequate service, which resulted in the Chartered Institute of Personnel and Development issuing a *Code for Career and Outplacement Consultants* (2003). This is a voluntary code of practice but gives some indication of the type of service and qualifications that an outplacement service should provide. It indicates that outplacement consultants should normally be able to demonstrate competence in 'the provision of career and outplacement consultancy services by possessing at least one of the following:

- chartered membership of the CIPD (Chartered MCIPD, Chartered FCIPD, Chartered CCIPD)
- registration with the British Psychological Society as a chartered psychologist
- other qualifications in psychology, vocational guidance or counselling recognised by a professional body
- psychometric testing and feedback must be conducted only by holders of the British Psychological Society Level A Statement of Certificate of Competence in Psychological testing. Those conducting personality testing should also hold the British Psychological Society Level B Statement or Certificate in Competence or the equivalent additional training specified by the supplier. Administration of psychological tests can also be carried out by members of the British Psychological Society Test Administration Certificate' (CIPD, 2003).

Ideally a firm of consultants would want people who had a range of qualifications in these areas. The CIPD (2003) differentiates between 'sponsored services where the client is an organisation paying for services provided to an individual or group of individuals' and 'private services where services are provided to clients as individuals for the services they personally receive'. All providers of whatever type of service should let the client know in advance, in writing, about the fees and terms of payment before the signing of any contract. They should also provide a written breakdown detailing exactly the service they will provide.

Survivor syndrome

While it is important to ensure excellent communication and to provide an outplacement service for those to be made redundant it is also of importance to pay attention to the feelings of those who have not been made redundant and to ensure that they do not suffer too great a lack of motivation.

Survivor syndrome refers generally to people who have suffered from witnessing traumatic events but has also come to be used in relation to those who have survived redundancy. While organisations plan for the reduction in staff, they do not always take into account how the feelings of those who survived may affect their productivity at work. The organisation will be concerned with retention of other staff and will want employees to be highly motivated, but according to Murphy (2009), 'the survivor syndrome can sabotage some of the effects of a downsizing operation.'

According to Murphy (2009) the most common symptoms of survivor syndrome include 'lower morale and commitment, breakdown of trust in management, increased stress and reduced motivation'. In this survey these four symptoms of survivor syndrome were also the four that exerted the most effect on employers. The survey found that it was important to communicate with all members of staff, not just those facing immediate threat of redundancy. 'According to employers that have emphasised the use of communication, the most effective means of doing so are: first holding general staff meetings (according to 39% of employers) and, second, ensuring that line managers provide briefings for their teams (34%)' (Murphy, 2009). This shows again the importance of good communication and emphasises once more the role of line managers as being crucial to maintaining morale and helping with retention of staff in such a difficult time.

Conclusion

A discussion of dismissal and redundancy may seem a rather depressing topic but they are not inevitable stages if earlier advice for good human resource practices and procedures is followed.

We have gone through the employment process in an almost chronological order, and examined the approaches of human resource practitioners to finding and selecting people by the use of human resource planning. We have also examined the employment relationship and how people should then be treated while they are working for the organisation, whether as employees or in some other capacity, how they should be trained and developed, and how they should be motivated and rewarded to achieve a high-performance organisation. We considered ways in which some problems may be prevented or, failing prevention, how they should be handled and we discussed this in relation to counselling and wellbeing, employee involvement, health and safety, and discipline and grievance handling. We have included dismissal and redundancy since it is likely that even with the best planning there will be occasional dismissals, as people operate from different standpoints and have different points of view, and will therefore not always act in the way in which the organisation hopes that they will act.

Dismissal and redundancy can be avoided to some extent by adopting good HRM techniques and programmes described in the rest of the text. Problems associated with redundancy and dismissal, both for employers and employees, will also be minimised by proper handling and by excellent communication to all employees as described in this chapter.

Just like any other area of HRM, this area is also subject to change, so one needs to be constantly vigilant.

All who are involved in the management of people, whether they call themselves HRM managers, personnel managers or line managers, must be aware of the need for strategic planning and clear links between everyone's work and the aims of the business even though most of you will not initially have the opportunity to operate at a strategic level.

All who are involved in human resource management also need to be aware of the law, and although this may be dealt with in more detail in other specialist modules in your course, we have felt it necessary to include brief summaries of relevant legislation in appropriate chapters for those of you who do not have the opportunity to study employment law modules. As you will have discovered by now, the law is always changing and varies from one country to another, so it is very important to ensure that you know how to find information about the current state of legislation.

REVIEW QUESTIONS

Brief answers to the review questions are provided on pages 497–8.

1 Discuss the measures that should be taken to ensure that both workers who have been selected for redundancy and those who have not remain motivated at work.

2 Outline the circumstances that are considered to constitute fair dismissal and comment on the extent to which an organisation should be expected to avoid dismissing employees.

SELF-CHECK QUESTIONS

Answer the following multiple-choice questions. The answers are provided on page 498 for you to check your understanding of this chapter.

1 Constructive dismissal is said to occur in which of the following circumstances?
  (a) The employer constructs a false case against the employee in order to dismiss them.
  (b) A fixed-term contract expires and is not renewed.
  (c) The employee leaves, with or without giving notice, in circumstances such that they are entitled to go without notice by reason of the employer's conduct.
  (d) The employment is terminated by the employer, with or without notice.
  (e) The employee is encouraged to take early retirement.

2 Which of the following is not a potentially fair reason for dismissal?
  (a) misconduct
  (b) lack of capability
  (c) lack of a qualification
  (d) a statutory restriction placed on the employer or on the employee
  (e) the employee has only worked for the organisation for six months.

3 Which of the following is a good definition of outplacement?
  (a) The employee is placed temporarily in another organisation with a view to improving their job chances.
  (b) The employee is actively helped by the employer to come to terms with the redundancy and assisted in finding a new job or developing a new career.
  (c) A form of job share that is introduced to minimise the need for redundancies.

(d) It is another word for the redundancy process.

(e) A service provided by consultants to employers to help them out when faced with redundancies.

4 Which of the following should *not* be one of the steps to take to minimise the need for redundancy?

(a) Give people the option of early retirement packages.

(b) Use natural wastage over a period of time instead of making employees redundant.

(c) Dismiss all employees who do not have the necessary length of employment to bring a case for unfair dismissal.

(d) Terminate the use of non-employees such as self-employed or agency staff.

(e) Ask for voluntary redundancies.

5 An employer must disclose certain information to the trade unions before making people redundant. Which of the following is not one of the things that the employer must disclose at this stage?

(a) the names of the people to be made redundant

(b) the reasons for the dismissals

(c) the proposed method of selection for redundancy

(d) the method of carrying out the redundancies

(e) the number and description of employees likely to be involved in redundancy.

HR IN THE NEWS

The safe way to sack a baby boomer

By Patti Waldmeir

The first American baby boomer registered for her government pension earlier this month, and there are 76m more where she came from. Corporate America is terrified that the postwar birth boom could fuel a 21st century lawsuit explosion, as more and more geriatrics cling to jobs they can no longer perform – and then sue the boss that fires them.

The statistics are enough to give a thirty-something human resources manager premature arrhythmia: recent studies suggest that nearly three-quarters of American workers intend to work past retirement age – and 12 per cent say they will never retire.

Since other studies show that 40 per cent of workers over the age of 65 have some kind of disability, the boom generation could easily provoke a perfect storm of liability: those who do not sue under age discrimination laws (which protect workers over 40) can try their luck with the Americans with Disabilities Act. Small wonder that corporate America seems to be developing a boomer phobia.

The Conference Board, the leading US business research group, is worried that US managers will be paralysed at the thought of all that risk, and just avoid dealing with anyone who is, to coin a politically incorrect phrase, old. The group recently published a corporate guide to dealing with 'mature workers'*. It offers lots of sage advice on how to keep older workers productive – by offering 'phased retirement' (flexi-time or reduced hours), lifetime training, and perks such as eldercare for their parents or daycare for their grandkids.

But, inevitably, much of the guide deals with how to avoid getting sued by boomers – whether the geriatric in question is a vibrant, vital, vivacious seventy-something with decades of experience to contribute to the corporation, or someone who is truly old, in the traditional sense of the word: intolerant, inflexible, and twice the price of a youngster.

Avoiding such lawsuits, it seems, requires a feat of double-think, for, in a world where 60 is the new 40, old people no longer consider themselves old – and employers had better not do so either. The guide cites a study by the Society of Human Resource Management that says only 4 per cent of American workers describe someone over 40 as 'older' – even though anyone over that age is protected by federal anti-discrimination law.

It warns managers against asking about retirement plans – even for those who are over 65 with fully vested pensions and a low handicap on the golf course.

Birthdays, it seems, are particularly dangerous territory: the guide includes a 'sample birthday celebrations policy' that warns 'careful attention should be made to the tone of and content of the celebrations to be respectful of . . . employees of all ages'. The policy sternly notes that "over-the-hill", "it's all downhill from here", "next stop – the grave", etc themes should be avoided', and that 'supervisors should be careful to avoid discussions of employees' ages at these celebrations'. And by all means, managers must not talk about 'work and/or career plans in relation to a particular birthday'. They must stick to 'the usual small-talk topics' – though it is hard to imagine what those might be, if one cannot mention the grandkids or the golf game.

The bad news is that the Conference Board thinks we all need sensitivity training to purge our minds of negative stereotypes about older workers. The good news is that, if a worker happens to act out those stereotypes, he can still safely be sacked. Nobody has to keep a worker on the payroll just because he is old: the key – as in any other potential case involving racial minorities, women or anyone else protected by anti-discrimination law – is to document what they have done wrong, give them a chance to remedy it, and be ready to prove they are being punished for how they do their job and not who or how old they are.

Most American companies cannot force employees to retire at a certain age, but maybe with the help of the Conference Board, and an army of sensitivity trainers, we can all survive the 'R' era.

Financial Times, 30/10/2007 (Patti Waldmeir), Reproduced with permission. © The Financial Times Ltd.

Questions

1 To what extent do you think that the abolition of the default retirement age in the UK will lead to similar problems to those experienced in the USA?

2 What methods are listed here as ways of keeping older workers productive?

3 To what extent do you think each of these methods will be useful?

WHAT NEXT?

1 Go to www.acas.org.uk and view the short video about the role that ACAS conciliation officers play prior to a case going to an employment tribunal.

2 Visit an employment tribunal to hear a case of alleged unfair dismissal. Assess the merits of each side's case and decide whether or not you think the participants in the case followed the statutory disciplinary dismissal and grievance procedures. A list of employment tribunals and further guidance about bringing cases to employment tribunals can be found at: **www.employmenttribunals.gov.uk.**

References

Advisory, Conciliation and Arbitration Service (n.d.) *The ACAS arbitration scheme for the resolution of unfair dismissal disputes (England and Wales)*, ACAS.

Advisory, Conciliation and Arbitration Service (2009) *Annual Report and Accounts 2008–2009*, ACAS.

Chartered Institute of Personnel and Development (2003) *Code for Career and Outplacement Consultants*, CIPD.

Chartered Institute of Personnel and Development (2007) *Unfair Dismissal: Member Resource*, CIPD (www.cipd.co.uk/EmploymentLaw/FAQ/_Redundancy/Redundancy.htm; accessed 5.6.2010).

Chartered Institute of Personnel and Development (2010a) *Age Discrimination and Retirement: Member Resource*, CIPD (www.cipd.co.uk; accessed 03.04.10).

Chartered Institute of Personnel and Development (2010b) *Wrongful Dismissal*, CIPD (www.cipd.co.uk; accessed 05.04.10).

Chartered Institute of Personnel and Development (2010c) *Redundancy Fact Sheet*, CIPD (www.cipd.co.uk; accessed 03.04.10).

European Industrial Relations Observatory online (2001) Industrial relations aspects of mergers and takeovers, February (www.eurofound.europa.eu/eiro/2001/02/study/tn0102401s.html; accessed 6.5.10).

HR Zone online (2010) *Lessons to be Learned from Facebook Sacking*, 25 March (www.HRzone.co.uk/topic/managing-people/lessons-be-learned-facebook-sacking/101835; accessed 4.4.2010).

Jones, A. (1994) *Delivering In-House Outplacement. A Practical Guide for Trainers, Managers and Personnel Specialists*, McGraw-Hill.

Monks, J. (2001) TUC welcomes French decision, TUC press release, 9 April (www.tuc.org.uk/international/tuc-3030-f0.cfm; accessed 6.5.10).

Murphy, N. (2009) *Survey: managing the survivor syndrome during and after redundancies*, *IRS Employment Review*, Issue 921, 26 May, IRS (www.xperthr.co.uk; accessed 7.4.2010).

PM online (2010) 'HR handles redundancy badly', say a third of job seekers, 12 March (www.peoplemanagement.co.uk; accessed 7.4.2010).

Sage, G. (1998) Health warning, *People Management*, 16 April, Vol. 4, No. 8, 23.

Simpson, S. (2010) Default retirement age proposals: 10 things employers need to know, *XpertHR*, 4 August (www.xperthr.co.uk; accessed 5.8.2010).

Sweeney, E. (2010) More employers using conciliation, ACAS figures show, PM online, 18 March (www.peoplemanagement.co.uk/pm/articles/2010/03; accessed 3.4.10).

Wise, A. (2009) Good practice: assisting redundant employees, *XpertHR*, 15 October (www.xperthr.co.uk; accessed 7.4.2010).

Further study

Books

Advisory, Conciliation and Arbitration Service (2010) Advisory booklet, *Redundancy Handling*, ACAS.

An excellent, clear guide to good practice (available at www.acas.org.uk/index.aspx?articleid=747; accessed 6.5.10).

Sen, A. (2010) *The Role of ACAS in Dispute Resolution*, IDS Pay report 1054, August.

This has been written by a member of ACAS staff who provides a clear account of the role of ACAS in the resolution of disputes (http://www.acas.org.uk/CHttpHandler.ashx?id=2864&p=0; accessed 19.9.2010).

Articles

Chartered Institute of Personnel and Development (2010) *Redundancy Fact Sheet*, CIPD.

This provides a useful summary of the key issues affecting redundancy.

Chiumento, R. (2003) How to support the survivors of redundancy, *People Management*, Vol. 9, No. 3, 48–9.

This discusses what to do to help motivate those who have not been made redundant.

Other sources

ACAS telephone advice service.

There are ACAS offices in most large towns and you should be able to find them in the telephone book. Alternatively, Department for Business, Innovation and Skills offices such as Job Centres should be able to give you their telephone number.

Internet

Advisory, Conciliation and Arbitration Service   **www.acas.org.uk**
A very useful source of information relating to dismissal and redundancy in Britain.

Business Link   **www.businesslink.gov.uk**
Useful information for employers relating to redundancy and dismissal and other HR topics.

Department for Business, Innovation and Skills   **www.bis.gov.uk**
Many useful publications relating to redundancy and dismissal in Britain can be found on this site.

Employment tribunals   **www.employmenttribunals.gov.uk**
A useful site for everything to do with tribunals.

European Industrial Relations Observatory   **www.eiro.eurofound.ie**
This has up-to-date information about issues in industrial relations, including redundancy and dismissal, throughout the EU member states and Norway.

European Trade Union Confederation   **www.etuc.org**
This provides information from the unions' and workers' perspective but in a European dimension.

Trades Union Congress (TUC)   **www.tuc.org.uk**
Lots of information from the perspective of the unions and employees relating to redundancy and dismissal. This also has a useful section for students.

Answers to review and self-check questions

We have provided a skeleton guide to issues you might address in answering review questions. In an exam or for an assignment, you would be expected to develop the ideas more fully to show your understanding of the topic. You can also enhance your response by making references to further reading.

Chapter 1 Introducing human resource management

Answers to review questions

It is not possible to provide model answers to the review questions for Chapter 1 because you will all have arrived at very individual answers to the activities suggested.

Answers to self-check questions

1 (c). 2 (d). 3 (b). 4 (d). 5 (a).

Chapter 2 Human resource strategy and planning

Answers to review questions

1
  - The levels of strategy are corporate, business and functional.
  - You might wish to review the generic strategies associated with the corporate level (growth; stability; retrenchment) and the business level (cost competitiveness; differentiation of products or services; focus on a niche in the market). In general, it is expected that business strategies will grow out of corporate strategies and functional strategies will grow out of business strategies. However, each level can provide useful information for the others. Human resource strategies will have a direct impact on all the other functional strategies, and conversely cannot be formulated without knowledge of what the other functional goals are.

2
  - Name the major stages and describe how each is carried out.
  - Development of the corporate plan: issues and information to be considered.
  - Estimate demand for human resources: techniques such as work study.
  - Estimate the internal supply of human resources: skills inventory; effects of labour turnover.
  - Gather and analyse information about the external labour market. Labour force issues.
  - Formulate human resource action plans: describe the functional areas.
  - Comment on the need for evaluation and feedback into the corporate objectives.

3 ● Comment on the decisions made throughout the human resource planning process: what the corporate objectives are to be; what skills are required to achieve these objectives; how the organisation decides whether it has these skills; what action is to be taken.

● Describe the sources of information for each of these areas: knowledge of product and market developments; the need for environmental scanning; managerial judgement; HRIS; statistical information about the labour force.

4 Skills shortages occur when employers have vacancies they have difficulty in filling. Skills gaps occur within the existing workforce.

Skills shortages may mean that the desired competencies are not available in the labour market, but it may also be that people with those skills are not attracted to the particular employer or do not wish to take on that type of job for some reason. Employers have a number of options: provide training; review pay and terms and conditions; develop and promote their employer brand; recruit overseas; focus on diversity if this has previously limited their recruitment practices.

Answers to self-check questions

1 Growth; stability; retrenchment. **2** Cost leadership; differentation, focus. **3** 50%. **4** 80%. **5** Problems or success with keeping long-term employees. **6** Estimate the supply of human resources. **7** Operational. **8** UK; other countries in the EU; USA; Australia. You should be able to find more examples of countries with the same issue.

● Chapter 3 High-performance working: employee engagement through involvement and participation

Answers to review questions

1 ● Outline the concepts of unitarism and pluralism.
  ● Outline the concepts of participation and involvement; state how they differ from each other; identify each concept correctly as a unitary or pluralist idea.

2 ● Define employee involvement and give examples of individual techniques such as quality circles.
  ● Define commitment as an attitude; explain how this attitude might motivate towards more productive behaviour.
  ● Explain that engagement is identified when employees in fact do deliver the sought-after discretionary effort.
  ● Link the involvement initiatives you have described with motivation concepts; e.g. quality circles provide employees with feelings of responsibility and achievement because they see they can contribute their ideas. This in turn should contribute to the development of a high-performance workplace.

3 You will have to read some of the references in order to gather more information for this question. Your answer should address developments on both a national and EU-wide scale.

4 You should have identified elements such as employment security, and information for employees and consultation with them to ensure an adequate channel for employee voice. Partnership recognises that employees are stakeholders in an organisation and have an interest in its success.

The aim of partnership is to improve productivity and competitiveness by fully engaging the capabilities of employees.

Answers to self-check questions

1 (c). **2** False. **3** At least 1,000 employees within the member states and at least 150 employees in each of any two member states. **4** (b). **5** (b). **6** False. **7**. Save As You Earn. **8** Team briefing; employer and employee publications; company videos; electronic news systems; roadshows. **9** (d). **10** Communication and evidence that it is sincere; managers who promote EI and adopt an appropriate style.

● Chapter 4 The employment relationship

Answers to review questions 1–3

1. It is not possible to forecast what you may discover when perusing recent articles or court cases because although some issues remain contentious for many years, there are always new issues arising too. However, you will probably notice that some new issues can be directly linked to new legislation which needs to be interpreted. The meaning of new employment legislation is often tested in employment tribunals and the appeal courts.

Through doing this exercise, you will have further developed your competence in finding information. We hope you will also reflect on your learning. If you have done so, you may have realised a few implications, including the following:

- New issues are constantly arising in the HRM field, and practitioners need to stay abreast of developments by engaging in activities similar to the one you have just completed.
- You can adapt this activity to other issues too, such as unlawful discrimination, unfair dismissal, redundancy.

2 Annual leave; paternity leave: number of days/weeks allowed; may pay during paternity leave; may give more notice or termination of employment; maternity pay provisions may be more generous than the statutory minimum.

3 Employers use flexible working arrangements to minimise the amount of time that employees are underemployed and yet being paid. Employers also benefit from being able to call on different people at different times if they approach diversity in a strategic fashion, and this may also lead to a good employer image and a more creative workforce with high levels of job satisfaction. Employees look for flexible working arrangements in order to achieve an acceptable balance between personal and work commitments.

Flexible working arrangements include part-time work, annualised hours, teleworking, job sharing and fixed-term contracts. Go back and review Chapter 4 to ensure you have a good grasp of the pros and cons of these arrangements. There are many possible arrangements that can be made, and we have referred you to some sources if you are interested in following this up.

Answers to self-check questions

1 (c). **2** Express terms are those that are addressed directly; implied terms are those that are not expressed directly but are taken as assumed. **3** Fidelity; obedience of lawful and reasonable orders; and working with due diligence and care. **4** Nine weeks. **5** One week. **6** Employment Rights Act. **7** 26 weeks. **8** False. **9** False. **10** Isolation of employees; difficulties with supervision.

● Chapter 5 Diversity and equality

Answers to review questions

1 Diversity is about celebrating the differences between people, and using these to enhance creativity, problem-solving, productivity and responsiveness to customer needs. A well-managed diverse group of people should experience greater job satisfaction and appreciate their employer for their commitment to equality. Being known as an employer who promotes equality should enhance the employer brand.

2 Managing a diverse group of people calls for managers to recognise the value of what each person can bring to the workplace and to adopt a style which will encourage all members of the workforce to reach their full potential. In order to obtain and retain a diverse workforce, organisations will have to develop flexible working arrangements to suit the needs of various workers. Communication of goals is important.

3 Check your answer with the information on pages 142–4 to ensure you have correctly identified and described the protected characteristics.

4 *Direct discrimination* occurs when someone is treated less favourably for a reason directly to do with his or her sex, race or racial origin, etc.

Indirect discrimination occurs when someone is treated unfairly because of some provision, criterion or practice that would disproportionately exclude the particular group that person belongs to, and when the requirement cannot be objectively justified.

Victimisation occurs when someone is treated less favourably because that person has made a complaint or indicated an intention to make a complaint about sex or race discrimination.

Harassment is defined as unwanted conduct that intimidates or humiliates an individual, affecting his or her dignity or creating a hostile work environment.

Answers to self-check questions

1 False. **2** Equality and Human Rights Commission. **3** 9. **4** (*b*). **5** False.

Chapter 6 Recruitment

Answers to review questions 2 and 4

2 ● Explain how each section of these documents is part of a systematic approach to recruitment and can help in designing a job advertisement.
● Comment on the need to give information of this kind so prospective applicants can engage in an informed process of self-selection.

4 ● Effects of an internal recruitment policy; the message that the employer rewards good performance.
● Adoption of, and commitment to, an equality policy.
● Treating people well and with respect in any telephone, written or personal contact.
● Include positive messages in recruitment advertising to strengthen public perceptions of the employer brand.

Answers to self-check questions

1 Is the post necessary at all? Can the tasks be distributed among other employees? Can the post be filled as a job share position? **2** Local or national newspapers; professional journals; online. **3** Company name; job title; tasks expressed as opportunities; competencies required; how to apply and by when. **4** No. **5** False.

Chapter 7 Selection: interviews and tests

Answers to review questions

1 The aim of selection is to 'choose the best person for the job'. Selectors gather and analyse information in an attempt to predict the performance of applicants in the job. This must be done as objectively as possible by matching evidence of the knowledge, skills and personal qualities of applicants with the requirements outlined in the person specification and/or competency framework. The selection process must also be fair, avoiding any unlawful discrimination in terms of sex, race and disability etc.

   Methodical approaches include:

   - having a selection policy and procedure which define the steps that will be followed in filling any vacancy
   - using the person specification/competency framework as a checklist when screening and shortlisting applicants
   - devising a set of standard questions to cover all the requirements on the person specification or the required competencies
   - gathering a full set of information from all candidates and using this information to assess their suitability for the post.

   Making sure that candidates can assess their own suitability for a post is also part of effective selection. Employers should therefore ensure that there is adequate opportunity for applicants to gather information about the organisation and the post during the selection process.

2 Validity and reliability are terms used in statistics to report on the results of tests. If a test consistently produces similar results when used at different times and administered by different people, then it would score high in reliability. Thus if an applicant was interviewed for a particular post by Mr Smith on Monday morning, and the same applicant was interviewed for the same post by Mrs Jones on Friday afternoon, we would expect the same result if we thought that the interview was a reliable test. Research has, however, shown that interviews can be low in reliability.

   Validity is an indicator of how well the test measures what it purports to measure. How well do interviews predict good performance on the job? Again, research has indicated that interviews can be low in validity. It must, however, be noted that a structured approach to interviewing can raise the level of both the reliability and the validity of employment interviews.

3 Employment interviews run a particular risk of being low in validity if they are approached in an unstructured fashion with the interviewers not properly prepared, and simply asking whatever they think is relevant in an impromptu manner. In these circumstances, interviewers are more likely to fall prey to perceptual errors than if they were conducting a structured interview.

   Perceptual errors include the halo effect, the contrast effect, hiring in one's own image, and quite simply not gathering sufficient and relevant data.

   These perceptual errors can be avoided simply by being aware of them and making a conscious effort to resist them. If a structured interview is conducted using a set of questions which is designed to elicit full information related to the person specification/competency framework, and an attempt is made to assess all candidates objectively against these criteria, then the validity of the interview process should also increase.

4 The different types of questions that can be asked include open, closed, leading, probing, situational, and behavioural (or competency-based) questions. Each kind of question will typically elicit a different sort of response from applicants, so interviewers should carefully design their questions to gain the specific information they are seeking.

Closed questions can be used to confirm information. However, the interview is an opportunity to gain as much information as possible, and open questions are more likely to encourage applicants to talk freely. Most questions used in an interview should therefore be open questions. Probing questions can also be used to clarify points or seek more in-depth information.

Leading questions, which indicate to the interviewee what the expected response is, are not useful.

Experienced interviewers can make good use of situational and behavioural (or competency-based) questions. These require applicants to address their own behaviour in incidents which are typical of the post. Behavioural questions assume that applicants have previous related experience, whereas situational questions address what an applicant *would do* if faced with a particular situation in the future.

5 Tests can secure additional objective information about applicants, but they must be relevant to the job and they must be administered properly. The costs of running tests must be weighed against the costs of making poor selection decisions.

Answers to self-check questions

1 (c). 2 False. 3 (d). 4 (d). 5 (i) (c). 5(ii) (b). 6 (b). 7 (b). 8 False. 9 False. 10 (b).

Chapter 8 Performance management and appraisal

1 Line managers may be reluctant to get involved with performance management as they may not perceive this to be a part of their job, or feel that they are too busy and there is insufficient time or they may not have been adequately trained.

They may just regard it as something that HR wants and think they should be doing this. Line managers would have to see the benefits of performance management and its relevance to them and their jobs and that it could help them achieve their targets. They also need to be made aware that it is their responsibility to manage their own team. It would need to be explained to them that potential benefits of performance appraisal should be to motivate employees and improve relations: to provide a better understanding of, and agreement on, goals; to give opportunities for praise/positive feedback; to encourage agreement on training needs/use of appraisal for staff development, and for improved communication. Performance management should therefore help individuals and their team to contribute to the organisation's goals.

Line managers will also need to be trained in relevant skills such as coaching, giving feedback and counselling.

2 There are many benefits to using a 360-degree form of appraisal as it is extremely thorough and information is collected about the individual from a number of contacts of the person being appraised. This may include their subordinates, their colleagues and their managers. In most organisations the appraisee is able to choose who will provide the feedback about their performance and in some organisations they can nominate up to 30 people.

This is useful as in many organisations nowadays each individual will have a number of roles which they may perform to different levels of satisfaction. This form of appraisal should provide good clear information for development purposes in all aspects of the individual's roles.

With the use of computers it is now possible to collect a wide range of information quite quickly.

There can also be disadvantages if those giving feedback have not been trained adequately or if they do not give fair comments because of dislike or jealousy of that person.

It can also be cumbersome to collect so much information and could be very daunting for the individual concerned to have such a thorough analysis of their performance, particularly if there are several areas in which they appear to be underperforming.

3 Reasons for failure:

These could include a lack of clarity about the reason for the performance appraisal and a lack of training for those conducting the appraisal and for those being appraised. You should also address the use of appraisal systems for different purposes: appraising for developmental reason and to make decisions about pay may conflict. In some organisations there is also a lack of involvement from the employees in the performance appraisal system.

The skills needed:

Lack of managerial skill and training in areas such as an inability to give critical feedback in a positive way could prevent this working as well as it should. This could be in relation to lack of planning and preparation, poor interpersonal skills such as interview skills, poor communication skills, inability to build and develop teams and give feedback to individuals and teams, etc. Sometimes the processes themselves can be counterproductive if the targets are unreasonable and have not been agreed or are poorly defined. There is a need for managerial training and commitment to the system.

4 (a) Evaluate current performance levels for the organisation, the team and for the individual.

Decide what levels of performance are required in order to contribute effectively to the organisation's strategic objectives and what measures will be used to evaluate then.

Assess what performance levels are required in the future for each of these groups and if there is a gap between these and the actual current levels of performance, then decide on the best approaches to achieve these and any rewards to give if they are achieved.

Implement these methods and review whether or not the required performances have been achieved. Then agree objectives for the next period of time.

4 (b) For the organisation the following approaches could be useful:

Measures such as productivity, absence, quality, complaints, etc.
Agreed measures of performance.
Ongoing assessments of the whole organisation's performance.
Use of the balanced scorecard approach to measuring performance.
Coaching
Mentoring
Line manager involvement
Learning and talent development initiatives, etc.

For the team:

Objective on-going regular assessments of performance.
Agreed measures of performance.
Team reviews.
Team incentives.
Coaching.
Learning and talent development initiatives, etc.

For the individual:

Objective performance appraisal and assessment.
360-degree feedback.
Regular performance and development reviews.
Clear measures for performance.
Learning and talent development.
Coaching, etc.

5 You should identify and describe three different approaches to performance management, e.g. individual appraisal conducted by the manager/supervisor, peer appraisal and 360-degree appraisal.

The general benefits relate to improved performance, motivation, communication and relationships. The actual nature of these benefits will need to be discussed in relation to the specific approach used.

Other general benefits include the opportunity to focus on future developments and to achieve organisational goals.

You might also mention some of the pitfalls, such as problems if there is a lack of clarity in the purpose of the appraisal, e.g. reward or development. You could also mention skills needed in giving feedback and discuss these in relation to the approaches used, e.g. in peer appraisal or 360-degree appraisal, would everyone involved have the required levels of skills and not be influenced by any personal vendettas they might want to settle?

There is also, regardless of the approach chosen, a need to encourage ownership and participation.

Answers to self-check questions

1 (c). **2** (a). **3** (c). **4** (a). **5** (b). **6** (a).

Chapter 9 Learning and talent development

Answers to review questions

1 There is a huge amount of information on the Internet relating to these topics. Once you have chosen your topic and found information you will need to list all the key benefits from the introduction of that topic if you are to persuade a line manager about it. Consider the benefits to the organisation and the individual, and particularly the potential benefits to the line manager, such as greater efficiency and higher productivity, and an easier job with a more highly trained workforce.

2 If you interview someone from a large organisation you are likely to find that learning and talent development is tied in very clearly with the strategic plan and objectives of the organisation. There are also likely to be clear objectives set for the learning and talent development department which clearly contribute to the overall objectives of the workplace. This is not the case in all organisations and some may still operate without making these links.

3 Answers should include comments on the cost involved in designing and running an induction programme, but should generally identify the benefits of easing a new employee into the workforce and how this is likely to result in a speedier route to full productivity, less labour turnover and fewer bad work habits being acquired. There should then be an outline of a suitable induction programme spread over some time.

4 Answers should define each concept and list the pros and cons of each, e.g. learning-by-doing in a realistic environment versus cost of errors and distractions. You should explain which technique you feel is the more successful overall.

Answers to self-check questions

1 (a). **2** (a). This effect is known as a *conditioned response*. (b) The cat food is the *stimulus* for Caroline's cats to make an appearance. (c) *Association*. The cats have started to associate the sound of the kettle with the cat food being put out. (d) In time the sound of the kettle becomes the *conditioned stimulus*, and the cats' response to it becomes the *conditioned response*. **3** No. **4** (b). **5** No. **6** (b). **7** (c). **8** (b). **9** Yes. **10** (d).

Chapter 10 Pay and reward systems

Answers to review questions

1 and **2** provide you with the opportunity to practise skills and seek relevant, up-to-date information for yourself and so it is impossible to provide guideline answers here. The 'Pay and benefits bulletin', contained in the *IRS Employment Review*, is published twice a month and is an extremely useful source of articles and up-to-date information about pay and benefits in various sectors and organisations. This may be of help in getting the latest information on the minimum wage or rates paid to people on apprenticeships or New Deal. Publications such as *People Management* or *Personnel Today* may also prove useful, as should quality newspapers.

3 Your answer should define job evaluation as a method of deciding on the value of a job and address the need for a methodical approach. The points rating method and its main benefits should then be outlined. Benefits of the points rating approach to job evaluation include the fact that all jobs are rated using the same method and that these must be perceived to be fair. It is comparatively simple to use and understand and is analytical in nature.

The second part of your answer should examine perceptions of fairness. Involvement of representatives of the workforce in the design and implementation of job evaluation is likely to improve employees' perceptions of whether or not the system is fair. The points rating method is an analytical approach to job evaluation and so does break each job into parts rather than analysing the whole job. This is generally regarded as being more objective and hence fairer than non-analytical schemes. It is also more likely that this system could be justified in a tribunal if an equal pay/value claim was brought against the organisation.

4 Your answer will describe issues such as internal and external relativities and differentials. You will also include and take account of the issues raised by legislation such as the Equality Act 2010. Systems of job evaluation which try to ensure that fair systems of pay are in place need to be discussed. Those based on analytical methods of job evaluation are likely to result in fairer systems and it will be easier to prove the fairness, if necessary. Involvement of representatives of the workforce in the design and implementation of job evaluation is likely to improve employees' perceptions of whether or not the system is fair.

Better answers will also comment on issues such as performance-related pay and how this may affect perceptions of fairness. Issues relating to gender pay reporting should also be fully discussed.

5 Your answer should be in report form as if you are a consultant employed to advise this organisation. You need to describe various forms of both the analytical and non-analytical types of job evaluation and outline the advantages and disadvantages of each. You should then decide on a scheme that you feel is most suitable for this organisation and make recommendations about its use. You are more likely to recommend an analytical form of job evaluation such as the points rating system. This would have benefits of being easy to justify but may be time-consuming to introduce. However, since we are making recommendations for a fairly small organisation, cost is also likely be an issue here and this form of analytical job evaluation will probably be cheaper to install than any designed or provided by a firm of consultants. Better answers would also refer to the need for fairness in whatever scheme is introduced and the need to involve members of the workforce in decisions about which scheme should be chosen. Reference should also be made to the need to take into account legislation, for example the Equality Act 2010, and also the issues of gender pay reporting raised in that Act.

Answers to self-check questions

1 No. 2 No. 3 No. 4 Yes. 5 Yes. 6 No. 7 No. 8 No. 9 Yes. 10 No.

Chapter 11 Health, safety and wellbeing

Answers to review questions

It is once again impossible to give ideal answers to the review questions here as your answers will depend on who you talk to or the organisations you analyse.

Answers to self-check questions

1 (d). 2 (d). 3 (c). 4 (b). 5 (d). 6 (d).

7 The safety committee should have been a means of ensuring cooperation between management and the workforce and also as a method of ensuring improvements in health and safety in the workplace. In particular, the committee should:

Study figures and trends for accidents and notifiable diseases so that they have raised the issue or are aware and involved in the decision to introduce new safety equipment to prevent accidents happening.

Examine safety audit reports so that they are aware of the main areas where accidents are occurring and can make recommendations for improvements and the introduction of new safety equipment.

Consider reports and factual information provided by inspectors. At this point there has not been any report from the inspectors for them to study.

Consider the reports of safety representatives. Once again, they should have been aware from the reports that the safety representatives had made of the need for improvements in health and safety and for the need for suitable safety equipment.

Assist in the development of safety rules and safe systems of work. On the basis of the evidence collected from the various sources already mentioned, they should be helping the management to formulate disciplinary rules and to choose appropriate safety equipment and assess its suitability for use in the workplace. They should also be involved in publicising the changes, assist in the provision of advice and help the management with training, if required to do so.

Monitor the effectiveness of safety training in the workplace. The safety committee should be concerned to make comparisons after new safety procedures are introduced, and they should compare accident rates. If the procedures are inadequate, as in this case, they should be pressing the management to obtain more appropriate safety equipment.

Monitor the effectiveness of the safety and health communication in the workplace. The safety committee should be checking to ensure that the communication about the new safety equipment is adequate and should assist the management in designing new materials if it is inadequate.

Encourage publicity for health and safety programmes in the workplace. Support the management's efforts and publicity and encourage competitions to publicise health and safety changes.

Provide a link with the appropriate inspectorates. In this case, the inspectorates have not yet become involved. The committee could get further information from them and if the management do not handle the situation in a reasonable manner, they could inform the inspectorates of the dangers in the workplace and ask them to inspect.

8 Improvements that a consultant might advise should be introduced at the Sheffley Company are likely to include the following:

Improve training for the supervisors and management in health and safety and wellbeing.

Appoint a trained safety officer.

Improve communication methods.

Encourage managers and supervisors to set a good example to the workforce.

Encourage managers and supervisors to investigate all accidents fully and to examine the statistics to identify trends.

Involve groups from the workforce including safety representatives and members of the safety committee in the design of a safety policy.

Publicise the policy.

Carry out exercises to assess risks in various parts of the workplace.

Appoint a competent person besides the safety officer to assess risks.

Introduce control measures in order to eliminate or minimise risks, e.g. substitute safer equipment or materials, improve design, replan procedures, and use protective clothing.

Monitor systems that are introduced.

Chapter 12 Discipline and grievance

Answers to review questions

It is impossible to give model answers for questions 1–3 as these require you to conduct your own research, so you may all have slightly different findings.

4 Your answer should be in the form of a report addressed to the general manager. When the organisation only employed 18 staff there was no legal requirement for it to have a grievance procedure, although it would still have been good practice to have had one. Now, since there are 100 employees, there is a legal requirement to produce a grievance procedure (Employment Rights Act 1996).

You should explain not only the importance of the legal situation to the general manager, but also make clear that grievance procedures provide a useful way for employees to express their grievances, rather than becoming dissatisfied and expressing the grievance by poor-quality work or by leaving the organisation altogether.

A model grievance procedure should be described in order to show what the grievance procedure should contain. This should be modelled on sample documents in ACAS (2009b) *Discipline and Grievances at Work: The ACAS Guide* and should include key features from the ACAS Code of Practice on disciplinary and grievance procedures 2009. Key features should include the following: an informal stage before the formal procedure is reached; grievances should be settled as near to the source of grievance as possible, at the lowest level; a small number of stages involving different people; time limits for responding at each stage and a right of appeal at each stage. There should also be a right to be accompanied by a friend or trade union official.

Answers to self-check questions

1 (c). 2 (b). 3 (c). 4 (c). 5 (d). 6 (c). 7 (e). 8 (b). 9 (e). 10 (e).

Chapter 13 Dismissal, redundancy and outplacement

Answers to review questions

1 You should discuss outplacement activities for those who are to be made redundant and activities relating to overcoming the survivor syndrome for those who have not been selected but who still may feel demotivated.

Typical outplacement activities would include the following:

- Counselling about the feelings brought about by the redundancy itself. This may sometimes involve also counselling the partner of the person who has been made redundant.
- Counselling about career or other options.
- Provision of facilities for conducting a job search.
- Provision of facilities for writing letters of application or curriculum vitae.
- Help with writing curriculum vitae and applications for jobs.
- Psychological tests to assist in career choice.
- Opportunities for practising interview skills.
- Possible direct contact with prospective employers.
- There may be provision of facilities in which interviews can be conducted.

It is also good practice for employers to continue to provide support even after the date of termination of employment.

Typical activities to overcome survivor syndrome and motivate those not selected for redundancy would include the following:

- The provision of an outplacement service for those facing redundancy does much to reassure the survivors so is important for them too.
- Excellent communication is really important and meetings should be held with all staff to explain what is happening.
- Excellent communication from line managers is also really important if the survivors are to be motivated during these difficult times.

2 You should outline the five main grounds for potentially fair dismissal as: misconduct, lack of capability, redundancy, statutory bar, or some other substantial reason. Better answers are likely to give examples of these types of potentially fair reasons for dismissal and to show awareness that until October 2011 retirement was also a potentially fair reason for dismissal.

You should also explain that the process followed for dismissal is as important as the reason for the dismissal and that the employer must act reasonably. This means that they must carry out a full investigation and follow the ACAS Code of Practice. Better answers are also likely to mention that some forms of dismissal are considered to be automatically unfair and for these there is only a one-stage process undertaken by the employment tribunals. You should outline some of the automatically unfair reasons for dismissal and indicate why these are designated as such.

You should express some considered opinion about the extent to which you feel that employers should try to avoid dismissals of employees. This is likely to include comment about managers taking early action to avoid the development of problems; the use of counselling skills by managers; the use of HRM planning to help avoid the need for redundancies; planned retirements and following 'the duty to consider' a request to work beyond normal retirement; the training and development of employees if skills need change; a proper recruitment and selection process to help minimise numbers of dismissals. Following good HRM policies and procedures should help to minimise costs involved. Sometimes, however, it is still necessary to dismiss and then it must be for a fair reason and must be handled reasonably in accordance with the ACAS Code of Practice.

Answers to self-check questions

1 (c). 2 (e). 3 (b). 4 (c). 5 (a).

Author index

Subject index

Quick guide to employment legislation and related documents